Defending possession proceedings

seventh edition

Jan Luba QC is a barrister in the housing team at Garden Court Chambers in London. He was called to the Bar in 1980 and was made Queen's Counsel in 2000. He is one of the leading authorities on housing law and practice. Jan is co-author of a number of housing law titles including *Repairs: tenant's rights* (LAG, 4th edn, 2010) and *Housing Allocations and Homelessness* (Jordans, 2nd edn, 2010), and he writes, with Nic Madge, the monthly series 'Recent developments in housing law' in *Legal Action.* Jan sits as a Recorder in the civil and criminal courts and as an additional judge of the Employment Appeal Tribunal. He is a patron of the Croydon Housing Aid Society.

John Gallagher is Principal Solicitor with Shelter, and has specialised in housing and homelessness law for over 20 years. He previously worked at SHAC (the London Housing Aid Centre), at Nottingham Law Centre and in private practice in Liverpool. He is an executive member of the Housing Law Practitioners' Association.

Derek McConnell is a solicitor at South West Law in Bristol. Since 1978 he worked in a number of law centres, and then in private practice, specialising in housing law. He writes the regular 'Owner-occupier' updates in *Legal Action.*

Nic Madge is a Circuit Judge. He was formerly a recorder and district judge and head of the Housing Department at Bindman and Partners, London. He is a long standing member of the Judicial Studies Board tutor team. Nic is co-author of *Housing Law Casebook* (LAG, 4th edn, 2008), *Annotated Housing Statutes* (Sweet and Maxwell, 2005) and a member of the senior editorial board of *Civil Procedure* ('the White Book') (Sweet & Maxwell). He writes regularly on housing law and procedure and co-authors 'Recent developments in housing law' in *Legal Action.* Nic is a founder member of the Housing Law Practitioners' Association. His personal web site can be seen at www.nicmadge.co.uk.

The Legal Action Group is a national, independent charity which campaigns for equal access to justice for all members of society. Legal Action Group:
- provides support to the practice of lawyers and advisers
- inspires developments in that practice
- campaigns for improvements in the law and the administration of justice
- stimulates debate on how services should be delivered.

Defending possession proceedings

SEVENTH EDITION

Jan Luba QC, John Gallagher,
Derek McConnell and Nic Madge

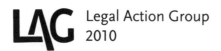

Legal Action Group
2010

This edition published in Great Britain 2010
by LAG Education and Service Trust Limited
242 Pentonville Road, London N1 9UN
www.lag.org.uk

© Jan Luba, John Gallagher, Derek McConnell and Nic Madge 2010

First edition 1987
Second edition 1989
Third edition 1993
Fourth edition 1997
Fifth edition 2002
Sixth edition 2006
Sixth edition reprinted 2009

First to fifth editions © Jan Luba, Nic Madge and Derek McConnell
Sixth edition © Nic Madge, Derek McConnell, John Gallagher and
Jan Luba

British Library Cataloguing in Publication Data
a CIP catalogue record for this book is available from the British Library.

Crown copyright material is produced with the permission of the
Controller of HMSO and the Queen's Printer for Scotland.

ISBN 978 1 903307 75 5

Typeset by Regent Typesetting, London
Printed by Hobbs the Printers, Totton, Hampshire

Preface

Legislation designed to protect residential tenants should be clear, simple and consistent in its effects, not dubious, complex and arbitrary.

These words of Baroness Hale, taken from her judgment in the case of *Austin v London Borough of Southwark*,[1] are as music to the ears of all residential occupiers (including, by extension, owner-occupiers), their lawyers and advisers. Too often, housing law is anything but clear, simple and consistent. Root and branch reform of housing law and procedure is long overdue. In the preface to the last edition of this book, we commended the work of the Law Commission in its well-received proposals for the simplification and codification of housing law.[2] It is shameful and short-sighted that the political will has not been found to implement those proposals. It is a fundamental pillar of access to justice that people should know their rights and obligations in respect of something as important as the roof over their heads, and that they should be able to obtain redress where those rights are denied.

The aim of *Defending possession proceedings* is to assist advice workers, solicitors, barristers and others called upon to help defendants or potential defendants to possession claims. This book is not, and could not be, a treatise on all the relevant law of tenancies and mortgages. There are other weighty tomes, some comprising several volumes, which fulfil that function. *Defending possession proceedings* is essentially a practical book. We concentrate on matters of practice and procedure and relevant substantive law. We have aimed to write it in a user-friendly way, so that it contains information which is of use to the most experienced legal practitioners, yet is still understandable to the least experienced housing advisers.

The task of advisers and lawyers helping those facing possession proceedings has become increasingly difficult in the 23 years since

1   [2010] UKSC 28; [2010] 3 WLR 144 at para [53].
2   *Renting Homes* (Law Com No 297), Cm 6781, May 2006.

we started writing the first edition of this book. The number of possession claims is again rising. In 2008, the latest full year for which records are available, a total of 290,958 claims for possession were started in county courts throughout England and Wales, of which 142,741 were mortgage-related. In the same year, 212,566 possession orders were made, of which 97,184 were suspended.[3] In the first quarter of 2010, 51,684 possession claims were begun, including 18,504 mortgage possession claims. In the same period 36,062 orders were made.[4] With reductions in housing benefit entitlement due to be implemented in April 2011 and the likelihood of an increase in mortgage interest rates alongside the effects of greater economic stringency, it seems inevitable that many more householders will find themselves involved in, or at risk of, possession proceedings. The availability of legal aid has become more and more restricted, and as we go to press solicitors' firms, law centres and advice agencies are in a state of turmoil, awaiting the outcomes of the tendering process in which they have been compelled by the Legal Services Commission to bid against one another for contracts for a limited number of 'matter starts'. It is difficult to reconcile a policy of rationing the numbers of cases in which advice and assistance are available under the 'Legal Help' scheme, whereby problems can be solved without resort to court proceedings, with the Commission's concern that litigation should be avoided where possible.

On the other hand, the law has become more and more complex – demonstrated by the fact that this seventh edition is more than three times longer than the first edition. Since publication of the first edition, the pace of change in housing law has become ever more rapid. As a result, this edition contains seven new chapters: on family intervention tenancies; replacement tenancies; public law defences; human rights defences; disability discrimination defences; rent arrears and bankruptcy; and Islamic home purchase, as well as separate chapters on introductory tenancies and demoted tenancies.

Some of the changes which have occurred since the last edition deserve particular comment. The profusion of case law which has sought to explore the interface between administrative law and possession proceedings has given rise to the new chapters on public law defences (chapter 25) and human rights defences (chapter 26). In

---

3 Table 4.3, *Judicial and Court Statistics* 2008, Cm 7697, Ministry of Justice, September 2009.

4 Ministry of Justice Statistics Bulletin, May 2010: www.justice.gov.uk/publications/docs/stats-mort-land-ql-2010.pdf.

the judgment of the European Court of Human Rights (Fourth Section) in *McCann v United Kingdom*[5] the Court stated:

> The loss of one's home is a most extreme form of interference with the right to respect for the home. Any person at risk of an interference of this magnitude should in principle be able to have the proportionality of the measure determined by an independent tribunal in the light of the relevant principles under Article 8 of the Convention, notwithstanding that, under domestic law, his right of occupation has come to an end.

The judgment in *McCann* was considered by the House of Lords in *Doherty v Birmingham CC*, [6] and in a succession of subsequent decisions of the High Court and the Court of Appeal: see chapters 25 and 26. In *R (Weaver) v London & Quadrant Housing Trust*,[7] the Court of Appeal held that the housing trust, as a hybrid public authority, was carrying out an act of a public, not a private, nature for the purposes of section 6(5) of the Human Rights Act 1998 when it took steps to terminate a tenancy, and its decision to do so was subject to scrutiny on public law principles.

As the Court of Appeal noted in *Central Bedfordshire Council v Taylor and others*[8], there is a continuing tension between ECtHR decisions and those of the domestic courts.[9] As this book went to press, the appeal in the case of *Manchester City Council v Pinnock* was being heard by the Supreme Court. Other cases relating to potential public law defences in cases concerning introductory tenancies and non-secure tenancies are due to come before the Supreme Court in November 2010, while the case of *Kay v United Kingdom* is pending in the European Court of Human Rights. Readers are recommended to refer to para 26.51 for details of a supplementary note on the outcomes of these cases, to be posted on the Legal Action Group website www.lag.org.uk, in addition to keeping abreast of all other housing law developments through *Legal Action* (see below).

The most prominent legislative change since publication of the last edition in 2006 is to be found in Schedule 11 of the Housing and Regeneration Act 2008, which came into effect from 20 May 2009. On that happy day, the concept of the tolerated trespasser ceased to exist, and many occupiers who had lost their secure tenancies had

5   Application no 19009/04, 13 May 2008, (2008) 47 EHRR 40, ECtHR.
6   [2008] UKHL 57; [2009] 1 AC 367; [2008] HLR 45.
7   [2009] EWCA Civ 587.
8   [2009] EWCA Civ 613; [2010] 1 WLR 446; [2010] HLR 12.
9   See Nic Madge, 'Article 8: La Lutta Continua?' [2009] JHL 43.

tenancy status restored to them, mostly without knowing it. The tolerated trespasser was a familiar figure in previous editions of this book. Advisers and lawyers struggled to make sense of the twilight existence of this legal oxymoron throughout the 23 years from its conception to its demise, which encompassed such abominations as the 'entrenched tolerated trespasser' and featured the Biblical imagery of 'Lazarus' applications for court orders which would restore defunct tenancies to life. For those who have laboured in these vineyards, the recent decision of the Supreme Court in *Austin* (see above) will have been greeted in equal measure with satisfaction and with frustration. For we now know what we long suspected, that the concept of the tolerated trespasser need not, and should not, have existed at all. Hundreds of hours of forensic argument, countless learned articles and innumerable training courses have been wasted in attempting to interpret what, in her trenchant judgment, Baroness Hale called 'all of this nonsense'. More importantly, an unknown number of people have lost their homes when they should not have done, particularly those who would have qualified to succeed a deceased 'tolerated trespasser'. These consequences could not of course be undone by the Supreme Court. It is a sobering reflection on our system of precedent and the accidents of litigation that the tolerated trespasser should effectively have been abolished twice over within twelve months, once by Parliament and subsequently on being relegated by the Supreme Court in *Austin* to a state of jurisprudential illegitimacy.

When the last edition was published, a series of decisions appeared to have established a defence to possession proceedings based on the Disability Discrimination Act 1995 in circumstances of indirect discrimination. However, in *London Borough of Lewisham v Malcolm and Disability Rights Commission (Intervener)*,[10] the House of Lords by a majority held that the Council's action in seeking possession of a tenant's flat for reasons which were arguably related to his disability did not amount to 'less favourable treatment' under the Disability Discrimination Act 1995. The decision in *Malcolm* will, however, be superseded by section 15 of the Equality Act 2010, when brought into force, which will again offer a tenant the basis for a defence, subject to certain conditions, where the reason for the possession proceedings derives from, or is associated with, the tenant's disability (see paras 27.9–27.16).

The Equality Act received Royal Assent on 8 April 2010, in common with a short but much-needed statute, the Mortgage Repossessions

---

10 [2008] UKHL 43; [2008] 1 AC 1399; [2008] HLR 41.

(Protection of Tenants etc) Act 2010, the purpose of which is to provide basic protection for unauthorised tenants of landlord borrowers in mortgage default. When in force, the Act will give the court power, in mortgage possession proceedings, to postpone the date of possession for up to two months in favour of an 'unauthorised tenant' of the mortgagor (see para 42.25). The Act will come into effect on 1 October 2010.

The last edition of this book coincided with the introduction of the Rent Arrears Protocol on 2 October 2006. There is now a counterpart protocol in mortgage possession proceedings. Lenders under residential mortgages who bring mortgage possession proceedings must, as from 16 November 2008, comply with the Mortgage Arrears Pre-action Protocol: see paras 42.3–42.10.

As ever, we are very grateful to those colleagues who have written to us with suggestions and comments on earlier editions. We have taken them into account where possible. Comments on this edition (addressed to us c/o the Legal Action Group) are warmly welcomed.

Many of the issues dealt with in this book are the subject of regular discussions at the meetings of the Housing Law Practitioners' Association (see www.hlpa.org.uk). In addition, the material in this book can be updated by reference to Nic Madge and Jan Luba's 'Recent developments in housing law', a monthly column in *Legal Action*, and to Derek McConnell's annual review 'Owner-occupiers: recent developments' which also appears in *Legal Action* in April each year.

We wish to express our thanks to Sam Madge-Wyld for reading this edition in draft and for his comments and suggestions. That this edition has been produced at all is a tribute to the formidable skills and indomitable efficiency of our editor at LAG, Esther Pilger, whose deep reserves of patience have once again been mined to the full, and of Lesley Exton at Regent Typesetting, who has yet again performed Herculean feats in assimilating major changes and updating at page proof stage. Their contribution has been incalculable. Any remaining mistakes are ours.

The law in England and Wales is stated as at 1 July 2010.

Jan Luba QC
John Gallagher
Derek McConnell
Nic Madge

Contents

How to use this book

Since the publication of the first edition in January 1987, *Defending possession proceedings* has been a practical reference handbook dealing with all aspects of the law and practice relating to possession proceedings pursued against occupiers of *residential* property. It seeks to guide occupiers and their advisers in dealing with possession claims. It goes through the process, from the initial notice given to the occupier to the aftermath of the bailiff's eviction. The main content of the book deals with three principal types of occupier, namely, the social housing tenant, the private tenant and the mortgage-borrower.

The starting point for making best use of this book is to establish what form of right to occupation of the property the occupier enjoys (if any). For owner-occupiers, the reader needs to go straight to Part IV except in relation to shared ownership leaseholders (see chapter 22) or rental purchasers (chapter 21). If the occupier has, at the other end of the spectrum, no legal right of occupation at all; go to chapter 29. In between ownership and trespass the most common form of occupation will be under a tenancy. To make best use of this book in those cases, the *type* of tenancy will first need to be identified

Relatively few tenants will still be protected by the Rent Acts (see chapter 15). The great bulk will either be *secure* (chapter 1), *assured shorthold* (chapter 11) or full *assured* (chapter 12) tenants. Others will be *introductory, demoted, family intervention, replacement* or *wholly unprotected* tenants and chapters 7, 8, 9, 10 and 18 deal with them respectively.

Where an adviser is clear as to the type of tenancy which an occupier has, then reference should be made to the relevant part or chapter of the book. However, where it is unclear, the brief introduction to the types of tenancy, found at the beginning of each Part, should be considered. A particular difficulty in the recent past has been to identify the correct form of occupation of a resident of *social* housing. That has not been helped by recent changes in the descriptions given to particular types of social housing provider and to the arrangements for the regulation of that sector. The book uses the modern statutory terms 'private registered provider' (PRP) for non-local authority social landlords in England and 'registered social landlords' (RSL) for those same landlords in Wales (and these terms are more fully explained in chapter 6). Wherever possible, 'social housing' is used to describe the whole class of rented accommodation outside the *private* rented accommodation sector.

Although the focus of the book is on possession proceedings, the text also covers the critical related issues that may trigger or affect possession claims. For example, chapter 20 deals with *death* of the occupier. chapter 30 tackles *bankruptcy*. The issues of *domestic violence, homelessness* and *housing benefit* are covered in chapters 35, 36 and 37 respectively. For the termination of accommodation linked to *employment* see chapter 19.

Part III of the book contains a discussion of possession procedure and related points as they affect residential tenants and other occupiers. Part IV deals with the procedure and other issues as they affect mortgage borrowers.

The relatively 'modern' defences to possession claims which rely on (1) *public law principles* or (2) *human rights* or (3) *disability discrimination* are described in chapters 25, 26 and 27 respectively. The law relating to all three was in ferment as the text of this edition was being prepared and advisers will need to note the references within them to relevant developments

The appendices contain a set of precedents which practitioners might find useful. An instructions checklist is provided as an aide-memoire. This edition also includes the texts of the two Protocols for claims based on rent arrears and claims based on mortgage arrears. The appendices also set out the text of the procedural rule governing possession cases – CPR Part 55 – and the practice directions to it.

For reasons of space, it has been impossible to include a complete range of citations of cases in individual footnotes. However, citations in all major law reports are included in the table of cases. Any reader who does not have access to the law reports referred to in a footnote citation should therefore refer to the table of cases.

Table of cases

References in the right-hand column are to paragraph numbers.

Table of statutes

References in the right-hand column are to paragraph numbers.

Table of statutory instruments

References in the right-hand column are to paragraph numbers.

Table of European legislation

References in the right-hand column are to paragraph numbers.

European Convention on Human Rights	2.31, 3.92, 5.34, 7.66, 23.12, 26.1, 26.2, 26.8, 29.14, 34.39
article 6	7.66, 8.58, 12.74, 23.44, 23.45, 24.13, 26.2, 26.6, 26.31, 29.35, 34.39, 34.40, 34.41, 42.62
article 6(1)	7.45, 23.44
article 8	2.30, 2.31, 3.92, 5.34, 7.66, 3.200, 8.58, 11.3, 12.74, 12.76, 12.78, 12.79, 13.21, 23.44, 26.2, 26.3 ,26.6, 26.23, 26.31, 26.33, 26.36 ,26.37, 26.38, 26.39, 26.40, 26.41, 26.43, 26.45, 27.6, 34.16, 34.39, 34.40, 34.41 34.51, 40.36, 49.19
article 8(2)	12.74, 26.31, 26.33, 26.37, 26.38, 26.45
article 14	7.7, 7.66, 12.74, 26.2, 26.6, 26.23, 26.31, 34.40, 34.41
First Protocol	
article 1	2.30, 2.31, 12.74, 26.2, 26.6, 39.4, 40.24, 40.36, 49.19

Abbreviations

AJA	Administration of Justice Acts
ASBO	Anti-social behaviour order
BC	Borough Council
BRMA	Broad rental market area
CA	Court of Appeal
CC	City Council
CCA	Consumer Credit Act
CCR	County Court Rules
ChD	Chancery Division
CLG	Department for Communities and Local Government
CML	Council of Mortgage Lenders
CPR	Civil Procedure Rules
DC	District Council
DoE	Department of the Environment
DWP	Department for Work and Pensions
ECHR	European Convention on Human Rights
ECtHR	European Court of Human Rights
FOS	Financial Ombudsman Service
FSA	Financial Services Authority
FSMA	Financial Services and Markets Act
H&RA	Housing & Regeneration Act
HA	Housing Act
HAT	Housing action trust
HB Regs	Housing Benefit Regulations 2006 SI No 213
HCA	Homes and Communities Agency
HL	House of Lords
HMO	House in multiple occupation
HRA	Human Rights Act
IA	Insolvency Act
IPO	Interim possession order
IS Regs	Income Support (General) Regulations 1987 SI No 1967
ISA	Individual savings account
JSA Regs	Jobseeker's Allowance Regulations 1996 SI No 207
LBC	London Borough Council
LHA	Local Housing Allowance
LPA	Law of Property Act
LSC	Legal Services Commission

LSVT	Large Scale Voluntary Transfer scheme
LVT	Leasehold Valuation Tribunal
MBC	Metropolitan Borough Council
MCOB	Mortgage: conduct of business sourcebook
NSP	Notice Seeking Possession
ODPM	Office of the Deputy Prime Minister
OFT	Office of Fair Trading
PCOL	Possession Claims Online
PEA	Protection from Eviction Act 1977
PEP	Personal Equity Plan
PRP	Private registered provider
RA	Rent Act
RPSH	Registered provider of social housing
RSC	Rules of the Supreme Court
RSL	Registered social landlord
SMI	Support for mortgage interest
TSA	Tenant Services Authority

Occupiers of social housing

Introduction to Part I

I.1 Part I of this book is concerned with defending possession proceedings brought against occupiers living in the rented social housing sector. Its main focus is on tenants and licensees of the 150 or so local housing authorities in England and Wales which retain and manage their own housing stock or which have retained ownership but contracted out the management of their homes (for example, to 'arms length management organisations').

I.2 For the three decades since 1980, most occupiers of such accommodation have enjoyed security of tenure as *secure* tenants or licensees. Their code of protection, now set out in the Housing Act 1985 Part IV, prevents their landlords from ending their tenancies or recovering possession except by establishing before a county court judge that grounds set out in the 1985 Act can be proved. In most cases, occupiers are further protected by a discretion the court exercises as to whether the particular circumstances justify the making of the order. On paper, therefore, these occupiers have considerable protection against loss of their homes. The focus of Part I of this book is accordingly on the defence of proceedings against occupiers in that part of the social housing sector where security of tenure is regulated by the Housing Act 1985. The first chapter provides a short summary of security in this sector. Chapter 2 deals with the situations in which security is threatened or lost. The third chapter deals with the grounds for possession that apply to proceedings against secure occupiers and chapter 4 deals with preparation of defences. Chapter 5 covers a miscellany of other situations affecting secure occupiers.

I.3 For the period from 1980 to 1989 the secure tenancy regime applied across the social housing rented sector and most tenants of housing associations, housing trusts and housing co-operatives were covered by the same tenancy regime as tenants of local housing authorities. The issues arising under that regime and reviewed in this Part still 3 apply to those other social landlords in the management of, and their dealings with, those occupiers who have been secure tenants or licensees for over 20 years. Chapter 6 deals with the special position of associations, trusts and co-operatives. However, since 1989 most new tenancies of housing association and other non-local-authority social housing stock have fallen within the Housing Act 1988 regime, as *assured* tenancies. The defence of possession proceedings against these more recent tenants of housing associations, trusts and co-operatives is now dealt with in Part II of this book.

I.4   Although *secure* tenants enjoy, as this Part explains, the highest level of statutory security of tenure available in the rented sector, this statutory protection has not led to any perceptible containment of landlords' attempts to recover possession. The county courts in England and Wales deal with tens of thousands of possession claims against secure tenants each year. Research has repeatedly shown that these possession cases receive insufficiently thorough attention in some county courts. Researchers have suggested that in some parts of the country the speed with which possession cases are heard indicates little regard for security of tenure and, rather, an emphasis on quick disposal. Despite the presence of 'secure' status, possession orders are made in the majority of cases and thousands of occupiers are actually evicted each year as a result. The research has emphasised the need for more secure tenants to attend court and urged more consistent handling of housing possession cases by the courts.[1]

I.5   Most of these cases are – in reality – 'debt collecting' actions. The main function of the proceedings is to threaten repossession on the ground of rent arrears unless the occupier resumes regular and full payment of rent due and owing. This happens notwithstanding the UK government's repeated exhortations to social landlords to see possession proceedings only as the last resort in recovering arrears.[2] Social landlords presumably regard possession proceedings as a 'bigger stick' to wield against defaulting tenants than other available recovery procedures. This practice, which might appear to some to verge on an abuse of the process of the court, received critical scrutiny from Lord Woolf's review of civil justice,[3] but appears not to have abated. It was hoped that the introduction of a new Rent Arrears

---

1   C Hunter et al, *The exercise of judicial discretion in rent arrears cases*, Department of Constitutional Affairs, Research Series 6/05, 2005.

2   *The use of possession actions and evictions by social landlords*, ODPM, June 2005 and see too Pawson et al, *Rent arrears management practices in the housing association sector*, TSA, February 2010.

3   Woolf, *Access to Justice: Final Report*, HMSO, 1996, ch 16.

Pre-Action Protocol (see para 3.38) would lead to a reduction in the overall number of possession proceedings and a sharper focus on the statutory criteria limiting the circumstances in which possession orders can be made. But after an initial post-protocol 'blip', numbers are on the increase again.

I.6   Concern that the 'secure' status makes it too difficult for social landlords to recover possession has led to the creation of an increasing number of exceptions to such status. For example, following a very effective lobbying campaign by landlords of secure tenants, the Housing Act 1996 introduced a new reduced form of security of tenure for most new tenants who would otherwise have been secure. That is because since 1997 local housing authorities have had power to elect to put these new tenants 'on probation' for their first year – now extendable to 18 months – by the grant of 'introductory tenancies' (considered in chapter 7). Also in 1997, the grounds for possession against secure tenants were added to and existing grounds were broadened: see, for example, grounds 2 and 2A discussed at paras 3.72 and 3.108 respectively. The safeguard that there must usually be a 'notice seeking possession' before court proceedings are commenced was punctured by a new provision allowing such notice to be dispensed with (see para 4.45).

I.7   But these are far from the only inroads. Since June 2004, following further amending legislation in the form of the Anti-Social Behaviour Act 2003, social landlords have been able to apply to the courts for 'demotion orders', whereby the security of tenure of a secure (or assured) tenant can be removed by the county court and the tenancy reduced to probationary status for a period of one year. These demoted tenancy arrangements are described in chapter 8. The Housing and Regeneration Act 2008 introduced yet another form of social housing tenancy which does not enjoy security of tenure – the family intervention tenancy. The defence of possession proceedings brought against those tenants is discussed in chapter 9.

I.8   Much of Part I of the book is concerned with advising in the statistically most common case – a rent arrears possession action brought against a secure occupier. Over the past 30 years the mass use of possession claims to secure conditional possession orders in such cases – placing the prospect of eviction over the tenants unless conditions for payment of rent plus arrears were scrupulously met, while in the meantime permitting them to remain in occupation – triggered the loss of tenancy status for hundreds of thousands of occupiers on wilful or unintended non-compliance. They remained in possession as 'tolerated trespassers' with bewildering legal and practical consequences. In May 2009 most were given a new tenancy status as *replacement* tenants. Their circumstances are addressed in chapter 10.

CHAPTER 1

Secure occupiers

Introduction

1.1   The rights to security of tenure of those living in the social housing rented sector operate as a supplement to the ordinary common law rules of landlord and tenant. Under those ordinary rules, the landlord needed only to bring the contractual arrangement to an end in accordance with its terms and the occupier's right to possession then ceased. The highest form of security of tenure in the social housing sector is the secure tenancy. It was first introduced by the Housing Act (HA) 1980, now derives from HA 1985 Part IV and operates by way of providing the contractual tenant with a 'cloak' of security of tenure. As will be seen, in an ordinary case, the social landlord can bring the tenancy to an end only by making an application to a court.

Secure tenancies

1.2   The greatest security of tenure available in the social housing rented sector is accorded to those who are 'secure tenants'. Most council tenants and many other social housing sector tenants are secure tenants. However, it is always important to check that all the hallmarks of a secure tenancy, as set out below, are present in each case.

1.3   A secure tenancy exists at any time when the conditions set out in HA 1985 ss79–81 are *all* satisfied. The general conditions are given in section 79. Then section 80 contains a 'landlord condition' and section 81 a 'tenant condition'. Combining the three provisions produces the following list of requirements for a 'secure' tenancy:

- the property is a 'dwelling-house';
- the landlord is a prescribed social landlord;
- the tenant is an individual;
- the tenant occupies the property as his or her only or principal home;
- the property was let 'as a separate dwelling'; and
- the tenancy is not in an excluded category.

Each of these requirements is discussed in turn below.

The property is a 'dwelling-house'

1.4   The term 'dwelling-house' covers both houses and parts of houses[1] and extends to any land let together with the dwelling-house other

---

1   HA 1985 s112(1).

than agricultural land exceeding two acres.[2] Neither of the words 'house' or 'dwelling-house' is further defined in HA 1985 Part IV. The phrase 'part of a house' is sufficiently broad to include flats, rooms, apartments and bed-sitting rooms and possibly accommodation in some hostels.

1.5 It was previously thought that a single room let furnished, without cooking facilities and situated in a hostel was not a 'dwelling-house' for the purposes of the security of tenure provisions.[3] However, it is now clear that a 'dwelling-house' is simply a house or part of a house in which a person lives.[4]

The landlord is a prescribed social landord

1.6 The 'landlord condition' for the tenancy to be secure is that the landlord must be one of the authorities or bodies within the list set out in HA 1985 s80, as amended. The section has been rendered so long and complex by multiple amendments that it cannot conveniently be set out here. Although the precise wording must always be checked, the landlords within the statutory list include:

- local authorities;
- development corporations;
- housing action trusts;
- some housing co-operatives;
- some housing associations; and
- a variety of other public bodies and authorities.

If there are joint landlords they must *all* be in the statutory list.[5] For the position of tenants of fully mutual housing co-operatives, see para 6.32.

1.7 The most significant changes to the list were made by the Housing Act 1988 but the process of constant revision has continued up to and including changes made by the Housing and Regeneration Act 2008.

1.8 These changes reflect the general policy intention that most *modern* lettings (ie, those made since 15 January 1989) by housing associations, trusts and other such social landlords should *not* come

---

2 HA 1985 s112(2).

3 *Central London YMCA Housing Association Ltd v Goodman* (1992) 24 HLR 109, CA and *Central London YMCA Housing Association Ltd v Saunders* (1991) 23 HLR 212, CA.

4 *Uratemp Ventures Ltd v Collins* [2001] UKHL 43; [2002] 1 AC 301; (2001) 33 HLR 972.

5 *R v Plymouth CC and Cornwall CC ex p Freeman* (1987) 19 HLR 328, CA.

within the secure tenancy regime. Secure tenancies granted by such landlords *before* that date retain their secure status and such landlords may grant some new secure tenancies but only in very narrowly defined circumstances.[6] Surprisingly, it is still possible for a non-secure tenancy held from such a landlord automatically to 'become' secure. This occurs when a social landlord acquires property with sitting Rent Act tenants[7] or if the transitional provisions in HA 1988 Sch 18 para 4 are activated by some change in the landlord's status.[8]

1.9   Secure tenants are most commonly tenants of a 'local authority'. That term is widely defined by HA 1985 s4(1)(e) to include a whole range of local government bodies and statutory authorities.[9] For discussion of the special position of housing association, housing co-operative and housing trust occupiers, see chapter 6.

1.10   If the interest of the landlord is transferred after the grant of the secure tenancy to a social landlord not in the section 80 list, for example, by the sale of council property into the private sector or to a housing association, any sitting secure tenants lose secure status although they may become 'assured' tenants under provisions regulating private sector tenancies.[10] For the circumstances in which a social housing sector landlord may seek to recover possession before such a sale, see para 3.165.

1.11   Since 1993, well over one million dwellings have been transferred out of council ownership through the Large Scale Voluntary Transfer (LSVT) scheme. That scheme applies where units of more than 500 council homes have been acquired, with central government approval, by other social landlords. As a result, there are now more tenants of housing associations in the social housing sector in England than there are tenants of local authorities. The Homes and Communities Agency (HCA) maintains a map of England indicating which areas have experienced an LSVT and publishes a list of all LSVTs in England to date.[11] In an LSVT, all sitting tenants will have ceased to be secure tenants at completion of the sale of their council landlord's stock.[12]

6   HA 1988 s35(4).

7   HA 1988 s35(5).

8   *Bhai v Black Roof Community Housing Association* [2001] 2 All ER 865; (2001) 33 HLR 607, CA.

9   It is essential to refer to a fully revised and updated version of section 4(1)(e) to check whether a particular social landlord is a 'local authority'.

10 See HA 1985 Pt II and HA 1988 s38.

11 Details available from the HCA website at www.homesandcommunities.co.uk/ Transferring_stock.

12 *Knowles HA v Miller* 2001 SLT 1326, Court of Session.

1.12   Housing action trusts (HATs) were set up to take over, revitalise, improve and regenerate certain specific areas of run-down local authority housing. The statutory basis of their operation is to be found in HA 1988 Part III. Only six[13] were in fact created, owing in part to the substantial finances that need to be raised for them to be able to undertake their work successfully. The sixth and last – Stonebridge HAT – was wound down and dissolved in 2007.[14]

The tenant is an individual

1.13   The tenant must be an individual person[15] or a group of individuals holding as joint tenants. Therefore, a tenancy cannot be secure if the tenant is a company, a charity, a short-life housing association,[16] a co-operative, a statutory authority or a statutory corporation. The subtenants of such bodies may of course themselves be secure tenants as against their immediate landlords. If a tenancy is purportedly granted to a company but both parties understand that the true occupier with possession will be an individual, that individual holds as a secure tenant because any other agreement would be a 'sham'.[17]

The 'only or principal home' rule

1.14   The 'tenant condition' is that the tenant must occupy the property as his or her only *or* principal home.[18] A secure tenant may, therefore, have more than one home but can usually have a 'secure' tenancy only in relation to the principal one: see para 2.73. Where there are joint tenants, at least one of them must occupy as his or her only or principal home in order to retain the 'secure' status.[19]

1.15   Temporary absences caused by holidays, stays in hospital, working abroad, etc, do not affect security, but a permanent absence will lead to loss of security. For the difficulties which arise from extended absences, see the discussion at paras 2.47–2.73.

---

13 North Hull HAT, Waltham Forest HAT, Liverpool HAT, Castle Vale HAT, Tower Hamlets HAT and Stonebridge HAT.
14 The Stonebridge Housing Action Trust (Dissolution) Order 2007 SI No 1862.
15 HA 1985 s81.
16 *Camden LBC v Shortlife Community Housing Ltd* (1993) 25 HLR 330; (1992) 90 LGR 358, HC, *Kay and others v Lambeth LBC* [2006] UKHL 10; [2006] 2 AC 465.
17 *City of London v Ukpoma* (1996) 1 L & T Rev D8; September 1996 *Legal Action* 11.
18 HA 1985 s81.
19 HA 1985 s81.

1.16   If an absent tenant is married or has a registered civil partner and the home has been the shared home, his or her spouse or civil partner can preserve the security of the tenancy by continuing in occupation during the tenant's absence.[20] There is no equivalent automatic provision for cohabitants or other family members to be deemed to be preserving the absent tenant's security of tenure, but if a cohabitant or former cohabitant successfully applies for an 'occupation order' under the Family Law Act 1996 s36(1) he or she will be treated as satisfying the 'only or principal home' rule on behalf of the absentee tenant (see chapter 35).[21]

The 'let as a separate dwelling' requirement

1.17   This has three components: the letting must have been a letting of the premises 'as' a separate dwelling; the premises let must be a 'dwelling' (in a 'dwelling-house', see para 1.4); and the dwelling must have been let as a 'separate' dwelling.[22]

1.18   The first of these components deals with the nature of the letting. Were the premises let 'as' a separate dwelling? In *Webb v Barnet LBC*,[23] the council let a house, yard, workshop and associated buildings as premises for use by a motor repair business. The tenant used them in this way until retirement and continued in occupation of the house once the business had closed. It was held that the tenancy was not secure. The original letting had been for commercial use, not for use 'as' a separate dwelling. In *Tomkins v Basildon DC*,[24] the tenant had a lease of a bungalow and kennels. The authorised use of the premises was for the training of greyhounds, and the letting was accordingly a business tenancy under the Landlord and Tenant Act 1954 Part II. Eventually, commercial activity ceased and the premises were used only as a residence. On the expiry of the lease, the tenant continued to live in the bungalow and claimed housing benefit in respect of the rent. However, the property had not been let 'as' a separate dwelling and the tenancy was not, therefore, a secure tenancy. The landlord had been content not to enforce the tenant's covenant

---

20 Family Law Act 1996 s30(4)(b), amended by Civil Partnership Act 2004 Sch 9 para 1, with effect from 5 December 2005. See para 2.71.

21 Family Law Act 1996 s36(13) and see *Gay v Sheeran and Enfield LBC* (2000) 32 HLR 1126, CA.

22 HA 1985 s79(1).

23 (1988) 21 HLR 288, CA.

24 [2002] EWCA Civ 876; [2003] L&TR 7.

for business use, but this was not sufficient to amount to an agreed variation of the letting condition.

1.19   It should be noted that the security of tenure provisions only cover 'a' separate dwelling, ie, one unit of accommodation. It may, however, be possible for two adjoining units let to the tenant to be combined to form a single dwelling for these purposes.[25]

1.20   The second component deals with the subject of the letting. It must be a 'dwelling'. This is something more than simply a physical unit of four walls, a floor and a ceiling (because that test would be satisfied by a garage or storeroom) but it can be difficult to identify or define a 'dwelling' with precision. In *Uratemp Ventures Ltd v Collins*,[26] the subject of the letting was a single room in a hotel. The House of Lords decided that a 'dwelling' was the place in which a person lived, or had his 'home'. It was no requirement of the concept of 'dwelling' that it should be a place where the tenant cooked or ate, although it would be the place where he usually slept. The room was a 'dwelling'.

1.21   Third, the premises must have been let to the tenant as a 'separate' dwelling.[27] Usually this condition is satisfied because the tenant and his or her family are the only intended occupiers of the property concerned. If, however, parts of a building are shared with other tenants this does not affect security unless the sharing is of living accommodation (kitchen,[28] lounge, dining room or bedroom).[29] Such sharing means that the tenant has not been let a 'separate' dwelling. Thus, in the case of an ordinary residential house or flat, a tenant or licensee of a single bedroom in the property who shares the kitchen, living room, etc, with the occupiers of the other bedrooms will not have a 'separate dwelling' for these purposes.[30]

1.22   Obviously, secure status is not lost just because living accommodation is shared by the tenant with other members of the tenant's own household or with the tenant's lodgers.

---

25 *Jenkins v Renfrew DC* 1989 SLT (Lands Tr) 41, but cf *Kavanagh v Lyroudias* [1985] 1 All ER 560, CA.

26 [2001] UKHL 43; [2002] 1 AC 301; (2001) 33 HLR 972.

27 HA 1985 s79(1).

28 Note the important distinction for these purposes between the shared occupation of a kitchen and the sharing of limited use of a kitchen (eg, to wash up or cook) described in *Uratemp Ventures Ltd v Collins* [2001] UKHL 43; [2002] 1 AC 301; (2001) 33 HLR 972 at [58] of the judgment.

29 See *Kensington and Chelsea RBC v Haydon* (1984) 17 HLR 114, CA on the effect of sharing with a hostel worker, and generally *Thomson v Glasgow CC* 1986 SLT 6, noted at December 1986 *Legal Action* 165, Lands Tr.

30 *Parkins v Westminster CC* (1998) 30 HLR 894; [1998] 1 EGLR 22, CA and *Smith v Hackney LBC* August 1998 *Legal Action* 21, CA.

The tenancy is not in an excluded category

1.23   Certain categories of tenancy are excluded from the full security of tenure provided by 'secure' status. They are:

- Tenancies in one of the classes exempted from protection by HA 1985 Sch 1, as amended.[31] Detailed consideration of each of the classes set out in the Schedule is beyond the scope of this work, but the categories may be broadly summarised as:
  - long tenancies (defined in HA 1985 s115);
  - introductory tenancies (see chapter 7);
  - demoted tenancies (see chapter 8);
  - family intervention tenancies (see chapter 9);
  - premises occupied in connection with employment;[32]
  - tenancies of land acquired for development;[33]
  - accommodation provided for homeless people in performance of statutory functions (see para 5.20);
  - temporary accommodation for people taking up employment;[34]
  - 'private sector leasing' accommodation (see para 5.25);
  - temporary accommodation provided during works to a tenant's home;
  - tenancies of agricultural holdings and licensed premises;
  - student lettings by educational institutions;
  - Landlord and Tenant Act 1954 Part II tenancies (business tenancies);
  - almshouses;

---

31 HA 1985 s79(2)(a).
32 HA 1985 Sch 1 para 2; *Hughes v Greenwich LBC* [1994] 1 AC 170; (1994) 26 HLR 99, HL; *Elvidge v Coventry CC* [1994] QB 241; (1994) 26 HLR 281, CA; *South Glamorgan DC v Griffiths* (1992) 24 HLR 334; [1992] 2 EGLR 232, CA; *Surrey CC v Lamond* (1999) 31 HLR 1051, CA; *Brent LBC v Charles* (1997) 29 HLR 876, CA; and *Greenfield v Berkshire CC* (1996) 28 HLR 691, CA. For modern illustrations see: *Lee v Neath & Port Talbot CC* June 1998 *Legal Action* 10; *Coleman v Ipswich BC* [2001] EWCA 852; August 2001 *Legal Action* 23; *Godsmark v Greenwich LBC* [2004] HLR 53; *Holmes v South Yorkshire Police Authority* [2008] EWCA Civ 51; [2008] HLR 32 and *Wragg v Surrey CC* [2008] EWCA Civ 19; [2008] HLR 30.
33 HA 1985 Sch 1 para 3; *Attley v Cherwell DC* (1989) 21 HLR 613, CA; *Harrison v Hyde Housing Association Ltd* (1991) 23 HLR 57; [1991] 1 EGLR 51, CA; *London & Quadrant Housing Trust v Robertson* (1991) unreported, but noted at September 1991 *Legal Action* 15 and *Lillieshall Road Housing Co-operative v Brennan* (1992) 24 HLR 195; [1991] EGCS 132, CA.
34 HA 1985 Sch 1 para 5; *Campbell v Western Isles Island Council* 1989 SLT 602, CS, noted at December 1989 *Legal Action* 13.

- accommodation provided to asylum-seekers;[35] and
- temporary accommodation for displaced persons.[36]
- Tenancies which ceased to be secure after the death of the secure tenant[37] (see para 2.37).
- Tenancies which ceased to be secure following assignment, parting with possession or full subletting (see chapter 2).
- Tenancies at will.[38]

Tenancies in equity

1.24   Most secure tenancies are tenancies valid at law as between landlord and tenant. There are, however, circumstances in which a landlord purports to grant the occupier a tenancy valid in law but cannot in fact do so. For example, a tenant may die leaving no will and no successor. In such circumstances the legal tenancy devolves in the unadministered estate of the deceased to the Public Trustee. A landlord, unaware that this has occurred, may 're-let' the empty property to someone else. This new tenant cannot be given the deceased's legal tenancy because that remains held by the Public Trustee. In such circumstances the 'new' tenant holds a tenancy taking effect in equity only.[39]

1.25   Likewise, a landlord may purport to grant a tenancy to a person under 18. That person cannot hold a legal tenancy but he or she has a right to occupy in equity.[40] Indeed, in the case of a purported grant of a tenancy to a minor, the landlord may find that it holds the tenancy on trust for the young person and is unable to terminate it.[41]

1.26   A tenancy in equity enjoys security of tenure just as much as a legal tenancy if all the hallmarks of secure status (described above) are in place.

---

35 HA 1985 Sch 1 para 4A, inserted by Immigration and Asylum Act 1999 Sch 14 para 81.

36 HA 1985 Sch 1 para 4B, inserted by the Displaced Persons (Temporary Protection) Regulations 2005 SI No 1379.

37 HA 1985 s79(2)(b).

38 *Banjo v Brent LBC* [2005] EWCA Civ 287; [2005] 1 WLR 2520; [2005] 37 HLR 32.

39 *Epping Forest DC v Pomphrett* (1990) 22 HLR 475, CA.

40 *Kingston upon Thames RLBC v Prince* (1999) 31 HLR 794; [1999] 1 FLR 593, CA; *Newham LBC v Ria* [2004] EWCA Civ 41; (2004) 148 SJLB 113 and *Hammersmith and Fulham LBC v Alexander-David* [2009] EWCA Civ 259; [2009] 3 All ER 39; [2009] HLR 39.

41 *Hammersmith and Fulham LBC v Alexander-David* [2009] EWCA Civ 259; [2009] 3 All ER 39; [2009] HLR 39.

Secure 'licensees'

1.27   Although it is not a common occurrence, the occupier of council or other social housing may be granted a licence rather than a tenancy (for example, because the occupier is under 18 years of age and thus incapable at law of holding a tenancy: see para 1.25). Whether or not the occupier pays 'rent' or a 'licence fee' or any other charge, such a licence is secure if all the hallmarks outlined above in relation to a secure tenancy apply.[42] Such licences can be granted quite casually and almost inadvertently.[43]

1.28   This extension of security to licensees of social housing renders substantially less significant the distinction, still important in some circumstances in the private sector, between those with licences and those with tenancies.

1.29   Ordinarily, what distinguishes a licence from a tenancy is that the former does not give the occupier exclusive possession but the latter does. Unusually, and for reasons largely of historical accident,[44] for a licence to be a 'secure' licence, the licence agreement must have conferred on the occupier the exclusive right to occupy a separate dwelling. Thus, a resident in a hostel – with specialist support facilities under a licence agreement permitting the owners unrestricted access to the room and containing power to require the occupier to share (and/or to move to another room) – does not have a right to exclusive occupation of any separate dwelling and does not therefore have security of tenure.[45] Similarly, a licence which is simply a subsidiary agreement associated with a secure tenancy of a dwelling (such as permission temporarily to use additional rooms during building work) does not itself amount to a licence to occupy premises as a 'separate dwelling'.[46] However, a 'licence' to occupy self-contained property will be a tenancy even if the social landlord had only intended the arrangement to be temporary.[47]

1.30   Occupiers who initially enter the property as trespassers and are then given a licence to remain as a temporary expedient do not

---

42   HA 1985 s79(3).

43   See, eg, *Lambeth LBC v Stroud*, September 1991 *Legal Action* 14.

44   Described by Lord Templeman in *Westminster CC v Clarke* [1992] 2 AC 288; [1992] 2 WLR 229; (1992) 24 HLR 360, HL.

45   *Westminster CC v Clarke* [1992] 2 AC 288; [1992] 2 WLR 229; (1992) 24 HLR 360, HL.

46   *Tyler v Kensington & Chelsea RLBC* (1991) 23 HLR 380, CA, but cf *Mansfield DC v Langridge* [2008] EWCA Civ 264; [2008] HLR 34.

47   *Mansfield DC v Langridge* [2008] EWCA Civ 264; [2008] HLR 34.

benefit from security of tenure.[48] Thus, even squatters whom it is not proposed to evict for some time are outside the protection of 'secure' status (for their situation, see chapter 29). It should be noted that if a licence is granted to the squatter other than as a temporary expedient, the licensee immediately benefits from security. Alternatively, the squatter could acquire security from being granted a tenancy of the property.

Going in and out of secure status

1.31   Housing Act 1985 s79(1) accords a contractual tenancy or a licence 'secure' status '... at any time when ...' all the hallmarks of security set out at para 1.3 above are satisfied. A tenancy or licence may lose security for want of satisfaction of one of the conditions but later become secure again on its subsequent fulfilment. The section is aptly described as having 'ambulatory' effect.[49]

1.32   Therefore, if a landlord seeks possession on the basis that the tenancy has lost protection and the contractual tenancy has been determined by notice to quit, it is crucial to consider whether the tenancy was in or out of the protection of the Act at the date of expiry of that notice.[50] If the tenancy was secure at the date of its expiry, the notice to quit will have been of no effect.

1.33   If a check through this chapter has revealed that the occupier is *not* a secure tenant or licensee and is not an assured tenant (see chapter 12), go directly to para 5.32 (non-secure tenants) or para 5.35 (non-secure licensees).

48   HA 1985 s79(4). See *R v Southwark LBC ex p Bannerman* (1990) 22 HLR 459, QBD.
49   *Basingstoke & Deane BC v Paice* (1995) 27 HLR 433; [1995] 2 EGLR 9, CA and *Manchester CC v Finn* [2002] EWCA Civ 1998; [2003] HLR 41 at [32].
50   *Hussey v Camden LBC* (1995) 27 HLR 5, CA.

CHAPTER 2

Security threatened

Introduction

2.1   This chapter considers the circumstances in which the landlord or the occupier can place the security of tenure of a secure tenancy in jeopardy. The initial focus is, of course, on the typical case of landlord-initiated action. Throughout this chapter the term 'secure tenancy' is used to refer to both secure tenancies and secure licences (see para 1.27) unless the contrary is expressed.

Landlord-initiated

Landlord threatens possession proceedings

2.2   A secure tenancy cannot be brought to an end lawfully by a landlord otherwise than by obtaining a court order for possession.[1] The landlord must therefore initiate court proceedings to recover possession unless the occupiers themselves have brought to an end the security of tenure, in one of the ways described below (para 2.17 onwards), and even in those cases a landlord is likely to need a court order before recovering possession[2] unless the premises have been left vacant, in the sense that there is no one in residence.

2.3   Usually, the landlord gives the tenant some informal notice by letter, interview or home visit, that possession proceedings may be taken unless the tenant remedies a specific default, for example, pays any outstanding rent, ceases to commit nuisances, etc.[3] In rent arrears cases, these steps are required by the Rent Arrears Pre-Action Protocol (see para 3.38).

2.4   The first formal step the landlord must usually take if intending to press ahead to recover possession is service of a notice, commonly known as 'notice seeking possession'. The purpose of the notice is, in summary: to inform the tenant of the matters the landlord will rely on; to identify for the tenant the legal ground on which possession will be sought; and to set out the date after which possession proceedings may be started. This is not a 'notice to quit' and therefore does not attract the requirements for such a notice set out in the Protection from Eviction Act (PEA) 1977 (described at para 14.6). Nor does the notice seeking possession operate to end the tenancy on its

---

1   HA 1985 s82(1).
2   PEA 1977 s3.
3   *Possession actions and evictions by social landlords*: Housing Research Summary 219 (ODPM, June 2005).

expiry. Only a subsequent possession order can end the tenancy. If the tenant in receipt of a notice seeking possession decides to leave, he or she must bring the tenancy to an end by service of a notice to quit or by agreeing a surrender of the tenancy with the landlord.

2.5 In order to be effective the notice must meet the requirements of the Housing Act (HA) 1985 s83(2):

> (2) A notice under this section shall –
>> (a) be in a form prescribed by regulations made by the Secretary of State,
>> (b) specify the ground on which the court will be asked to make the order, and
>> (c) give particulars of that ground.

Each of the requirements of HA 1985 s83(2) is considered in chapter 4 (see paras 4.12–4.35).

2.6 The Act also requires the notice to specify certain *dates*. If the notice sets out ground 2 (nuisance) as one of the grounds for possession, then the notice must also state: (1) that possession proceedings may be begun immediately; and (2) the date sought by the landlord as the date on which the tenant is to give up possession.[4] In any other case, the date specified should be the date after which possession proceedings may be begun.[5]

2.7 In respect of any notice, unless the exception relating to ground 2 applies, the 'specified date' is to be no earlier than the date on which the tenancy could, under common law or in contract, have been brought to an end by notice to quit served on the tenant that day. For a weekly periodic tenancy that means that the date specified cannot be less than four weeks from the date on which the notice is given.[6]

2.8 Where the tenancy is a periodic tenancy the notice ceases to be effective 12 months from the specified date.[7] This means that, if the landlord wishes to proceed to recover possession on the basis of the notice, possession proceedings must be begun within 12 months of the specified date.[8] Note that this is a longer period than simply 12 months running from the date of service of the notice.

2.9 Special provision is made for notices given in respect of fixed-term secure tenancies.[9]

---

4 HA 1985 s83(3)(a).
5 HA 1985 s83(4).
6 PEA 1977 s5.
7 HA 1985 s83(3)(b) and (4)(b).
8 HA 1985 s83A(1) and (2).
9 HA 1985 s83(6).

2.10   Failure to comply with any of these strict procedural requirements may give rise to a defence to any proceedings brought on the
basis of that notice (see chapter 4). However, it is open to a landlord
to commence possession proceedings without serving a notice and
then seek to rely on the court's discretionary power to dispense with
the requirement for a notice.[10] The exercise of the same power may
be sought by a landlord who serves a defective notice. The scope of
this power is considered in chapter 4. Most landlords would prefer
the assurance of serving a proper notice at the outset and it is likely
to be only in the most urgent or unusual circumstances that the landlord starts proceedings without having served a notice of seeking possession at all.

2.11   The procedure to be followed by a landlord in seeking to recover
possession through the courts is outlined in chapter 23. What the
landlord needs to prove is discussed in chapter 3. The defences available to secure occupiers are reviewed in chapter 4.

2.12   Occasionally, even the landlords of secure tenants seek to recover possession unlawfully without first taking proceedings. The
relevant law on securing remedies for unlawful eviction is reviewed
in Arden and Partington's *Quiet Enjoyment*.[11] The 'penal' damages
awarded under HA 1988 s28 arising from the tort of statutory unlawful eviction are available as much against social landlords as private
landlords.[12]

Landlord proposes to sell the property

2.13   A secure tenancy remains secure only for so long as the landlord
condition remains satisfied, ie, the landlord is a prescribed social
landlord.[13] Once the interest of the landlord is transferred to a body
other than one of those prescribed in HA 1985 s80(1) (see para 1.6),
security of tenure under the Housing Act 1985 is lost, although the
contractual tenancy itself continues and binds the new landlord. In
recent years, many local housing authorities have transferred all or
part of their housing stock to housing associations or other such
social landlords. In these circumstances, the sitting tenants usually

10 HA 1985 s83(1)(b).
11 Arden, Partington, Carter and Dymond (6th edn, Legal Action Group, 2002).
12 See *White v Lambeth LBC* September 1995 *Legal Action* 20 (£18,000) and *Osei-
    Bonsu v Wandsworth LBC* [1999] 1 WLR 1011; (1999) 31 HLR 515, CA (£30,000
    reduced on appeal to £10,000).
13 HA 1985 s80(1) and see para 1.6.

obtain protection against the new owners as assured tenants under HA 1988 Part I.[14]

2.14   A proposal by a prescribed social landlord to sell or transfer the whole or part of its housing stock thus threatens the 'secure' status of the tenants of dwellings to be disposed of. Once the proposal becomes a positive decision to sell to a particular buyer, the secure tenants must be consulted.[15] The consultation procedure for disposal of the stock is governed by the requirements of HA 1985 s106A and Sch 3A,[16] which make more detailed provision than the general consultation arrangements made under HA 1985 s105.[17]

2.15   The landlord may not wish to sell with 'sitting' tenants but may prefer to sell with vacant possession. Such a landlord may attempt to secure vacant possession by taking possession proceedings against those who will not vacate voluntarily. In such cases, the procedures as to a notice seeking possession (see above) and grounds for possession (see chapter 3) must be satisfied. The Housing and Planning Act 1986 introduced ground 10A to HA 1985 Sch 2 to allow landlords a limited opportunity to recover possession in such circumstances (see para 3.165). However, the secretary of state's consent is required to such a proposed disposal and the landlord must undertake a consultation exercise with the tenants to be displaced before seeking such consent.[18]

Landlord seeks a demotion order

2.16   A secure tenancy can be terminated on the making of a demotion order by a county court.[19] The procedure by which a landlord may apply for and obtain such an order is described in chapter 8.

---

14 HA 1988 s38 and see para 1.11.
15 *Short v Tower Hamlets LBC* (1986) 18 HLR 171, CA.
16 Added by Housing and Planning Act 1986 s6.
17 See *The Housing Act 1985: Schedule 3A – consultation before disposal to private sector landlord Statutory guidance – paragraph 3: requirements as to consultation* Communities & Local Government, July 2009.
18 HA 1985 Sch 2 Pt V. If the landlord is a housing association, the consent of the appropriate regulator is required.
19 HA 1985 s82, as amended.

Tenant-initiated

Tenant surrenders the tenancy or gives notice to quit

2.17 Nothing in the Housing Act 1985 restricts the ability of secure tenants to determine their own tenancies. Termination can be achieved by either surrender or notice to quit. These are considered in turn.

Surrender

2.18 A secure tenant may end his or her own fixed-term or periodic tenancy by *surrender*. Surrender is the termination of a tenancy by mutual agreement between landlord and tenant. If the tenancy is a joint tenancy, all the joint tenants must agree to the surrender.[20] Agreement between landlord and tenant to a termination of the tenancy is best demonstrated by a deed of surrender.[21] If there is no deed, surrender can be achieved by operation of the common law. A surrender by operation of law arises where the tenant plainly acts so as to offer the landlord possession (for example, by emptying the property and returning the keys and rent book) and the landlord responds by accepting possession (for example, by acknowledging that the tenancy is over and by taking steps to re-let). The conduct of the parties creates an estoppel preventing either from asserting the continuation of the tenancy. The concept of surrender by operation of law in the general landlord and tenant context is more fully described in paras 14.34–14.43.[22]

2.19   Several cases have illustrated the surrender of secure tenancies by operation of law. In *Brent LBC v Sharma and Vyas*,[23] the tenant wrote to her landlord stating that she was no longer living in the property and would not be returning. The landlord responded by closing the rent account. This was held to amount to a concluded surrender by operation of law. In *Camden LBC v Alexandrou*,[24] the tenant had moved out of his flat and written to the landlord that he was unable to pay for the upkeep and considered it no longer his responsibility. Acting on that, the landlord had granted a tenancy of the flat to the tenant's estranged wife. The Court of Appeal refused permission

---

20 *Leek and Moorlands Building Society v Clark* [1952] 2 QB 788; [1952] 2 All ER 492, CA.

21 Law of Property Act 1925 ss52–53.

22 For a useful modern statement of the law of 'surrender by operation of law' see *QFS Scaffolding Ltd v Sable* [2010] EWCA Civ 682.

23 (1993) 25 HLR 257, CA.

24 (1998) 30 HLR 534, CA.

to appeal from a finding that the husband's tenancy had ended by surrender.

2.20 However, in order to establish the surrender, the party asserting it must demonstrate both unequivocal conduct of the secure tenant in offering up the tenancy and unequivocal conduct on the part of the landlord in accepting that offer. In *R v Hammersmith & Fulham LBC ex p Quigley*,[25] the judge summarised the law in these terms:

> The court must, adopting an objective approach, ask itself the following two questions. First, does the conduct of the tenant on his or her part drive the court objectively to the conclusion that he or she has surrendered his or her tenancy and ... is it demonstrated, on the other hand, that the landlord for his or their part has unequivocally accepted that act of surrender?[26]

Ms Quigley's partner fled his flat, abandoning their children there. The council claimed that his tenancy had been determined by surrender at that point. The assertion of surrender failed because the council's conduct in later serving a notice to quit and possession proceedings (contending that the tenancy had continued until expiry of the notice) was inconsistent with unequivocal acceptance of the implied offer of surrender.

2.21 In *Hackney LBC v Ampratum*,[27] a secure tenant left her family in occupation of her home when she was deported. During her six-year absence, the council consented to the assignment of her tenancy to someone else. A claim that the tenancy had been surrendered by operation of law prior to the assignment was rejected. The fact that the tenant was absent by reason of her deportation was not unequivocal conduct on her part demonstrating that she was treating her tenancy as at an end. Likewise, in *Sanctuary HA v Baker*,[28] the acts of a tenant in leaving a property, ceasing to pay the rent and handing in the keys to her landlord were not sufficient to amount to unequivocal evidence of surrender because those acts were all consistent with her belief that the tenancy had been assigned to an assignee (who had been a secure tenant) who was to collect the keys from the landlord. In *Newham LBC v Phillips*,[29] Miss Phillips had become a sole secure tenant by succession on the death of her mother. She later agreed that her sister's name could be added to the rent book provided that

25 (2000) 32 HLR 379, QBD.
26 (2000) 32 HLR 379, QBD at 383.
27 September 2003 *Legal Action* 25, Central London Civil Trial Centre, Bell J.
28 (1998) 30 HLR 809, CA.
29 (1998) 30 HLR 859, CA.

she remained the sole successor tenant. The council subsequently argued that this amounted to the surrender of the sole tenancy and grant of a joint tenancy. The Court of Appeal held that the express statement by Miss Phillips that she wished to remain the sole successor tenant was inconsistent with the assertion that there had been an unequivocal act of surrender of that tenancy by her.

2.22   Exceptionally, it may be possible to imply a surrender from circumstances in which the tenant abandons the premises and the landlord, finding them empty, simply secures them (see further para 2.68). A landlord relying on what seems to be such an implied offer of surrender by a secure tenant must, however, expect to exercise some caution, given that a secure tenancy is a valuable asset not likely to be given up lightly by some informal act by the tenant. For example, in *Zionmor v Islington LBC*,[30] the tenant – in an attempt to gain relief from harassment by his neighbours – posted on a communal noticeboard a notice that he had ceased to reside in his flat. He then went away for a while, leaving a friend in occupation. The council, on finding the flat apparently empty, changed the locks. It was held that: (1) the tenant's leaving a friend in possession was inconsistent with a suggestion that he wished to bring the tenancy to an end; and (2) changing the locks and boarding up were not unequivocal acts of acceptance of surrender: they might equally be explained by an intention to protect the council's stock during the tenant's temporary absence. On the facts, there had been no surrender.

2.23   Particular difficulties can arise in applying the concept of surrender by operation of law where the secure tenant's alleged unequivocal conduct is departure from the premises but where the tenant's spouse or former partner is left in occupation. The courts have historically been reluctant to permit surrender[31] to be used as a device to overcome 'home rights', that is, the rights of occupation of a spouse or civil partner (arising under the Family Law Act 1996 as amended by the Civil Partnership Act 2004[32]). If the sole tenant spouse or civil partner has purported to surrender, it may be argued by the non-tenant spouse or civil partner that there can have been no termination by operation of law because the tenant cannot give possession so long as he or she remains in residence. However, a surrender effective to terminate a sole secure tenancy was identified

30   (1997) 30 HLR 822, CA.
31   See *Hoggett v Hoggett* (1980) 39 P&CR 121, CA.
32   Schedule 9 para 1, amending Family Law Act 1996 s30.

in *Sanctuary Housing Association v Campbell*.[33] In that case the wife – a sole secure tenant – left the property, taking her children, and was rehoused. Her husband remained in possession. The Court of Appeal found that the tenancy had been determined by the wife's unequivocal conduct in writing to inform the landlords that she was leaving, that she would not be paying the rent and that she was returning the keys. She had done all she could, short of taking proceedings against her husband, to give back vacant possession. The landlords impliedly accepted that position by treating the tenancy as terminated and seeking possession against the husband. Similarly, in *Ealing FHA v McKenzie*,[34] a sole secure tenant left her home but her husband remained in occupation. The council agreed to rehouse her on condition that she would give up her tenancy. On being rehoused, she gave notice to quit her former home and the council treated the tenancy as ended by closing the rent account of the former home and opening a rent account for the new one. Although the notice to quit was invalid, the Court of Appeal found the conduct of landlord and tenant sufficient to amount to a surrender of the secure tenancy of the former home.

Notice to quit

2.24 In the case of a *fixed-term* secure tenancy, the tenant may bring the tenancy to an end by giving such notice as may be required by any *break clause* in the contractual tenancy agreement. Unless the tenancy agreement provides to the contrary, a fixed-term joint secure tenancy can only be ended within that term by a notice given by *all* the joint tenants. Once the term has expired, any periodic joint tenancy arising can be terminated by notice given by any one of the joint tenants (see para 2.30).

2.25 *Periodic* secure tenancies can be ended by the tenant's service on the landlord of a valid *notice to quit*. Such a notice operates unilaterally and brings to an end both security of tenure and the tenancy itself. To be effective, any such notice must be in writing and meet contractual,[35] common law and statutory requirements.[36] For example, the tenancy agreement may: specify a minimum amount of notice; stipulate that any notice to be given expires on a particular day or date;

---

33 [1999] 1 WLR 1279; (2000) 32 HLR 100, CA.
34 [2004] 36 HLR 313, CA.
35 *Community Housing Association v Hoy* December 1988 *Legal Action* 18.
36 The main statutory requirements are contained in PEA 1977 s5, reproduced at para 14.8.

or require service by delivery of the notice to particular premises. At common law, the minimum period of notice is a period of the tenancy and the notice must expire on the first or last day of such a period.[37] The primary statutory requirement, contained in PEA 1977 s5, is that at least 28 days' notice in writing must be given.

2.26   A valid notice to quit will end the tenancy on expiry. An otherwise invalid notice can also operate to determine the tenancy on expiry if the parties agree to waive the invalidity. For example, in *Hackney LBC v Snowden*,[38] the secure tenant gave a notice to quit expressed to take effect only three days later. The council acted on the notice, rehoused the former tenant, sought no further rent for the property and voided the rent account. The Court of Appeal held that the tenancy had terminated on expiry of the notice because the council had agreed to waive non-compliance with the requirements of PEA 1977 s5. However, in *Hounslow LBC v Pilling*,[39] the invalid notice to quit had been given by a joint secure tenant. The Court of Appeal held that such a notice could determine the tenancy only if both the landlord and the other joint tenant(s) were prepared to waive the invalidity. Once the landlord has accepted and acted upon the invalid notice to quit, and thus treated the tenancy as at an end, it will be too late for the tenant to assert the invalidity in support of an argument that the tenancy is continuing.[40]

2.27   A *sole* tenant is free to end his or her tenancy by notice to quit irrespective of the concerns or interests of other occupiers, including any family members. This may cause particular difficulties if the property has been the matrimonial home, the non-tenant spouse or civil partner remains in occupation, and a consequence of the termination is to render that person a trespasser in what had been their home. The courts have historically been reluctant to uphold notices[41] which are being used as devices to overcome 'home rights', that is, the rights of occupation of a spouse or civil partner (arising under the Family Law Act 1996 as amended by the Civil Partnership Act 2004[42]) in this way, but most modern statutory schemes enabling the family courts to regulate the disposal, occupation or use of the family home require that a tenancy is still extant when the jurisdiction comes to be exercised.

37   *Crate v Miller* [1947] KB 946; [1947] 2 All ER 45, CA.
38   (2001) 33 HLR 554; [2001] L&TR 60, CA.
39   [1993] 1 WLR 1242; (1993) 25 HLR 305, CA.
40   *Lewisham LBC v Lasisi-Agiri* [2003] EWHC 2392 (Ch); [2003] 45 EGCS 175.
41   See *Griffiths v Renfree* (1989) 21 HLR 338; [1989] 2 EGLR 46, CA.
42   Schedule 9 para 1, amending Family Law Act 1996 s30.

2.28   If a sole secure tenant has given notice to quit in these circumstances, the non-tenant spouse or civil partner may be able to show that there is still a tenancy by asserting the invalidity of the notice, for example, if it can be shown that the notice failed to comply with the contractual, common law or statutory requirements (see para 2.25 above). However, in such a case the landlord could waive a deficiency in the notice and thus restore its validity.[43]

2.29   If the notice given by a sole secure tenant is in valid form and is effective to end the tenancy, the non-tenant spouse or civil partner is not able to apply in family proceedings for the setting aside of a disposal of the home in that way.[44] The giving of a notice to quit is not a 'disposal' for these purposes.[45] Everything will therefore turn on the ability of the non-tenant to restrain the sole secure tenant from actually giving notice to quit (see para 2.35 below).

2.30   The position is broadly the same if there is a *joint tenancy*. If one joint tenant to a *periodic* secure tenancy gives a valid notice to quit to the landlord, the whole tenancy determines on its expiry even if the effect will be to leave the other joint tenant as a trespasser in the former home.[46] It has been suggested that this rule (sometimes referred to as the rule in *Monk*) may fall foul of the terms of the Human Rights Act 1998 Sch 1 which provide for respect for a home (article 8) and the prevention of arbitrary interference with property rights (article 1 of Protocol 1).[47] In *Dixon v Wandsworth LBC*,[48] one of two joint secure tenants gave a valid notice to quit and left. The remaining tenant asserted that the rule in *Monk* was incompatible with article 8. The judge said:

> I am satisfied, for the reasons expounded by Lord Bridge in *Monk*, which appear to have been accepted by all in *Qazi, Kay* and *Doherty* as being compatible with article 8, that the domestic law strikes a proper and unassailable balance between the rights of joint tenants and their landlords and that it is not arguable that the rule in *Monk* is incompatible with article 8. (at para [58])

---

43 *Hackney LBC v Snowden* (2001) 33 HLR 49; [2001] L&TR 60, CA.

44 Matrimonial Causes Act 1973 s37 and see, generally, chapter 35.

45 *Newlon Housing Trust v Al-Sulaimen* [1999] 1 AC 313; (1998) 30 HLR 1132, HL.

46 *Hammersmith & Fulham LBC v Monk* [1992] 1 AC 478; (1992) 24 HLR 207, HL, approving *Greenwich LBC v McGrady* (1982) 6 HLR 36; 81 LGR 288, CA.

47 As to human rights generally, see chapter 26. On the notice to quit by one joint tenant aspect, see Ian Loveland, 'After Qazi: 1 – Sole tenant termination of joint tenancies and article 8 ECHR' [2005] 69 Conv 123 and 'Beating the rule in *Hammersmth & Fulham v Monk*' September 2008 *Legal Action* 22.

48 [2009] EWHC 27 (Admin); [2009] L&TR 28.

Mr Dixon failed to secure permission to appeal to the Court of Appeal.[49]

2.31   In *R (Husband) v Solihull MBC*,[50] permission to seek judicial review was sought in order to contend that the rule in *Monk* was inconsistent with the European Convention on Human Rights. Refusing that application, the judge said (at [8]):

> ... the submissions based on *Monk* have been determined in other cases, including the decision of the House of Lords in *Doherty v Birmingham CC* [2008] UKHL 57 and the decision of HHJ Bidder QC in *Wandsworth LBC v Dixon* [2009] EWHC 27 (Admin). In my judgment, it is not, in the state of English law now, arguable that the unqualified right to possession by a landlord is incompatible with Article 8; or indeed, in the light of *Sheffield CC v Smart* [2002] HLR 34, with Article 1 Protocol 1 of the Convention.

2.32   Attempts to establish that the rule in *Monk* can operate only where one joint tenant has at least *consulted* the other(s) before giving notice have also failed.[51] At present, the law remains that one of the joint secure tenants can give notice to quit entirely unilaterally with the effect that, if the notice is valid, the whole tenancy ends. Indeed, a joint tenant is free to give such a notice to quit even if he or she is the subject of an order of the court not to 'exclude' the other tenant(s).[52]

2.33   One joint tenant may be able to demonstrate that the tenancy subsists if the notice given by another joint tenant was invalid due to failure to comply with contractual, common law or statutory requirements (see para 2.25): for example, the notice is ineffective if given in respect of a weekly tenancy for a shorter period than the four weeks prescribed by PEA 1977 s5[53] or if it fails to provide for expiry at the end of a period of a periodic tenancy.[54]

---

49 *Dixon v Wandsworth LBC* [2009] EWCA Civ 821.

50 [2009] EWHC 3673 (Admin). A renewed application for permission was refused by the Court of Appeal: [2010] EWCA Civ 684. See too, the subsequent decisions to the same effect in *Poplar HARCA v Howe* [2010] EWHC 1745 (QB) and *Harrow LBC v Wilson* [2010] EWHC 1574 (QB).

51 See *Crawley BC v Ure* [1996] QB 13; (1995) 27 HLR 524, CA and *Notting Hill Housing Trust v Brackley* [2001] EWCA Civ 601; [2002] HLR 10.

52 *Harrow LBC v Johnstone* [1997] 1 WLR 459; (1997) 29 HLR 475, HL.

53 *Hounslow LBC v Pilling* [1993] 1 WLR 1242; [1994] 1 All ER 432, CA (see para 2.26), and see *Fletcher v Brent LBC* [2006] EWCA Civ 960; [2007] HLR 12, in which a joint secure tenant gave a notice expressed to take effect on that day or 'on the first Monday after that date being at least 4 clear weeks after service'.

54 *Camden LBC v Lahouasnia* March 1998 *Legal Action* 12, Central London County Court (the notice given by one joint tenant and held to be invalid simply said 'I hereby give notice of 28 days that I am relinquishing my tenancy').

2.34 But again, the service of a valid notice by a joint secure tenant causes particular difficulty in the context of relationship breakdown where the effect is to leave family members as trespassers in the former family home. If the notice is valid, the other joint tenant, even if a spouse or civil partner, is not able to apply in family law proceedings for the setting aside of disposal of the home in this way.[55] This is again because the giving of a notice is not a 'disposal' of family assets.[56]

2.35 The occupier who believes that a notice to quit may be about to be given by his or her (former) partner would be best advised to make a 'without notice' application for an injunction to restrain the giving of such notice (see chapter 35). It has been suggested that such an injunction may be granted under the court's inherent jurisdiction in matrimonial matters or in proceedings brought under the Matrimonial Causes Act 1973 s37[57] (or the Children Act 1989 Sch 1 where there are children of the family).[58] Alternatively and additionally, it may be possible to apply for a transfer of the tenancy from sole to joint names and to seek an injunction in those proceedings.[59] See further chapter 35.

2.36 Once the notice to quit validly given by a sole (or a joint) secure tenant has expired, the former landlord can physically retake possession if the premises are empty. Otherwise, straightforward possession proceedings can be taken against anyone left in occupation (such as any partner or former joint tenant). They will be trespassers at common law and will have no defence to the possession claim unless exceptionally it may be seriously arguable that the social housing provider has acted unlawfully in bringing the possession proceedings (see chapter 25) or that the making of a possession order would amount to a breach of the defendant's Convention rights (see chapter 26) or that a new tenancy has been granted.

Tenant dies[60]

2.37 If one *joint secure tenant* dies, and the other remains in occupation, the tenancy devolves by survivorship and the last remaining joint tenant becomes a sole secure tenant by operation of law (albeit one

---

55 Matrimonial Causes Act 1973 s37.
56 *Newlon Housing Trust v Al-Sulaimen* [1999] 1 AC 313; (1998) 30 HLR 1132, HL.
57 *Bater v Greenwich LBC* (2000) 32 HLR 127, CA.
58 *Re F (minors)* [1994] 1 WLR 370; (1993) 26 HLR 354, CA.
59 Family Law Act 1996 s53 and Sch 7.
60 See also chapter 20.

treated as a 'successor' so that there can be no further succession on his or her own death).[61]

2.38   If a *sole secure tenant* (or the last remaining joint tenant) dies, neither the tenancy itself nor security of tenure automatically ends.[62] If there is a person in occupation entitled to succeed the tenant – and the tenant was not him or herself a 'successor'[63] – the secure tenancy automatically vests in the successor: HA 1985 s89(2).

2.39   In summary, those entitled to succeed are: (1) the spouse or civil partner[64] of the tenant; or (2) another member of the tenant's family. In both cases the successor must have been occupying the dwelling as his or her only or principal[65] home at the time of the tenant's death. In the case of family members other than spouses or civil partners, the potential successor must additionally have lived with the tenant throughout the 12-month period ending with the tenant's death.[66] The full 12 months need not have been spent in the property to which succession is claimed.[67] But the successor must have been residing with the tenant (as opposed to simply visiting or acting as carer for the tenant while maintaining a home elsewhere) throughout the 12 months.[68] The situation where there is more than one potential successor is dealt with by HA 1985 s89(2).[69]

2.40   The phrase 'member of the family' is defined by HA 1985 s113 as amended by the Civil Partnership Act 2004 Sch 8 para 27:

(1) A person is a member of another's family within the meaning of this Part if –
    (a) he is the spouse or civil partner of that person, or he and that person live together as husband and wife or as if they were civil partners, or
    (b) he is that person's parent, grandparent, child, grandchild, brother, sister, uncle, aunt, nephew or niece.

---

61 HA 1985 s88(1)(b).
62 Unless the tenancy agreement expressly provides otherwise: *Youngmin v Heath* [1974] 1 WLR 135; [1974] 1 All ER 461, CA.
63 Defined in HA 1985 s88.
64 HA 1985 s87(a) as amended by Civil Partnership Act 2004 Sch 8 para 20.
65 *Peabody Donation Fund Governors v Grant* (1982) 6 HLR 41; (1982) 264 EG 925, CA.
66 HA 1985 s87(b); see *Camden LBC v Goldenberg* (1996) 28 HLR 727, CA and *Wandsworth LBC v Morgan* January 2000 *Legal Action* 25, CA.
67 *Waltham Forest LBC v Thomas* [1992] 2 AC 198; (1992) 24 HLR 622, HL.
68 *Freeman v Islington LBC* [2009] EWCA Civ 536; [2010] HLR 6.
69 Succession by more than one person (eg, by two daughters of the deceased) is not possible: *Newham LBC v Phillips* (1998) 96 LGR 788; (1997) 30 HLR 859, CA.

(2) For the purpose of subsection (1)(b) –

    (a) a relationship by marriage or civil partnership shall be treated as a relationship by blood,

    (b) a relationship of the half-blood shall be treated as a relationship of the whole blood,

    (c) the stepchild of a person shall be treated as his child, and

    (d) an illegitimate child shall be treated as the legitimate child of his mother and reputed father.

2.41   The list in section 113 exhaustively defines the family members who may succeed.[70] It will be seen that HA 1985 s113(1)(a) applies to a cohabitant of the deceased who has lived with the deceased in a co-habiting relationship, whether heterosexual or same sex, for at least 12 months.[71] Cousins[72] or foster children[73] are not in the prescribed list, but a minor who fulfils the statutory conditions can succeed to a tenancy in equity.[74]

2.42   Where there is no person entitled to succeed, the tenancy ceases to be a secure tenancy either (a) when it is vested or otherwise disposed of in the course of the administration of the tenant's estate (unless the vesting or other disposal is in pursuance of one of a prescribed list of family court orders) or (b) when it is known that when the tenancy is so vested or disposed of it will not be in pursuance of such an order.[75] The newly non-secure tenancy itself vests in the estate of the deceased. Thereafter it will be disposed of in the administration of the estate, usually by being surrendered to the landlord by the executors or administrator.[76] If the deceased tenant did not leave a will, the tenancy vests in the Public Trustee until such time as letters of administration are taken out by the next of kin: see chapter 20.[77] However, special provision is made to deal with the situation which arises if a court exercising family law jurisdiction has earlier directed what is to happen to the tenancy in the event of the tenant's death.[78]

2.43   Following the death of a secure tenant, a dispute may arise between the landlord and an occupier about whether the occupier is

---

70 *Michalak v Wandsworth LBC* [2002] EWCA Civ 282; [2003] 1 WLR 617.

71 *Westminster City Council v Peart* (1992) 24 HLR 389, CA.

72 *Brent LBC v Fofana* September 1999 *Legal Action* 28, CA.

73 *Sheffield CC v Wall* [2006] EWCA Civ 495; May 2006 *Legal Action* 31.

74 *Kingston upon Thames RLBC v Prince* [1999] LGR 333; (1999) 31 HLR 794, CA and *Newham LBC v Ria* [2004] EWCA Civ 41; and see para 1.24 above.

75 HA 1985 s89(3).

76 See M Lee, 'The periodic tenancy and death of a tenant' (1983) 80 LS Gaz 883.

77 Law of Property (Miscellaneous Provisions) Act 1994 s14.

78 HA 1985 s89(3), as substituted by HA 1996 Sch 18 para 10 and as amended by Civil Partnership Act 2004 Sch 8 and Sch 30.

entitled to succeed to the tenancy. In such cases, if the landlord is satisfied that there has been no statutory succession, it may determine the tenancy by notice to quit (by service of such notice on the executor or administrator or the Public Trustee[79]) and start ordinary possession proceedings against the occupier. (It would be unusual for the landlord to serve a notice seeking possession while asserting that the occupier has not become the secure tenant but such a notice might be expressed to be served without prejudice to the notice to quit.) Non-statutory guidance is available to social landlords on the process of recovering possession from those considered to be 'unauthorised successors'.[80] The occupier may then defend the claim on the basis that he or she is a secure tenant having properly 'succeeded' the deceased tenant, in which case an adjournment of what appeared to be straightforward possession proceedings may be necessary.[81] The burden of proof is on the occupier to establish the right to succeed, including the requirement, if he or she is claiming succession as a family member, that he or she lived with the deceased tenant throughout the 12-month period before the latter's death.[82] The occupier claiming to have succeeded would be well advised to make arrangements to put aside sums equivalent to the rent or to make a claim for housing benefit because, if he or she is successful in establishing succession, he or she will be liable to pay the rent from the moment of death.

2.44   If the landlord admits that a succession has taken place but claims that the successor is under-occupying, see para 3.190.

2.45   More unusually, those in occupation following the death of a tenant may defend on the basis that since the death of the tenant they have been accepted as tenants in their own right. However, it has been held that the making and acceptance of payments while a disputed issue of succession is resolved are insufficient on their own to show an intention on the landlord's part to create a tenancy.[83] If the landlord is asserting that the occupier is a trespasser (often described

---

79 See the Public Trustee (Notices Affecting Land) (Title on Death) Regulations 1995 SI No 1330. As to service of such notice, see *Practice Direction (Probate: Notice to Quit)* [1995] 1 WLR 1120.

80 *Tackling unlawful subletting and occupancy: Good practice guidance for social landlords* (Communities and local Government, November 2009), pp69–72.

81 *Camden LBC v Hall* March 1998 *Legal Action* 11, CA.

82 *Peabody Donation Fund Governors v Grant* (1982) 6 HLR 41; (1982) 264 EG 925, CA.

83 See *Hammersmith and Fulham LBC v Jastrzebska* May 2001 *Legal Action* 22, ChD and *Hammersmith & Fulham LBC v Jastrzebski* [2001] EWCA Civ 431.

as an 'unauthorised occupier') it cannot simply rush into proceedings on the basis that it has a right to possession against the alleged trespasser (see chapter 29). The occupier who is able to show, in such proceedings, that the deceased tenant's tenancy has not been properly determined (for example, by service of notice on the executor/administrator or the Public Trustee[84]) has a complete defence to the action.[85] Alternatively, it may be possible to defend the claim if he or she can show that it is seriously arguable that the decision to take possession proceedings was reached in breach of public law principles (see chapter 25) or of human rights (see chapter 26).

2.46   Once the landlord has served an effective notice to quit on the person responsible for the deceased tenant's estate it may, if there is no occupier, simply take possession.

Absentee tenant

2.47   A secure tenant's absence from the property, however lengthy, does not of itself bring the *tenancy* to an end. However, the *security of tenure* of the secure tenant may be placed in jeopardy by a long-term absence.

2.48   That is because, as already mentioned above (para 1.14), a secure tenancy remains secure only for so long as the tenant (or one of the joint tenants) 'occupies the dwelling-house as his only or principal home'.[86] A very prolonged absence may indicate that the tenant no longer occupies the property as a home and thus the security of tenure may lapse. A landlord may then seize the opportunity of such a lapse by serving a notice to quit to bring to an end the then insecure tenancy. For the requirements of a valid notice to quit, see paras 14.6–14.22. (The landlord may face considerable difficulties in serving the true tenant with notice to quit – see para 2.74.) Even a notice to quit expressed to expire only one day short of the necessary minimum period will be invalid and insufficient to end a non-secure tenancy.[87]

2.49   There are several possible variations on the scenario of the absentee tenant.

---

84 See the Public Trustee (Notices Affecting Land) (Title on Death) Regulations 1995 SI No 1330. As to service of such notice, see *Practice Direction (Probate: Notice to Quit)* [1995] 1 WLR 1120.

85 *Wirral BC v Smith and Cooper* (1982) 4 HLR 81; (1982) 43 P&CR 312, CA.

86 HA 1985 s81.

87 *Southwark LBC v Jackson* April 2009 *Legal Action* 18, Lambeth County Court.

The tenant has 'assigned' the tenancy to a new tenant and left

2.50   For discussion of this variation see para 2.76.

The tenant has sublet, or otherwise parted with possession of, the whole property to others

2.51   Here the security of tenure is brought to an end not only by the tenant's own failure to occupy but also by the specific provision that subletting or parting with possession of the whole of the property let to the secure tenant causes loss of security.[88] This loss of security cannot be repaired by the tenant ousting the subtenants and returning to the property because HA 1985 s93(2) provides that the tenancy cannot again become a secure tenancy.[89] Security may even be lost inadvertently by the unintentional creation of what is later held to be a true subtenancy.[90]

2.52   Whether there has been a subletting of the whole will be a matter for determination by a court on the evidence. For example, in one case where there was evidence that all the rooms in a property were occupied by persons other than the tenant or her family and most doors had separate locks, the court was entitled to conclude that there had been an unlawful subletting of the whole of the premises.[91] In another, a tenant's advertisement of their home to let had provided powerful evidence of subletting.[92] In some cases the judge will need to resolve a conflict of evidence between the tenant and the occupier as to whether there was a true subletting or a simple temporary licence.[93] It seems particularly common for secure tenancies to be sublet in the run-up to a right to buy purchase.[94]

2.53   If there has been a true subletting of the whole, then security is plainly lost.[95] But it does not necessarily follow that, just because as a matter of fact the tenant is absent and others are in occupation,

---

88   HA 1985 s93(2).
89   *Merton LBC v Salama* June 1989 *Legal Action* 25, CA.
90   *Brent LBC v Cronin* (1998) 30 HLR 43, CA.
91   *Lambeth LBC v Vandra* [2005] EWCA Civ 1801; [2006] HLR 19.
92   *Luton BC v Menni* [2006] EWCA Civ 1850.
93   *Brent LBC v Smart (Mark)* [2005] EWCA Civ 434.
94   As in *Sutton LBC v Swann* (1985) 18 HLR 140, CA; *Muir Group Housing Association Ltd v Thornley* (1993) 25 HLR 89, CA; *Jennings v Epping Forest DC* (1993) 25 HLR 241 and *Lewisham LBC v Malcolm* [2008] UKHL 43; [2008] 1 AC 1399.
95   *Muir Group Housing Association Ltd v Thornley* (1993) 25 HLR 89, CA.

security has been lost by 'parting with possession'.[96] It may be that those in occupation are mere 'house-sitters' or other licensees simply taking care of the premises pending the return of the tenant and there has been no parting with possession at all.[97]

2.54 As already noted, even subletting the whole does not bring the tenancy to an end – only security of tenure is lost. If the landlord considers that there has been a parting with possession or subletting of the whole it may serve an ordinary notice to quit on the true tenant to determine that tenancy[98] and, once that has expired, start possession proceedings to recover possession against both the true tenant and the actual occupiers. (The landlord may face considerable difficulties in serving the true tenant with notice to quit – see para 2.74.) If there is simply a suspicion that the tenant may have sublet, a letter before action seeking information about the true position may protect the landlord in costs if it is later unsuccessful in establishing full subletting.[99]

2.55 On 30 November 2009, the Minister for Housing in England launched a major initiative to encourage social landlords to take firmer action against tenants believed to be subletting and to recover those properties for allocation to families in housing need.[100] It has been estimated that as many as 50,000 social housing properties may be in use by unauthorised occupiers.[101] To assist in the task of recovering possession of those properties, detailed but non-statutory guidance has been drafted by the Chartered Institute of Housing: *Tackling unlawful subletting and occupancy: Good practice guidance for social landlords*.[102] The position of any subtenants in properties let by secure tenants is considered at para 5.2.

---

96 *Hussey v Camden LBC* (1995) 27 HLR 5, CA. For a modern restatement of the law on breach of an obligation not to 'part with possession', see *Clarence House Ltd v National Westminster Bank plc* [2009] EWCA Civ 1311; [2010] 1 WLR 1230.

97 *Basildon DC v Persson* September 1995 *Legal Action* 13 and *Islington LBC v LaMarque* September 1991 *Legal Action* 14.

98 Some landlords react to such situations by serving a notice seeking possession as well as ordinary notice to quit, each expressed to be without prejudice to the other.

99 *Brent LBC v Aniedobe* January 2000 *Legal Action* 25, CA.

100 For an outline of the Social Housing Fraud initiative see www.communities. gov.uk/housing/housingmanagementcare/socialhousingfraud/.

101 *Protecting the public purse: Local government fighting fraud*, Audit Commission, September 2009, para 18.

102 Communities and Local Government, November 2009, available at www. communities.gov.uk/publications/housing/housingfraudguidance.

The tenant is absent for a long period (but intends to return)

2.56   Most tenants are temporarily away from their homes from time to time – on holiday, receiving medical treatment, working away from home, and such like. Some tenants may be absent for long periods, perhaps many years, through working abroad, travelling, visiting relatives overseas, or otherwise. In such cases, furniture and other belongings are usually left in the property and, in the case of prolonged absence, a informal 'caretaker' (usually a friend or relative) may have been let into occupation to take care of the property and to ensure that the rent is paid.

2.57   However, long absences may give rise to the suggestion that security of tenure has been lost because the secure tenant is no longer occupying the property in question as his or her principal home and thus satisfying the 'tenant condition' in HA 1985 s81 (see para 1.14).

2.58   The true questions in a case where there has been a significant period of absence are: (1) whether the absence is temporary, in the sense that the tenant intends to return, and (2) whether that intention is manifest from the physical signs of continued occupation. The Court of Appeal has held that the correct approach in secure tenancy cases where the tenant has been absent is to consider all the surrounding circumstances to determine whether those conditions are fulfilled. In *Crawley BC v Sawyer*,[103] a tenant was away from his home for over a year. The gas and electricity were disconnected. The tenant had moved in with his girlfriend and they intended to buy a property together. The council served a notice to quit. The couple's relationship broke down and the tenant moved back to his home. The county court judge held that the council property had throughout remained his principal home and the tenant had always intended to return to it. The Court of Appeal did not interfere with that finding.

2.59   In contrast, in *Jennings v Epping Forest DC*,[104] the tenants, an elderly couple in failing health, left their council home and took a flat near to their daughter's home. Once there, the husband's health deteriorated and he was admitted to a residential care home. His wife stayed in the new flat to be near him. The trial judge (the point not being in issue in the appeal) had no difficulty in finding that security of tenure had been lost. There was no prospect of, or intention to, return to the original home.

103 (1988) 20 HLR 98; (1988) 86 LGR 629, CA.
104 (1993) 25 HLR 241, CA.

2.60 In *Lewisham LBC v Robinson*,[105] the secure tenant was not found at home on repeated visits by housing staff. On each occasion the property was found to be occupied by persons who said that they paid rent to Mr Robinson who lived elsewhere. Upholding an appeal by the council against a refusal to grant possession, the appeal court said:

> The judge was ... required to consider whether, given that he may have continued to have occupation of No 50, that occupation was either as his main or as his principal home. The mere fact, as the judge found, that Mr Robinson kept keys to the property, that he had clothing in the property and that he had never given up a bedroom of his own in the property does not answer that enquiry.

2.61 The overwhelming evidence of long-term residence by other occupiers who had claimed to be tenants, the absence of the secure tenant and his residence elsewhere and the judge's finding that the secure tenant was a dishonest and unbelievable witness, should have led the judge to find that he was no longer occupying as his only or principal home. The appeal was allowed.

2.62 The most common situations of long-term absence arise from: tenants going abroad for indeterminate periods to visit relatives or to travel; tenants serving terms of imprisonment; tenants receiving long-term hospital treatment;[106] and tenants moving into residential care or nursing homes.[107]

2.63 The case of the secure tenant who becomes a *prisoner* is relatively straightforward because he or she can be promptly located, will have left belongings at the property and usually asserts an intention to return even when serving a lengthy term.[108] The case of a very elderly or mentally ill tenant in a caring institution is more problematic, as it can be difficult to establish that he or she has both the intention and the prospect of returning to resume occupation (but see cases in the Rent Act context, discussed at para 16.7). There may well be difficulties with 'fleeting changes of mind' in such cases, which makes a focus on the real or 'enduring' intention of the tenant all the more important.[109]

---

105 [2003] EWHC 2630 (Ch).
106 See *McLoughlin's Curator Bonis v Motherwell DC* 1994 SLT (Lands Tr) 31.
107 *Hammersmith and Fulham LBC v Clarke* (2001) 33 HLR 77, CA and *Braintree DC v Vincent* [2004] EWCA Civ 415, CA.
108 See *Notting Hill Housing Trust v Etoria* April 1989 *Legal Action* 22; *Oldham MBC v Walker* January 1999 *Legal Action* 26 and *Amoah v Barking and Dagenham LBC* (2001) 81 P&CR D12; March 2001 *Legal Action* 28, ChD.
109 *Hammersmith and Fulham LBC v Clarke* (2001) 33 HLR 77, CA and see *McLoughlin's Curator Bonis v Motherwell DC* 1994 SLT (Lands Tr) 31.

2.64   In the tenant's absence, the landlord may find either an apparently empty property or a 'caretaker' in occupation. A landlord not satisfied that the secure tenant remains in occupation of the property as his or her principal home and wishing to recover possession may serve an ordinary notice to quit on the absentee tenant (on the basis that security has lapsed) and physically recover possession – if there is no one in occupation – or start possession proceedings. (The landlord may face considerable difficulties in serving the true tenant with notice to quit – see para 2.74.) A tenant who can show that, notwithstanding prolonged 'temporary' absence, he or she continues to occupy the property as his or her principal home, retains security of tenure and may successfully defend the action or secure reinstatement.

2.65   For the position of a tenant clearly having two homes, see para 2.73.

The tenant has 'disappeared'

2.66   It is not unusual, particularly in serious rent arrears cases, for the landlord to find that the tenant has abandoned the premises, leaving them vacant or with 'unauthorised' occupiers in possession. The landlord will want to regularise the position quickly and to re-let.

2.67   However, if the landlord commences proceedings to recover possession against the 'trespassers' (see chapter 29) too hastily, without first determining the tenancy at common law, the occupiers will have a complete defence to the action on the basis that the landlord does not have an immediate right to possession.[110] (The landlord may face considerable difficulties in serving the true tenant with notice to quit – see para 2.74.)

2.68   In certain limited circumstances, it may be possible for the landlord to show that the tenant has, by his or her action, surrendered the tenancy, thus entitling the landlord to recover possession (see para 2.18). In order for this to be established the court must be satisfied that, at the very least, 'a tenant had left owing a very substantial sum of money and had been absent for a substantial time'.[111] The burden of proof is on the landlord.

2.69   The courts have varied in their approach as to whether a simple abandonment is sufficient, on the particular facts, to amount to

---

110   *Preston BC v Fairclough* (1982) 8 HLR 70, CA and *Braintree DC v Vincent* [2004] EWCA Civ 415; [2004] All ER (D) 167 (Mar).

111   *Preston BC v Fairclough* (1982) 8 HLR 70, CA, per Griffiths LJ at 73. See too, *R v Croydon LBC ex p Toth* (1988) 20 HLR 576, CA.

an offer by the tenant to surrender the secure (or newly insecure) tenancy. In *Preston BC v Fairclough*[112] the secure tenants had left another family in occupation but there was no evidence of the tenants' own date of departure or the amount of rent in arrears, if any. The court held that surrender was not established. In *R v Croydon LBC ex p Toth*,[113] the premises had been left empty for several weeks, all furniture had been removed and £488 rent was outstanding. It was held that termination by surrender was made out when the landlord simply took possession of the empty flat.

2.70 If the landlord deals with a case of 'abandonment' by serving notice to quit, it may recover possession of the vacant property on expiry or commence summary proceedings for possession against any occupiers. The difficulties of serving notice on the absentee tenant are discussed at para 2.74.

The tenant has left a non-tenant spouse/civil partner/cohabitant in occupation

2.71 During a tenant's temporary absence or following a permanent departure, the presence of a spouse or registered civil partner in the property makes good the tenant's failure to occupy and is treated as occupation by him or her (see para 1.16).[114] That situation continues for so long as the parties are married or their civil partnership subsists and lasts up to decree absolute or dissolution order.

2.72 Other cohabitants – whether heterosexual or same sex – may also be able to claim that their partner's tenancy remains secure. Depending on the specific facts, they may argue that their occupation is indicative of the tenant's intention to return and thereby the security of the absent tenant's tenancy is preserved (see para 2.56). Otherwise, former spouses and cohabitants can apply under the Family Law Act 1996 for court orders permitting them to occupy. Any such order works as a 'deemed' occupation by the departed tenant (see, generally, chapter 35).[115]

---

112 (1982) 8 HLR 70, CA.
113 (1988) 20 HLR 576, CA.
114 Matrimonial Homes Act 1983 s1(6), as amended by Housing (Consequential Provisions) Act 1985 Sch 2 para 56(2), and Family Law Act 1996 s30(4)(b), as amended by Civil Partnership Act 2004 Sch 9 para 1.
115 Family Law Act 1996 ss35(13)(a) and 36(13)(a), as amended by Civil Partnership Act 2004 Sch 9 para 6, and *Gay v Enfield and Sheeran* [2000] 1 WLR 673; (1999) 31 HLR 1126, CA.

The tenant has two homes

2.73   The tenant loses the benefit of secure status in a dwelling if it is neither his nor her *only* or *principal* home.[116] It is a question of fact, in relation to secure tenants with two homes, which of them is the principal home.[117] In *Sutton LBC v Swann*,[118] the tenant of a council flat purchased another home. At the other home, he registered as a residential customer with the telephone company, gave that address to his bank and mortgage lenders, gave that address as his residence to the local police and had the address on his firearms certificate changed to that address. The trial judge's finding that his council flat had ceased to be his 'principal' home was not disturbed by the Court of Appeal. The practical application of the tenant condition in HA 1985 s81 to a two-home tenant is well demonstrated by a series of noted first-instance decisions.[119]

Notice to the absent tenant

2.74   If the secure tenancy has lost 'secure' status as a result of the failure to fulfil the tenant condition (see para 1.14) in any of the circumstances described above, the landlord may end the non-secure tenancy by service of a valid notice to quit.

2.75   At common law, such a notice is proved to have been served only if the landlord can show actual personal delivery (to the tenant, his wife or 'servant') or that the notice has otherwise actually come to the attention of the tenant. Plainly, this can prove difficult if the whereabouts of the absent tenant are unknown. If the tenancy agreement expressly makes provision for service of notice to quit by simple delivery to the premises or in some other way, then such notice may be effectively given in that way.[120] If there is no such provision in the agreement, there is at present no alternative statutory basis for even a local authority landlord to serve such a notice to quit other

---

116   HA 1985 s81.

117   See Thompson, 'The two-home tenant' (1986) 83 LS Gaz 2073 and the case-law on the two-home tenant under the Rent Acts discussed at para 16.14.

118   (1985) 18 HLR 140, CA.

119   *Camden LBC v Coombs* March 1988 *Legal Action* 17; *Marsh v Lewisham LBC* December 1989 *Legal Action* 14; *Miller v Falkirk DC* 1990 SLT (Lands Tr) 111; *Roxburgh DC v Collins* 1991 SLT (Sh Ct) 49 and (1991) 8 GWD 483; *Lambeth LBC v Gent* July 2001 *Legal Action* 32 and *Johnson v Dundee CC* (2006) Hous LR 68, Lands Tribunal.

120   *Wandsworth LBC v Atwell* (1995) 27 HLR 536, CA and *Lambeth LBC v Davies* March 1998 *Legal Action* 11.

than in one of the ways sufficient at common law (see also paras 4.40–4.44).[121]

Tenant assigns

2.76 Security of tenure may be threatened if a secure tenant seeks to transfer the whole tenancy to a third party. As seen above (at para 2.51), *subletting* of the whole property brings to an end the security of tenure of the secure tenant (although not the tenancy itself).[122] The same provision operates to deprive the tenancy of secure status if the tenant 'parts with possession' otherwise than by subletting. However, if the tenancy is effectively transferred by an *assignment* there is no subletting and no parting with possession.[123]

2.77 Housing Act 1985 s91 provides that, except in prescribed cases, a secure tenancy is not capable of assignment *at all*. The three prescribed cases are:

- assignment by way of mutual exchange (in these circumstances the strict provisions of HA 1985 s92 and Sch 3 must be complied with);
- assignment pursuant to a property transfer order made under the Matrimonial Causes Act 1973 s24, the Matrimonial and Family Proceedings Act 1984 s17, the Civil Partnership Act 2004 Sch 5 Part 2 or Sch 7 or the Children Act 1989 Sch 1;
- assignment to a person who would have been qualified to succeed to the tenancy if the tenant had died immediately before the assignment (for the persons who may succeed a secure tenant, see para 2.39).

2.78 The prohibition is one of substance rather than form. Thus, where two joint secure tenants purport, by deed of release, to transfer the tenancy from joint names into the sole name of one of them, that will be an attempted assignment and will fail.[124]

2.79 If an assignment takes place in one of the three prescribed circumstances, the assignee receives the full secure tenancy (notwithstanding any prohibition on assignment in the tenancy agreement

---

121 *Enfield LBC v Devonish and Sutton* (1997) 29 HLR 691; (1996) *Times* 12 December, CA.

122 HA 1985 s93(2).

123 *Clarence House Ltd v National Westminster Bank plc* [2009] EWCA Civ 1311; [2010] 1 WLR 1230.

124 *Burton v Camden LBC* [2000] 2 AC 399; (2000) 32 HLR 625, HL.

itself).[125] The landlord can then obtain possession only by serving a notice seeking possession (see above) on the new secure tenant and commencing possession proceedings on one of the grounds applicable to a secure tenant. In *Peabody Donation Fund Governors v Higgins*, the tenant assigned the tenancy to his daughter, who was his potential successor. The landlord claimed possession on the basis that the assignment was in breach of a specific clause in its tenancy agreement which prohibited assignment without the landlord's consent. While accepting that the secure tenancy had been transferred to the assignee, the Court of Appeal left open whether the assignment would give rise to a ground for possession on the basis of a breach of obligation of the tenancy.[126]

2.80   However, in the above circumstances, there is considerable doubt whether it is open to a landlord to grant a secure tenancy subject to a covenant against entering into any one of the three classes of statutorily permitted assignment, since such a covenant arguably offends the Unfair Terms in Consumer Contracts Regulations 1999.[127] In any event, it is unlikely that the court would consider it reasonable to enforce a tenancy condition which appears to be at variance with the statutory purpose.

2.81   If the assignment is not made within the permitted three classes or the purported assignment is ineffective (for example, because no deed of assignment was used[128]), the tenancy is not transferred.

2.82   If the true tenant has left and the assignment was ineffective, the assignee will be without any right to occupy. He or she will be able to remain only until the landlord has taken the appropriate steps to recover possession. The landlord must first determine properly the tenancy of the original tenant (usually by service of a valid notice to quit, since the tenancy will no longer be secure) and then take proceedings for possession against the assignee as a trespasser.

---

125 *Peabody Donation Fund Governors v Higgins* [1983] 1 WLR 1091; [1983] 3 All ER 122; (1983) 10 HLR 82, CA.

126 *Peabody Donation Fund Governors v Higgins* [1983] 1 WLR 1091; [1983] 3 All ER 122; (1983) 10 HLR 82, CA.

127 SI No 2083. The regulations apply to tenancy agreements: *R (Khatun and others) v Newham LBC and Office of Fair Trading* [2004] EWCA Civ 55; [2005] QB 37; [2004] HLR 29. See also Office of Fair Trading, *Guidance on unfair terms in tenancy agreements*, OFT 356, September 2005.

128 *Croydon LBC v Bustin and Triance* (1991) 24 HLR 36, CA; *Newham LBC v Bennett* [1984] CLY 1960 (both cases of ineffective transfer from mother to son) and *Crago v Julian* [1992] 1 WLR 372; [1992] 1 All ER 744, CA (spouse to spouse).

CHAPTER 3

Grounds for possession against secure occupiers

continued

Introduction

3.1   A landlord can bring a secure tenancy or secure licence to an end only by successful application to a court.[1] The prerequisite of a successful claim for possession is service of a notice seeking possession in the prescribed form unless the court is prepared retrospectively to dispense with service of such a notice (see paras 4.45–4.48).[2]

3.2   The landlord brings the claim for possession in the local county court (using Civil Procedure Rules (CPR) Part 55) because no costs can be recovered if the claim against a secure tenant is started in the High Court.[3] The process starts with the issue of a claim form and particulars of claim (see chapter 23 for a full description of the procedure). Proceedings must be issued at a time when the notice seeking possession is still effective (see para 4.36).

3.3   At the hearing of the claim the landlord must show that the necessary ground (or grounds) and conditions for obtaining a possession order are made out. Before considering those matters and the substantive merits, the court must also be satisfied about a number of technical issues (for example, that the notice was properly served). These are dealt with at para 4.11.

3.4   In this chapter references to secure tenancies also include secure licences (see para 1.27) unless the contrary is stated.

Possession by consent

3.5   The concept of a 'consent order' is not applicable in the case of secure tenants or licensees. The Housing Act (HA) 1985 s84(1) prevents the making of any form of possession order until the court is satisfied that a ground and a condition for ordering possession are made out. The court can be so satisfied only if it hears the evidence or is presented with express admissions by the tenant.[4] For these purposes simple assent to a suspended possession order is not an admission

1   HA 1985 s82(1).
2   HA 1985 s83(1).
3   HA 1985 s110(3). In addition, CPR 55.3(2) and PD 55A para 1.1 provide that claims will only exceptionally be issued in the High Court.
4   *Wandsworth LBC v Fadayomi* (1987) 19 HLR 512; [1987] 3 All ER 474, CA and see *R v Bloomsbury and Marylebone County Court ex p Blackburne* (1984) 14 HLR 56; (1985) 2 EGLR 157, CA. Even where specific admissions have been made as to the facts necessary to found a ground for possession, the issue of reasonableness must be specifically considered: see *Cobalt Housing Ltd v Devine* January 2005 *Legal Action* 28, Liverpool County Court.

of the landlord's grounds and any such order obtained 'by consent' should be set aside.[5] Setting aside a possession order said to have been made by 'consent' may be achieved either on appeal or on an application for judicial review.[6] However, where the trial of a claim for possession is under way and evidence has been given, the tenant may, by agreeing to a consent order, impliedly admit that the tenancy is not a secure tenancy or that the grounds and conditions are made out on the evidence the court has heard.[7]

Grounds and conditions

3.6   Once the court is seised of the substance of the claim for posses-sion (in the sense that all the technical requirements scrutinised in chapter 4 have been met) it must first be satisfied that a *ground* for possession is made out. HA 1985 s84(1) provides that:

> The court shall not make an order for the possession of a dwelling-house let under a secure tenancy except on one or more of the grounds set out in Schedule 2.

3.7   If a ground within HA 1985 Sch 2 cannot be established, the pro-ceedings must inevitably be dismissed. Each of the grounds is separ-ately considered below (para 3.10 onwards). The burden of proof is on the landlord throughout to show that the ground is made out on the balance of probabilities. Even if the court is satisfied that a ground is made out, possession is not to be ordered unless the par-ticular ground has been specified in the notice seeking possession (which was served before the proceedings were commenced) or the need for a notice seeking possession has been dispensed with. The routes available to a landlord who makes out an alternative ground are either: (1) to seek permission of the court to amend the notice seeking possession to embrace the new ground;[8] or (2) to adjourn the proceedings and serve a new notice seeking possession based on the new ground (perhaps with the intention of then consolidating the new proceedings with the current proceedings);[9] or (3) to seek

---

5   *Hounslow LBC v McBride* (1999) 31 HLR 143, CA.

6   *R v Birmingham CC ex p Foley* March 2001 *Legal Action* 29, QBD (Admin Ct).

7   *R v Worthing BC ex p Bruce* (1994) 26 HLR 223, CA and *Morris v Barnet LBC* December 1995 *Legal Action* 18, CA.

8   HA 1985 s84(3).

9   *City of London v Devlin* (1997) 29 HLR 58, CA.

permission of the court to dispense with the requirement for a notice seeking possession altogether.[10]

3.8   Furthermore, no order for possession may be made simply because a ground for possession has been established. The landlord must also prove that any relevant *conditions* are made out. Each ground for possession carries with it a condition or set of conditions which must be satisfied before possession is ordered. Indeed, HA 1985 s84(2) provides:

> (2) The court shall not make an order for possession –
> (a) on the grounds set out in Part I of that Schedule (grounds 1 to 8), unless it considers it reasonable to make the order,
> (b) on the grounds set out in Part II of that Schedule (grounds 9 to 11), unless it is satisfied that suitable accommodation will be available for the tenant when the order takes effect,
> (c) on the grounds set out in Part III of that Schedule (grounds 12 to 16), unless it both considers it reasonable to make the order and is satisfied that suitable accommodation will be available for the tenant when the order takes effect;
> and Part IV of that Schedule has effect for determining whether suitable accommodation will be available for a tenant.

3.9   Each of these conditions is considered below in relation to the relevant ground. If the landlord cannot show on the balance of probabilities that the conditions relevant to the particular ground are satisfied, the claim for possession should be dismissed even though the grounds have been proved.

Ground 1 (first limb): rent arrears

3.10   This is the most common ground on which possession is sought against secure occupiers.[11] The first part of ground 1 of HA 1985 Sch 2 will be satisfied only if the landlord proves that:

> rent lawfully due from the tenant has not been paid.

3.11   In order to recover possession the landlord must also satisfy the court that the appropriate condition is met – in this case that it is reasonable

---

10 HA 1985 s83(1)(b). See para 4.45.
11 It accounts for the vast majority of possession claims: see *The use of possession actions and evictions by social landlords* (ODPM, June 2005) and *Rent arrears management practices in the housing association sector* (Tenant Services Authority, March 2010).

to make the order.[12] Each element of both the ground and condition must to be proved to the satisfaction of the court.

3.12   So many possession claims based rent arrears are brought in the county court that serious attempts have been made in recent years to encourage social landlords and their tenants to resolve difficulties well before court action becomes necessary. The most significant was publication of a Pre-Action Protocol which came into force in October 2006. Its requirements are discussed at para 3.38 below.

The ground

3.13   In the usual case, the landlord proves the ground by putting in evidence of the rent payable under the tenancy agreement, particulars of the current rent due, the record of payments made by the tenant and copies of demands made for payments of arrears. The first Practice Direction to CPR Part 55 (Possession claims) requires that detailed particulars of the rent and the arrears accrued over the past two years be included in the Particulars of Claim (see para 23.15).[13] If the landlord wants to rely on a history of arrears going back beyond two years, that fact should be stated in the particulars of claim and a full (or longer) schedule should be exhibited to a witness statement.[14]

3.14   For the purpose of preparing a secure tenant's defence to a rent arrears possession claim, almost every word of ground 1 requires careful consideration.

'rent'

3.15   The rent in question is the rent due in respect of the relevant property under the secure tenant's tenancy agreement. However, the term 'rent' is not defined in HA 1985 Part IV. It is suggested that 'rent' for these purposes does not include – in the absence of express provision to the contrary – service charges, water rates,[15] other amenity

---

12   HA 1985 s84(2)(a).
13   CPR PD 55A para 2.3. This Practice Direction is reproduced in appendix E.
14   CPR PD 55A para 2.3A.
15   The opportunity to determine finally whether water rates were part of rent arose in *Lambeth LBC v Thomas* (1997) *Times* 31 March; (1998) 30 HLR 89, CA, but was not taken by the Court of Appeal although that court gave a strong indication that it would have found that 'rent' included water rates had it been necessary to decide the question.

payments, insurance premiums, overpaid housing benefit[16] or any other indebtedness which is not strictly rent.[17]

3.16 In addition to collecting basic 'rent', social landlords have a tendency to use the rent payment system to collect a variety of charges from tenants, ranging from fees for communal TV aerials to tenants' association membership subscriptions, and from rent for separate garages to heating charges. It must be doubted whether all or any of these charges can properly be said to be part of the 'rent' for the premises let unless so described or defined expressly in the tenancy agreement.

3.17 On the other hand, in the Rent Act jurisdiction, where the amount of 'rent' has historically been crucial to the existence of security of tenure, courts have inclined to the view that 'rent' embraces the total monetary payment made to the landlord.[18] In *Dudley MBC v Bailey*,[19] it was hoped that the Court of Appeal would provide an authoritative definition of 'rent' in the context of a secure tenancy. However, the council in that case conceded that general rates owed by the tenant and usually collected with the rent were *not* part of the rent and the case turned on other issues. The concession was in line with earlier decisions in the lower courts.[20] A subsequently noted county court decision has preferred the Rent Act 'total indebtedness' approach[21] and that may be the approach which proves most attractive to the Court of Appeal when the issue arises directly for determination.[22]

'lawfully due'

3.18 Rent must be lawfully due from the tenant. It is therefore open to the tenant to assert in a defence that the rent has been improperly fixed or increased and that accordingly the amount claimed is not 'lawfully' due. That involves a careful consideration of the contractual

16 See *Complaint against Wychavon DC*, Local Government Ombudsman Investigation 90/B/2514, 23 March 1992.
17 See Ann McAllister and Siobhan McGrath, 'Grounds for possession: rent lawfully due' Parts 1–3 in December 1985 *Legal Action* 169, January 1986 *Legal Action* 9 and February 1986 *Legal Action* 21.
18 *Sidney Trading Co v Finsbury Corp* [1952] 1 All ER 460 at 461 and *Markworth v Hellard* [1921] 2 KB 755.
19 (1990) 22 HLR 424; [1991] 1 EGLR 53, CA.
20 See, eg, *Trafford BC v Mullings* March 1990 *Legal Action* 12.
21 *Lewisham LBC v Simba-Tola* June 1993 *Legal Action* 14, Bromley County Court (where the amount said to be 'arrears of rent' included general rates, water rates and other sundry charges).
22 See *Lambeth LBC v Thomas* (1998) 30 HLR 89, CA.

provisions for rent and rent increases in the tenancy agreement. Where the landlord is a local housing authority there may properly be an assertion that in breach of its statutory duty the council has not fixed a reasonable rent.[23] Although this is a straightforward assertion to make, it is exceptionally difficult to prove.[24] A successful defence of not 'lawfully' due may be raised if the rent increase was based on some misinterpretation by the landlord of the relevant housing finance legislation (as in *R v Ealing LBC ex p Lewis*[25]).

3.19   Similarly, the rent claimed is not lawfully due if the landlord has failed to observe any contractual or statutory requirements as to notice of increase.[26] Such requirements are strictly construed.[27] Furthermore, rent cannot usually be lawfully increased on account of any improvement work by the tenant.[28] In the case of a secure housing association tenant with a registered fair rent, the maximum rent recoverable will be that so registered. Any excess will not be 'lawfully due'.

3.20   Likewise, a rent is not payable and accordingly not lawfully due unless the landlord has given an address for service of notices in accordance with Landlord and Tenant Act 1987 s48 (see para 17.12). However, the outstanding rent will immediately become lawfully due on the provision of such an address.

'from the tenant'

3.21   Only the rent due from the tenant is relevant. Any rent owed by a previous occupier, former tenant or spouse/civil partner/cohabitant of the current tenant is irrelevant. For example, in *Notting Hill Housing Trust v Jones*,[29] the defendant had received the secure tenancy on its transfer to her from her former husband pursuant to an order made in family proceedings. He owed arrears of rent. The tenant agreed to clear those arrears by instalments. Thereafter, she paid her current rent but failed to clear the arrears. The housing trust brought possession proceedings based on non-payment of the old 'arrears'. The

23   HA 1985 s24. See *Wandsworth LBC v Winder (No 1)* [1985] AC 461; (1985) 17 HLR 196, HL.

24   *Wandsworth LBC v Winder (No 2)* (1987) 20 HLR 400, CA.

25   (1992) 24 HLR 484; (1992) 90 LGR 571, QBD.

26   HA 1985 s102. For the correct approach to construction of tenancy agreement provisions relating to rent increases see *Riverside HA v White* [2007] UKHL 20; [2007] HLR 31.

27   *Clements & O'Boyle v Brent LBC* March 1990 *Legal Action* 12.

28   HA 1985 s101.

29   [1999] L&TR 397, CA.

Court of Appeal dismissed the proceedings – the amount outstanding was not rent due from the defendant, the present tenant.

3.22   Likewise, a secure tenant who acquired the tenancy by way of statutory succession following the death of a secure tenant, or by an assignment, is only liable for rent accruing from the date of succession or assignment and thus starts with a 'clean slate' for the purpose of ground 1 possession proceedings brought by the present landlord.[30] It should be noted, however, that any one of a number of joint secure tenants may be sued for the whole rent due from the commencement of their joint tenancy. There is no legal concept of one joint tenant's 'part' or 'proportion' of the rent. The whole rent is 'lawfully due' from each of them.

'has not been paid'

3.23   If all arrears are cleared before the issue of proceedings, the court is not able to order possession under ground 1.[31] This is so, even if the landlord can prove that there were arrears at the date of the notice seeking possession or that there is a history of poor payment. The landlord cannot seek to avoid this consequence by refusing to accept or by returning payments tendered shortly before the issue of proceedings, even if they are substantially late.[32] There is no freestanding ground for possession in the case of secure tenants comparable to that available against assured tenants in HA 1988 Sch 2 ground 11 (persistent late payment).

3.24   If arrears were outstanding at the date of issue of the proceedings but are cleared before the hearing or on the hearing date, the court may still find the ground made out but is unlikely also to be satisfied that it is reasonable to make the order (see below).[33]

3.25   In spite of apparent arrears shown on the (often computer-generated) rent account, it may be that there are in fact no true arrears of rent or only a lesser amount than that shown. A number of possibilities should be carefully checked.

3.26   First, the tenant may have made payments not in fact recorded as received. These may either be very recent payments that had not reached the rent account by the date it was printed or earlier payments

---

30 *Tickner v Clifton* [1929] 1 KB 207, CA and *Notting Hill Housing Trust v Jones* [1999] L&TR 397, CA.

31 *Bird v Hildage* [1948] 1 KB 91, CA.

32 *Bird v Hildage* [1948] 1 KB 91, CA.

33 *Dellenty v Pellow* [1951] 2 KB 858, CA and *Haringey LBC v Stewart* (1991) 23 HLR 557, CA.

that the landlord has attributed to the wrong account. Many large social landlords have an account holding substantial amounts in 'unattributed' receipts from current or former tenants.

3.27   Second, the housing benefit authority (which might also be the landlord) may have awarded and paid housing benefit (see chapter 37) which has not been credited to the account. If the landlord is the benefit authority, the effect of an award of housing benefit will have been to 'rebate' the rent (ie, reduce the amount of it) whether or not the reduced level of rent has actually been adjusted on the rent account.

3.28   Third, if the tenant has been having deductions made from welfare benefits by the Department for Work and Pensions (see para 3.48) those monies deducted may have been received by the landlord direct from the benefits office, but not yet applied to the account. Such 'direct deductions' are usually paid in a lump sum every four weeks in arrears.

3.29   Fourth, the landlord may be charging an incorrect (higher) rent than that actually payable under the tenancy.[34] All these possibilities repay careful consideration.

3.30   It is important to note that an entitlement to *housing benefit* does not, of itself, serve to reduce or eliminate liability for rent. It is only when such benefit is awarded by the benefit authority, and (if the rent is not a rebated council rent) actually paid to the landlord, that liability for rent is satisfied (see chapter 37). From that point in time the rent will have been 'paid' even if there is an administrative delay in attributing it to the particular tenant's rent account. If the landlord is the benefit authority itself, 'payment' is made by rebating the rent otherwise payable and showing only a net amount to be paid as rent. It appears from the forms of 'payment' listed in the Social Security Administration Act 1992 s134(2)[35] that the tenant's liability for the rent is satisfied by such a rebate, even if the local authority subsequently decides that there has been an overpayment of housing benefit. If the authority debits the amount of the overpaid housing benefit to the rent account, this sum should not be treated as rent arrears and should be kept separate in the account.[36] However, the council may recover the overpayment by weekly deductions from current housing benefit entitlement, so that the tenant will have to

---

34   See para 3.18 and *Riverside HA v White* [2007] UKHL 20; [2007] HLR 31.
35   As amended by the Welfare Reform Act 2007.
36   See *Complaint against Wychavon DC*, Local Government Ombudsman Investigation 90/B/2514, 23 March 1992.

make up the shortfall in the rent from other resources.[37] Where the secure tenant of a social landlord other than the benefit authority has been overpaid housing benefit and the overpayment has been recovered directly from that landlord by the benefit authority, the landlord may seek to debit the amount of the overpayment to the tenant's rent account, with the result that the tenant will be placed in rent arrears and will be vulnerable to possession proceedings: see para 32.27.

3.31   However, there are other respects in which housing benefit issues may arise in ground 1 possession claims. First, delay in payment of benefit to the landlord by the benefit authority is, of course, material in considering the reasonableness condition (see para 3.35). Second, delay by the landlord in processing the benefit claim – where the landlord is also the benefit authority – is likewise relevant to reasonableness. Third, 'arrears' may in fact have arisen where, after satisfaction of the rent liability by payment or credit of housing benefit, the benefit authority (which may or may not also be the landlord) has been advised of, or discovered, an overpayment and has sought to recover the overpayment by adjusting the tenant's rent account. It was previously arguable, in such a case, that there were no arrears of rent because the rent had already been paid[38] but the position would appear to have been settled by amendments to the Housing Benefit Regulations made in April 1997 and now incorporated in the consolidated Housing Benefit Regulations 2006, at least in relation to rent allowance payments as opposed to rent rebates (see further para 37.27).

3.32   It is strongly arguable that a court should delay considering whether or not a possession order should be made until outstanding housing benefit issues have been resolved since it is not possible to consider whether or not it is reasonable to make a possession order until the true figure for arrears is known. If it is the benefit authority itself claiming possession, it cannot expect the repeated indulgence of the court in granting adjournments while the benefit position is resolved. The court might well strike out a case in which the tenant had done everything he or she could to resolve a housing benefit problem but the landlord authority itself was not in a position to explain clearly what the true rent outstanding was.[39] It is, however, not

---

37 Housing Benefit Regulations 2006 SI No 213 reg 102.

38 See *Thamesmead Town v Mighty* March 1998 *Legal Action* 12; *Church Commissioners v Akindele* March 1998 *Legal Action* 12 and *Hyde Housing Association v Brown* October 1999 *Legal Action* 24.

39 *Lambeth LBC v Tagoe* August 2000 *Legal Action* 24.

for the judge in possession proceedings to determine entitlement to housing benefit.[40]

3.33   Even if there is prima facie an amount of rent owing, that may be matched or exceeded by an amount which the tenant is entitled to set off, for example, the cost of repair work which the tenant has had to undertake because of the landlord's default in undertaking repairs or the damages awarded to the tenant on a counterclaim.[41] Such a set-off will act as a complete defence to the claim for rent. These possibilities are discussed further at para 4.53.

3.34   If a landlord fails to prove any element of ground 1, proceedings founded solely on that ground must be dismissed.

The condition

3.35   Even if the court is satisfied that there has been a failure to pay rent lawfully due, it cannot make a possession order of any description (including a 'suspended' or 'postponed' order) unless it is also satisfied that in all the circumstances of the case it would be reasonable to do so.[42]

3.36   In rent arrears cases, if there is no evidence as to why it is reasonable for possession to be granted over and above the ordinary relief of a money judgment for the outstanding amount due, any form of possession order must be resisted. The tenant could invite the court to dismiss the possession claim but enter a judgment for the money claim made by the landlord, if the amount of the arrears claimed is agreed or has been proved. This gives the landlord the satisfaction of an order against the tenant in default, but it is arguable that no order for costs should be made against the tenant because a money claim could have been brought by a small claim rather than by possession proceedings.

3.37   However, if the landlord contends that it would be reasonable to order possession, then in applying the 'reasonableness' test the court is required to have regard to all relevant factors. These will include the duration of the tenancy, the past rent record of the tenant, whether the failure to pay rent is persistent, whether there have been earlier agreements to clear arrears, the conduct of the landlord in seeking or waiving amounts due and the personal circumstances of the tenant.

40 *Southwark LBC v Kofi-Adu* [2006] EWCA Civ 281; [2006] HLR 33.
41 See the 'forensic disaster' (of commencement of possession proceedings based on rent arrears against a secure tenant who then recovered over £50,000 on her counterclaim for damages for disrepair) in *Brent LBC v Carmel Murphy* (1996) 28 HLR 203, CA.
42 HA 1985 s84(2)(a).

Woodspring DC v Taylor[43] provides a good example of the application of these principles. The Court of Appeal held that it was not appropriate for an order to be made against long-standing tenants with a previous good rent record presently in temporary financial difficulties, even though arrears of over £700 (in 1982) were proved. Where the root cause of the arrears of rent is the low income of the defendant, the court will need to consider the availability of, and entitlement to, social security benefits. In *Second WRVS Housing Society v Blair*,[44] the Court of Appeal set aside an order for possession made against a young, single man who owed £1,200 rent (in 1985) and had been a tenant for only eight years. The county court judge had not adequately considered: (a) the possibility of arranging direct payment from the housing benefit authority to the landlord of current rent; (b) the possibility of the social security office deducting small amounts from the tenant's welfare benefits and paying them direct to the landlord towards the arrears (see para 3.48 below); and (c) the tenant's medical condition.

3.38   The *Protocol for Possession Claims based on Rent Arrears* ('Rent Arrears Protocol') has been in force since 2 October 2006. The text of the protocol is set out in full in appendix D to this book. The protocol is a critical document for both the parties and the court in relation to any action for possession brought by a social landlord on the basis of rent arrears.

3.39   The aim of the Rent Arrears Protocol is to encourage more pre-action contact between the parties and to enable court time to be used effectively. The protocol requires landlords to:

- contact the tenant as soon as reasonably possible once he or she falls into rent arrears to discuss the cause of the arrears, the tenant's financial circumstances, his or her entitlement to benefits and payment of the arrears;
- attempt to agree an affordable sum for the tenant to pay off the arrears and (where appropriate) assist in arranging for direct payments to be made towards the arrears from the tenant's benefit entitlement (see para 3.48 below);
- provide the tenant with a full rent statement;
- take reasonable steps to ensure that information has been appropriately communicated;
- assist the tenant in connection with his or her claim for housing benefit and establish effective liaison with the housing benefit department (see chapter 37 on housing benefit);

43 (1982) 4 HLR 95, CA.
44 (1986) 19 HLR 104, CA.

- refrain from taking possession action where the tenant has a reasonable expectation of eligibility for housing benefit and has provided all the evidence necessary for the claim to be processed;
- if a possession claim must be brought, contact the tenant before the court hearing to discuss the current position with regard to the arrears and housing benefit;
- postpone the court proceedings where the tenant has reached an agreement to pay the current rent and arrears, so long as the tenant keeps to the agreement; and
- encourage the tenant to attend the court hearing.

3.40   If a landlord unreasonably fails to comply with the terms of the Rent Arrears Protocol the court may impose a sanction or sanctions in the form of costs and/or adjournment of the proceedings or may strike out or dismiss the claim. If the tenant unreasonably fails to comply with the terms of the protocol, the court may take such failure into account when considering whether it is reasonable to make a possession order.

3.41   Whether it is reasonable to make a possession order in a rent arrears case may well be influenced by the landlord's conduct both in relation to the protocol and in the management of the arrears issue in the particular case. Social landlords are expected to abide by guidance on the management of rent arrears issued by central government and by the Tenant Services Authority (TSA) and reference can usefully be made to this guidance when defending possession proceedings.

3.42   Extensive good practice guidance has been published by the Department for Communities and Local Government. For example, the document *Improving the Effectiveness of Rent Arrears Management: Good Practice Guidance*[45] 'sets out the Government's view ... which emphasises that social landlords should seek to maintain and sustain tenancies rather than terminate them, and that eviction should only be used as a last resort'. The guidance states that landlords can and should actively assist tenants with claims for housing benefit, including helping them to complete forms. Housing officers should work with housing benefit colleagues to establish access to information systems and case records. Tenants should never be served with a notice seeking possession where there are unresolved housing benefit claims, unless it is clear that this is due to the tenant's failure to supply necessary information or unless the tenant is failing to pay elements of the rent not covered by benefits.

45 CLG, June 2005. Now out of print but available to download at www.communities.gov.uk/publications/housing/improvingeffectiveness.

3.43   That guidance was supplemented in August 2006 by publication of *Guide on Effective Rent Arrears Management*[46] intended to be read with the (then) new Rent Arrears Protocol. 'The guidance is aimed at social landlords and all levels of a landlord's rent arrears management service ... It sets out clearly the DCLG view ... that social landlords should seek to maintain and sustain tenancies, rather than terminate them and that eviction should be used as a last resort.' In respect of court action for possession based on arrears of rent it states at para [11]:

- Tenants should never be served with a Notice Seeking Possession (NOSP) until the landlord has established personal contact or exhausted all possible means of doing so.
- NOSPs should be served on tenants with unresolved Housing Benefit claims only where it has been established beyond doubt that the claim remains outstanding due to the tenant's failure to supply requested information or provide requested documents or if the tenant is failing to pay agreed personal contributions.
- Existing regulatory and good practice guidance for registered social landlords stresses that eviction is the last resort.
- Prior to court action landlords should seek a meeting with the tenant and agencies supporting them if appropriate, whilst also reviewing the tenant's personal circumstances and actions taken.
- Landlords taking tenants to court should encourage and assist the tenant to contact agencies providing relevant advice, and/or counselling services, as well as to access legal advice and to attend hearings.
- During court proceedings, and where a repayment agreement has already been struck, it is good practice to seek an adjournment on terms rather than a postponed Possession Order (*note:* following the introduction of an amended possession procedure in July 2006, as a result of the decision in *Harlow DC v Hall*, a possession order where possession is deferred will be called a 'postponed possession order', replacing the previous widely used but incorrect 'suspended possession order' and this replacement term should be read into the guidance).

3.44   The court's attention should be drawn to the guidance where the landlord's practices do not meet these standards or where proceedings have been brought without trying other methods of rent recovery. Particular emphasis might be placed on the three concluding paragraphs of the *Guide* which state:

12. Social landlords should seek to maintain and sustain tenancies and should only seek to terminate a tenancy and evict as a last resort.

---

46 CLG, August 2006.

13. Landlords should have in place a clear strategy for preventing and managing rent arrears, produce clear guidance for officers and have in place robust systems for prevention and management. They should put in place measures to prevent arrears accruing and seek to maximise rental income.

14. Where arrears have accrued landlords should seek early intervention through personal contact with the tenant, offering support and advice and agreeing a way forward for recovering the arrears. These strategies should be evaluated for cost-effectiveness and overall effectiveness.

3.45   On 1 April 2010 the Tenant Services Authority adopted a new statutory National Tenancy Standard applicable to local housing authorities and all other social landlords which are registered providers of social housing. The 'required outcome' in respect of tenure states:[47]

3. Tenure

3.1 Registered providers shall publish clear and accessible policies which outline their approach to tenancy management. They shall develop and provide services that will support tenants to maintain their tenancy and prevent unnecessary evictions. The approach should set out how registered providers will make sure that the home continues to be occupied by the tenant they let the home to.

3.46   The TSA expects that the policies described in para 3.1 of the Tenancy Standard will be developed in consultation with tenants' representatives and that, where appropriate, locally agreed Local Standards ('local offers') will supplement the National Standards. Advisers defending possession claims will wish to check for compliance with the National and any Local Standards and with the particular landlord's own policies on rent arrears management and then draw any shortcomings to the attention of the court.

3.47   Where the rent has been *withheld* by the secure tenant because the amount due or outstanding is genuinely disputed, or because the tenant has a legitimate grievance over disrepair, the court would not usually find it reasonable to make an order, but is more likely to adjourn the proceedings with directions (for example, that a defence and counterclaim be filed in respect of the dispute or alleged repairing default). In *Haringey LBC v Stewart*,[48] the secure tenant withheld rent on account of alleged disrepair. At trial, his counterclaim for damages for disrepair was dismissed. In relation to the possession

---

47 *The Regulatory Framework for Social Housing in England from April 2010* (TSA, March 2010) at p25.
48 (1991) 23 HLR 557, CA.

claim, the tenant was then unable to repay the withheld rent amounting to over £1,000 (because it had been spent rather than set aside) and made no proposals as to payment of current rent or payment of the arrears. The Court of Appeal declined to interfere with a decision that it was reasonable to make an outright possession order.

3.48   Notwithstanding the guidance described at para 3.42, social landlords frequently bring possession proceedings in respect of rent arrears owed by secure tenants on very low incomes, including those on welfare benefits. The key issues on reasonableness in such cases are likely to be:

- Why did the landlord (if not itself a housing benefit authority) not arrange direct payment of housing benefit from the benefit authority to meet current rent, either with the tenant's consent or (once eight weeks' worth of arrears had accrued) as of right?[49]
- Why did the landlord not arrange with the Department for Work and Pensions the deduction at source of a small amount from the tenant's welfare benefit to pay off the arrears[50] instead of bringing possession proceedings?
- Whether the landlord could have offered advice and assistance with claiming benefits, maximising other income and debt control, and failed to do so.

3.49   The most powerful submission available to the defendant in such a case is that the secure tenant is paying (and is willing to keep paying) current rent and is paying (and willing to keep paying) whatever can reasonably be afforded towards the arrears. Where such a submission can be joined with an assertion that the arrears are in part the result of genuine housing benefit problems, possession is unlikely to be ordered.[51] Indeed, in these and other situations where the tenant is making genuine efforts to reduce the arrears, or where there have been difficulties with housing benefit, the court should be asked to consider granting a general adjournment of the claim, on the basis that it is not necessary, and therefore cannot be reasonable, to make any order for possession in the circumstances (see para 4.56). The landlord may argue that it needs the potential sanction of a postponed possession order to secure continuing payment. However, unless the tenant has a history of broken arrangements to pay, the court may well accept that the landlord's interests are sufficiently protected by

---

49   Housing Benefit Regulations 2006 SI No 213 regs 95–96 and see para 37.35.
50   Social Security (Claims and Payments) Regulations 1987 SI No 1968 reg 35 and Sch 9.
51   *Islington LBC v LaMarque* September 1991 *Legal Action* 14.

having liberty to restore the proceedings in the event of the tenant's breach of the terms of an adjournment.

3.50   A good example of the courts' approach to possession claims for arrears of rent brought against secure tenants is afforded by *Brent LBC v Marks.*[52] In that case the secure tenant, having earlier fallen into arrears, was receiving housing benefit by way of rent rebate in respect of almost all her rent. The shortfall (water rates), together with a weekly sum of £2.50 in respect of the arrears, were, from September 1996, being deducted at source from her welfare benefits and paid over quarterly in arrears to the council landlord. In January 1997 the council served notice seeking possession and claimed possession under ground 1. In June 1997, HHJ Krikler granted possession, suspended on payment of current rent plus £2.50 per week to meet the arrears of £1,500. On appeal, the Court of Appeal set the order aside and remitted the claim for rehearing. As it was clear that the social security office was paying the deducted amounts quarterly in arrears, the terms of the order requiring weekly payment unnecessarily put the tenant at risk of breach of the order. The relevant material about the history of the reduction of the arrears had not been properly put before the judge. As to the retrial, Butler-Sloss LJ indicated that the first main matter for the judge to deal with would be 'whether there should be an order for possession at all'. The council failed to recover its costs both in the county court and in the Court of Appeal.

3.51   The case also illustrates that in the social housing sector, if a possession order for arrears is to be made at all, an order may be postponed on terms requiring payment by the tenant of small instalments towards the arrears over a very long period. In *Lambeth LBC v Henry,*[53] the Court of Appeal declined to set aside a suspended order made on terms as to payment of arrears by instalments which would need to run for over 20 years in order to clear the arrears.

3.52   Where a tenant has had difficulty in managing his or her financial affairs owing to a mental illness, he or she may be able to raise a defence under the Disability Discrimination Act 1995: see chapter 27.

3.53   A tenant repeatedly facing unmeritorious claims for possession based on rent arrears, which are repeatedly dismissed by the courts, may well have a claim for harassment against the landlord.[54]

---

52 (1999) 31 HLR 343, CA.
53 (2000) 32 HLR 874, CA.
54 *Allen v Southwark LBC* [2008] EWCA Civ 1478; January 2009 *Legal Action* 25.

Ground 1 (second limb): other breach of the tenancy agreement

3.54 Ground 1 of HA 1985 Sch 2 further provides that (subject to it being reasonable in all the circumstances to grant possession) an order for possession can be made if

an obligation of the tenancy has been broken or not performed.

3.55 One of the most common obligations relied on in such cases is an obligation in the tenancy agreement to pay additional sums together with the rent, such as water rates.[55] However, the obligation which is relied on by the landlord must arise from an express or implied term of the tenancy agreement itself, and not from some collateral agreement (for example, the separate renting of a garage or a free-standing agreement to clear a previous tenant's arrears of rent[56]). A failure to comply with the conditions attached to a separate grant of permission to carry out improvements is, however, specifically brought within ground 1.[57]

3.56 The term breached must be a term of the tenancy itself, not a matter of mere personal obligation on the part of the tenant. As a result, landlords are unable to use this ground in respect of such matters as failure to comply with requirements to remain in the landlord's employment[58] or to participate in counselling, treatment or resettlement programmes.[59]

3.57 In preparing the defence, the tenancy terms should be carefully checked to see whether the term relied on by the landlord is in fact a term of the agreement applicable to the tenant's present tenancy. Landlords often produce to the court the 'current version' of their standard tenancy agreement. However, the true tenancy agreement is the one originally entered into by the tenant, subject to any statutory or contractual procedure for variation.[60] A variation cannot be achieved simply by sending the tenant a 'fresh' tenancy agreement, even if after having received such a document the tenant remains in occupation and pays the rent.[61]

---

55 *Lambeth LBC v Thomas* (1998) 30 HLR 89, CA.
56 *Notting Hill Housing Trust v Jones* [1999] 1 L&TR 397, CA.
57 HA 1985 s99(4).
58 *RMR Housing Society v Combs* [1951] 1 KB 486, CA.
59 *Paddington Churches Housing Association v Boateng* January 1999 *Legal Action* 27.
60 HA 1985 ss102 and 103.
61 *Palmer v Sandwell MBC* (1988) 20 HLR 74, CA and *Carolan and Hamnett v Warrington BC* June 2000 *Legal Action* 24.

3.58   Once the correct document has been identified, it is necessary to check the precise wording to see whether the conduct alleged against the tenant has actually been prohibited by the agreement.[62] The details of the conduct alleged to amount to a breach of the agreement must be given in the particulars of claim.[63]

3.59   In addition, the term relied on by the landlord should be scrutinised carefully to see whether it is 'fair' for the purposes of the Unfair Terms in Consumer Contracts Regulations 1999.[64] Useful guidance as to 'fairness' in this context is provided by the Office of Fair Trading (OFT) in its *Guidance on Unfair Terms in Tenancy Agreements*.[65] If the term is unfair the court should reject any attempt to rely on it in ground 1 proceedings.[66]

3.60   Many social landlords have in recent years introduced provisions into tenancy agreements which expressly prohibit acts of anti-social behaviour, domestic violence or racial harassment.[67]

3.61   Some social landlords have included among the obligations of their tenancy agreements for secure tenants a requirement to desist from particular activity at the premises which might amount to a crime, for example, having controlled drugs in the premises. This allows possession to be claimed under the second limb of ground 1 even if the tenant is not actually prosecuted for or convicted of an offence (in which case ground 2 below could have been relied on). If it is made out, the usual order would be for possession.[68] However, a landlord should not usually be permitted to use this limb of ground 1 to obtain possession in reliance on a tenancy term which has been designed to avoid the need to rely on another ground for possession specifically dealing with the issue. For example, the landlord should not be permitted to rely on ground 1 in respect of breach of a covenant not to allow premises to be statutorily overcrowded because there is a specific ground for possession covering overcrowding (see para 3.151 below) and that ground carries an obligation to supply suitable alternative accommodation.[69]

---

62 *Lewisham LBC v Simba-Tola* (1992) 24 HLR 644, CA.
63 CPR PD 55A para 2.4A.
64 SI No 2083.
65 OFT paper 356, September 2005. www.oft.gov.uk/advice_and_resources/ publications/guidance/unfair-terms-consumer/oft356.
66 *R (Khatun Zeb and Iqbal) v Newham LBC* [2005] QB 37; [2004] HLR 29, CA and *Camden LBC v McBride* January 1999 *Legal Action* 26.
67 See *Kensington Housing Trust v Borkwood* July 2005 *Legal Action* 28.
68 *Bristol CC v Mousah* (1998) 30 HLR 32, CA and *Sandwell MBC v Hensley* [2007] EWCA Civ 1425; [2008] HLR 22, CA.
69 *Newham LBC v Anwar Ali* February 2004 *Legal Action* 31, Bow County Court.

3.62   Another common provision contained in secure tenancy agreements is the prohibition against the keeping of pets or other animals on the premises let. Proceedings under ground 1 based on this particular breach provide a good illustration of the distinction between the ground for possession and the reasonableness requirement. The tenant may well admit a clear and continuing breach of the agreement by keeping an 'animal companion' but a possession order may be refused where, in the particular circumstances, it would not be reasonable to order possession (notwithstanding that the tenant intends to continue keeping the pet at the premises).[70] This may be the case particularly if there is good medical or social evidence of the effect that loss of the animal companion will have on the tenant.[71] In the absence of any such evidence, however, the court is likely to take the view that it is reasonable to evict a tenant who, despite having entered into a plain 'no pets' agreement, and having been given appropriate notice that the landlord intends to enforce the agreement, will not get rid of the animal.[72]

3.63   In other cases where the ground is proved, the condition of reasonableness is affected by considerations such as: whether the breach is continuing, persistent or repeated; the seriousness of the breach; its implications for the landlord; and the personal circumstances of the tenant. In *Wandsworth LBC v Hargreaves*[73] the tenant had allowed visitors to assemble fire bombs in his flat and throw them from the windows, in clear breach of an express term of the tenancy (as to the keeping of 'combustible materials' in the flats). Spilt petrol caused a fire which seriously damaged the flat. The Court of Appeal was not prepared to upset the trial judge's conclusion that, notwithstanding the breach and the damage caused, it was not reasonable to evict the tenant in the particular circumstances of that case.

3.64   It is, however, no part of the court's function in determining reasonableness to investigate whether the landlord's policy justification for including a particular term in a tenancy agreement is a good or valid one.[74]

3.65   Advisers may find it helpful to draw the attention of the court to the landlord's readily available alternative remedy for breach of the contractual agreement – an order for specific performance to enforce

---

70 *Bell London and Provincial Properties Ltd v Reuben* [1947] KB 157, CA.
71 *Corporation of London v Prior* (1996) 1 L&T Rev 1 pD8.
72 *Sheffield City Council v Jepson* (1993) 25 HLR 299, CA and *Green v Sheffield City Council* (1994) 26 HLR 349, CA.
73 (1994) 27 HLR 142, CA.
74 *Barking and Dagenham LBC v Hyatt* (1992) 24 HLR 406, CA.

compliance or an injunction to restrain further breach.[75] Where a member of the tenant's household is the main party responsible for the conduct amounting to the alleged breach of the tenant's tenancy agreement, it might be suggested that the more sensible course is for the landlord to seek an injunction or other relief against that person – rendering the grant of possession against the tenant unnecessary. However, tenants' advisers will need to be prepared to tackle the reverse contention – that there are circumstances in which a conditional possession order can be more appropriate than an injunction enforceable by committal.[76]

3.66   Those defending secure tenants in these ground 1 cases should always argue against the apparently attractive option of an order postponed or suspended on terms that there be no further breach. Any form of order can be resisted on the basis that it would not be reasonable in the circumstances to make any order at all. Alternatively, as in the case of rent arrears (see para 3.49), that the same objective can be met by adjourning the proceedings on terms (see para 4.56), giving the landlord liberty to restore in the event of a further alleged breach. Even a postponed possession order would usually attract an award of costs against the tenant.

3.67   Those representing secure tenants should argue that a conditional order in a 'breach of obligation' case should, where appropriate, only be made on terms that it is not to be enforced without a prior finding by the court that there has been a breach of the conditions.[77] Without such an express restriction the landlord could obtain a warrant for possession, without a further hearing, simply by alleging breach. If the court is minded to make a conditional order at all it should be urged to adopt the form of postponed possession order (form N28A) suitably adapted for the purposes of a 'behaviour' case.

Ground 2: overview

3.68   Ground 2 (which deals with nuisance and criminal activity) was substituted in its present wording – set out below – by HA 1996 s144. The revised wording was intended to make it easier to recover possession from those guilty of anti-social behaviour. The ground is

---

75 *Sutton Housing Trust v Lawrence* (1987) 19 HLR 520, CA.
76 See Ralph Gibson LJ in *Sheffield City Council v Jepson* (1993) 25 HLR 299, CA, at 303.
77 See *Solon Co-op Housing Services Ltd v Headly* March 1997 *Legal Action* 11 and *Knowsley Housing Trust v McMullen* [2006] EWCA Civ 539; [2006] HLR 43.

identical to ground 14 of the assured tenancy grounds for possession in HA 1988 Sch 2, discussed below at para 12.135.

3.69   Because the factual background causing claims to be brought against secure tenants under this ground may require swift action by landlords, special provisions are made in relation to notices seeking possession which specify ground 2 among the grounds to be relied on (see para 2.6). Proceedings can be commenced immediately after such a notice has been served[78] and possession can be ordered as early as the date on which the landlord has claimed for possession in the notice (ie, the date on which the tenancy could have been brought to an end if it had not been secure). In a case of really serious nuisance or criminality a landlord may simply issue proceedings immediately and invite the court to exercise its power to dispense with any notice seeking possession at all (see para 4.45).

3.70   A tenant might attempt to frustrate the landlord's intention to gain possession under ground 2 by exercising the statutory right to buy. If the application to buy has reached the stage at which the tenant would be enabled to compel completion, the tenant will ordinarily be entitled to apply for an injunction requiring the landlord to complete the sale before the trial of any claim for possession under ground 2.[79] This could lead to a race between the secure tenant and the landlord to obtain a hearing for their respective claims first. It has been held that if the tenant's application falls for hearing on the same date as the possession claim, it will be for the judge to exercise a discretion as to which case to hear first;[80] and that the sequence of events and the seriousness of the allegations of misbehaviour are relevant factors which the court must take into account when considering whether the possession action or the injunction application should prevail.[81]

3.71   However, such 'races' are unlikely to recur because parliament has resolved the balance in such cases in favour of the landlord by enacting HA 1985 ss121A[82] and 138(2A)–(2D).[83] Section 121A permits the court to make an order suspending the right to buy (a 'suspension order') for such period as is specified in the order. The grounds that need to be established for making such an order are the same

78 HA 1985 s83A(1).
79 HA 1985 s138(3).
80 *Bristol CC v Lovell* [1998] 1 WLR 446; [1998] 1 All ER 775, HL.
81 *Tandridge DC v Bickers* (1999) 31 HLR 432, CA.
82 Inserted by HA 2004 s192(2), with effect from 6 June 2005.
83 Inserted by HA 2004 s193, with effect from 6 June 2005.

as the grounds for making a demotion order (see chapter 8). Further orders can be made extending the period of suspension.[84] Where a suspension order has not been made and the process of completing the right to buy is already well advanced, the landlord can still prevent the purchase from taking place. Section 138(2A) provides that, where an application is pending before any court for a possession order under ground 2, a demotion order or a suspension order, the landlord is not bound to transfer the property to the tenant until the court application is determined.

Ground 2 (first limb): nuisance or annoyance

3.72   The first part of ground 2 of HA 1985 Sch 2 is satisfied where:

> The tenant or a person residing in or visiting the dwelling-house
> (a) has been guilty of conduct causing or likely to cause a nuisance or annoyance to a person residing, visiting or otherwise engaging in a lawful activity in the locality ...

3.73   Note that the ground imputes the secure tenant with responsibility for the actions of *any* others living in *or* visiting the property – not just members of the same household. In this sense the ground is one of 'strict liability' – its terms may be satisfied even in a case where the tenant did not know that a co-resident or visitor was causing a nuisance or where, if the secure tenant had known, he or she would have been powerless to stop it.[85]

3.74   However, a casual caller to tenant's home who is guilty of causing annoyance while there may arguably not be 'visiting the dwelling-house' for the purposes of the ground if his or her visit is uninvited or positively unwelcome to the tenant. Otherwise, a tenant may be faced with a claim for possession based on the activities of a person actually coming to the property for the purpose of causing nuisance to him or her, such as a violent ex-partner.

3.75   Each of the words in this limb of ground 2 require consideration. The meaning of 'nuisance' is not restricted in this context to the narrow legal meaning of the terms 'public nuisance' and 'private nuisance'.[86] Indeed, the words 'or annoyance' add to and broaden the concept of nuisance. Both words are given their ordinary rather than their technical legal meanings. The necessary 'conduct' to be proved

---

84   HA 1985 s121A(6).
85   *Portsmouth CC v Bryant* (2000) 32 HLR 906, CA.
86   *Harlow DC v Sewell* [2000] EHLR 122; February 2000 *Legal Action* 25, CA.

may possibly be constituted by one single act but is more likely to be shown through a number of examples of similar behaviour. The particulars of claim must detail the 'conduct' alleged.[87]

3.76 The use of the term 'guilty' does not impose a requirement that conduct be deliberate or culpable. In *Kensington and Chelsea RLBC v Simmonds*,[88] the tenant's teenage son, who resided with her, had deliberately engaged in conduct amounting to nuisance. He was therefore 'guilty' of such conduct and ground 2 was satisfied. The Court of Appeal rejected the contention that the ground could be satisfied only if there was also some fault on the tenant's part, although it did hold that the existence or extent of any personal blame on the tenant's part would be relevant to the question of 'reasonableness' discussed below. That approach has likewise been applied to the current wording of ground 2 by the Court of Appeal in *Portsmouth CC v Bryant*.[89]

3.77 In *Croydon LBC v Moody*,[90] a point was taken that the defendant tenant was so affected by mental illness as to have been incapable of being 'guilty' of the conduct complained of, which was simply a manifestation of his illness. However, as the conduct was also a breach of a tenancy term and the landlord was relying on ground 1 (which makes no reference to 'guilty' – see above), as well as ground 2, the issue did not need to be resolved. For a possible defence under the Disability Discrimination Act 1995 in these circumstances, see chapter 27.

3.78 There is no need for the landlord to prove that any person was actually the victim of nuisance or annoyance – it is sufficient if there is evidence of conduct that was *likely* to cause such nuisance or annoyance (so that no victim need give evidence). Thus, the landlord may prove the ground using the evidence of those who simply saw or heard the misconduct complained of, for example, a police officer, an environmental health patrol team, the caretaker or other 'professional' witnesses. Indeed, if the judge is prepared to give it sufficient weight, even pure hearsay evidence may satisfy the court that the ground is made out.[91]

---

87 CPR PD 55A para 2.4A.
88 (1997) 29 HLR 507, CA.
89 (2000) 32 HLR 906, CA. See too, *Bedfordshire Pilgrims HA v Khan* [2007] EWCA Civ 1445.
90 (1999) 31 HLR 738, CA.
91 *Leeds City Council v Harte* April 1999 *Legal Action* 27, CA. See also *Solon South West Housing Association Ltd v James* [2004] EWCA Civ 1847; [2005] HLR 24 and *Washington Housing Company Ltd v Morson* [2005] EWHC 3407 (Ch). On the caution which must be exercised in reliance on hearsay in residential tenancy cases see *Moat Housing v Harris and Hartless* [2005] EWCA Civ 287; [2006] QB 606.

3.79   A much wider group of potential victims than simply 'neighbours' is embraced by the ground. It extends to the protection of others living in, visiting or otherwise lawfully conducting themselves in the locality. The term 'locality' is not defined by the Act. It was substituted for the word 'vicinity' which appeared in earlier drafts of the legislation and was thought too narrow. It is an ordinary English word requiring no special elaboration or definition. Any issue as to whether the matters complained of took place within the 'locality' of the dwelling is to be resolved as a question of fact on all the evidence.[92]

3.80   The existence of this wide ground for possession does not mean that a victim can always expect it to be used by a social landlord. Even if its terms are satisfied, the landlord cannot be required to instigate proceedings in reliance on it unless there is an express term in the victim's own tenancy agreement that this landlord will bring such proceedings on request. There is certainly no implied term which requires the landlord to take action under ground 2 in the case of neighbour nuisance. The victim cannot compel the landlord to act under this ground in the absence of an express agreement to do so.[93]

3.81   Even if the first limb of ground 2 is made out, the landlord must go on to prove that it is reasonable that possession of the tenant's home should be ordered.[94] This is the 'reasonableness condition' and must always be satisfied before an order under ground 2 can be made. There may be cases in which a judgment proceeds from a finding that ground 2 is made out directly to a conditional possession order, thus missing the vital issue of whether it is reasonable for *any* order to be made. The Court of Appeal has repeatedly emphasised the importance of the judge indicating in the judgment that the question of reasonableness has been expressly considered.[95]

3.82   In determining 'reasonableness' in ground 2 cases, the court is directed by HA 1985 s85A(2)[96] to consider in particular:

(a) the effect that the nuisance or annoyance has had on persons other than the person against whom the order is sought;
(b) any continuing effect the nuisance or annoyance is likely to have on such persons;

92 *Manchester City Council v Lawler* (1999) 31 HLR 119, CA.
93 *O'Leary v Islington LBC* (1983) 9 HLR 81, CA; *Hussain v Lancaster City Council* (1999) 31 HLR 164, CA and *Mowan v Wandsworth LBC* [2001] LGR 228; (2001) 33 HLR 56, CA.
94 HA 1985 s84(1).
95 For an example see *Manchester City Council v Green* January 1999 *Legal Action* 26, CA.
96 Inserted by Anti-Social Behaviour Act 2003 s16.

(c) the effect that the nuisance or annoyance would be likely to have on such persons if the conduct is repeated.

3.83 Essentially, this provision, which has the effect of structuring the court's discretion towards the interests of the victims or potential victims of the alleged behaviour, gives statutory effect to the approach of the Court of Appeal in anti-social behaviour cases in recent years (see para 3.88). Although the rubric is of strict application only when the court is considering 'reasonableness', much the same factors will be taken into account in considering whether to postpone any order for possession.[97]

3.84 But while the court must give special prominence to the interests of the victims of the behaviour complained of, it nevertheless retains its discretion to consider other factors. It should also be invited to consider, among other issues: the seriousness and frequency of the nuisance; whether it is continuing, persistent or recently abated; warnings issued by the landlord; and the relevant personal circumstances of the tenant.[98] In *Woking BC v Bistram*,[99] the nuisance proved was foul, abusive and menacing language. The trial judge refused to order possession, on the basis that such language was commonplace in areas of council housing. The Court of Appeal held that: (a) the finding as to use of similar language elsewhere was not supported by any evidence; and (b) as the abuse had been continuing right up to trial it was reasonable for the protection of other tenants to grant possession. In *Solihull MBC v Reeman*,[100] the trial judge had been satisfied that the tenant had caused nuisance and annoyance but found it not reasonable to order possession in view of the steps the tenant had taken to abate the nuisance and the fact that the tenant was an epileptic single man whom the council did not propose to rehouse if possession were granted. In *Stonebridge Housing Action Trust v Gabbidon*,[101] where the home had been used for dealing in drugs, the judge found it reasonable to grant possession but was persuaded to suspend the order because the female defendant had not personally been involved in the dealing and there was no evidence of recent incidents. The judge also took into account the fact that there was a seven-month-old child in the household, The High Court on appeal

---

97 *Lambeth LBC v Debrah* [2007] EWCA Civ 1503; May 2008 *Legal Action* 44.
98 *Darlington BC v Sterling* (1997) 29 HLR 309, CA.
99 (1995) 27 HLR 1, CA.
100 June 1994 *Legal Action* 10.
101 [2002] EWHC 2091 (Ch); (2003) 100(5) LSG 30; (2002) *Times* 13 December; cf *Sandwell MBC v Hensley* [2007] EWCA Civ 1425; [2008] HLR 22.

refused to interfere with the judge's ruling: the landlord's contention that allowing the family to remain in occupation would set a precedent for other tenants was not supportable.

3.85   The court's attention on the 'reasonableness' issue might also be directed to the landlord's (and the victim's) alternative available remedies for nuisance, including injunctions – especially in the light of the availability of draconian orders to control anti-social behaviour available under HA 1996 Part V Ch 3, the Protection from Harassment Act 1997 s2 and the Crime and Disorder Act 1998 s1 (anti-social behaviour orders (ASBOs)). However, the mere existence of these alternative remedies is no bar to the landlord seeking possession under ground 2 instead of, or in addition to, such other relief.[102] The fact that an ASBO has been made against the tenant or a member of his or her family can point in either direction, depending on the circumstances. In one case, the conduct which gave rise to the ASBO may be so serious that the making of an outright possession order, rather than a postponed or suspended order, may be self-evident, while in another case the ASBO may have served its purpose of restraining future misbehaviour, so that suspension might still be possible.[103] See para 3.90.

3.86   In considering 'reasonableness' where the nuisance has been caused not by the tenant but by another resident or a visitor, the court will need to be fully appraised of the extent to which the tenant has sought to modify or control that behaviour, whether by excluding the perpetrator or otherwise.[104]

3.87   Similarly, where the conduct on which the landlord relies is said to be a manifestation of the tenant's mental illness or personality disorder, the extent of those conditions and their 'treatability' will be crucial on the question of 'reasonableness' and the court will obviously need to have regard to medical evidence tendered.[105] Where it can be shown that such conduct was caused by a disability within the meaning of the Disability Discrimination Act 1995, this may be a powerful factor in persuading the court that it would not be

---

102 *Newcastle upon Tyne City Council v Morrison* (2000) 32 HLR 891, CA.

103 *Manchester City Council v Higgins* [2005] EWCA Civ 1423; [2006] 1 All ER 841; [2006] HLR 14 and *Knowsley Housing Trust v McMullen* [2006] EWCA Civ 539; [2006] HLR 43.

104 See *Kensington and Chelsea RLBC v Simmonds* (1997) 29 HLR 507, CA; *Gallagher v Castle Vale Housing Trust* [2001] EWCA Civ 944; (2001) 33 HLR 810; *Portsmouth City Council v Bryant* (2000) 32 HLR 906, CA and *Knowsley Housing Trust v McMullen* [2006] EWCA Civ 539; [2006] HLR 43.

105 *Croydon LBC v Moody* (1999) 31 HLR 738, CA and *Southwark LBC v Kennedy* [1998] CLY 2988.

reasonable to make a possession order: see chapter 27. Nevertheless, if bizarre behaviour by the tenant (however explained) is putting the welfare and safety of that tenant or their neighbours at risk, an order for possession may well be appropriate.[106]

3.88   Historically, the Court of Appeal has been unwilling to interfere with the decisions of trial judges on 'reasonableness' issues in nuisance-related cases.[107] But in the context of modern concerns about anti-social behaviour, the Court of Appeal has, in a series of decisions, reversed the decisions of judges who have not been satisfied that it was reasonable to order possession in secure tenancy 'nuisance' cases or who have made only postponed or suspended orders rather than outright orders.[108] The position may now be fairly said to have been reached that if ground 2 is made out in a serious case, something exceptional will be required on the part of the tenant to show why it would be unreasonable to order possession.

3.89   Instead, the focus in such anti-social behaviour cases is nowadays on whether the court can be persuaded to make a conditional rather than an outright order. The court will pay particular heed to whether the tenant acknowledges the seriousness of the conduct in question and, particularly where the behaviour is that of a young person, to his or her efforts to co-operate with other agencies in seeking to bring about change. If there is real hope for the future that the tenant will 'turn a corner', a postponed order may well be appropriate.[109] On the other hand, a tendency to minimise the alleged behaviour and its effects and to show no remorse will inevitably pre-dispose the court against postponing the order.[110] Where there have been serious acts of harassment or intimidation, even a subsequent improvement in the conduct of the tenant's family will not prevent the court from making an outright order.[111] Again, the Court of Appeal has been prepared to upset suspended orders in such cases and replace them with outright orders[112] and (only very exceptionally) to substitute

106 *CDS Housing v Bellis* [2008] EWCA Civ 1315; February 2009 *Legal Action* 28.
107 *Ealing LBC v Jama* [2008] EWCA Civ 896; August 2008 *Legal Action* 40.
108 *Woking BC v Bistram* (1993) 27 HLR 1; *Darlington BC v Sterling* (1997) 29 HLR 309; *Bristol City Council v Mousah* (1998) 30 HLR 32; *West Kent Housing Association v Davies* (1999) 31 HLR 415 and *Newcastle upon Tyne City Council v Morrison* (2000) 32 HLR 891.
109 *High Peak BC v Purser* August 2008 *Legal Action* 40.
110 See, eg, *Merton LBC v Mitchell* [2005] EWCA Civ 678 and *Manchester CC v Higgins* [2005] EWCA Civ 1423; [2006] 1 All ER 841.
111 *Solon South West Housing Association Ltd v James* [2004] EWCA Civ 1847; [2005] HLR 24.
112 *Canterbury CC v Lowe* (2001) 33 HLR 583, CA.

suspended orders for absolute orders.[113] It has repeatedly backed county court judges who have made outright possession orders in serious nuisance cases.[114]

3.90   The general approach of the Court of Appeal to possession claims based on anti-social behaviour is evident from the case of *Manchester City Council v Higgins*.[115] Ms Higgins was a secure tenant and a single mother of three children, aged 15, 13 and 2. Her son and, to a lesser extent, her elder daughter caused distress to a widow who lived nearby with three sons, all of whom suffered from a mental disability. They swore at the neighbour and her children, bullied the children and damaged her property. The council warned the tenant that if her son's behaviour did not change, it would have no alternative but to begin proceedings. That had no effect and the council obtained a 'without notice' injunction. Subsequently, the council obtained an ASBO against the son. He was then arrested after a further incident involving criminal damage, following which he was placed under supervision for two years for the offences of criminal damage and assault, but he continued to harass the neighbouring family.

3.91   The council began possession proceedings under grounds 1 and 2. In the county court, a recorder made a possession order, but suspended it for 18 months. The Court of Appeal allowed the council's appeal. The discretion of the court to make a possession order under HA 1985 s85 is unfettered, but it has to be exercised judicially. It follows that all the circumstances of the case which are material are to be borne in mind. If the misconduct by the tenant or by a member of the household is serious and persistent enough to justify an ASBO, that is strong but not conclusive evidence that the tenant would have forfeited any entitlement to retain possession. In one case, the facts giving rise to the making of an ASBO might be so serious that both the making of a possession order and the refusal to suspend it would be self-evident. In another case, the making of an ASBO might have served its purpose of restraining future misbehaviour, so that, in spite of past conduct, postponement of the order might still be

---

113 *Greenwich LBC v Grogan* (2001) 33 HLR 12, CA; *Gallagher v Castle Vale Housing Action Trust* [2001] EWCA Civ 944; (2001) 33 HLR 810 and *Moat Housing Group South Ltd v Harris and Hartless* [2004] EWCA Civ 1852; [2006] QB 606; [2005] HLR 33.

114 *Camden LBC v Gilsenan* (1999) 31 HLR 81, CA; *Waltham Forest LBC v Partridge* July 2000 *Legal Action* 28; *Westminster City Council v Garcia* August 2000 *Legal Action* 24, CA and *Lambeth LBC v Howard* [2001] EWCA Civ 468; (2003) 33 HLR 58.

115 [2005] EWCA Civ 1423; [2006] 1 All ER 841; [2006] HLR 14.

possible. Since the court would already have found that it was reasonable to make a possession order, the question whether or not to defer its execution has to be very much a question of the future. Previous unheeded warnings point one way, genuine remorse the other.

3.92 The level of support available to a parent who is making proper efforts to control an errant child is relevant. However, there has always to be a sound basis for the hope that the anti-social behaviour will cease. Ultimately, given the respect for a tenant's home guaranteed by article 8 of the European Convention on Human Rights (ECHR), the question is whether an immediate possession order is necessary in order to protect the rights and freedoms of others, and is proportionate.

3.93 In this case, the behaviour of Ms Higgins and her children, especially the son, had been quite intolerable. The son had shown himself unrepentantly anti-social. The mere fact that the ASBO would remain in force until the son attained the age of 16 would not give the neighbours sufficient protection. In the absence of any expression of remorse or any well-founded expectation of improvement, it was disproportionate not to make an immediate possession order. Ms Higgins was without remorse and totally indifferent to the effect her children's behaviour was having on her neighbours. She had forfeited her right to respect for her home. The recorder should have made an order for possession in 28 days.

3.94 On the other hand, in *Moat Housing Group South Ltd v Harris and Hartless*,[116] where the anti-social behaviour was far less serious, the Court of Appeal considered the absence of any prior warning or complaint by the landlord together with good school reports received by the tenant's children, the absence of any criminal records or any serious record of police involvement with the family and favourable testimonies which were given about the defendant, and suspended the outright possession order made in the county court. Plainly, where it is put to the court by the landlord that the tenant is responsible for behaviour which has founded an *un*successful prosecution for breach of an ASBO, the court would be wrong to make a possession order primarily based on that conduct.[117]

3.95 If the judge is satisfied that it is reasonable to grant an order for possession in a ground 2 case, it is not part of his or her function to require the housing authority to set out what arrangements will be available for the rehousing of the family after eviction.[118]

116 [2004] EWCA Civ 1852; [2006] QB 606; [2005] HLR 33.
117 *Wandsworth LBC v Webb* [2008] EWCA Civ 1643; January 2009 *Legal Action* 23; (2009) *Times* 5 January.
118 *Watford BC v Simpson* (2000) 32 HLR 901, CA.

3.96   It is clear that ground 2 cases involving alleged nuisance can give rise to difficult issues of fact and law and that the risk of a possession order being made is such that the tenant should have a proper opportunity to prepare a defence and secure representation.[119]

3.97   Whether it is reasonable to grant possession in a claim based on this limb of ground 2 may turn, particularly where other aspects are finely balanced, on the conduct of the social *landlord*. In particular those advising a secure tenant might usefully review whether the landlord has complied with its own policies and procedures for handling anti-social behaviour cases and has treated the secure tenant in accordance with them.[120] Section 218A of the Housing Act 1996[121] requires every landlord of secure tenants to prepare, maintain and keep under review a policy in relation to anti-social behaviour and procedures for dealing with occurrences of anti-social behaviour. Those documents must be published and available at the landlord's offices. A free summary of them must be available on request.[122] The policy and procedures (and any review of them) must have regard to the content of relevant statutory guidance.[123]

3.98   In addition to establishing their own in-house policies and procedures, many social landlords are signatories to the *Respect Standard for Housing Management.*[124] Section 6 of that document particularly addresses cases where the tenant could benefit from support to sustain a tenancy and avoid eviction. It provides that signatory landlords are committed to:

---

119 *Bates v Croydon LBC* [2001] EWCA Civ 134; (2001) 33 HLR 792.

120 See *Croydon LBC v Barber* [2010] EWCA Civ 51; (2010) *Times* 24 March, in which failure to follow its own policy proved fatal to the council's possession claim against a non-secure tenant.

121 Inserted by the Anti-Social Behaviour Act 2003 s12.

122 HA 1996 s218A(6).

123 HA 1996 s218A(7). There are three separate statutory guidance documents: (1) *Anti-social Behaviour: Policy and Procedure – Code of guidance for local housing authorities and housing action trusts in England* (CLG, August 2003) available at www.communities.gov.uk/publications/housing/antisocialbehaviourpolicy; (2) *Anti-social behaviour: policies and procedures – code of guidance for local authorities and housing associations in Wales* (Welsh Assembly Government, July 2005) available at http://new.wales.gov.uk/topics/housingandcommunity/housing/publications/antisocialbehaviour/?lang=en and (3) *Statutory Housing Management Guidance on policies and procedures on tackling anti-social behaviour for housing associations in England* (Housing Corporation, August 2004) available at www.housingcorp.gov.uk/server/show/conWebDoc.3311.

124 *Respect Standard for Housing Management – A Guide for Landlords* (CLG, August 2006) available at www.communities.gov.uk/publications/housing/respectstandard2.

- Ensure staff are fully aware of the range of support provision available and are able to identify how each approach should be used as a core component of case management.
- Ensure staff have a clear understanding of how support provision should be linked with triggers (eg early intervention measures or use of enforcement action such as demotion).
- Ensure Policies and Procedures state clearly how support provision will be provided or accessed and the triggers/process by which support needs will be identified.
- A clear focus on delivering support and challenge solutions (ie linking support with enforcement at an early stage) rather than crisis-based interventions where problems have escalated.
- Making it clear to residents that enforcement action may be considered where suitable offers of support are refused and their behaviour does not improve.
- Clear policies and procedures on dealing with vulnerable residents (eg mental health issues and drug and alcohol problems).
- Following assessment (involving multi-agency case conferening where appropriate) deployment of 'floating support' designed to work with residents in stopping anti-social behaviour and where possible, maintaining a tenancy.
- Where available and appropriate, referral to Family Intervention Programmes for residents with complex support needs who are causing anti-social behaviour in the community.
- Negotiate with local Supporting People teams in order to build on existing floating and residential housing related support schemes to ensure that the appropriate support is available for those residents/ families with complex needs. Where no support currently exists explore possible opportunities for Supporting People to fund new support projects.

3.99   Advisers assisting tenants in cases where support has not been forthcoming to help them address anti-social behaviour should obviously check whether the landlord was a signatory to the Standard at the time that there was need for support. For the future, the Tenant Service Authority has adopted a new statutory National Neighbourhood and Community Standard for social landlords with effect from 1 April 2010. The first 'specific expectation' under the standard in respect of anti-social behaviour provides at para 3.1 that:

> Registered providers shall publish a policy on how they work with relevant partners to prevent and tackle anti-social behaviour in areas where they own properties.[125]

---

125 *The regulatory framework for social housing in England from April 2010* (TSA, March 2010) p30.

3.100   The courts have shown a readiness to measure the landlord's perform-ance in a particular case against its published policies and procedures even in cases where the tenants do not enjoy security of tenure.[126] The relevance of such materials must be even greater where the tenant is a secure tenant.

Ground 2 (second limb): criminal activity

3.101   A landlord may additionally or alternatively rely on ground 2 where:

> The tenant or a person residing in or visiting the dwelling-house ...
> (b) has been convicted of –
>   (i) using the dwelling-house, or allowing it to be used, for im-moral or illegal purposes, or
>   (ii) an indictable offence committed in, or in the locality of, the dwelling-house.

3.102   Again, the precise words of the ground require careful attention. Note, for example, that the ground is satisfied by the conviction (not mere ar-rest) of any of the tenant, a co-resident or a visitor. There is no definition of 'locality' for the purposes of the ground (see para 3.79 for discussion of its meaning in this context). The word 'indictable' replaced 'arrestable' on 1 January 2006.[127] The term 'indictable offence' has a specific defin-ition in criminal law.

3.103   There was little or no experience of use of the first part of this limb of ground 2 (illegal or immoral user) in the social housing sector in the early years following the introduction of security of tenure in 1980. However, in more recent years, convictions for use of premises to manufacture, store or trade illicit drugs have led to greater use of the ground by social landlords. For guidance on judicial considera-tion of 'immoral' or 'illegal' purpose, reference may usefully be made to the developed case-law on the almost identically expressed word-ing found in the Rent Act 1977 for private tenants (para 17.21) and the Housing Act 1988 for assured tenants (see para 12.138).

3.104   The latter part of the second limb of ground 2 (conviction of an indictable offence) was an innovation introduced by the Housing Act 1996. It breaks the link between the acts of criminality and use of the dwelling which is the criminal's home. Guidance published by cen-tral government at the time of its enactment suggested that it may be particularly useful for a landlord 'which is concerned about drug

---

126 *Croydon LBC v Barber* [2010] EWCA Civ 51; (2010) *Times* 24 March.
127 Substitution made by Serious Organised Crime and Police Act 2005 s111 and Sch 7 Pt 3 para 45.

dealing where the trafficking is taking place in the common parts of the estate rather than a house or flat'.[128]

3.105 The second limb of ground 2 is also subject to the condition that it must be shown to be reasonable in all the circumstances for a possession order to be made.[129] Here again, the court is directed to pay special attention to the effects of the behaviour in question on other people (see para 3.82), in so far as this consideration is relevant to the second limb. Other factors on reasonableness will include: the seriousness of the offence; the pattern of offending (if any); previous good character; the circumstances of the non-offending occupiers; and the relationship (or lack of one) between the offence and the landlord–tenant relationship.

3.106 Where there has been a conviction and sentence, the offender will have received as much punishment as the criminal justice system thought appropriate. A secure tenant's representative might pray that point in aid on the question of reasonableness in particular ground 2 cases. Such a case is likely to arise where a long-standing tenant (or fellow resident) has been found guilty of a one-off offence highly unlikely to be repeated.[130] However, if there has been a conviction of an offence or offences of any real seriousness, it would be an exceptional case in which not even a conditional order for possession were made, whatever sentence the criminal court imposed.[131]

3.107 In a case where the issue is as stark as whether the possession order should be outright or suspended, it is worth the tenant's adviser drawing the attention of the court to the increased risk of further offending if the criminal is evicted to live an insecure life on the streets or in transient accommodation as opposed to receiving the benefit of support services (such as that of the probation service), which can be more straightforwardly supplied to those with a fixed address.[132] Alternatively, a critical feature in such cases will often be that the tenant has the capacity to reform and has stated an intention to 'mend [his or her] ways'.[133]

---

128 DoE Circ 2/97 para 28(iii).
129 HA 1985 s84(2)(a).
130 *Tower Hamlets LBC v Kellum* November 2000 *Legal Action* 22.
131 *Bristol City Council v Mousah* (1998) 30 HLR 32, CA and *Sandwell MBC v Hensley* [2007] EWCA Civ 1425; [2008] HLR 22.
132 *Greenwich LBC v Grogan* (2001) 33 HLR 140, CA.
133 *Sheffield CC v Shaw* [2007] EWCA Civ 42; [2007] HLR 25.

Ground 2A: domestic violence

3.108   Ground 2A was introduced into Schedule 2 to the Housing Act 1985 by HA 1996 s145 and has subsequently been amended by the Civil Partnership Act 2004. The ground can be satisfied where:

> The dwelling-house was occupied (whether alone or with others) by a married couple, a couple who are civil partners of each other, a couple living together as husband and wife or a couple living together as if they were civil partners and –
> (a) one or both of the partners is a tenant of the dwelling-house,
> (b) one partner has left because of violence or threats of violence by the other towards –
>   (i) that partner, or
>   (ii) a member of the family of that partner who was residing with that partner immediately before the partner left, and
> (c) the court is satisfied that the partner who has left is unlikely to return.

3.109   The ground is designed to deal with what might be broadly described as 'domestic violence', particularly where this has housing management implications for the landlord. The ground is most commonly relied on where the landlord has re-housed the departed victim of violence, leaving the perpetrator under-occupying the former family home.

3.110   The ground has no application where there is no 'couple', as defined by the wording of the ground, for example, where the violence of a child causes a parent to leave. It must be a partner who leaves.

3.111   The landlord must be able to prove not only that the dwelling had been home to a couple but that both: (1) the partner who left did so because of violence or the threat of violence (as distinct from some other unreasonable conduct[134]); *and* (2) he or she is unlikely to return. As to the first of these, it is not necessary for the landlord to establish that the violence was the sole cause of the partner's departure. However, it will not suffice simply to demonstrate that the violent behaviour was one of a number of factors that caused the departed

---

134   'Violence' requires physical contact, ie, something more than emotional or psychological abuse: 'when an ordinary English word is used, one is entitled to assume that, in the absence of good reason to the contrary, it should be given its primary natural meaning, and to my mind, when one is talking of violence to a person, it involves physical contact' per Neuberger LJ in *Kensington & Chelsea RLBC v Danesh* [2006] EWCA Civ 1404; [2007] 1 WLR 69 at [15], followed and applied in *Yemshaw v Hounslow LBC* [2009] EWCA Civ 1543.

partner to leave. It must be the main, substantive or significant reason why the victim left.[135]

3.112   The second of the conditions (unlikelihood of return) will be particularly difficult to satisfy if the departed partner wants to return when the partner remaining is evicted.

3.113   If the departed partner is him or herself unwilling to give evidence the landlord may need to rely on hearsay evidence – rendered admissible by the Civil Evidence Act 1995 – to establish these matters.

3.114   The ground arises not only where there has been violence or threat of violence directed to the departed partner but also where there has been violence or threat of violence directed to other family members that has caused the partner to leave. The term 'member of the family' is defined in HA 1985 s113 (reproduced at para 2.40).

3.115   The strict wording of the ground would not be satisfied if the family member was driven to leave ahead of the departing partner who only left sometime later. The requirement that the family member must be residing with the partner 'immediately' before the latter's departure suggests that only departure en masse is within the ground.

3.116   Special requirements concerning service of notices seeking possession apply if possession is to be sought on ground 2A. If the partner who has left is not the tenant (or one of the joint tenants), the landlord must serve a copy of the notice on that partner or show that it has 'taken all reasonable steps' to do so.[136] Likewise, if permission is given to add ground 2A to a notice seeking possession after proceedings have started, the landlord must serve a special notice (complying with HA 1985 s83A(6)) on the departed partner if he or she is not a party in the proceedings, or show that it has 'taken all reasonable steps' to do so.[137] The court cannot entertain a ground 2A claim unless these requirements are met. They can be dispensed with only if (a) the landlord has also specified ground 2 (nuisance – see above) in the notice seeking possession and (b) it is just and equitable to do so.[138]

3.117   Presumably, the rationale for providing the departed partner with these copy notices is that in all save the most urgent cases the departed partner should be forewarned that the former family home is at risk so that he or she might make any appropriate application under the Family Law Act 1996 Part IV for occupation or transfer orders before the tenancy is lost (see chapter 35).

135   *Camden LBC v Mallett* (2001) 33 HLR 20, CA.
136   HA 1985 s83A(3).
137   HA 1985 s83A(4).
138   HA 1985 s83A.

Ground 3: deterioration in condition

3.118   Housing Act 1985 Sch 2 ground 3 provides a ground for possession to the landlord of a secure tenant where:

> The condition of the dwelling-house or any of the common parts has deteriorated owing to acts of waste by, or the neglect or default of, the tenant or a person residing in the dwelling-house and, in the case of an act of waste by, or the neglect or default of, a person lodging with the tenant or a sub-tenant of his, the tenant has not taken such steps as he ought reasonably to have taken for the removal of the lodger or sub-tenant.

3.119   The ground is subject to the condition that an order for possession may be made only if it would be reasonable to do so.[139]

3.120   Useful guidance on the construction of this provision is to be derived from cases on the Rent Act 1977 Sch 15 case 3 (see para 17.23) and HA 1988 Sch 2 ground 13 (see para 12.132). However, unlike the Rent Act case, ground 3 embraces deterioration in the condition of 'common parts' within its terms. This phrase is defined[140] as meaning:

> ... any part of a building comprising the dwelling-house and any other premises which the tenant is entitled under the terms of the tenancy to use in common with the occupiers of other dwelling-houses let by the landlord ...

and the ground may therefore cover the situation in which the secure tenant or another person residing in the dwelling-house has been responsible for damaging the lifts, stairways, rubbish chutes, communal lighting, etc, in the block of flats of which the dwelling-house forms part. The acts or omissions must be proved on the balance of probabilities to have been the responsibility of the tenant or co-resident.

3.121   Note that in contrast to the amendments made by the Housing Act 1996 relating to ground 2 above, the wording of ground 3 has not been enlarged to make tenants responsible for damage caused by 'visitors' (although it does cover visitors who can properly be considered to be 'residing in' the dwelling or 'lodging with the tenant').

---

139   HA 1985 s84(2)(a).
140   HA 1985 s116.

Ground 4: deterioration of furniture

3.122 Housing Act 1985 Sch 2 ground 4 provides:

> The condition of furniture provided by the landlord for use under the tenancy, or for use in the common parts, has deteriorated owing to ill-treatment by the tenant or a person residing in the dwelling-house and, in the case of ill-treatment by a person lodging with the tenant or a sub-tenant of his, the tenant has not taken such steps as he ought reasonably to have taken for the removal of the lodger or sub-tenant.

3.123 Although they have power to provide furniture for tenants,[141] local authority landlords rarely do so. Most social housing is let unfurnished. However, the ground extends to furniture provided by the landlord in the common parts of the property. Given the extended definition of 'common parts' in HA 1985 s116 (set out at para 3.120 above), this would embrace vandalism by the tenant or co-resident in such places as the communal laundry or children's playing area.

3.124 Note that, in contrast to the amendments made by HA 1996 relating to ground 2 above, the wording of ground 4 has not been enlarged to make tenants responsible for damage caused by 'visitors' although it will extend to those 'lodging with' the tenant.

3.125 Ground 4 is subject to the condition that, even if the terms of the ground are established, an order may be granted only if it would be reasonable in all the circumstances.[142]

Ground 5: tenancy obtained by deception

3.126 Housing Act 1985 Sch 2 ground 5 is satisfied if:

> The tenant is the person, or one of the persons, to whom the tenancy was granted and the landlord was induced to grant the tenancy by a false statement made knowingly or recklessly by –
> (a) the tenant, or
> (b) *a person acting at the tenant's instigation.*

3.127 The ground is basically designed for those cases in which the tenancy has been obtained by deception. It extends not only to the making of false representations known to be false at the time of their making, but also to the 'reckless' making of statements which turn out to be false. Where a person completes an application form for allocation of housing on the basis that he or she will inform the prospective

---

141 HA 1985 s10.
142 HA 1985 s84(2)(a).

landlord of any changes in their circumstances which might affect their need for housing, the subsequent failure to disclose new information to the prospective landlord may amount to a false statement which induces the grant of a tenancy.[143] On the other hand, it cannot be applied where the landlord's essential complaint is that it would not have granted the tenancy if the tenant had given information for which in fact the landlord had failed to ask.[144]

3.128   The words in italics were added on 12 February 1997 by HA 1996 s146. Previously, only statements attributable to the *tenant* (or one of the joint tenants) could satisfy the ground, so that if a partner induced the landlord to let the accommodation in the sole name of the other partner, the ground could not be relied on. The effect of the amendment is to close that lacuna and enable the landlord to rely on the ground in respect of a representation made by a third party. It is not enough, however, for the landlord just to prove that a third party made the relevant representation – it must additionally be shown that this was done at the instigation of the tenant.[145] Note also that ground 5 is not available where the current tenant is not the person to whom the tenancy was granted (so, for example, it cannot be made out where a tenant obtained the tenancy by deception and then lawfully assigned it to an innocent party).[146]

3.129   In order to prove a ground 5 case the landlord must establish not only a false statement but also that the statement *induced* the grant of the tenancy. It is not necessary for the landlord to produce evidence from the actual decision-maker who granted the tenancy. In *Waltham Forest LBC v Roberts*,[147] the tenant had stated in her application for housing that she did not own any property, whereas she was in fact the joint owner of an undisclosed property. The Court of Appeal held that the correct approach was to ask whether the misstatement was material to the landlord's discharge of its social housing functions. Once the materiality of the misstatement had been established, it was a 'fair inference' of fact that the decision-maker had been influenced by it.

3.130   Even if the ground is proved, the landlord must also show that it is reasonable for possession to be ordered.[148]

143   *North Hertfordshire DC v Carthy* [2003] EWCA Civ 20.
144   *Peterborough CC v Moran* September 1993 *Legal Action* 13.
145   *Merton LBC v Richards* [2005] EWCA Civ 639; [2005] HLR 44.
146   *Islington LBC v Uckac* [2006] EWCA Civ 340; [2006] 1 WLR 1303.
147   [2004] EWCA Civ 940; [2005] HLR 2.
148   HA 1985 s84(2)(a).

3.131   When defending on reasonableness in such a case, a tenant's advocate may wish to remind the court that a *local authority* landlord already has a specific remedy if induced to grant the tenancy by the deception of an applicant for housing – prosecution under HA 1996 s171 (where the application was made under the allocation scheme) or s214 (where application was made under homelessness provisions). The loss of the home, it may be argued, would be 'excessive punishment' in all but the most exceptional cases. On the other hand, the argument may itself prompt the landlord to prosecute.

3.132   In *Rushcliffe BC v Watson*,[149] the tenant recorded on her application form that she had been a lodger in her former home. The landlord subsequently discovered that she had held a housing association tenancy elsewhere. The entry on the form was unquestionably 'false' for the purposes of ground 5. The county court judge was satisfied that all the other elements of the ground were similarly proven, and ordered possession. An appeal on the basis, inter alia, that it was not reasonable to render the tenant homeless by repossession was dismissed but the court stressed that a high burden of proof as to the ground itself was appropriate in view of the seriousness of an allegation that a tenant had made a knowing or reckless false statement.[150]

3.133   If it is clear that there has been flagrant and deliberate lying and deceitfulness, the expectation will be that possession will be ordered. In such a case it would be 'an affront to those who put forward their claims honestly, wait patiently and rely on the local housing authority to deal fairly with their claims' if a judge in such a case was not satisfied that it was reasonable to order possession.[151] Nevertheless, even in a case where the tenant has been successfully prosecuted and received a custodial sentence in respect of the deception, it will not always be reasonable to make a possession order.[152] The possibility that the evicted tenant may be faced with a subsequent finding of intentional homelessness is no impediment to the court holding that it is reasonable to order possession in a ground 5 case.[153]

3.134   The requirements of ground 5 cannot be avoided by the landlord seeking possession on the basis that the secure tenancy falls to be rescinded on account of fraud or deception.[154] Even if the tenancy was

---

149 (1992) 24 HLR 123, CA. See also *Camden LBC v Burrell* June 1997 *Legal Action* 19.
150 The reasoning in relation to the burden of proof may need to be reconsidered in the light of *Re B (children)* [2008] UKHL 35, especially para [15].
151 *Shrewsbury and Atcham BC v Evans* (1998) 30 HLR 123, CA.
152 *Southwark LBC v Erekin* [2003] EWHC 1765 (Ch).
153 *Lewisham LBC v Akinsola* (2000) 32 HLR 414, CA.
154 *Islington LBC v Uckac* [2006] EWCA Civ 340; [2006] 1 WLR 1303.

granted to a person who would not have been entitled to be allocated it under the terms of a relevant housing allocation scheme, it will not be ultra vires and therefore void.[155]

3.135   As a result of the launch of a major initiative in November 2009 to address social housing fraud in England (see para 2.55), the number of claims brought under ground 5 might be expected to increase. As part of that initiative, social landlords in England were supplied with non-statutory guidance designed to assist with evidence gathering and case preparation in ground 5 cases.[156]

Ground 6: payment of a premium

3.136   The Housing Act 1985 permits assignment by way of exchange of tenancies between secure occupiers[157] but payment of a premium as part of such a transaction renders both parties to the exchange exposed to possible possession proceedings based on HA 1985 Sch 2 ground 6. This applies where:

> The tenancy was assigned to the tenant, or to a predecessor in title of his who is a member of his family and is residing in the dwelling-house, by an assignment made by virtue of section 92 (assignments by way of exchange) and a premium was paid either in connection with that assignment or the assignment which the tenant or predecessor himself made by virtue of that section. In this paragraph the word 'premium' means any fine or other like sum and any other pecuniary consideration in addition to rent.

3.137   The wide definition of premium was presumably intended to catch not only those tenants who are induced to agree to 'swap' their homes by outright cash payments but also those offered other financial inducements by the other party to the swap – such as the purchase (at inflated values) of curtains and carpets left behind or the payment of removal expenses.

3.138   In order to recover possession the landlord must, in addition to proving the ground, show that it would be reasonable for an order for possession to be made.[158]

---

155 *Birmingham CC v Qasim* [2009] EWCA Civ 1080; [2010] LGR 253.

156 *Tackling unlawful subletting and occupancy: Good practice guidance for social landlords* (CLG, November 2009).

157 HA 1985 s92, and in some cases between secure occupiers and other tenants of social housing: see para 2.76.

158 HA 1985 s84(2)(a).

3.139   It should be noted that the ground is met whichever party to the assignment pays a premium and extends to the current tenant where the assignment was carried out by a predecessor in title. In the latter case, the predecessor must be a member of the tenant's family still living in the tenant's home. Thus if a notice seeking possession is served relying on this latter aspect of the ground, the claim can be defeated if the family member responsible moves permanently out of residence prior to the issue of proceedings.

3.140   Those defending tenants should carefully examine whether the mutual exchange in relation to which a premium was paid or received was in fact achieved by way of assignment under HA 1985 s92 at all. Many social landlords still undertake exchanges by inviting each tenant to surrender his or her existing tenancy in order to take a fresh tenancy of his or her exchange-partner's home.[159] Such an exchange would plainly not be within the reach of this ground at all. Nor can it be relied on where, although the administrative records of the landlord appear to show an assignment by way of mutual exchange, there is – as a matter of fact – no assignment at all.[160]

Ground 7: non-housing accommodation

3.141   Ground 7 of HA 1985 Sch 2 makes very specific provision for recovery of possession from those secure tenants residing in non-housing accommodation (for example, in a social service or educational facility) who are guilty of inappropriate conduct. It is met where:

> The dwelling-house forms part of, or is within the curtilage of, a building which, or so much of it as is held by the landlord, is held mainly for purposes other than housing purposes and consists mainly of accommodation other than housing accommodation, and –
> (a) the dwelling-house was let to the tenant or a predecessor in title of his in consequence of the tenant or predecessor being in the employment of the landlord, or of –
>   a local authority,
>   a development corporation,
>   a housing action trust,
>   an urban development corporation,

---

159 As in *Merton LBC v Richards* [2005] EWCA Civ 639; [2005] HLR 44.
160 *Birmingham CC v Qasim* December 2008 *Legal Action* 24, Birmingham County Court. Not appealed on this point: see *Birmingham CC v Qasim* [2009] EWCA Civ 1080; [2010] LGR 253.

... or

the governors of an aided school,

and

(b) the tenant or a person residing in the dwelling-house has been
guilty of conduct such that, having regard to the purpose for which
the building is used, it would not be right for him to continue in
occupation of the dwelling-house.

3.142   The examples that parliament presumably had in mind were of 'misbehaviour' by resident staff (or their successors) accommodated within
the buildings or grounds of schools, colleges and residential homes.

3.143   Note that the misconduct must be related to the purpose for which
the main building is generally used. Note also that the dwelling occupied by the tenant must either be within the same building as the
workplace or be within the 'curtilage' of that building. It is not sufficient simply to show that the tenanted dwelling is within the same
grounds as that building.[161]

3.144   Whether the dwelling is within the 'curtilage' of another building
is largely an issue of fact. Advisers will find helpful guidance in the
case-law relating to applications for exercise of the right to buy which
turn on whether the property sought to be purchased is within the
curtilage of another.[162]

3.145   Likewise, assistance may be derived from judicial consideration
of the term 'curtilage' in planning cases.[163]

3.146   If the accommodation has been provided to an employee who is
required to occupy it for the better performance of his or her duties,
the tenancy or licence may not be secure at all.[164]

3.147   Possession may be ordered under ground 7 only if in all the circumstances it is reasonable for an order to be made.[165]

Ground 8: temporary accommodation

3.148   Not infrequently, landlords temporarily rehouse secure tenants while
works of repair or improvement are in progress at their homes. If the

---

161 *Dyer v Dorset CC* [1989] QB 346; (1988) 20 HLR 490, CA and *Burns v Central
Regional Council* 1988 SLT (Lands Tr) 46.

162 HA 1985 Sch 5 para 5. See in particular *Barwick v Kent CC* (1992) 24 HLR
341, CA.

163 See, eg, *Skerritts of Nottingham Ltd v Secretary of State for the Environment* [2001]
QB 59, CA and *Morris v Wrexham BC* December 2001 *Legal Action* 22.

164 HA 1985 Sch 1 para 2 (see para 1.23 above).

165 HA 1985 s84(2)(a).

secure tenant is offered and accepts an alternative secure tenancy or licence of such accommodation while work is in progress, ground 8 of HA 1985 Sch 2 deals with the situation if that tenant or his or her successor refuses to return 'home' once the work is completed. The ground will be satisfied where:

> The dwelling-house was made available for occupation by the tenant (or a predecessor in title of his) while works were carried out on the dwelling-house which he previously occupied as his only or principal home and –
>
> (a) the tenant (or predecessor) was a secure tenant of the other dwelling-house at the time when he ceased to occupy it as his home,
> (b) the tenant (or predecessor) accepted the tenancy of the dwelling-house of which possession is sought on the understanding that he would give up occupation when, on completion of the works, the other dwelling-house was again available for occupation by him under a secure tenancy, and
> (c) the works have been completed and the other dwelling-house is so available.

3.149   Note that ground 8 is not concerned with requiring the tenant to move *out* for works to be undertaken – that is covered by ground 10 (see para 3.156). Ground 8 concerns the scenario of a tenant refusing to move *back* to the former home when the work on that home is completed. It must be shown both that the tenant had agreed to move back (the term 'understanding' is used in the ground) and that the works have been completed. For an example of the factual circumstances in which ground 8 could have been (but was not) deployed, see *Lambeth LBC v Gent*.[166] The ground can be satisfied only if the tenant will be returning to the former home which is to be let under a secure tenancy. Therefore, it cannot apply if, after the tenant was temporarily decanted, the former home was subject of a sale or other transfer to a landlord other than one capable of granting a secure tenancy (see para 1.6). Of course, if the tenant's current temporary home was also transferred, the tenant will no longer be a secure tenant and the ground cannot be relied upon at all.

3.150   The ground is subject to the condition that the grant of an order must be reasonable in all the circumstances.[167] Relevant factors on reasonableness will include: the circumstances under which the tenant was initially required to move; the terms of any understanding reached at that time with the landlord; and the length of time the tenant has been in the present property. The court may be particularly reluctant

166 July 2001 *Legal Action* 32.
167 HA 1985 s84(2)(a).

to disturb the tenant if works at the former home were scheduled to take a few months and were only completed some years later.

Ground 9: overcrowding

3.151   Housing Act 1985 Sch 2 ground 9 will be made out where:

> The dwelling-house is overcrowded, within the meaning of Part X, in such circumstances as to render the occupier guilty of an offence.

3.152   On what may constitute 'overcrowding' for these purposes, see the extracts from HA 1985 Part X reproduced at para 17.61.

3.153   Overcrowding is generally prohibited by HA 1985 Part X, but not all overcrowding renders the occupier guilty of an offence. In particular, overcrowding caused by visiting family members[168] or by a natural growth in family size[169] is excepted and a local council may, in any event, license what would otherwise be illegal overcrowding[170] to prevent the occupier being liable to conviction. However, a council which places secure tenants in overcrowded property may itself be liable to conviction.[171]

3.154   If this ground is made out, the landlord need not also satisfy the court on 'reasonableness' but must show that suitable alternative accommodation will be available to the tenant if an order is made.[172] Housing Act 1985 Sch 2 Part IV para 3 makes special provision as to what is 'suitable alternative accommodation' for those against whom possession is sought on overcrowding grounds, in the following terms:

> 3. Where possession of a dwelling-house is sought on ground 9 (overcrowding such as to render occupier guilty of offence), other accommodation may be reasonably suitable to the needs of the tenant and his family notwithstanding that the permitted number of persons for that accommodation, as defined in section 326(3) (overcrowding: the space standard), is less than the number of persons living in the dwelling-house of which possession is sought.

3.155   Of course, the accommodation must also be suitable in the other respects referred to in Housing Act 1985 Sch 2 Part IV (see para 3.205).

---

168   HA 1985 s329.
169   HA 1985 s328.
170   HA 1985 s330.
171   See *DPP v Carrick DC* (1985) 31 *Housing Aid* 5.
172   HA 1985 s84(2)(b).

Ground 10: landlord's works

3.156   Possession proceedings may be brought on ground 10 of Housing Act 1985 Sch 2 where:

> The landlord intends, within a reasonable time of obtaining possession of the dwelling-house –
> (a) to demolish or reconstruct the building or part of the building comprising the dwelling-house, or
> (b) to carry out work on that building or on land let together with, and thus treated as part of, the dwelling-house,
> and cannot reasonably do so without obtaining possession of the dwelling-house.

3.157   The landlord must not simply intend to carry out substantial work but, in order to satisfy this ground, must also show that the work *cannot* be carried out without obtaining possession of the dwelling-house. The landlord needs to establish that legal possession of the property and termination of the tenancy is necessary, not simply access to, or temporary occupation of, the premises by the landlord's contractors.[173]

3.158   Unless the case is one of prospective complete demolition, it must be proved that either the tenant has refused to co-operate with the landlord's proposals for temporary displacement to other accommodation or that the landlord does not have and cannot supply any accommodation to provide a temporary dwelling for the tenant while works are in progress. That is because the ground cannot be made out if the tenant demonstrates a willingness to move out of the premises (for example, to stay with relatives or in temporary accommodation supplied by the landlord) while work is in progress.

3.159   On the other hand, there will be cases in which the proposed works are so extensive as to amount to reconstruction, in which circumstances the recovery of possession seems sensible and the ground will be satisfied.

3.160   The Court of Appeal has held that in order to establish ground 10, the landlord must be in a position to: (a) identify specifically the proposed works and (b) show why it is necessary to recover possession in order for the works to be carried out.[174]

3.161   Even if the ground is made out, possession cannot be ordered unless suitable alternative accommodation is available to the tenant and

---

173   See *Sugarwhite v Afridi* [2002] CLY 3013, Central London Civil Justice Centre (where possession was unsuccessfully sought from an assured tenant on a similarly worded ground) and the discussion of *Heath v Drown* [1973] AC 498, at para 12.54.

174   *Wansbeck DC v Marley* (1988) 20 HLR 247, CA.

his or her family.[175] There is, however, no requirement that the land-lord also prove 'reasonableness', whether in the sense that it is reasonable for the landlord to want to carry out the particular works or that it is reasonable for the particular tenant to be compulsorily moved.

3.162   If the tenant is forced to give up possession, he or she will usually seek to move to permanent suitable alternative accommodation rather than to negotiate an 'understanding' with the landlord for return to the original accommodation once work is completed because such an understanding opens the way to later proceedings under ground 8 (see para 3.148).

3.163   Tenants displaced as a result of ground 10 proceedings may be entitled to home loss payments.[176] A check should also be made to see if there is any specific provision in the tenancy agreement about the compensation which may be payable.[177]

3.164   Before the introduction of the Housing Act 2004, a tenant attached to his or her home in its present condition could frustrate the land-lord's intentions for demolition or reconstruction by exercising the statutory right to buy. If the application to buy reached the stage at which the tenant would be enabled to compel completion by injunction, the tenant would be entitled to complete the purchase if the application for the injunction was heard before the trial of any claim for possession under ground 10.[178] If the injunction application and trial were listed on the same date, it would be for the judge to decide which matter to take first.[179] However, in order to prevent the purchase of properties obviously scheduled for future redevelopment, the right to buy provisions have now been extensively modified in such cases by HA 2004 ss182–183.

Ground 10A: landlord seeking to sell with vacant possession

3.165   The Housing and Planning Act 1986 s5 inserted ground 10A into HA 1985 Sch 2.[180] It assists landlords who want to achieve vacant

---

175 HA 1985 s84(2)(b). See para 3.203.
176 Land Compensation Act 1973 s29, as amended by Housing and Planning Act 1986 s5(3).
177 *Borg v Southwark LBC* June 1987 *Legal Action* 19, CA.
178 *Dance v Welwyn Hatfield DC* [1990] 22 HLR 339, CA.
179 *Bristol City Council v Lovell* [1998] 1 WLR 446; [1998] 1 All ER 775, HL.
180 Housing and Planning Act 1986 Commencement (No 5) Order 1987 SI No 754. Effective date 13 May 1987; see DoE Circ 14/87.

possession and thereafter sell property for redevelopment. Ground 10A provides that a court may order possession if suitable alternative accommodation is available to the secure tenant (see para 3.203) and:

> The dwelling-house is in an area which is the subject of a redevelopment scheme approved by the Secretary of State[181] or the Regulator of Social Housing[182] or Scottish Homes in accordance with Part V of this Schedule and the landlord intends within a reasonable time of obtaining possession to dispose of the dwelling-house in accordance with the scheme.

> or

> Part of the dwelling-house is in such an area and the landlord intends within a reasonable time of obtaining possession to dispose of that part in accordance with the scheme and for that purpose reasonably requires possession of the dwelling-house.

3.166   In order for the ground to become available, the dwelling must be in a 'redevelopment' area. Housing Act 1985 Sch 2 Part V sets out the terms under which the secretary of state, the regulator of social housing or the Welsh Assembly Government may designate such an area. The procedure requires an element of prior consultation with tenants[183] and allows the secretary of state, the regulator or the Welsh Assembly Government to require information from the relevant landlord,[184] take into account a variety of factors[185] and grant conditional or outright approval.[186] If the scheme is approved conditionally, the landlord may rely on a notice seeking possession served on ground 10A even though the conditions are not satisfied at the date of service, so long as they are fulfilled at the date of the hearing.[187] Where the landlord is a local housing authority or registered provider of social housing, the Part V functions fall on the new regulator of social housing.[188] The secretary of state's approach to Part V applications for

---

181   Functions of the secretary of state, so far as exercisable in relation to Wales, were transferred to the National Assembly for Wales, by the National Assembly for Wales (Transfer of Functions) Order 1999 SI No 672 art 2 and Sch 1.

182   From 1 April 2010 the Regulator of Social Housing replaced the Housing Corporation for these purposes: Housing and Regeneration Act 2008 (Consequential Provisions) Order 2010 SI No 866 Sch 2 para 37(2). The regulator in England is the Tenant Services Authority.

183   HA 1985 Sch 2 Pt V para 2.

184   HA 1985 Sch 2 Pt V para 3(2).

185   HA 1985 Sch 2 Pt V para 3(1).

186   HA 1985 Sch 2 Pt V para 5(1).

187   HA 1985 Sch 2 Pt V para 5(3).

188   HA 1985 Sch 2 Pt V para 6.

England was set out in DoE (former Department of the Environment) Circular 14/87 but applications from social landlords in England which are decided on or after 1 April 2010 will be determined by the regulator of social housing.

3.167　In order to obtain possession on ground 10A, the landlord need not satisfy the court that an order is reasonably required. The only relevant condition is that suitable alternative accommodation is available.

3.168　Tenants displaced as a result of ground 10A proceedings may be entitled to home loss payments.[189] A check should also be made to see if there is any specific provision in the tenancy agreement about the compensation which may be payable.[190]

Ground 11: charitable landlords

3.169　Housing Act 1985 Sch 2 ground 11 provides that a ground for possession arises where:

> The landlord is a charity and the tenant's continued occupation of the dwelling-house would conflict with the objects of the charity.

3.170　The condition which the landlord must also satisfy is that suitable alternative accommodation is available to the tenant[191] (see para 3.203). However, the landlord need not also show that it is reasonable to require the tenant to move.

3.171　If the conflict with the objects of the charity is caused by the tenant's breach of the tenancy agreement, the tenant runs the risk that the landlord may in the alternative rely on ground 1 and secure possession without being required to provide alternative accommodation (see para 3.54).

3.172　In other cases, the ground is likely to be satisfied as a result of a change in the tenant's circumstances (for example, where the charity's object is the provision of accommodation for single people and the tenant marries or has children) or by a change in the charity's objects.

189　Land Compensation Act 1973 s29, as amended by Housing and Planning Act 1986 s5(3).
190　*Borg v Southwark LBC* June 1987 *Legal Action* 19, CA.
191　HA 1985 s84(2)(b).

Ground 12: tied accommodation

3.173 Housing Act 1985 Sch 2 ground 12 relates to what might be described as 'tied' or 'employment-related' accommodation. It requires the landlord to prove that:

> The dwelling-house forms part of, or is within the curtilage of, a building which, or so much of it as is held by the landlord, is held mainly for purposes other than housing purposes and consists mainly of accommodation other than housing accommodation, or is situated in a cemetery, and –
>
> (a) the dwelling-house was let to the tenant or a predecessor in title of his in consequence of the tenant or predecessor being in the employment of the landlord or of –
> a local authority,
> a development corporation,
> a housing action trust,
> an urban development corporation,
> ..., or
> the governors of an aided school,
> and that employment has ceased,
> and
>
> (b) the landlord reasonably requires the dwelling-house for occupation as a residence for some person either engaged in the employment of the landlord, or of such a body, or with whom a contract for such employment has been entered into conditional on housing being provided.

3.174 Clearly the ground is not restricted to the situation in which the same body is both landlord and employer. It expressly incorporates situations where the landlord is a prescribed social landlord (see para 1.6) and the tenant is an employee of another or different authority of the type mentioned in the body of the ground.

3.175 It is not sufficient that the tenant (or the person from whom the tenant derived title) is an ex-employee of the landlord: the original letting must have been 'in consequence' of that employment. See the discussion on the similar Rent Act ground (para 17.33) and generally chapter 19 (Premises occupied by employees). For the meaning of 'within the curtilage of' see paras 3.143–3.144.

3.176 Note that the landlord must already be employing the next person for whom the property is required or have a contract for the employment of that person. The property must also be 'reasonably required' by the landlord.[192]

---

192 Compare with Rent Act 1977 Sch 15 case 8 discussed at para 17.33.

3.177   In addition, the landlord must satisfy the dual conditions that: (a) there will be suitable alternative accommodation (see para 3.203) for the tenant and any family and (b) it is reasonable to order possession in all the circumstances of the case.[193]

3.178   In considering whether it would be reasonable to order possession, the court should have regard to issues including: the ex-employee's age; his or her length of service; other accommodation possibilities for the new employee; and the nature of the accommodation of which possession is sought.

Ground 13: accommodation for the disabled

3.179 Special provision is made for the recovery of premises adapted for the disabled. Housing Act 1985 Sch 2 ground 13 applies where:

> The dwelling-house has features which are substantially different from those of ordinary dwelling-houses and which are designed to make it suitable for occupation by a physically disabled person who requires accommodation of a kind provided by the dwelling-house and –
> (a) there is no longer such a person residing in the dwelling-house, and
> (b) the landlord requires it for occupation (whether alone or with members of his family) by such a person.

3.180 Note that the special features must be 'substantially' different from those of an ordinary dwelling and they must have been 'designed' (in the technical sense) for the special needs of the physically disabled. A simple additional ground-floor lavatory does not fulfil those requirements.[194]

3.181   It should also be noted that the ground is not available where the premises are adapted for use by a mentally disabled tenant (recovery of possession in such cases would be sought under grounds 14 or 15 discussed below). Furthermore, the landlord must show that possession is required for a new prospective tenant who is a physically disabled person with requirements for all or any of the particular special features presently provided.

3.182   If the ground is made out, the landlord must prove, in addition, that: (a) suitable alternative accommodation is available (see para

---

193 HA 1985 s84(2)(c).
194 *Freeman v Wansbeck DC* (1983) 10 HLR 54; [1984] 2 All ER 746, CA.

3.203); and (b) it would be reasonable for a possession order to be made.[195]

Ground 14: special needs accommodation provided by housing associations and trusts

3.183 Housing Act 1985 Sch 2 ground 14 applies where:

> The landlord is a housing association or housing trust which lets dwelling-houses only for occupation (whether alone or with others) by persons whose circumstances (other than merely financial circumstances) make it especially difficult for them to satisfy their need for housing, and –
> (a) either there is no longer such a person residing in the dwelling-house or the tenant has received from a local housing authority an offer of accommodation in premises which are to be let as a separate dwelling under a secure tenancy, and
> (b) the landlord requires the dwelling-house for occupation (whether alone or with members of his family) by such a person.

3.184 Note that the limbs of paragraph (a) are expressed in the alternative. The second limb makes special provision for those reluctant to move on from 'half-way' houses or 'bridging' accommodation into permanent social housing sector tenancies. That limb cannot be satisfied by the association or trust making available a secure or an assured tenancy with the same or another association or trust – only a local authority secure tenancy (and not an introductory tenancy) satisfies the provision. Whichever limb is relied on, the landlord must also show that a person with the appropriate special housing need would take the tenant's place.

3.185   In order to succeed in recovering possession in reliance on this ground, the landlord must show that both the 'suitable alternative accommodation' (see para 3.203) and 'reasonableness' conditions are satisfied.[196]

3.186   For the position of housing association and housing trust tenants generally, see chapter 6.

195 HA 1985 s84(2)(c).
196 HA 1985 s84(2)(c).

Ground 15: special needs accommodation

3.187 Provision is made by HA 1985 Sch 2 ground 15 for recovery of possession of one of a group of dwellings let to those with special needs. It applies where:

> The dwelling-house is one of a group of dwelling-houses which it is the practice of the landlord to let for occupation by persons with special needs and –
> (a) a social service or special facility is provided in close proximity to the group of dwelling-houses in order to assist persons with those special needs,
> (b) there is no longer a person with those special needs residing in the dwelling-house, and
> (c) the landlord requires the dwelling-house for occupation (whether alone or with members of his family) by a person who has those special needs.

3.188 The special needs dwellings must be in a 'group' within the ordinary meaning of that term. It is suggested that this requirement would not be met where the relevant dwellings said by the landlord to comprise the 'group' were spread throughout the area of the landlord's ordinary housing stock.[197]

3.189 Limbs (a), (b) and (c) must all be satisfied. In order to succeed in recovering possession the landlord must also show that 'suitable alternative accommodation is available' (see para 3.203) and that the making of an order would be reasonable in all the circumstances.[198]

Ground 16: under-occupation

3.190 No ground for possession is available to the landlord in HA 1985 Sch 2 simply on the basis that the original tenant no longer requires such extensive accommodation as was needed at the date of the original letting. Extensive non-statutory guidance is available to help landlords encourage secure tenants to move voluntarily from under-occupied homes.[199]

---

197 *Martin v Motherwell DC* 1991 SLT (Lands Tr) 4, noted at September 1991 *Legal Action* 15.

198 HA 1985 s84(2)(c).

199 *Overcrowding and under-occupation: Self-assessment for social landlords* (TSA, November 2009) and *Managing underoccupation: A guide to good practice in social housing* (DETR, April 2001).

3.191 However, if the present tenant has become a secure tenant on a statutory succession (as described at para 2.39 above) and was not the deceased tenant's spouse or registered civil partner, ground 16 makes limited provision for recovery of the property by the landlord where:

> The accommodation afforded by the dwelling-house is more extensive than is reasonably required by the tenant and –
> (a) the tenancy vested in the tenant by virtue of section 89 (succession to periodic tenancy), the tenant being qualified to succeed by virtue of section 87(b) (members of family other than spouse or civil partner), and
> (b) notice of the proceedings for possession was served under section 83 *(or, where no such notice was served, the proceedings for possession were begun)* more than six months but less than twelve months after the date of the previous tenant's death.

> The matters to be taken into account by the court in determining whether it is reasonable to make an order on this ground include
> (a) the age of the tenant,
> (b) the period during which the tenant has occupied the dwelling-house as his only or principal home, and
> (c) any financial or other support given by the tenant to the previous tenant.

3.192 Note therefore that ground 16 does not provide for recovery of possession from a widow or widower or surviving civil partner of the deceased tenant who is under-occupying. Nor does it apply to the under-occupying successor to a fixed-term tenancy.[200]

3.193 It can also be avoided if the late tenant had sufficient foresight to assign the tenancy to the successor in advance of his or her death rather than leaving it to be transmitted on death.[201] In such a case, the new assignee tenant cannot be ousted under ground 16 (although ground 1 may be applicable if the assignment was made in breach of a prohibition against assignment: but see para 2.80 on the possible unfairness of such a restriction).[202]

3.194 Ground 16 sets a specific timetable for action by the landlord. The notice seeking possession must be served no earlier than six months from the date of death of the former tenant and no later than 12 months after the death. Note that the time runs from the actual date of death, not the date on which the landlord learned of the death

200 HA 1985 s90.
201 HA 1985 s91(3)(c).
202 *Peabody Donation Fund Governors v Higgins* [1983] 3 All ER 122; (1983) 10 HLR 82, CA.

(contrast this with HA 1988 Sch 2 ground 7 – see para 12.57). This requirement cannot be avoided by the landlord inviting the court to dispense with a notice altogether[203] because the ground itself provides that where no notice is served, the proceedings for possession must still have been commenced within the same six month 'window'.

3.195   If the first information about the death of the secure tenant reaches the landlord only after the first anniversary of the tenant's death (perhaps because the successor has misrepresented the position), it will be too late for a possession claim to be based on this ground, however great the extent of the under-occupation and however great the needs of other families for social housing accommodation. This factual scenario has been judicially described as 'unjust' because

> it frustrates the statutory purpose of ground 16. It means that this family house cannot at any rate for the present be released for use by a family who need it ... I hope that the legislature may find an early opportunity to alleviate the difficulty ... perhaps by amending the Housing Act.[204]

3.196   The words italicised in ground 16 were added by HA 1996 s147(3). It seems difficult to envisage a case in which the court could be persuaded in a ground 16 situation to exercise its discretion and dispense with a notice seeking possession when no notice had been given to the bereaved successor at all. More likely the new words will be relied on by a landlord which is found to have served a technically defective notice (see para 4.11) but has nevertheless brought the claim in time.

3.197   The ground requires the landlord to prove that the dwelling *is* more extensive than *is* reasonably required. It is not sufficient to show that the dwelling was more extensive than the successor reasonably required at the date of succession. The question is to be addressed by the judge on the facts as the date of the hearing.[205]

3.198   The landlord must not only satisfy each limb of ground 16 but also show that: (a) suitable alternative accommodation is available (see para 3.203 onwards) and (b) it would be reasonable for an order to be made.[206] Indeed, the fact that suitable alternative accommodation is available to the tenant is a factor that goes to the 'reasonableness' of making an order in this class of case.[207]

---

203 HA 1985 s83(1).
204 *Newport CC v Charles* [2008] EWCA Civ 1541; [2009] HLR 18 at [28].
205 *Wandsworth LBC v Randall* [2007] EWCA Civ 1126; [2008] 1 WLR 359.
206 HA 1985 s84(2)(c).
207 *Bracknell Forest BC v Green* [2009] EWCA Civ 238; [2009] HLR 38.

3.199   As to (a), because the present tenant is a successor, he or she will take the fresh secure tenancy of alternative accommodation also as a successor unless the landlord can be persuaded to agree otherwise.[208] The possibility of such an agreement may be raised in negotiations designed to achieve a compromise in a ground 16 case where the defence is not strong and the successor is attracted by the offer of alternative accommodation which is not only suitable but which will (if agreement can be reached) also provide the opportunity for a further succession within the family. Alternative accommodation will usually be suitable if, like the secure tenant's present tenancy, it will offer the opportunity to exercise the right to buy. Whether it can be a suitable alternative where the tenant will lose the right to buy was canvassed in, but not resolved by, the Court of Appeal in *Manchester CC v Benjamin*.[209]

3.200   As to (b), the reasonableness test, note that the second paragraph of ground 16 makes specific provision for identified factors to be taken into account by the court. In addition, the successor tenant may argue that account should be taken of his or her rights under article 8 of the ECHR to respect for home, family and private life in relation to what may have been a lifetime home (although the reliance on the right to respect will not amount to a defence in itself: see chapter 26).[210]

3.201   It has been held that if the successor tenant has claimed a right to buy, the court, in considering reasonableness, should take into account the reasons why the landlord wishes to recover possession and the fact that the tenant may have established a right to purchase.[211] For the specific factors which the court should consider in weighing the legitimate claim by a tenant to exercise the right to buy against the landlord's well-founded claim for possession, see *Kensington and Chelsea RLBC v Hislop*[212] and *Basildon DC v Wahlen*.[213] Both cases were reviewed and discussed by the Court of Appeal in *Manchester CC v Benjamin*.[214] Ultimately, it is a matter for the judge who has heard the evidence to balance the various factors.

---

208   HA 1985 s88(4).
209   [2008] EWCA Civ 189; [2009] 1 All ER 798.
210   *Newham LBC v Neal* [2003] EWCA Civ 541. But cf *Gangera* [2003] EWHC 794 (Admin); *Michalak* [2002] EWCA 271 Civ and *Coombes* [2010] EWHC 666 (Admin).
211   *Enfield LBC v McKeon* [1986] 2 All ER 730; (1986) 18 HLR 330, CA.
212   [2003] EWHC 2944 (Ch); [2004] 1 All ER 1036; [2004] HLR 26.
213   [2006] EWCA Civ 326; May 2006 *Legal Action* 32.
214   [2008] EWCA Civ 189; [2009] 1 All ER 798.

3.202 More commonly the issues on reasonableness will come down to a fine balance between the tenant's understandable desire to remain in what may have been their lifetime home against the housing needs of others on the landlord's list who could fully utilise the presently under-occupied accommodation. The classic example is provided by *Bracknell Forest BC v Green*.[215] In that case, the Court of Appeal said that:

> Taking into account all the factors relevant to the reasonableness of making a possession order, the Recorder was entitled to conclude that the combination of factors relied on by the council, including the offer of suitable accommodation, was outweighed by the length of Mr Green's occupation of the house, his personal and family circumstances, his age and the permanently destabilising effect of a possession order on him. (at [35])

and that

> The judicial process of balancing the circumstances, some pointing one way and some the other way, is for the lower court, not for the council nor for this court on an appeal. The terms of the 1985 Act expressly contemplate cases in which the tenant's personal circumstances, such as Mr Green's age and his unusually long period of occupation, may outweigh the pressures on public housing and other factors. (at [37])

Suitable alternative accommodation

3.203 In any proceedings based on grounds 9 to 16 the landlord must show that suitable alternative accommodation will be available to the tenant and his or her family if a possession order is made.[216]

3.204 Where the landlord is not the local housing authority, the obligation is satisfied by production of a certificate issued by the housing authority to the effect that it will provide suitable accommodation before a specified date.[217]

3.205 Where the landlord is the housing authority or there is no certificate, the landlord must prove at the hearing of the claim that suitable accommodation within the terms of HA 1985 Sch 2 Part IV paras 1 and 2 is going to be available to the tenant if a possession order is made (earlier offers of other accommodation being irrelevant save

215 [2009] EWCA Civ 238; [2009] HLR 38.
216 HA 1985 s84(2)(b) and (c).
217 HA 1985 Sch 2 Pt IV para 4. As to such certificates see para 12.89.

possibly to any consideration of 'reasonableness').[218] Those paragraphs provide:

1. For the purposes of section 84(2)(b) and (c) (case in which court is not to make an order for possession unless satisfied that suitable accommodation will be available) accommodation is suitable if it consists of premises –

(a) which are to be let as a separate dwelling under a secure tenancy, or

(b) which are to be let as a separate dwelling under a protected tenancy, not being a tenancy under which the landlord might recover possession under one of the Cases in Part II of Schedule 15 to Rent Act 1977 (cases where court must order possession), or

(c) which are to be let as a separate dwelling under an assured tenancy which is neither an assured shorthold tenancy, within the meaning of the Housing Act 1988, nor a tenancy under which the landlord might recover possession under any of Grounds 1 to 5 in Schedule 2 to that Act

and, in the opinion of the court, the accommodation is reasonably suitable to the needs of the tenant and his family.

2. In determining whether the accommodation is reasonably suitable to the needs of the tenant and his family, regard shall be had to –

(a) the nature of the accommodation which it is the practice of the landlord to allocate to persons with similar needs;

(b) the distance of the accommodation available from the place of work or education of the tenant and of any members of his family;

(c) its distance from the home of any member of the tenant's family if proximity to it is essential to that member's or the tenant's well-being;

(d) the needs (as regards extent of accommodation) and means of the tenant and his family;

(e) the terms on which the accommodation is available and the terms of the secure tenancy;

(f) if furniture was provided by the landlord for use under the secure tenancy, whether furniture is to be provided for use in the other accommodation, and if so the nature of the furniture to be provided.

218 In *Wandsworth LBC v Randall* [2007] EWCA Civ 1126; [2008] HLR 24; [2008] 1 WLR 359, Dyson LJ said at [18]: 'the language of section 84(2)(c) clearly provides that the date when the order takes effect is the date at which the court must be satisfied that the suitable accommodation "will be available". On its face, that date is a date later than the date of the hearing. It certainly is not the date of succession, which will always be more than 6 months earlier than the date of the hearing. As a matter of ordinary language, I find it impossible to construe section 84(2)(c) as requiring a consideration of whether the accommodation is reasonably suitable to the needs of the tenant and his family as they were at the date of succession'.

3.206   The words in italics were added by HA 1988 Sch 17 para 65. On the quality of security offered by an assured tenancy, compared with the secure status that the tenant enjoys, see chapter 12.

3.207   In applying these provisions, note that:

- 'Family' is defined broadly in HA 1985 Part IV.[219]
- If family members have different or conflicting views about the suitability of the alternative accommodation offered, the court should grant permission for them to be joined as parties to the proceedings in addition to the tenant.[220]
- The list of factors set out in paragraph 2 is not exhaustive.[221]
- The listed factors are not identical to those set out for Rent Act tenants in similar circumstances (although case-law developed in the Rent Act jurisdiction may provide useful aids to construction (see para 17.4), the Rent Act authorities must be approached with some caution).[222]
- Nor are the listed factors identical to those set out for the recovery of possession against assured tenants in similar circumstances (although case-law developed in that jurisdiction may provide useful aids to construction (see para 12.86)).
- It may be helpful to invite the judge to view the present home and the alternative accommodation offered.
- If the alternative accommodation will be provided by a different landlord, and that landlord is a housing association or other registered provider of social housing, the court should be invited to direct that the tenancy of the accommodation be a secure rather than an assured tenancy.[223]
- Paragraph 2(a) has no parallel in the grounds for possession against Rent Act or assured tenants. It allows the court to consider the landlord's usual allocation policy for families of the same size etc as that of the tenant. Thus, it will be open to the landlord to suggest in the case of a single person that its usual policy is to provide a small flat or bedsitter. The defence for a tenant faced with such an assertion relies on showing that it is an unreasonable rule or that an exception should be made.

219   HA 1985 s113, as amended by Civil Partnership Act 2004 Sch 8 para 27, reproduced at para 2.40; and see *Stonebridge HAT v McKay* June 2006 *Legal Action* 37 (in which accommodation was held not to be suitable because it did not enable the tenant's grandchildren to stay with her).
220   *Wandsworth LBC v Fadayomi* [1987] 3 All ER 474, CA.
221   *Enfield LBC v French* (1984) 17 HLR 211, CA.
222   *Enfield LBC v French* (1984) 17 HLR 211, CA at 216–217.
223   HA 1988 s35(4)(e).

- Where the alternative accommodation is council housing and that local authority landlord has elected to operate an introductory tenancy regime, it will be necessary for the tenant's adviser to ensure that the new tenancy is secure rather than introductory (see HA 1996 s124(2)).

Appeals[224]

3.208   The procedure for pursuing an appeal against a possession order is described below at para 34.1. Those advising secure tenants should be aware that, although a general right of appeal lies from the making of a possession order (from district judge to circuit judge or circuit judge to High Court judge), the appeal court is likely to be singularly reluctant to disturb findings made at first instance on issues of fact as to whether a ground of possession was made out, on reasonableness, and/or on suitability of alternative accommodation.

3.209   Appeal court pronouncements such as 'this court will only interfere with the exercise of the trial judge's discretion in such a case, if it can be shown to be plainly and utterly wrong'[225] are to be found liberally in reported cases. In addition, permission to appeal is required either from the judge who made the order or from the appeal court.[226]

3.210   There can be no appeal on any matter of fact in a case turning on grounds 1 to 8,[227] although that is no impediment to an appeal under one of those grounds on the basis that the judge failed to consider reasonableness or failed to consider whether the order for possession made should be something other than an outright order.[228] Challenges to decisions that, on particular facts, it was 'reasonable' to make a possession order are particularly difficult to pursue.[229]

3.211   For all these reasons every effort should be put into ensuring a successful outcome at the first hearing (or subsequent trial of) a possession claim.

224 The procedure for appeals is regulated by CPR Part 52, discussed in more detail at paras 34.1 onwards.

225 Per Simon Brown LJ in *Kensington and Chelsea RLBC v Simmonds* (1997) 29 HLR 507.

226 CPR 52.3.

227 County Courts Act 1984 s77(6)(e), discussed in *Croydon LBC v Crawford* [2010] EWCA Civ 618.

228 *Gallagher v Castle Vale Action Trust Limited* [2001] EWCA Civ 944; (2001) 33 HLR 72.

229 *Bracknell Forest BC v Green* [2009] EWCA Civ 238; [2009] HLR 38.

Preparing the defence

General preparation

4.1   The preparation of a defence to the possession claim for a secure occupier[1] should take place at the earliest possible opportunity. If instructed *at the last minute*, go immediately to para 4.79.

4.2   If instructed *well in advance* of any prospective or actual court hearing date, the adviser will need to take full instructions from the client (see the instructions checklist at appendix C).

4.3   In addition to taking the client's statement and assembling background material relating to the particular possession proceedings, the adviser will wish to gather together:

- the claim form and particulars of claim;
- a copy of the tenancy agreement;
- a copy of the notice seeking possession – if any (see para 2.4);
- the rent book/rent account/schedule of arrears; and
- other relevant documents.

4.4   An early opportunity might usefully be taken to inspect the tenant's housing management file as held by the landlord, in order to secure copies of the above and any other relevant documents. In the case of a local authority landlord an application for such access should:

- be made in writing;
- make reference to the Data Protection Act 1998;
- enclose a signed authority from the client;
- enclose a cheque for £10 (being the maximum fee currently payable for access).

4.5   Most local authority landlords will respond to such a request either by simply forwarding a photocopy of the entire file or by making it available at their offices with a copying facility. Other social landlords make similar provision for tenants (or their advisers) to inspect housing files. If the possession proceedings have already started (and will proceed beyond the first hearing), such documents would in any event eventually be obtained in the course of disclosure.[2] If the proceedings have not yet started but are contemplated, early disclosure of the documents would certainly accord with the principles of the Practice Direction on Pre-Action Protocols[3] and, in a rent arrears case, with the Rent Arrears Pre-Action Protocol (see para 3.38 and appendix D).

---

1   References in this chapter to a 'secure tenant' should be treated as including a 'secure licensee' (see para 1.27) unless the contrary is stated.

2   CPR Part 31.

3   See para 4 of the CPR Practice Direction on Pre-Action Protocols.

4.6 Depending on the issues which arise in the client's statement, and after consideration of the documents, it may be necessary to undertake a housing benefit (or general welfare benefit) assessment and/or obtain an expert's report on the condition of the property.

4.7 Many defendants will qualify for initial advice under the Legal Help and Legal Help at Court schemes (see chapter 28) but a full certificate for publicly funded legal representation should be applied for immediately if the tenant might meet the financial criteria and some prospect of resisting possession can be shown. The usual rules governing public funding are modified because the litigation concerns an issue of vital importance, ie, the tenant's continued occupation of his or her home.[4] Indeed, the Legal Services Commission's Funding Code – Decision-Making Guidance para 19.7(4) states:

> Legal Representation is likely to be granted where there is a substantive defence to the possession action, including a defence as to reasonableness of the possession order being made, ie, where the ground for possession has been made out but where the court must also assess whether it is reasonable in all the circumstances to make an order for possession.

4.8 If the adviser is instructed only a few days prior to the hearing, an emergency certificate for legal representation should be obtained or granted under devolved powers (see chapter 28).

4.9 If a defence is to be submitted this should be in the appropriate variant of the defence form (N11), filed with the court, and properly served on the landlord in advance of the hearing date (see chapter 23 for possession procedure and appendix B for a precedent defence). The adviser instructed at a late stage will simply have to pass a copy to the landlord at court (if it has been possible to file a defence at all) or apply for an extension of time in which to file a defence. In the latter case, it would be sensible to have an outline or early draft of the defence available at court.

4.10 The following pages set out the so-called 'technical' defences and then the 'substantive' defences. Either or both can be successfully deployed to resist or defeat possession proceedings.

---

4 See Legal Services Commission Funding Code – criteria para 10.3.

Technical defences

4.11   Although these defences are described as 'technical', at least in the short term[5] they have the potential to be as effective as the substantive defences in preventing the landlord from obtaining an order for possession against a secure occupier.

Defective notice

4.12   As seen above (at para 2.4) the proper notice – a notice seeking possession – must usually be served on the secure tenant as a prerequisite to the commencement of possession proceedings. If the notice is deficient, the proceedings must fail unless in the particular case the court exercises its discretion to dispense with notice (see para 4.45). In this chapter, each potential irregularity in a notice seeking possession is considered before a review of the circumstances in which the court may exercise its power to dispense with the need for a valid notice.

4.13   A sample copy of a notice seeking possession in the current prescribed form for periodic secure tenancies is reproduced in appendix A. (The different prescribed form for fixed-term secure tenancies is not reproduced.) Every notice seeking possession relied on by a landlord should be carefully inspected with a view to discovering any possible deficiency that might render it invalid.

Form

4.14   The notice must usually be in the form prescribed in regulations made by the secretary of state.[6] Those regulations are made by statutory instrument.

4.15   The current prescribed form of notice is contained in the Secure Tenancies (Notices) Regulations 1987,[7] as amended by the Secure Tenancies (Notices) (Amendment) (England) Regulations 1997,[8] and

---

5   See *City of London v Devlin* (1997) 29 HLR 58, CA.
6   HA 1985 s83(2)(a).
7   1987 SI No 755. The earliest prescribed form was contained in Secure Tenancies (Notices) Regulations 1980 SI No 1339, as amended by SI 1984 No 1224 and upheld in *Wansbeck DC v Charlton* 79 LGR 523; (1981) 42 P&CR 162, CA. Those regulations were saved for the purposes of the Housing Act 1985 by Housing (Consequential Provisions) Act 1985 s2(2). A revised form was prescribed by Secure Tenancies (Notices) Regulations 1987, which came into force on 13 May 1987.
8   1997 SI No 71.

subsequently by the Secure Tenancies (Notices) (Amendment) (England) Regulations 2004[9] and the Secure Tenancies (Notices) (Amendment) (Wales) Regulations 2005.[10]

4.16 These numerous references to regulations simply serve to demonstrate the importance of checking the actual notice relied on by the landlord against the prescribed form which was required on the date on which the notice was given.

4.17 If the notice is *not* in the form prescribed at the date of service it may[11] be ineffective. However, because minor technical deficiencies would otherwise invalidate notices, the 1987 Regulations contain a 'saving provision' that a notice seeking possession not in the prescribed form will be valid if it is 'in a form substantially to the same effect'.[12] The use of delegated legislation in this way to save otherwise faulty notices has been held to be within the relevant powers of the secretary of state: *Dudley MBC v Bailey*.[13]

4.18 As that case was fought entirely on the point of the lawfulness of the saving power (rather than on the faults in the notice actually served), there is little judicial guidance from it about the degree of error necessary to remove a form from the category of 'substantially to the same effect' as that prescribed and into a category of invalidity.[14]

4.19 Arguably, a notice would differ in substance if the 'Notes for Guidance' contained in the body of the prescribed form were omitted from the notice actually served[15] or were only set out on the reverse[16] or on a separate sheet without (at the very least) an indication to 'see overleaf' or 'see attached'.

4.20 Similarly, the words 'name(s) of secure tenant(s)' in paragraph 1 of the prescribed form are crucial, because the guidance notes on the prescribed form distinguish secure tenants from other tenants and licensees. It should also be noted that the words 'Notice of Seeking

---

9 2004 SI No 1627.

10 2005 SI No 1226.

11 In *Swansea CC v Hearn* (1991) 23 HLR 284, CA, a notice to quit served without the latest version of the statutorily prescribed information set out on it, but with the earlier version endorsed, was held effective.

12 Secure Tenancies (Notices) Regulations 1987 reg 2(1).

13 (1990) 22 HLR 424, CA.

14 But see *Tadema Holdings v Ferguson* (2000) 32 HLR 866, CA, in which a notice of rent increase was held to be 'substantially to the same effect' as the prescribed form after an examination of its alleged defects.

15 See *Manel v Memon* (2001) 33 HLR 24, CA.

16 But see *Swansea CC v Hearn* (1991) 23 HLR 284, CA, in which prescribed particulars were given on the reverse of a notice to quit, although this particular point does not appear to have been taken.

Possession' and the statutory reference at the head are themselves important parts of the prescribed form. They enable the tenant to identify the statutory power under which it is alleged the notice has been given.

4.21   On the other hand, simple 'slips' such as the omission of a manuscript signature above the typescript job title of the officer authorising the giving of the notice, will not prevent the form being substantially to the same effect as the prescribed form and thus valid.[17]

4.22   For guidance on the situation which arises when the landlord has transferred its interest to a new landlord *after* serving a notice, see *Knowsley Housing Trust v Revell, Helena Housing Limited v Curtis*.[18]

Name of tenant

4.23   The prescribed form has a space for the insertion of the tenant's name and the notice must be served on *that tenant*.[19] Practical difficulties may arise over the misspelling of names or the use of former names where the tenant has changed his or her name following marriage or otherwise. To guard against this difficulty most landlords will use the name as it appears on the original tenancy agreement.

4.24   If the tenancy is a joint tenancy then the reference on the prescribed form to the 'tenant' is a reference to all the joint tenants. All must therefore be named in the notice even if some are no longer in residence.[20]

Ground

4.25   The notice must 'specify the ground on which the court will be asked to make an order for possession'.[21] The ground specified must therefore correspond with the ground that is (1) pleaded in the particulars of claim and (2) relied on in court.

4.26   As to (1), landlords sometimes fail to set out in their particulars of claim the ground on which possession is being sought, contrary to the requirements of the Civil Procedure Rules (see chapter 23). As to (2), if a different ground for possession is made out at trial from that shown in the notice seeking possession, the proceedings must

---

17   *City of London v Devlin* (1997) 29 HLR 58, CA.
18   [2003] EWCA Civ 496; [2003] HLR 63,CA.
19   HA 1985 s83(1)(a). See *Enfield LBC v Devonish and Sutton* (1997) 29 HLR 691, CA.
20   *Newham LBC v Okotoro* March 1993 *Legal Action* 11.
21   HA 1985 s83(2)(b).

be dismissed[22] unless the court gives permission for an alternative ground to be read into the notice seeking possession by alteration or addition, or the court exercises a discretion to dispense with the requirement of notice altogether.[23]

4.27 Although neither the Housing Act (HA) 1985 nor the regulations which prescribe the form of notice define what is meant by 'specify', courts should interpret this to mean that the actual words of the ground as they appear in the statute must be set out or, in default, at least words giving all the salient elements of the ground relied on.[24] The case for requiring the exact text in a notice seeking possession served on a secure tenant is strengthened by the use of the marginal note in the prescribed form which directs the landlord to 'give the text in full of each ground which is being relied on'. It follows that the words used in the notice seeking possession must always be carefully checked against the actual statutory formulation of the ground in each case. If they are significantly different this may well invalidate the notice.

Particulars

4.28 The notice must, on its face, give 'particulars' of the ground for possession specified in it.[25] These particulars must give the tenant sufficient details of the circumstances that the landlord relies upon in asserting that a ground for possession is made out, since the function of the notice is to fire a 'warning shot' telling the tenant what the complaint is against him or her so as to enable the tenant to rectify it.[26] Clearly, the simple statement 'arrears of rent' is an insufficient particular.[27] Similarly 'various acts of nuisance' or 'instances of dilapidation' would be inadequate.[28] In a nuisance case, the Court of Appeal described the following particulars as 'obviously' insufficient:[29]

> The tenant frequently disturbs his neighbour, and on one occasion has threatened his neighbour with physical violence.

22 See *Midlothian DC v Tweedie* 1993 GWD 1068, Sh Ct.
23 HA 1985 ss83–84 and see *Gedling BC v Brener* September 2001 *Legal Action* 23.
24 *Mountain v Hastings* (1993) 25 HLR 427, CA.
25 HA 1985 s83(2)(c).
26 *Torridge DC v Jones* (1986) 18 HLR 107; [1985] 2 EGLR 54, CA. See too *Marath v MacGillivray* (1996) 28 HLR 484, CA.
27 *Torridge DC v Jones* (1986) 18 HLR 107; [1985] 2 EGLR 54, CA.
28 *South Buckinghamshire DC v Francis* [1985] CLY 1900 and *Slough BC v Robbins* [1996] CLY 3832; December 1996 *Legal Action* 13.
29 *Camden LBC v Oppong* (1996) 28 HLR 701, CA, at 703.

4.29   Likewise the use of the simple words 'major refurbishment scheme' in a claim for possession under ground 10 is deficient,[30] as is the bare repetition of the terms of a tenancy agreement where the ground alleged is breach of those terms.[31] Neither can simple repetition of the text of the statutory ground amount to 'particulars'.

4.30   If insufficient particulars are given, the court cannot entertain the proceedings, which must, therefore, be struck out unless the notice is amended or the court finds it just and equitable to dispense with notice.[32] The court can give the landlord permission to amend the notice seeking possession for the purpose of improving the particulars,[33] but it should not be assumed that the discretion will be exercised in favour of such an amendment if application is made at a late stage in the proceedings.[34]

4.31   If particulars are given but they are *inaccurate*, the court may (according to the degree of inaccuracy) permit the claim to proceed or allow amendment of the notice seeking possession. For example, if the notice gives particulars that the 'arrears of rent are £x' and it is shown at trial that the landlord has innocently and in error included in that figure amounts which are not arrears of rent, the action can proceed, but the judge will take into account the nature and extent of the error in determining whether possession should be given.[35]

The dates

4.32   The prescribed form contains a space for completion of the specified date (see para 2.7) and for entry of the date of the notice itself (which should be the date of service). It is vital that these dates are carefully checked, first, to ensure that the dates have been entered and, second, to identify any errors. A form is not in the prescribed form or in a form to substantially the same effect if a material date has either been omitted[36] or incorrectly stated.[37]

4.33   The specified date must be no earlier than the date on which the tenancy or licence could have been brought to an end by notice to

---

30   *Waltham Forest LBC v England* March 1994 *Legal Action* 11.

31   *East Devon DC v Williams* December 1996 *Legal Action* 13.

32   *Torridge DC v Jones* (1986) 18 HLR 107; [1985] 2 EGLR 54, CA.

33   *Camden LBC v Oppong* (1996) 28 HLR 701, CA.

34   *Merton LBC v Drew* July 1999 *Legal Action* 22.

35   *Dudley MBC v Bailey* (1990) 22 HLR 424, CA.

36   *Patel v Rodrigo* June 1997 *Legal Action* 23.

37   *Panayi v Roberts* (1993) 25 HLR 421, CA.

quit or notice to determine given by the landlord on the same date that the notice seeking possession was served.[38]

4.34   Accordingly, the adviser should check carefully the date of service and the minimum period of notice the landlord would have been required to give under the provisions of the tenancy agreement, statute or common law. In the ordinary case of a weekly periodic tenancy, the specified date must be no earlier than four weeks after the next rent day.[39] If the 'specified date' is too early, the notice is bad on its face and the proceedings should be dismissed unless the court exercises a discretion to dispense with service of the notice in the landlord's favour. The Housing Act 1985 does not give the court power to amend the dates set out in the notice.

4.35   Unless the notice included ground 2 (nuisance) as one of the grounds specified in it, proceedings issued before the specified date should also be dismissed, as no claim should be issued until after the specified date has passed.[40]

Has the notice lapsed?

4.36   The notice is valid for only 12 months from the specified date.[41] It must be noted that the 12 months runs *not* from the date of service but from the specified date it contains.

4.37   As the specified date is usually at least 28 days after the notice was served, it should be at about the end of the thirteenth month after service that the notice lapses (contrast the position for the notice seeking possession served in respect of an assured tenancy, para 12.20).

4.38   No proceedings can be brought in respect of a notice that has lapsed.[42] Thus, an action for possession started more than 12 months after the specified date is defective and should be struck out unless the court decides that it is just and equitable to dispense with notice.[43]

4.39   For these purposes, the proceedings 'begin' on the date the relevant county court issues the claim.[44] A notice might be treated as

---

38 HA 1985 s83(5). See too para 2.6 if the notice relies on ground 2.

39 Protection from Eviction Act 1977 s5, as amended.

40 HA 1985 s83(4)(a). But see *City of London v Devlin* (1997) 29 HLR 58, CA, in which the claim was issued three days before the specific date but a further claim was issued after that date and consolidated with the first claim.

41 HA 1985 s83(3)(b) and (4)(b).

42 HA 1985 s83(4).

43 *Edinburgh City Council v Davis* 1987 SLT 33, noted at June 1987 *Legal Action* 19.

44 *Shepping v Osada* (2001) 33 HLR 13, CA. See also *Salford City Council v Garner* [2004] EWCA Civ 364; [2004] HLR 35, in relation to introductory tenancies.

'spent' once it has been used to found a claim for possession. A court is unlikely to allow a second set of proceedings to be issued within the period of validity of a single notice[45] except, perhaps, where the two sets of proceedings based on the same notice are to be consolidated.[46]

Service

4.40   The Housing Act 1985 requires that the notice seeking possession has been served by the landlord 'on the tenant'.[47] It is for the landlord to prove that the notice was served on the secure tenant. There is, of course, no difficulty if the secure tenant admits service.

4.41   Nothing in HA 1985 Part IV or in s617 (service of notices) assists with the form that service of the notice must take.[48] It has been held that 'serve' is an ordinary English word connoting the delivery of a document to a particular person.[49] For the rules on acceptable proof of service developed by the courts in relation to methods of service of notices to quit (in summary: personal service on the tenant, service on a wife of the tenant or service on the servant of the tenant), see para 14.25.[50] The common law acceptance of service on the tenant's wife as service on the tenant must presumably now be taken to extend to service on the husband or registered civil partner of the tenant.

4.42   In the absence of an express admission by the tenant of service of the notice seeking possession, the burden of proof remains on the landlord to show that the notice was properly served.

4.43   Although the surest route to proving service is personal delivery to the tenant, many landlords seek to rely on postal service, putting the notice through a letterbox or giving it to someone at the property to pass on to the tenant. None of these is reliable or offers conclusive evidence that the tenant was served. Local authority landlords are not assisted in establishing service by the Local Government Act 1972 s233 (which permits service by post or hand delivery of statutory notices to the 'proper address', usually the last known address), because

---

45   See *Shaftesbury HA v Rickards* December 2005 *Legal Action* 20.
46   *City of London v Devlin* (1997) 29 HLR 58, CA.
47   HA 1985 s83(1).
48   See January 1982 *Housing* 27.
49   *Tadema Holdings v Ferguson* (2000) 32 HLR 866 at 873.
50   See *Enfield LBC v Devonish and Sutton* (1997) 29 HLR 691, CA.

a notice seeking possession is not served by the authority in its capacity as a local authority but rather in the capacity of landlord.[51]

4.44　　To avoid these difficulties, the Court of Appeal has encouraged landlords of secure tenants to ensure that express provision for appropriate methods of service is made in the tenancy agreement itself.[52]

Dispensing with notice

4.45　Until the changes introduced by the Housing Act 1996, a successful argument that a notice seeking possession was defective was fatal to the landlord's case. However, HA 1985 s83(1)(b), as amended by the 1996 Act,[53] now provides the court with the power to dispense with the need for a valid notice where it is 'just and equitable to do so'. An application to dispense should be entertained only if the secure tenant has been given full notice of it and of the basis on which the exercise of the power is sought.[54]

4.46　　On whether the application should be allowed, the approach taken is that:

> Every case will depend upon its own facts and the pleaded ground or grounds relied on in the notice. The court must take all the circumstances into account, both from the view of the landlord and the tenant, and decide whether it is just and equitable to dispense with the required particulars.[55]

4.47　In *Braintree DC v Vincent*,[56] the secure tenant was in a nursing home and her sons were occupying the property. The landlord brought possession proceedings against the sons as trespassers. The judge joined the tenant to the proceedings, and a possession order was made on the basis that the property had ceased to be her only or principal home and on the alternative statutory ground of rent arrears. In relation to the statutory ground, the judge considered that it was just and equitable to dispense with a notice seeking possession. This decision was upheld in the Court of Appeal. Although it was 'obviously only

---

51　See *Chesterfield BC v Crossley* June 1998 *Legal Action* 10 and *Eastbourne BC v Dawson* June 1999 *Legal Action* 23.

52　*Wandsworth LBC v Atwell* (1995) 27 HLR 536, CA and *Enfield LBC v Devonish* (1997) 29 HLR 691, CA.

53　HA 1996 s147.

54　*Knowsley Housing Trust v Revell, Helena Housing Limited v Curtis* [2003] EWCA Civ 496; [2003] HLR 63.

55　*Kelsey Housing Association v King* (1995) 28 HLR 270, CA, at 276.

56　[2004] EWCA Civ 415.

in relatively exceptional cases where the court should be prepared to dispense with a section 83 notice', the circumstances were unusual in procedural terms. The tenant was added as defendant only at the insistence of the judge, and a notice of seeking possession would have been of no benefit to her. See also para 12.24, concerning the same power as it applies to assured tenancies (under HA 1988 s8), and in particular: *North British HA v Sheridan.*[57]

4.48   See too the linked cases of *Curtis v Helena Housing Association Ltd* and *Revell v Knowsley Housing Trust,*[58] in which the claimants sought to dispense with the notice requirement following a large-scale transfer of council housing stock to other social landlords. The Court of Appeal gave general guidance in the handling of applications to dispense with notices seeking possession (although in the context of possession claims against assured tenants).

Defective claims

4.49   The usual rules on drafting claims in civil litigation apply to possession proceedings against secure occupiers in the county court (see chapter 23). Common technical deficiencies in landlords' claims for possession against secure tenants include:

- failure to join all joint tenants;
- failure to set out the landlord's title;
- failure to refer to the notice seeking possession;
- insufficient particulars given (particularly of 'reasonableness');[59] and
- failure to restrict the claim to the ground in the notice seeking possession.

4.50   The claim for possession must be brought in accordance with the provisions of CPR 55 and the Practice Directions to that rule (each of which is reproduced in appendix E).The particulars of claim in possession proceedings must contain prescribed basic information about the premises and the tenancy agreement.[60] Moreover, if the claim is on the ground of non-payment of rent the particulars of claim should

---

57 [2000] L&TR 115; (2000) 32 HLR 346, CA.

58 [2003] EWCA Civ 496; [2003] HLR 63, CA.

59 See *Midlothian DC v Brown* 1990 SCLR 765 and *Renfrew DC v Inglis* 1991 SLT (Sh Ct) 83.

60 CPR PD 55A para 2.1.

be in the relevant court form[61] and must contain prescribed particulars concerning the arrears and the circumstances of the parties.[62]

4.51   However, as landlords can generally apply for and obtain permission to amend, reliance on defects in the claim will rarely provide a long-term defence. It has nevertheless been possible in some cases to have the whole proceedings struck out for failure to use and complete the usual form of particulars of claim for use in 'arrears' cases or otherwise give the prescribed particulars. The application to strike out a defective claim is likely to have greater prospects of success if there has also been a failure to comply with the Practice Direction on Pre-Action Protocols or a specific protocol such as the Rent Arrears Protocol (reproduced at appendix D).

Action improperly brought

4.52   If the possession proceedings against the secure tenant have been improperly brought (for example, the decision to bring them has been motivated by bad faith, abuse of power or malice by landlord), the county court may be invited to strike out the action as an abuse of process or the tenant could set up the unlawful action of the landlord by way of defence to the claim.[63] The possibility of such a 'public law' defence to a possession claim is explored further in chapter 25.

Set-off

4.53   Secure tenants have a complete defence to an action for possession based on a failure to pay monies due to the landlord if they can properly set off (for example, by a successful counterclaim under CPR Part 20) an amount payable to them by the landlord and equal to or greater than the amount the landlord has claimed. Such circumstances usually arise from success on a counterclaim for disrepair (see para 23.35) or a failure to pay housing benefit (see chapter 37). However, reliance should not be placed solely on a defence by way of set-off which presupposes a successful counterclaim, because there is never a guarantee that the counterclaim will succeed.[64]

---

61 Form N119.
62 CPR PD 55A paras 2.1–2.4A.
63 The repeated issue of unjustified proceedings may even amount to 'harassment': *Allen v Southwark LBC* [2008] EWCA Civ 1478; January 2009 *Legal Action* 25.
64 *Haringey LBC v Stewart* (1991) 23 HLR 557, CA.

Substantive defences

Ground not made out

4.54   The first substantive line of defence for the secure tenant, assuming that the technical defences mentioned above have proved insufficient, is to demonstrate that the ground asserted by the landlord is not made out on the evidence and on the balance of probabilities. The usual issues dealt with in possession proceedings on the grounds available against secure tenants, and common methods of defending such cases, are set out in the discussion of the individual grounds (see chapter 3).

Condition not made out

4.55   The second line of defence, assuming that the landlord has proved (or the tenant admits) that a ground has been made out, is to demonstrate that there is insufficient evidence to establish on the balance of probabilities that a necessary condition is satisfied. The conditions are discussed in chapter 3 together with the respective grounds to which they relate. The most common condition is that it is reasonable to order possession and it is for the landlord to satisfy the court that it would be reasonable to make a possession order.

Possession orders and eviction

Adjournment on terms

4.56   It need not inevitably follow that, because both a ground and the necessary condition can be made out, a possession order (whether outright or conditional) should be made against a secure tenant. Indeed, there are cases in which, despite it being shown that the landlord has acted reasonably in bringing possession proceedings and has established both the ground and its associated condition, it is nevertheless worthwhile to give the tenant another 'chance'. That may be appropriate even in a serious case, for example, where a young tenant has been convicted of a drug offence relating to use of the premises.[65] The mechanism readily available to the court is the adjournment of the proceedings[66] in all cases except those brought

---

65 *Glasgow HA v Hetherington* September 2009 *Legal Action* 32, Sheriff Court.
66 HA 1985 s85(1).

under grounds 9 to 11 inclusive (to which the statutory power to adjourn does not apply).

4.57   The statutory power to adjourn (additional to any other discretion in the court) arises in all cases relying on grounds 1 to 8 or grounds 12 to 16 contained in HA 1985 Sch 2. In any of these cases, the court may adjourn the proceedings for such period or periods as it thinks fit.[67] This has the substantial benefit to the secure tenant of not simply avoiding a possession order but, in most cases, of avoiding an adverse costs order. The costs of the claim are not usually awarded to one party or the other if the matter is adjourned.

4.58   The safeguard for the landlord is that the court is free to make the adjournment conditional.[68] For example, the adjournment may be conditional on the tenant paying the current rent plus £x towards the arrears. The check on excessive conditions is HA 1985 s85(3)(a), which provides that conditions are not to be imposed if they would cause exceptional hardship to the tenant or would otherwise be unreasonable. A form of order for adjournment on terms meeting these points was first published almost 20 years ago.[69] An example of such an order is given in appendix B.

4.59   If the court cannot be persuaded to deal with the matter by way of adjournment, and it decides to make a possession order, the adviser must seek to avoid the making of an absolute or outright order for possession.

Resisting an absolute/outright possession order

4.60   There are, of course, many cases in which the landlord establishes both the grounds and conditions for possession against a secure tenant and the court is satisfied that a possession order must be made. If a possession order is made, the secure tenancy continues only until the order is executed (by a bailiff evicting the tenant pursuant to a warrant granted in execution of the order).[70]

4.61   Prior to amendments introduced on 20 May 2009, the Housing Act 1985 provided that the tenancy ended on the date on which the tenant was to give up possession in pursuance of the order. This meant that the secure tenancy would end on the date for possession

---

67 HA 1985 s85(1).
68 HA 1985 s85(3).
69 See J Platt and N Madge, 'Suspended Possession Orders' (1991) 141 NLJ 853.
70 HA 1985 s82(1) and (1A), as amended by Housing and Regeneration Act 2008 Sch 11 para 2(3).

stated in the order or on breach of any terms on which an order had been suspended. The result was that many tens of thousands of secure tenants lost their tenancies but nevertheless remained in possession (often indefinitely) unless and until the former landlord obtained execution of the order. They were described by the courts as 'tolerated trespassers'. As a result of the amendments made in 2009, no further secure tenants will become tolerated trespassers. Those who were tolerated trespassers have become 'replacement tenants' (see chapter 10).

4.62   The tenant's adviser will nevertheless want to persuade a court to make a form of possession order that will not be capable of execution (and thus termination of the tenancy) in the near future. The court has a wide discretion as to the form of order to be made and can postpone the date for delivery of possession (the earliest date after which execution can be sought) for such period as it thinks fit.[71] It also has power to add provisions to the order which suspend or stay the execution of the order.[72] The tenant's adviser will therefore be seeking to persuade the court either (1) that the date for possession should be postponed, usually on condition that the tenant complies with certain specified terms, or (2) if the court is not prepared to postpone the possession date conditionally, that execution of the order on or after the date stated for possession should be stayed on terms. For a general discussion of the jurisdiction of the court to postpone the date for possession and suspend or stay execution of possession orders, and for more on the available forms of order, see chapters 33 and 34.

Postponed conditional possession orders

4.63   These orders have in the past, indeed even very recently, been described as 'suspended possession orders'.[73] The better view is that they should be called 'postponed possession orders', since HA 1985 s85(2) provides that the court may '*postpone* the date of *possession*' but may only 'stay or *suspend* the *execution* of the order'. The term 'suspension' is therefore used only in relation to enforcement of the possession order, not in relation to the order itself.

4.64   The court will usually accede to an application to 'postpone' the order only where postponement is on the basis of specified terms

---

71   HA 1985 s85(2)(b).
72   HA 1985 s85(2)(a).
73   The court form N28 is still entitled *Order for possession (rented residential premises) (suspended)*.

being complied with during the period of postponement. The court must impose conditions on any postponement relating to payment of rent and such further conditions as it thinks fit unless that would cause exceptional hardship or would otherwise be unreasonable.[74] The conditions imposed should, of course, relate to the subject-matter of the claim.[75]

4.65 Even though a postponed conditional possession order will mean that, at least for the time being, the tenant retains the secure tenancy and occupation of his or her home, wherever possible tenants' advisers should seek to avoid the making of *any* form of possession order. Even a postponed order gives rise to adverse consequences. First, *costs* are usually awarded against the tenant on the making of the order for possession, whether postponed or otherwise. Although a tenant with a legal aid funding certificate for legal representation has some protection against an award of costs, such protection is not absolute (see chapter 28) and for those without such protection, costs may cause considerable hardship. Second, the postponement may be on terms which – although they must not be unreasonable or cause exceptional hardship – may nevertheless cause some hardship. Third, in the event of a breach of the conditions, the landlord may proceed to apply for a warrant for execution of the possession order.

4.66 If a postponed possession order is to be made, the form of wording of the order is critical. The court's practice may be to use the court form N28 (March 2006 template, which contains a date for delivery of possession) or form N28A (July 2006 template, which does not contain a date for delivery of possession). However, in *Bristol CC v Hassan; Bristol CC v Glastonbury*,[76] the Court of Appeal made it clear that a judge is not obliged to set out the terms of a possession order in any particular form. The wording of the actual order the court may make is at large.

4.67 The requirements of modern IT systems are such that, unless care is taken, whatever the judge manually records as to the terms of the order made, the wording may be electronically transposed by the court's administrative staff into one of the standard templates. Advisers seeking to avoid that occurring should furnish the judge with a typescript or manuscript of the actual order sought/made that can be approved by the judge and sealed by the court.

---

74 HA 1985 s85(3).
75 *Lambeth LBC v Hama* January 2008 *Legal Action* 34.
76 [2006] EWCA Civ 656; [2006] 1 WLR 2582; [2006] HLR 31.

4.68   In July 2006, a new Section IV ('Orders fixing a date for possession') was added to CPR PD 55A to deal with postponed conditional
possession orders made in form N28A which do not contain a specified date for giving possession. Where an order has been made in
this form, and the conditions of postponement are alleged to have
been breached, CPR PD 55A para 10.2 provides that the landlord may
apply to the court for an order fixing the date on which the tenant has
to give up possession. At least 14 days before making such an application, the landlord must give written notice to the tenant of its intention to do so, and of its reasons for doing so. The notice must record,
by reference to a copy of the rent account, in what respect the tenant has failed to comply with the order and must invite the tenant's
response within seven days. The application itself may be made without notice, but the landlord must attach a copy of the tenant's reply (if
any) and must state whether there is any outstanding housing benefit
claim by the tenant. A district judge should usually determine the
application without a hearing by fixing the date for possession as the
next working day, unless he or she considers that a hearing is necessary, in which case a date of hearing will be arranged.

4.69   The exercise of fixing a date for possession on such an application
is usually a paper procedure, although the judge may refer the landlord's application for an oral hearing where appropriate (for example,
where the tenant has responded to the landlord's notice and has denied the alleged breach or explained the reason for the breach). That is
particularly true of cases in which allegations of anti-social behaviour
in breach of conditions of the order are denied.[77] Only if the court
then fixes a date will it become possible for the landlord to seek execution of the order and (on execution) bring the tenancy to an end.

4.70   It is clearly important for advisers and legal representatives to
attempt to persuade the court that it should use the form N28A
rather than N28. Where an order is made in form N28 (March 2006),
the order becomes capable of enforcement on a single breach of the
terms of the order. Where form N28A is used, the landlord cannot
seek execution of the order in the event of a breach or breaches unless and until the court fixes a date for possession on an application by the landlord. In *Croydon LBC v Crawford*[78] the judge made an
order that possession be suspended on conditions for two years in
an anti-social behaviour case. The order was in a form prepared by
the council's advocate and the Court of Appeal refused permission to

77 *Wandsworth LBC v Whibley* [2008] EWCA Civ 1259; [2009] HLR 26.
78 [2010] EWCA Civ 618.

appeal on the ground that a postponed order in form N28A should have been made

4.71 Any postponed order should preferably be expressed to provide for automatic discharge on compliance with all its specified terms or on the expiry of a particular period from the date it is made.[79]

4.72 In any event, the tenant can always apply for the discharge or rescission of the possession order if the conditions are complied with,[80] even if they were not complied with punctiliously.[81] When amended by provisions yet to be commenced, the Housing Act 1985 will provide that the court may at any time discharge or rescind a possession order if it thinks it appropriate to do so having had regard to (1) any conditions imposed under by the order and (2) the conduct of the tenant in connection with those conditions.[82] As is obvious, the prospects of a successful application to discharge or rescind the order will be greater the more that the tenant is able to show some substantive efforts at compliance with the original conditions.

Preventing an eviction

4.73 Where an order for possession has been made, secure occupiers retain their tenancy or licence and their secure status until the date they give up possession on execution of the order.[83] It is on that date that both the security and the tenancy or licence end.

4.74 In the case of an *absolute or outright order* for possession, the date on which the tenant is to give up possession will be clearly shown in the order itself or identified by a reference to 'X days from today's date' (often 28 days from the date of hearing). From that date, the landlord can seek execution of the order. An adviser instructed for the secure tenant who is subject of such an order should always consider (1) whether an appeal can be justified (see para 3.208), (2) whether an application can be made to set it aside (see para 34.7) or (3) whether circumstances have changed sufficiently since the order was made to enable a successful application to be made to postpone the date for possession, on terms if necessary.[84]

---

79 *Blaenau Gwent BC v Snell* March 1990 *Legal Action* 13 and see *Merton LBC v Hashmi* September 1995 *Legal Action* 13, CA.

80 HA 1985 s85(4).

81 See *Knowsley Housing Trust v White* [2008] UKHL 70; [2009] 1 AC 636.

82 HA 1985 s85(4), as substituted by Housing and Regeneration Act 2008 s299 and Sch 11 Pt 1 paras 1 and 3.

83 HA 1985 s82(1) and (1A), as amended by Housing and Regeneration Act 2008 Sch 11 para 2(3).

84 *Ujima Housing Association v Smith* April 2001 *Legal Action* 21.

4.75   In the case of a *conditional order* for possession made in court form N28 (see para 4.66), the landlord can apply for execution of the order as soon as any date stated in it has passed and the terms have not been complied with.[85] Where the order was a *postponed conditional order* in court form N28A (see para 4.66), the landlord will first need to obtain a fixed date for possession using the procedure described above (para 4.72) before seeking execution of the order.

4.76   Once the date fixed by an order has passed, the landlord may apply to the court (by completing a simple form) for the issue of a warrant for possession and its execution by a bailiff. The occupier should receive notice from the bailiffs (form N54) giving the time and date on which they will attend to take possession.

4.77   Whether the order was expressed to be absolute/outright or was postponed, the court can suspend or stay *execution* of the order or further postpone the date for possession on any grounds that it 'thinks fit'.[86] This can be done at any time before the moment of execution of the order by the bailiffs, even a matter of hours or minutes beforehand.[87] The procedure for making an application for a stay, suspension or postponement is described in chapter 34. Note that this procedure is not available where the possession order has been obtained under ground 9, 10, 10A or 11 contained in HA 1985 Sch 2, but that in all other cases it is available even if the original date for possession has passed or the terms of a conditional order have been breached.

Reinstating the tenant after eviction

4.78   Even if the order has been executed by the bailiff taking possession, it may still not be too late to set aside the possession order or the warrant or both. See para 34.54 for a full description of what can be done to reinstate the former tenant after eviction.

'Duty advocate' plan

4.79   Almost every county court now has a 'help desk' or 'duty representation scheme' available to a tenant who attends court unrepresented on the date fixed for hearing of a possession claim. Such schemes are funded by the Legal Services Commission (LSC), central government

---

85 *Thompson v Elmbridge BC* [1987] 1 WLR 1425; (1987) 19 HLR 526, CA and *Leicester CC v Aldwinkle* (1992) 24 HLR 49, CA.

86 HA 1985 s85(2).

87 *Islington LBC v Harridge* (1993) *Times* 30 June, CA.

(Department for Communities & Local Government) or operated by volunteers. This section of this chapter illustrates how an adviser on such a scheme might respond to the type of secure tenancy possession case which occurs with greatest frequency – a claim based on rent arrears – and where instructions are received *at the door of the court*.

4.80 The proper preparation of a defence in a rent arrears possession case usually requires careful consideration. In particular, all the documents must be examined, statements taken and negotiations with the landlord pursued and, where appropriate, a fully pleaded defence filed (possibly including a counterclaim).

4.81 If instructed at 'the door of the court' the adviser should avoid the temptation of immediately negotiating or advocating for a postponed conditional possession order requiring payment of current rent and a modest level of weekly payment off the arrears. After all, closer examination may establish that there are in fact no arrears at all or (if there are arrears) that the tenant has a defence as described earlier in this chapter.

4.82 If instructions are received literally at the last moment, the adviser should make an initial application for the case to be put back in the list of cases awaiting hearing and then take some brief particulars from the client. Although the court list may contain dozens of cases, it does not always follow that there will be the opportunity to have a lengthy discussion – these cases can be processed very quickly in some courts.

4.83 The adviser should try to take a preliminary statement from the tenant covering the duration of the tenancy, the personal circumstances of the tenant, the circumstances surrounding the 'arrears', details of income and details of housing benefit received (see appendix C for a useful checklist).

4.84 If the tenant has any documents with him or her, or if copies can be obtained from the landlord's representative at court, the adviser should inspect:

- the notice seeking possession (see para 4.12);
- the claim form and the particulars of claim (see paras 4.49–4.51);
- the rent book/rent account schedule; and
- any correspondence or other relevant documents.

4.85 If there is time and if necessary, Legal Help or Help at Court forms should be completed at this stage so that on return to court the adviser can undertake funded representation (see chapter 28).

4.86 If it emerges that the arrears are disputed, or there is disrepair which may sustain a counterclaim, or simply that more time is needed to ensure that the defence can be put fairly, the immediate objective should be to secure an adjournment to another date. Before returning to make such an application in court the adviser should be prepared to deal with:

- the likely eventual defence;
- the tenant's circumstances;
- the possibility of an agreement to pay current rent during the adjournment;
- the possibility of an agreement to pay something off the alleged arrears during that time (without prejudice to any contention that nothing, or not the amount claimed, is owed);
- the reason why advice was not sought earlier; and
- the minimum case management directions necessary to achieve the next stage in the claim (for example, date by which a defence should be served).

4.87   The adviser may then indicate to the landlord's representative that a request for an adjournment will be made. If the application is opposed, the adviser may need to explain to the court that:

- he or she has just been instructed;
- those instructions reveal that the client has an arguable defence (for example, that the arrears are disputed or it would not be reasonable to order possession and/or that the tenant has a potential counterclaim and defence by way of set-off based on disrepair or failure to pay housing benefit, etc);
- the tenant will immediately be directed to a legal adviser to draft the defence; and
- an adjournment is sought for that purpose.

4.88   It is usually helpful to be able to indicate that the tenant will submit to a condition that current rent be paid throughout the period of the adjournment.[88] The court may be tempted to impose a requirement for additional modest payments towards the arrears but (where appropriate) the adviser may respond that further conditions would be unreasonable or would cause excessive hardship.[89] The adviser should invite the making of directions for a defence to be filed within (say) 21 days and for such other steps as may be appropriate, for example, disclosure, experts' reports, etc. The court should be addressed on the proper order as to the costs of the adjournment.

---

88 HA 1985 s85(3).
89 HA 1985 s85(3)(a).

4.89   In most cases, the above procedure ought to achieve an adjournment. If not, the adviser has to do his or her best to defend successfully on the day and obtain permission to appeal any adverse order made. In an appropriate case, an appeal may be entered against the refusal to adjourn, in addition to an appeal against the order made.[90]

4.90   Once the adjournment is secured, the adviser should make the necessary arrangements for full legal representation to be obtained and for all technical and substantive defences and counterclaims to be considered. If the matter is to be conducted by a solicitor, advisers should bear in mind the possible delays in obtaining a full funding certificate for legal representation and the importance of not exceeding the time allowed by the court for filing and service of the defence.

---

90   See *Janstan Investments Ltd v Corregar* (1973) 21 November, unreported, CA; *Spitaliotis v Morgan* [1986] 1 EGLR 51; (1985) 277 EG 750, CA and *Bates v Croydon LBC* [2001] EWCA Civ 134; (2001) 33 HLR 70.

CHAPTER 5

Subtenants, homeless persons and non-secure occupiers

Introduction

5.1   This chapter considers the position of four classes of occupier in social housing accommodation:

- subtenants of secure occupiers;
- homeless persons;
- non-secure tenants;
- non-secure licensees;

and outlines in each case the prospects for defending possession proceedings brought against them.

Subtenants of secure occupiers

5.2   In November 2009 the Minister for Housing in England launched a major new initiative on 'social housing fraud' designed to encourage social landlords to recover possession of properties sublet by secure tenants (see para 2.55). As a result there are likely to be far more requests for advice from those who claim to be, or are alleged to be, subtenants of secure occupiers. In such cases it is necessary to identify correctly the true legal status of those persons living in the secure tenant's property.

5.3   An occupier may indeed be the *subtenant* of a secure tenant. But it is more often the case that the person is let into occupation as a *lodger*. In any event, this is usually what the secure tenant will assert because that tenant requires no permission from the head landlord to allow lodgers on to the premises[1] but may be in difficulties with his or her own landlord if he or she has truly sublet. The correct analysis of the legal position is therefore important and the first step is to determine whether the occupier is a lodger (or some other licensee) or a true subtenant.

Lodgers and other licensees

5.4   The occupier is a lodger in the secure tenant's home if he or she has *not* been provided with any exclusive part of the tenant's home for his or her own use. Even if the occupier does have his or her 'own room', he or she is a lodger if the secure tenant provides services which require unrestricted access to the occupier's room (such as changes

---

1   HA 1985 s93(1)(a).

of bed-linen, cleaning, removing refuse, etc).[2] Where the tenant exercises a high degree of control over the occupier's use of the room – for example, regarding decoration or visitors – this will also point towards a lodging situation. A true lodger is not a subtenant because he or she has no exclusive occupation of any property – such 'exclusive possession' is one of the key hallmarks of a (sub)tenancy.[3] In law, the lodger is a mere licensee of the tenant.

5.5 Secure tenants are free to take lodgers if they wish[4] but are usually required by the terms of their own tenancy agreements to inform the landlord if they do so.

5.6 The secure tenant may have allowed visiting family members to come and stay in his or her home or have had such people sharing with him or her from the outset of the tenancy. None of these occupiers has a subtenancy. That is either because they do not have exclusive possession (a prerequisite of tenancy – see above) or because there has been no intention to create a legal relationship,[5] or both.

5.7 The true lodger's position is precarious. He or she is liable to exclusion by the tenant at the end of any period of lodging without the need for a formal notice in any prescribed form. For example, a lodger allowed to 'stay for a week' can be turned out at the end of the week and a lodger staying on a weekly basis can be given as little as a week's notice. This results from the exclusion of the lodger from the scope of the Protection from Eviction Act (PEA) 1977 and is a consequence of the lodger sharing use of the premises with his or her licensor, the true tenant.[6]

5.8 In *Monmouth BC v Marlog*,[7] a woman and her two children moved into a council house with its new tenant and she paid him £20 per week. She and her children had two of the three bedrooms, the tenant had his own bedroom and the use of the other rooms was shared. The Court of Appeal refused to disturb the county court judge's finding that the woman was only a licensee. The court described as 'ludicrous' any suggestion that the parties might have intended the creation of a subtenancy.

---

2 *Huwyler v Ruddy* (1996) 28 HLR 550, CA. See also *Aslan v Murphy (No 2)* [1990] 1 WLR 766; [1989] 3 All ER 130, CA and *Crancour v De Silvaesa* (1986) 18 HLR 265, CA.

3 See, generally, *Street v Mountford* [1985] AC 809; (1985) 17 HLR 402, HL.

4 HA 1985 s93(1)(a).

5 *Errington v Errington* [1952] 1 KB 290; [1952] 1 All ER 149, CA.

6 PEA 1977 s3A(2)(a).

7 (1995) 27 HLR 30, CA.

5.9   The lodger's right to remain is subsidiary to the tenant's own continuing tenancy and, as a result, the lodger cannot be ousted by the head landlord for as long as that tenancy remains in place. For example, in *Braintree DC v Vincent*,[8] the secure tenant left the premises and went to live in a nursing home. The tenant's sons, her licencees, remained in occupation. The council claimed possession against the sons and the judge granted a possession order on the basis that the tenant was no longer fulfilling the tenancy condition (see para 1.14) and so was no longer a secure tenant. The Court of Appeal held that to have been an error because nothing had been done – by notice to quit or otherwise – to end the mother's non-secure tenancy. Only if and when that tenancy was determined would the licencees become trespassers capable of being ousted by the council.

Subtenants of part

5.10   Secure tenants are free to sublet parts of their homes with the written consent of their landlord.[9] In practice, many do not seek or obtain such consent even though it may not be unreasonably withheld.[10] That may expose a secure tenant to a claim for possession for breach of an obligation (to seek consent before subletting) of his or her own tenancy under the second limb of ground 1: see para 3.54. However, whether or not consent of the head landlord has been obtained, any subletting is valid and enforceable as between the secure tenant and the subtenant.

5.11   Such a true subletting does not usually give the subtenant any security of tenure or protection under the Protection from Eviction Act 1977 because the 'landlord' (the secure tenant) will be resident in the part not sublet and will therefore be sharing living accommodation with the tenant.[11]

Subtenants of the whole

5.12   It is not uncommon for secure tenants to move out of their homes and put others in exclusive occupation on long-term or short-term arrangements. Even if the secure tenant intends to return and resume occupation at a later date, security of tenure is lost by the *subletting or*

---

8   [2004] EWCA Civ 415.
9   HA 1985 s93(1)(b).
10 HA 1985 s94.
11 PEA 1977 s3A(2)(a).

notice to quit is defective or has not been served. The circumstances in which these defences can be established are set out at paras 14.6–14.26.

• *Administrative law grounds.* The non-secure tenant may be able to defend on the ground that the proceedings have been improperly brought by the landlord. Examples would include bad faith, malice or otherwise acting unreasonably.[47] The onus is on the tenant to make out the allegation of abuse of power or breach of duty.[48] For more on 'public law' defences see chapter 25.

• *Human rights grounds.* This will arise if the non-secure tenancy is the occupier's home and it is claimed that eviction would interfere with the right to respect for that home provided by the European Convention on Human Rights article 8. See chapter 26.

5.34   Although usually an allegation that a social housing provider is acting unlawfully on administrative law grounds should be made in proceedings brought by way of judicial review,[49] that requirement does not apply where the social housing body has brought the proceedings itself and the illegality of the claimant's own action is being relied on by the defendant.[50] See chapter 25.

Non-secure licensees

5.35   Some licensees in social housing never acquire secure status (for example, because they do not enjoy exclusive possession of their accommodation[51] or they are excepted by HA 1985 Sch 1 – see the list in para 1.23) or lose it in one of the ways described above in chapter 2. They remain contractual licensees liable to pay their licence fee and the other contractual obligations of both parties continue to bind them and be enforceable by either licensor or licensee.

5.36   The licensor seeking to recover possession must therefore determine the contractual licence and bring proceedings for possession

---

47 *Bristol DC v Clark* [1975] 3 All ER 976, CA; *Bristol CC v Rawlins* (1977) 34 P&CR 12, CA; *Sevenoaks DC v Emmott* (1979) 39 P&CR 404, CA; *McGlynn v Welwyn Hatfield District Council* [2009] EWCA Civ 285; [2010] HLR 10; *Croydon LBC v Barber* [2010] EWCA Civ 51; (2010) *Times* 24 March; *Manchester CC v Mushin* (reported sub nom *Salford CC v Mullen*) [2010] EWCA Civ 336.

48 *Cannock Chase DC v Kelly* [1978] 1 All ER 152, CA.

49 CPR Part 54.

50 *Wandsworth LBC v Winder* [1985] AC 461, HL and *Kay v Lambeth LBC* [2006] UKHL 10; [2006] 2 AC 465.

51 *Westminster City Council v Clarke* (1992) 24 HLR 360, HL, and see paras 1.27–1.30.

(except where the accommodation is a room in a 'public sector' hostel – see para 5.24 – or where the licence was granted to squatters as a temporary expedient[52]).

5.37   Possession proceedings brought against non-secure licensees may be defended on only one of three grounds:

- *Insufficient notice.* A licence can be determined only by the giving of contractual or reasonable notice.[53] 'What is a reasonable time depends on all the circumstances of the case and where the licence has been to occupy premises for residential purposes the reasonable time has reference to enabling the licensee to have an opportunity of taking his effects away from the property.'[54] The licensee given insufficient notice may have a defence that longer notice should have been given and that the notice relied on is insufficient. Any proceedings to recover possession on the basis that the licensee has become a trespasser (see chapter 29) can be started only *after* reasonable notice has expired.[55] Any notice given to determine a non-secure licence has to (i) be in writing; (ii) contain the prescribed information; and (iii) be given not less than four weeks before it takes effect.[56] The only relevant licences not covered by the statutory rules are those granted to squatters as a temporary expedient[57] or to licensees of hostels provided by social landlords.[58]

- *Administrative law grounds.* The non-secure licensee is as able as the non-secure tenant to argue that the proceedings are improperly brought by the licensor if it is a social landlord (see above).[59] For more on 'public law' defences see chapter 25.

- *Human Rights grounds.* See chapter 26.

---

52 PEA 1977 s3A.

53 *Minister of Health v Bellotti* [1944] KB 298, CA.

54 *GLC v Jenkins* [1975] 1 All ER 354 at 357C per Diplock LJ.

55 *GLC v Jenkins* [1975] 1 All ER 354 at 357C per Diplock LJ.

56 PEA 1977 s5(1B), as inserted by HA 1988 s32(2).

57 PEA 1977 s3A(6).

58 PEA 1977 s3A(8) and see *Brennan v Lambeth LBC* (1998) 30 HLR 481, CA.

59 *Cleethorpes BC v Clarkson* (1978) 128 NLJ 860, noted at July 1978 *LAG Bulletin* 166, CA; *R v Wear Valley DC ex p Binks* [1985] 2 All ER 699; *Kensington and Chelsea RLBC v Haydon* (1984) 17 HLR 114, CA and *Wandsworth LBC v A* [2000] 1 WLR 1246, CA.

CHAPTER 6

Housing associations and other non-council social landlords

Introduction

6.1   In recent years, the terms in which non-council social landlords are referred to in housing legislation have been repeatedly modified. From 1996, 'registered social landlord' (RSL) was the term used to describe those social landlords which were registered with, and regulated by, the Housing Corporation, or Housing for Wales, pursuant to the statutory scheme established by the Housing Act (HA) 1996 Part 1. Most such landlords were housing associations and housing trusts. On 1 April 2010 the scheme in HA 1996 Part 1 was replaced in England by new arrangements contained in the Housing and Regeneration Act 2008. Under the new arrangements, such landlords had to register with the regulator of social housing, the Tenant Services Authority (TSA), as a 'registered provider of social housing' (RPSH). Non-council RPSHs are known as private registered providers (PRPs). For the time being, the scheme of HA 1996 Part 1 continues in operation in Wales, although the Welsh Assembly Government is considering plans for a new system of registration and regulation of housing associations in Wales. Indeed, at the time of writing, the future of the TSA as regulator in England was under review.

6.2   Although there are important differences between the legal meanings of 'housing association', 'registered social landlord' and 'registered provider of social housing' for other purposes, the differences have limited (if any) significance for possession proceedings and are not explored further here. The terms are used interchangeably in this chapter and no significance should be attached to the label used in the text unless otherwise indicated.

6.3   Those who occupy housing association-owned property may do so as tenants or licensees and may fall within either the 'secure tenancy' regime for security of tenure (described in chapters 1–5 of this book) or the 'assured tenancy' or 'assured shorthold tenancy' regimes (see chapters 11 and 12). This chapter explains the protection available according to the type of arrangement under which the occupier is living in a housing association property.

Tenants of housing associations

6.4   Under the provisions of HA 1985 s80, as originally enacted, tenants of all housing associations (whether registered or unregistered) were within the 'secure tenancy' regime described in chapter 1. However, the intention behind the changes made by the Housing Act 1988 was to produce a situation in which all *new* housing association lettings from 15 January 1989 would be on assured tenancies rather than secure tenancies. Assured tenants have a more limited form of security of tenure than that enjoyed by secure tenants and are placed in the same category of protection as tenants of private sector landlords – albeit that most private sector landlords now grant assured *shorthold* tenancies (see chapter 11).

6.5   Subject to the limited exceptions described below, all housing association tenancies granted on or after 15 January 1989 are assured rather than secure tenancies.[1] They may be full assured tenancies or assured shorthold tenancies at the election of the housing association.[2] From 1996 to 2009 the Housing Corporation, in its then statutory role of guiding the activities of housing associations in England,[3] repeatedly indicated that housing associations which use assured shorthold tenancies (sometimes referred to as 'starter' tenancies) should do so only as part of a managed strategy for dealing with anti-social behaviour in limited geographic areas for limited periods with regular reviews of the necessity for maintaining the practice.[4] The widespread use of assured shorthold tenancies by very many housing associations would suggest that this statutory guidance was often ignored. From 1 April 2010 housing associations in England have been required to comply with the new National Tenancy Standard adopted by the TSA. It provides:

3. Tenure

Registered providers shall offer and issue the most secure form of tenure compatible with the purpose of the housing and the sustainability of the community.

They shall meet all applicable statutory and legal requirements in relation to the form and use of tenancy agreements.

6.6   That very broadly worded statutory standard is unlikely to produce any dramatic change in the widespread use of assured shorthold tenancies by housing associations in England. In Wales, the Assembly Government's *Regulatory Code for Housing Associations Registered in*

---

1   HA 1988 s35(4).

2   By default, the tenancy will be an assured shorthold unless the housing association indicates by notice in writing that the tenancy will be a full assured tenancy: HA 1988 Sch 2A para 1.

3   HA 1996 s36.

4   See, eg, *Regulatory Circular 07/04*, para 3.3.3, *Regulatory Code and Guidance* August 2005, para 3.5.2 and *Good Practice Note 14: Tenure* November 2007.

Wales[5] states that housing associations 'should ensure that residents are offered the most secure form of occupancy'.[6]

6.7   The key to determining whether the tenant of a housing association is assured or secure is usually the date of grant of the tenancy. If that date falls on or after 15 January 1989 then the tenancy is likely to be assured. If that date falls on or before 14 January 1989 it will probably be secure. However, housing association tenancies granted on or after 15 January 1989 will be secure rather than assured in any one of the following situations:

- The tenant was previously a secure occupier (whether as sole or joint secure tenant or as sole or joint secure licensee) of the same housing association.[7] Therefore a secure tenant can transfer to other property within the same housing association's stock without loss of secure status.
- The tenancy was granted following the re-acquisition of defective property (which a former secure tenant had bought) under the procedure set out in HA 1985 Part XVI (formerly the Housing Defects Act 1984) pursuant to HA 1985 s554(2A).[8] This embraces not only the original tenant who bought the defective house from the association, but also certain members of his or her family.[9]
- The tenancy was granted pursuant to a contract to let made before 15 January 1989.[10] This exception demonstrates the importance of ascertaining not merely the date the tenancy commenced but also the date the agreement for the letting was made.
- The tenancy is offered as 'suitable alternative accommodation' to a former secure occupier against whom a possession order has been made in proceedings taken under HA 1985 s84(2)(b) or (c) and the court has directed that the new tenancy or licence should be secure.[11] This exception will be relevant to secure tenants of any landlord who are being rehoused by a housing association in accommodation arranged by the former landlord (see para 3.203).
- The tenant was a private sector protected or statutory tenant and the housing association has acquired the interest of the private sector landlord.[12]

---

5   Published by the Welsh Assembly Government, June 2006.
6   Key Expectation 1.4.1.
7   HA 1988 s35(4).
8   HA 1988 s35(4)(f).
9   HA 1988 Sch 17 para 61.
10   HA 1988 s35(4)(c).
11   HA 1988 s35(4)(e).
12   HA 1988 s34(5).

6.8   Further modifications to the usual rules on whether the tenancy is secure or assured apply where the association is housing homeless families or is a housing co-operative. These are discussed separately below.

6.9   Of course, the general exceptions to secure or assured status (that prevent certain tenancies from enjoying security of tenure) also apply in the housing association sector. However, if one of those exceptions ceases to apply, whether the tenancy thereupon becomes secure or assured is determined according to the date of the original letting and the application of any relevant transitional provisions.[13]

Defending housing association tenants

6.10   The first step is to work out (using the preceding paragraphs) whether the tenant facing a claim for possession holds an assured tenancy (possibly an assured shorthold) or a secure tenancy or has no security of tenure under either regime.

6.11   Wherever possible it should be argued that the tenancy is secure (rather than assured or unprotected) as this confers a greater degree of security of tenure (as well as the possibility of enjoying the full 'right to buy', etc).

6.12   The second step is to consider whether the association is acting in accordance with (or in breach of) the standards expected by the regulatory body, presently the TSA in England and the Welsh Assembly Government in Wales, in relation to the recovery of possession from the class of tenant in question.[14]

6.13   If a check of this material suggests that the association has not acted properly or fairly, that point can be raised with (1) the association itself under its complaints procedure, (2) the appropriate regulator – the TSA in England or the Welsh Assembly Government in Wales, (3) the Housing Ombudsman Service, and/or (4) the court considering the possession claim (for the last, see chapters 25 and 26).

6.14   Most particularly, where proceedings are brought under any of the discretionary grounds against a secure or assured tenant, the attention of the court can usefully be drawn to any relevant part of the regulatory guidance as part of the courts consideration of 'reasonableness'. Until April 2010 much useful regulatory guidance was

---

13 See *Bhai v Black Roof Community Housing Association Limited* [2001] 2 All ER 865; (2001) 33 HLR 55, CA.
14 See Introduction to Part II.

contained in the Housing Corporation's various publications. For example, the *Regulatory Code and Guidance* required (in para 3.5c) that 'legal repossession of a property is sought as a last resort'. *Regulatory Circular 07/04* stated that 'associations should act to support and sustain, rather than terminate, a tenancy: early intervention is essential' (para 1.2).

6.15   This detailed guidance has now been withdrawn and replaced by the much more generally expressed statutory standards and guidance issued by the TSA for social housing providers in England (see para 6.1).[15] In Wales, the Assembly Government's *Regulatory Code for Housing Associations Registered in Wales*[16] states that housing association performance will be assessed by asking, among other matters: 'Does the association initiate possession action for breaches of tenancy agreements only as a last resort and when other avenues have been exhausted? Does the association use mandatory possession only in exceptional individual circumstances?'[17]

6.16   Note also the Rent Arrears Protocol which ensures that all social landlords offer tenants information, advice and assistance in applying for housing benefit, so that court proceedings are avoided wherever possible (see para 3.38). As to housing association practice in relation to rent arrears possession proceedings, see *Housing associations and rent arrears: attitudes, beliefs and behaviour*,[18] *The use of possession actions and evictions by social landlords*[19] and *Rent arrears management practices in the housing association sector.*[20]

6.17   Demonstrating a failure to comply with any of this guidance may be useful in persuading the court that it is not reasonable in all the circumstances to grant an order for possession. Where that question will not arise, because possession is being sought on a mandatory ground, a failure to comply with guidance may well support a 'public law' defence.[21] For public law defences, see chapter 25.

---

15 *The regulatory framework for social housing in England from April 2010* TSA, March 2010.
16 Published by the Welsh Assembly Government, June 2006.
17 Key Expectation 1.4.1, p8.
18 Published by the Chartered Institute of Housing, 1998.
19 ODPM, June 2005.
20 TSA, March 2010.
21 See, eg, *Eastlands Homes Partnership Ltd v Whyte* [2010] EWHC 695 (QB).

Assured tenants

6.18   The principles for defending possession proceedings brought against assured tenants are set out in detail in chapter 12 (and see chapter 11 for assured shorthold tenants).

Secure tenants

6.19   The approach to defending secure tenants of housing associations and other social landlords is discussed in chapters 3 and 4.

Unprotected tenants

6.20   For the defences open to a tenant or licensee of a housing association facing eviction and unable to rely on any security of tenure, see paras 5.32–5.36.

Housing association licensees

6.21   Some housing associations make property available to occupiers on licence rather than by way of tenancy.[22] The first step for an adviser assisting such an occupier is to determine whether what has been granted is truly a licence or is in law a tenancy. If, despite its description, the licence is a tenancy (because it provides exclusive possession in return for periodic payment and there are no special circumstances),[23] see para 6.4.

6.22   If the arrangement is a true licence (for example, because services provided to the occupier by the association require unrestricted access to the premises occupied), then the security of tenure it attracts is determined by the date on which it was granted. A licence granted by a housing association on or before 14 January 1989 may be a secure licence attracting considerable security of tenure (see para 1.27 for a discussion of the conditions for such a licence being secure). If the licence was granted on or before 14 January 1989 but does not fulfil the conditions for being a secure licence, see para 5.35 which deals with non-secure licensees.

---

22   See *Bruton v London & Quadrant Housing Trust* [2000] 1 AC 406; (1999) 31 HLR 902, HL and *Kay v Lambeth LBC* [2006] UKHL 10; [2006] 2 AC 465; [2006] HLR 22.

23   *Street v Mountford* [1985] AC 809; [1985] 17 HLR 402, HL.

6.23   If the licence was granted on or after 15 January 1989 it cannot be secure (unless it falls into one of the excepted categories set out at para 6.7). Nor can it be 'assured'. There is no such concept as an 'assured licence'.[24] The occupier has only the most limited protection. See para 5.35 for the conditions governing the recovery of possession from such licensees. For the circumstances in which such an occupier might rely on a 'public law' defence see chapter 25.

Housing associations and the homeless

6.24   In discharging their statutory duties toward the homeless, local authorities are encouraged to seek the help and co-operation of housing associations[25] and housing associations are obliged by statute to provide reasonable help on request.[26] As a result, in many areas of the country, housing associations provide short-term temporary accommodation for homeless people where:

- investigations by the local authority under HA 1996 Part 7 (Homelessness) are under way; or
- the person became homeless intentionally and is entitled only to short-term temporary accommodation;
- the person is awaiting acceptance of a referral by a different housing authority to which he or she has been referred under the local connection provisions; or
- accommodation is being provided pursuant to the exercise of other local authority powers or duties under HA 1996 Part 7.

6.25   The occupier does not gain *secure* status in any of these situations as against the housing association landlord (see further para 6.7 for the exceptional circumstances in which a post-1989 tenancy granted by a housing association can now be secure). Nor, even if the accommodation is first provided on or after 15 January 1989 by way of grant of a tenancy, is it immediately *assured*. Such a tenancy is assured or an assured shorthold only if either (a) the tenant is so notified by the association[27] or (b) 12 months have expired since service on the tenant of the local authority's decision on the homelessness application or decision on review or appeal.[28]

24   *Black Roof Community Housing Association Ltd v Lanipekun* [1999] EWCA Civ 1592.
25   *Homelessness Code of Guidance* CLG, July 2006.
26   HA 1996 s213.
27   HA 1996 s209, as substituted by the Homelessness Act 2002.
28   HA 1996 s209.

6.26   In order to avoid the possible accrual of secure or assured status, many associations purport to grant licences, rather than tenancies, of temporary accommodation to homeless people. If the licence was granted before 15 January 1989 and it conferred rights of exclusive occupation, it will have long since become secure. If granted on or after 15 January 1989 it is neither secure nor assured and attracts only the limited protection indicated at para 6.27.

6.27   Whether what has been granted to the homeless person pursuant to a temporary obligation under HA 1996 Part 7 is a licence or a tenancy is to be determined according to the usual legal principles.[29] The Court of Appeal has[30] resiled from the view that the usual principles can be modified in these cases.[31] Whether the arrangement is in law a tenancy or a licence can have important implications, principally because only a tenancy can have assured or assured shorthold status, but also in determining the correct method by which it may be ended.

Housing co-operatives and housing trusts

6.28   A tenancy or licence granted before 15 January 1989 is secure and covered by the provisions described in chapter 1 of this book if it is granted by:

- a housing trust which is a charity; or
- an unregistered housing association which is a co-operative housing association; or
- a registered housing association other than a co-operative housing association;[32] or
- a management co-operative exercising the functions of a social housing landlord.[33]

6.29   Accordingly, even longstanding pre-1989 occupiers of property held by housing trusts which are not charities or by registered housing co-operatives (particularly 'fully mutual' housing co-operatives) are

---

29 *Street v Mountford* [1985] AC 809; [1985] 17 HLR 402 and *Eastleigh BC v Walsh* [1985] 1 WLR 525; [1985] 2 All ER 112, HL.

30 *Family Housing Association v Jones* [1990] 1 WLR 779; (1990) 22 HLR 45, CA, expressly not following *Ogwr BC v Dykes* [1989] 1 WLR 295; [1989] 2 All ER 880, CA.

31 *Ogwr BC v Dykes* [1989] 1 WLR 295; [1989] 2 All ER 880, CA.

32 HA 1985 s80(1) and (2) as enacted.

33 HA 1985 s80(4).

not within the secure status regime. If a registered housing co-operative deregisters, however, the tenants must be notified that they have become secure.[34]

6.30   This requirement to notify a change of status simply illustrates the fact that the security of tenure of the occupiers may change from time to time depending on which variant of association their landlord is at any particular time: see *Bhai v Black Roof Community Housing Association Limited.*[35]

6.31   Each of the above-mentioned variations in landlord type is closely defined by the Housing Act 1985 and the technical definitions may be found in the Act as follows:

- 'charity' (s622);
- 'co-operative housing association' (s5(2));
- 'housing association' (s5(1));
- 'housing trust' (s6);
- 'registered' (s5(4)).

6.32   For tenancies granted on or after 15 January 1989, those granted by housing trusts, co-operatives and associations usually attract assured or assured shorthold status and so are governed by the regimes described in Part II of this book. However, a 'fully mutual housing association' cannot grant an assured tenancy[36] and after 15 January 1989 it cannot grant a secure tenancy either. Tenants of fully mutual housing associations are therefore outside both schemes of security and are unprotected tenants (see para 5.32 for their protection against eviction).[37] The term 'fully mutual' is defined by HA 1985 s5(2).

6.33   The tenants and licensees of housing management co-operatives and other similar bodies administering council property under arrangements made within HA 1985 s27B continue to be secure whatever the date of grant of their tenancies.

---

34 HA 1985 s80(3).
35 [2001] 2 All ER 865; (2001) 33 HLR 55, CA.
36 HA 1988 Sch 1 para 12(1)(h).
37 *Mexfield Housing Co-Operative Ltd v Berrisford* [2010] EWCA Civ 811. For an example of the issues which may arise in possession claims against tenants of fully mutual housing co-ops, see *Nettleton Road Housing Co-operative Ltd v Joseph* [2010] EWCA Civ 228, CA.

Other social landlords

6.34 As explained above, most RSLs and most PRPs are, in fact housing associations and other similar bodies. However, it was also open to not-for-profit private companies to apply for registration as RSLs under the Housing Act 1996 and now as PRPs under the Housing and Regeneration Act 2008. The tenants and licensees of these social landlords will have broadly the same security of tenure (or lack of it) as would be granted to new tenants and licensees of private landlords. It may be expected, however, that the TSA will insist on the grant of full assured tenancies wherever possible and the use of comparatively 'generous' terms and conditions of tenancy in order to ensure compliance with its National Tenancy Standard (see para 6.5).

Human Rights Act 1998

6.35 Advisers defending occupiers in any of the circumstances described in this chapter will wish to consider whether the housing association or other social housing provider with which they are dealing is a 'public authority' for the purposes of the Human Rights Act 1998 s6 and what implications the answer to that question might have for possession proceedings. See further, chapter 26.

Introductory tenancies

Background

7.1   In 1995 the concerted efforts of some local authority landlords produced a commitment from central government to increase legal powers available to those landlords to deal with errant tenants guilty of 'anti-social' behaviour towards others.[1] The result was an array of new measures and amendments to existing housing law enacted in Housing Act (HA) 1996 Part 5, which bears the title 'Conduct of Tenants'.

7.2   Chapter I of HA 1996 Part V set out the arrangements for a new regime of 'introductory tenancies'. It was brought into force on 12 February 1997. It is not of universal application – each local housing authority in England and Wales is free to choose whether to apply its provisions in its area. Voluntary adoption of the provisions by a local housing authority allows it to offer all its future lettings to new tenants on a 'probationary' or 'trial' basis. If the tenancy endures for 12 months (or, exceptionally, for 18 months where the trial period has been extended – see para 7.24), it becomes a 'secure' tenancy if it otherwise fulfils the requirements for attracting that status.

7.3   In the 'probationary' or 'trial' period, the introductory tenant enjoys no security of tenure and only modified statutory rights. The tenancy can be ended by a process which starts with the landlord giving a notice. Once that has expired, possession can be recovered virtually 'as of right'. The underlying intention of the provisions is to enable local authority landlords to 'nip in the bud' anti-social behaviour among new tenants.

7.4   In the event, there is nothing in HA 1996 Part V Chapter I (save its title) which confines the operation of the introductory tenancy scheme to a context of nuisance or nuisance-related issues. A local authority landlord may perfectly lawfully adopt the introductory scheme for other reasons (for example, to achieve quicker possession against new tenants in early default with rent) and may seek possession during the trial or probationary period for any reason at all. Not all local authorities have elected to adopt the introductory tenancy regime but the majority have done so.

7.5   To accompany the introduction of HA 1996 Part V, considerable guidance was prepared about the operation of introductory tenancy schemes for those authorities choosing to adopt them. Just before their amalgamation into the Local Government Association, the representative associations for local authorities published *Introductory*

---

1   Department of the Environment, *Anti-social behaviour on council estates*, April 1995.

tenancies: guidance for local authorities,[2] with the intention of assisting those councils which had decide to operate introductory tenancies with practical matters of implementation. That guidance was expressly endorsed by central government (the then Department of the Environment (DoE)) in its own circular[3] outlining the new provisions. The circular does not appear to have been withdrawn or superseded and may usefully be referred to by an adviser asked to assist an introductory tenant.

7.6   This chapter does not purport to offer a description of every facet of the introductory tenancy, the specific rights that attach to it, or the more general rights of introductory tenants.[4] Its aim is to provide assistance in those circumstances where a person alleged to be an introductory tenant is faced with the prospect of repossession by his or her landlord. All references are to sections of the Housing Act 1996 unless otherwise stated.

7.7   The introductory tenancy scheme, by its very nature, creates the opportunity for discrimination in local authority housing. Two tenants of identical houses in the same street and paying the same rent may hold very different tenancies from their council landlord – one may have long-term security of tenure as a 'secure' tenant, the other may be (for an initial 12, or possibly 18, months) at risk of dispossession as an introductory tenant. The argument that this discrimination is in unlawful breach of article 14 of the European Convention on Human Rights has, however, been rejected by the courts.[5]

Strategy for defending possession proceedings

7.8   The adviser faced with a prospective or actual claim for possession against a person alleged to be an introductory tenant should consider first whether the tenancy is 'introductory' at all and (if it is), second, how best to use the procedures available to delay or prevent repossession. What steps to take should then be determined by the results of that consideration. If the possession proceedings have not yet been

2 AMA/ADC/ALG, February 1997.

3 DoE Circ 2/97, *Introductory tenancies and repossession for secure tenancies,* 31 January 1997.

4 Although the term 'tenancy' is used throughout this chapter it is possible to have an 'introductory licence' to which the provisions described in the chapter apply with like effect: HA 1996 s126.

5 *R (McLellan) v Bracknell Forest DC* [2001] EWCA Civ 1510; [2002] QB 1129 at para 104.

issued, the tenant will need advice and assistance (under the Legal Help scheme) but once proceedings are issued he or she should be able to obtain full publicly funded representation if financially eligible: see chapter 28.

Is the tenancy 'introductory'?

7.9   First, the tenant's adviser needs to establish whether the tenancy really is 'introductory', if that is the description being used by the landlord. Working through the following headings should enable that issue to be resolved. If this 'checking process' gives rise to an issue as to whether the tenancy is introductory, that could be resolved by proceedings issued by the tenant in the county court.[6] Such proceedings may take so long to resolve that the alleged introductory tenant remains in possession beyond the expiry of the trial period and moves into secure status by default (but see para 7.52 on the effect of the landlord starting possession proceedings before the expiry date).

The landlord

7.10   Only a local housing authority may operate an introductory tenancy regime.[7] If the landlord claiming possession is a housing association or any other form of landlord,[8] the tenancy cannot be 'introductory' at all (although it may be some other form of tenancy enjoying reduced statutory protection, such as an assured shorthold tenancy). Thus, if a housing association or other social landlord acquires council stock with sitting introductory tenants, the tenancies will cease to have that status.

The election

7.11   The landlord must have 'elected' to operate the introductory tenancy regime.[9] That requires a decision of the full council of the local authority. No such election can have been made before 12 February 1997 when the statutory provisions were commenced and, accordingly, the fact of the making of an election and the date of the election should be identified and checked.

6 HA 1996 s138.
7 HA 1996 s124(1).
8 It is possible for a housing action trust (HAT) to operate an introductory tenancy regime but the six HATs previously operating have been wound up (see para 1.12) and there are no plans to introduce new ones.
9 HA 1996 s124(1).

7.12 A tenancy can be introductory only if it is granted by that council *after* the election and at a date when the election is still in force. An election can be revoked at any time and can even be adopted again later.[10]

7.13 If it can be shown that the election was made improperly or is otherwise invalid or has been revoked, that would provide a complete defence to any assertion that the tenant is an introductory tenant. The issue might be canvassed in judicial review proceedings or be raised by the tenant in defence to any actual proceedings for possession (for public law defences, see chapter 25).[11]

7.14 A tenancy entered into (or adopted) *before* the date of the election cannot be an introductory tenancy.[12] For these purposes a tenancy is 'adopted' if the council becomes the landlord under the tenancy following a disposal or surrender to it of the former landlord's interest.[13]

The tenant

7.15 A tenant who is a secure tenant at the date of any election to operate an introductory tenancy regime retains that status. Indeed, a secure tenant will not become an introductory tenant of the same landlord on subsequently moving to alternative accommodation, by way of a transfer, after the election.[14]

7.16 Those becoming new tenants of a local authority landlord which has adopted an introductory regime will also not be introductory tenants if, immediately before the new tenancy is entered into (or adopted), they were secure tenants of another landlord or assured tenants (not assured shorthold tenants) of another social landlord.[15]

7.17 If any one of several joint tenants satisfies any of the above conditions then the new tenancy will not be an introductory tenancy.[16]

The tenancy

7.18 Both periodic tenancies and periodic licences can be introductory.[17] A fixed-term tenancy or licence cannot be introductory.[18]

---

10 HA 1996 s124(5).
11 See *Wandsworth LBC v Winder (No 1)* [1985] AC 461, HL.
12 HA 1996 s124(3).
13 HA 1996 s124(4).
14 HA 1996 s124(2)(a).
15 HA 1996 s124(2).
16 HA 1996 s124(2).
17 HA 1996 s126.
18 HA 1996 s124(2).

7.19   The tenancy is only an introductory tenancy if it would otherwise have been a *secure* tenancy but for the extant election to operate the introductory scheme.[19] Thus, the landlord and tenant conditions of the Housing Act 1985[20] must be satisfied and the tenancy must not come within any of the exceptions to secure tenancy status in that Act.[21] For the prerequisites of 'secure' status see chapter 1.

7.20   Similarly, if an event occurs which would cause a secure tenancy to lose its status as such (for example, subletting the whole – see para 2.51), any introductory tenancy loses that status and reverts to being a bare contractual tenancy.[22] In contrast to the position with secure tenants, introductory tenants cannot pass in and out of introductory status (see the 'ambulatory' nature of protection for secure occupiers described at para 1.31 above). Once a tenancy has lost introductory status that status cannot apply to it again later.[23]

The trial period

7.21   A tenancy usually remains an introductory tenancy only until the end of the 'trial period' of one year. At the end of that period it ordinarily becomes a secure tenancy without the need for further action by landlord or tenant (but see para 7.24). It is therefore crucial to establish the date on which the one year starts to run.

7.22   In the case of a tenancy which was granted by the council itself, the period begins with whichever is the later of:

- the date on which the tenancy was entered into; or
- the date on which the tenant was first entitled to possession under the tenancy.[24]

7.23   Thus, if a tenancy agreement is signed on 14 August 2010 which entitles the tenant to possession on 20 August 2010, the trial period runs from the latter date and expires on 19 August 2010. However, if on 14 August 2010 the tenant not only signs the agreement but also moves in (for example, to start decorating and installing furniture), the trial period runs from that date even if the first rent payable under the agreement is expressed to be due from 20 August 2010.[25]

---

19 HA 1996 s124(2).
20 HA 1985 ss80–81; see also para 1.3.
21 HA 1985 s79(4) and Sch 1; see also para 1.23.
22 HA 1996 s125(5)(a).
23 HA 1996 s125(6).
24 HA 1996 s125(2).
25 *Salford City Council v Garner* [2004] EWCA Civ 364; [2004] HLR 35.

7.24 Where the introductory tenancy started on or after 6 June 2005, the landlord has a power to extend the trial period by a further six months.[26] Where the landlord wishes to exercise this power, presumably because there has been some breach of tenancy obligations but the landlord is prepared to give the tenant a chance to remedy the situation, it must serve a notice of extension on the tenant at least eight weeks before the original one-year expiry date. The notice must set out the reasons for the landlord's decision and inform the tenant of his or her right to request a review of that decision and the time allowed for making the request. The request must be made within 14 days beginning with the day when the notice of extension is served. The procedure on review is similar to that on review of a decision to seek possession (see para 7.39). The review is to be carried out – and the tenant notified of the review decision – before the original one-year expiry date.

7.25 An introductory tenant may of course be offered a further introductory tenancy by the same or another council before the year expires (for example, as a result of a successful early request for a transfer). In such circumstances the time served under the former tenancy counts towards the trial period of the new tenancy, providing that the former tenancy ended immediately before the grant of the new one.[27]

7.26 If a tenant has held more than two successive introductory tenancies then each period counts towards the trial period providing that:

- the most recently completed period ended immediately before the new introductory tenancy was entered into (or was adopted); and
- each period succeeded the other without interruption.[28]

7.27 Where the new introductory tenancy is held by joint tenants, time towards the trial period is calculated by reference to the tenant who has been an introductory tenant, without interruption, for the longest period.[29]

7.28 A housing association's assured shorthold tenant might successfully apply for a transfer to a local authority which is operating the introductory tenancy regime. Providing the housing association is a registered social landlord (RSL) or private registered provider of social housing (PRP), the time served under the assured shorthold tenancy counts towards the trial period so long as the former assured

26 HA 1996, s125A, inserted by HA 2004 s179.
27 HA 1996 s125(3).
28 HA 1996 s125(3)(b).
29 HA 1996 s125(4).

shorthold tenancy ends immediately before the grant of the new tenancy.[30]

Loss of introductory status

7.29   An introductory tenancy ceases to be an introductory tenancy even before the end of the trial period if one of the following occurs:

- the circumstances are or become such that the tenancy could not otherwise be secure;
- the landlord ceases to be a local authority;
- the election in force when the tenancy was entered into (or adopted) is revoked; or
- the tenant dies and there is no one qualified to succeed.[31]

7.30   In any of these circumstances (other than revocation of the election), the tenancy itself continues but only as a bare contractual tenancy and it cannot later resume introductory status.[32] Where the election is revoked, the tenancy may become secure.

7.31   However, if by the date of the occurrence of one of these developments listed in para 7.29 the landlord has already started possession proceedings, the tenancy has a deemed introductory status until those proceedings are concluded.[33]

7.32   Of course, the most common cause for the loss of introductory status is automatic conversion into a secure tenancy at the end of the one-year trial period or 18-month extended trial period. The landlord can only prevent that happening by the actual *issue* of possession proceedings before the trial period expires. The date when the proceedings are issued by the court is crucial, and this will often be a few days later than the date when the landlord lodged the claim form with the court.[34] The issue of proceedings serves to preserve introductory status until the proceedings are determined.[35]

The repossession procedure

7.33   Assuming that consideration of the above factors has shown that the tenancy is indeed 'introductory', it will be necessary next for the

---

30 HA 1996 s125(3).
31 HA 1996 s125(5).
32 HA 1996 s125(6).
33 HA 1996 s130(1)(b).
34 *Salford City Council v Garner* [2004] EWCA Civ 364; [2004] HLR 35.
35 HA 1996 s130(1)(a).

adviser to check for proper observance by the landlord of the prescribed steps for recovery of possession. Those steps should be examined in turn and carefully scrutinised for error which may be relied on in defence of any proceedings. Particular care is needed if the tenant is vulnerable. Local authorities have been advised by central government that:

> Landlords should ensure that introductory tenancies can never be used as a weapon against vulnerable individuals and ensure that there are safeguards to protect such tenants ... It is essential that landlords are fully alive to the special needs of vulnerable tenants and their relationship with the community as a whole.

7.34 Where problems have arisen between a vulnerable tenant and neighbours, eviction may not necessarily be the most appropriate action to take.[36]

Preliminary notice

7.35 Before issuing possession proceedings, the landlord must serve a notice on the tenant. The reference to 'service' would suggest that only a written notice suffices. Without service of such a notice the landlord cannot bring proceedings for possession and there is no jurisdiction in the court to dispense with service of such a notice or waive any defect in it.[37]

7.36 No form of notice is prescribed but the notice must:[38]

- state that the court will be asked to make a possession order;
- set out the reasons for the landlord's decision to apply for a such an order;
- specify a date after which possession proceedings may be begun;
- inform the tenant of the right to request a review of the decision to seek an order;
- inform the tenant of the time within which such a request must be made; and
- inform the tenant that, if he or she needs help or advice about the notice, and what to do about it, he or she should take it immediately to a citizen's advice bureau, a housing aid centre, a law centre or a solicitor.

36 See Department of the Environment Circular 2/97 paras 10–15. See also the joint DoH/DoE guidance *Housing and community care: establishing a strategic framework*, January 1997.
37 HA 1996 s128(1).
38 HA 1996 s128(2)–(7).

Reasons ②

7.37   Where no reasons, inadequate reasons or plainly wrong reasons are given, the notice is invalid and the court cannot entertain the possession proceedings.[39] A notice with no reasons at all is plainly defective. A notice which is factually incorrect or contains sparse reasons (for example, 'because you have proved an unsatisfactory tenant') may be held invalid for non-compliance with the statutory requirements. In *Lambeth LBC v Dearie*,[40] a possession order granted against an introductory tenant was set aside by a district judge. The reasons given in the notice were 'the tenant has failed to pay the rent due'. The court held this to be insufficient. These reasons did not enable the tenant to know precisely what had to be done to rectify the position or to exercise properly the right to review which was referred to in the notice.

7.38   Generally a statutory duty to give reasons is construed to mean that the reasons given must be proper, intelligible and adequate.[41] The government circular on introductory tenancies advises landlords to give a 'full statement of reasons' which should include 'a case history of the sequence of events'.[42]

Dates ③

7.39   The date stated in the notice as the date after which possession proceedings may be begun must not be earlier than the date on which the tenancy could, if it were not an introductory tenancy, be brought to an end by notice to quit given on the same date as the notice of proceedings.[43] For a weekly periodic tenancy, the earliest date is a date at least 28 days after service and that date must be the first or last day of a period of the tenancy.[44] The notice must also comply with any express terms of the tenancy as to the period of notice.

---

39 See by analogy *Torridge DC v Jones* (1986) 18 HLR 107, CA and *Dudley MBC v Bailey* (1990) 22 HLR 424, CA.

40 April 2001 *Legal Action* 20.

41 Per Megaw J in *Re Poyser and Mills' Arbitration* [1964] 2 QB 467; [1963] 2 WLR 1309, approved by the House of Lords in *Save Britain's Heritage v Number1 Poultry Ltd* [1991] 1 WLR 153, HL.

42 DoE Circ 2/97 para 16. It also advises (para 17) that an explanation in a covering letter is not an adequate substitute.

43 HA 1996 s128(4).

44 Protection from Eviction Act 1977 s5.

The request for review ④

7.40 Within 14 days of being served with the notice the tenant may request that the landlord reviews the decision to seek possession. The request need not be made in writing (although it would be sensible to ensure it was recorded in writing). There is no prescribed form, and no requirement to make the request in any particular manner.[45] There is no requirement to give grounds for seeking a review.

7.41 The period of 14 days begins with the day on which the notice is served.[46] Accordingly, if the notice is served on a Thursday the request for a review must be made by a week next Wednesday.[47] This 14-day time period cannot be extended by the landlord nor on application to a county court because a court has no discretion to extend a statutory time limit.[48]

Timing and procedure on review ⑤

7.42 The review must be dealt with speedily. It must be concluded (which includes notification of the result to the tenant) within the period between the service of the notice and the date specified in it for earliest commencement of proceedings.[49] That may be as short as 28 days. If the landlord misses this window of opportunity the chance may be lost – possibly for good if the trial year (or 18-month period) has meantime expired. If it has not expired the landlord can start again with a new notice. However, failure to conclude a review within the statutory period may not be fatal to the council's case. In *R (Chelfat) v Tower Hamlets LBC*,[50] the court in its discretion refused relief where the council had not conducted a review within the prescribed timescale because the tenant's request for a review had been directed to the housing benefits section of the council and not to the housing officer named in the notice. The council had subsequently agreed to a warrant of possession being suspended by consent to enable a review to be carried out, and against that background it would have been wholly unjust to allow the tenant's application for judicial review.

7.43 Since section 129(6) is silent as to the consequences of any failure to carry out a review within the time specified, the question of

45 *R (Chelfat) v Tower Hamlets LBC* [2006] EWHC 313 (Admin); April 2006 *Legal Action* 32.
46 HA 1996 s129(1).
47 *Trow v Ind Coope (West Midlands) Ltd* [1967] 2 QB 899; [1967] 3 WLR 633.
48 *Honig v Lewisham LBC* (1958) 122 JPJ 302, CA.
49 HA 1996 s129(6).
50 [2006] EWHC 313 (Admin); April 2006 *Legal Action* 32.

whether such a delay was fatal to the council's decision to seek possession would turn on the facts. If the failure was due to a genuine oversight capable of being remedied, there would seem to be no good reason to prevent a landlord from remedying the position and bringing a possession claim. In particular, if the reason that the time limit for completion of the review has been exceeded is because the landlord acceded to a tenant's request to adjourn or postpone a review hearing, it is unlikely that a court would hold that the landlord had thereby lost the possibility of proceeding with a possession claim.)

7.44   The Introductory Tenants (Review) Regulations 1997[51] are concerned with the procedure that is to be followed on a review. In summary:

- Regulation 2 provides that there is to be no oral hearing unless one has been expressly requested by the tenant within 14 days of the service of the notice of intention to seek possession. There is no power to extend that time limit. That notice need not advise the tenant of this right to request an oral hearing (see the requirements at para 7.36). The request for an oral hearing need not be made in writing.

- Regulation 3 provides that the review is to be carried out by a person who was not involved in the decision to apply for possession and if that person is an officer it must be a person senior to the officer who took the decision to serve the notice of intention to seek possession.

- Regulation 4 provides that, if no oral hearing has been requested in time, the tenant has a right to submit written representations within a fixed period of being notified of that right. This is based on the premise, therefore, that on receipt of a request for review the landlord will acknowledge it and invite written representations by a fixed date which must not be earlier than five clear days from the date the tenant receives this notice of the right to make representations.

- Regulations 5 and 6 deal with oral hearings. Where a request for an oral hearing has been made in time, the landlord must give the tenant notice of the date, time and place of the hearing, which cannot be less than five days after the landlord receives the tenant's request. If the notice is defective or short then the hearing may only proceed with the consent of the tenant or his or her representative. At a hearing the tenant has a right to:

51   SI No 72.

- be heard and to be accompanied and represented by another person (professional or otherwise);
- call people to give evidence;
- put questions to any person who gives evidence; and
- make written representations.)

The tenant should be given sufficient opportunity to read any written material relied on by the council and to prepare his or her own case.[52]

- (Regulations 7 to 10 deal with such matters as adjournments, postponements and non-attendance.)

7.45 As is apparent from this description of the statutory review scheme, and of the regulations which flesh it out, the scheme makes no pretence of 'independence'. The review is carried out by the very landlord that has decided to give notice of intention to claim possession.) In *R (McLellan) v Bracknell Forest BC*,[53] it was contended that the review scheme was incompatible with the right to a fair and impartial determination of civil rights guaranteed by article 6(1) of the European Convention on Human Rights. The Court of Appeal decided that the requirements of article 6 were met because the Administrative Court's judicial review jurisdiction could be invoked to cure any deficiency in the review process in any particular case.)

Outcome of the review

7.46 (After the review has been completed, the landlord must notify the tenant of its decision and, if the decision to take possession proceedings still stands, then the landlord must give reasons for that decision.[54] The use of the word 'notify' would suggest that the notice and the reasons both have to be in writing.)

7.47 (Where the landlord decides, following a review, to allow the tenant an opportunity to remedy any breach of tenancy obligations, but the tenant does not do so, the landlord may take proceedings for possession without the need to serve a fresh notice.) In *Cardiff City Council v Stone*,[55] the tenant had fallen into rent arrears. The council issued a notice of intention to take proceedings for possession. Following a review, the tenant was informed that proceedings would not be taken if she cleared the arrears at the rate of £3 per week. The arrears later

---

52 *R (McDonagh) v Salisbury DC* September 2001 *Legal Action* 23.
53 [2001] EWCA Civ 1510; [2002] QB 1129.
54 HA 1996 s129(5).
55 [2002] EWCA Civ 298; [2003] HLR 47.

increased, and the council claimed possession on the basis of the original notice. The Court of Appeal rejected the argument that a second notice should have been served: this might deter a landlord from taking a humane 'wait and see' approach before issuing proceedings. In these circumstances, the landlord should make it clear that on the review it has upheld the decision to seek possession and is merely deferring proceedings to give the tenant a further chance to save his or her home.[56]

7.48   Where the landlord serves a notice of intention to seek possession and the tenant then commits breaches of a different nature from those specified in the notice, the landlord will usually be required to serve a second notice and hold a further review (if requested). This requirement may, however, be waived if the landlord has acted fairly and the tenant has suffered no prejudice.[57]

Possession proceedings

7.49   The landlord can only bring an introductory tenancy to an end (while it is an introductory tenancy) by obtaining a possession order and then executing that order.[58]

7.50   Before commencing possession proceedings the landlord does *not* need to serve a notice to quit or a notice seeking possession (under the Housing Act 1985) – the notice procedure described at para 7.35 above substitutes for those requirements. The landlord should use the usual procedure for possession in the county court set out in CPR Part 55 (see chapter 23).

Defending the proceedings

7.51   The court shall not make an order for possession unless satisfied that the provisions of HA 1996 s128 apply.[59] To meet that requirement the landlord needs to prove that:

- the tenancy was an introductory tenancy at the time when possession proceedings were begun; and
- a valid HA 1996 section 128 notice (para 7.35) has been served; and

---

56   *R (Forbes) v Lambeth LBC* [2003] EWHC 222 (Admin); [2003] HLR 49.
57   *R (Laporte) v Newham LBC* [2004] EWHC 227 (Admin); [2004] 2 All ER 874.
58   HA 1996 s127(1) and (1A), as substituted by Housing and Regeneration Act 2008 s299 and Sch 11 Pt 1 paras 10 and 11(1) and (2), on 20 May 2009.
59   HA 1996 s127(2).

- the proceedings were begun after the date specified in that notice (para 7.39).)

7.52   The effect of commencing the proceedings is to keep the introductory tenancy alive until the conclusion of the proceedings.[60]

7.53   It should be noted that the landlord does not need to prove that the post-notice review procedure has been properly observed or completed in order to recover possession(If the landlord can prove the three above-mentioned matters on the balance of probabilities, possession *must* be granted.)

7.54   Advisers will want to explore the possibilities of running defences based on either or any of the following: *Defences*

- the tenancy was not 'introductory' at the date the proceedings were issued (see para 7.9);
- the HA 1996 section 128 notice is defective or was not served (see paras 7.35–7.39);
- the proceedings were begun prematurely (see para 7.39);
- the proceedings were begun too late (ie, after the trial period had expired) (see para 7.21–7.28).[61]

7.55   If any of these defences succeeds, the proceedings should be dismissed, usually with costs.

Adjourning the proceedings

7.56   Subject to para 7.57, it is no part of the county court's function, in possession proceedings against an introductory tenant, to inquire into the reasons for the decision to give notice or the merits of the decision to take proceedings. Likewise, the court is not concerned with the review process, its conduct or outcome – it has no statutory jurisdiction to investigate compliance or otherwise with the review process or the general merits of the landlord's claim.[62]

7.57   (In those circumstances, a tenant wishing to challenge the initial decision to give notice, to challenge a decision on review or to take issue with the procedure followed on review must do so by way of judicial review in the Administrative Court (complaint might, of course, also be made to the local government ombudsman). Given the procedural complexity of the review procedure and the haste with which reviews are to be conducted, it is inevitable that mistakes will

60   HA 1996 s130.
61   *Salford CC v Entwhistle* October 2002 *Legal Action* 28; *Salford CC v Garner* [2004] EWCA Civ 364; [2004] HLR 35.
62   *Manchester City Council v Cochrane* [1999] 1 WLR 809; (1999) 31 HLR 810, CA.

be made. To avoid any such challenge becoming 'academic', the tenant will have to hold up the possession proceedings in the county court. That court has jurisdiction to grant a short adjournment if satisfied that there is a real chance of permission to proceed by way of judicial review being granted.[63])

7.58   (Where an application may be made to adjourn possession proceedings in these circumstances, the court will need to assess the basis for the potential judicial review claim. Indeed, the court has a general duty to consider the procedure that has been followed by the landlord of an introductory tenant and has power to draw the tenant's attention to matters that may give rise to a claim for judicial review.[64] To enable the court to take an informed view on this question, the local authority landlord should provide evidence to the county court judge setting out how the review procedure was operated in the individual case. Such evidence should deal with the degree of independence of the review body from the person who took the original decision; the way the hearing was conducted; and the reason for taking the decision to continue the proceedings.[65])

7.59   (If granted an adjournment, the tenant will need to apply quickly for permission to proceed by way of judicial review (CPR Part 54) and make an urgent application for a further stay of any possession proceedings until the full hearing of the judicial review.[66]

7.60   Even if there may be flaws in the decision-making procedure in the particular case, the court on judicial review will not grant a remedy where there is a lack of merit in the tenant's application.[67] Where a tenant fell into rent arrears as a result of failing to provide information to support a housing benefit claim, in the absence of good reasons for the failure, his claim for judicial review was dismissed.) (The court noted that the role of a tenant was not a passive one. If he ignored correspondence and requests for further information, the failure lay at his door.[68])

---

63 *Manchester City Council v Cochrane* [1999] 1 WLR 809; (1999) 31 HLR 810, CA, at 819. See also *R (McLellan) v Bracknell Forest DC* [2001] EWCA Civ 1510; [2002] QB 1129 at para 103 and *Salford CC v Mullen* [2010] EWCA Civ 336.

64 *Merton LBC v Williams* [2002] EWCA Civ 980; [2003] HLR 20.

65 *R (McLellan) v Bracknell Forest DC* [2001] EWCA Civ 1510; [2002] QB 1129.

66 Such a stay will probably be granted as a matter of course if the tenant is given permission to pursue the judicial review claim.

67 *R (Swindells) v Greenwich LBC* [2008] EWCA Civ 244; June 2008 *Legal Action* 31, upholding the dismissal of a claim for judicial review (see [2007] EWHC 2131 (Admin)).

68 *R (Chowdhury) v Newham LBC* [2003] EWHC 2837 (Admin). See also *Merton LBC v Williams* [2002] EWCA Civ 980; [2003] HLR 20.

Bad Outcome

7.61 (If the application for judicial review fails, the possession proceedings are generally restored and possession granted. If the application *Good* for judicial review succeeds, the relevant decision to take the proceed-*Outcome* ings should be quashed and the authority directed to reconsider. If it then decides to withdraw the proceedings the tenant will become 'secure' (as more than 12 months will inevitably have passed since the grant of the tenancy). If it decides, this time lawfully, to proceed to recover possession, it may apply for the proceedings in the county court to be restored. Any such reconsideration can take account of developments since the initial decision to evict.[69])

7.62 (This procedure for adjournment and judicial review requires two courts to become involved in adjudicating on the question of whether the landlord should have possession against a single introductory tenant.) The Court of Appeal has called in vain for Parliament to legislate so as to enable the county court to deal with the whole claim, including any public law defence.[70] At the time of writing, the Supreme Court was scheduled to consider at a hearing in late 2010 whether, where an introductory tenant asserts that the decision to recover possession is improper or irrational, such matters may be raised in the county court by way of a defence – see further chapter 25 – enabling all relevant matters to be adjudicated by the county court within the possession proceedings. Pending the Supreme Court judgment, judges in the county court[71] and in the High Court[72] have held that it is open to the introductory tenant to run a public law defence to a possession claim but that view was disapproved in *Salford CC v Mullen*.[73]

The possession order

7.63 (If the court makes a possession order against an introductory tenant it cannot postpone the date for giving of possession for more than 14 days unless:

- possession by that date would cause exceptional hardship, in which case the postponement can be for up to six weeks;[74] or
- the landlord consents to a longer period.

Except by consent, there is no scope for the making of other forms of possession orders.)

69 *R (McDonagh) v Salisbury DC* September 2001 *Legal Action* 23.
70 *Manchester City Council v Cochrane* [1999] 1 WLR 809; (1999) 31 HLR 810, CA.
71 See, eg, *Bristol CC v McCalla* June 2009 *Legal Action* 32, Bristol County Court.
72 See, eg, *R (Constantiou) v Sandwell MBC* March 2008 *Legal Action* 18, Mitting J.
73 [2010] EWCA Civ 336.
74 HA 1980 s89.

7.64   The court has no discretion to stay or suspend execution of the possession order beyond the periods mentioned above.[75] The introductory tenancy will, however, only come to an end with the eviction of the tenant on execution of the possession order.

7.65   Notwithstanding that the whole point of the introductory tenancy regime is to enable the local authority landlord to achieve the swift eviction of introductory tenants where that proves necessary, many local authorities – having obtained possession orders – do not immediately proceed to execute them. Before 20 May 2009,[76] a possession order against an introductory tenant took effect to end his or her tenancy on the date stated in the order.[77] The former introductory tenant remained in possession as a 'tolerated trespasser' unless and until evicted pursuant to the order. Any such tolerated trespassers still in occupation became replacement tenants on 20 May 2009 (see chapter 10). It remains to be seen whether local authorities will continue the past practice of obtaining orders against introductory tenants and then not executing those orders.

Human Rights Act 1998

7.66   The Court of Appeal has held that the introductory tenant regime and its operation are not incompatible with articles 6, 8 or 14 of the European Convention on Human Rights.[78] The remaining scope for an introductory tenant to place any reliance on the Human Rights Act 1998 is explored in chapter 26.

> **SPECIAL NOTE:** The Supreme Court is scheduled to hear appeals at the end of November 2010 which raise the questions of whether (1) the introductory tenancy regime is compatible with articles 6 and 8 of the ECHR and (2) whether a public law defence to a possession claim against an introductory tenant can be pursued in the county court proceedings. Readers will need to annotate this chapter with reference to the outcome in those appeals. The introductory tenancy appeals are *Birmingham CC v Frisby* and *Leeds CC v Hall*.

75   HA 1980 s89 and *Plymouth CC v Hill* January 2010 *Legal Action* 31.
76   When HA 1996 s127 was amended by Housing and Regeneration Act 2008 s299 and Sch 11.
77   See *Lambeth LBC v Azu* June 2002 *Legal Action* 25.
78   *R (Mclellan) v Bracknell Forest BC* [2001] EWCA Civ 1510; [2002] QB 1129; (2001) 33 HLR 989 and *Salford MBC v Mullen* [2010] EWCA Civ 336.

Demoted tenancies

Background

8.1   The Anti-Social Behaviour Act 2003 introduced a new weapon in the armoury of social landlords to deal with serious nuisance behaviour. Section 14 of the 2003 Act gave the power to some social landlords to ask courts to 'demote' secure or assured tenancies to 12-month probationary tenancies.[1] If during that year the social landlord has cause for complaint about the tenant's behaviour, the tenancy can be terminated by court order following a notice of proceedings, but without the need to prove a ground for possession.

8.2   A local authority, a registered social landlord (RSL) or a private registered provider of social housing (PRP) can apply to a county court for a demotion order, under:

- Housing Act (HA) 1985 s82A (where the tenancy is a secure tenancy); or
- HA 1988 s6A (where the tenancy is an assured tenancy).[2]

8.3   Demotion involves the court making an order that:

- ends an existing secure or assured tenancy; and
- replaces it with a new tenancy which gives the tenant reduced security of tenure for a fixed period of time; and
- carries forward any rent arrears or credits from the old rent account on to the new rent account.[3]

8.4   This chapter deals with the rules on demotion of both secure and assured tenancies. While the grounds for demotion are identical in respect of both types of tenancy, there are major differences in the nature of the demoted tenancy which is created in each case.

'Relevant landlord'

8.5   Demotion can only be sought by a relevant landlord. Only a local housing authority, a RSL or a PRP is a 'relevant landlord' for these

---

1   The provisions were brought into effect in England from 30 June 2004 and in Wales from 30 September 2004. See generally Jon Holbrook and Dean Underwood, 'Defending demoted tenancy claims' September 2004 *Legal Action* 27 and October 2004 *Legal Action* 23; and Christopher Baker, 'Demoting tenancies: innovation or exasperation?' Parts 1 and 2 *Journal of Housing Law*, September 2004 and November 2004.

2   Both sections were inserted in the respective Acts by Anti-Social Behaviour Act 2003 s14(2).

3   HA 1985 s82A(3); HA 1988 s6A(3).

purposes, that is, one which can apply to demote a secure or assured tenancy.[4] No private sector landlord can apply for a demotion order and not all of the various types of landlord that can grant a secure tenancy (see para 1.6) can apply for demotion.[5]

Grounds for a demotion order

8.6 The court must not make a demotion order unless it is satisfied that (1) the tenant or a person residing in or visiting the tenant's home has engaged in or threatened to engage in conduct which falls within *either* of the limbs set out below *and* (2) it is reasonable to make the order.[6] The same two-stage test applies in all cases.

The first limb: nuisance and annoyance

8.7 This limb relates to conduct. The landlord must show that the tenant, co-resident or visitor has engaged or threatened to engage in 'housing-related anti-social conduct'.[7]

8.8 That term is defined[8] as having the same meaning as the identical term used in HA 1996 s153A, ie, conduct

(a) which is capable of causing nuisance or annoyance to any person;
and
(b) which directly or indirectly relates to or affects the housing management functions of a relevant landlord.

8.9 It is immaterial where the conduct in question occurs.[9] Conduct which causes harassment to 'any person' – not only a neighbour – is included, but there must be a connection between the conduct and

4 HA 1985 s82A(1); HA 1988 s6A(1) (in each case amended by Housing and Regeneration Act 2008 (Consequential Provisions) Order 2010 SI No 866 art 5 and Sch 2).

5 Although housing action trusts are a type of landlord capable of applying for demotion of a secure tenancy under HA 1985 s82A(1), all the housing action trusts have now been wound up.

6 HA 1985 s82A(4) in respect of secure tenancies; HA 1988 s6A(4) in respect of assured tenancies.

7 HA 1985 s82A(4)(a) in respect of secure tenancies; HA 1988 s6A(4)(a) in respect of assured tenancies.

8 HA 1985 s82A(7A) in respect of secure tenancies; HA 1988 s6A(7A) in respect of assured tenancies, inserted by Police and Justice Act 2006 s52 and Sch 14 para 12(1) and (3).

9 HA 1996 s153A(5), inserted by Anti-Social Behaviour Act 2003 s13(3).

the landlord's 'housing management functions'. Housing management functions are defined broadly to include:

(a) functions conferred by or under any enactment; and
(b) the powers and duties of the landlord as the holder of an estate or interest in housing accommodation.[10]

8.10   Clearly, any behaviour which adversely affects tenants of the landlord or their household members or visitors, or the landlord's staff, relates to housing management functions. Despite the reference to conduct which affects functions conferred by any enactment, it is suggested that the scope of this provision does not extend to the non-housing functions of a local authority, for example, in its capacity as highways authority. However, the phrase has been given the widest possible interpretation by the courts. In *Swindon BC v Redpath*,[11] Rix LJ said that the tenant's conduct had to be viewed as a whole:

> Viewed as a whole ... the council's housing management functions easily embrace its sense of responsibility to its continuing tenants and also to owner-occupiers [in the same street] for the conduct of its former tenant, ... who has pursued his vendetta against his former neighbours irrespective of the loss of his tenancy. (para 55)

Lord Neuberger said that it was clear that the definition was intended 'to have a broad sweep' (para 62). He said that 'housing related' conduct

> can clearly be engaged in by someone who is not a tenant or an occupier of property owned by the relevant landlord; equally, it can be engaged in by someone who neither resides nor works within the area in which the conduct occurs. (para 64)

The second limb: use of premises for unlawful purposes

8.11   Under this limb the landlord must establish conduct by the tenant, co-resident or visitor to which to HA 1996 s153B (use of premises for unlawful purposes) applies.[12] That is conduct which consists of or involves using or threatening to use housing accommodation owned or managed by a relevant landlord (see para 8.5) for an unlawful purpose.[13]

---

10   HA 1996 s153E(11).
11   [2009] EWCA Civ 943; [2010] 1 All ER 1003; [2010] HLR 13.
12   HA 1985 s82A(4)(a) in respect of secure tenancies; HA 1988 s6A(4)(a) in respect of assured tenancies.
13   HA 1996 s153B, inserted by Anti-Social Behaviour Act 2003 s13(3).

8.12   It is not necessary to prove a conviction for the unlawful use of the accommodation (in contrast with the second limb of the comparable ground for possession for secure and assured tenancies – see paras 3.101 and 12.135).

Reasonableness

8.13   The court cannot grant a demotion order unless it is satisfied that it is reasonable to do so.[14] The court has a broad exercise of judgment to undertake in assessing reasonableness, and some guidance may be derived from case-law under the 'nuisance or annoyance' ground for possession in relation to secure and assured tenancies (see paras 3.81–3.100 and 13.10–13.14). In *Washington Housing Company Ltd v Morson*,[15] the landlord sought a demotion order based on evidence of the misconduct of the tenant's children. Refusing permission to appeal against a finding that it was reasonable to make the order, the appeal court said that the order was 'a reasonable way of balancing the parents' right and entitlement to a secure home with the public interest in preventing this sort of behaviour in future'.[16]

Notice of intention to apply for a demotion order

8.14   Before applying for a demotion order, the landlord must serve a notice of its intention to do so. The procedure differs according to whether the tenancy is a secure tenancy or an assured tenancy.

Demotion claims against secure tenants

8.15   The landlord must first serve a notice in the prescribed form.[17] Where the landlord also intends to seek possession, in the alternative to a demotion order, there is no need for two separate notices to be served: the notice of seeking possession and the notice seeking

---

14 HA 1985 s82A(4)(b) in respect of secure tenancies; HA 1988 s6A(4)(b) in respect of assured tenancies.

15 *Washington Housing Company Ltd v Morson* [2005] EWHC 3407 (Ch).

16 *Washington Housing Company Ltd v Morson* [2005] EWHC 3407 (Ch) at [67].

17 HA 1985 s83(2), as amended by Anti-Social Behaviour Act 2003 s14(3). See also Secure Tenancies (Notices) (Amendment) (England) Regulations 2004 SI No 1627 and Secure Tenancies (Notices) (Amendment) (Wales) Regulations 2005 SI No 1226.

demotion can be given in a single notice and the prescribed form has been adapted to accommodate that possibility.[18]

8.16   The notice of intended demotion must contain particulars of the conduct which has caused the landlord to seek to demote the tenancy. It must also specify a date after which proceedings may be begun.[19] That date must not be earlier than the date on which a notice to quit would expire.[20] Since most secure tenants are weekly periodic tenants, a notice to quit would need to give at least 28 days following the date of service and expire on the first or last day of a tenancy period.[21] There is no provision allowing proceedings to be begun immediately after service of the notice, as there is with regard to possession claims on nuisance grounds, but there is provision for the court to dispense with notice altogether.[22]

8.17   The notice has a 'life span' of 12 months beginning with the date specified in it.[23] During that calendar year, proceedings may be issued based on the notice. After that period, a fresh notice must be issued, unless the court agrees to dispense with the notice requirement if it considers it 'just and equitable' to do so.

Demotion claims against assured tenants

8.18   In the case of an assured tenant, the landlord must serve a notice of intention to apply for demotion before the court can entertain proceedings,[24] but there is no prescribed form of notice. However, the notice must:

- give particulars of the conduct complained of;
- state that proceedings will not begin before the date specified in the notice; and
- state that proceedings will not begin later than 12 months after the date of service.[25]

---

18 See Secure Tenancies (Notices) (Amendment) (England) Regulations 2004 SI No 1627 and Secure Tenancies (Notices) (Amendment) (Wales) Regulations 2005 SI No 1226.
19 HA 1985 s83(4A)(a).
20 HA 1985 s83(5).
21 Protection from Eviction Act 1977 s5.
22 HA 1985 s83(1)(b).
23 HA 1985 s83(4A)(b).
24 HA 1988 s6A(5).
25 HA 1988 s6A(6).

8.19 The notice period is shorter than that for secure tenancies: the date specified in the notice must be at least two weeks from the date of service of the notice and the specified date need not be the first or last day of a tenancy period.[26] The 'life span' of the notice dates from the date of service, not from the date specified.

8.20 As with applications in relation to secure tenancies, the court may dispense with the notice requirements in an assured tenancy case if it considers it just and equitable to do so.[27]

Applying for a demotion order

8.21 A landlord can seek a demotion order in possession proceedings as an alternative to a possession order, in which case the landlord should use the claim form N5 (for possession). The claim will be governed by CPR Part 55 and the procedure described in chapter 23.

8.22 Alternatively, a landlord may make a free-standing application for a demotion order without seeking possession. In this situation the landlord should use form N6 (claim form for demotion of a tenancy) and specific particulars of claim (form N122). The conduct of these stand-alone claims is governed by CPR 65 Part III and the associated Practice Direction 65 Part III. The procedure is described in paras 8.23–8.24.

8.23 Claims for demotion orders must be made in the county court for the district in which the property to which the claim relates is situated.[28] However, in the light of CPR 3.10, issue in the wrong court is likely to be seen as an error of procedure which does not invalidate the step taken. In most cases, judges would correct the error by transferring the claim to the appropriate court.[29]

8.24 The claim form seeking demotion and the form of defence sent with it must be in the forms set out in the relevant Practice Direction.[30] Particulars of claim in form N122 must be filed and served with the claim form.[31] The particulars of claim must:

- state whether the demotion claim is made under HA 1985 s82A(2) or HA 1988 s6A(2);

26 HA 1988 s6A(7).
27 HA 1988 s6A(5)(b).
28 CPR 65.12 and PD 65 para 6.1.
29 See, in another context, *Gwynedd County Council v Grunshaw* [2000] 1 WLR 494; [1999] 4 All ER 304, CA.
30 PD 65 para 6.2 and PD 4 Table 1. The forms are N6 and N11D.
31 CPR 65.15.

- state whether the claimant is a local housing authority, RSL or PRP;
- identify the property to which the claim relates;
- provide details about the tenancy, including the parties, the period of the tenancy, the rent, the dates on which the rent is payable and any statement of express terms of the tenancy served on the tenant; and
- state details of the conduct alleged.[32]

8.25   Courts should fix hearing dates when they issue the claim forms. The hearing date should be not less than 28 days from the date of issue of the claim form. The standard period between the issue of the claim form and the hearing should be not more than eight weeks. Defendants must be served with claim forms and particulars of claim not less than 21 days before the hearing date.[33] Courts may extend or shorten these times.[34] Particular consideration should be given to abridging time between service and the hearing if:

- the defendant has assaulted or threatened to assault the claimant, a member of the claimant's staff or another resident in the locality;
- there are reasonable grounds for fearing such an assault; or
- the defendant has caused serious damage or threatened to cause serious damage to the property or to the home or property of another resident in the locality.[35]

8.26   Defendants should file defences within 14 days after service of the particulars of claim, but they may still take part in any hearing even if they do not do so. However, courts may take such a failure to do so into account when deciding what order to make about costs.[36] It is not possible for landlords to enter judgment in default if a tenant fails to file a defence.[37]

8.27   At the hearing, the court may decide the demotion claim, or give case management directions. Where the demotion claim is genuinely disputed on grounds which appear to be substantial, case management directions should be given. They should include the

---

32 PD 65 para 7.1. See too PD 65 para 9.1, which provides that each party should wherever possible include all the evidence he or she wishes to present in his or her statement of case, verified by a statement of truth.

33 CPR 65.16.

34 CPR 3.1(2)(a).

35 PD 65 para 8.2.

36 CPR 65.17(1).

37 CPR 62.17(2); cf CPR Part 12.

allocation of the demotion claim to a track or directions to enable it to be allocated.[38]

8.28　Any fact that needs to be proved by the evidence of witnesses may be proved by evidence in writing unless the demotion claim has been allocated to the fast or multi-track or the court directs otherwise.[39] The claimant's evidence should include details of the conduct alleged.[40] All witness statements should be filed and served at least two days before the hearing.

8.29　District judges have jurisdiction to try demotion claims.[41]

Defending the proceedings

8.30　The court shall not make an order for demotion unless satisfied that the provisions of HA 1985 s82A(4) (in the case of secure tenancies) or HA 1988 s6A(4) (in the case of assured tenancies) are satisfied. Accordingly, the landlord needs to prove that:

- the proper notice of intention to bring proceedings has been served (or the court agrees to dispense with such a notice);
- the proceedings were begun after the specified date and within the appropriate 12-month period;
- the tenant or a person residing in or visiting the dwelling has engaged or has threatened to engage in conduct which falls within one of the statutory limbs – see paras 8.7–8.12 above; and
- it is reasonable for a demotion order to be made.

8.31　Advisers should initially check that the form of the notice complies with the statutory requirements, that it was properly served and that the proceedings were not begun prematurely. Any irregularity in any of these respects may provide sufficient defence to the claim.

Substantive defences

8.32　Assuming that none of the more technical defences mentioned above is available, it may be open to the tenant to defend the claim on the basis that neither limb of the statutory ground has been made out on the evidence and on the balance of probabilities. Advisers may find

38　CPR 65.18(1).
39　CPR 65.18(3). See too CPR 32.2.
40　PD 65 para 6. See too *Washington Housing Company Ltd v Morson* [2005] EWHC 3407, ChD.
41　PD 2B para 11.1(b).

it helpful, in preparing a defence, to refer to the non-statutory guidance directed to landlords in *Demotion Orders: Anti-social behaviour fact-sheet 3*.[42]

8.33   The first line of defence is to test the evidence concerning the alleged misconduct. As in possession proceedings based on anti-social behaviour, the adviser will need to take detailed instructions from the tenant and any other witnesses on every allegation particularised in the landlord's statement of case, and prepare the defence and witness statements accordingly. Where the tenant accepts general responsibility for the behaviour complained of, he or she should make the necessary admissions, explain any mitigating factors and emphasise his or her willingness to change his or her behaviour. Where the tenant has not personally been responsible for the nuisance but the conduct is that of a household member or visitor, the tenant should clearly set out the steps that he or she has taken to address the problem, including co-operating with any statutory or other agencies involved.

8.34   The second line of defence, assuming that the landlord has proved (or the tenant admits) that one of the limbs has been made out, is to assert that it is not reasonable to order demotion. It is for the landlord to satisfy the court that it would be reasonable to grant a demotion order. In applying the 'reasonableness' test, the court is required to have regard to all relevant factors. The defence and the witness statements should deal in detail with the tenant's own personal circumstances, including any health problems or other life experiences which have contributed to the present situation. In deciding whether to make an order, the court will be influenced by the tenor of Court of Appeal decisions in relation to the 'nuisance' ground for possession and anti-social behaviour injunctions, and in particular the need to consider the interests of those affected by the behaviour. Even so, the objective will be to convince the court that demotion would be unnecessary and disproportionate, and that alternative measures – such as an undertaking to the court, or a willingness to engage in an acceptable behaviour contract – are sufficient to deal with the situation.

8.35   Assuming that the tenant is financially eligible, he or she may be able to obtain a public funding (legal aid) certificate for legal representation in defending the proceedings. See generally chapter 28.

8.36   Where the application for demotion is made in possession proceedings, it will be one of the options which the court is considering at the conclusion of the evidence. In some cases, the range of choices

42 Home Office and ODPM, October 2004.

will effectively be between a demotion order and a postponed possession order. A demotion order may be presented by the landlord
as a less drastic alternative to a postponed possession order. On the
other hand, it must be remembered that, under a postponed possession order, the court retains its discretion up to the date of eviction,
whereas it has no discretion to refuse a possession order sought
against a demoted tenant (see below). In *Manchester CC v Pinnock,*
the Court of Appeal said:

> A demotion order is a drastic measure: it deprives the tenant of his
> security of tenure for the period of the demotion order and, as will
> be seen, removes from the county court the jurisdiction to examine
> whether the making of an order evicting the tenant, if it comes to
> that, is reasonable or proportionate. It is a far more drastic step than
> the making of a suspended possession order, following which the
> county court retains supervision of the landlord's claim, and may vary
> the conditions of the order or in due course discharge or rescind the
> order: section 85 of the 1985 Act.[43]

Another judge has said of demotion orders:[44]

> Although that is obviously a Draconian sanction, it is not as Draconian
> as an immediate order for possession ...

The effect of a demotion order

8.37   A demotion order – whether made in respect of a secure or assured
tenancy – has the following effects:

- the former secure or assured tenancy is terminated with effect
  from the date specified in the order;
- if the tenant remains in occupation of the dwelling after that date,
  a demoted tenancy is created with effect from that date;
- it is a term of the demoted tenancy that any rent in arrears or rent
  paid in advance at the termination of the secure or assured tenancy
  becomes payable or is credited under the demoted tenancy;[45]
- the parties to, and period of, the tenancy, the amount of the rent
  and the dates on which rent is payable are the same as under the
  former tenancy.[46]

---

43 [2009] EWCA Civ 852; [2010] HLR 7 at [27].
44 *Washington Housing Company Ltd v Morson* [2005] EWHC 3407 (Ch) at [67].
45 HA 1985 s82A(3); HA 1988 s6A(3).
46 HA 1985 s82A(5); HA 1988 s6A(8).

8.38   However, the nature of the demoted tenancy is different depending on whether the former tenancy was secure or assured. When a secure tenancy is demoted and the landlord is a local authority,[47] it becomes a *demoted tenancy* governed by HA 1996 ss143A–143P.[48] When an assured tenancy, or a secure tenancy with a non-local authority social landlord, is demoted, it becomes a *demoted assured shorthold tenancy* governed by HA 1988 s20B.

Demoted tenancies (former secure tenancies)

8.39   The framework for demoted tenancies inserted at HA 1996 ss143A–143P follows much the same model as the introductory tenancy provisions in Part V of the same Act. The two statutory schemes are very similar, as the demoted tenancy scheme has been closely modelled on the introductory tenancy regime. The statutory framework also deals with matters such as succession, assignment, the right to carry out repairs and the provision of information in respect of demoted tenancies.

8.40   The demoted tenancy will start on the date specified in the demotion order. It will only remain a demoted tenancy if the landlord's interest remains held by a local housing authority *and* the tenant continues to occupy the premises as his or her only or principal home.[49] If, after one year from that date, the landlord has not given notice of proceedings for possession, the tenancy will cease to be a demoted tenancy and will become secure again.[50]

8.41   However, the landlord may give notice of possession proceedings at any time within the one-year period, for any reason. There is no prescribed form, but the notice of proceedings must:

- state that the court will be asked to make an order for possession;
- set out the landlord's reasons for seeking the order;
- specify the date after which possession proceedings may begin; and
- inform the tenant of his or her right to request a review of the landlord's decision and the time within which the request must be made (ie, 14 days from the date of service).[51]

---

47   HA 1996 s143A(2).
48   Inserted by Anti-Social Behaviour Act 2003 Sch 1.
49   HA 1996 s143A.
50   HA 1996 s143B.
51   HA 1996 s143E(2).

8.42 Although the basis for the demotion order in the first place lay in the anti-social behaviour of the tenant, the landlord's reasons for seeking possession of the demoted tenancy need not be related to such behaviour. They can relate to any breach of the tenancy conditions, such as rent arrears, or indeed to any other factor, such as under-occupation.

8.43 The date specified in the notice must be not earlier than the date on which the tenancy could be brought to an end by a notice to quit.[52] In the usual case of a weekly tenancy, the earliest date will be the first or last day of a tenancy period which follows a period of 28 days from the date of the notice. The notice must also advise the tenant to take the notice immediately to a citizen's advice bureau, housing aid centre, law centre or solicitor if he or she needs help or advice.[53]

8.44 Where a landlord serves a notice of proceedings for possession on a demoted tenant, the tenancy will continue as a demoted tenancy even if the 12-month anniversary of the start date goes by, until any of the following events occur:

- the notice of proceedings is withdrawn by the landlord;
- the proceedings are determined in favour of the tenant;
- a period of six months has gone by since the notice was served and no proceedings for possession have been brought;[54] or
- the proceedings are determined in favour of the landlord (when the tenancy will come to an end on the date on which the possession order is executed[55]).

8.45 The effective extension of the demotion period by six months is achieved solely by the service of a valid notice of intended proceedings and is not dependent (as in the case of introductory tenancies) on the service of a special notice of extension: see para 7.24.

8.46 The tenant has 14 days beginning with the date of service of the notice to request the landlord to review its decision[56] (the fourteenth day effectively being two calendar weeks less one day). If a tenant so requests, the landlord must carry out a review of the decision to seek an order for possession and notify the tenant of the outcome along with its reasons for the decision on review. The review must take place, and the decision must be notified, before the date specified in

---

52 HA 1996 s143E(3).
53 HA 1996 s143E(5).
54 HA 1996 s143B(4).
55 HA 1996 s143D(1A), inserted by Housing and Regeneration Act 2008 s299 and Sch 11 Pt 1 paras 10 and 13(1) and (3).
56 HA 1996 s143F(1).

the notice as the date after which proceedings may be begun.[57] The decision on review must be made by a person of appropriate seniority who was not involved in the original decision, and the review must be conducted in accordance with the Demoted Tenancies (Review of Decisions) (England) Regulations 2004[58] or the Demoted Tenancies (Review of Decisions) (Wales) Regulations 2005.[59] In particular, the tenant may request an oral hearing. This procedure does not provide an independent or impartial consideration of the decision to seek possession but the Court of Appeal has held that it does not infringe the Human Rights Act 1998 Sch 1 articles 6 or 8 (see chapter 26).[60]

8.47   If the tenant does not request a review within the 14-day period, or if the landlord on review decides to confirm its decision to seek possession, the landlord may thereafter start possession proceedings. The court must make an order for possession unless it thinks that the procedure relating to either the notice of proceedings or the review 'has not been followed'.[61] It has no power to investigate the landlord's reasons for bringing the proceedings. But, in contrast to the position in respect of introductory tenancies, where the court's role is restricted to ensuring that the correct notice has been served, here it appears that the court must be satisfied that all aspects of the procedure have been correctly observed, including the conduct of the review process. Beyond that, the court cannot go:

> Section 143D of the 1996 Act restricts the county court to considering whether the procedure under sections 143E and 143F has been followed. If the court concludes the procedure has not been followed, it will not make an order for possession. If it has been followed, it must make the order. I emphasise the word procedure. The court's review is limited to matters of procedure, and the county court cannot review the substance or rationality of the landlord's decision, or whether or not it is consistent with the tenant's or other occupiers' Convention rights.[62]

8.48   A demoted tenant may therefore have a defence to the claim for possession if:

---

57   HA 1996 s143F(6).

58   SI No 1679.

59   SI No 1228.

60   *R (Gilboy) v Liverpool City Council* [2008] EWCA Civ 751; [2009] QB 699; [2009] 3 WLR 300; [2009] HLR 11.

61   HA 1996 s143D(2).

62   *Manchester City Council v Pinnock* [2009] EWCA Civ 852, [2010] HLR 7 at [50]. At the time of writing, the judgment on an appeal against this decision was pending from the Supreme Court.

- the notice of proceedings did not contain the requisite information;
- the notice was not served on the tenant;
- the period of the notice was insufficient;
- proceedings were started before the specified date;
- the landlord has not held a review despite the fact that the tenant requested one within the 14-day period allowed;
- the review has not been conducted by a person of appropriate seniority; or
- there has been some other material breach of the review regulations.[63]

8.49   Where the tenant wishes to challenge the fairness or rationality of the decision to terminate the demoted tenancy, this should generally be done by proceedings for judicial review. In this event, the tenant should seek advice and legal representation as a matter of urgency and should make an application for public funding (legal aid) to cover the cost of the judicial review proceedings. It will be necessary to ask the county court to adjourn the possession claim to await the outcome of an application to the Administrative Court for permission to apply for judicial review. The Court of Appeal has held that the 'public law defence' (see chapter 25) is not available to a demoted tenant[64] but the Supreme Court has granted permission to appeal from that decision.

8.50   Where, however, the court makes an order for possession, it cannot postpone the date for giving of possession for more than 14 days unless:

- possession by that date would cause exceptional hardship, in which case the postponement can be for up to six weeks;[65] or
- the landlord consents to a longer period.

8.51   The court has no power to suspend a possession order or the execution of it beyond those periods unless the landlord consents. The demoted tenancy ends on the date on which the order is executed by the bailiffs.

---

63   In *Brighton & Hove CC v Knight* June 2009 *Legal Action* 33, Brighton County Court, the notice of outcome of a review was given one day outside the time limit prescribed by HA 1996 s143F and the court dismissed the possession claim against the demoted tenant.

64   *Manchester City Council v Pinnock* [2009] EWCA Civ 852; [2010] HLR 7.

65   HA 1980 s89(1).

Demoted assured shorthold tenancies

8.52   Former *secure* tenants of RSLs or PRPs (demoted under HA 1985 s82A) and former *assured* tenants of such landlords (demoted under HA 1988 s6A) will have demoted assured shorthold tenancies governed by HA 1988 s20B. This form of tenancy is in most respects similar to a standard assured shorthold tenancy: see chapter 11.

8.53   The demoted assured shorthold tenancy will start on the date specified in the demotion order. If within one year from that date the landlord has not given notice of proceedings for possession, the tenancy will cease to be an assured shorthold tenancy.[66] The tenancy will then become *assured*, even where the original tenancy was a secure tenancy.

8.54   Where notice of proceedings has been given within the one-year demotion period, the tenancy continues to be a demoted assured shorthold tenancy even after the 12-month anniversary of the start date has gone by, and will remain such until one of the following events occurs:

- the landlord withdraws the notice of proceedings;
- the proceedings are determined in favour of the tenant (for example, where the possession claim is dismissed because the landlord has served an invalid notice);
- a period of six months from the date of the notice has gone by and no proceedings for possession have been brought;[67] or
- the proceedings result in a possession order in favour of the landlord (as they usually will).

8.55   Where the landlord wishes to bring a demoted assured shorthold tenancy to an end, it may serve a notice requiring possession. The procedure governing such notices is much less regulated than that governing notices served on demoted tenants of local authorities. The notice given to a demoted assured shorthold tenant will be a two months' notice under HA 1988 s21(4), which must expire on the last day of a period of the tenancy: see para 11.21. Moreover, the landlord is not obliged to offer its demoted assured shorthold tenants a right to a review of its decision to seek possession. In practice, it is to be expected that landlords will in fact offer a review in order to provide at least a sufficiently fair procedure to avoid a possible public law defence (see chapter 25) or a human rights defence (see chapter 26).

66   HA 1988 s20B(2).
67   HA 1988 s20B(4).

8.56   Where the landlord brings proceedings for possession of a demoted assured shorthold tenancy, the court's role is restricted to examining the validity of the section 21 notice and, if satisfied on that matter, it must make an order for possession. Where the court makes an order for possession, it cannot postpone the date for giving possession for more than 14 days unless:

- possession by that date would cause exceptional hardship, in which case the postponement can be for up to six weeks;[68] or
- the landlord consents to a longer period.

8.57   If the demoted assured shorthold tenant believes that the landlord has made its decision to bring possession proceedings without sufficient evidence, or has failed to take account of relevant matters, or has failed to give the tenant the chance to respond to allegations against him or her, or has otherwise acted unfairly, there may be a challenge to the landlord's decision by way of a claim for judicial review in the Administrative Court. Any possession claim would need to be adjourned while the application for judicial review was being determined (see para 8.49).

8.58   The more practical alternative would be for the demoted assured shorthold tenant to raise these matters in the county court by way of a public law defence to the landlord's claim (see chapter 25). Although the Court of Appeal has held that such a defence is not available in this class of case,[69] the judgment on an appeal against that decision was pending at the time of writing.

SPECIAL NOTE: The Supreme Court heard an appeal in early July 2010 which raised the questions of whether (1) the demoted tenancy regime is compatible with articles 6 and 8 of the ECHR and (2) whether a public law defence to a possession claim against a demoted tenant can be pursued in the county court proceedings. Readers will need to annotate this chapter with reference to the outcome in that appeal when judgments have been delivered. The appeal was *Manchester CC v Pinnock*.

---

68 HA 1980 s89.
69 *Manchester City Council v Pinnock* [2009] EWCA Civ 852; [2010] HLR 7.

CHAPTER 9

Family intervention tenancies

Introduction

9.1 Since 1 January 2009 it has been possible for social landlords in England to grant a new form of tenancy – the family intervention tenancy. This is a non-secure[1] non-assured,[2] usually periodic, social housing tenancy. A family intervention tenancy gives no long term security of tenure and can be terminated by simple notice to quit given by the social landlord (or by the tenant). Although the description contains the word 'family', the tenancies can be granted to an individual or individuals. There need not be a family (in the sense of dependent children) at all.

9.2 The new form of tenancy has been created by legislation made in a somewhat indirect fashion. Both the Housing Act (HA) 1985 (which deals with secure tenancies) and the Housing Act 1988 (which deals with assured tenancies) contain a list – in Schedule 1 – of those tenancies which are not, respectively, 'secure' or 'assured' despite fulfilling all the usual requirements for such tenancies. In each case Schedule 1 was amended on 1 January 2009 by the Housing and Regeneration Act (H&RA) 2008 s297 to add family intervention tenancies as a further type of tenancy which is not 'secure' or 'assured'.[3] The new paragraph inserted in each schedule fleshes out the detailed requirements for family intervention tenancies – discussed in turn below. But the provisions regulating termination of a family intervention tenancy are to be found in the body of the Housing and Regeneration Act 2008 itself.[4] Although those provisions expressly apply only to family intervention tenancies granted by local housing authorities, the expectation is that they will also be voluntarily applied by other social landlords when they are terminating family intervention tenancies. This method of making legislative provision for a new form of tenancy by an indirect route is striking.

9.3 Family intervention tenancies are designed to be granted to tenants who are to be provided with 'behaviour support services' after entering into agreements to receive such support.[5] Those services are intended to help people who have previously been evicted from their homes (or who face the prospect of eviction) as a result of their

---

1 For secure tenancies see chapters 1–4.
2 For assured tenancies see chapters 11 and 12.
3 In HA 1985, provision is made by Sch 1 para 4ZA. In HA 1988, it is Sch 1 para 12ZA.
4 H&RA 2008 s298.
5 See Jill Morgan, 'Family intervention tenancies: the de(marginalisation) of social tenants' [2010] 32 *Journal of Social Welfare Law* 37.

anti-social behaviour. Such services are usually provided by, or in association with, local family intervention projects.[6] As the UK government has made clear,

> Family Intervention Tenancies are usually offered to residents in specialist or purpose built accommodation, and are likely to be located away from the tenant's previous home. Distance between old and new homes is necessary to establish a new start and remove links with previous surrounding factors that may have encouraged the family's anti-social behaviour, such as friends, peer groups and local connections.[7]

9.4 The policy intention is that the behaviour support services will help address the root causes of such past anti-social behaviour. At the end of the period of support, it is hoped that the tenant will no longer be inclined towards anti-social behaviour and will be ready to move on to other social housing[8] or to an alternative long-term home. The family intervention tenancy can then be ended by surrender. If the period of support is disrupted by the tenant or is unproductive, the tenancy can be ended for those – or any other – reasons by the landlord.

9.5 The UK government has issued non-statutory guidance to social landlords covering the grant and termination of family intervention tenancies.[9] The guidance contains a useful set of appendices reproducing the legislation, statutory instruments and a glossary. If the landlord under a family intervention tenancy is a non-local authority

---

6 An early evaluation of the effectiveness of family intervention projects (FIPs) reported that 60% of families surveyed were subject to one or more housing enforcement actions when they started working with a FIP but that this had reduced to 18% for families leaving the schemes. The results of research into intensive family support projects, which seek to provide families at risk of eviction because of anti-social behaviour with intensive support to address their often multiple and complex needs, suggest that 70% of families using the schemes had managed to sustain or achieve positive change with no further complaints about their behaviour: *CLG Housing Research Summary 240* Communities and Local Government (CLG), January 2008. The very latest evaluation of outcomes is given in *ASB family intervention projects: monitoring & evaluation* National Centre for Social Research, March 2010.

7 *Tackling anti-social behaviour: tools and powers – toolkit for social landlords* CLG, April 2010, para 4.134.

8 If an occupier is moving from a family intervention tenancy to a new home in social housing, the usual rules for allocation of social housing are disapplied: Allocation of Housing (England) (Amendment) (Family Intervention Tenancies) Regulations 2008 SI No 3015. The policy intention is that unfettered access to offers of social housing – without having to go through the usual housing allocation scheme procedure – will ensure that social housing can be available at the earliest time when the tenant is ready to move on.

9 *Guidance on the use of family intervention tenancies* CLG, January 2009.

landlord, useful guidance may be obtained from the National Housing Federation's Briefing Note *Guidance on the use of family intervention tenancies.*[10] It is estimated that between 150 and 600 households in England and Wales will hold such tenancies at any one time.[11]

9.6   The intention is that a tenant will occupy under a family intervention tenancy for only a temporary short-term period while engaged in the behaviour support programme. Although the tenancy will often be a periodic (usually, weekly) tenancy, 'the typical length of tenancy would be expected to be between six months and a year or possibly longer'.[12] However, a social landlord can at any time convert a family intervention tenancy into a secure or assured tenancy, as appropriate, by serving a notice to that effect on the tenant in writing.[13]

Preliminaries to claiming possession

9.7   Family intervention tenancies are simply unprotected contractual tenancies. To end them, social landlords need to serve a notice to quit. Once the notice to quit has expired, if the former tenant does not leave the property, the social landlord should seek possession in court proceedings but need not prove any specific grounds for possession.

9.8   However, there are special additional preliminary requirements before notice to quit can be served.

Local housing authorities

9.9   If the family intervention tenancy landlord is a local housing authority then, before it can give notice to quit, it must first serve a 'minded-to' notice.[14] There is no prescribed form of that notice.

9.10   The notice must be in writing and state[15]:

•   that the local housing authority has decided to serve a notice to quit on the tenant;
•   the effect of serving a notice to quit;

10 NHF, April 2009.
11 *Housing and Regeneration Act – impact assessment* CLG, December 2008, p235 para 25.
12 *Guidance on the use of family intervention tenancies* CLG, 2009, para 15.
13 HA 1985 Sch 1 para 4ZA(2) and HA 1988 Sch 1 para 12(ZA)(2).
14 H&RA 2008 s298(1)(a).
15 H&RA 2008 s298(2).

tenants who would have faced eviction on those grounds but agreed to surrender their tenancies when offered the option of a behaviour support programme and a family intervention tenancy. Yet others may have previously been tenants who would have faced eviction on the stipulated grounds had they been secure or assured tenants at that time.

9.25 **Condition 3**: the purpose of the letting must have been to provide 'behaviour support services'.[32] This term means: relevant support services to be provided by any person to –

- the new tenant, or
- any person who is to reside with the new tenant

for the purpose of addressing the kind of behaviour which led to the new tenant falling within the 'behaviour' condition described above.

9.26 The phrase 'relevant support services' means support services of a kind identified in a behaviour support agreement and designed to meet such needs of the recipient as are identified in the agreement.[33]

9.27 It follows that with every family intervention tenancy there must be a tailor-made behaviour support agreement. Such an agreement must be in writing and be made between the parties who are the landlord and the tenant under the family intervention tenancy.[34] Additionally, if the landlord is not a local housing authority, the local housing authority for the area in which the property to be occupied under a family intervention tenancy is situated must also be a party to the behaviour support agreement.[35] The behaviour support agreement should be separate from, but probably referred to in, the tenancy agreement for the family intervention tenancy itself.

9.28 **Condition 4**: the landlord must have served the tenant with a pre-letting notice before the tenant entered into the family intervention tenancy.[36] This notice is intended to ensure that the prospective tenant is made fully aware of the nature of the decision he or she is being asked to make, in order that he or she might properly reflect on it before reaching a decision to accept a family intervention tenancy.[37]

---

32 HA 1985 Sch 1 para 4ZA(3)(b) and HA 1988 Sch 1 para 12ZA(3)(b).

33 HA 1985 Sch 1 para 4ZA(12) and HA 1988 Sch 1 para 12ZA(12).

34 HA 1985 Sch 1 para 4ZA(12) and HA 1988 Sch 1 para 12ZA(12).

35 HA 1988 Sch 1 para 12ZA(12).

36 HA 1985 Sch 1 para 4ZA(4) and HA 1988 Sch 1 para 12ZA(4).

37 *Guidance on the use of family intervention tenancies* CLG, 2009, para 27.

The form of notice is not prescribed. But what it must contain is pre-scribed.[38] It must set out:

(a) the reasons for offering the tenancy to the new tenant;

(b) the dwelling-house in respect of which the tenancy is to be granted;

(c) the other main terms of the tenancy (including any requirements on the new tenant in respect of behaviour support services);

(d) the reduced security of tenure available under the tenancy and any loss of security of tenure which is likely to result from the new tenant agreeing to enter into the tenancy;

(e) that the new tenant is not obliged to enter into the tenancy or (unless otherwise required to do so) to surrender any existing tenancy or possession of a dwelling-house;

(f) any likely action by the social landlord if the new tenant does not enter into the tenancy or surrender any existing tenancy or possession of a dwelling-house; and

(g) advice to the prospective tenant as to how he or she may be able to obtain assistance in relation to the notice.[39]

9.29   Note that the notice must be given *before* the family intervention tenancy is entered into. That requirement cannot be complied with by giving the notice at the same time as the agreement is made, or at some time between sign-up and the first day of the commencement of tenancy, or after the tenant has taken up occupation.

9.30   Given the importance of the pre-tenancy notice and the likelihood that some vulnerable tenants may be among those entering into family intervention tenancies, the guidance suggests that 'efforts should be made to ensure any information is presented in a user-friendly format ... If a landlord is aware that the tenant has difficulty in reading or understanding printed information, the landlord should take reasonable steps to address this. This should include consideration of mental capacity and the Disability Discrimination Act'.[40]

9.31   A regulation-making power enables the secretary of state to change, add to or remove the required contents of the pre-tenancy notice but that power has not been exercised.[41]

9.32   If the defendant demonstrates that the claimant in the possession claim cannot make out all four of the conditions, the claim should be dismissed.

---

38 HA 1985 Sch 1 para 4ZA(5) and HA 1988 Sch 1 para 12ZA(5).

39 HA 1985 Sch 1 para 4ZA(7) and HA 1988 Sch 1 para 12ZA(7).

40 *Guidance on the use of family intervention tenancies* CLG, 2009, para 30. The Equality Act 2010 was passed after the guidance was issued.

41 HA 1985 Sch 1 para 4ZA(6) and HA 1988 Sch 1 para 12ZA(6).

Defence (2): the family intervention tenancy has not been lawfully terminated

9.33 If the tenancy is (or is found by the court to be) a family intervention tenancy, the second available line of defence is that the family intervention tenancy has not been lawfully terminated.

9.34 The termination must have been by service of a valid notice to quit.

9.35 If the landlord was a local housing authority, the minded-to notice procedure above must have been complied with (and the requirements in relation to review must have been complied with) before notice to quit was given.[42]

9.36 In addition to the usual checks to see whether the form and content of the notice to quit are in order, the notice given by a local housing authority landlord should be examined to see whether it contains 'advice to the tenant as to how the tenant may be able to obtain assistance in relation to the notice.'[43] If it does not, it is invalid. The expectation is that such advice should be a good deal fuller than the detail already required by the prescribed information[44] which any notice to quit must contain. Otherwise the special statutory provision will have achieved nothing. There is a reserve power to make regulations about the type of advice that a notice to quit must contain when given in respect of a family intervention tenancy but it has not been exercised.[45]

9.37 If the notice to quit was given by a local housing authority, it will be invalid if served prematurely, ie, before the dates mentioned in para 9.12.

Other defences

9.38 If a tenant considers that the landlord under the family intervention tenancy has not lawfully complied with the requirements for a review of the decision to give a notice to quit, the usual course would be to seek a judicial review in the Administrative Court. However, if the complaint is about the validity of the notice to quit itself, that

---

42 H&RA 2008 s298(1).
43 H&RA 2008 s298(7).
44 Protection from Eviction Act 1977 s5 and the regulations made thereunder. See para 14.14.
45 H&RA 2008 s298 (8).

point can be taken in the family intervention tenant's defence. For example, if the landlord is a local housing authority and the tenant has requested a review of the decision to serve a notice to quit, a valid notice to quit cannot be served until the review decision has been notified. Such a notification must itself contain reasons in order to be valid. If no reasons were included, the review decision notice would be invalid and any notice to quit served on the strength of it would likewise be invalid.

9.39   As explained in chapter 25 on public law defences, there may be circumstances in which a tenant may wish to challenge the legality of both the notice to quit and the review decision. In such circumstances reference should be made to the advice given in that chapter.

9.42   If the tenancy is a family intervention tenancy and there is no doubt that the notice to quit is valid, the former tenant under the family intervention tenancy may need to have recourse to a public law or human rights defence.[46] In pursuing any such defence, reference may usefully be made to para 9.16 and to the further non-statutory guidance which advises landlords under family intervention tenancies that a 'key consideration in any decision to terminate the tenancy is what will happen to the family afterwards. The local authority homelessness and housing options teams need to be involved at or before the point at which the [landlord] decides to terminate the tenancy.'[47]

---

46 See chapters 25 and 26 respectively.
47 *Guidance on the use of family intervention tenancies* CLG, 2009, para 47.

Replacement tenancies

Introduction

10.1   On 20 May 2009 hundreds of thousands of occupiers of residential
properties in England and Wales became replacement tenants of their
homes on the commencement of the Housing and Regeneration Act
(H&RA) 2008 s299 and Schedule 11.[1] This happened 'automatically'
in the sense that it required no action on the part of either the landlord or the tenant under the replacement tenancy and in most cases
there was no new document reflecting the fact that a replacement
tenancy had arisen. The Housing and Regeneration Act 2008 simply
provides that, if certain conditions are fulfilled, a replacement tenancy relationship arose between the parties on or after 20 May 2009.[2]

10.2   For the assistance of social housing providers in England, the
Department for Communities and Local Government (CLG) produced non-statutory guidance on the operation of the replacement
tenancy regime.[3] References in this chapter to 'the *Guidance*' are references to that document.

10.3   To explain why the enactment of this new form of tenancy was
considered appropriate, the next few paragraphs offer a summary
of the developments that occurred in the social housing sector over
the three decades preceding the arrival of the replacement tenancy
regime.

10.4   It will be recalled that security of tenure for most social housing
tenants was conferred by the Housing Act (HA) 1980 which came
into force in October 1980. For both council and housing association tenants it introduced a 'secure' tenancy status.[4] The Housing Act
1988 enacted a different regime for most new housing association
tenants. Since the coming into force of that Act, in January 1989,
most new housing association tenants have been 'assured' tenants.[5]
The Housing Act 1996 introduced a new form of council house tenancy – the introductory tenancy – under which most council tenants

---

1   Housing and Regeneration Act 2008 (Commencement No 5) Order 2009 SI No
    1261.
2   In almost all cases, the replacement tenancy will have started on 20 May 2009.
    For a very small number of occupiers (those out of occupation on 20 May 2009
    but subsequently re-admitted on the setting-aside of a warrant for possession)
    the replacement tenancy will commence on a later date (the date on which they
    resume occupation): H&RA 2008 Sch 11 para 16(4) and (5).
3   *Tolerated Trespassers: guidance for social landlords* CLG, May 2009. See www.
    communities.gov.uk/publications/housing/toleratedtrespass.
4   See chapter 1 of this book.
5   See chapter 12 of this book.

occupy their homes for the first year or so.[6] The Anti-Social Behaviour Act 2003 enacted a status of 'demoted' tenancy to which a secure or assured tenancy can be reduced by court order.[7]

10.5 Despite the fact that the earliest of these provisions was intended to confer security of tenure on tenants, social landlords have actually been bringing tens of thousands of claims for possession every year for the past 30 years in respect of these tenancies. Most such claims have resulted in possession orders – either outright or conditional ('suspended') orders. But most of the defendants were not, in fact, evicted. Because most claims had been brought on grounds of rent arrears, the landlords were content for the defendants to remain in occupation if something was being paid regularly towards current charges and the arrears:

> The vast majority of landlords continue to make active efforts to negotiate repayment agreements after Notices have been served and even after a tenant has breached the terms of a Suspended Possession Order. At most stages of the process landlords are generally prepared to accept repayment agreements involving relatively small instalments, even if this implies that clearing the debt will be protracted.[8]

10.6 In 1987, the Court of Appeal decided that, where a possession order had been obtained against a secure tenant, the tenancy itself terminated either on the date for possession stipulated in the order or, where the order had been suspended, on breach of the conditions of suspension.[9] The occupier's continued occupation beyond that point was not as tenant but was contingent (usually) on the toleration of continued occupation by the former landlord. The tenancy had gone into a 'limbo' from which it might be restored by further order of the court.[10] Unless and until that happened, the occupier was a 'tolerated trespasser'.[11] In 2007, the Court of Appeal held that exactly the same process occurred on the making or breach of a possession order granted in respect of an 'assured' tenancy.[12] It was assumed that the same principles applied in respect of possession orders granted against 'introductory' and 'demoted' tenants.

6 See chapter 7 of this book.

7 See chapter 8 of this book.

8 Housing Research Summary 219: *Possession actions and evictions by social landlords* CLG, June 2005, p4.

9 *Thompson v Elmbridge BC* [1987] 1 WLR 1425; [1987] 19 HLR 526, CA.

10 HA 1985 s85.

11 *Burrows LBC v Brent* [1996] 1 WLR 1448; [1996] 29 HLR 167, HL.

12 *Knowsley HT v White* [2007] 1 WLR 2897; [2007] 39 HLR 610, CA.

10.7   In 2008, the government estimated that even in the relatively short period from October 2001 to July 2006, some 250,000 to 300,000 occupiers had lost their tenancies by the making of possession orders and had been reduced to the limbo status of tolerated trespassers.[13] The appellate courts were pressed to make a series of constantly more refined and rarified decisions about whether that status had arisen, what its nature was, and what consequences any dealings between the former landlord and former tenant, while the previous tenancy remained in limbo, might give rise to (in particular, whether a new tenancy might have been created).[14]

10.8   Following an extended consultation exercise,[15] government amendments designed to address the position of tolerated trespassers were moved during the parliamentary passage of what became the Housing and Regeneration Act 2008.

10.9   As enacted, H&RA 2008 Sch 11 serves two functions. Part 1 contains amendments to housing legislation, applicable to secure, assured, introductory and demoted tenancies, designed to ensure that any possession order made after 20 May 2009 does not end such a tenancy until the order is executed and the tenant actually evicted.[16] The intention was that no more 'tolerated trespassers' would be created.

10.10   But that left a legacy of hundreds of thousands of former tenants still occupying their homes – most commonly in social housing – with the limbo status of tolerated trespasser. Although some respondents to the consultation on how to tackle the problem of tolerated trespassers had urged that it be addressed by simply reviving the old tenancies that the occupiers had held, the government decided against that course.[17] Instead, H&RA 2008 Sch 11 Part 2 confers the status of 'replacement tenant' on those who had become tolerated trespassers but had remained in their homes.[18] It is with those new tenants that this chapter is concerned.

10.11   For most replacement tenants, the effect of this statutory regime is that they have a historic 'gap' between the termination of their old

---

13 *Housing and Regeneration Act – impact assessment* CLG, December 2008.

14 Nothing would now be served by setting out the extensive references to these numerous cases.

15 See *Tolerated trespassers – consultation* CLG, August 2007 and *Summary of responses to the consultation on tolerated trespassers* CLG, April 2008.

16 Care must be taken when applying H&RA 2008 Sch 11 Pt 1 because the provisions in paras 3(3), 8(3) and 14(3) have not been brought into force.

17 For the reasons given in the *Guidance* paras 58–59.

18 H&RA 2008 Sch 11 paras 15–16.

tenancy (perhaps years or even decades earlier) and the commencement of their new replacement tenancy on or after 20 May 2009. The Housing and Regeneration Act 2008 describes that gap as the 'termination period'.[19] It expressly provides that, for some specific purposes, the old tenancy will be deemed to have been running during the termination period.[20] The 2008 Act also confers on the county court a jurisdiction to treat an old tenancy as having been running during the termination period, most particularly for the purpose of reviving and giving effect to an obligation under the old tenancy (eg, a covenant to repair).[21] But for most replacement tenants the period immediately before 20 May 2009 will have been a termination period running back months or years during which they were *not* tenants.

10.12   Very shortly after parliament had enacted this new scheme of replacement tenancies, but before the provisions had been commenced, the House of Lords decided that in fact the concept of tolerated trespass had never applied to the assured tenancy regime at all.[22] It held that an assured tenancy made subject to a possession order only terminated on the execution of the possession order. Nevertheless, the government decided to bring the replacement tenancy regime into place in full, even though it had been rendered irrelevant for most assured tenants.[23]

10.13   In April 2010 the UK Supreme Court was invited to take the same approach to secure tenancies and to hold that the whole notion of 'limbo' status and tolerated trespass had been mistaken for secure tenants also. It decided that, in light of the new statutory regime of the 2008 Act, it would be wrong to overrule the previous line of authority with retrospective effect.[24]

10.14   Most replacement tenants would be better off, in terms of legal status, if they could recover and reinstate their 'old' tenancies which had been terminated by possession orders before 20 May 2009. In many cases that can be achieved by applying in the original possession proceedings for the variation or discharge of the old possession order.[25] A discharge of the possession order resurrects the old tenancy and the same effect can be achieved by varying the old order to

---

19 H&RA 2008 Sch 11 para 16(3).
20 H&RA 2008 Sch 11 para 21(1) and (2).
21 H&RA 2008 Sch 11 para 21(3)–(5).
22 *Knowsley HT v White* [2008] UKHL 70; [2009] AC 636.
23 It did so for the reasons given in the *Guidance* at paras 11 and 12.
24 *Austin v Southwark LBC* [2010] UKSC 28; [2010] 3 WLR 144.
25 Eg, for secure tenants who were subject to possession orders on discretionary grounds, by using HA 1985 s85.

extend the date of possession to a date that has yet to be reached. If the result of such a successful application is that the original tenancy has thus only been 'temporarily' terminated, the replacement tenancy provisions do not apply at all.[26] For more on the making of such applications see para 33.19. The remainder of the present chapter assumes that, for whatever reason, such an application is inappropriate, or has been made unsuccessfully,[27] and that possession is being sought against a tenant occupying under a replacement tenancy.

Identifying the type of replacement tenancy and its terms

10.15   Precisely because a replacement tenancy arises by virtue of statute rather than by grant between landlord and tenant – and because there is unlikely to be any document expressly stating that the tenancy is a replacement tenancy – a first step for anyone advising such a tenant on defending possession proceedings is to identify whether there is in fact a replacement tenancy and, if so, the type of replacement tenancy that it is and the terms on which it is held. Social landlords were 'strongly encouraged to issue former tolerated trespassers with a document confirming the terms of the new tenancy on commencement of these provisions' in May 2009 (*Guidance* para 37).

10.16   Importantly, if the landlord and tenant expressly entered into a new tenancy *after* the loss of the old one but *before* 20 May 2009, it is the new tenancy made by agreement that governs arrangements between them and no replacement tenancy has arisen.[28]

10.17   In the absence of any such express agreement, the starting point for advising on replacement tenancies is that there is a replacement tenancy only if the tenant was formerly a tenant under an earlier tenancy which was ended (before 20 May 2009) by a possession order.[29] Assuming that such an order is identified and it is clear that

---

26   H&RA 2008 Sch 11 para 25.

27   All such applications turn on the exercise of judicial discretion. An application might conceivably be refused if the judge considers that H&RA 2008 Sch 11 provides a complete code which supersedes previous authorities on the revival of old tenancies. Such a judge might refuse to vary orders in these circumstances, on the basis that it is not desirable to grant such applications when parliament's assumed intention in the 2008 Act was to provide a different solution.

28   H&RA 2008 Sch 11 para 16(1)(b).

29   H&RA 2008 Sch 11 para 15.

it operated to end the tenancy, in the absence of the agreement of any new tenancy, a replacement tenancy will have arisen on 20 May 2009, but only if on that date the occupier was still using the property as his or her only or principal home and had been so using it throughout the termination period.[30] If the old tenancy was a joint tenancy, the occupation condition will have been fulfilled if at least one former joint tenant was still using the property as his or her only or principal home on 20 May 2009 and had been so using it throughout the termination period.[31]

10.18   The type of replacement tenancy that has been created depends on what type of tenancy the tenant held when the old possession order was made. If the old tenancy was a sole tenancy, the new replacement tenancy is a sole tenancy. If the old tenancy was a joint tenancy, the new replacement tenancy is a joint tenancy (even if one of the joint tenants has left the premises since the old possession order was made). The *Guidance* advises that:

> This is something which the landlord should bring to the attention of the newly restored tenant who remains in the property and who may wish to take the necessary action to terminate the joint tenancy. Landlords are recommended to consider whether to take reasonable steps to bring the situation to the attention also of the tenant who has left the property, but it is recognised that frequently in such situations there are no contact details for that tenant. (para 41).

10.19   In broad terms, if the old terminated tenancy was a secure tenancy, the replacement tenancy will be a secure tenancy (and so on).[32] Likewise, the statutory provisions applicable to an ordinary secure tenancy will be applicable to a secure replacement tenancy (and so on).[33] Note that for replacement introductory tenancies and replacement demoted tenancies arising under the Housing and Regeneration Act 2008, the 'trial period' applies in full again from the date the new tenancy starts (*Guidance* para 47). Identifying the correct type of replacement tenancy should be relatively easy except where there has been a change of landlord between the loss of the old tenancy and the start of the new replacement tenancy. For that situation, see para 10.23.

---

30 H&RA 2008 Sch 11 paras 16(1)(a)(i) and 16(2). Any period during which the occupier was out of possession by virtue of a warrant for possession which is subsequently set aside is ignored: H&RA 2008 Sch 11 para 16(6).

31 H&RA 2008 Sch 11 para 21.

32 H&RA 2008 Sch 11 para 17.

33 H&RA 2008 Sch 11 para 19.

10.20   Much more difficult is the identification of the terms of the replacement tenancy itself. Unless the landlord and tenant agree new terms between them after commencement of the replacement tenancy, the terms and conditions are automatically those under which the tenant held the old tenancy prior to its termination – perhaps many years earlier.[34] To avoid the terms being simply the fossilised remnants of the old terminated tenancy, the Housing and Regeneration Act 2008 provides that the terms are treated as having been updated by any changes made during the termination period to the level of payments or other terms and conditions of the occupation.[35] These provisions are far from straightforward.[36] Not least, the statute fails to explain how any 'terms and conditions of occupation' will have arisen between the former landlord and the former tenant during a period of tolerated trespass – let alone how any 'changes' will have been made to those terms and conditions! The *Guidance* simply advises that:

> We would not expect this to be an issue in many cases, and where it is an issue we would recommend negotiation with the tenant to agree the relevant term. (para 51)

10.21   Given this uncertainty (in the absence of new terms agreed since the creation of any replacement tenancy), advisers need to check extremely carefully any assertion by a landlord of a replacement tenant that the tenant is in breach of the terms of the replacement tenancy. It is essential to ascertain exactly what those terms are.

10.22   Greater clarity is provided in respect of arrears of mesne profits that the replacement tenant was due to pay during the termination period. Such arrears become arrears of rent under the new replacement tenancy.[37]

'New landlord' cases

10.23   In the considerable period over which tolerated trespassers accumulated in the social housing stock, much of that housing stock changed hands. In particular, well in excess of a million homes in England were transferred from council to housing association ownership in the period from 1980 to 2009.

---

34 H&RA 2008 Sch 11 para 18(1).
35 H&RA 2008 Sch 11 para 18(1).
36 Note the special provisions in H&RA Sch 11 para 18(3)–(6).
37 H&RA 2008 Sch 11 para 18(3).

10.24   This has caused difficulty in situations in which the present land-lord under the replacement tenancy is different from the landlord under the old tenancy. In such circumstances, before the passage of H&RA 2008 Sch 11, it had been conceded that the powers of the court regulating the possession order would remain those of the tenancy regime applicable to the old tenancy.[38]

10.25   The Housing and Regeneration Act 2008 conferred new powers to make regulations to cover these change-of-landlord circumstances.[39] Following a further consultation exercise,[40] the powers have been exercised in both England[41] and Wales[42] and, in cases where the landlord has changed since the original possession order was made, reference should be made to the appropriate regulations and to section 5 of the *Guidance*.

Procedure for recovery of possession

10.26 An extraordinary feature of the replacement tenancy regime is that, although replacement tenancies are new tenancies created on or after 20 May 2009, they remain subject to the terms of possession orders made before they commenced. By definition, there is only a replacement tenancy if there was a possession order that ended the occupier's old tenancy. That order continues to have a 'life' in respect of the new tenancy.

10.27   Therefore a landlord of a replacement tenant who wishes to re-cover possession does not usually need to bring fresh possession proceedings. The possession order which brought the old tenancy to an end is treated, so far as practicable, as applying to the replacement tenancy.[43] Any other court orders made in connection with or in consequence of the possession order (for example, an order for stay or

---

38 *Lambeth LBC v O'Kane* [2005] EWCA Civ 1010; [2006] HLR 2 at [44].

39 H&RA 2008 Sch 11 para 24.

40 See *Tolerated trespassers: successor landlord cases – a consultation paper* CLG, September 2008, *Consultation on tolerated trespassers: successor landlord cases – summary of responses* CLG, March 2009 and *Tolerated trespassers: successor landlord cases – impact assessment* CLG, March 2009.

41 Housing (Replacement of Terminated Tenancies) (Successor Landlords) (England) Order 2009 SI No 1262.

42 Housing (Replacement of Terminated Tenancies) (Successor Landlords) (Wales) Order 2009 SI No 1260 (W 112).

43 H&RA 2008 Sch 11 para 20(1).

suspension of a possession warrant) are likewise to be treated, so far as practicable, as applying to the replacement tenancy.[44]

10.28   A landlord seeking possession against a replacement tenant needs to apply in the old possession proceedings for the variation and/or enforcement of the old possession order. Liberty to apply is deemed to exist even if the replacement tenant is once again in compliance with any conditions imposed by the old possession order or any warrant.[45] However, a prudent landlord is unlikely to make a simple administrative application for the issue of a warrant. Enforcement of the old possession order will probably be sought because of something that the replacement tenant has recently done or failed to do. In those circumstances, an appropriate application should be made to the court supported by evidence setting out the nature of the landlord's concerns.[46] In default of such an application for a hearing, any replacement tenant would be well advised to apply to stay or suspend any new order or warrant obtained by the landlord without a hearing. The result of such an application by the tenant should, again, produce a judicial consideration on the merits. The court's jurisdiction to grant relief to either party is governed by the terms of the earlier possession order and the relevant statutory regime which most approximates to the type of replacement tenancy concerned (see para 10.19).

10.29   Of course, if there has been a change of landlord since the old possession order was made, the present landlord's first or prior application should be for an order that it be substituted for the claimant in the old proceedings.[47] That application should be supported by evidence and would usually be made on notice to the new replacement tenant.[48]

Defending possession proceedings against replacement tenants

10.30   In the light of the above content of this chapter, the best form of defence in respect of a prospective or actual application for possession against a replacement tenant might well be to make an application

---

44   H&RA 2008 Sch 11 para 20(2).
45   *Manchester CC v Finn* [2002] EWCA Civ 1998; [2003] HLR 41.
46   *Sheffield CC v Hopkins* [2001] EWCA Civ 1023; [2002] HLR 12.
47   Civil Procedure Rules 19.4.
48   *Knowsley Housing Trust v Revell* [2003] EWCA Civ 496; [2003] HLR 63 at [23].

for discharge or variation of the original possession order with a view to the resurrection of the old tenancy. If such an application is successful, the replacement tenancy evaporates.

10.31 If that is neither possible nor appropriate, the following alternative variants – deployed where apt – may assist in at least securing a delay in the recovery of possession, if not in defeating the landlord's application:

- The old possession order did not, as a matter of law or fact, bring the old tenancy to an end and so that tenancy is still extant and no replacement tenancy has arisen (see para 10.17).
- After the old possession order was made, but before 20 May 2009, the landlord and tenant entered into a new tenancy agreement so that there is no replacement tenancy at all (see para 10.16).
- The landlord's issue of fresh possession proceedings is an abuse of process. The correct course was to apply in the old proceedings (see paras 10.27–10.28) and the new proceedings should be struck out.
- (If there has been a change of landlord) the current landlord has not applied to be substituted as claimant in the old proceedings and should have done so before issuing the application (see para 10.29).
- The matters relied on by the current landlord as constituting a breach of the tenancy are not in fact breaches of the terms of the present agreement because those terms are not part of the tenancy agreement (see paras 10.20–10.21).
- The landlord is a public body and its decision to recover possession against the replacement tenant was reached in breach of public law principles (see chapter 25).
- The landlord is a public authority for the purposes of the Human Rights Act 1998, as is the court, and eviction would be contrary to a Convention right protected by that Act (see chapter 26).

10.32 As in all possession cases, the best answer to the landlord's application is to satisfy the court that eviction from the home is not warranted on the facts of the case.

Independent sector tenants

Introduction to Part II

II.1
Outside the local authority sector, almost all new residential tenancies created on or after 15 January 1989 are assured or assured shorthold tenancies.[1] In practice, most private sector landlords create assured shorthold tenancies, whereas most landlords in the social sector wish to grant assured tenancies with security of tenure. There are, however, exceptions. Some social landlords grant assured shorthold tenancies in respect of temporary accommodation or as probationary tenancies. Also, before the implementation of the Housing Act (HA) 1988 s19A on 28 February 1997, some private sector landlords inadvertently created assured tenancies because they failed to comply with the requirements in HA 1988 s20. However, since 28 February 1997 almost all new tenancies are assured shorthold tenancies unless the landlord elects to create an assured tenancy (see para 11.6). In practice, in most cases, social landlords such as housing associations continue to grant assured tenancies with security of tenure.

II.2   Since 1 April 2010, housing associations and other 'private registered providers of social housing' (PRPs) in England have been regulated by the Tenant Services Authority (TSA), while in Wales 'registered social landlords' (RSLs) continue to be regulated by the Welsh Assembly Government (see paras 6.1–6.9). At the time of writing, however, the government has indicated that it intends to abolish the TSA and transfer some of its regulatory powers to the Homes and Communities Agency. In the meantime, in England the guidance and good practice notes published by the former regulator, the Housing Corporation, have been withdrawn. The regulatory framework established by the TSA identifies ten key principles and objectives, including the promotion of robust self-regulation and focusing on

---

1 For tenancies granted by local authorities, see Part I. Occupiers of agricultural accommodation may enjoy 'assured agricultural occupancy' status.

outcomes for tenants, which are to be judged against certain general standards.[2]

Rent Act transitional provisions

II.3   Tenancies granted before 15 January 1989 by private sector landlords either enjoyed security of tenure under the Rent Act 1977 or lacked long-term security of tenure. There are still many thousands of Rent Act protected or statutory tenants (see chapters 15 to 17).[3]

II.4   Housing Act 1988 s34 provides that no new Rent Act protected tenancies can be created after 15 January 1989, unless one of three exceptions applies:

- The tenancy was entered into in pursuance of a contract made before the Housing Act came into force.
- The tenancy was granted to an existing Rent Act protected or statutory tenant by the same landlord. If there are joint tenants or joint landlords, it is sufficient for only one of the joint tenants to have been a protected tenant and for only one of the joint landlords to have been the landlord of the existing tenant or tenants. Although the wording of this section is not very clear, it is plain that parliament's intention was that this exception should apply even if the tenant has moved from other accommodation.[4]
- Before the grant of the new tenancy an order for possession was made on the ground of suitable alternative accommodation against a protected or statutory tenant[5] and in the possession proceedings relating to the earlier tenancy, the court directed that the tenancy of the suitable alternative accommodation should be held on a protected tenancy. The court should consider whether an assured tenancy would 'afford the required security'. If it would not, it may

---

2   See para 6.15. The six standards currently govern the following areas: tenant involvement and empowerment; the condition and quality of the home; tenancy conditions, rent and allocations; neighbourhood and community; value for money; and governance and financial viability.

3   See *Cadogan Estates Ltd v McMahon* [2001] 1 AC 378; [2000] 3 WLR 1555; [2000] 4 All ER 897, HL, per Lord Millett.

4   See *Laimond Properties Ltd v Al-Shakarchi* (1998) 30 HLR 1099; (1998) *Times* 23 February, CA; *Kotecha v Rimington* March 1991 *Legal Action* 15; *Singh v Dalby* September 1992 *Legal Action* 22; *Gorringe v Twinsectra* June 1994 *Legal Action* 11; *Giddy v Murray* March 1995 *Legal Action* 12 and *Secretarial Nominee Co Ltd v Thomas* [2005] EWCA Civ 1008; (2005) *Times* 20 September.

5   Under Rent Act 1977 s98(1)(a) or Sch 16 case 1 or Rent (Agriculture) Act 1976 Sch 4 case 1.

direct that the suitable alternative accommodation should be held on a protected tenancy. It is obviously important that representatives of Rent Act tenants in suitable alternative accommodation cases do all they can to ensure that the court directs that the new tenancy should be held on a protected tenancy. The higher rent which would be recoverable under an assured tenancy may mean that the alternative accommodation would not be suitable 'to the means of the tenant' and/or it would be unreasonable to make a possession order.

CHAPTER 11

Assured shorthold tenancies

Introduction

11.1 ⎛Assured shorthold tenancies provide no long-term security of tenure
and are subject to minimal rent control.⎞Although, legally, they are
a kind of assured tenancy, the lack of security of tenure means that,
from a tenant's point of view, the adjective 'assured' is something of
a misnomer.⎞

11.2 Most private sector lettings since January 1989 have been assured
shorthold tenancies. Until 28 February 1997, when amendments
introduced by the Housing Act (HA) 1996 ss96–100 came into force,
landlords had to serve HA 1988 section 20 notices before the grant
of tenancies informing prospective tenants that tenancies were to be
assured shorthold tenancies⎞Failure to serve such notices, or service
of invalid notices, resulted in the creation of assured tenancies.⎞How-
ever, since 28 February 1997 the section 20 requirement has been
abolished and, subject to the exceptions set out at para 11.6, all new
tenancies are assured shorthold tenancies. This is the case even if
they are granted orally or are periodic tenancies.⎞Accordingly, when
advising, it is vital to determine when the tenancy was granted or, if
there has been a succession of tenancies, when the first tenancy was
granted. ⎞

11.3 It should be noted that the Court of Appeal has held that the
assured shorthold regime does not breach European Convention on
Human Rights article 8 (respect for the home).[1]

Tenancies granted before 28 February 1997

Requirements for assured shorthold tenancies

11.4 Housing Act 1988 s20 stipulated four requirements for the creation
of an assured shorthold tenancy:

- It must have been granted for a fixed term of not less than six
months.[2]
- It must not contain any provision enabling the landlord to terminate the tenancy within six months of the beginning of the tenancy.

---

1 *Poplar HARCA v Donoghue* [2001] EWCA Civ 595; [2002] QB 48.
2 *Bedding v McCarthy* [1994] 41 EG 151; (1995) 27 HLR 103, CA. A tenancy
granted for 'a term certain of one year ... and ... thereafter from month to
month' is a tenancy granted for a term certain within the meaning of s20(1)(a)
which was capable of being an assured shorthold tenancy: *Goodman v Evely*
[2001] EWCA Civ 104; [2002] HLR 53.

HA 1988 s45(4) provides that a power of re-entry or forfeiture for breach of condition does not count as a provision enabling the landlord to determine the tenancy for this purpose.[3]

- Notice in the prescribed form must have been served[4] before the commencement of the tenancy stating that the tenancy would be an assured shorthold tenancy. The court had no power to dispense with service of this notice.[5] The form of the notice was prescribed by the Assured Tenancies and Agricultural Occupancies (Forms) Regulations 1988.[6] The omission of certain words from the prescribed form or the inclusion of incorrect details may render the notice invalid.[7] However, in view of the purposive approach adopted and sanctioned in *Manel v Memon*[8] and *Mannai Investment Co Ltd v Eagle Star Life Assurance Co Ltd*,[9] a notice is likely to be valid if, notwithstanding any errors or omissions, it was substantially to the same effect in accomplishing the statutory purpose of telling the proposed tenant of the special nature of an assured shorthold tenancy.[10]

- It would be an assured tenancy but for the above requirements being satisfied.[11] See para 12.3.

3 See *Maryland Estates v Bar-Joseph* [1999] 1 WLR 83; [1998] 3 All ER 193, CA.

4 See *Yenula Properties Ltd v Naidu* [2002] EWCA Civ 719; [2003] HLR 18.

5 *Panayi v Roberts* (1993) 25 HLR 421; [1993] 28 EG 125, CA.

6 SI No 2203.

7 *Panayi v Roberts* (1993) 25 HLR 421; [1993] 2 EGLR 51 (notice failed to state date); *Clickex Ltd v McCann* (2000) 32 HLR 324; [1999] 30 EG 6, CA (dates in notice in conflict with dates in tenancy agreement); *Manel v Memon* [2000] 33 EG 74; (2001) 33 HLR 235, CA (omission of bullet points, exhortation to take legal advice and statement that tenant was not committed to take the tenancy); *London and Quadrant Housing v Robertson* September 1991 *Legal Action* 17; *Lomas v Atkinson* September 1993 *Legal Action* 16 (notice failed to include information about how to seek advice); *Mistry v Dave* June 1995 *Legal Action* 19 (notice gave no date for the end of the tenancy); *Symons v Warren* [1995] CLW 33/95 (failure to identify landlord properly and incorrect date); *Stevens v Lamb* March 1996 *Legal Action* 12 (failure to include landlord's name, address and telephone number); *Smith v Willson* November 1999 *Legal Action* 28 (error in date and use of notice of *protected* shorthold (HA 1980 s52)) and *Charalambous v Pesman* January 2001 *Legal Action* 26 (name and address of landlord omitted).

8 [2000] 2 EGLR 40; (2001) 33 HLR 223, CA.

9 [1997] AC 749; [1997] 3 ALL ER 352, HL.

10 *Ravenseft Properties Ltd v Hall; White v Chubb; Kasseer v Freeman* [2001] EWCA Civ 2034; [2002] HLR 33. See too *Osborn and Co Ltd v Dior* [2003] EWCA Civ 281; [2003] HLR 45 (even if the particulars of the landlord are absent, a notice is still substantially to the same effect where the agent has signed and given its particulars), cf *York and Ross v Casey* (1999) 31 HLR 209; [1998] 30 EG 110, CA.

11 This is analogous to HA 1980 s52 which referred to 'a protected shorthold tenancy' as being 'a protected tenancy' which satisfied certain criteria.

A further tenancy (or tenancies[12]) of the same or substantially the same premises granted to a former assured shorthold tenant is also an assured shorthold tenancy even if any of the first three requirements is no longer satisfied.

11.5   Housing Act 1988 s20(3) makes it impossible for a landlord to grant an assured shorthold tenancy to anyone who, immediately before the grant of a new tenancy, was already an assured tenant of the same landlord. This is the case even if the premises in question are different.

Tenancies granted on or after 28 February 1997

11.6   Housing Act 1996 s96 and Sch 7 introduced a new HA 1988 s19A and Sch 2A. They provide that all new tenancies entered into on or after 28 February 1997 which would otherwise have been assured tenancies are automatically assured shorthold tenancies lacking long-term security of tenure. This applies whether the tenancy is granted orally or by a written agreement. In other words, the requirement of an HA 1988 section 20 notice informing the tenant that the tenancy would be an assured shorthold tenancy has been abolished. There are, however, several exceptions which are set out in HA 1988 Sch 2A. A tenancy will not be an assured shorthold tenancy where one of the following applies:

- the new tenancy is granted pursuant to a contract made before the new provisions came into force;[13]
- the landlord serves a notice before entering into the tenancy stating that the tenancy is not to be an assured shorthold tenancy;[14]
- the landlord serves a notice after the grant of the tenancy stating that the tenancy is no longer an assured shorthold tenancy;[15]
- there is a provision in the tenancy agreement stating that the tenancy is not an assured shorthold tenancy;[16]

---

12 *Lower Street Properties Ltd v Jones* (1996) 28 HLR 877; [1996] 48 EG 154, CA.

13 HA 1988 s19A(a).

14 HA 1988 Sch 2A para 1. In *Andrews and Andrews (Executors of W. Hodges deceased) v Cunningham* [2007] EWCA Civ 762; [2008] HLR 13, it was held that the use of a rent book bearing the words 'Assured tenancy' on the cover was not sufficient to convert the tenancy from an assured shorthold tenancy to a fully assured tenancy. The words 'assured tenancy' were not a statement 'that the assured tenancy to which [the notice] relates is not to be an assured shorthold tenancy' within HA 1988 Sch 2A para 1(2) (c) because an assured shorthold tenancy was itself a type of assured tenancy.

15 HA 1988 Sch 2A para 2.

16 HA 1988 Sch 2A para 3.

- the tenancy is an assured tenancy by succession, ie, where a member of the family of a statutory tenant under the Rent Act 1977 or the Rent (Agriculture) Act 1976 became an assured tenant after the death of the original tenant;[17]
- the tenancy was formerly a secure tenancy and became an assured tenancy, for example, on transfer of housing stock from a local housing authority to a housing association or other landlord;[18]
- an assured tenancy came into existence on the ending of a long residential tenancy;[19]
- the tenancy is granted to someone who immediately before its grant was an assured tenant (as opposed to an assured *shorthold* tenant) and is granted by someone who was the landlord under the old tenancy;[20]
- a periodic tenancy arising after the expiry of a non-shorthold fixed term assured tenancy;[21]
- in some cases, the tenancy or licence is an assured agricultural occupancy.[22]

Termination of assured shorthold tenancies

11.7   Housing Act 1988 s21 as amended provides:

(1) Without prejudice to any right of the landlord under an assured shorthold tenancy to recover possession of the dwelling-house let on the tenancy in accordance with Chapter I above, on or after the coming to an end of an assured shorthold tenancy which was a fixed term tenancy, a court shall make an order for possession of the dwelling-house if it is satisfied –

(a) that the assured shorthold tenancy has come to an end and no further assured tenancy (whether shorthold or not) is for the time being in existence, other than an assured shorthold periodic tenancy (whether statutory or not); and

(b) the landlord or, in the case of joint landlords, at least one of them has given to the tenant not less than two months'

---

17 Rent Act 1977 s2(1)(b) and Sch 1, HA 1988 s39 and HA 1988 Sch 2A, para 4, as amended by Civil Partnership Act 2004 Sch 8.

18 HA 1985 Pt IV, HA 1988 s38 and HA 1988 Sch 2A para 5.

19 Landlord and Tenant Act 1954 Pt I, Local Government and Housing Act 1989 s186 and Sch 10 and HA 1988 Sch 2A para 6.

20 HA 1988 Sch 2A.

21 HA 1988 Sch 2A para 8.

22 Rent (Agriculture) Act 1976, HA 1988 s24 and Sch 3 and HA 1988 Sch 2A para 9.

notice *in writing* stating that he requires possession of the dwelling-house.

(2) A notice under paragraph (b) of subsection (1) above may be given before or on the day on which the tenancy comes to an end; and that subsection shall have effect notwithstanding that on the coming to an end of the fixed term tenancy a statutory periodic tenancy arises.

(3) Where a court makes an order for possession of a dwelling-house by virtue of subsection (1) above, any statutory periodic tenancy which has arisen on the coming to an end of the assured shorthold tenancy shall end (without further notice and regardless of the period) in accordance with section 5(1A).

(4) Without prejudice to any such right as is referred to in subsection (1) above, a court shall make an order for possession of a dwelling-house let on an assured shorthold tenancy which is a periodic tenancy if the court is satisfied –

(a) that the landlord or, in the case of joint landlords, at least one of them has given to the tenant a notice *in writing* stating that, after a date specified in the notice, being the last day of a period of the tenancy and not earlier than two months after the date the notice was given, possession of the dwelling-house is required by virtue of this section; and

(b) that the date specified in the notice under paragraph (a) above is not earlier than the earliest day on which, apart from section 5(1) above, the tenancy could be brought to an end by a notice to quit given by the landlord on the same date as the notice under paragraph (a) above.

(4A) Where a court makes an order for possession of a dwelling-house by virtue of subsection (4) above, the assured shorthold tenancy shall end in accordance with section 5(1A).

(5) Where an order for possession under subsection (1) or (4) above is made in relation to a dwelling-house let on a tenancy to which section 19A above applies, the order may not be made so as to take effect earlier than –

(a) in the case of a tenancy which is not a replacement tenancy, six months after the beginning of the tenancy, and

(b) in the case of a replacement tenancy, six months after the beginning of the original tenancy.

(5A) Subsection (5) above does not apply to an assured shorthold tenancy to which section 20B (demoted assured shorthold tenancies) applies.

(6) In subsection (5)(b) above, the reference to the original tenancy is –

(a) where the replacement tenancy came into being on the coming to an end of a tenancy which was not a replacement tenancy, to the immediately preceding tenancy, and

(b) where there have been successive replacement tenancies, to the tenancy immediately preceding the first in the succession of replacement tenancies.

(7) For the purposes of this section, a replacement tenancy is a tenancy –

    (a) which comes into being on the coming to an end of an assured shorthold tenancy, and

    (b) under which, on its coming into being –

        (i) the landlord and tenant are the same as under the earlier tenancy as at its coming to an end, and

        (ii) the premises let are the same or substantially the same as those let under the earlier tenancy as at that time.

11.8 Section 21(1)(b) and 21(4)(a) were amended by HA 1996 s98(2) and (3) to make it clear that notices under this section must be in writing. Subsections (5)– (7) were added by HA 1996 s99. Subsection (5A) was added by the Anti-Social Behaviour Act 2003.

11.9 If the assured shorthold tenancy is for a fixed term, the ability of a landlord to recover possession depends on whether or not the fixed term has expired.

During a fixed-term tenancy

11.10 During a fixed term, a landlord cannot successfully claim possession relying on HA 1988 s21 (automatic right to possession on giving two months' notice), unless there is a contractual break clause in the tenancy allowing the landlord to recover possession before the expiry of the term.[23] If there is a 'break clause' in an assured shorthold tenancy, allowing the landlord to terminate the tenancy on giving notice within the fixed term, service of a Housing Act 1988 section 21 notice may be sufficient to activate the break clause.[24]

11.11 Otherwise, however, the usual grounds for possession against assured tenants are available during the fixed term (see para 12.29). Although the wording of the Act is far from clear, it seems that for a landlord to regain possession during a fixed term tenancy:

- the tenancy must contain a term allowing the landlord to re-enter or terminate the tenancy for breach of any covenant in the tenancy or if one of the grounds for possession against assured tenants exists;
- the landlord must serve notice of proceedings for possession in accordance with HA 1988 s8 (see para 12.11); and

---

23 *Gloucestershire HA v Phelps* May 2003 *Legal Action* 35, Gloucester County Court.
24 *Aylward v Fawaz* (1997) 29 HLR 408; (1996) *Times* 15 July, CA.

- the landlord must prove the existence of any of the following grounds for possession, namely, 2, 8, 10, 11, 12, 13, 14, 14A, 15 or 17 (ie, essentially 'tenant's default' grounds), and, if appropriate, prove that it is reasonable for an order to be made.

11.12   The tenant cannot apply for relief from forfeiture. HA 1988 s5(1) sets out the only routes for bringing an assured tenancy to an end.[25] If the landlord is prepared to wait until the end of the fixed term to claim possession, reliance may be placed on a section 21 notice served during the currency of the term, subject to prior compliance with the landlord's obligation to protect the tenant's deposit under HA 2004 s213 (see paras 11.32–11.35).

During a periodic tenancy

11.13   Landlords may grant an assured shorthold tenancy for a fixed term such as six or 12 months, but then allow the tenant to 'hold over' after the end of that period. In those circumstances, if the tenant continues to occupy the premises as his or her only or principal home, a statutory periodic tenancy arises, but it remains an assured shorthold tenancy and lacks security of tenure. For tenancies which began before 28 February 1997, a tenancy could be an assured shorthold tenancy only if it began with a fixed term of at least six months. Alternatively, since 28 February 1997 the landlord may have granted an assured shorthold tenancy that was periodic from the outset.

11.14   All that a landlord need do to recover possession of a periodic assured shorthold tenancy (whether it is a contractually periodic tenancy from the start or a statutory periodic tenancy, following the expiry of a fixed term) is to:

- prove that any fixed-term tenancy has come to an end and that no new tenancy has been granted;
- give at least two months' notice to the tenant in accordance with HA 1988 s21 that the landlord requires possession; and
- take court proceedings.

11.15   If landlords comply with these requirements, they are automatically entitled to possession. The court has no power to suspend possession orders, apart from HA 1980 s89(1), which provides that orders for possession must take effect no later than 14 days after the court

---

25 See para 14.44. See also *Artesian Residential Investments Ltd v Beck* [2000] QB 541; [2000] 2 WLR 357, CA.

order unless exceptional hardship would be caused, in which case the maximum period which may be allowed is six weeks. See para 33.1.

11.16   The HA 1988 section 21 notice:

- may be given before any fixed term expires;[26]
- need not be in any particular form, although it must be in writing;[27]
- may be given by only one of several joint landlords.[28]

11.17   There is no power to dispense with service of the notice. Some landlords and agents have developd a practice of serving section 21 notices at the start of a tenancy. It is likely, however, that any such notice will now be invalid where the tenant has paid a deposit and the landlord has not already complied with the requirements of HA 2004 s213 for the protection of the deposit and notification of prescribed information (see para 11.32).[29]

11.18   It is important to check that the notice complies with the specifications in the following paras 11.19–11.28.

11.19   *The notice gives at least two months' notice*,[30] although no actual date need be specified, provided that 'the tenant knows or can easily ascertain the date referred to'. ('The word "specified" ... means no more than "made clear".'[31])

11.20   In *Notting Hill Housing Trust v Roomus*,[32] the Court of Appeal held that a section 21 notice which stated 'Possession is required (by virtue of section 21(4) of the Housing Act 1988) of [the property] which you hold as tenant at the end of the period of your tenancy which will end after expiry of two months from the service upon you of this notice' was valid because the phrase 'at the end of a tenancy' in a notice given pursuant to section 21 means 'after the end of the tenancy' and so the notice complied with the requirements of section 21(4)(a). The notice should strictly state that possession is required 'after', rather than 'on', the date in question, but a court is unlikely to consider that there is any substantial difference between the two prepositions.

---

26 HA 1988 s21(2).

27 HA 1988 s21(1)(b) and s21(4)(a), as amended by HA 1996 s98.

28 HA 1988 s21(1)(b) and s21(4)(a).

29 See eg *Delicata v Sandberg* August 2009 *Legal Action* 35, Central London County Court.

30 *Symons v Warren* [1995] CLW 33/95. See also *Mundy v Hook* (1998) 30 HLR 551; [1997] 3 CL 388.

31 *Lower Street Properties Ltd v Jones* [1996] 48 EG 154; (1996) 28 HLR 877, CA.

32 [2006] EWCA Civ 407; [2006] 1 WLR 1375. See too *Elias v Spencer* [2010] EWCA Civ 246.

11.21   *If the tenancy is a periodic tenancy, the date specified in the notice is (or the period of notice given in the notice expires on) must be 'the last day of a period of the tenancy'.* The last day of a period of the tenancy may be the day before rent is due, but this is not automatically the case because a tenancy may provide for payment of rent on a day which is not the first day of the period of the tenancy: the period of the tenancy does not necessarily run from the rent day.[33]

11.22   In *Salford CC v Garner*,[34] Chadwick LJ said:

> There is ... no conceptual difficulty in an obligation which requires a tenant to pay, on the Monday, rent for a period of seven days which commenced on the previous Friday. When the rent is paid is simply a matter of accounting convenience for the landlord.

Thus, where a fixed-term tenancy runs, for example, from 1 January to 30 June, but the rent is due on the 15th of the month, the statutory periodic tenancy begins on 1 July, and the last day of a tenancy period will be the last day of each month.

11.23   In the past, uncertainty was caused by the dichotomy between HA 1988 ss21(1)(b) and 21(4)(a). Section 21(1)(b) merely provides that the landlord must give the tenant 'not less than two months' notice stating that he requires possession of the dwelling-house'. However, section 21(4)(a) provides that the date specified in a notice where there is 'a periodic tenancy' shall be 'the last day of a period of the tenancy'. Where section 21(1)(b) applies, ie, (where the notice is served *during, or on the last day of*, a fixed-term assured shorthold tenancy, two calendar months' notice only is required, and there is no need for the two months' notice to expire on 'the last day of a period of the tenancy'.)

11.24   This requirement must be satisfied, however, if the notice is served during a periodic or statutory periodic assured shorthold tenancy. In *Fernandez v McDonald*,[35] after the expiry of a fixed-term assured shorthold tenancy, tenants remained in occupation as statutory periodic tenants from the 4th of each month to the 3rd of the following month. On 24 October 2002, the landlord gave them a notice headed 'Section 21(4)(a) Assured Shorthold Tenancy: Notice Requiring Possession of Periodic Tenancy' stating 'I give you notice that I require possession of the dwelling house known as ... on 4th January 2003'. The Court of Appeal held that the notice did not comply with section

---

33   See, eg, *Baynes v Hall and Thorpe* November 2005 *Legal Action* 21; 29 June 2005, Dewsbury County Court.

34   [2004] EWCA Civ 364; [2004] HLR 35.

35   [2003] EWCA Civ 1219; [2004] 1 WLR 1027.

21(4)(a) and was defective: its expiry date should have been the last day of a period of the tenancy, ie, the <u>3rd of the month</u>.[36])

11.25   In order to avoid the pitfalls of specifying the wrong date, landlords may serve notices which include, after the date given, a rider which provides that the notice may expire, in the alternative, 'at the end of the period of your tenancy which will end next after the expiration of two months from the service upon you of this notice', or which contains a similar 'saving clause'. In spite of the lack of clarity in a notice which gives an incorrect expiry date followed by such a saving clause, it is likely that a notice in this form will be effective.[37]

11.26   *The date specified 'is not earlier than the earliest day on which ... the tenancy could be brought to an end by a notice to quit given by the landlord on the same date as the notice ...'* (section 21(4)(b)). Accordingly, more than two months' notice is required where there is an express provision requiring a longer period of notice or the rental period is longer than two months, for example, where there is a quarterly tenancy, in which case three months' notice has to be given.

11.27   *If the notice relates to a periodic tenancy, the section 21(4) notice includes reference to section 21 itself,* since section 21(4) provides that the court must be 'satisfied ... that the landlord ... has given ... notice ...stating that ... possession ... is required *by virtue of this section'* (emphasis added). A district judge, dismissing a possession claim, has held that a notice which failed to do this was defective.[38]

11.28   *Proceedings have not been commenced before the date specified in the notice.* The claim for possession in *Lower Street Properties Ltd v Jones*[39] was dismissed because proceedings were started the day before the HA 1988 section 21 notice expired. Schiemann LJ stated that it 'is implicit that the landlord cannot bring proceedings until after [the date specified in the notice]', although Kennedy LJ reached his decision on the ground that the notice served stated that the 'landlord cannot apply for such an order before the notice has run out', and left open whether, with a different wording, proceedings could have been begun before expiry.

---

36   See too *Gracechurch International SA v Tribhovan and Abdul* (2001) 33 HLR 28, CA.

37   See *Hussain v Bradford Community Housing Ltd and Kauser* [2009] EWCA Civ 763, in relation to the use of a similar saving clause in a notice to quit, and *Elias v Spencer* [2010] EWCA Civ 246. See also para 14.19.

38   *Adamson v Mather* November 2004 *Legal Action* 25, Harrogate County Court.

39   (1996) 28 HLR 877; [1996] 2 EGLR 67.

11.29   If the tenancy is one to which HA 1988 s19A applies (ie, it was granted after 28 February 1997 and none of the exceptions in HA 1988 Sch 2A applies), then any possession order may not take effect earlier than six months after the grant of the original tenancy.[40]

11.30   There is no rule that section 21 notices expire or lapse or that landlords are deemed to waive their right to rely on them if proceedings are not issued within a particular period after service of the section 21 notice. There may in theory be a gap of several years between service of a secton 21 notice and the issue of possession proceedings.[41] A fresh section 21 notice will of course be necessary if a new tenancy has been granted to the tenant in the meantime. It is arguable that if the landlord and tenant agree a variation in the terms of the original tenancy, such as a rent increase, the landlord has acted in a manner inconsistent with a notice requiring possession and would be estopped from relying on an earlier section 21 notice.

Section 21 notices and premises subject to licensing requirements

11.31   Housing Act 2004 ss75 and 98 prevent section 21 notices being given where a house in multiple occupation (HMO) which is subject to mandatory licensing (section 75) or a property which is subject to selective licensing (section 98) is not licensed. These provisions came into force on 6 April 2006.

Section 21 notices and deposits

11.32   Housing Act 2004 s215(1) provides that if a tenancy deposit[42] has been paid in connection with an assured shorthold tenancy, no section 21 notice may be given in relation to the tenancy at any time when:

- the deposit is not being held in accordance with an authorised scheme;[43] or
- the initial requirements of such a scheme[44] have not been complied with in relation to the deposit; or

---

40   HA 1988 s21(5) as inserted by HA 1996 s99.
41   See, eg, *Paddington Churches HA v Khan* December 2004 *Legal Action* 18; 29 October 2003, Willesden County Court (HHJ Copley allowing an appeal against an earlier decision to the contrary noted at [2004] 3 CLD 328).
42   As defined in HA 2004 s212(8).
43   See HA 2004 s213(4).
44   See HA 2004 s213(4).

- the prescribed information (as to which scheme has been used to protect the deposit and as to the relevant procedures) has not been given to the tenant.

11.33   Section 215 provides:

Sanctions for non-compliance

(1) If a tenancy deposit has been paid in connection with a shorthold tenancy, no section 21 notice may be given in relation to the tenancy at a time when –

    (a) the deposit is not being held in accordance with an authorised scheme, or

    (b) the initial requirements of such a scheme (see section 213(4)) have not been complied with in relation to the deposit.

(2) If section 213(6) is not complied with in relation to a deposit given in connection with a shorthold tenancy, no section 21 notice may be given in relation to the tenancy until such time as section 213(6)(a) is complied with.

(3) If any deposit given in connection with a shorthold tenancy could not be lawfully required as a result of section 213(7), no section 21 notice may be given in relation to the tenancy until such time as the property in question is returned to the person by whom it was given as a deposit.

(4) In subsection (3) 'deposit' has the meaning given by section 213(8).

(5) In this section a 'section 21 notice' means a notice under section 21(1)(b) or (4)(a) of the Housing Act 1988 (recovery of possession on termination of shorthold tenancy).

11.34   These provisions came into force on 6 April 2007. The obligation to protect tenancy deposits imposed by HA 2004 s213 on landlords and anyone else who 'receives' deposit money applies only to assured shorthold tenancies which commenced after that date. Section 213 makes no transitional provision for successor tenancies granted on or after 6 April 2007, where the original tenancy began before that date and a deposit was paid at the start of the original tenancy. It is arguable that, on the 'renewal' of a tenancy after 6 April 2007, even though the landlord retains the deposit paid on the previous tenancy, there is a notional return and fresh receipt of the money by the landlord at the commencement date of the later tenancy, which would require the landlord to protect the deposit by using one of the authorised schemes.[45]

---

45 See *Saad v Hogan* June 2009 *Legal Action* 33, Brentford County Court (HHJ Oppenheimer).

11.35   Where section 215 operates to invalidate a section 21 notice, the terms of subsections (1) and (2) make it clear that notice is not validated by the landlord's subsequent compliance with the tenancy deposit rules. This has the effect that no claim for possession can be brought against an assured shorthold tenant in these circumstances unless and until the landlord has duly protected the deposit and has subsequently served a new, valid section 21 notice.

Assured tenancies

continued

Introduction

12.1   Assured tenancies are lettings at market rents with security of tenure. There is no control over the rents at which such tenancies are initially let and subsequent rent regulation is minimal. The security of tenure provided is different from that provided by the Housing Act (HA) 1985 and the Rent Act (RA) 1977 and in some cases the grounds for possession are more widely drafted.

12.2   Statutory references in this chapter are to the Housing Act 1988 unless otherwise stated.

Definition of 'assured tenancy'

12.3   Housing Act 1988 s1 contains three prerequisites for a tenancy to be an assured tenancy:

*   *The dwelling-house must be let as a separate dwelling.* This is the well-known phrase which appears in RA 1977 s1. The word 'dwelling' is not a term of art with a specialised legal meaning. It is 'the place where [an occupier] lives and to which he returns and which forms the centre of his existence ... No doubt he will sleep there and usually eat there; he will often prepare at least some of his meals there'.[1] However, there is no legislative requirement that cooking facilities must be available for premises to qualify as a dwelling. In deciding whether an occupant has security of tenure:

    > The first step is to identify the subject-matter of the tenancy agreement. If this is a house or part of a house of which the tenant has exclusive possession with no element of sharing, the only question is whether, at the date when proceedings were brought, it was the tenant's home. If so, it was his dwelling ... The presence or absence of cooking facilities in the part of the premises of which the tenant has exclusive occupation is not relevant.[2]

    If a tenancy comprises two or more separate units of accommodation which are let together to a tenant, there can be no assured tenancy.[3] Housing Act 1988 s3 provides that if a tenant enjoys exclusive occupation of some rented accommodation, with a right

---

1   *Uratemp Ventures Ltd v Collins and Carrell* [2001] UKHL 43; [2002] 1 AC 301.
2   *Uratemp Ventures Ltd v Collins and Carrell* [2001] UKHL 43; [2002] 1 AC 301.
3   See, eg, *Horford Investments Ltd v Lambert* [1976] Ch 39; *St Catherine's College v Dorling* [1980] 1 WLR 66 and *Kavanagh v Lyroudias* [1985] 1 All ER 560.

to share other accommodation with other people, apart from the landlord, the mere fact that the other accommodation is shared does not prevent the tenant from occupying the accommodation which is not shared 'as a separate dwelling'.

- *The tenant or, if there are joint tenants, each of the joint tenants, must be individuals.* A genuine letting to a company cannot be an assured tenancy.[4] In such cases, the tenancy is unprotected and may be terminated either by the passing of time or by service of a break notice (if it is a fixed-term tenancy) or by service of a notice to quit (if it is a periodic tenancy). If this is done, a landlord who brings possession proceedings is automatically entitled to possession without having to prove any ground for possession.

- *The tenant or, if there are joint tenants, at least one of them, must occupy the premises as his or her only or principal home.* This is the same wording as HA 1985 s81, the 'tenant condition', which applies to secure tenancies (see paras 1.14–1.16). It is a more restrictive definition than the comparable provision in RA 1977 s2(1)(a).[5] Although it is possible for tenants to occupy more than one home at the same time, a tenancy can only continue to be assured if it is in respect of the tenant's principal home. There is no reason why an assured tenant should not be temporarily absent from the premises in question, provided that they remain his or her main home.[6] If an assured tenant moves out permanently, the tenancy becomes unprotected and can be terminated by notice to quit. The landlord does not have to prove any ground for possession. This is well illustrated by *Ujima Housing Association v Ansah*,[7] where an assured tenant sublet the entire flat on an assured shorthold

---

4 *Hiller v United Dairies* [1934] 1 KB 57, CA; *Hilton v Plustitle Ltd and Rose* [1988] 3 All ER 1051, CA; *Kaye v Massbetter Ltd and Kanter* (1991) 39 EG 129; (1992) 24 HLR 28, CA and *Eaton Square Properties Ltd v O'Higgins* [2000] EGCS 118, CA. However, the court may decide that a letting to a company fails to represent the substance and reality of the transaction or is an artificial transaction or that the company is merely a nominee. See dicta in *Cove v Flick* [1954] 2 QB 326 (Note); [1954] 2 All ER 441; *Firstcross v East West Ltd* (1980) 7 HLR 577, CA and *Gisborne v Burton* (1988) 38 EG 129 and the passages in *AG Securities v Vaughan* [1990] 1 AC 417; [1988] 3 WLR 1205; February 1989 *Legal Action* 21, HL, concerning 'artificiality' and 'pretence'.

5 For more detailed consideration of these issues, see chapter 16.

6 *Crawley BC v Sawyer* (1987) 20 HLR 98, CA; *Sutton LBC v Swann* (1985) 17 HLR 140, CA; *Hussey v Camden LBC* (1995) 27 HLR 5, CA; *Hammersmith and Fulham LBC v Clarke* March 2001 *Legal Action* 28, CA and *Amoah v Barking and Dagenham LBC* March 2001 *Legal Action* 28, ChD.

7 (1998) 30 HLR 831, CA.

tenancy on terms which were inconsistent with his remaining in occupation as his only or principal home. He left furniture in the flat, but no personal possessions. Ujima served a notice to quit and brought possession proceedings. The Court of Appeal held that Ujima was entitled to a possession order. The 'only or principal home' test was strict and, since the defendant was no longer in physical occupation, the onus was on him to establish that he was still occupying the flat as his principal home. He had granted the right to immediate occupation of the flat to others and was unable to return unless they voluntarily surrendered it to him. Viewed objectively, the defendant did not have the intention to preserve his occupation of the flat as his principal residence.[8]

12.4   If one spouse or civil partner (A) is a sole assured tenant but moves out, occupation by the other spouse or civil partner (B) as his or her only or principal home may preserve the assured tenancy. This is provided for by the Family Law Act 1996 s30(4) as amended by the Civil Partnership Act 2004 Sch 9 para 1, which states:

> B's occupation by virtue of this section –
> (a) is to be treated for the purposes of ... the Rent Act 1977 ... as occupation by A as A's residence, and
> (b) if B occupies the dwelling-house as B's only or principal home, it is to be treated, for the purposes of Housing Act 1985, Part I of the Housing Act 1988 ... as occupation by A as A's only or principal home.

12.5   A tenancy cannot be an assured tenancy if any of the exceptions listed in HA 1988 Sch 1 applies. Many of these exceptions are similar to those set out in RA 1977 Part I.[9] They include:

- Tenancies at a high rent (ie, currently £25,000 per annum; from 1 October 2010, in England only, £100,000 per annum[10]), or, if granted before 1 April 1990, tenancies of premises with high rateable values (ie, over £1,500 in Greater London and over £750 elsewhere).[11]

- Tenancies at a low rent (ie, rent-free or at a rent of less than £1,000 per annum in London or less than £250 per annum elsewhere, or,

8 See also *Waltham Forest CBHA v Fanning* July 2001 *Legal Action* 33.

9 See, in particular, RA 1977 ss4, 5, 8, 9, 10, 11, 12 (and Sch 2), 13 and 14.

10 HA 1988 Sch 1 para 2(1)(b), amended in England by Assured Tenancies (Amendment) (England) Order 2010 SI No 908. The increase in the maximum rent threshold applies whether the tenancy began before or after 1 October 2010.

11 References to Rating (Housing) Regulations 1990 SI No 434.

if granted before 1 April 1990, at a rent less than two-thirds of the rateable value).[12]

- Business premises which are protected under the Landlord and Tenant Act 1954 Part II.
- Licensed premises such as public houses.
- Agricultural land or holdings.
- Lettings to students by specified educational institutions.[13]
- Holiday lettings where the tenant merely has 'the right to occupy the dwelling-house for a holiday'.[14]
- Lettings by resident landlords. (This exception does not apply to purpose-built blocks of flats. For the exception to apply, the tenancy must have been granted by a landlord who, both at the time of the grant of the tenancy and at all times since, has had his or her 'only or principal home' elsewhere in the building. The schedule, like RA 1977 Sch 2, provides that existing assured tenants cannot be deprived of security of tenure by accepting a new tenancy or moving to another part of the same building after a landlord has become a resident landlord. Similarly, there are periods of disregard after the sale of premises or the death of a landlord when the fact that there is no resident landlord living in the building does not mean that the 'resident landlord' exception ceases to apply.)
- Crown tenancies, but not premises managed by the Crown Estate Commissioners.
- Tenancies granted by private landlords under arrangements made by local housing authorities in accordance with their functions under HA 1996 s188, s190, s200 or s204 (interim duties towards the homeless) within 12 months of the date of notification of the local authority's decision or the determination of any HA 1996 section 202 review or section 204 appeal, unless the landlord notifies the tenant that the tenancy is to be an assured shorthold tenancy.[15]
- Tenancies granted by fully mutual housing associations.[16]

12.6   If one of these exceptions applies, the tenant has no security of tenure and the landlord does not need to prove a reason or ground for

---

12 Rating (Housing) Regulations 1990 SI No 434.

13 Assured and Protected Tenancies (Lettings to Students) Regulations 1998 SI No 1967 as amended.

14 But note *Buchmann v May* [1978] 2 All ER 993, CA and *R v Rent Officer for Camden ex p Plant* (1980) 257 EG 713; (1980) 7 HLR 15, QBD (where tenancies which were not genuine holiday lets were found to be protected tenancies).

15 HA 1996 s209, as substituted by Homelessness Act 2002 Sch 1 para 19.

16 HA 1988 Sch 1 para 12(1)(h). See *Berrisford v Mexfield Housing Co-operative Ltd* [2010] EWCA Civ 811.

possession. Once a notice to quit has been served and has expired, the tenant has no statutory protection, except for, in some cases, Protection from Eviction Act 1977 s3 which provides that it is unlawful for a landlord to evict such a tenant without taking court proceedings.[17] The landlord has to prove only that the contractual tenancy has been terminated.

12.7 In addition, HA 1988 Sch 1 lists another exception:

- Local authority tenancies, or tenancies granted by the Homes and Communities Agency or the Welsh Ministers, residuary bodies within the meaning of Local Government Act 1985, the Residuary Body for Wales (Corff-Gweddilliol Cymru), waste disposal authorities or development corporations.

If any of the categories in this exception applies, the tenancy may be a secure tenancy (see chapter 1).

Termination of assured tenancies

Security of tenure

12.8 Housing Act 1988 s5 provides:

(1) An assured tenancy cannot be brought to an end by the landlord except by –
    (a) obtaining –
        (i) an order of the court for possession of the dwelling-house under section 7 or 21, and
        (ii) the execution of the order,
    (b) obtaining an order of the court under section 6A (demotion order), or
    (c) in the case of a fixed term tenancy which contains power for the landlord to determine the tenancy in certain circumstances, by the exercise of that power,
    and, accordingly, the service by the landlord of a notice to quit is of no effect in relation to a periodic assured tenancy.
(1A) Where an order of the court for possession of the dwelling-house is obtained, the tenancy ends when the order is executed.
(2) If an assured tenancy which is a fixed-term tenancy comes to an end otherwise than by virtue of –
    (a) an order of the court, or
    (b) a surrender or other action on the part of the tenant,
    then, subject to section 7 and Chapter II below, the tenant shall be entitled to remain in possession of the dwelling-house let under that tenancy and, subject to subsection (4) below, his right to

17 See para 18.2.

possession shall depend upon a periodic tenancy arising by virtue of this section.

(3) The periodic tenancy referred to in subsection (2) above is one –

   (a) taking effect in possession immediately on the coming to an end of the fixed term tenancy;

   (b) deemed to have been granted by the person who was the landlord under the fixed term tenancy immediately before it came to an end to the person who was then the tenant under that tenancy;

   (c) under which the premises which are let are the same dwelling-house as was let under the fixed term tenancy;

   (d) under which the periods of the tenancy are the same as those for which rent was last payable under the fixed term tenancy; and

   (e) under which, subject to the following provisions of this Part of this Act, the other terms are the same as those of the fixed term tenancy immediately before it came to an end, except that any term which makes provision for determination by the landlord or the tenant shall not have effect while the tenancy remains an assured tenancy.

(4) The periodic tenancy referred to in subsection (2) above shall not arise if, on the coming to an end of the fixed term tenancy, the tenant is entitled, by virtue of the grant of another tenancy, to possession of the same or substantially the same dwelling-house as was let to him under the fixed term tenancy.

(5) If, on or before the date on which a tenancy is entered into or is deemed to have been granted as mentioned in subsection (3)(b) above, the person who is to be the tenant under that tenancy –

   (a) enters into an obligation to do any act which (apart from this subsection) will cause the tenancy to come to an end at a time when it is an assured tenancy, or

   (b) executes, signs or gives any surrender, notice to quit or other document which (apart from this subsection) has the effect of bringing the tenancy to an end at a time when it is an assured tenancy,

the obligation referred to in paragraph (a) above shall not be enforceable or, as the case may be, the surrender, notice to quit or other document referred to in paragraph (b) above shall be of no effect.

(5A) Nothing in subsection (5) affects any right of pre-emption –

   (a) which is exercisable by the landlord under a tenancy in circumstances where the tenant indicates his intention to dispose of the whole of his interest under the tenancy, and

   (b) in pursuance of which the landlord would be required to pay, in respect of the acquisition of that interest, an amount representing its market value.

'Dispose' means dispose by assignment or surrender, and 'acquisition' has a corresponding meaning.

(6) If, by virtue of any provision of this Part of this Act, Part I of Schedule 1 to this Act has effect in relation to a fixed-term tenancy as if it consisted only of paragraphs 11 and 12, that Part shall have the like effect in relation to any periodic tenancy which arises by virtue of this section on the coming to an end of the fixed term tenancy.

(7) Any reference in this Part of this Act to a statutory periodic tenancy is a reference to a periodic tenancy arising by virtue of this section.

Periodic tenancies

12.9 Housing Act 1988 s5 provides that a periodic assured tenancy can be brought to an end by a landlord only by means of an order of the court. HA 1988 s5(1) makes it clear that notices to quit served by landlords have no effect upon periodic assured tenancies. However, a notice to quit served by a tenant on the landlord terminates both the assured tenancy and the tenant's security of tenure.

Fixed-term tenancies

12.10 If a contractual, fixed-term assured tenancy comes to an end, other than by an order of a court or by surrender, either by the simple expiry of the term or by the landlord giving a break notice in accordance with the terms of the agreement, a periodic assured tenancy (called a 'statutory periodic tenancy') will generally come into existence immediately after the fixed-term tenancy ends. In some ways this is similar to a Rent Act statutory tenancy,[18] but there are significant differences. The most important of these is the provision for fixing the terms of the statutory periodic tenancy. The basic rule is that the terms will be the same as for the former contractual assured tenancy.[19] However, HA 1988 s6 provides a mechanism by which landlords and tenants may propose new terms.

Notice of intention to bring possession proceedings

12.11 Housing Act 1988 s8 as amended provides:

(1) The court shall not entertain proceedings for possession of a dwelling-house let on an assured tenancy unless –
(a) the landlord or, in the case of joint landlords, at least one of them has served on the tenant a notice in accordance with this

---

18 RA 1977 s2.
19 HA 1988 s5(3)(d) and (e).

section and the proceedings are begun within the time limits stated in the notice in accordance with subsections (3) to (4B) below; or

(b) the court considers it just and equitable to dispense with the requirement of such a notice.

(2) The court shall not make an order for possession on any of the grounds in Schedule 2 to this Act unless that ground and particulars of it are specified in the notice under this section; but the grounds specified in such a notice may be altered or added to with the leave of the court.

(3) A notice under this section is one in the prescribed form informing the tenant that –

(a) the landlord intends to begin proceedings for possession of the dwelling-house on one or more of the grounds specified in the notice; and

(b) those proceedings will not begin earlier than a date specified in the notice in accordance with subsections (4) to (4B) below; and

(c) those proceedings will not begin later than twelve months from the date of service of the notice.

(4) If a notice under this section specifies in accordance with subsection (3)(a) above Ground 14 in Schedule 2 to this Act (whether with or without other grounds), the date specified in the notice as mentioned in subsection (3)(b) shall not be earlier than the date of the service of the notice.

(4A) If a notice under this section specifies, in accordance with subsection (3)(a) above, any of Grounds 1, 2, 5 to 7, 9 and 16 in Schedule 2 to this Act (whether without other grounds or with any ground other than Ground 14), the date specified in the notice as mentioned in subsection (3)(b) above shall not be earlier than –

(a) two months from the date of service of the notice; and

(b) if the tenancy is a periodic tenancy, the earliest date on which, apart from section 5(1) above, the tenancy could be brought to an end by a notice to quit given by the landlord on the same date as the date of service of the notice under this section.

(4B) In any other case, the date specified in the notice as mentioned in subsection (3)(b) above shall not be earlier than the expiry of the period of two weeks from the date of service of the notice.

(5) The court may not exercise the power conferred by subsection (1)(b) above if the landlord seeks to recover possession on Ground 8 of Schedule 2 to this Act.

(6) Where a notice under this section –

(a) is served at a time when the dwelling-house is let on a fixed term tenancy, or

(b) is served after a fixed term tenancy has come to an end but relates (in whole or in part) to events occurring during that tenancy, the notice shall have effect notwithstanding that the tenant becomes or has become tenant under a statutory periodic tenancy arising on the coming to an end of the fixed term tenancy.

12.12 A landlord wishing to bring possession proceedings against an assured tenant should first serve a notice, in prescribed form, informing the tenant that it is the landlord's intention to bring proceedings on one or more grounds specified in the notice. Courts have no jurisdiction to entertain claims for possession against assured tenants unless section 8 notices are served, or the court exercises its power to dispense with notice under section 8(1)(b) (see para 12.24).[20] The form of the notice, which is similar to that of notices seeking possession used against secure tenants, is specified by the Assured Tenancies and Agricultural Occupancies (Forms) Regulations 1997[21] (Form 3) (see appendix A of this book). A Housing Act 1988 section 8 notice must specify the ground on which possession is sought and give particulars of the ground.

The ground

12.13 The regulations state that the landlord must 'give the full text of each ground which is being relied upon'. In *Mountain v Hastings*,[22] the notice given by the landlord, under the heading 'Ground 8' simply stated, 'At least three months rent is unpaid', although later, under 'Particulars of Ground', it did state the total of arrears claimed. Ralph Gibson LJ held that although the full text of the ground as set out in HA 1988 Sch 2 might not have to be repeated verbatim:

> ... the words used [must] set out fully the substance of the ground so that the notice is adequate to achieve the legislative purpose of the provision. That purpose ... is to give ... information ... to enable the tenant to consider what she should do and, with or without advice, to do that which is in her power and which will best protect her against the loss of her home.

The notice was defective because it had omitted the words, 'Both at the date of service of the notice ... and at the date of the hearing' and the explanation that 'rent' means 'rent lawfully due from the tenant'.

12.14 In the county court, it has been held that the omission of the words 'rent means rent lawfully due from the tenant' from a section

---

20 *Knowsley Housing Trust v Revell; Helena Housing Ltd v Curtis* [2003] EWCA Civ 496; [2003] HLR 63.

21 SI No 194.

22 (1993) 25 HLR 427; [1993] 29 EG 96, CA. (Note that ground 8 has since been amended – eight weeks' or two months' arrears is now sufficient: see para 12.60.)

8 notice in which the landlord sought to rely on ground 8 meant that the notice was not substantially to the same effect as that required by the prescribed form and the subsequent possession claim was dismissed.[23]

12.15   Although HA 1988 s8(2) provides that a court may alter or add to the grounds specified in a notice, in *Mountain v Hastings* (see para 12.13) the Court of Appeal held that there must be a valid notice before this power may be exercised. Section 8(2) is solely directed to the possibility of adding to or deleting grounds and cannot be used to cure a notice which is invalid because the only ground relied on has not been properly set out.

Particulars

12.16   Particulars of the ground(s) relied on have to be included, as well as reference to the ground itself. For example, if proceedings are to be issued under ground 11, it is not enough for the notice merely to state 'persistent rent arrears', without giving figures of arrears and dates of late payment.[24] A notice may, however, be valid even if it does not state a figure for the arrears if the amount due can be ascertained from the notice. In *Marath v MacGillivray*,[25] the Court of Appeal stated that a landlord claiming possession under ground 8 could rely on a section 8 notice which did not specify a figure for the arrears provided that:

> ... it is made clear ... that more than three months' rent is at the date of that notice unpaid and due and provided also that in some way or other that notice makes it clear either how much, or how the tenant can ascertain how much, is alleged to be due.

12.17   It is not necessary for the notice to contain a schedule of the arrears. The Protocol for Possession Claims based on Rent Arrears does, however, require social landlords to provide rent statements on a quarterly basis.[26]

12.18   Courts have power to allow a landlord to alter or add to the particulars relied on in a notice, although such permission should only

---

23 *Equity Housing Group Ltd v Boshir* March 2005 *Legal Action* 21, Stockport County Court.

24 *Torridge DC v Jones* (1985) 18 HLR 107 (arrears of rent); *Kelsey Housing Association v King* (1995) 28 HLR 270, CA; *South Bucks DC v Francis* [1985] CLY 1900 (various acts of nuisance); *East Devon DC v Williams and Mills* December 1996 *Legal Action* 13 and *Slough BC v Robbins* December 1996 *Legal Action* 13; but cf *Dudley MBC v Bailey* (1990) 22 HLR 424, CA.

25 (1996) 28 HLR 484, CA. (Note that ground 8 has since been amended – eight weeks' or two months' arrears is now sufficient – see para 12.60.)

26 Para 3. See appendix D.

be given in circumstances where it would be just to do so. The nature and the extent of the addition or alteration should always be critical factors.[27]

Length of notice

12.19 Usually, notices of intention to bring possession proceedings against assured tenants have to give two weeks' notice, but in the case of grounds 1, 2, 5, 6, 7, 9 and 16 at least two months' notice or notice equivalent to the contractual period of the tenancy, whichever is longer, must be given. If ground 14 (anti-social behaviour) is relied on, however, section 8(4) provides no minimum period of notice, merely that the date specified in the notice shall not be earlier than the date of service of the notice.

Commencement of proceedings

12.20 With most grounds, the period specified in the notice must have expired before proceedings may be commenced. However, proceedings may be begun immediately after service if ground 14 (anti-social behaviour) is relied on.[28] Proceedings must be started within 12 months of service of the notice, otherwise a new notice must be served.[29]

Service of notice

12.21 Housing Act 1988 s8(1)(a) provides that the notice must be 'served on the tenant'. If the tenancy agreement incorporates the Law of Property Act 1925 s196, service may be effected by delivery to the premises. However, landlords cannot rely on section 196 unless it is expressly incorporated into the tenancy agreement.[30] If there is no such provision in the tenancy agreement, the landlord must prove that the notice has been received by the tenant.

12.22 There is no need for a landlord of an assured tenant to serve a notice to quit as well as a notice of intention to bring proceedings.[31]

12.23 Housing Act 1988 s45(3) makes it clear that it is sufficient if just one out of two or more joint landlords gives notice.[32]

---

27 HA 1988 s8(2) and *Marath v MacGillivray* (1996) 28 HLR 484, CA. Cf HA 1985 s83(4) and *Camden LBC v Oppong* (1996) 28 HLR 701, CA (discussed at para 4.28).

28 HA 1988 s8(4).

29 HA 1988 s8(3)(c).

30 *Wandsworth LBC v Atwell* (1995) 27 HLR 536; [1996] 01 EG 100, CA and *Enfield BC v Devonish and Sutton* (1997) 29 HLR 691, CA.

31 HA 1988 s5(1).

32 See also HA 1988 Sch 2 Pt IV.

Dispensing with notice

12.24   Courts have power (except in relation to ground 8, ie, eight weeks' arrears) to dispense with service of a notice before the institution of possession proceedings if they consider it 'just and equitable' to do so.[33] This phrase is used in HA 1985 s83 and in different circumstances in HA 1988 Sch 2 Part I (see para 12.34) and RA 1977 Sch 15 Part II also (see para 17.48). It gives the court a wide discretion to review all factors which may affect or prejudice both the landlord and tenant, including matters which have occurred since the issue of proceedings.[34] In the context of secure tenancies, the Court of Appeal has stated that it is 'obviously only in relatively exceptional cases where the court should be prepared to dispense with' a notice seeking possession.[35] It may be that if a landlord has given written notice which does not comply with the regulations prescribing its form, or if oral notice is given, the court will consider that the tenant has not been prejudiced, and that it is 'just and equitable' to dispense with the requirement.[36] On the other hand, it may not be just and equitable if the tenant had no notification at all.

12.25   Applications to dispense with section 8 notices should not be heard without notice, since judges must be in a position to weigh up all factors from both points of view.[37] In *Knowsley Housing Trust v Revell; Helena Housing Ltd v Curtis,*[38] a case where there was a stock transfer from a local authority to a registered social landlord after the issue of proceedings, the Court of Appeal held that the discretion under section 8(1)(b) is wide enough to allow substitution of the new landlord as claimant in the proceedings and dispensation of the section 8 notice where the reality is that the new landlord relies on the same breach of the same term and the relief sought is no different. However, it is not legitimate for courts to dispense with

---

33   HA 1988 s8(1)(b). For a case in which the Court of Appeal decided that it was just and equitable to dispense with a notice, even though the trial judge was not asked to consider this, see *North British Housing Association v Sheridan* [2000] L&TR 115; (2000) 32 HLR 346, CA.

34   Cf *Bradshaw v Baldwin-Wiseman* (1985) 17 HLR 260, CA; *Fernandes v Parvardin* (1982) 264 EG 49, CA (Rent Act 1977 Sch 15 case 11 cases) and *Kelsey Housing Association v King* (1995) 28 HLR 270, CA.

35   *Braintree DC v Vincent* [2004] EWCA Civ 415, although in that case, where there were unusual facts, the Court of Appeal did find it just and equitable to dispense with a HA 1985 section 83 notice.

36   Cf *North British Housing Association v Sheridan* [2000] L&TR 115; (2000) 32 HLR 346, CA.

37   *Kelsey HA v King* (1996) 28 HLR 270, CA.

38   [2003] EWCA Civ 496; [2003] HLR 63.

large numbers of such section 8 notices in one hearing without giving some consideration to any objection which might be taken by tenants with reference to the facts of their individual cases.[39]

Fixed-term assured tenancies

12.26 A fixed-term assured or assured shorthold tenancy can be terminated by the court during the fixed term if the landlord can prove that any of grounds 2, 8, 10, 11, 12, 13, 14, 14A, 15 or 17 exists and provided that the tenancy contains a provision entitling the landlord to rely on that ground (see HA 1988 s7(6)).

12.27 In the past, a landlord wishing to determine a fixed-term tenancy would generally have relied on a forfeiture clause and the tenant would have been able to seek relief from forfeiture (for example, under the County Courts Act 1984 s138 (see para 14.61) or the Law of Property Act 1925 s146 (see para 14.49)). However, courts have no jurisdiction to grant relief from forfeiture where there is an assured tenancy. In *Artesian Residential Investments Ltd v Beck*,[40] a fixed-term assured tenancy agreement included a proviso for re-entry and determination if the rent was at any stage 14 days in arrears. The defendant fell into rent arrears before the expiry of the term and the landlord brought possession proceedings relying on HA 1988 Sch 2 grounds 8 and 10. A possession order was made, but the defendant later paid all the arrears and applied for suspension of the possession order, relying upon the relief from forfeiture provisions of the County Courts Act 1984 s138. The Court of Appeal held that HA 1988 s5(1) sets out the only routes for bringing an assured tenancy to an end. There is no need for a parallel claim for forfeiture to bring the contractual tenancy to an end after the granting of an order for possession under the Act. Housing Act 1988 s5(1A) makes it clear that an order for possession brings a tenancy to an end when the order is executed. This construction is also borne out by HA 1988 s7(7) which provides that, when the court makes an order for possession on grounds relating to a fixed-term tenancy which has come to an end, any ensuing statutory periodic tenancy which arises on the ending of the fixed-term tenancy also ends (without any notice or regardless of the period) on the execution of the order. Furthermore, HA 1988 s7(3) is explicit, obliging the court mandatorily to make an order for

---

39 See too *McShane v William Sutton Trust* (1997) 1 L&T Rev D67; December 1997 *Legal Action* 13.
40 [2000] QB 541; [2000] 2 WLR 357, CA.

possession if satisfied that any of the grounds in Sch 2 is established (other than those grounds excluded by section 7(6) (see para 12.29)). Section 7(6)(b) does no more than require provision for forfeiture to be included in the terms of the tenancy, and does not set up forfeiture as an independent ground for terminating the tenancy. As a matter of principle there is no room for applying HA 1988 s138.[41]

12.28   Grounds 1, 3, 4, 5, 6, 7, 9 and 16 cannot be used against fixed-term assured tenants whose tenancies have not expired by efflux-ion of time (HA 1988 s7(6)). Once the fixed term has expired and a statutory assured periodic tenancy has arisen, those grounds become available.

Grounds for possession

12.29   Housing Act 1988 s7 provides:

(1) The court shall not make an order for possession of a dwelling-house let on an assured tenancy except on one or more of the grounds set out in Schedule 2 to this Act; but nothing in this Part of this Act relates to proceedings for possession of such a dwell-ing-house which are brought by a mortgagee, within the meaning of the Law of Property Act 1925, who has lent money on the secu-rity of the assured tenancy.

(2) The following provisions of this section have effect, subject to sec-tion 8 below, in relation to proceedings for the recovery of posses-sion of a dwelling-house let on an assured tenancy.

(3) If the court is satisfied that any of the grounds in Part I of Sched-ule 2 to this Act is established then, subject to subsections (5A) and (6) below, the court shall make an order for possession.

(4) If the court is satisfied that any of the grounds in Part II of Sched-ule 2 to this Act is established, then, subject to subsections (5A) and (6) below, the court may make an order for possession if it considers it reasonable to do so.

(5) Part III of Schedule 2 to this Act shall have effect for supplement-ing Ground 9 in that Schedule and Part IV of that Schedule shall have effect in relation to notices given as mentioned in Grounds 1 to 5 of that Schedule.

(5A) The court shall not make an order for possession of a dwelling-house let on an assured periodic tenancy arising under Schedule 10 to the Local Government and Housing Act 1989 on any of the following grounds, that is to say –
(a) Grounds 1, 2 and 5 in Part I of Schedule 2 to this Act;
(b) Ground 16 in Part II of that Schedule; and

---

41 See also ground 8, para 12.60.

(c) If the assured periodic tenancy arose on the termination of a former 1954 Act tenancy, within the meaning of the said Schedule 10, Ground 6 in Part I of Schedule 2 to this Act.

(6) The court shall not make an order for possession of a dwelling-house to take effect at a time when it is let on an assured fixed term tenancy unless –

(a) the ground for possession is Ground 2 or Ground 8 in Part I of Schedule 2 to this Act or any of the grounds in Part II of that Schedule, other than Ground 9 or Ground 16; and

(b) the terms of the tenancy make provision for it to be brought to an end on the ground in question (whether that provision takes the form of a provision for re-entry, for forfeiture, for determination by notice or otherwise).

(7) Subject to the preceding provisions of this section, the court may make an order for possession of a dwelling-house on grounds relating to a fixed term tenancy which has come to an end; and where an order is made in such circumstances, any statutory periodic tenancy which has arisen on the ending of the fixed term tenancy shall end (without any notice and regardless of the period) on the day on which the order takes effect.

12.30 As well as serving a notice of intention to bring proceedings, or persuading the court to dispense with such a notice, a landlord must also satisfy the court that one of the grounds for possession set out in HA 1988 Sch 2 exists. Some of the grounds are similar in form to the Rent Act 1977 and Housing Act 1985 grounds,[42] but others are not. As in the Rent Act 1977 and the Housing Act 1985, some grounds for possession are mandatory, whereas others are discretionary, with a requirement that the landlord must convince the court that it is reasonable to make an order for possession as well as satisfying the ground for possession.

12.31 The jurisdiction of the court to make an order for possession under section 7 is limited. If the court is not satisfied that a ground under Sch 2 has been established it does not have jurisdiction to make the order. A court is under a duty to determine whether the relevant ground has been established, whether or not it has been raised by the parties. Where a court lacks jurisdiction, it cannot be conferred merely by consent. To confer jurisdiction, an admission that a ground is satisfied, either express or implied, has to be clearly shown. Any consent order should clearly spell out in express terms the admission made by the tenant, or the court should ask the tenant what admission is being made, so that there can be no room for confusion or doubt in the future.[43]

---

42 See chapters 3 and 17.
43 *Baygreen Properties Ltd v Gil* [2002] EWCA Civ 1340; [2003] HLR 12.

12.32   Some registered social landlords have standard form tenancy agreements which provide that they will only rely on certain grounds for possession. In *North British Housing Association v Sheridan*,[44] where such a tenancy agreement set out in full the wording of the grounds that the landlord might rely on, a tenant defended possession proceedings by arguing that the landlord could not rely on a ground that had been widened by the Housing Act 1996. The Court of Appeal rejected this argument, stating that it had not been the intention of the parties to the tenancy agreement 'to restrict the landlord for ever to the statutory grounds for possession as they stood in the 1988 Act and the intention must have been that, if the statutory grounds for possession (or other related provisions) were amended, neither party would be disentitled from relying on the amended provisions'. Any other construction 'would fossilise the agreement'.

Mandatory grounds for possession

Ground 1: Owner-occupiers

12.33   Not later than the beginning of the tenancy the landlord gave notice in writing to the tenant that possession might be recovered on this ground or the court is of the opinion that it is just and equitable to dispense with the requirement of notice and (in either case) –

(a) at some time before the beginning of the tenancy, the landlord who is seeking possession or, in the case of joint landlords seeking possession, at least one of them occupied the dwelling-house as his only or principal home; or

(b) the landlord who is seeking possession or, in the case of joint landlords seeking possession, at least one of them requires the dwelling-house as his, *his spouse's or his civil partner's* only or principal home and neither the landlord (or, in the case of joint landlords, any one of them) nor any other person who, as landlord, derived title under the landlord who gave the notice mentioned above acquired the reversion on the tenancy for money or money's worth.

12.34   This ground is similar to case 11 in RA 1977 Sch 15 (see para 17.46), but much wider in its ambit. A landlord must:

• *Prove that at, or before, the grant of the tenancy the landlord gave notice in writing that possession might be recovered on this ground.* The notice need not be in any particular form and may be included as

44   (2000) 32 HLR 346; [2000] L&TR 115, CA. See too *Charles Clay & Sons Ltd v British Railways Board* [1970] 2 All ER 463, ChD.

a recital in any tenancy agreement provided that the agreement does not operate retrospectively.

or

- *Satisfy the court that 'it is just and equitable to dispense with the requirement of notice'.* These words have 'a very wide importance' and mean that the court should take into account all of the circumstances, including questions of greater hardship, and not just the circumstances which surround a failure to give written notice.[45] If the court fails to consider relevant circumstances, any possession order may be set aside.[46] A tenant's persistent late payment of rent may be a relevant circumstance.[47] If oral notice was given when a tenancy was granted, it may be an important factor favouring dispensation, but it does not follow that oral notice is a prerequisite for such a decision. Absence of oral notice is not a reason for restricting dispensation to circumstances where there is an 'exceptional case'.[48] Courts may consider circumstances affecting the landlord, the landlord's successors in title, the tenant's circumstances and the effect of the failure to give notice.[49] In one Rent Act case, where, prior to the granting of a tenancy, tenants were told orally that the premises were the landlord's home, that the landlord would be returning and there was no misunderstanding about this, the court considered that oral notice was just as effective as written notice and so dispensed with the formal requirements.[50] However, in another Rent Act case where no formal notice was given at the beginning of the tenancy because at that time the landlord had no intention of returning to the premises,

---

45 *Bradshaw v Baldwin-Wiseman* (1985) 17 HLR 260, CA; *Fernandes v Parvardin* (1982) 264 EG 49, CA; *Boyle v Verrall* (1997) 29 HLR 436; [1997] 1 EGLR 25, CA and *Wynne v Egan* June 1997 *Legal Action* 15, CA.

46 *Hegab v Shamash* June 1998 *Legal Action* 13, CA (judge correctly considered the fact that no tenancy had been contemplated because the defendant had intended to purchase the premises from the plaintiff and the fact that the landlord had later 'behaved in a disgraceful way' by illegally evicting the tenant and disobeying an injunction, but failed to take into account two matters: (1) the tenant had paid a deposit of £4,000 in relation to the proposed purchase, which had not been refunded and (2) the landlord had not paid the costs of the earlier proceedings concerning the illegal eviction).

47 *Boyle v Verrall* (1997) 29 HLR 436; [1997] 1 EGLR 25, CA.

48 *Boyle v Verrall* (1997) 29 HLR 436; [1997] 1 EGLR 25, CA. See also *Mustafa v Ruddock* (1998) 30 HLR 495; [1997] EGCS 87, CA.

49 *Bradshaw v Baldwin-Wiseman* (1985) 17 HLR 260, CA.

50 *Fernandes v Parvardin* (1982) 264 EG 49, CA. Cf *White v Jones* (1994) 26 HLR 477, CA.

it was not just and equitable to dispense with the requirement.[51] The fact that the parties signed what purported (wrongly) to be a temporary 'licence' agreement is not enough to make it 'just and equitable' to dispense with the need for a notice.[52]

12.35   In addition, one of the following must be satisfied:

- *At some time before the grant of the tenancy, the landlord, or if there are joint landlords, at least one of them, had occupied the dwelling-house as his or her only or principal home.*[53] A landlord's previous occupation may suffice even if it was only temporary or intermittent.[54] To satisfy this limb, the landlord need not give any reason for requiring possession.

or

- *The landlord (or at least one of them) 'requires the dwelling-house as his or his spouse's only or principal home'.* The landlord need not show that the premises are 'reasonably' required, merely that the landlord 'bona fide wants' or 'genuinely has the immediate intention' of occupying the premises.[55] Premises need not be required as a permanent residence and fairly intermittent residence will be sufficient.[56]

12.36   This ground for possession is not available to a new landlord who acquired the premises 'for money or money's worth' from an original landlord who gave a notice that possession might be recovered under this ground. There is an equivalent provision in RA 1977 Sch 15 case 11 (see para 17.46). All of the relevant case-law relates to RA 1977 Sch 15 case 9 (para 17.35), but exactly the same principles apply. The purpose of this provision is to prevent an outsider buying up tenanted property and then evicting the tenant.[57] In this connection the word 'purchasing' means 'buying'.[58] It does not include

---

51 *Bradshaw v Baldwin-Wiseman* (1985) 17 HLR 260, CA.

52 *Ibie v Trubshaw* (1990) 22 HLR 191, CA.

53 Note the contrast with the wording under RA 1977 Sch 15 case 11 (discussed at para 17.46).

54 *Naish v Curzon* (1984) 17 HLR 220, CA; *Mistry v Isidore* (1990) 22 HLR 281; [1990] 2 EGLR 97, CA and *Ibie v Trubshaw* (1990) 22 HLR 191, CA.

55 Cf RA 1977 Sch 15 case 9. See *Kennealy v Dunne* [1977] QB 837.

56 *Naish v Curzon* (1984) 17 HLR 220, CA and *Davies v Peterson* (1989) 21 HLR 63; [1989] 06 EG 130, CA.

57 *Fowle v Bell* [1946] 2 All ER 668 and *Epps v Rothnie* [1945] KB 562; [1946] 1 All ER 146.

58 *Powell v Cleland* [1948] 1 KB 262; [1947] 2 All ER 672.

'inheriting',[59] acquiring through a family settlement,[60] a transfer to a family member 'in consideration of mutual love and affection'[61] or the granting of an intermediate lease with no premium.[62]

12.37 A tenant will have a defence to proceedings under this ground if his or her tenancy was in existence at the date when the premises were bought. The relevant date is the date of exchange of contracts, and not the date of completion.[63] However, owners are entitled to rely on ground 1 if they buy premises with vacant possession and subsequently let to tenants,[64] or if they buy premises with one sitting tenant who leaves and is then replaced by another tenant.[65]

12.38 If landlords become 'landlords by purchase' they do not acquire the right to bring proceedings under ground 1 even if a new contractual tenancy on different terms is created or there are minor changes in the subject matter of the tenancy, for example, by the addition or deduction of rooms.[66] Similarly if a 'landlord by purchase' dies, the person to whom the property is transferred acquires no greater right under ground 1 than the original landlord by purchase.[67]

Ground 2: Mortgagees

12.39 The dwelling-house is subject to a mortgage granted before the beginning of the tenancy and –
(a) the mortgagee is entitled to exercise a power of sale conferred on him by the mortgage or by section 101 of the Law of Property Act 1925; and

---

59 *Baker v Lewis* [1946] 2 All ER 592, CA. Note, though, that where an owner said, before she died, that she wished her executors to offer a property for sale to the plaintiff, who then bought it, he was 'a landlord by purchase' and was not entitled to possession: *Amaddio v Dalton* (1991) 22 HLR 332.

60 *Thomas v Fryer* [1970] 1 WLR 845; [1970] 2 All ER 1, even though money was paid by one beneficiary under the will to the others.

61 *Mansukhani v Stanley* (1992) *Times* 17 April.

62 *Powell v Cleland* [1948] 1 KB 262; [1947] 2 All ER 672.

63 *Emberson v Robinson* [1953] 1 WLR 1129 and *Newton and Wife v Biggs* [1953] 2 QB 211; [1953] 1 All ER 99.

64 *Epps v Rothnie* [1945] KB 562; [1946] 1 All ER 146.

65 *Fowle v Bell* [1947] KB 242; [1946] 2 All ER 668. See also *Newton and Wife v Biggs* [1953] 2 QB 211; [1953] 1 All ER 99, where the former owner sold premises to the plaintiff on condition that he was granted a tenancy. The new landlord was not a landlord by purchase.

66 *Wright v Walford* [1955] 1 QB 363; [1955] 1 All ER 207.

67 *Littlechild v Holt* [1950] 1 KB 1; [1949] 1 All ER 933.

    (b) the mortgagee requires possession of the dwelling-house for the purpose of disposing of it with vacant possession in exercise of that power; and

    (c) either notice was given as mentioned in Ground 1 above or the court is satisfied that it is just and equitable to dispense with the requirement of notice;

    and for the purposes of this ground 'mortgage' includes a charge and 'mortgagee' shall be construed accordingly.

12.40   This ground applies if, for example, the landlord/mortgagor has defaulted on instalments of the mortgage. The purpose of this ground is to enable the landlord's mortgagee, who has consented to a borrower letting or where the mortgage deed does not prohibit letting, to obtain the full vacant possession value when exercising a power of sale. Note, though, the suggestion by Lord Denning MR that the court's equitable powers may prevent a lender from obtaining possession, 'except when it is sought bona fide and reasonably for the purpose of enforcing the security'.[68] In practice, the ground is rarely needed, since the tenant will usually be an assured shorthold tenant rather than a fully assured tenant, though it may be used by a mortgagee who wishes to bring a fixed-term assured shorthold tenancy to an end before the contractual term has expired (see para 12.26).

12.41   Note that an 'owner-occupier' notice under ground 1 must be given for this ground to apply. For the principles to be applied when a landlord seeks to persuade the court to dispense with service of a notice prior to commencement of the tenancy see para 12.34.

Ground 3: Tenancy preceded by 'holiday let'

12.42   The tenancy is a fixed-term tenancy for a term not exceeding eight months and –

    (a) not later than the beginning of the tenancy the landlord gave notice in writing to the tenant that possession might be recovered on this ground; and

    (b) at some time within the period of twelve months ending with the beginning of the tenancy, the dwelling-house was occupied under a right to occupy it for a holiday.

12.43   This ground was designed to enable landlords who let premises on holiday lets during, for example, the summer, to be able to recover possession if they let them on longer lets during the winter. However,

---

68 *Quennel v Maltby* [1979] 1 WLR 318, CA, approved in *Albany Home Loans v Massey* [1997] 2 All ER 609; (1997) 29 HLR 902, CA.

the ground as enacted operates in far wider circumstances than that. To rely on ground 3, a landlord must prove that:

- The premises were occupied at some time during the preceding 12 months for the purpose of 'a holiday'. Even if a landlord produces a copy of a 'holiday let agreement' relating to such a period, it may be possible for the tenant to prove that that agreement was 'a sham' or 'did not reflect the intention of the parties' to it.[69] However, it should be remembered that the burden of proving this lies on the tenant.
- The relevant tenancy was granted for a fixed period of not more than eight months. It is, however, arguable that ground 3 is available even where a tenant who initially agreed to rent the premises for eight months has held over and occupied the premises for a far longer period.
- Not later than the commencement of the tenancy the landlord gave written notice to the tenant that this ground for possession might be relied upon.

12.44　The court has no power to dispense with service of the notice required prior to the grant of the tenancy.[70]

Ground 4: Educational institutions

12.45　The tenancy is a fixed-term tenancy for a term not exceeding twelve months and –

(a) not later than the beginning of the tenancy the landlord gave notice in writing to the tenant that possession might be recovered on this ground; and

(b) at some time within the period of twelve months ending with the beginning of the tenancy, the dwelling-house was let on a tenancy falling within paragraph 8 of Schedule 1 to this Act.

12.46　This ground applies where, during the 12 months preceding the tenancy, the premises were let by a specified educational institution.[71] The term 'specified educational institution' includes universities, any other publicly funded institution providing further education and a number of associations and companies which have been specifically

---

69　See para 12.5 and *Buchmann v May* [1978] 2 All ER 993 and *R v Rent Officer for Camden ex p Plant* (1980) 257 EG 713; (1980) 7 HLR 15, QBD.

70　Cf *Fowler v Minchin* (1987) 19 HLR 224, CA and *Springfield Investments v Bell* (1990) 22 HLR 440, CA.

71　See Assured and Protected Tenancies (Lettings to Students) Regulations 1998 SI No 1967, as amended.

designated as such for Rent Act and Housing Act purposes, and for this purpose any private registered providers of social housing (PRP) or registered social landlord (RSL).

12.47   As with ground 3 above, notice stating that this ground may be relied on has to be served before the commencement of the tenancy.

Ground 5: Ministers of religion

12.48   The dwelling-house is held for the purpose of being available for occupation by a minister of religion as a residence from which to perform the duties of his office and –

(a) not later than the beginning of the tenancy the landlord gave notice in writing to the tenant that possession might be recovered on this ground; and

(b) the court is satisfied that the dwelling-house is required for occupation by a minister of religion as such a residence.

12.49   This ground applies to premises which are 'held for the purpose of being available for occupation by a minister of religion as a residence from which to perform the duties of his office'. Notice that possession might be required under this ground must be served before the grant of the tenancy, and the landlord must satisfy the court that the property is required for occupation by a minister of religion as a residence. It is similar to RA 1977 Sch 15 case 15.[72]

Ground 6: Demolition or reconstruction

12.50   The landlord who is seeking possession or, if that landlord is a non-profit registered provider of social housing, registered social landlord or charitable housing trust or, (where the dwelling-house is social housing within the meaning of Part 2 of the Housing and Regeneration Act 2008) a profit-making registered provider of social housing, a superior landlord intends to demolish or reconstruct the whole or a substantial part of the dwelling-house or to carry out substantial works on the dwelling-house or any part thereof or any building of which it forms part and the following conditions are fulfilled –

(a) the intended work cannot reasonably be carried out without the tenant giving up possession of the dwelling-house because –

(i)   the tenant is not willing to agree to such a variation of the terms of the tenancy as would give such access and other facilities as would permit the intended work to be carried out, or

---

72 See para 17.53.

(ii) the nature of the intended work is such that no such variation is practicable, or

(iii) the tenant is not willing to accept an assured tenancy of such part only of the dwelling-house (in this sub-paragraph referred to as 'the reduced part') as would leave in the possession of his landlord so much of the dwelling-house as would be reasonable to enable the intended work to be carried out and, where appropriate, as would give such access and other facilities over the reduced part as would permit the intended work to be carried out, or

(iv) the nature of the intended work is such that such a tenancy is not practicable; and

(b) either the landlord seeking possession acquired his interest in the dwelling-house before the grant of the tenancy or that interest was in existence at the time of that grant and neither that landlord (or, in the case of joint landlords, any of them) nor any other person who, alone or jointly with others, has acquired that interest since that time acquired it for money or money's worth; and

(c) the assured tenancy on which the dwelling-house is let did not come into being by virtue of any provision of Schedule 1 to the Rent Act 1977, as amended by Part I of Schedule 4 to this Act or, as the case may be, section 4 of the Rent (Agriculture) Act 1976, as amended by Part II of that Schedule.

For the purposes of this ground if, immediately before the grant of the tenancy, the tenant to whom it was granted or, if it was granted to joint tenants, any of them was the tenant or one of the joint tenants of the dwelling-house concerned under an earlier assured tenancy or, as the case may be, under a tenancy to which Schedule 10 to the Local Government and Housing Act 1989 applied, any reference in paragraph (b) above to the grant of the tenancy is a reference to the grant of that earlier assured tenancy, or as the case may be, to the grant of the tenancy to which the said Schedule 10 applied.

For the purposes of this ground 'registered social landlord' has the same meaning as in the Housing Act 1985 (see section 5(4) and (5) of that Act) and 'charitable housing trust' means a housing trust, within the meaning of Housing Associations Act 1985, which is a charity, within the meaning of the Charities Act 1993.

12.51 This ground is available for a landlord who 'intends to demolish or reconstruct the whole or a substantial part of the dwelling-house or to carry out substantial works'. It is very similar to the Landlord and Tenant Act 1954 s30(1)(f), which allows landlords of business tenants to oppose the grant of a new tenancy in similar circumstances.

12.52 It has been held that 'reconstruction' means 'a substantial interference with the structure of the premises and then a rebuilding, in probably a different form, of such part of the premises as has been demolished by reason of the interference with the structure'.[73]

12.53　The landlord must show that the intention to demolish or reconstruct will be fulfilled shortly after the date of the hearing.[74] There are two elements to the concept of intention: first, a genuine desire that the result will come about and, second, a reasonable prospect of bringing about that result. For example, in *Edwards v Thompson*,[75] the landlord failed to prevent the grant of a new tenancy because she had not found a developer at the time of the hearing and 'there was a real possibility that [she] would not be in a position to carry out the entire development on the termination of the current tenancy ... She had failed to show that she had the means and ability; she had not established the necessary intention'. A landlord's case is stronger if planning permission has been obtained in advance of the institution of possession proceedings, but this is not essential if it can be shown that there is a reasonable prospect of getting consent.[76]

12.54　The landlord must also show that, because of one of four specified reasons, the intended work cannot reasonably be carried out without the tenant giving up possession of the premises. 'Possession' means 'putting an end to legal rights of possession' and not merely access. For example, in *Heath v Drown*,[77] a business tenant successfully defeated the landlord's claim even though the front wall of the premises had to be entirely rebuilt and it would not be possible to occupy the premises while such work was carried out. It is not enough for the landlord to say that access is required, since most tenancies contain an express or implied[78] right of access to carry out repairs. The landlord must show that the work cannot be carried out while the tenancy still exists.

12.55　This ground for possession is not available to a landlord who has acquired his or her interest in the property by purchasing it after the grant of the tenancy.[79]

73　*Joel v Swaddle* [1957] 1 WLR 1094; [1957] 3 All ER 325 at 329 (removal of internal walls and replacement with reinforced steel joists amounted to reconstruction of a substantial part). See also *Barth v Pritchard* [1990] 20 EG 65 and *Cook v Mott* (1961) 178 EG 637, CA.

74　*Betty's Cafes Ltd v Phillips* [1959] AC 20; [1958] 2 WLR 513, HL.

75　[1990] 29 EG 41, CA. See also *Capocci v Goble* (1987) 284 EG 230, CA.

76　*Gregson v Cyril Lord* [1963] 1 WLR 41; [1962] 3 All ER 907, CA.

77　[1973] AC 498; [1972] 2 WLR 1306, CA and, for an example in the county court, *Sugarwhite v Afridi* [2002] 5 CL 425, Central London Civil Justice Centre. See too HA 1988 s16.

78　HA 1988 s16.

79　See discussion in relation to ground 1(b), para 12.36.

12.56   When a possession order is made under this ground the landlord must pay a sum equal to the tenant's reasonable removal
expenses.[80]

Ground 7: Death of the tenant

12.57   The tenancy is a periodic tenancy (including a statutory periodic tenancy) which has devolved under the will or intestacy of the former
tenant and the proceedings for the recovery of possession are begun
not later than twelve months after the death of the former tenant or,
if the court so directs, after the date on which, in the opinion of the
court, the landlord or, in the case of joint landlords, any one of them
became aware of the former tenant's death.

For the purposes of this ground, the acceptance by the landlord of
rent from a new tenant after the death of the former tenant shall not
be regarded as creating a new periodic tenancy, unless the landlord
agrees in writing to a change (as compared with the tenancy before
the death) in the amount of the rent, the period of the tenancy, the
premises which are let or any other term of the tenancy.

12.58   Although an assured tenancy may pass by will or on intestacy after the
death of the tenant, the landlord may obtain possession if proceedings
are brought within 12 months of the death of the tenant or the date on
which the landlord became aware of the death. 'Proceedings' means
the issue of a court claim, not merely the service of a notice seeking
possession.[81] No other reason for seeking possession need be given.

12.59   This ground does not apply if a spouse or or civil partner, or person
living with the tenant 'as his or her wife or husband or civil partner'
succeeds to the tenancy as a result of the statutory succession provisions in HA 1988 s17. The Act specifies that acceptance of rent after
the death of the former tenant should not be regarded as creating a
new tenancy unless the landlord has agreed in writing to a change
in the terms of the tenancy, such as an increase in rent. The ground
does not apply where the deceased tenant had a fixed-term tenancy.

80   HA 1988 s11(1).
81   *Shepping v Osada* (2001) 33 HLR 13; [2000] 30 EG 125, CA. See also *Tunbridge
     and Malling Housing Association v Reed* September 2001 *Legal Action* 24.

Ground 8: Eight weeks' or two months' rent arrears

12.60   Both at the date of the service of the notice under section 8 of this Act relating to the proceedings for possession and at the date of the hearing –

(a) if rent is payable weekly or fortnightly, at least *eight* weeks' rent is unpaid;

(b) if rent is payable monthly, at least *two* months' rent is unpaid;

(c) if rent is payable quarterly, at least one quarter's rent is more than three months in arrears; and

(d) if rent is payable yearly, at least three months' rent is more than three months in arrears;

and for the purpose of this ground 'rent' means rent lawfully due from the tenant.

12.61   This is the first of three distinct grounds for possession based on rent arrears, although in practice many landlords plead all three in the alternative. Ground 8 was amended by HA 1996 s101 to substitute eight weeks and two months in place of 13 weeks and three months.

12.62   Under ground 8, two months' rent arrears (or eight weeks' arrears in the case of a weekly tenancy) give a landlord an automatic right to a possession order. However, the landlord must prove that there were eight weeks' or two months' arrears, both at the time when the notice of the landlord's intention to bring proceedings was served and at the date of the hearing. 'The date of the hearing' is the date when the claim is heard. It is not the date fixed for the hearing if, on that date, an adjournment is granted without a hearing taking place at all.[82]

12.63   A possession order cannot be made under ground 8 unless the landlord proves that a valid HA 1988 section 8 notice has been served.[83] There is no discretion to dispense with a section 8 notice if ground 8 is relied on – see section 8(5) (para 12.11).

12.64   Money which a defendant has been ordered to pay into court to await the outcome is available 'on account of rent arrears' and ignoring such money would lead to an artificial and inequitable result when calculating arrears for the purpose of ground 8.[84] In *Day v Coltrane*,[85] a case where possession was sought under ground 8, the Court of Appeal held that an uncleared cheque which was delivered

---

82 *North British Housing Association Limited v Matthews* [2004] EWCA Civ 1736; [2005] 1 WLR 3133.

83 *Capital Prime Plus plc v Wills* (1999) 31 HLR 926, CA.

84 *Etherington v Burt* [2004] EWHC 95, QBD (Fulford J).

85 [2003] EWCA Civ 342; [2003] 1 WLR 1379. See too *Homes v Smith* [2000] Lloyd's Law Rep Banking 139.

to the landlord at or before the hearing and accepted by him, or which he was bound by an earlier agreement to accept, was to be treated as payment on the date of delivery provided that it was subsequently paid on first presentation.

12.65   Delays on the part of a local authority in making housing benefit payments do not provide a defence to proceedings brought under ground 8.[86] In cases where arrears have been caused by delays in paying housing benefit, it is worth considering issuing a witness summons to compel the appropriate official to attend at court to explain personally the reason for any delay.[87]

12.66   In a case where an outright order for possession was made under HA 1988 Sch 2 ground 8, but the landlord subsequently accepted the tenant's offer to pay rent and £100 per month off arrears, the Court of Appeal held that the landlord had done nothing to affect the legal relations between the parties.[88] No new or different terms were come to. The landlord had no intention to create a new tenancy. The legal relations between the parties were governed by the terms of the order until the landlord took a position inconsistent with the order.

12.67   As ground 8 is mandatory, once the court is satisfied that the ground is proved, there is no power to adjourn or suspend.[89] In practice, where a tenant faces a claim for possession under ground 8, the only way for him or her to obtain time to pay the rent arrears (or to sort out housing benefit) is to apply for an adjournment *before* evidence has been heard. The Court of Appeal considered such applications in *North British Housing Association Limited v Matthews*.[90] It held that:

• There is no doubt that it is a perfectly proper exercise of the court's discretion to adjourn, if a case has to be taken out of the list because there is no judge available, or because there has been over-listing, or because the defendant is prevented by ill health from attending court.

---

86 *Marath v MacGillivray* (1996) 28 HLR 484, CA.

87 See further chapter 37.

88 *Stirling v Leadenhall Residential 2 Ltd* [2001] EWCA Civ 1011; [2002] 1 WLR 499; [2001] 3 All ER 645.

89 HA 1988 s9(6).

90 [2004] EWCA Civ 1736; [2005] 1 WLR 3133. See too cf *Razack v Osman* [2001] 9 CL 426; December 2001 *Legal Action* 22. Cf, eg, *R v A Circuit Judge ex p Wathen* (1976) 33 P&CR 423, QBD; *Birmingham Citizens Permanent Building Society v Caunt* [1962] Ch 883, ChD; *Bristol CC v Lovell* [1998] 1 WLR 446, HL and *Hoffman v Cueto-Corondo and Filipe* April 2000 *Legal Action* 32.

- The court retains jurisdiction to grant an adjournment before it is satisfied that the landlord is entitled to possession. It may be a proper exercise of discretion to adjourn the hearing before the court is satisfied that the landlord is entitled to possession, for example, where there is an arguable claim for damages which can be set off against arrears or where the tenant shows that there is an arguable defence based on accord and satisfaction or estoppel arising from an agreement whereby the landlord accepts an offer by the tenant to pay off the current rent and arrears at a certain rate in return for not pursuing the claim for possession.

- An adjournment may also be granted where the court is satisfied that there is a seriously arguable case on public law grounds for challenging the landlord's decision to claim possession: such a challenge may be based either on conventional judicial review grounds or on the basis that the decision to take proceedings on a mandatory ground amounts to a breach of the tenant's rights under the European Convention on Human Rights (see para 12.74).

- However, it is not legitimate to adjourn to enable the tenant to pay off arrears and so defeat the claim for possession, unless there are exceptional circumstances, for example, if a tenant is robbed on the way to court, or if a computer failure prevents the housing benefit authority from being able to pay benefit due until the day after the hearing date. The fact that arrears are attributable to maladministration on the part of the housing benefit authority is not an exceptional circumstance.

- Once the court has expressed the conclusion that it is satisfied that the landlord is entitled to possession, there is no power to grant an adjournment in any circumstances (see sections 7(3) and 9(6)). However, the court cannot be 'satisfied' within the meaning of section 9(6) until the judge has given a judgment and effect is given to that judgment in a perfected order of the court.

12.68   As with all rent arrears grounds, it is important for advisers to consider whether or not there has been any breach of repairing obligations on the landlord's part. If there has, any damages awarded on a counterclaim based on the disrepair may be set off against arrears of rent and may result in the arrears being wiped out or reduced below the level of two months' arrears.

12.69   Where the tenancy is an assured shorthold tenancy, if the landlord has not protected the tenant's deposit in an authorised scheme in accordance with HA 2004 s213, he or she may become liable to pay to the tenant a sum equal to three times the amount of the deposit.[91] Such an award may reduce or even exceed the rent arrears, and it may be argued that the award should be set against the 'rent lawfully due' for the purposes of ground 8.

12.70   It is also important to check that the claimant has complied with the provisions of the Landlord and Tenant Act 1987 s48, which require demands for rent to include the landlord's name and address, and that landlords supply tenants with details of an address in England and Wales where notices may be served. If landlords fail to comply with these provisions, rent is not due until the failure has been rectified.[92]

12.71   Assured tenancies may include contractual provisions for rent reviews. However, if such a clause is not in substance or reality a provision for the fixing of rent, but a provision for the landlord to recover possession otherwise than in accordance with the statutory scheme, it may not be enforceable. This is a question of fact. In *Bankway Properties v Penfold-Dunsford*,[93] the Court of Appeal found that such a clause permitting a landlord to increase the rent of a tenant in receipt of housing benefit to £25,000 per annum was a mere device, which enabled the landlord, effectively when it chose, to recover possession. In those circumstances it was unenforceable and the landlord's claim based upon arrears was dismissed.

12.72   A rent review clause in a fixed-term assured tenancy which purports to continue to apply once the fixed term has ended and has been superseded by a statutory periodic tenancy is of no effect.[94] In order to increase

91   HA 2004 s214(4).

92   See *Dallhold Estate (UK) Pty Ltd v Lindsay Trading Properties Inc* [1994] 17 EG 148, CA and *Hussain v Singh* [1993] 31 EG 75, CA, but cf *Rogan v Woodfield Building Services Ltd* (1995) 27 HLR 78; [1995] 20 EG 132, CA and *Drew-Morgan v Hamid-Zadeh* (2000) 32 HLR 216; [1999] 26 EG 156, CA.

93   [2001] EWCA Civ 528; [2001] 26 EG 164. See too *Home 4 Rent Ltd v Killelea Housing Aid Update*, Issue 136, April 2004; June 2004 *Legal Action* 30, St Helens County Court and *Shah v Mori* January 2004 *Legal Action* 30.

94   *London District Properties Management Ltd and others v Goolamy* [2009] EWHC 1367 (Admin). HA 1988 s13(1)(b) provides that, where a contractual periodic tenancy contains its own rent review clause, it is not necessary for the landlord to use the notice of increase procedure under s13(2) and the tenant will be unable to make a reference to the Rent Assessment Committee. Where the agreement provides for a simple form of notice of variation of the rent, this will suffice for the purposes of s13(1)(b): it is not necessary for the rent review provision to provide a fixed agreed uplift or formula for the determination of the new rent in order to oust the jurisdiction of the Rent Assessment Committee: *Contour Homes v Rowen* [2007] EWCA Civ 842; (2007) *Times* 13 July.

the rent in the absence of agreement, the landlord must therefore serve a valid notice of increase under HA 1988 s13(2), which may be referred by the tenant to the Rent Assessment Committee[95] within the period specified in the notice. However, if the landlord has requested a rent increase otherwise than through the statutory procedure and the tenant has paid the higher amount, he or she may be treated as having agreed to a variation of the rent.[96]

12.73   In *Riverside Housing Association v White*,[97] the tenancy agreement provided that the landlord association 'may increase the rent by giving the tenant four weeks' notice in writing ...'. The agreement went on to state: 'The rent payable will be increased annually with effect from the first Monday of June each year.' The landlord in fact served notices of increase in successive years to take effect in the first week of April. The House of Lords held that, on a fair reading, the effect of the review clauses was that the landlord was entitled to increase the rent once a year on 28 days' notice, but that such a notice could take effect any time on or after the first Monday in June. The rent had therefore been lawfully increased on the April dates.

12.74   There remains an argument that ground 8 may conflict with articles 6, 8 and 14 of the European Convention on Human Rights ('the Convention'/ECHR) and article 1 of the First Protocol to the Convention. This is especially so when ground 8 proceedings are brought by a PRP/RSL, as a social landlord. In many cases rent arrears are caused by housing benefit problems, sometimes without the tenant being at fault, for example, where housing benefit forms or supporting documentation are mislaid by the local authority. It is hard to see how, in such circumstances, it is 'necessary', within the meaning of article 8(2), to deprive tenants of their homes. Furthermore, the legislation lacks any procedural safeguards which would allow tenants to challenge the decision to bring or continue proceedings.[98] Such a contention would be strengthened by reliance on article 14 and a comparison with the rights of secure tenants under the Housing Act 1985, who are not subject to a mandatory ground for possession

95 HA 1988 s13(4)(a).

96 HA 1988 s13(4)(b).

97 [2007] UKHL 20; [2007] 4 All ER 97.

98 See *Lambeth LBC v Kay; Leeds CC v Price* [2006] UKHL 10; [2006] 2 WLR 570, in which Lord Hope said that the making of a possession order in *Connors v UK* Application no 66746/01; [2004] HLR 52; (2004) *Times* 10 June, ECtHR failed to meet the third requirement in article 8(2). 'It failed to do so in that case because the making of the order was not attended by the procedural safeguards that were required to establish that there was a proper justification for the interference with the applicant's right to respect for his private and family life and his home.'

based on rent arrears. What is the 'objective and reasonable justification' for the distinction between assured and secure tenants of PRPs/RSLs? How does it pursue a 'legitimate aim'? The position is less clear cut if the claimant is a private landlord because the court would then have to balance the landlord's rights under article 1 of the First Protocol against the tenant's article 8 rights.

12.75   Ultimately, the question is whether it is legitimate for a registered social landlord to seek to deprive the court of a discretion which it would otherwise have. Any challenge to the use of ground 8 on these principles requires consideration of two major preliminary issues. First, can a decision to bring proceedings on ground 8 be challenged on public law grounds or human rights grounds and, if so would such a challenge be by way of a defence in the county court or by an adjournment of the possession claim followed by an application for judicial review? Second, is a housing association or other PRP/RSL a body which is amenable to challenge on public law grounds? Only if these questions may be answered affirmatively will it be possible to examine the merits of such a challenge in specific cases.

12.76   For a full discussion of these questions, see chapters 25 and 26. For present purposes, the starting point is the decision of the House of Lords in *Kay v Lambeth LBC*,[99] in which the majority held that there were only two possible 'gateways' for a potential defence to a claim for summary judgment in possession cases, namely:

(a) a seriously arguable challenge under Article 8 ECHR to the law itself under which the possession order was made, but only where it is possible to adapt the domestic law to make it more compliant with Convention rights; and

(b) a seriously arguable challenge on conventional judicial review grounds to the local authority's decision to recover possession.

12.77   Following the decision of the Lower Chamber of the European Court of Human Rights in *McCann v UK*,[100] the House of Lords revisited its decision in *Kay* in *Doherty v Birmingham CC*[101] and held that the formulation adopted in *Kay* needed to be modified to some extent. It was open to a defendant to argue under gateway (b) that a possession order should not be made unless the court is satisfied that the decision to seek a possession order was not unreasonable. Lord Hope said:

I think that in this situation it would be unduly formalistic to confine the review strictly to traditional *Wednesbury* grounds. The

99 [2006] UKHL 10; [2006] 2 WLR 570.
100 European Court of Human Rights Application no 19009/04, 13 May 2008.
101 [2008] UKHL 57.

considerations that can be brought into account in this case are wider. In my opinion, the test of reasonableness should be ... whether the decision to recover possession was one which no reasonable person could reach. (para 55)

12.78   Lord Scott agreed that the test was whether the decision was one to which the council could not reasonably have come but, in applying that test, there was no disharmony between conventional judicial review grounds and the occupier's rights under article 8. He stated:

> [Local authorities] are obliged when deciding to terminate tenancies and recover possession of residential properties to act consistently with article 8. If a decision, for example to serve a notice to quit, is inconsistent with the article 8 rights of the person on whom it is served, the decision would be unlawful and the notice to quit devoid of effect...Such a defence would, if raised, be dealt with by a county court judge as part of the possession proceedings. A separate judicial review application to the High Court is not necessary. If factual issues need to be resolved in order for the article 8 defence to be dealt with, that can be done before the county court judge ... (para 84)

12.79   Lord Mance considered that the modification which Lord Hope had proposed (above) would create a category of case 'in which review on traditional *Wednesbury* grounds was relaxed to become a more straightforward examination of reasonableness' (para 163). It seems clear that the courts expect article 8 principles to form an integral part of a public authority's decision-making process, such that a failure to have regard to those principles will arguably constitute a conventional ground of judicial review, and in some circumstances provide a basis for a public law defence.

12.80   It is evident from *Kay* and *Doherty* that – at least in cases concerning non-secure tenancies or where there is no longer a right to occupy – public law defences on traditional judicial review grounds may now be raised and decided in the county court, with evidence as to factual disputes where appropriate. Where, however, statute provides that the county court must grant possession on the landlord's proof of compliance with certain procedural steps, there is (at the time of publication) some uncertainty about whether a challenge of this kind may be brought by way of defence in the county court. In *Manchester CC v Pinnock*,[102] the Court of Appeal held in relation to demoted tenancies that the county court's powers were restricted to considering whether the statutory procedure had been followed, and did not extend to reviewing the substance of a decision on judicial

102 [2009] EWCA Civ 852.

review principles or its consistency with Convention rights. Such a challenge could be raised only by an application for judicial review in the Administrative Court, and it would be necessary to ask the county court to adjourn the claim for possession for this purpose.

12.81 A similar conclusion was reached in relation to introductory tenancies in *Mullen v Salford CC*,[103] in which the Court of Appeal held that the language of the Housing Act 1996 was clear and mandatory, and excluded consideration by the court of 'gateway (b)' defences. The Court of Appeal's decision in *Manchester CC v Cochrane*[104] remained good law, and an adjournment of possession proceedings should be granted if a public law point is seriously arguable. If the decisions in *Pinnock* and *Mullen* are upheld by the Supreme Court, the same reasoning is likely to apply to ground 8 claims. The tenant who wishes to challenge a decision to bring proceedings on ground 8 would therefore need to request an adjournment of the county court hearing in order to bring judicial review proceedings.

12.82 Second, any challenge to a decision to bring a ground 8 claim on public law grounds depends on the status of a housing association or other PRP/RSL as a 'public body' or as performing 'public functions' for the purposes of the Human Rights Act 1998 s6. The law is currently in a state of development. In *R (Weaver) v London & Quadrant Housing Trust and Equality & Human Rights Commission (Intervenor)*,[105] the use of ground 8 by the housing trust was challenged by the tenant as being in breach of a 'legitimate expectation'. It was argued for the tenant that because the trust had stated in the tenancy agreement that it would comply with guidance issued by the Housing Corporation,[106] its decision to use ground 8 rather than a discretionary ground for possession was unlawful. The Administrative Court accepted that that the housing trust's function of allocating and managing social housing was a function of a public nature, with the effect that the Trust was to be regarded as a public authority for the purposes of the Human Rights Act 1998 s6(3)(b). However, the tenant's application

---

103 [2010] EWCA Civ 336.

104 (1999) 31 HLR 810.

105 [2009] EWCA Civ 587; [2010] 1 WLR 363.

106 Housing Corporation Regulatory Circular 02/07 gave the following guidance: 'Ground 8 of Schedule 2 of the Housing Act 1988 is a mandatory ground that can be used to seek possession of an assured tenancy where a tenant has arrears of more than eight weeks' rent. *Before using Ground 8, associations should first pursue all other reasonable alternatives to recover the debt.* Where the use of Ground 8 forms part of an arrears and eviction policy, tenants should have been consulted and governing board approval for the policy should have been given' (emphasis added).

for judicial review was dismissed. The court held that the guidance was in the nature of a 'target duty' only; it was not the equivalent of a statutory rulebook. Moreover, the tenant did not have any personal awareness of the guidance, and hence had no legitimate expectation,

12.83   On the housing trust's appeal against that decision (there being no cross-appeal by the tenant), the Court of Appeal held that the Administrative Court had asked itself the wrong question in considering whether the function of housing management was a public function. The court and the parties were in agreement that the trust was a 'hybrid body' falling within the Human Rights Act 1998 s6(3)(b) (ie, a body with a mixture of private and public functions). The question was whether the act of terminating a tenancy or evicting a tenant amounted to an act of a private or public character. If the act was merely a private act, then the trust would not be considered a public authority for these purposes.[107] By a majority, the court dismissed the appeal. It held that, when terminating the tenancy, the housing trust was carrying out a public, rather than a private, act. The act of termination was not merely a private law contractual act. The context in which the act took place was crucial and termination was inextricably bound up with the housing trust's public functions. The functions of allocating and terminating tenancies were each part of deciding who in society should receive the public benefit of social housing; they were in essence two sides of the same coin.

12.84   Thus, in the present state of the law, it seems that most housing associations and other PRPs/RSLs will be amenable to challenge on conventional judicial review grounds incorporating ECHR principles in respect of decisions concerning the allocation of social housing or in relation to the eviction of a tenant or other person from his or her home.[108]

12.85   While the challenge in *Weaver* to the use of ground 8 on the basis of a breach of legitimate expectation failed, this should not discourage advisers from using other arguments in this context. Such contentions may be based on the landlord's policy of using ground 8 without genuine consideration of alternative means of recovery or on the decision in an individual case, as being disproportionate and unnecessary in all the circumstances of the case.

---

107 Human Rights Act 1998 s6(5).

108 See also *R (McIntyre) v Gentoo Group Limited* [2010] EWHC 5 (Admin) (mutual exchange refused because of rent arrears: public law arguments could be raised in a private law claim in the county court on the ground of unreasonable refusal of consent); and *Eastlands Homes Partnership Limited v Whyte* [2010] EWHC 695 (QB).

Discretionary grounds for possession

Ground 9: Suitable alternative accommodation

12.86   Suitable alternative accommodation is available for the tenant or will be available for him when the order for possession takes effect.

12.87   As with the Rent Act 1977,[109] the availability of suitable alternative accommodation, either at the time of the hearing or when the order is to take effect, is a ground for possession. Housing Act 1988 Sch 2 Part III[110] gives further clarification of the matters to be taken into account when determining whether or not accommodation is suitable.

1.   For the purposes of Ground 9 above, a certificate of the local housing authority for the district in which the dwelling-house in question is situated, certifying that the authority will provide suitable alternative accommodation for the tenant by a date specified in the certificate, shall be conclusive evidence that suitable alternative accommodation will be available for him by that date.

2.   Where no such certificate as is mentioned in paragraph 1 above is produced to the court, accommodation shall be deemed to be suitable for the purposes of ground 9 above if it consists of either –

(a) premises which are to be let as a separate dwelling such that they will then be let on an assured tenancy, other than –

(i) a tenancy in respect of which notice is given not later than the beginning of the tenancy that possession might be recovered on any of Grounds 1 to 5 above, or

(ii) an assured shorthold tenancy, within the meaning of Chapter II of Part 1 of this Act, or

(b) premises to be let as a separate dwelling on terms which will, in the opinion of the court, afford to the tenant security of tenure reasonably equivalent to the security afforded by Chapter I of Part I of this Act in the case of an assured tenancy of a kind mentioned in sub-paragraph (a) above, and, in the opinion of the court, the accommodation fulfils the relevant conditions as defined in paragraph 3 below.

3.   (1) For the purposes of paragraph 2 above, the relevant conditions are that the accommodation is reasonably suitable to the needs of the tenant and his family as regards proximity to place of work, and either –

(a) similar as regards rental and extent to the accommodation afforded by dwelling-houses provided in the neighbourhood by

---

109 Section 98(1)(a), see para 17.1.

110 Cf RA 1977 Sch 15 Pt IV. HA 1988 Sch 2 Pt III is very similar to the comparable Rent Act provisions, although the alternative accommodation should be let on an assured tenancy, rather than on a protected tenancy.

any local housing authority for persons whose needs as regards extent are, in the opinion of the court, similar to those of the tenant and his family; or

(b) reasonably suitable to the means of the tenant and to the needs of the tenant and his family as regards extent and character; and

that if any furniture was provided for use under the assured tenancy in question, furniture is provided for use in the accommodation which is either similar to that so provided or is reasonably suitable to the needs of the tenant and his family.

(2) For the purposes of subparagraph (1)(a) above, a certificate of a local housing authority stating –

(a) the extent of the accommodation afforded by dwelling-houses provided by the authority to meet the needs of tenants with families of such number as may be specified in the certificate, and

(b) the amount of the rent charged by the authority for dwelling-houses affording accommodation of that extent,

shall be conclusive evidence of the facts so stated.

4. Accommodation shall not be deemed to be suitable to the needs of the tenant and his family if the result of their occupation of the accommodation would be that it would be an overcrowded dwelling-house for the purposes of Part X of the Housing Act 1985.

5. Any document purporting to be a certificate of a local housing authority named therein issued for the purposes of this Part of this Schedule and to be signed by the proper officer of that authority shall be received in evidence and, unless the contrary is shown, shall be deemed to be such a certificate without further proof.

6. In this Part of this Schedule 'local housing authority' and 'district' in relation to such an authority, have the same meaning as in the Housing Act 1985.

12.88   When a possession order is made under this ground, the landlord must pay a sum equal to the tenant's reasonable removal expenses.[111]

Local authority certificate that accommodation available

12.89   Housing Act 1988 Sch 2 Part III para 1 provides that a certificate from a local housing authority confirming that it will provide suitable alternative accommodation for the tenant is conclusive evidence that suitable alternative accommodation will be available[112] at the date specified in the certificate. The certificate must be from the housing authority for the area in which the relevant premises are situated,

---

111 HA 1988 s11(1).
112 *Wallasey v Pritchard* (1936) 3 LJNCCR 35.

otherwise it is totally ineffective.[113] It seems that there is no requirement that the certificate provide details of the address or size of the
suitable alternative accommodation. If, after issuing a certificate, a
local authority failed to provide suitable alternative accommodation,
the court would have power under HA 1988 s9(2) to stay execution
of the order on an application by the tenant. There is no requirement that the certificate be in any particular form: a signed letter will
suffice.

12.90 In view of the shortage of local authority accommodation, it is
extremely rare for local authorities to provide certificates under paragraph 1. Accordingly, whether or not suitable accommodation is
available is usually decided in the light of the guidelines in Schedule
2 Part III paras 2–6.

No local authority certificate that accommodation available

12.91 If there is no local authority certificate the landlord must prove that
the requirements set out below are satisfied (see HA 1988 Sch 2 Part
III paras 2–4).

12.92 **Equivalent security of tenure**

> 2 ... (a) ... premises which are to be let as a separate dwelling ... on an
> assured tenancy, other than [one under which] possession might be
> recovered on any of Grounds 1 to 5 above, or ... an assured shorthold
> tenancy ... or ... premises ... let as a separate dwelling on terms which
> will ... afford to the tenant security of tenure reasonably equivalent to
> ... an assured tenancy ...

12.93 It is clear that the accommodation offered must be in a single building:
accommodation offered in two separate houses cannot be suitable.[114]
Similarly, the requirement is not satisfied if the premises offered consist
of two separate parts of a building which are separated by another flat[115]
or if the alternative accommodation involves sharing a kitchen.[116]

12.94 Housing Act 1988 Sch 2 Part III para 2(b) provides that accommodation may be suitable even if it is not let on an assured tenancy,
if the security of tenure provided is 'reasonably equivalent' to that
provided by HA 1988 Part I Chapter I. In determining whether this
condition is satisfied it is necessary to look strictly at the rights which
the landlord of the alternative accommodation has to terminate the

---

113 *Sills v Watkins* [1956] 1 QB 250, CA.
114 *Sheehan v Cutler* [1946] KB 339.
115 *Selwyn v Hamill* [1948] 1 All ER 70, CA.
116 *Cookson v Walsh* (1954) 163 EG 486.

tenancy and not at common practice or the assurances given by the new landlord.[117] What is 'reasonably equivalent' security will depend on the facts. In one Rent Act case an unprotected fixed-term tenancy of 16 years was held to provide reasonably equivalent security.[118] In another, an unprotected fixed-term tenancy of ten years offered to a tenant aged 57 and her husband aged 58 was held to provide reasonably equivalent security.[119] It is not necessary for the alternative accommodation to be let by the same landlord. It is enough that it is available and suitable.

12.95   If the tenant against whom possession is sought occupies premises as a sole tenant, a joint tenancy or even joint ownership of a house cannot be suitable alternative accommodation since the other joint tenant or joint owner may unilaterally terminate the tenancy or force a sale.[120] It is not clear whether other premises owned by the tenant can amount to suitable alternative accommodation.[121]

12.96   **Closeness to workplace**

> 3. (1) ... the accommodation is reasonably suitable to the needs of the tenant and his family as regards proximity to place of work ...

12.97   A 'place of work' need not be a factory or an office. It can be an area or the location in which the tenant's work is based.[122] The court should consider not only distance from work, but also the time which it would take to travel, the means of transport available and any inconvenience which would be caused.[123] The work may be unpaid.[124]

---

117   Eg, *Sills v Watkins* [1956] 1 QB 250, CA, where the offer of alternative accommodation was a council tenancy with no security of tenure (prior to the advent of secure tenancies introduced by HA 1980) . Although in practice the council did not evict tenants without reason, this offer did not comply with the statutory requirements.

118   *Fulford v Turpin* [1955] CLY 2324.

119   *Edwards v Cohen* (1958) 108 LJ 556.

120   *Barnard v Towers* [1953] 1 WLR 1203; [1953] 2 All ER 877, CA; *Greenwich LBC v McGrady* (1982) 6 HLR 36, CA; *Hammersmith and Fulham LBC v Monk* (1992) 39 EG 135; (1992) 24 HLR 203, HL and *Notting Hill Housing Trust v Brackley* [2001] EWCA Civ 601; [2001] 35 EG 106.

121   See the conflicting dicta in *Barnard v Towers* [1953] 1 WLR 1203; [1953] 2 All ER 877, CA and *Standingford v Probert* [1950] 1 KB 377, CA.

122   *Yewbright Properties Ltd v Stone* (1980) 40 P&CR 402, CA.

123   *Yewbright Properties Ltd v Stone* (1980) 40 P&CR 402, CA. See also *Minchburn Ltd v Fernandez* (1987) 19 HLR 29; May 1985 *Legal Action* 66, CA, where alternative accommodation was held not to be suitable because it would have doubled the tenant's 30-minute walk to work to one hour. The needs of the particular tenant count, not those of a reasonable tenant.

124   *Dakyns v Pace* [1948] 1 KB 22.

12.98 When considering the workplaces of other members of the tenant's family, the court can consider only those members actually residing with the tenant. The phrase 'member of family' is given its ordinary meaning as understood by an ordinary person.[125] It has been held to include a son, daughter-in-law[126] and mother-in-law.[127] It will also now include a long-term gay or lesbian partner.[128] It is possible that a lodger may be counted as a member of the family.[129]

12.99 **Rental and size**

> 3. (1) ... the accommodation is... (a) similar as regards rental and extent to the accommodation afforded by dwelling-houses provided in the neighbourhood by any local housing authority for persons whose needs as regards extent are ... similar to those of the tenant and his family; or (b) reasonably suitable to the means of the tenant and to the needs of the tenant and his family as regards extent and character ...

12.100 The landlord can satisfy this test in either of two ways. First, the landlord may produce a certificate from the local authority for the area in which the tenant rents his or her current accommodation setting out the kind of accommodation which would be provided for people of similar needs. The certificate should probably state the number of rooms which would be provided and give some indication of the dimensions of such rooms.[130] A certificate which stated that local authority rents would be more than twice as high as the alternative accommodation offered did not show that the accommodation offered was similar as regards rental.[131] It is for a judge to decide, after considering the certificate, whether or not the accommodation offered is similar to that which the local authority would provide. In *Jones v Cook*,[132] the Court of Appeal set aside a possession order where

---

125 *Standingford v Probert* [1950] 1 KB 377, CA; *Scrace v Windust* [1955] 1 WLR 475, CA. See also, in another context, *Fitzpatrick v Sterling Housing Association* [2001] 1 AC 27; [1999] 3 WLR 1113, HL and *Ghaidan v Godin-Mendoza* [2004] UKHL 30; [2004] 3 WLR 113.

126 *Standingford v Probert* [1950] 1 KB 377, CA.

127 *Scrace v Windust* [1955] 1 WLR 475, CA.

128 *Fitzpatrick v Sterling Housing Association* [2001] 1 AC 27; [1999] 3 WLR 1113; [1999] 4 All ER 705 and *Ghaidan v Godin-Mendoza* [2004] UKHL 30; [2004] 3 WLR 113.

129 *Standingford v Probert* [1950] 1 KB 377, CA, cf *Stewart v Mackay* 1947 SLT 250.

130 Per Edmund Davies LJ in *Macdonnell v Daly* [1969] 1 WLR 1482, CA, cf *Wallasey v Pritchard* (1936) 3 LJNCCR 35.

131 *Turner v Keiller* 1950 SC 43 and *Robert Thackeray's Estate Ltd v Kaye* (1989) 21 HLR 160, CA.

132 (1990) 22 HLR 319, CA.

a judge had simply accepted the contents of a certificate which had stated that the property offered by the landlord was 'similar in extent to council-owned dwelling-houses which may be provided in the neighbourhood for families consisting of husband, wife and three children'.

12.101   If there is no local authority certificate (and it is comparatively rare for a landlord to obtain such a certificate), the court should consider whether the property offered is reasonably suitable. Accommodation may be suitable even though it is inferior to the accommodation currently occupied by the tenant.[133] It may also be suitable even though it is considerably smaller.[134] Part only of the accommodation currently rented by the tenant may amount to suitable alternative accommodation if at the time of the hearing the tenant is not occupying all of the accommodation let (for example, because part is sublet[135]) or because it is larger than the tenant requires.[136]

12.102   When the court considers the 'needs' of the tenant and the tenant's family, it should primarily consider their housing needs and not incidental advantages, such as the use of a stable and paddock.[137] The court may, however, take into account a tenant's professional needs, such as an artist using a room as a studio[138] or the need for a tenant to entertain business associates.[139] Accommodation may be unsuitable if it is too large,[140] if it is in disrepair,[141] if it lacks a bathroom and

133 Per Lord Asquith in *Warren v Austen* [1947] 2 All ER 185, CA.

134 *Quick v Fifield* (1982) 132 NLJ 140 (less than half the size) and *Hill v Rochard* [1983] 1 WLR 478, CA.

135 *Parmee v Mitchell* [1950] 2 KB 199, CA; *Thompson v Rolls* [1926] 2 KB 426; [1926] All ER 257 and *Yoland v Reddington* (1982) 263 EG 157, CA.

136 *Macdonnell v Daly* [1969] 1 WLR 1482, CA (two out of three rooms) and *Mykolyshyn v Noah* [1970] 1 WLR 1271, CA (current accommodation less sitting room).

137 *Hill v Rochard* [1983] 1 WLR 478, CA, although such matters will be relevant when considering reasonableness. See also *Montross Associated Investments v Stone* March 2000 *Legal Action* 29, CA ('magnificent views' overlooking Hyde Park). On tenants' 'needs' generally, see H W Wilkinson, 'What does a tenant need?' (1985) 135 NLJ 933, where there is a summary of the facts of some of the cases noted in the following footnotes.

138 *Macdonnell v Daly* [1969] 1 WLR 1482, CA.

139 *De Markozoff v Craig* (1949) 93 SJ 693, CA. Cf *Stewart v Mackay* 1947 SLT 250 (tenant's inability to take in lodgers); *Wilcock v Booth* (1920) 122 LT 678 (loss of off-licence) and *Warren v Austen* [1947] 2 All ER 185, CA (unreasonable to make order where alternative accommodation not large enough to enable tenant to continue to take lodgers).

140 *Islington LBC v Metcalfe and Peacock* August 1983 *LAG Bulletin* 105.

141 If there is any question of disrepair in the alternative accommodation it is always wise for the tenant to obtain a full survey report.

toilet,[142] if it means the tenant living with his estranged wife[143] or if it does not have a garden in which the tenant's children can play.[144] Accommodation in a shared house may be unsuitable for a tenant currently living alone.[145]

12.103 The court should take into account environmental factors. For example, in *Redspring Limited v Francis*,[146] the alternative accommodation was on a busy traffic thoroughfare, had no garden, was next door to a fish shop and was near to a hospital, cinema and public house with the result that there were people 'coming and going' at all hours of the day and night, whereas the tenant's current accommodation was in a quiet and secluded residential street. However, environmental factors can be taken into account only so far as they relate to the character of the property. The proximity of the tenant's friends and cultural interests are not relevant here, although they clearly are relevant when the court comes to consider reasonableness.[147]

12.104 Furniture

3. (1) ... if any furniture was provided for use under the assured tenancy in question, furniture is provided for use in the accommodation which is either similar to that so provided or is reasonably suitable to the needs of the tenant and his family ...

12.105 Availability

... accommodation is available for the tenant or will be available for him when the order in question takes effect (see ground 9).

12.106 The suitable alternative accommodation must be available for the particular tenant.[148] In determining whether it is available, accommodation which was previously available is completely irrelevant,[149] although refusals by the tenant of previous offers of other accommodation may be considered when the court decides the question of reasonableness and may be relevant when the court considers costs. It is sufficient for the landlord to show that such accommodation is

---

142 *Esposito v Ware* (1950) 155 EG 383.
143 *Heglibiston Establishments v Heyman* (1977) 246 EG 567, CA.
144 *De Markozoff v Craig* (1949) 93 SJ 693, CA, cf in the public sector, *Enfield LBC v French* (1984) 17 HLR 211, CA.
145 *Barnard v Towers* [1953] 1 WLR 1203; [1953] 2 All ER 877, CA.
146 [1973] 1 WLR 134. See also *Dawncar Investments Ltd v Plews* [1993] 13 EG 110; (1993) 25 HLR 639, CA.
147 *Siddiqu v Rashid* [1980] 1 WLR 1018, CA.
148 *Topping v Hughes* [1925] NI 90.
149 *Kimpson v Markham* [1921] 2 KB 157.

available even if it is to be rented from another person. It need not have been available when the Housing Act 1988 section 8 notice was served or when proceedings were issued, although such circumstances would no doubt be relevant to costs.

12.107 **Overcrowding**

> 4. Accommodation shall not be deemed to be suitable to the needs of the tenant and his or her family if the result of their occupation of the accommodation would be that it would be an overcrowded dwelling-house for the purposes Part X of the Housing Act 1985.

12.108 For the definition of overcrowding, see para 17.60.

Reasonableness

12.109 It should be remembered that even if the court is satisfied that suitable alternative accommodation exists, the court must still consider whether it is reasonable to make a possession order. Failure to do this makes the possession order a nullity.[150]

12.110   The correct approach to reasonableness in this context was considered by the Court of Appeal in the Rent Act case of *Whitehouse v Loi Lee*.[151] Here, the landlord wished to obtain possession and sell the property in order to fund her pension. The tenant did not wish to move as she had lived in her existing home for 45 years and had many associations with the immediate locality. The county court judge made a possession order. However, the Court of Appeal held that:

> the decision ... required the judge to look at the question from all angles, in particular by considering the effect on the parties if an order was made and also if an order was not made.

Although the judge had considered the effects on both parties of making an order, he had only considered the effect on the tenant of making no order. The judge had accepted that the landlord was financially secure and there was no suggestion she would suffer financial hardship if she were unable to sell the flat with vacant possession. Consequently, considering the effects on both parties if an order was made, and also if an order was not made, it was not reasonable to make an order for possession.

---

150 See chapter 13 and *Minchburn Estates v Fernandez (No 2)* (1986) 19 HLR 29, CA; *Treismann v Cotterell* September 1996 *Legal Action* 14 and *Hildebrand v Constable* September 1996 *Legal Action* 14.

151 [2009] EWCA Civ 375; [2009] L&TR 29.

Ground 10: Rent arrears

12.111   Some rent lawfully due from the tenant –
(a) is unpaid on the date on which the proceedings for possession are begun; and
(b) except where subsection (1)(b) of section 8 of this Act applies, was in arrears at the date of the service of the notice under that section relating to those proceedings.

12.112   A landlord must prove that there were rent arrears both at the date when proceedings were begun and (unless the court considers it 'just and equitable' to dispense with service of a notice seeking possession) when the notice was served. In theory, a possession order may be made even if the arrears are paid off before the hearing, although in most circumstances there would be strong grounds for arguing that it would not be reasonable to make an order.[152]

12.113   If rent has been tendered to the landlord on a regular basis when it has become due, but has not been accepted by the landlord, there is a complete defence to the proceedings based on alleged rent arrears if the tenant pays into court all the rent which is due.[153] Accordingly, if a landlord refuses to accept rent, it is important that the tenant continues to tender rent regularly (for example, by sending cheques by recorded delivery) and saves any rejected rent in a separate bank or building society account so that the rent can be paid into court as soon as proceedings are issued.[154] Failure to provide a rent book does not disentitle the landlord from claiming that rent is lawfully due.[155]

12.114   When advising a tenant who faces a claim for possession based on rent arrears, it is important to check exactly what rent is lawfully recoverable, and, in particular, whether the landlord has been claiming too much rent. Note that if a landlord has failed to furnish the tenant with an address at which notices may be served, Landlord and Tenant Act 1987 s48 provides that any rent which would otherwise be due is to be treated as not being due before the landlord has rectified the failure.[156]

---

152 *Hayman v Rowlands* [1957] 1 WLR 317; [1957] 1 All ER 321, CA; *Sopwith v Stutchbury* (1983) 17 HLR 50, CA, but see *Lee-Steere v Jennings* (1988) 20 HLR 1, CA.

153 *Bird v Hildage* [1948] 1 KB 91, CA.

154 See CPR 37.2 which states that a defence of tender can only be relied on if the amount tendered is paid into court.

155 *Shaw v Groom* [1970] 2 QB 504, CA.

156 See *Dallhold Estates (UK) Pty Ltd v Lindsay Trading Properties Inc* [1994] 17 EG 148, CA; *Hussain v Singh* [1993] 31 EG 75, CA, but cf *Rogan v Woodfield Building Services Ltd* (1994) 27 HLR 78; [1995] 20 EG 132, CA and *Drew-Morgan v Hamid-Zadeh* (2000) 32 HLR 316; [1999] 26 EG 156, CA.

12.115   Advisers should also check whether there is any possibility of a counterclaim for breach of repairing obligations (see para 23.33), or whether there has been any failure by the relevant authorities to make payments of housing benefit (see para 37.18).

12.116   In considering whether it is reasonable to make an order under this ground, and under ground 11, and if so what order to make, the court should bear in mind the Protocol for Possession Claims based on Rent Arrears (see appendix D). The Protocol applies to possession claims made by social landlords in respect of secure and assured (but not assured shorthold) tenancies, which are based solely on rent arrears. The aim of the Protocol is to 'encourage more pre-action contact between landlords and tenants and to enable court time to be used more effectively'. Among the requirements of the Protocol are:

- early contact by the landlord to discuss the cause of arrears;
- landlord and tenant to agree affordable sums for the tenant to pay towards arrears;
- landlord to provide tenant with detailed rent statements at least every 13 weeks, and also on request;
- landlord to attempt to identify any particular difficulties which the tenant has, such as poor literacy, possible issues of mental capacity, disability or vulnerability for other reasons such as youth or age, and to consider the need for a community care assessment;
- consideration of direct deductions from benefits, where possible;
- landlord to offer assistance to the tenant with any problems in claiming housing benefit, and with the tenant's consent to make direct contact with the council's housing benefit department before beginning proceedings;
- landlord to advise tenant of sources of assistance with general debt problems;
- tenant to comply with any agreement to pay current rent and reasonable instalments towards the arrears.

12.117   Even after notices have been served, the landlord should make efforts to contact the tenant to discuss the cause of the arrears and to attempt to reach agreement on repayment. If nevertheless it is necessary to bring a claim for possession, the landlord must inform the tenant of the hearing date and advise him or her to attend court; and must, at least ten days before the hearing, provide the tenant with up-to-date rent statements and disclose what information the landlord has about the tenant's housing benefit claim.

12.118   Where a landlord unreasonably fails to comply with the terms of the Protocol, this should be taken into account by the court in deciding:

- whether it is reasonable to make a possession order;
- (in cases where the court has a discretion) whether a claim should be adjourned, struck out or dismissed; and
- who should pay the costs.

Ground 11: Persistent delay in paying rent

12.119 Whether or not any rent is in arrears on the date on which proceedings for possession are begun, the tenant has persistently delayed paying rent which has become lawfully due.

12.120 Even if there are no arrears on the date when possession proceedings are issued, persistent delay in paying rent that is due is a ground for possession. The phrase 'persistent delay' is not defined but is likely to have the same meaning as in the Landlord and Tenant Act 1954 s30(1)(b), ie, one instalment of rent has been in arrears for a significant period of time or instalments have persistently been paid late, or both.[157]

12.121 It is important to check that the rent claimed was lawfully due – see paras 12.68 onwards (compliance with the Landlord and Tenant Act 1987 s48, the possibility of a set-off for breach of repairing obligations, etc).

Ground 12: Breach of any obligation

12.122 Any obligation of the tenancy (other than one related to the payment of rent) has been broken or not performed.

12.123 The obligation must be one which is binding on tenants in their capacity as tenants and not one of a personal nature or collateral to the agreement.[158] This can be determined by asking whether the obligation would be equally applicable if the tenancy were assigned to another person. For example, an obligation to remain in the employment of the landlord is a personal one, and breach of it cannot give rise to grounds for possession under ground 12. Similarly, a covenant that the tenant should give up possession by a particular date cannot be relied on by a landlord since it is inconsistent with the provisions of the Housing Act 1988.[159]

---

157 See *Hopcutt v Carver* (1969) 209 EG 1069, CA and *Horowitz v Ferrand* [1956] CLY 4843.

158 *RMR Housing Society v Combs* [1951] 1 KB 486; [1951] 1 All ER 16, CA and *Paddington Churches Housing Association v Boateng* January 1999 *Legal Action* 27.

159 *Barton v Fincham* [1921] 2 KB 291; *Hunt v Bliss* (1919) 89 LJKB 174 and *Artizans, Labourers and General Dwellings Company Ltd v Whitaker* [1919] 2 KB 301.

12.124   A court can make an order for possession provided that there has been a breach of an obligation under the tenancy agreement, even if the breach no longer exists at the date of the hearing. It is not confined to considering breaches which are persisting at the time of the hearing.[160]

12.125   It is outside the scope of this book to consider in detail the meaning of covenants which may be found in tenancy agreements. The following brief points should, however, be noted.

Covenants against subletting

12.126   The exact wording of the covenant is important because the three forms of phraseology frequently used have different meanings. A 'covenant against subletting' without any further qualification is merely a prohibition against subletting the whole of the premises which are let.[161] It does not prohibit subletting of part or sharing the premises with licensees. A 'covenant against subletting the whole or any part of the premises' does prohibit the subletting of the whole or any part of the premises, but does not cover taking in lodgers or sharing the premises with anyone else who is not a formal subtenant. A covenant which is wide enough to cover all of these activities is one to the effect that the tenant 'cannot sublet the whole or any part of the premises or share occupation with any other person', or that 'the tenant can only use the premises as a private residence in his sole occupation'.[162] A tenant who has friends who share living expenses staying in the premises is not in breach of a covenant against parting with possession, taking lodgers or using premises for business purposes.[163] The mere fact that a name other than that of the tenant appears on the electoral register relating to the premises is not by itself evidence that anyone other than the tenant is living in the accommodation.[164]

12.127   Housing Act 1988 s15(1) provides that it is an implied term of every *periodic* assured tenancy that, except with the consent of the landlord, the tenant shall not assign the tenancy in whole or in part, or sublet or part with possession of the whole or any part of the dwelling. There is no provision that the landlord's consent is not to be

---

160 *Brown v Davies* [1958] 1 QB 117; [1957] 3 All ER 401, CA.

161 *Cook v Shoesmith* [1951] 1 KB 752, CA.

162 *Falgor Commercial SA v Alsabahia* (1986) 18 HLR 123, CA.

163 *Heglibiston Establishments v Heyman* (1977) 246 EG 567, CA. See also *Blanway Investments Ltd v Lynch* (1993) 25 HLR 378, CA.

164 *Metropolitan Properties Co Ltd v Griffiths* (1982) 43 P&CR 138, CA.

unreasonably withheld,[165] and the landlord therefore has an absolute right to refuse consent. Where the periodic tenancy is *contractual* (ie, it did not come into being at the end of a fixed-term assured tenancy), the implied term is excluded if either (a) there is an express provision in the agreement governing the conditions on which the tenant may assign, sublet, etc or (b) the tenant paid a premium on the grant or renewal of the tenancy.[166] The implied term under section 15(1) will, however, apply to statutory periodic tenancies. Where the tenancy is a fixed-term tenancy, the tenant's rights to assign, sublet, etc will depend on the terms of the agreement and, if assignment or subletting is permitted with consent, the Landlord and Tenant Act 1927 s19 will operate to ensure that consent may not be unreasonably withheld.

Covenant against user for immoral purposes

12.128 This is basically designed to prevent prostitution. It does not prohibit two unmarried people living together.[167]

Covenant against business user

12.129 This can have a wide meaning. It may include the carrying out of the activities of a political organisation on the premises[168] and the taking in of two paying lodgers.[169]

Unfair terms

12.130 If a term is unfair, it may breach the Unfair Terms in Consumer Contracts Regulations 1999.[170] These regulations (unlike the Unfair Contract Terms Act 1977) apply to tenancy agreements because landlords and tenants may be 'suppliers' and 'consumers' within the meaning of the regulations.[171] A term is unfair if it has not been 'individually negotiated' and 'contrary to the requirement of good faith, it causes a significant imbalance in the parties' rights and obligations arising under the contract, to the detriment of the consumer'. Such a term

---

165 Landlord and Tenant Act 1927 s19 is excluded from this implied term.

166 HA 1998 s15(3).

167 *Heglibiston Establishments v Heyman* (1977) 246 EG 567, CA.

168 *Florent v Horez* (1983) 268 EG 807, CA.

169 *Tendler v Sproule* [1947] 1 All ER 193, CA. Cf *Lewis v Weldcrest Ltd* [1978] 1 WLR 1107; (1978) 247 EG 211, CA.

170 SI No 2083.

171 *R (Khatun) v Newham LBC* [2003] EWHC 2326 (Admin); [2005] QB 37.

is not binding on the tenant.[172] In *Peabody Trust Governors v Reeve*,[173] a clause in the landlord's standard assured tenancy agreement provided that the terms of the tenancy could be varied unilaterally by the landlord on notice to the tenant. It was held that the clause created a significant imbalance in the parties' rights and obligations, and was not enforceable. The fact that the landlord was a social landlord and a charity was a factor to be taken into account, but did not make it fair that the landlord should be able to change any term of the tenancy. The court referred to guidance[174] produced by the Office of Fair Trading, according to which a term giving the landlord a wide discretion to impose new burdens on the tenant was likely to fall foul of the 1999 Regulations.

Waiver of a breach of a tenancy term

12.131   See para 17.17.

Ground 13: Waste or neglect

12.132   The condition of the dwelling-house or any of the common parts has deteriorated owing to acts of waste by, or the neglect or default of, the tenant or any other person residing in the dwelling-house and, in the case of an act of waste by, or the neglect or default of, a person lodging with the tenant or a subtenant of his, the tenant has not taken such steps as he ought reasonably to have taken for the removal of the lodger or subtenant.

For the purposes of this ground, 'common parts' means any part of a building comprising the dwelling-house and any other premises which the tenant is entitled under the terms of the tenancy to use in common with the occupiers of other dwelling-houses in which the landlord has an estate or interest.

12.133   This ground is similar to RA 1977 Sch 15 case 3 (para 17.23) but slightly wider, in that it applies not only to the premises let, but also to common parts.

12.134   It may apply even though there has been no breach of any term of the tenancy or of any common law duty.[175] The court should, however, take into account only neglect or waste which has taken place

---

172   Unfair Terms in Consumer Contracts Regulations 1999 SI No 2083 regs 5(1) and 8.

173   [2008] EWHC 1432 (Ch); [2009] L&TR 6.

174   OFT 356: *Guidance on unfair terms in tenancy agreements*, Office of Fair Trading, November 2001.

175   *Lowe v Lendrum* (1950) 159 EG 423, where it was also said that 'neglect' is used in the context of tenant-like conduct.

since the tenant became tenant of the premises. For example, in a Rent Act case where a son who was living with aged parents became a statutory tenant by succession after their death, it was wrong for the court to take into account his failure to do any works in the garden before their death.[176]

Ground 14: Nuisance or annoyance or criminal conviction

12.135 The tenant or a person residing in *or visiting* the dwelling-house –
   (a) has been guilty of conduct causing or likely to cause a nuisance or annoyance to a person residing, visiting or otherwise engaging in lawful activity in the locality, or
   (b) has been convicted of –
      (i) using the dwelling-house or allowing it to be used for immoral or illegal purposes, or
      (ii) an indictable offence committed in, or in the locality of, the dwelling-house.

12.136 This ground is identical in form to HA 1985 Sch 2 ground 2 – see para 3.68 onwards for a fuller discussion than can be provided here. It applies to both the conduct of the tenant and the conduct of any person residing in or visiting the premises. There is no requirement that any person visiting the premises and causing a nuisance should be there lawfully (although it would rarely be reasonable for the court to make a possession order where the perpetrator's visits were against the wishes of the tenant). The widening of the original ground in the 1988 Act[177] from conduct which *is* a nuisance or annoyance to neighbours to conduct which *is likely to cause nuisance or annoyance to others* is designed to meet two problems. First, the new ground avoids the apparent need for the landlord to produce victims as witnesses to whom nuisance or annoyance has been caused.[178] Second, the ground covers nuisance or annoyance to people who are not neighbours, such as housing officers.

12.137 Section 12 of the Anti-Social Behaviour Act 2003 places a statutory duty on housing associations to publish policies and procedures for tackling anti-social behaviour. Guidance formerly issued by the late Housing Corporation[179] advised that such policies should

---

176 *Holloway v Povey* (1984) 15 HLR 104, CA.

177 By HA 1996 s148.

178 But cf *Frederick Platts Co v Grigor* [1950] 1 All ER 941, CA, where it was held that the court can infer that nuisance or annoyance has been caused without hearing evidence from anyone affected.

179 Regulatory Circular 07/04, *Tenancy Management: Eligibility and Evictions*, para 3.

show a commitment to using the full range of tools now available to tackle anti-social behaviour, and that eviction should be considered only when other interventions have failed to protect the wider community.

12.138   In *Raglan Housing Association Ltd v Fairclough*,[180] the landlord sought possession under ground 14(b)(ii) on the basis of offences which had occurred while the tenant had a tenancy of another property owned by the same housing association. The Court of Appeal considered that it was arguable that the first limb of ground 14(b) – conviction for using the dwelling-house or allowing it to be used for immoral or illegal purposes – related only to the use the tenant had made of the premises during the current tenancy. However, the second limb of ground 14(b) – conviction of an indictable offence committed in, or in the locality, of the dwelling-house – was broader and was related to behaviour in the locality in general. The tenant could properly be held responsible for the way in which he had behaved in the locality both before he became a tenant and afterwards.

Ground 14A: Violence to occupier

12.139   The dwelling-house was occupied (whether alone or with others) by *a married couple, a couple who are civil partners of each other,* a couple living together as husband and wife, *or a couple living together as if they were civil partners* and –

(a) one or both of the partners is a tenant of the dwelling-house,

(b) the landlord who is seeking possession is a non-profit registered provider of social housing, a registered social landlord or a charitable housing trust or, where the dwelling-house is social housing within the meaning of Part 2 of the Housing and Regeneration Act 2008, a profit-making registered provider of social housing,

(c) one partner has left the dwelling-house because of violence or threats of violence by the other towards –

(i) that partner, or

(ii) a member of the family of that partner who was residing with that partner immediately before the partner left, and

(d) the court is satisfied that the partner who has left is unlikely to return.

For the purposes of this ground 'registered social landlord' and 'member of the family' have the same meaning as in Housing Act 1996 Part I and 'charitable housing trust' means a housing trust, within the meaning of the Housing Associations Act 1985, which is a charity within the meaning of the Charities Act 1993.

180 [2007] EWCA Civ 1087; [2008] HLR 21.

12.140 This ground was introduced by HA 1996 s149. It does not apply to private landlords, and is designed to enable registered social landlords or charitable housing trusts to recover possession where one partner has left because of violence or threats of violence and is unlikely to return. It is identical to HA 1985 Sch 2 ground 2A in respect of secure tenants – see para 3.108.

12.141 There is no requirement that the partner who has left should give evidence to the effect that he or she is unlikely to return. It may be that such evidence would be advisable from the landlord's point of view unless the period of absence is long or there is other evidence which enables the court to draw that inference.

12.142 The ground applies where the landlord is a non-profit registered provider of social housing (in England) or a registered social landlord (in Wales) or a charitable housing trust. See para 6.1.

12.143 'Member of another's family' includes spouses, civil partners, people who live together as husband and wife or as if they were civil partners, parents, grandparents, children, grandchildren, brothers, sisters, uncles, aunts, nephews and nieces. Relationships of 'half-blood' are to be treated as relationships of the 'whole blood' and stepchildren are to be treated as children.[181]

12.144 A landlord seeking to rely on this ground must satisfy the court that notice of proceedings for possession has been served on the partner who has left the home or that it has taken reasonable steps to do so or that it is just and equitable to dispense with the requirement of such a notice (see para 12.24).[182]

12.145 Where possession is sought under ground 14A, it is not sufficient that the alleged violence or threats of violence were merely one of a range of causes of equal efficacy in the victim's departure from the property. For the ground to be made out it has to be established that the alleged violence or threat of violence was the dominant, principal and real cause of the departure.[183]

Ground 15: Deterioration of furniture

12.146 The condition of any furniture provided for use under the tenancy has, in the opinion of the court, deteriorated owing to ill-treatment by the tenant or any other person residing in the dwelling-house and, in the case of ill-treatment by a person lodging with the tenant or by

181 HA 1996 s62, as amended by Civil Partnership Act 2004 Sch 8 para 51.
182 HA 1988 s8A, as inserted by HA 1996 s150.
183 *Camden LBC v Mallett* (2001) 33 HLR 20, CA.

a subtenant of his, the tenant has not taken such steps as he ought reasonably to have taken for the removal of the lodger or subtenant.

Ground 16: Premises let to employees

12.147   The dwelling-house was let to the tenant in consequence of his employment by the landlord seeking possession or a previous landlord under the tenancy and the tenant has ceased to be in that employment.

12.148   This ground for possession is wider than case 8, the comparable Rent Act ground (see para 17.33). It applies whether or not the employer requires the premises for another employee. Usually, the employer and the landlord have to be the same person. However, if health service employees are employed by a health service body (for example, a health authority) but live in premises owned by the Department of Health, the secretary of state, when bringing possession proceedings, may rely on ground 16.[184]

Ground 17: Tenancy induced by false statement

12.149   The tenant is the person, or one of the persons, to whom the tenancy was granted and the landlord was induced to grant the tenancy by a false statement made knowingly or recklessly by –
(a) the tenant, or
(b) a person acting at the tenant's instigation.

12.150   This ground was introduced by Housing Act 1996 s102 and is identical to Housing Act 1985 Sch 2 ground 5 as amended (see para 3.126).

Prohibition orders, demolition orders, etc

12.151   A tenant is not entitled to rely on the protection of the Housing Act 1988 or the Rent Act 1977 when a prohibition order under the Housing Act 2004[185] or a demolition order[186] is in force in relation to the premises. The effect of such orders is to remove security of tenure.[187] They do not, however, provide landlords with an automatic right to

---

184 National Health Service and Community Care Act 1990 s60(6) and Sch 8 para 10.

185 HA 2004 s33 (provided that possession is necessary for the purpose of complying with the order).

186 HA 1985 s270(3), as amended (recovery of possession after the making of a demolition order) and *Marela v Machorowski* [1953] 1 QB 565.

187 *Johnson v Felton* (1994) 27 HLR 65, CA.

possession. Any tenancy must still be terminated in the usual way (for example, by notice to quit).[188] Local authorities have a statutory duty to rehouse residential occupiers who have been displaced from residential accommodation as a result of such housing orders, irrespective of whether they come within the category of 'priority need' within the meaning of HA 1996 s189.[189] However, the making of a management order under the Housing Act 2004 does not prevent the continuance of an assured tenancy or the continued operation of the Housing Act 1988.[190]

12.152   Housing Act 1985 s582 restricts the recovery of possession of tenanted premises in a HMO or renewal area which have been compulsorily purchased by a local authority. The execution of any possession order may be suspended for a period of three years after the making of the compulsory purchase order – although this provision does not apply where it is the local authority that is seeking possession.[191]

Reasonableness

12.153 The criteria for establishing whether or not it is reasonable to make an order for possession against an assured tenant are the same as those used in proceedings against Rent Act protected tenants or Housing Act secure tenants (see chapter 13).

Other court orders

Removal expenses

12.154 Housing Act 1988 s11 provides:

(1) Where a court makes an order for possession of a dwelling-house let on an assured tenancy on Ground 6 or Ground 9 in Schedule 2 to this Act (but not on any other ground), the landlord shall pay to the tenant a sum equal to the reasonable expenses likely to be incurred by the tenant in removing from the dwelling-house.
(2) Any question as to the amount of the sum referred to in subsection (1) above shall be determined by agreement between the landlord and the tenant or, in default of agreement, by the court.

188 *Aslan v Murphy (No 2)* [1990] 1 WLR 766; [1989] 3 All ER 130, CA.
189 Land Compensation Act 1973 s39(1).
190 HA 2004 s124.
191 HA 1985 s582(7).

(3) Any sum payable to a tenant by virtue of this section shall be recoverable as a civil debt due from the landlord.

12.155 A landlord can be compelled to pay removal expenses only where possession is obtained on the ground that the landlord wishes to demolish or reconstruct premises (ground 6) or where suitable alternative accommodation is available (ground 9).

Misrepresentation and concealment

12.156 If, after a possession order has been made, the court is satisfied that the landlord obtained the order 'by misrepresentation or concealment of material facts', the court may order the landlord to pay 'such sum as appears sufficient as compensation for damage or loss sustained ... as a result of the order'.[192] Generally, a landlord who deprives a tenant of an assured tenancy by deceit is liable to a claim for damages,[193] and the tenant may be able to apply to set aside the possession order. However, HA 1988 s12 provides additional remedies where a landlord has obtained possession by misrepresentation or concealment. The section applies not only to misrepresentations made during the course of the hearing, but also to any made earlier which result in a tenant consenting to a possession order.[194]

12.157   There are few reported cases dealing with the quantum of damages. In *Neil v Kingsnorth*,[195] a case decided in 1988, a landlord converted a property into four flats and sold them off immediately after obtaining a possession order under RA 1977 Sch 15 case 9. The tenant, who had found better accommodation by the date of the court hearing, obtained special damages of £180, general damages of £750 for worry and inconvenience and exemplary damages of £5,000.

12.158   It seems that, unlike a claim founded in deceit, the court may, unless exemplary or aggravated damages are awarded, be limited by the wording of the section to considering the loss suffered by the tenant, and not any benefit accruing to the landlord, although tenants' advisers should bear in mind Lord Denning's comments that a statutory tenancy (under the Rent Act 1977) is a valuable asset[196] and the

---

192 HA 1988 s12.
193 Under the tort of deceit. See *Mafo v Adams* [1970] 1 QB 548, CA.
194 *Thorne v Smith* [1947] KB 307, CA.
195 March 1988 *Legal Action* 21.
196 See remarks by Lawton LJ in *Drane v Evangelou* [1978] 1 WLR 455; [1978] 2 All ER 437 at 443, that to deprive a tenant of the roof over his or her head is one of the most serious torts imaginable. See also Clayton and Tomlinson, 'Damages for loss of a Rent Act tenancy' January 1986 *Legal Action* 10.

decision in *Murray v Lloyd*,[197] where, in another context, damages for the loss of a statutory tenancy were assessed at a quarter of the vacant possession freehold value of the premises.

Adjournment, stays and suspension

12.159 If a court is satisfied that one of the mandatory grounds for possession applies, it has only the very limited power to adjourn,[198] stay or suspend an order for possession which is provided for by HA 1980 s89(1), ie, for 14 days, unless exceptional hardship would be caused, in which case the time for giving up possession may be delayed for up to six weeks. 'Exceptional hardship' is not defined by the Act and there have been no reported cases on its meaning.

12.160 Otherwise, where the ground(s) proved against the tenant is subject to the test of reasonableness, HA 1988 s9 (see para 33.13) gives the court a discretion to adjourn proceedings, stay or suspend the execution of any order or postpone the date of possession for such period or periods as the court thinks fit, although when doing so the court must impose conditions relating to the payment of rent or rent arrears unless doing so would 'cause exceptional hardship ... or would otherwise be unreasonable'. This means that if a landlord satisfies the court that one of the discretionary grounds is proved, the court has exactly the same discretion as it has when making an order against a tenant enjoying the protection of the Rent Act 1977 or the Housing Act 1985.

12.161 A spouse or former spouse or civil partner or former civil partner who remains in occupation has the same rights in relation to adjournments, stays, suspensions and postponements as the tenant.[199]

---

197 [1989] 1 WLR 1060; [1990] 1 EGLR 274, ChD.
198 For the power to adjourn in exceptional circumstances before a mandatory ground is satisfied, see para 12.67.
199 HA 1988 s9(5). See chapter 35.

Reasonableness

Introduction

13.1   Issues concerning the reasonableness of the making of a possession order on discretionary grounds against a secure tenant are considered in detail in chapter 3 – see especially paras 3.35 and 3.81. Readers are advised to consult that chapter first. This chapter considers particular factors concerning reasonableness which apply to claims for possession on discretionary grounds against assured and Rent Act tenants.

13.2   Landlords seeking possession on any of the discretionary grounds in the Housing Act (HA) 1988 Sch 2 Part II or the Rent Act (RA) 1977 Sch 15 Part I, as well as proving the ground for possession, must also satisfy the court that it is reasonable to make an order for possession. The question of reasonableness, which is an 'overriding requirement',[1] gives the court a very wide discretion.[2] Reasonableness must always be considered where a landlord has pleaded one of the discretionary grounds, so judgment cannot be entered in default in such cases.[3] Failure to consider reasonableness means that the judgment is a nullity,[4] even where the tenant consents to the possession order.[5] If the case is appealed because the county court judge failed to consider the question of 'reasonableness', it should usually be sent back to the county court for a new trial.[6]

---

1   See Megarry, *The Rent Acts*, 11th edn, Stevens, 1988, p387 and *Smith v McGoldrick* (1976) 242 EG 1047, CA.

2   *Bell London and Provincial Properties Ltd v Reuben* [1947] KB 157; [1946] 2 All ER 547, CA and *Plaschkes v Jones* (1982) 9 HLR 110, CA.

3   CPR 55.7(4). See too *Peachey Property Corporation Ltd v Robinson* [1967] 2 QB 543, CA; *Smith v Poulter* [1947] KB 339 and *Salter v Lask (No 1)* [1924] 1 KB 754.

4   *Shrimpton v Rabbits* (1924) 131 LT 478; *Minchburn v Fernandez (No 2)* (1987) 19 HLR 29, CA and *Verrilli v Idigoras* [1990] EGCS 3, CA.

5   See para 33.45 and *R v Bloomsbury and Marylebone CC ex p Blackburne* (1985) 275 EG 1273, CA (where a tenant consented to an order for possession in return for a payment of £11,000 – the order was set aside because the judge had not considered the question of reasonableness); *Hounslow LBC v McBride* (1999) 31 HLR 143, CA (in a rent arrears case 'by consent' suspended possession order made without hearing evidence set aside); *R v Birmingham City Council ex p Foley* March 2001 *Legal Action* 29, QBD (nuisance suspended possession order 'by consent' set aside) and *Baygreen Properties Ltd v Gil* [2002] EWCA Civ 1340; [2002] 49 EG 126; [2003] HLR 12 (possession claim against assured shorthold tenant compromised at court by a consent order which provided that the landlord recover possession, all future proceedings be stayed, and the landlord pay the tenant £2,500 before she left the property: order set aside).

6   *Smith v McGoldrick* (1976) 242 EG 1047, CA, but see a number of the cases noted at notes 46–50. The Court of Appeal is increasingly substituting its own judgment as to reasonableness. See also *Richmond Housing Partnership v Green* January 2010 *Legal Action* 31.

In *Cumming v Danson*,[7] Lord Greene MR said:

> ... in considering reasonableness ... it is, in my opinion, perfectly clear
> that the duty of the Judge is to take into account all relevant circum-
> stances as they exist at the date of the hearing. That he must do in
> what I venture to call a broad commonsense way as a man of the
> world, and come to his conclusion giving such weight as he thinks
> right to the various factors in the situation. Some factors may have
> little or no weight, others may be decisive, but it is quite wrong for
> him to exclude from his consideration matters which he ought to take
> into account.

Relevant considerations

13.3   In considering reasonableness, courts should not be concerned with
the propriety or impropriety of a landlord's policy or rules, but rather
with 'the reasonableness in the particular case of ordering possession'.[8] Every case turns on its own facts. Cases on reasonableness
should be seen as examples. They rarely lay down prescriptive rules.

13.4   It has, however, been said that judges should consider only matters that have been expressly pleaded when taking into account reasonableness. In *Laimond Properties Ltd v Raeuchle*,[9] the Vice-Chancellor
indicated that a judge had been wrong to take into account matters
which had not been pleaded. He should have constrained himself to
those matters properly pleaded by the landlord to establish whether
the order for possession should have been suspended. The Vice-
Chancellor said:

> In considering whether it is reasonable to make an order ... the judge
> should consider all the relevant circumstances: but that is not a con-
> sideration at large. It is, or should be, a consideration in accordance
> with the pleadings. In my judgment, the matters proposed to be relied
> upon by the landlord in support of the contention that it would be
> reasonable to make an order for possession ... must be pleaded by the
> landlord.

However, in practice landlords rarely follow this guidance and courts
rarely penalise them for failing to do so.

13.5   There are many examples of circumstances which can be relevant:

- *The financial position of the parties.* For example, a financial gain
  which the landlord would receive from a possession order and the

---

7 [1942] 2 All ER 653 at 655.
8 *Barking and Dagenham LBC v Hyatt* (1992) 24 HLR 406, CA.
9 (2001) 33 HLR 113; April 2000 *Legal Action* 31, CA.

financial loss resulting to the tenant,[10] the fact that the landlord's only motive is pecuniary gain,[11] loss of income to the tenant from subletting[12] or from taking paying guests.[13]

- *Hardship to people living with either party.* For example, overcrowding affecting the landlord's invalid sister and refugees living with them,[14] although the court may inquire as to the cause of such overcrowding.[15]
- *The length of time the tenant has lived in the premises.*[16]
- *Previous warnings by the landlord, breaches of agreements with the landlord, and earlier possession orders.*[17]
- *The landlord's reasons for wishing to obtain possession.*[18]
- *The health of the parties and their relatives.*[19]
- *The age of the parties.*[20]
- *In suitable alternative accommodation cases, the effects on both parties respectively of making an order, and of making no order.*[21]
- *In suitable alternative accommodation cases, the loss of amenities.* For example, a garden,[22] the importance of leisure activities and spiritual needs.[23]

---

10 *Cresswell v Hodgson* [1951] 1 All ER 710, CA and *Williamson v Pallant* [1924] All ER 623.

11 *Battlespring Ltd v Gates* (1983) 268 EG 355, CA.

12 *Yoland v Reddington* (1982) 263 EG 157, CA and *Amrit Holdings Co Ltd v Shahbakhti* [2005] EWCA Civ 339; [2005] HLR 30.

13 *Warren v Austen* [1947] 2 All ER 185, CA.

14 *Cumming v Danson* [1942] 2 All ER 653, CA. See also *Rhodes v Cornford* [1947] 2 All ER 601, CA.

15 *Wint v Monk* (1981) 259 EG 45, CA. See also *Hardie v Frediani* [1958] 1 WLR 318, CA.

16 *Battlespring v Gates* (1983) 268 EG 355, CA; *Minchburn v Fernandez (No 2)* (1986) 19 HLR 29, CA; *Hildebrand v Constable* September 1996 *Legal Action* 14; *Laimond Properties Ltd v Raeuchle* [2000] L&TR 319; December 1999 *Legal Action* 21; (2001) 33 HLR 113, CA and *Gallagher v Castle Vale Housing Action Trust* [2001] EWCA Civ 944; (2001) 33 HLR 72, CA.

17 *Laimond Properties Ltd v Raeuchle* December 1999 *Legal Action* 21; (2001) 33 HLR 113, CA and *Manchester City Council v Higgins* [2005] EWCA Civ 1423; [2006] 1 All ER 841.

18 *Minchburn v Fernandez (No 2)* (1986) 19 HLR 29, CA.

19 *Briddon v George* [1946] 1 All ER 609; *Hensman v McIntoch* (1954) 163 EG 322; *Williamson v Pallant* [1924] 2 KB 173; [1924] All ER 623 and *Croydon LBC v Moody* (1999) 31 HLR 738, CA.

20 *Battlespring v Gates* (1983) 268 EG 355, CA.

21 *Whitehouse v Loi Lee* [2009] EWCA Civ 375.

22 *Warren v Austen* [1947] 2 All ER 185, CA.

23 *Siddiqu v Rashid* [1980] 1 WLR 1018, CA.

- *The public interest.* In particular, in cases involving anti-social behaviour, the effect of the tenant's behaviour on adjoining occupiers and the obligation of landlords towards other tenants.[24]
- *The conduct of the parties.* For example, a tenant's past failure to decorate or tend the garden,[25] or lies told by parties in court to substantiate their claim.[26] Where there is an admitted breach of covenant and the tenant intends to continue breaching the covenant, possession should be refused only in 'very special cases'.[27] It may be reasonable to make a possession order where the behaviour complained of is not that of the tenant, but that of other family members where the tenant has failed to prevent that behaviour,[28] but not necessarily against a tenant who is powerless to rectify the situation,[29] or where the person responsible for the anti-social behaviour has left.[30]
- *In rent arrears cases, whether or not the tenant is entitled to welfare benefits and, if so, whether or not they have been paid.*[31]

13.6 Particular factors relating to reasonableness apply to the various grounds for possession.

Rent arrears

13.7 In proceedings based on rent arrears, a judge who has found that a ground for possession is proved should first ask whether it is reasonable to make a possession order at all and then ask whether the order

---

24 *West Kent Housing Association v Davies* (1999) 31 HLR 415, CA; *Cresswell v Hodgson* [1951] 2 KB 92; [1951] 1 All ER 710, CA; *Woking BC v Bistram* (1995) 27 HLR 1, CA; *Wandsworth LBC v Hargreaves* (1994) 27 HLR 142, CA; *Grogan v Greenwich LBC* (2001) 33 HLR 140; (2000) *Times* 28 March, CA; *Portsmouth City Council v Bryant* [2000] EHLR 287; (2000) 32 HLR 906, CA and *Wallasey v Pritchard* (1936) 3 LJNCCR 35. See too the cases listed at note 47.

25 *Brown v Davies* [1958] 1 QB 117; [1957] 3 All ER 401, CA and *Holloway v Povey* (1984) 15 HLR 104, CA.

26 *Yelland v Taylor* [1957] 1 WLR 459; [1957] 1 All ER 627, CA.

27 *Sheffield CC v Green* (1994) 26 HLR 349, CA and *Accent Peerless Ltd v Kingsdon* [2007] EWCA Civ 1314.

28 *Kensington and Chelsea RLBC v Simmonds* [1996] 3 FCR 246; (1997) 29 HLR 507, CA; *West Kent Housing Association v Davies* (1999) 31 HLR 415, CA and *Newcastle upon Tyne CC v Morrison* (2000) 32 HLR 891; [2000] L&TR 333, CA.

29 *Portsmouth City Council v Bryant* (2000) 32 HLR 906; [2000] EHLR 287, CA; cf *Knowsley HT v McMullen* [2006] EWCA Civ 539; (2006) *Times* 22 May.

30 *Gallagher v Castle Vale Housing Action Trust* [2001] EWCA Civ 944; (2001) 33 HLR 810, CA.

31 *Brent LBC v Marks* (1999) 31 HLR 343, CA and *Second WRVS Housing Society v Blair* (1987) 19 HLR 104, CA.

should be postponed or execution stayed or suspended under HA 1988 s9 or RA 1977 s100(2).[32]

13.8   In practice it is rare for the court to consider it reasonable to make an absolute order for possession unless there are substantial arrears. See, for example, *Woodspring DC v Taylor*,[33] at para 3.37. It is very unusual for any order for possession to be made if all the arrears have been paid into court before the hearing or if the arrears are very low,[34] although it may be reasonable to make an order if the tenant has a bad history of payment and, in particular, if proceedings based on rent arrears have been issued in the past.[35] The possibility of payment of housing benefit direct to the landlord may be an important factor when a tenant argues that it is not reasonable to make a possession order.[36] If arrears are in the region of a few hundred pounds, the court may adjourn on terms or make a suspended or postponed order for possession.[37] In *Laimond Properties Ltd v Raeuchle*,[38] where, at the date of trial, there were arrears of £511.10 and the tenant had offered to pay £10 per week, Sedley LJ on granting permission to appeal, said that, in his experience:

> ... it would have been unique to find an outright order made in circumstances such as these, even against a tenant as difficult as this one where there was no history (and there was none) of breaches of the conditions upon which previous orders have been suspended. There was indeed no history of suspended possession orders.

13.9   If tenants have withheld rent because they believed that they had a counterclaim based on breach of the landlord's repairing obligations, but at court they lose on that issue, it is usually not reasonable for the court to make an absolute order without giving tenants the opportunity to pay the arrears, although the position may be different if they fail to make any offer to pay off the arrears and have a history of non-payment.[39]

---

32 *Laimond Properties Ltd v Raeuchle* (2001) 33 HLR 113; April 2000 *Legal Action* 31, CA.

33 (1982) 4 HLR 95, CA.

34 *Hayman v Rowlands* [1957] 1 WLR 317; [1957] 1 All ER 321, CA and *Sopwith v Stutchbury* (1985) 17 HLR 50, CA, but see *Lee-Steere v Jennings* (1988) 20 HLR 1, CA.

35 *Dellenty v Pellow* [1951] 2 KB 858; [1951] 2 All ER 716, CA.

36 Cf *Second WRVS Housing Society v Blair* (1987) 19 HLR 104, CA. See para 37.35.

37 Suspended possession orders were described by Lord Denning MR as 'everyday practice' in *Hayman v Rowlands* [1957] 1 WLR 317; [1957] 1 All ER 321, CA.

38 [2000] L&TR 319; December 1999 *Legal Action* 21, CA.

39 *Lal v Nakum* (1982) 1 HLR 50, CA. See also *Lombard Realty Co v Shailer* [1955] CLY 2366 and *Haringey LBC v Stewart* [1991] 2 EGLR 252; 23 HLR 557, CA.

Breaches of obligation and anti-social behaviour

13.10 If possession proceedings are brought on the ground of breach of an obligation of the tenancy, much depends on the seriousness of the breach and the tenant's intention. For example, if there is a breach which is 'trivial' and which 'cannot injure the plaintiff in any way at all' it will not be reasonable to make any order.[40] The same applies if a breach is committed in innocence, with the tenant believing that no breach was being committed.[41] Very occasionally, if the breach has little or no effect on neighbours, it may be unreasonable for the court to make an order for possession even if the tenant intends to continue breaching the covenant, despite the fact that the covenant itself is reasonable.[42] Usually, however, tenants indicate that they will not breach the particular covenant in future and, if the past breaches have not been serious, the court may accept an undertaking from the defendant[43] or may make an order which is suspended or postponed on condition that the tenant does not commit further breaches.[44]

13.11 Housing Act 1988 s9A[45] provides:

> (1) ... if the court is considering ... whether it is reasonable to make an order for possession on ground 14 ...
> (2) The court must consider, in particular –
>   (a) the effect that the nuisance or annoyance has had on persons other than the person against whom the order is sought;
>   (b) any continuing effect the nuisance or annoyance is likely to have on such persons;
>   (c) the effect that the nuisance or annoyance would be likely to have on such persons if the conduct is repeated.

No equivalent amendment has been made to the Rent Act 1977.

13.12 In serious anti-social behaviour cases involving nuisance to other tenants and/or drug-dealing, courts are increasingly making absolute

---

40 *Upjohn v MacFarlane* [1922] 2 Ch 256.

41 *Upjohn v MacFarlane* [1922] 2 Ch 256.

42 *Bell London and Provincial Properties Ltd v Reuben* [1947] KB 157; [1946] 2 All ER 547, CA and *Metropolitan Properties v Crawford and Wetherill* March 1987 *Legal Action* 20. See also *Tideway Investment and Property Holdings Ltd v Wellwood* [1952] Ch 791; [1952] 2 All ER 514, CA. Cf *Sheffield City Council v Jepson* (1993) 25 HLR 299, CA.

43 See *Hastoe Housing Association Ltd v Ellis* [2007] EWCA Civ 1238 (undertaking coupled with two-year adjournment).

44 See, eg, *Norwich City Council v Famuyiwa* [2004] EWCA Civ 1770; (2005) *Times* 24 January.

45 Introduced by Anti-Social Behaviour Act 2003 s16.

300 Defending possession proceedings / chapter 13

possession orders.[46] In such cases, if the court is to consider postponing or suspending a possession order, it will expect the defendant to acknowledge the seriousness of his or her behaviour and its effects on others, to express remorse and to undertake not to repeat the behaviour.[47] It is for the trial judge to form an opinion on the sincerity of expressions of remorse and assurances about future conduct.[48] It has been said that courts should not force neighbours to live alongside people who behave in a grossly offensive manner.[49] However, an outright possession order may not be appropriate where the antisocial behaviour was not caused by the tenant, but by a member of the tenant's family who has since left the premises, with the result that

---

46 *Bristol City Council v Mousah* (1997) 30 HLR 32, CA; *Kensington and Chelsea RLBC v Simmonds* (1997) 29 HLR 507, CA; *West Kent Housing Association v Davies* (1999) 31 HLR 415; [1998] EGCS 103, CA; *Newcastle upon Tyne City Council v Morrison* (2000) 32 HLR 891; [2000] L&TR 333, CA; *Canterbury City Council v Lowe* (2001) 33 HLR 583; [2001] L&TR 14; January 2001 *Legal Action* 26, CA; *London and Quadrant Housing Trust v Root* [2005] EWCA Civ 43; [2005] HLR 28; *New Charter Housing (North) Ltd v Ashcroft* [2004] EWCA Civ 310; [2004] HLR 36 and *Manchester City Council v Higgins* [2005] EWCA Civ 1423; [2006] 1 All ER 841, cf *Arena HA v Crossland* June 2002 *Legal Action* 26, Wigan County Court (assured tenant, arrested for possession of cannabis with intent to supply; district judge satisfied that the grounds for possession were proved but not that it was reasonable to order possession) and *Tai Cymdogaeth Cyfngedig v Griffiths* February 2003 *Legal Action* 36, Swansea County Court (defendant convicted of possessing significant amounts of amphetamine and cannabis resin on four occasions between July 2000 and May 2001 and once in November 2000 of possessing cannabis resin with intent to supply; HHJ Hickinbottom rejected the suggestion that any burden moves to the tenant to prove 'exceptional circumstances' to avoid a possession order, and, allowing the tenant's appeal, made a suspended possession order).

47 See *Sandwell MBC v Hensley* [2007] EWCA Civ 1425; [2008] HLR 22; *Fletcher v Sheffield CC* [2007] EWHC 419 (Ch) and *Knowsley Housing Trust v Prescott* [2009] EWHC 924 (QB); [2009] L&TR 24. But in *North Devon Homes Ltd v Batchelor* [2008] EWCA Civ 840, the tenant, who was aged 61 and in poor health, was involved in drug-related activities and was convicted of possession of cocaine with intent to supply, possession of cannabis and money laundering, for which she received a sentence of 18 months' imprisonment. It was accepted that she was looking after the drugs for her son. The judge held that it was not reasonable to make a possession order. The Court of Appeal declined to interfere with his decision.

48 *Sheffield CC v Shaw* [2007] EWCA Civ 42; [2007] HLR 25.

49 *Devon and Cornwall HA v Morgan* [2002] 3 CL 418, Plymouth County Court (campaign of bullying behaviour against neighbours, including threatening behaviour and throwing paint, rubbish and excrement into their garden. The existence of an ASBO was not a sufficient reason for declining to make a possession order).

the chances of recurrence are reduced.[50] Even though the defendants have community care needs, if they refuse to undergo treatment for their condition, and there is a likelihood of recurrence of their behaviour, the court may be compelled to make an outright order.[51]

13.13　Another exception to the practice of making suspended or postponed orders occurs where there has been breach of a covenant against immoral user (ie, prostitution). In such cases it has been held that it is prima facie reasonable to make an immediate order for possession.[52]

13.14　Where allegations that the tenant has neglected premises have been substantiated, it may be unreasonable to make an order for possession without giving the tenant an opportunity to put matters right.[53]

Landlord requiring occupation

13.15　In proceedings brought under RA 1977 Sch 15 case 9, the overriding question of reasonableness has to be considered separately and independently from the question of whether or not the premises are reasonably required by the landlord (see para 17.36). The mere fact that it has been found that the landlord reasonably requires the premises does not mean that it is reasonable to make an order for possession: 'because a wish is reasonable, it does not follow that it is reasonable in a court to gratify it'.[54]

Reasonableness and disability discrimination

13.16　The fact that the tenant suffers from a disability is clearly relevant to the question of whether it is reasonable to make an order for possession. Where the reason for the possession claim is arguably related to the tenant's disability, he or she may additionally contend, in relation to reasonableness, that the claim amounts to disability discrimination

---

50 *Gallagher v Castle Vale Housing Action Trust* [2001] EWCA Civ 944; (2001) 33 HLR 810. Cf *London and Quadrant Housing Trust v Root* [2005] EWCA Civ 43; [2005] HLR 28 and *New Charter Housing (North) Ltd v Ashcroft* [2004] EWCA Civ 310; [2004] HLR 36.
51 *Accent Peerless Ltd v Kingsdon and Kingsdon* [2007] EWCA Civ 1314.
52 *Yates v Morris* [1951] 1 KB 77, CA, at 80 and 81 – although in *Yates* the order was in fact suspended.
53 *Holloway v Povey* (1984) 15 HLR 104, CA.
54 *Shrimpton v Rabbits* (1924) 131 LT 478.

under the Disability Discrimination Act 1995 or (when in force) the
Equality Act 2010: see paras 27.4 and 27.9.

Appeals on questions of reasonableness

13.17   Although the County Courts Act 1984 s77(6) excludes appeals against
judges' findings of fact, it does not exclude, in a proper case, the possibility of an appeal against a finding of reasonableness.[55]

13.18   Reasonableness is above all a question of judgment based on the
particular circumstances of each case. In the past it was generally
difficult for a party who was dissatisfied with a judge's determination
in respect of reasonableness to succeed on appeal[56] unless it could be
shown that:

• there was no evidence to support the judge's determination; or
• the judge took into account irrelevant considerations or failed to
take into account relevant considerations;[57] or
• no reasonable judge could have made such a finding.[58]

In *Bracknell Forest BC v Green*,[59] Mummery LJ said:

> ... the appeal process is not there merely for having another go
> at the kind of fact-based issue that the lower court is often bet-
> ter placed to assess than a law-oriented appellate court is ... [The
> Court of Appeal] should be slow to upset [a county court judge's]
> evaluation of reasonableness on the possession order issue, unless

---

55   *Castle Vale Housing Action Trust v Gallagher* [2001] EWCA Civ 944; (2001) 33
HLR 810.

56   Eg, *Pazgate Ltd v McGrath* (1984) 17 HLR 127, CA, at 134; *Lee-Steere v Jennings*
(1988) 20 HLR 1, CA; *Rushcliffe BC v Watson* (1992) 24 HLR 124, CA; *Dawncar
Investments Ltd v Plews* [1993] 13 EG 110; (1993) 25 HLR 639, CA; *Dame
Margaret Hungerford Charity Trustees v Beazeley* [1993] 29 EG 100, CA; *Moray
DC v Lyon* [1992] GWD 14–824, *Haringey LBC v Stewart* (1991) 23 HLR 557;
[1991] 2 EGLR 252, CA and *Bristol CC v Grimmer* [2003] EWCA Civ 1582; 22
October 2003, where Hale LJ said that whether or not to make an outright
possession order 'is pre-eminently a difficult judgment that has to be made by
the judge who is hearing the evidence and seeing the parties'. Cf *Mathews v
Ahmed* (1985) CAT No 2, noted at (1985) 7 CL 3; *Sheffield CC v Jepson* (1993) 25
HLR 299, CA; *Westminster City Council v Garcia* August 2000 *Legal Action* 24,
CA and *Ealing LBC v Jama* [2008] EWCA Civ 896. See also County Courts Act
1984 s77(6).

57   See, eg, *Barking and Dagenham LBC v Hyatt and Hyatt* (1992) 24 HLR 406, CA
and *Croydon LBC v Moody* (1999) 31 HLR 738, CA.

58   *Yoland v Reddington* (1982) 263 EG 157, CA.

59   [2009] EWCA Civ 238; [2009] HLR 38 at paras 29 and 30.

it is clear that he acted under an error of principle or unless his decision was obviously wrong.

13.19 In recent years, however, there has been an increasing tendency for the Court of Appeal to overturn first instance decisions on reasonableness, even when they do not come within these limited categories.[60]

13.20 Where evidence has been given in a county court hearing which is relevant to the question of reasonableness, the Court of Appeal assumes that the judge had that evidence in mind when making an order even if it was not expressly referred to in the judgment.[61]

Article 8 and reasonableness

13.21 The Court of Appeal has doubted whether article 8 of the European Convention on Human Rights makes any difference to the way in which courts have always approached questions of the reasonableness of making a possession order. The concepts of reasonableness and proportionality are similar, but article 8 does reinforce the importance of making an order depriving someone of his or her home only in circumstances where a clear case is made out and the outcome is proportionate to the matters complained of.[62]

---

60 See, eg, *Bristol City Council v Mousah* (1997) 30 HLR 32, CA; *Grogan v Greenwich LBC* (2001) 33 HLR 140; (2000) *Times* 28 March, CA; *Taj v Ali* [2000] 43 EG 183; (2001) 33 HLR 253, CA; *Newcastle upon Tyne City Council v Morrison* (2000) 32 HLR 891; [2000] L&TR 333, CA and *Knowsley Housing Trust v Prescott* [2009] EWHC 924 (QB); [2009] L&TR 24.

61 *Tendler v Sproule* [1947] 1 All ER 193, CA. See *Rhodes v Cornford* [1947] 2 All ER 601, CA, but cf *Minchburn v Fernandez (No 2)* (1986) 19 HLR 29, CA and *Dame Margaret Hungerford Charity Trustees v Beazeley* [1993] 29 EG 100, CA, but see *Richmond Housing Partnership v Green* January 2010 *Legal Action* 31.

62 *Gallagher v Castle Vale Housing Action Trust* [2001] EWCA Civ 944; (2001) 33 HLR 810.

Termination of contractual tenancies

continued

Introduction

14.1 This chapter is relevant whenever a landlord is seeking a possession order against:

- unprotected tenants who lack any statutory security of tenure; or
- Rent Act (RA) protected tenants.

The chapter is mostly not relevant to secure or assured tenants who continue to occupy their homes as their only or principal residences. However, the following topics are relevant to secure and assured tenancies:

- tenant's notice to quit;
- surrender.

14.2 Before a landlord can succeed in obtaining a possession order against an unprotected tenant or a Rent Act protected tenant, the original contractual tenancy must be terminated. If a landlord fails to prove that this has happened, the tenant has a complete defence to possession proceedings,[1] even if the landlord has grounds[2] for possession. If tenants have full Rent Act protection (ie, as protected tenants) and occupy the premises as their residence, the effect of the termination is to convert the tenancy into a statutory tenancy.[3]

14.3 The most common ways in which a contractual tenancy can be terminated are by expiry of a fixed term, service of a notice to quit by a landlord or tenant, surrender, forfeiture and, in some circumstances, service of a notice of increase of rent. These various methods are considered in more detail in the following sections.

Expiry of fixed-term tenancies

14.4 If a tenancy is initially granted for a fixed period ('a fixed term') such as six months or one year, the contractual tenancy usually ends at the expiry of that period by the passing of time. If the tenancy is a protected tenancy,[4] any tenant who still occupies the premises as his or her residence automatically becomes a statutory tenant. If a fixed-term tenancy has expired, a landlord usually need not serve a notice to quit before bringing possession proceedings because the

---

1 *Wallis v Semark* [1951] 2 TLR 222, CA.
2 See below and RA 1977 Sch 15 cases 1 to 20.
3 RA 1977 s2(1)(a).
4 RA 1977 s1 and see para 15.4.

contractual tenancy has already been terminated.[5] Occasionally, however, the terms of the original contractual tenancy may be such that it continues even after the expiry of the initial fixed-term period. For example, if the tenancy agreement states that the tenancy is for a term 'of one year, and thereafter from month to month until determined by notice to quit', the landlord will have to terminate the contractual tenancy after the expiry of the initial year before bringing possession proceedings.

14.5   Once a fixed-term tenancy has come to an end by the passing of time, the courts generally lean against implying a new contractual tenancy, unless there has been an express agreement for a new tenancy. The fact that a tenant continues to pay rent does not by itself imply a new contractual tenancy.[6] Occasionally, however, a landlord and a tenant may make an express agreement which will be construed either as commencing a new contractual tenancy or as a variation of the original tenancy, which means that a contractual tenancy continues to exist.[7] In such a case a landlord has to serve a notice to quit before starting possession proceedings.

Notice to quit by landlord or tenant

14.6   The most common way of terminating a contractual periodic[8] tenancy is by either the landlord or the tenant serving a notice to quit. Unlike surrender (see para 14.34), when both parties agree to the tenancy coming to an end, a notice to quit operates to terminate the contractual tenancy whether or not the other party agrees. If the tenancy has not been terminated in any other way, failure to serve a valid notice to quit is a complete defence to possession proceedings.[9] Similarly tenants have a complete defence to possession claims if court proceedings are issued before the expiry of the notice to quit.[10]

---

5   RA 1977 s3(4) and *Morrison v Jacobs* [1945] KB 577.

6   *Morrison v Jacobs* [1945] KB 577; cf *Hartell v Blackler* [1920] 2 KB 161. See also *Longrigg, Burrough and Trounson v Smith* (1979) 251 EG 847; *Cardiothoracic Institute v Shrewdcrest Ltd* [1986] 3 All ER 633; *Westminster City Council v Basson* (1991) 23 HLR 225; [1991] 1 EGLR 277 and *Burrows v Brent LBC* [1996] 1 WLR 1448; [1996] 4 All ER 577, HL.

7   *Bungalows (Maidenhead) Ltd v Mason* [1954] 1 WLR 769.

8   That is, a tenancy which was not originally granted for a fixed period of time, such as a weekly or monthly tenancy.

9   See, eg, *Plaschkes v Jones* (1982) 9 HLR 110 and *Franklyn v Tingey* (1975) BLT No 441A; (1976) 120 NLJ 767.

10   *Beaney v Branchett* [1987] 2 EGLR 115.

A notice to quit should be strictly construed by the court. If invalid, it cannot be amended.[11] It is for a landlord seeking possession to prove that a valid notice to quit has been served.[12]

14.7 Notices to quit have no application during a fixed-term tenancy unless the tenancy agreement contains a 'break clause' which expressly provides that the term may be terminated prematurely by a notice. The usual method for a landlord to terminate a fixed-term tenancy before it expires is by forfeiture (see below). There is no need for a notice to quit where the tenancy has already become a Rent Act statutory tenancy.[13]

Protection from Eviction Act 1977 s5

14.8 A notice to quit must comply both with the statutory requirements of Protection from Eviction Act (PEA) 1977 s5 and with common law requirements. Section 5 states:

> (1) Subject to subsection (1B) below no notice by a landlord or a tenant to quit any premises let (whether before or after the commencement of this Act) as a dwelling shall be valid unless –
>   (a) it is in writing and contains such information as may be prescribed, and
>   (b) it is given not less than 4 weeks before the date on which it is to take effect.
> (1A) Subject to subsection (1B) below, no notice by a licensor or licensee to determine a periodic licence to occupy premises as a dwelling (whether the licence was granted before or after the passing of this Act) shall be valid unless –
>   (a) it is in writing and contains such information as may be prescribed, and
>   (b) it is given not less than 4 weeks before the date on which it is to take effect.
> (1B) Nothing in subsection (1) or subsection (1A) above applies to –
>   (a) premises let on an excluded tenancy which is entered into on or after the date on which the Housing Act 1988 came into force unless it is entered into pursuant to a contract made before that date; or
>   (b) premises occupied under an excluded licence.
> (2) In this section 'prescribed' means prescribed by regulations made by the Secretary of State by statutory instrument, and a statutory instrument containing any such regulations shall be subject to annulment in pursuance of a resolution of either House of Parliament.

11 *Precious v Reedie* [1924] 2 KB 149.
12 *Lemon v Lardeur* [1946] KB 613.
13 RA 1977 s3(4) and *Morrison v Jacobs* [1945] KB 577.

(3) Regulations under this section may make different provision in relation to different descriptions of lettings and different circumstances.

Subsections (1A) and (1B) were inserted by the Housing Act (HA) 1988 s32. Note that PEA 1977 s5 does not apply to an agricultural holding, even if it includes a dwelling.[14]

14.9   Section 5 now applies to:

- all Rent Act or unprotected tenancies granted before 15 January 1989;
- all such tenancies granted on or after 15 January 1989, apart from excluded tenancies;
- all licences whenever created, apart from excluded licences.

14.10   Tenancies and licences are excluded if:

- *The occupier shares with the landlord or licensor accommodation which is part of his or her 'only or principal home'.* However, a tenancy or licence is not 'excluded' if the accommodation shared consists only of storage areas or means of access, such as corridors or staircases.
- *The occupier lives in the same building as the landlord or licensor and shares accommodation with a member of the landlord's or licensor's family.* The definition of 'member of the family' which appears in HA 1985 s113 applies. This includes spouses or civil partners, people living together as husband and wife or as civil partners, parents, children, grandparents, grandchildren, siblings, uncles and aunts.
- *The tenancy or licence is granted as a temporary expedient to a person who entered the premises as a trespasser.*
- *The tenancy or licence merely confers the right to occupy for a holiday.*
- *The tenancy or licence is not granted for money or money's worth.*
- *A licensee occupies a room in a hostel provided by a local authority, development corporation, the Regulator of Social Housing, a housing trust or PRP/RSL.*[15]
- *The tenancy or licence is granted to provide accommodation to an asylum-seeker under Immigration and Asylum Act 1999 Part VI.*[16]

---

14 *National Trust v Knipe* [1997] 4 All ER 627; (1998) 30 HLR 449, CA.

15 PEA 1977 s3A, as amended by Housing and Regeneration Act 2008 (Consequential Provisions) Order 2010 SI No 866 Sch 2 para 13.

16 See Immigration and Asylum Act 1999 Sch 14 para 73.

14.11 Case-law has determined that other categories of letting are also excluded from PEA 1977 ss3 and 5. Where a homeless person has been placed in interim accommodation[17] pending the local authority's decision, or in temporary accommodation for other purposes, it is considered that such accommodation is not let or occupied 'as a dwelling'[18] and so does not attract the limited protection of the Act. Such lettings may be terminated by contractual notice only. If the agreement does not specify the length of notice, this will usually be equivalent to the length of the rental period or (in the case of a licence) will consist of reasonable notice.

14.12 Protection from Eviction Act 1977 s5 applies to notices served by both landlords and tenants. However, the Notices to Quit etc (Prescribed Information) Regulations 1988,[19] which specify what information must be included, apply only to landlords. Tenants' notices to quit must accordingly give four weeks' notice and be in writing, but need not follow any particular form.[20]

14.13 The requirement for a minimum of four weeks' notice does not mean 28 'clear' days.[21] In calculating the four weeks, one should include the day on which the notice to quit is served, but not the last day referred to in the notice to quit. A notice served on a Friday complies with PEA 1977 s5 if it expires on a Friday four weeks later.[22]

14.14 The 'prescribed information' to be included in notices served by landlords is contained in the Schedule to the Notices to Quit etc (Prescribed Information) Regulations 1988:

> 1 If the tenant or licensee does not leave the dwelling, the landlord or licensor must get an order for possession from the court before the tenant or licensee can lawfully be evicted. The landlord or licensor cannot apply for such an order before the notice to quit or notice to determine has run out.
>
> 2 A tenant or licensee who does not know if he has any right to remain in possession after a notice to quit or notice to determine runs out can obtain advice from a solicitor. Help with all or part of the cost of legal advice and assistance may be available under the Legal

---

17 Under HA 1996 s188(1).

18 *Mohammed v Manek and Kensington and Chelsea RLBC* (1995) 27 HLR 439.

19 SI No 2201.

20 See *Hounslow LBC v Pilling* [1993] 1 WLR 1242; [1994] 1 All ER 432, CA and *Laine v Cadwallader* [2001] L&TR 77; (2001) 33 HLR 397, CA.

21 *Schnabel v Allard* [1967] 1 QB 627.

22 *Schnabel v Allard* [1967] 1 QB 627, where a notice given on Friday 4 March to expire on Friday 1 April was held to be good.

Aid Scheme. He should also be able to obtain information from a Citizens' Advice Bureau, a Housing Aid Centre or a Rent Officer.

14.15   It has been held that an old, standard-form notice to quit, which complied with the former regulations[23] but which was served after the introduction of the Notices to Quit etc (Prescribed Information) Regulations 1980,[24] was effective in terminating a tenancy, even though it did not follow the precise wording of the current regulations. Similarly, a notice to quit served on a tenant in 1989 which complied with the 1980 Regulations but not the 1988 Regulations was also held to be valid. The position might well be different if, for some reason, confusion or uncertainty was caused by using the old form rather than the current form.[25]

14.16   It has been held that it is possible for a landlord and tenant to waive the requirements of PEA 1977 s5.[26]

Common law

14.17   A notice to quit must comply with the common law rules relating to validity. The first such requirement is that the notice must comply with any express provisions relating to service or validity which are contained in the tenancy agreement. In general, any such express provision overrides the common law rules, but cannot override the provisions of PEA 1977 s5.[27] An express provision may, however, state that a notice to quit should give more notice than usual.[28] Similarly an express provision may provide that a notice to quit may be validly served in the middle of a rental period.[29]

Clarity and timing

14.18   The main common law requirement is that a notice to quit should state with certainty when the notice expires. Landlords have a duty:

---

23   Notices to Quit (Prescribed Information) (Protected Tenancies and Part VI Contracts) Regulations 1975 SI No 2196.

24   SI No 1624.

25   *Beckerman v Durling* (1981) 6 HLR 87, CA and *Swansea CC v Hearn* (1991) 23 HLR 284, CA. Cf *Shah v Emmanuel* December 1988 *Legal Action* 17.

26   *Hackney LBC v Snowden* (2001) 33 HLR 49, CA and *Lewisham LBC v Lasisi-Agiri* [2003] EWHC 2392 (Ch); [2003] 45 EGCS 175.

27   Cf *Prudential Assurance Co v London Residuary Body* [1992] 2 AC 386.

28   *Doe d Peacock v Raffan* (1806) 6 Esp 4.

29   *Charles Clay & Sons Ltd v British Railways Board* [1970] 2 All ER 463, ChD.

... to give notices in terms which are sufficiently clear and unambiguous in that the right date is either stated or can be ascertained by the tenant by reference to his tenancy agreement with the terms of which he must be taken to be familiar ...[30]

14.19 The time between the date on which notice is served and the date on which it purports to take effect should be at least as long as the rental period of the tenancy.[31] If the tenancy is a monthly tenancy, the notice to quit should give at least one month's notice. If the tenancy is a quarterly tenancy, the notice should give at least three months' notice.[32] However, in addition to giving the correct length of time, it is vital that the notice expires on the correct day. A notice to quit a weekly tenancy may expire either on the same day as the date on which the tenancy commenced or on the date on which the rent is paid[33] or on the day before.[34] In respect of a monthly tenancy, if the tenancy began on the first day of the month or rent is payable on the first day of the month, the notice may validly expire on the first or last day of the month.[35] Any notice to quit expiring on any other day is completely invalid and the tenant will have a complete defence to possession proceedings.[36] As a safeguard against this eventuality, most standard form notices to quit contain a 'saving clause' (see para 14.20). The usual rule is that a contractual tenancy ends at midnight on the date on which the notice to quit expires.[37] The Civil Procedure Rules (CPR) do not apply when calculating time in relation to service of a notice to quit. Possession proceedings cannot be issued until the notice to quit has expired.

14.20 It is usual for landlords to serve notices to quit which, as well as giving a specific date, also include a formula such as the following: 'or at the end of the period of your tenancy which will end next after the expiration of four weeks from the service upon you of this

---

30 *Addis v Burrows* [1948] 1 KB 444; [1948] 1 All ER 177 at 182 per Evershed LJ.
31 *Doe d Peacock v Raffan* (1806) 6 Esp 4. See also *Manorlike Ltd v Le Vitas* [1986] 1 All ER 573, CA for the meaning of 'within three months'.
32 *Lemon v Lardeur* [1946] KB 613. A yearly tenancy can be determined by six months' notice.
33 *Crane v Morris* [1965] 1 WLR 1104 and *Harley v Calder* (1989) 21 HLR 214; [1989] 1 EGLR 88, CA. For a yearly tenancy, see *Sidebotham v Holland* [1895] 1 QB 378.
34 *Newman v Slade* [1926] 2 KB 328 and *Harley v Calder* (1989) 21 HLR 214; [1989] 1 EGLR 88, CA.
35 *Precious v Reedie* [1924] 2 KB 149 and *Queen's Club Gardens Estates v Bignell* [1924] 1 KB 117. Note the definition of 'month' in LPA 1925 s61(a).
36 *Precious v Reedie* [1924] 2 KB 149 and *Queen's Club Gardens Estates v Bignell* [1924] 1 KB 117.
37 *Bathavon RDC v Carlile* [1958] 1 All ER 801.

notice'. Such a saving clause is valid[38] provided that proceedings are not issued before the date on which the tenancy could have been validly determined. In spite of the lack of clarity in a notice which gives an incorrect expiry date followed by a saving clause, it has been held that this kind of ambiguity does not invalidate a notice.[39]

14.21   Although the overriding consideration is that a notice to quit must be clear and unambiguous, it may well be that minor misdescriptions are not fatal. The question which a court should ask is: 'Is the notice quite clear to a reasonable tenant reading it? Is it plain that he cannot be misled by it?'[40] For example, a notice referring to 'The Waterman's Arms' which should have referred to 'The Bricklayer's Arms' has been held to be valid.[41] Similarly, a notice served in 1974 stating that the tenant should give up possession in 1973 rather than 1975 has been held to be valid because it was clear to the tenant that there was a clerical error and the landlord intended the notice to refer to 1975.[42]

14.22   There are no common law requirements relating to signature of notices to quit. It is necessary only that a tenant should be able to ascertain who has sent the notice to quit. A notice to quit must include all of the premises let under the particular tenancy agreement. A notice to quit which purports to terminate a tenant's interest in only part of the property covered by the tenancy is completely ineffective.[43]

Service

14.23   A notice to quit may be served either by a landlord or tenant or by an authorised agent. In some circumstances a notice to quit may be given in the name of the agent[44] but it is more usual for notice served by an agent to state that it is served 'for and on behalf of' the landlord'. One joint owner may validly serve notice to quit on behalf of other

---

38 *Addis v Burrows* [1948] 1 All ER 177; *Bathavon RDC v Carlile* [1958] 1 All ER 801; *Queen's Club Gardens Estates v Bignell* [1924] 1 KB 117; *Fletcher v Brent LBC* [2006] EWCA Civ 960; [2007] HLR 12 and *Bradford Community Housing Ltd v Hussain* [2009] EWCA Civ 763.

39 *Hussain v Bradford Community Housing Ltd and Kauser* [2009] EWCA Civ 763.

40 *Carradine Properties Ltd v Aslam* [1976] 1 All ER 573 at 576 per Goulding J, approved in *Mannai Investment Co Ltd v Eagle Star Life Assurance Co Ltd* [1997] AC 749, HL.

41 *Doe d Armstrong v Wilkinson* (1840) 1 A & E 743. Cf *Jankovitch v Petrovitch* August 1978 *LAG Bulletin* 189, CA.

42 *Carradine Properties Ltd v Aslam* [1976] 1 All ER 573.

43 *Woodward v Dudley* [1954] Ch 283.

44 See *Lemon v Lardeur* [1946] KB 613.

joint owners even if they are not named in the notice.[45] Similarly, one joint tenant may serve a notice to quit on the landlord and so determine the contractual tenancy even if the other joint tenant does not agree.[46] A notice to quit served by a landlord on only one out of several joint tenants is sufficient to determine the joint contractual tenancy.[47] It is not possible for a landlord to purport to terminate one joint tenant's interest in the premises without determining the interest of the other joint tenants.[48]

14.24 The notice to quit must be served on or before the date in the notice from which time starts to run, otherwise it is invalid and totally ineffective. It need not be served personally by handing it to the tenant. However, the common law rules on what is otherwise valid service are far from clear. There are few recent cases and many of the reported cases appear to conflict. It has been held sufficient to leave a notice to quit with a tenant's wife or servant even though it did not actually come to the tenant's attention before the time started running. On the other hand, service on a tenant's wife when she was not on the premises rented has been held to be bad service. The modern view seems to be that, unless the Law of Property Act (LPA) 1925 s196 applies (see para 14.25), a landlord must prove that any notice to quit left at the premises came to the attention of the tenant.[49]

14.25 If the tenancy was created by a written agreement it may provide that LPA 1925 s196 applies. Section 196 provides that a notice is 'sufficiently served if ... left at the last-known place of abode or business in the United Kingdom of the lessee ... [or] if it is sent by recorded delivery addressed to the lessee at his abode or business, office or counting house' if that letter is not returned through the Royal Mail

---

45 *Doe d Aslin v Summersett* (1830) 1 B & Ad 135 and *Annen v Rattee* (1984) 17 HLR 323, CA. Cf *Jacobs v Chaudhuri* [1968] 2 All ER 124; *Featherstone v Staples* [1986] 2 All ER 461, CA and *Leckhampton Dairies Ltd v Artus Whitfield* (1986) 130 SJ 225.

46 *Hammersmith LBC v Monk* [1992] 1 AC 478, HL; *Greenwich LBC v McGrady* (1982) 6 HLR 36; *Crawley BC v Ure* (1995) 27 HLR 524, CA and *Notting Hill Housing Trust v Brackley* [2001] EWCA Civ 601; [2002] HLR 212. Cf *Harrow LBC v Johnstone* (1996) 28 HLR 83, CA; *Hounslow LBC v Pilling* 1993] 1 WLR 1242; [1994] 1 All ER 432, CA; *Hackney LBC v Snowden* (2001) 33 HLR 554; [2001] L&TR 60, CA; *Fletcher v Brent LBC* [2006] EWCA Civ 960; [2007] HLR 12 and *Bradford Community Housing Ltd v Hussain* [2009] EWCA Civ 763.

47 *Doe d Bradford v Watkins* (1806) 7 East 551 and *Hammersmith and Fulham LBC v Monk* [1992] 1 AC 478; [1991] 3 WLR 1144; [1992] 1 All ER 1; (1992) 39 EG 135; (1992) 24 HLR 206.

48 *Greenwich LBC v McGrady* (1982) 6 HLR 36.

49 *Wandsworth LBC v Atwell* (1995) 27 HLR 536; [1996] 01 EG 100, CA and *Enfield BC v Devonish and Sutton* (1997) 29 HLR 691; (1997) 75 P&CR 288, CA.

undelivered. Section 196 does not apply to notices to quit unless the tenancy agreement expressly incorporates it.[50] Service is deemed to be made at the time at which the recorded delivery letter would arrive in the ordinary course of the post. Where LPA 1925 s196 applies, a notice may be validly served even though it is not actually received by the addressee.[51] Where a tenant rents a bed-sitting room, there is no need for the notice to be delivered to or fixed to the door of that room. It is sufficient for it to be delivered through the letter box in the main door on the ground floor of the building.[52]

14.26   The notice should be addressed to the tenant of the premises, and not to a subtenant, although it will operate to determine the sub-tenancy as well as the head tenancy.[53] If a tenant has died, the notice must be served either on the person who becomes legally entitled to the tenancy or, if the tenant died without making a will, on the Public Trustee[54] or administrator of the estate (see para 20.1).

Statutory tenants and notices to quit

14.27   Although there is no need for landlords to serve notices to quit on Rent Act statutory tenants before starting possession proceedings, such tenants remain liable for rent until any statutory tenancy has been validly determined,[55] even if they have moved out of the premises. This liability can be ended only by a possession order, voluntary agreement of landlord and tenant or a notice to quit served by the tenant.

14.28   Rent Act 1977 s3(3) provides:

> Subject to section 5 of the Protection from Eviction Act 1977 (under which at least 4 weeks' notice to quit is required), a statutory tenant of a dwelling-house shall be entitled to give up possession of the dwelling-house if, and only if, he gives such notice as would have been required under the provisions of the original contract of tenancy,

---

50 Cf though, *Wandsworth LBC v Atwell* (1995) 27 HLR 536; [1996] 01 EG 100, CA and *Enfield BC v Devonish and Sutton* (1997) 29 HLR 691; (1997) 75 P&CR 288, CA.

51 *Re 88 Berkeley Road, London NW9, Rickwood v Turnsek* [1971] Ch 648. See also *Cannon Brewery Co Ltd v Signal Press Ltd* (1928) 139 LT 384.

52 *Trustees of Henry Smith's Charity v Kyriacou* [1989] 2 EGLR 110; (1990) 22 HLR 66, CA.

53 *Mellor v Watkins* (1874) LR 9 QB 400 per Blackburn J. Cf the effect of RA 1977 s137.

54 Law of Property (Miscellaneous Provisions) Act 1994 s14 and Public Trustee (Notices Affecting Land) (Title on Death) Regulations 1995 SI No 1330. See also *Wirral BC v Smith and Cooper* (1982) 43 P&CR 312; (1982) 4 HLR 81, CA.

55 *Trustees of Smith's (Henry) Charity v Willson* [1983] 1 All ER 73, CA.

or, if no notice would have been so required, on giving not less than 3 months' notice.

14.29 A tenant cannot unilaterally determine a Rent Act statutory tenancy without serving a notice to quit and the usual strict requirements relating to notices apply (although a landlord may be prepared to agree to waive them).[56] Advisers should therefore caution tenants against simply departing without giving notice or reaching agreement with the landlord.

Acceptance of rent after service of a notice to quit

14.30 Acceptance of rent after a notice to quit has been served does not usually operate to create a new contractual tenancy.[57] In order to establish that a new contractual tenancy has been created a tenant has to show that this was the intention of both landlord and tenant.[58] Payment and acceptance of rent may, however, operate as a waiver on the landlord's part of any breach of any clause in the tenancy agreement.

Notice of increase of rent

14.31 In some circumstances a notice of increase of rent may terminate a periodical Rent Act protected contractual tenancy in exactly the same way as a notice to quit. Rent Act 1977 s49(4) provides:

> Where a notice of increase is served during a contractual period and the protected tenancy could, by a notice to quit served by the landlord at the same time, be brought to an end before the date specified in the notice of increase, the notice of increase shall operate to convert the protected tenancy into a statutory tenancy as from that date.

14.32 If a landlord wishes to increase the rent to take into account a new registration by the rent officer,[59] a notice of increase in the prescribed form must be served.[60] In addition, such an increase can usually take

---

56 *King's College Cambridge v Kershman* (1948) 64 TLR 547; *Boyer v Warbey* [1953] 1 QB 234 and RA 1977 s5(1).

57 *Clarke v Grant* [1950] 1 KB 104; *City of Westminster v Basson* (1991) 23 HLR 225; [1991] 1 EGLR 277 and *Burrows v Brent LBC* [1996] 1 WLR 1448; [1996] 4 All ER 577, HL. An invalid agreement for an irrecoverable rent increase does not vary an existing tenancy agreement or amount to a new contractual tenancy: *Sopwith v Stutchbury* (1983) 17 HLR 50.

58 *Vaughan Armatrading v Sarsah* (1995) 27 HLR 631, CA.

59 See RA 1977 s72 and Pt III.

60 RA 1977 s49(2).

effect only if the tenancy is already a statutory tenancy or if the landlord can convert the contractual tenancy into a statutory tenancy. Rather than requiring the landlord to serve both a notice to quit and a notice of increase, a notice of increase which gives at least as much notice as would be necessary in a notice to quit fulfils both functions.

14.33   If the notice of increase is invalid (for example, because it fails to comply with statutory requirements, purports to operate retrospectively, or does not give sufficient notice), it is ineffective in converting a contractual tenancy into a statutory tenancy. If tenants pay increases in rent after the service of invalid notices of increase, they are not estopped from maintaining that there is still a contractual tenancy.[61]

Surrender

Surrender by express agreement

14.34   A surrender is a voluntary agreement of both landlord and tenant that the tenancy should come to an end without the service of a notice to quit. An express surrender must state an immediate intention that the tenancy should come to an end. It cannot operate to take effect in the future. Surrenders by express agreement must be made by deed,[62] although in some circumstances an oral agreement may be effective as a surrender by operation of law (see below).

14.35   If there are joint tenants all tenants must agree to the surrender.[63] A husband has no implied authority to surrender a tenancy on behalf of his wife.[64]

Surrender by operation of law

14.36   Even if there is no express surrender by deed, the law may consider that the landlord and tenant have behaved in an unequivocal way which is inconsistent with the continuance of the contractual tenancy. In such circumstances, if their behaviour makes it inequitable for one of the parties to claim that the tenancy still exists, the law will

---

61 *Wallis v Semark* [1951] 2 TLR 222, CA.
62 See LPA 1925 s52; Law of Property (Miscellaneous Provisions) Act 1989 s2 and *Ealing Family Housing Association v McKenzie* [2003] EWCA Civ 1602; [2004] 36 HLR 21.
63 *Leek and Moorlands Building Society v Clark* [1952] 2 QB 788.
64 *Re Viola's Indenture of Lease, Humphrey v Stenbury* [1909] 1 Ch 244.

imply a surrender. In *Foster v Robinson*,[65] Sir Raymond Evershed MR stated:

> It has been laid down that in order to constitute a surrender by operation of law there must be, first, an act or purported surrender invalid per se by reason of non-compliance with statutory or other formalities, and secondly, some change of circumstances supervening on, or arising from, the purported surrender, which, by reason of the doctrine of estoppel or part performance, makes it inequitable and fraudulent for any of the parties to rely upon the invalidity of the purported surrender.[66]

14.37   In *Mattey Securities Ltd v Ervin*,[67] when considering the circumstances in which a surrender by operation of law may occur, Bracewell J said:

> The conduct of the parties must unequivocally amount to an acceptance that the tenancy is ended for the doctrine to apply. Although a surrender by operation of law does not require that there is an intention of the parties to surrender the lease, it does however require that there is some unequivocal act which has the effect of estopping the parties from asserting that the lease is still extant.

14.38   In *Chamberlain v Scally*,[68] it was held that for there to be an implied surrender there must be unequivocal conduct on the part of both the landlord and the tenant which is inconsistent with the continuance of the tenancy. There are three main examples of situations where there may be an effective surrender by operation of law.

14.39   First, where there is an agreement that the tenant should abandon the tenancy and that the landlord should resume possession of the premises.[69] It is necessary for the tenant to hand back the premises to the landlord. In *Hoggett v Hoggett and Wallis*,[70] the tenant tried to surrender premises to the landlord while his wife was still living in them. This was not a valid surrender. Similarly, the mere departure by a tenant from the premises while rent is owing is not an

---

65 [1950] 1 KB 148, CA.
66 [1950] 1 KB 148, CA, at 155, quoting from Foa, *General Law of Landlord and Tenant*, 7th edn, Hamish Hamilton, 1947, pp617–618. See also *Dibbs v Campbell* (1988) 20 HLR 374, CA.
67 [1998] 34 EG 91, CA.
68 (1992) 26 HLR 26, CA. See too *Andre v Robinson* [2007] EWCA Civ 1449.
69 *Phene v Popplewell* (1862) 12 CBNS 334.
70 (1980) 39 P&CR 121, CA. See too *Ealing Family Housing Association v McKenzie* [2003] EWCA Civ 1602; [2004] HLR 21 and *Hackney LBC v Ampratum* September 2003 *Legal Action* 25, Central London Civil Trial Centre.

implied surrender unless there is agreement.[71] In *Belcourt Estates Ltd v Adesina*[72] the Court of Appeal stated that there must either be relinquishment of possession and its acceptance by the landlord, or other conduct consistent only with the cesser of the tenancy and the circumstances must be such as to render it inequitable for the tenant to dispute that the tenancy has ceased or such as to render it inequitable for the landlord to dispute that the tenancy has ceased. Mere inaction or omissions cannot be unequivocal conduct. The position may be different if there has been a long absence and there are substantial rent arrears outstanding.[73]

14.40   Second, where there is a delivery of the key. Delivery of the key to the premises by the tenant to the landlord and its acceptance by the landlord may be a surrender by operation of law. However, it depends on the circumstances. In *Furnivall v Grove*,[74] there was a surrender where a tenant handed back the key and a few days later the landlord demolished the building. On the other hand, in *Boynton-Wood v Trueman*,[75] a tenant handed the key of a cottage to his landlord so that repairs could be carried out. The court held that there was no surrender because there was 'no unequivocal act on the part of the tenant ... which would indicate that he was surrendering his tenancy'. In *Laine v Cadwallader*,[76] tenants left and put the keys through the landlord's letter box. The landlord sued, among other things, for four weeks' rent in lieu of notice. The Court of Appeal held that the dropping off of the keys was not a surrender, but an offer to surrender. There had been no acceptance of the offer by the landlord.

14.41   Third, where there is an agreement for a new lease. The creation of a new lease between landlord and tenant, or between the landlord and some third party with the agreement of the tenant, determines

---

71 *Preston BC v Fairclough* (1982) 8 HLR 70, CA.

72 [2005] EWCA Civ 208. Cf *Artworld Financial Corporation v Safaryan* [2009] EWCA Civ 303; [2009] L&TR 20, where Jacob LJ said 'Going in and living in the property is, in effect, taking over it and treating it as your own, which is inconsistent with the continuance of a lease.' (para 25).

73 *Preston BC v Fairclough* (1982) 8 HLR 70, CA; *R v Croydon LBC ex p Toth* (1986) 18 HLR 493 and *Chamberlain v Scalley* (1992) 26 HLR 26, CA.

74 (1860) 8 CB(NS) 496. See also *Phene v Popplewell* (1862) 12 CBNS 334, where the tenant delivered the key to the landlord who then painted out the tenant's name above the premises and instructed an auctioneer to put up a 'To let' sign.

75 (1961) 177 EG 191. See also *Proudreed Ltd v Microgen Holdings* [1996] 12 EG 127; (1995) *Times* 17 July, CA and *Borakat v Ealing LBC* [1996] EGCS 67, QBD.

76 [2001] L&TR 8, CA.

the original contractual tenancy.[77] This is the case even if the new lease is for a shorter period than the old lease[78] or if there is an agreement that instead of a tenancy the tenant should enjoy a rent-free licence for the rest of his or her life.[79] If the new lease is for some reason invalid, there is no surrender of the earlier lease unless the surrender has been effected by deed.[80] The new agreement must be more than a variation of the terms of the existing tenancy,[81] although an agreed increase in rent may, depending on the circumstances, take effect either as an implied surrender and regrant of a new lease, or as a variation of the terms of the existing lease.[82] A request by the tenant that the landlord should relet the premises to someone else does not operate as a surrender if his wife is still in occupation of the premises.[83]

14.42   If a tenancy is surrendered and the tenant moves out with an intention to cease residing at the premises, that is the end of the tenancy. In these circumstances a surrender by operation of law takes effect irrespective of the parties' intentions.[84] No statutory tenancy can arise and there is no need for the landlord to bring possession proceedings. If, however, a landlord and a contractual protected

---

77 Eg, *Climping Park Ltd v Barritt* (1989) *Independent* 15 May, CA. In these circumstances a tenant is estopped from denying the validity of the new lease and so cannot deny the implied surrender of the old lease, for a landlord cannot validly grant a new lease without first procuring a surrender of the old lease: *Jenkin R Lewis & Son Ltd v Kerman* [1970] 1 All ER 833, but cf *Rhyl UDC v Rhyl Amusements Ltd* [1959] 1 All ER 257 and *Ashton v Sobelman* [1987] 1 WLR 177 (agreement between freeholder and subtenant alone not sufficient).

78 *Phene v Popplewell* (1862) 12 CBNS 334.

79 *Foster v Robinson* [1951] 1 KB 149; [1950] 2 All ER 342, provided that it is a genuine transaction.

80 *Rhyl UDC v Rhyl Amusements Ltd* [1959] 1 All ER 257 and the cases reviewed therein by Harman J at 267.

81 *Smirk v Lyndale Developments* [1975] 1 All ER 690, although an agreement that a tenant will rent additional land or an extra part of premises and that the total should be held as one parcel with an increased rent does operate as an implied surrender and regrant: *Jenkin R Lewis & Son Ltd v Kerman* [1970] 1 All ER 833. Similarly the variation of the term (ie, length) of a lease so that it subsists for a longer period also operates as an implied surrender and regrant: *Re Savile Settled Estates, Savile v Savile* [1931] 2 Ch 210.

82 Cf *Jenkin R Lewis & Son Ltd v Kerman* [1970] 1 All ER 833 and *Gable Construction Co Ltd v Inland Revenue Commissioners* [1968] 2 All ER 968.

83 *Hoggett v Hoggett and Wallis* (1979) 39 P&CR 121, CA. See also *Fredco Estates v Bryant* [1961] 1 All ER 34 (where the landlord said that the tenant could use three extra rooms with no increase in rent; it was held there was no surrender) and *Coker v London Rent Assessment Panel* [2006] All ER (D) 297 May.

84 *Jenkin R Lewis & Son Ltd v Kerman* [1970] 1 All ER 833.

tenant agree to the surrender of a tenancy, but the tenant continues to occupy the premises as a residence, the only effect of the surrender is to convert the contractual tenancy into a statutory tenancy.[85] The landlord still has to prove a Rent Act ground for possession, and, if appropriate, that it is reasonable for the court to make an order for possession (see chapter 17). This is the case even if the landlord, the tenant and a prospective purchaser all agree that the purchaser will acquire the property with vacant possession and that the tenant will not make any claim to occupy the premises against the purchaser.[86]

14.43   A surrender of a tenancy does not terminate any subtenancy which the tenant has previously created. The subtenant becomes a direct tenant of the landlord[87] even if the head tenancy contained a covenant against subletting without the landlord's consent.[88] However, service by the tenant of a notice to quit will bring the subtenancy to an end.[89]

Forfeiture

Nature of forfeiture

14.44   Forfeiture is the procedure which allows a landlord to bring to an end a contractual fixed-term tenancy or lease before expiry of the fixed period of time for which the lease was originally granted. Forfeiture of a fixed-term tenancy has the same effect as a notice to quit on a periodic tenancy (see para 14.6). If the tenancy is outside statutory protection, forfeiture means that the landlord is entitled to repossess the premises.[90] If the tenancy has full Rent Act protection, forfeiture merely converts the contractual protected tenancy into a statutory tenancy. Forfeiture can take place only if there is an express provision in the lease allowing the landlord to 're-enter' or forfeit. In practice all leases contain such clauses.

14.45   At common law there was no need for a landlord to bring court proceedings to forfeit a lease: an unequivocal act on the part of the

---

85   RA 1977 s2(1)(a) and *R v Bloomsbury and Marylebone CC ex p Blackburne* (1985) 275 EG 1273, CA.
86   *Appleton v Aspin and Plane* (1987) 20 HLR 182, CA.
87   *Mellor v Watkins* (1874) LR 9 QB 400.
88   *Parker v Jones* [1910] 2 KB 32.
89   *Pennell v Payne* [1995] 2 All ER 592, CA.
90   Subject, where applicable, to any restraint imposed by PEA 1977.

landlord sufficed.[91] Most commonly this consisted of the landlord entering the premises and taking possession. However, PEA 1977 s2 provides:

> Where any premises are let as a dwelling on a lease which is subject to a right of re-entry or forfeiture it shall not be lawful to enforce that right otherwise than by proceedings in the court while any person is lawfully residing in the premises or part of them.

On whether premises are 'let as a dwelling', see *Pirabkaran v Patel*,[92] in which the premises consisted of a ground floor shop and first floor flat. When the tenant fell into arrears with his rent, the landlords exercised their right of re-entry to take possession of the shop premises. They argued that the premises were not 'let as a dwelling' and, as they had exercised their right of re-entry, the lease had become forfeit. However, the Court of Appeal held that the premises fell within section 2: for the purposes of the section, 'let as a dwelling' meant 'let wholly or partly as a dwelling'.

14.46   The service of court proceedings claiming forfeiture is an unequivocal act which amounts to forfeiture.[93] In view of the various forms of relief available to lessees (see para 14.58), the lease is not actually terminated until a court order is made, but the effect of an order is that forfeiture takes effect from the date when proceedings were served.[94] If proceedings include a claim for an injunction to restrain the lessee from future breaches of covenant, however, the issue and service of proceedings is not an unequivocal act and so does not give rise to forfeiture.[95] A landlord claiming forfeiture in the county court must use a claim form in Form N6 and specify the daily rate of rent accruing.[96] When issuing proceedings, a landlord must notify any person who may be entitled to relief from forfeiture.[97]

14.47   Even before issuing proceedings for forfeiture, a landlord may have to comply with various requirements. If the landlord is claiming forfeiture due to rent arrears, the general rule is that there must

---

91 An agreement with an existing subtenant that the subtenant will change the locks is not sufficient to forfeit the headlease: *Ashton v Sobelman* [1987] 1 WLR 177.

92 [2006] EWCA Civ 685; [2006] 1 WLR 3112.

93 *Grimwood v Moss* (1872) LR 7 CP 360 and *Canas Property Co Ltd v KL Television Services Ltd* [1970] 2 QB 433; [1970] 2 WLR 1133.

94 *Borzak v Ahmed* [1965] 2 QB 320.

95 *Moore v Ullcoats Mining Co* [1908] 1 Ch 575.

96 CPR PD 55A para 2.3 and *Canas Property Co Ltd v KL Television Services Ltd* [1970] 2 QB 433; [1970] 2 WLR 1133.

97 CPR PD 55A para 2.4 (cf CCR Ord 6 r3(2)).

be a formal written demand before proceedings are issued. In practice, however, this rule is usually excluded by a provision in the lease which gives the landlord a right to re-enter if there are arrears 'whether the rent has been lawfully demanded or not'. In addition, the County Courts Act 1984 s139(1) provides that if six months' rent is owing at the commencement of the action and if there are insufficient goods on the premises to cover the arrears, proceedings may be issued without a formal demand for rent even if there is no corresponding provision in the lease. See too the special restrictions on the forfeiture of long leases for arrears of rent and service charges described in paras 14.56 (service charges) and 14.59 (rent).

14.48　　If forfeiture proceedings are issued for breach of any other covenant in the lease, a notice must be served pursuant to LPA 1925 s146 before the issue of proceedings. Service of an LPA 1925 section 146 notice by sending it to the property in question is effective, even if it does not actually come to the attention of the lessee.[98]

14.49　　Section 146 provides:

> *Restrictions on and relief against forfeiture of leases and underleases*
> (1) A right of re-entry or forfeiture under any proviso or stipulation in a lease for a breach of any covenant or condition in the lease shall not be enforceable, by action or otherwise, unless and until the lessor serves on the lessee a notice –
> (a) specifying the particular breach complained of; and
> (b) if the breach is capable of remedy, requiring the lessee to remedy the breach; and
> (c) in any case, requiring the lessee to make compensation in money for the breach;
> and the lessee fails, within a reasonable time thereafter, to remedy the breach, if it is capable of remedy, and to make reasonable compensation in money, to the satisfaction of the lessor, for the breach.
> (2) Where a lessor is proceeding, by action or otherwise, to enforce such a right of re-entry or forfeiture, the lessee may, in the lessor's action, if any, or in any action brought by himself, apply to the court for relief; and the court may grant or refuse relief, as the court, having regard to the proceedings and conduct of the parties under the foregoing provisions of this section, and to all the other circumstances, thinks fit; and in case of relief may grant it on such terms, if any, as to costs, expenses, damages, compensation, penalty, or otherwise, including the granting of an injunction to restrain any like breach in the future, as the court, in the circumstances of each case, thinks fit.

98　*Van Haarlam v Kasner* [1992] 36 EG 135, ChD (lessee in prison).

(3) A lessor shall be entitled to recover as a debt due to him from a lessee, and in addition to damages (if any), all reasonable costs and expenses properly incurred by the lessor in the employment of a solicitor and surveyor or valuer, or otherwise, in reference to any breach giving rise to a right of re-entry or forfeiture which, at the request of the lessee, is waived by the lessor, or from which the lessee is relieved, under the provisions of this Act.

(4) Where a lessor is proceeding by action or otherwise to enforce a right of re-entry and forfeiture under any covenant, proviso, or stipulation in a lease, or for non-payment of rent, the court may, on application by any person claiming as under-lessee any estate or interest in the property comprised in the lease or any part thereof either in the lessor's action (if any) or in any action brought by such person for that purpose, make an order vesting, for the whole term of the lease or any less term, the property comprised in the lease or any part thereof in any person entitled as under-lessee to any estate or interest in such property upon such conditions as to execution of any deed or other document, payment of rent, costs, expenses, damages, compensation, giving security, or otherwise, as the court in the circumstances of each case may think fit, but in no case shall any such under-lessee be entitled to require a lease to be granted to him for any longer term than he had under his original sub-lease.

(5) For the purposes of this section –

(a) 'Lease' includes an original or derivative under-lease; also an agreement for a lease where the lessee has become entitled to have his lease granted; also a grant at a fee farm rent, or securing a rent by condition;

(b) 'Lessee' includes an original or derivative under-lessee, and the persons deriving title under a lessee; also a grantee under any such grant as aforesaid and the persons deriving title under him;

(c) 'Lessor' includes an original or derivative under-lessor, and the persons deriving title under a lessor; also a person making such grant as aforesaid and the persons deriving title under him;

(d) 'Under-lease' includes an agreement for an under-lease where the under-lessee has become entitled to have his under-lease granted;

(e) 'Under-lessee' includes any person deriving title under an under-lessee.

(6) This section applies although the proviso or stipulation under which the right of re-entry or forfeiture accrues is inserted in the lease in pursuance of the directions of any Act of Parliament.

(7) For the purposes of this section a lease limited to continue as long only as the lessee abstains from committing a breach of covenant shall be and take effect as a lease to continue for any longer term for which it could subsist, but determinable by a proviso for re-entry on such a breach.

(8) This section does not extend –
    (i) To a covenant or condition against assigning, underletting, parting with the possession, or disposing of the land leased where the breach occurred before the commencement of this Act; or
    (ii) In the case of a mining lease, to a covenant or condition for allowing the lessor to have access to or inspect books, accounts, records, weighing machines or other things or to enter or inspect the mine or the workings thereof.

(9) This section does not apply to a condition for forfeiture on the bankruptcy of the lessee or on taking in execution of the lessee's interest if contained in a lease of –
    (a) Agricultural or pastoral land;
    (b) Mines or minerals;
    (c) A house used or intended to be used as a public-house or beer-shop;
    (d) A house let as a dwelling-house, with the use of any furniture, books, works of art or other chattels not being in the nature of fixtures;
    (e) Any property with respect to which the personal qualifications of the tenant are of importance for the preservation of the value or character of the property, or on the ground of neighbourhood to the lessor, or to any person holding under him.

(10) Where a condition of forfeiture on the bankruptcy of the lessee or on taking in execution of the lessee's interest is contained in any lease, other than a lease of any of the classes mentioned in the last subsection, then –
    (a) if the lessee's interest is sold, within one year from the bankruptcy or taking in execution, this section applies to the forfeiture condition aforesaid;
    (b) if the lessee's interest is not sold before the expiration of that year, this section only applies to the forfeiture condition aforesaid during the first year from the date of the bankruptcy or taking in execution.

(11) This section does not, save as otherwise mentioned, affect the law relating to re-entry or forfeiture or relief in case of non-payment of rent.

(12) This section has effect notwithstanding any stipulation to the contrary.

...

14.50 Law of Property Act 1925 s146 gives tenants two opportunities to resist forfeiture: first, an opportunity to remedy any breach which is capable of remedy and, second, to apply for relief from forfeiture.[99] It

---

99 *Expert Clothing Service and Sales v Hillgate House Ltd* [1986] Ch 340; [1985] 2 All ER 998 per Slade LJ.

applies to breaches of all covenants except for non-payment of rent.[100] A landlord cannot avoid these provisions by dressing up a forfeiture as a surrender of the lease.[101] It should be noted that there are special provisions relating to service of notices where a landlord alleges that a lessee has been in breach of the lessee's repairing covenant.[102]

14.51   If the notice given under LPA 1925 s146(1) (see para 14.49) does not state whether or not the breach is capable of remedy or, if it is remediable, does not require the lessee to remedy it within a reasonable time, the notice is invalid.[103] Breaches of 'positive covenants' (for example, to keep premises in repair) are usually capable of remedy if the lessee can comply with them within a reasonable time.[104] This applies even if the lessee is in breach of a continuing positive covenant. However, it is often more difficult to remedy a breach of a negative covenant.[105] For example, a breach of a covenant not to assign, sublet or part with possession is incapable of remedy because the assignment or subletting has already taken place and cannot be undone.[106] Breaches of covenant against immoral user (prostitution) cannot usually be remedied owing to the stigma which attaches to the premises and the possible effect on property values,[107] although this is not an automatic rule,[108] particularly if the tenant does not know about the breach. A breach involving a criminal conviction cannot be remedied.[109]

14.52   Commonhold and Leasehold Reform Act 2002 s168 provides that a landlord under a long lease of a dwelling may not serve a notice under s146(1) unless:

- it has been finally determined on an application under s168(4) that the breach has occurred; or

100 LPA 1925 s146(11).

101 *Plymouth Corporation v Harvey* [1971] 1 WLR 549.

102 Leasehold Property (Repairs) Act 1938.

103 *Expert Clothing Service and Sales v Hillgate House Ltd* [1985] 2 All ER 998.

104 *Rugby School (Governors) v Tannahill* [1935] 1 KB 87 and *Expert Clothing Service and Sales v Hillgate House Ltd* [1985] 2 All ER 998.

105 But cf *Savva v Houssein* [1996] 47 EG 138; (1997) 73 P&CR 150; (1996) *Times* 6 May, CA.

106 *Scala House and District Property Co v Forbes* [1974] QB 575.

107 *Rugby School (Governors) v Tannahill* [1935] 1 KB 87; *British Petroleum Pension Trust v Behrendt* (1985) 276 EG 199 and *Egerton v Jones* [1939] 2 KB 702.

108 *Glass v Kencakes Ltd* [1966] 1 QB 611.

109 *Hoffmann v Fineberg* [1949] Ch 245 (gaming club, no licence); *Ali v Booth* (1966) 110 SJ 708; (1966) 199 EG 641, CA (food hygiene offences) and *Dunraven Securities Ltd v Holloway* (1982) 264 EG 709 (Obscene Publications Act offences).

- the tenant has admitted the breach; or
- a court in any proceedings, or an arbitral tribunal in proceedings pursuant to a post-dispute arbitration agreement, has finally determined that the breach has occurred.

Commonhold and Leasehold Reform Act 2002 s76 defines 'a long lease'. The most common 'long leases' are shared ownership leases, leases granted for a term of years certain exceeding 21 years and leases granted under the right to buy provisions of HA 1985 Part V and the right to acquire provisions of HA 1996 s17.

Waiver of breach

14.53   If landlords waive particular breaches of covenant, they cannot rely on those breaches to bring proceedings for forfeiture. A landlord may waive a breach expressly or by implication. Waiver takes place where the landlord does an unequivocal act which recognises the continued existence of the lease after having knowledge of the ground for forfeiture. There are certain actions which amount to waiver of breach irrespective of the landlord's intention,[110] for example, a demand for or receipt of rent which accrues after knowledge of a breach giving a right to forfeit[111] even if the demand is made 'without prejudice'[112] or the commencement of proceedings seeking access to premises.[113] The knowledge or actions of agents[114] or employees such as porters[115] are deemed to be equivalent to direct knowledge of the landlord. Suspicion that there is a breach without actual knowledge of the facts is not enough to constitute waiver.[116]

14.54   No demand for rent after proceedings have been issued can amount to waiver because the landlord has already acted unequivocally in issuing those proceedings. Similarly, there is no waiver of a breach even if the landlord knows about it but merely stands by without interfering while the lessee carries on with the conduct which amounts to the breach.

---

110 *Central Estates (Belgravia) v Woolgar (No 2)* [1972] 3 All ER 610.
111 *Blackstone Ltd v Burnetts* [1973] 1 WLR 1487; *Van Haarlam v Kasner* [1992] 36 EG 135, ChD; *Iperion Investments Corporation v Broadwalk House Residents* [1992] EGLR 235, ORB and *Thomas v Ken Thomas Ltd* [2006] EWCA Civ 1504; [2006] L&TR 21.
112 *Segal Securities v Thoseby* [1963] 1 QB 887; [1963] 1 All ER 500.
113 *Cornillie v Saha and Bradford and Bingley BS* (1996) 28 HLR 561; 72 P&CR 147, CA.
114 *Central Estates (Belgravia) v Woolgar (No 2)* [1972] 3 All ER 610.
115 *Metropolitan Properties Co Ltd v Cordery* (1979) 251 EG 567.
116 *Chrisdell Ltd v Johnson and Tickner* (1987) 19 HLR 406, CA.

14.55 A continuing breach of covenant continually gives rise to new rights to forfeit and so waiver cannot affect future breaches.[117] Waiver operates to prevent a landlord from relying on a particular breach only, not on subsequent future breaches. Subletting is a 'one off' breach which only occurs at the time when premises are initially sub-let. However, sharing premises may be a continuing breach which persists even after waiver.[118]

Service charges

14.56 Housing Act 1996 s81 prevents landlords from exercising a right of re-entry or forfeiture of premises let as a dwelling for failure to pay service charges unless the amount claimed is either agreed or admitted by the lessee or has been determined by a court or an arbitral tribunal in accordance with Arbitration Act 1996 Part I. 'Service charge' has the same meaning as in the Landlord and Tenant Act 1985 s18(1), ie, sums payable 'directly or indirectly, for services, repairs, maintenance, improvements or insurance or the landlord's costs of management' and which vary according to the relevant costs. The importance of this provision is that it prevents freeholders from pressurising lessees who have a genuine dispute about service charges (or their mortgagees) into paying up rather than face forfeiture proceedings.

14.57 The court has power to transfer a claim involving the reasonableness of service charges[119] to a leasehold valuation tribunal.[120]

Relief from forfeiture

14.58 Even if a landlord establishes that a tenant has breached a covenant, the tenant may still be entitled to apply for relief from forfeiture. If the court grants relief, the tenant's contractual tenancy is restored to full effect and continues as if the landlord had not sought to forfeit.[121] Relief from forfeiture may be expressed to be conditional, for example, on the tenant not committing future breaches of covenant. There are several forms of relief which operate in different ways. The county court and High Court powers to grant relief from forfeiture differ.

---

117 *Segal Securities v Thoseby* [1963] 1 All ER 500 and *Houghton v Kemp* [1996] 12 CL 348.
118 *Metropolitan Properties Co Ltd v Crawford and Wetherill* March 1987 *Legal Action* 20.
119 Landlord and Tenant Act 1985 s19.
120 Landlord and Tenant Act 1985 s19(2A).
121 *Hynes v Twinsectra* (1996) 28 HLR 183; [1995] 35 EG 136, CA.

Arrears of rent – long lessees

14.59 Commonhold and Leasehold Reform Act 2002 s166 provides that a tenant under a long lease[122] is not liable to pay rent unless the landlord has given a notice demanding payment. The notice must specify the amount of the payment and the date on which the tenant is liable to make it. The date on which the tenant is liable to make the payment must not be either less than 30 days or more than 60 days after the day on which the notice is given, or before the date on which payment would have been due under the lease. Any notice must be in the prescribed form, but may be sent by post instead of personal service.[123]

14.60 Landlords of long lessees[124] may not forfeit for failure to pay rent, service charges or administration charges unless the total amount unpaid exceeds 'the prescribed sum', or consists of or includes an amount which has been payable for more than 'a prescribed period'. The prescribed sum is currently £350 and the prescribed period is currently three years.[125]

Arrears of rent – county court

14.61 Procedure for forfeiture for non-payment of rent in the county court is governed by County Courts Act 1984 s138. The 1984 Act was amended by the Administration of Justice Act 1985 s55. Section 138 as amended provides:

Forfeiture for non-payment of rent

Provisions as to forfeiture for non-payment of rent

138(1) This section has effect where a lessor is proceeding by action in a county court (being an action in which the county court has jurisdiction) to enforce against a lessee a right of re-entry or forfeiture in respect of any land for non-payment of rent.

---

122 For the meaning of 'long lease' see Commonhold and Leasehold Reform Act 2002, summarised at para 14.52.

123 See too Landlord and Tenant (Notice of Rent) (England) Regulations 2004 SI No 3096 and Landlord and Tenant (Notice of Rent) (Wales) Regulations 2005 SI No 1355 (W.103) which contain additional requirements, namely notes for both lessees and lessors.

124 For the meaning of 'long lease' see the Commonhold and Leasehold Reform Act 2002, summarised at para 14.52.

125 See Rights of Re-entry and Forfeiture (Prescribed Sum and Period) (England) Regulations 2004 SI No 3086 and Rights of Re-entry and Forfeiture (Prescribed Sum and Period) (Wales) Regulations 2005 SI No 1352 (W.100).

(2) If the lessee pays into court or to the lessor not less than 5 clear days before the return day all the rent in arrear and the costs of the action, the action shall cease, and the lessee shall hold the land according to the lease without any new lease.

(3) If –

  (a) the action does not cease under subsection (2); and
  (b) the court at the trial is satisfied that the lessor is entitled to enforce the right of re-entry or forfeiture,

  the court shall order possession of the land to be given to the lessor at the expiration of such period, not being less than 4 weeks from the date of the order, as the court thinks fit, unless within that period the lessee pays into court or to the lessor all the rent in arrear and costs of the action.

(4) The court may extend the period specified under subsection (3) at any time before possession of the land is recovered in pursuance of the order under that subsection.

(5) ... if –

  (a) within the period specified in the order; or
  (b) within that period as extended under subsection (4),

  the lessee pays into court or to the lessor –

    (i) all the rent in arrear; and
    (ii) the costs of the action,

  he shall hold the land according to the lease without any new lease.

(6) Subsection (2) shall not apply where the lessor is proceeding in the same action to enforce a right of re-entry or forfeiture on any other ground as well as for non-payment of rent, or to enforce any other claim as well as the right of re-entry or forfeiture and the claim for arrears of rent.

(7) If the lessee does not –

  (a) within the period specified in the order; or
  (b) within that period as extended under subsection (4),

  pay into court or to the lessor –

    (i) all the rent in arrear; and
    (ii) the costs of the action,

  the order shall be enforceable in the prescribed manner and so long as the order remains unreversed the lessee shall, subject to subsections (8) and (9A), be barred from all relief.

(8) The extension under subsection (4) of a period fixed by a court shall not be treated as relief from which the lessee is barred by subsection (7) if he fails to pay into court or to the lessor all the rent in arrear and the costs of the action within that period.

(9) Where the court extends a period under subsection (4) at a time when –

  (a) that period was expired; and
  (b) a warrant has been issued for the possession of the land,

  the court shall suspend the warrant for the extended period; and, if, before the expiration of the extended period, the lessee pays into court or to the lessor all the rent in arrear and all the costs of the action, the court shall cancel the warrant.

(9A) Where the lessor recovers possession of the land at any time after the making of the order under subsection (3) (whether as a result of the enforcement of the order or otherwise) the lessee may, at any time within six months from the date on which the lessor recovers possession, apply to the court for relief; and on any such application the court may, if it thinks fit, grant to the lessee such relief, subject to such terms and conditions, as it thinks fit.

(9B) Where the lessee is granted relief on an application under subsection (9A) he shall hold the land according to the lease without any new lease.

(9C) An application under subsection (9A) may be made by a person with an interest under a lease of the land derived (whether immediately or otherwise) from the lessee's interest therein in like manner as if he were the lessee; and on any such application the court may make an order which (subject to such terms and conditions as the court thinks fit) vests the land in such a person, as lessee of the lessor, for the remainder of the term of the lease under which he has any such interest as aforesaid, or for any lesser term.

In this subsection any reference to the land includes a reference to a part of the land.

(10) Nothing in this section or section 139 shall be taken to affect –

(a) the power of the court to make any order which it would otherwise have power to make as respects a right of re-entry or forfeiture on any ground other than non-payment of rent; or

(b) section 146(4) of the Law of Property Act 1925 (relief against forfeiture).

14.62   County Courts Act 1984 s138 provides three different forms of relief from forfeiture:

- *If all the rent arrears and costs are paid to the lessor or into court at least five days before the return day, the action automatically ceases and the lease continues as if no proceedings had been issued.*[126] The 'return day' is the date on the claim form even if that hearing is in fact only treated as a directions hearing and the action is adjourned for a full hearing at a later date.[127] If all arrears and costs are paid at least five days before the return day, the tenancy remains a contractual tenancy.

- *At the hearing, if there is a claim based on arrears of rent, the court must automatically delay possession for at least four weeks.* If during

---

126 County Courts Act 1984 s138(2).

127 *Swordheath Properties Ltd v Bolt* [1992] 38 EG 154, CA. See also County Courts Act 1984 s147.

this period the lessee pays to the lessor or into court all the arrears and costs, there is again complete relief from forfeiture[128] and the tenancy continues as a contractual tenancy. The Court of Appeal has held that the words 'the lessee pays into court … all the rent in arrear' used in County Courts Act 1984 s138(3) do not mean that the court can order payment of the rent in arrears only at the date of issue of the claim form. It is to be assumed that the lease continues after service of the claim, that the tenant remains under an obligation to pay the sum reserved in the lease as rent and that 'all the rent in arrear' means the rent payable up to the date stated in the order.[129] The court may, of its own motion, adjourn the hearing once for enquiry to ascertain the lessee's ability to pay rent, but it is usually wrong for there to be two such adjournments without the lessor's consent.[130] The period of postponement may be extended at any time before possession is actually recovered.[131]

- *The lessee may apply to the court within six months of the landlord recovering possession (for example, by sending in the bailiff or otherwise) for relief against forfeiture.*[132] Similar applications for relief where there has been peaceable re-entry may be made under County Courts Act 1984 s139(2), although in view of PEA 1977 s2 (see above) this will rarely be applicable to residential premises.

Other breaches of covenants – county court

14.63   Law of Property Act 1925 s146(2) (reproduced at para 14.49) provides that a lessee may apply for relief from forfeiture and that the court may grant such relief, subject to whatever conditions it thinks fit. This does not apply where there are arrears of rent.[133] Although the most common way for lessees to apply for relief from forfeiture is to counterclaim in forfeiture proceedings which the landlord has issued, it is possible for lessees themselves to issue proceedings in

128 County Courts Act 1984 s138(3).
129 *Maryland Estates v Bar-Joseph* [1998] 3 All ER 193; (1999) 31 HLR 269, CA.
130 *R v A Circuit Judge ex p Wathen* (1976) 33 P&CR 423 (tenant admitted arrears of rent, but said that he had an expectancy of money under a trust at an unknown future date).
131 County Courts Act 1984 s138(4) – see para 14.61.
132 County Courts Act 1984 s138(9A) (para 14.61), reversing the effect of *Di Palma v Victoria Square Property Co Ltd* [1985] 2 All ER 676. Cf *Jones v Barnett* [1984] Ch 500; [1984] 3 All ER 129.
133 LPA 1925 s146(11); see para 14.49.

which they claim relief. Indeed, that is the only way in which relief may be sought if a landlord peaceably re-enters premises which are 'not let as a dwelling' and so not protected by PEA 1977 s2. Lord Templeman summarised the law in *Billson v Residential Apartments*[134] by stating:

> A tenant may apply for ... relief from forfeiture under section 146(2) after the issue of a section 146 notice but he is not prejudiced if he does not do so. A tenant cannot apply for relief after a landlord has forfeited a lease by issuing and serving a writ, has recovered judgment and has entered into possession pursuant to that judgment. If the judgment is set aside or successfully appealed the tenant will be able to apply for relief in the landlord's action but the court in deciding whether to grant relief will take into account any consequences of the original order and repossession and the delay of the tenant. A tenant may apply for relief after a landlord has forfeited by re-entry without first obtaining a court order for that purpose, but the court in deciding whether to grant relief will take into account all the circumstances including delay on the part of the tenant.

14.64   Underlessees have, in all cases, including rent arrears cases, the right to apply for relief and to have leases vested in themselves instead of the lessees.[135] This operates by granting a new lease which comes into effect from the date when relief is given.[136]

14.65   If there are joint lessees of premises, all must apply together for relief under LPA 1925 s146.[137] The court may grant relief in respect of part only of premises if, for example, the breaches of covenant are confined to one distinct part of the building.[138]

Equitable jurisdiction – county court

14.66   The court has a further equitable jurisdiction, wider than LPA 1925 s146(4), to grant relief to underlessees or mortgagees.[139] This jurisdiction does not, however, extend to lessees in rent arrears cases because of the inclusion of the words 'shall be barred from all relief' in County Courts Act 1984 s138(7) (see para 14.61).[140]

---

134 [1992] 1 AC 494; [1992] 2 WLR 15, HL.
135 LPA 1925 s146(4).
136 *Cadogan v Dimovic* [1984] 1 WLR 609.
137 *Fairclough (TM) and Sons v Berliner* [1931] 1 Ch 60.
138 *GMS Syndicate Ltd v Gary Elliott Ltd* [1982] Ch 1.
139 *Abbey National BS v Maybeech* [1985] Ch 190; [1984] 3 All ER 262.
140 *Di Palma v Victoria Square Property Co Ltd* [1985] 2 All ER 676.

The High Court

14.67 Proceedings for forfeiture of leases of residential premises are usually brought in the county court, however large the arrears of rent,[141]
because costs are not recoverable in the High Court[142] and because
of the restrictions contained in the Civil Procedure Rules Part 55.[143]
Briefly, the High Court's powers to grant relief are contained in the
Common Law Procedure Act 1852 ss210–212. These provisions state
that a lessee must seek relief within six months of the execution of
judgment, although it appears that there is an equitable jurisdiction for the court to grant relief outside that period if there has been
peaceable re-entry.[144] LPA 1925 s146 (para 14.49) applies equally to
High Court proceedings.

Principles on which relief is granted

14.68 The circumstances in which relief is granted vary considerably and
the courts are reluctant to lay down general principles.[145] It is clear,
however, that courts must take into account all relevant circumstances. The harm caused to a landlord by breach of covenant (for
example, the effect on the value of the property[146]) is important. For
this reason, relief was frequently refused where an unlawful subletting or assignment led to the creation of a Rent Act statutory tenancy (where there would not otherwise have been one and where it
would have been reasonable for a landlord to refuse consent to the
subletting or assignment).[147] Similarly, it is rare for relief to be given
where the covenant broken is a covenant against immoral user, since
the courts take the view that a 'stigma' may attach to the property.[148]
If a breach has been brought to an end, or ended some time ago,
the court is more likely to grant relief.[149] If the breach complained
of would not have been a breach if the landlord had consented, it

141 RA 1977 s141(3) and (5).
142 RA 1977 s141(4).
143 CPR 55.3 and PD 55A para 1.1.
144 *Thatcher v Pearce and Sons* [1968] 1 WLR 748.
145 *Leeward Securities Ltd v Lilyheath Properties* (1983) 271 EG 279; (1983) 17
     HLR 35, CA and *Bickel v Duke of Westminster* [1977] QB 517 at 524 per Lord
     Denning MR.
146 *Central Estates (Belgravia) v Woolgar (No 2)* [1972] 3 All ER 610.
147 *Leeward Securities Ltd v Lilyheath Properties* (1983) 271 EG 279; (1983) 17 HLR
     35, CA and *West Layton Ltd v Ford* [1979] QB 593.
148 *British Petroleum Pension Trust v Behrendt* (1985) 276 EG 199.
149 *Scala House and District Property Co v Forbes* [1974] QB 575.

is relevant to consider whether the landlord could reasonably have withheld consent.[150] Similarly, the intention of the lessee at the time of committing the breach is important (for example, where the lessee had no intention of breaching the lease, but the breach was brought about by a solicitor's mistake, relief was granted[151]). The landlord's conduct is also relevant and, in a case where the conduct of the landlord throughout had been to harass the lessee and in which the court held that the landlord's conduct was unreasonable, relief was given without hesitation.[152] The tenant's age and health may be relevant.

Forfeiture and Rent Act protection

14.69   A landlord who wishes to evict a Rent Act protected tenant for breach of a covenant during a fixed-term tenancy has to go through two stages, although both may be dealt with at the same hearing. First, the court must consider whether the lease should be forfeited and, if appropriate, whether relief against forfeiture should be given.[153] If the lease is forfeited, the tenancy becomes a statutory tenancy. The court has then to consider whether a Rent Act ground for possession exists (most commonly under case 1: see para 17.9) and, if so, whether it is reasonable to make an order for possession.[154]

---

150 *Scala House and District Property Co v Forbes* [1974] QB 575.

151 *Scala House and District Property Co v Forbes* [1974] QB 575.

152 *Segal Securities v Thoseby* [1963] 1 All ER 500.

153 *Central Estates (Belgravia) v Woolgar (No 2)* [1972] 3 All ER 610. The position is very different if the tenant is an assured tenant – see para 12.27.

154 See chapter 13 and *Wolmer Securities v Corne* [1966] 2 QB 243; [1966] 2 All ER 691.

CHAPTER 15

The Rent Acts

15.1   This chapter applies only to tenancies granted before 15 January 1989, or, after that date, in the limited circumstances provided for by the Housing Act (HA) 1988 s34 – see Introduction to Part II. There are nevertheless still many Rent Act regulated tenancies still in existence.[1]

15.2   The law relating to protected and statutory tenants' security of tenure and to possession proceedings brought against them is an amalgam of the common law and protection superimposed on it[2] by the Rent Acts. Before the passing of the first Rent Act, landlords bringing possession proceedings had to prove only that they owned or had an interest in the premises in question and that they were entitled to possession. Usually, this involved proving that any occupant had never had permission to be on the premises or, alternatively, that any such permission had been terminated in accordance with the provisions of the licence or tenancy. Apart from when landlords sought to forfeit fixed-term tenancies for breach of covenant, there was no question of a landlord having to prove any ground or reasons for seeking possession or that it was reasonable for the court to make an order.

15.3   Although landlords' and tenants' rights were very greatly modified by the Rent Acts, the old common law rules remain highly relevant to residential occupiers who wish to defend possession proceedings. If occupiers are outside full Rent Act or Housing Act protection the only defence that they may have to possession proceedings is likely to

---

1   See *Cadogan Estates Ltd v McMahon* [2001] 1 AC 378; [2000] 3 WLR 1555, HL, per Lord Millett.

2   Common law rules have themselves been considerably modified, eg, the restrictions on forfeiture in Law of Property Act 1925 s146 and County Courts Act 1984 s138. See paras 14.49 and 14.61.

be that the landlord has failed to terminate the tenancy or licence in the proper way. Even if a tenant has full Rent Act protection, a landlord must prove that any occupant's contractual tenancy has been determined properly before relying on the Rent Act grounds for possession.[3] A landlord's failure to determine a contractual tenancy, for example, by serving an invalid notice to quit (see paras 14.8–14.22), provides a complete defence even though there may be unanswerable Rent Act grounds for possession. For this reason, the common law rules relating to determination of tenancies have been dealt with in detail (see chapter 14).

15.4   The effect of most of the Rent Acts passed between 1915 and 1977 was to provide tenants who enjoyed full Rent Act status with two forms of rights, namely, control over recoverable rents and security of tenure. Rent Act (RA) 1977 s1 defines a protected tenancy as follows:

> Subject to this Part of this Act, a tenancy under which a dwelling-house (which may be a house or part of a house) is let as a separate dwelling is a protected tenancy for the purposes of this Act.

> Any reference in this Act to a protected tenant shall be construed accordingly.

15.5   The opening words of RA 1977 s1 refer to the various exceptions to full Rent Act protection which are listed in RA 1977 Part I. Although it is outside the scope of this book to deal in detail with Rent Act security of tenure, the exceptions (in summary) are as follows:

- dwelling-houses with rateable values above certain limits (if granted before 1 April 1990) or where the rent is more than £25,000 per annum (if granted after 1 April 1990) (s4);[4]
- tenancies where no rent is payable or the rent is less than two-thirds of the rateable value (if granted before 1 April 1990) or less than £1,000 per annum in Greater London or £250 elsewhere (if granted after 1 April 1990) (s5);[5]
- some dwelling-houses let with other land (s6);
- tenancies where the tenant is obliged to pay for board or substantial attendances (s7);
- lettings by certain educational establishments to students (s8);
- holiday lettings (s9);

---

3   RA 1977 Sch 15 (see chapter 17). The position is different for assured and assured shorthold tenants. See chapters 11 and 12.

4   As amended by the References to Rating (Housing) Regulations 1990 SI No 434.

5   As amended by the References to Rating (Housing) Regulations 1990 SI No 434.

- agricultural holdings (s10);
- licensed premises (s11);
- some lettings by resident landlords (s12);
- landlord's interest belonging to the Crown, but not to the Crown Estates Commissioners (s13);
- landlord's interest belonging to a local authority, etc (s14);
- landlord's interest belonging to a housing association or housing co-operative (ss15 and 16); and
- assured tenancies (s16A): see chapters 11 and 12.

15.6 Full Rent Act protection gives residential tenants the right to continue as 'statutory tenants'[6] even after their contractual tenancy has terminated, provided that they continue to occupy the premises 'as a residence'. However, this status of 'virtual irremovability' is qualified – landlords are given various 'grounds for possession'[7] which, if proved, may enable the county court to make a possession order.

15.7 A landlord must always terminate a tenant's contractual tenancy (for example, by serving a valid notice to quit) *before* issuing proceedings. Unless a tenant is already a statutory tenant, failure by a landlord to terminate the contractual tenancy provides a complete defence, even if the tenant is outside the protection of the Rent Act 1977 or however overwhelming the Rent Act grounds for possession may be. This is not, however, the case if the contractual tenancy has been terminated at some time in the past and the tenant is already a statutory tenant (see chapter 16).

15.8 If statutory tenants cease to 'occupy premises as a residence', they lose their Rent Act protection, and a landlord then has to prove only that the contractual tenancy has, at some stage, been terminated. However, statutory tenants are not treated as ceasing to occupy as a residence (and so may keep Rent Act protection) even though they may be temporarily absent or live in two different homes (see chapter 16).

15.9 There are two categories of grounds for possession: 'discretionary grounds'[8] and 'mandatory grounds'.[9] If a landlord proves that a tenant's contractual tenancy has been terminated and that one of the *mandatory* grounds for possession exists, there is an automatic entitlement to an order for possession. However, where a contractual tenancy has been terminated and one of the *discretionary* grounds for

---

6 See RA 1977 s2.
7 RA 1977 Sch 15.
8 RA 1977 cases 1 to 10 and the availability of suitable alternative accommodation.
9 RA 1977 cases 11 to 20.

possession exists, the landlord must, in addition, satisfy the court that it is reasonable to make an order for possession (see chapter 13).

15.10　The Rent Act 1977 also provided for an intermediate category of tenants and licensees who have the benefit of 'restricted contracts'.[10] They are tenants and licensees who do not have full Rent Act security, usually because their landlord comes within the 'resident landlord exception'[11] or because their landlord provides board or substantial attendances.[12] Tenants or licensees with restricted contracts enjoy only minimal rights to delay the operation of a possession order (see Rent Act 1977 ss102A–106A). Very few restricted contracts still exist (see para 17.67).

15.11　Even after a possession order has been made, the court may still have power to vary, stay, suspend or set aside the order (see chapter 34).

15.12　In chapters 16 and 17 of this book dealing with tenancies created before 15 January 1989 (or, exceptionally, after 15 January 1989 in the circumstances explained at para II.4), all references are to the Rent Act 1977 unless otherwise stated.

10　RA 1977 s19.
11　RA 1977 s12.
12　RA 1977 s7. See, eg, *Otter v Norman* [1989] AC 129; [1988] 3 WLR 321, HL.

Statutory tenants ceasing to reside

General principles

16.1 After a contractual Rent Act (RA) protected tenancy has been determined, it becomes a statutory tenancy with continuing Rent Act protection provided that the tenant occupies the premises 'as his residence'.[1] Although there is no requirement in the Act that a contractual tenant should occupy premises as a residence, this is crucial for statutory tenants.

16.2 If a statutory tenant ceases to reside in the premises, Rent Act protection is lost completely and a landlord bringing possession proceedings need prove only ownership of the premises, the termination of the contractual tenancy and that the tenant no longer resides in the premises.[2] On the other hand, if a statutory tenant does not give up possession and cease to live in the premises, the only way in which the landlord can repossess is to prove one of the Rent Act grounds for possession, and, if appropriate, that it is reasonable to make an order for possession.[3]

16.3 Rent Act 1977 s2 provides for the creation of statutory tenancies:

2 (1) Subject to this Part of this Act –
(a) after the termination of a protected tenancy of a dwelling-house the person who, immediately before that termination, was the protected tenant of the dwelling-house shall, if and so long as he occupies the dwelling-house as his residence, be the statutory tenant of it; and
(b) Part I of Schedule 1 to this Act shall have effect for determining what person (if any) is the statutory tenant of a dwelling-house or, as the case may be, is entitled to an assured tenancy of a dwelling-house by succession at any time after the death of a person who, immediately before his death, was either a protected tenant of the dwelling-house or the statutory tenant of it by virtue of paragraph (a) above.
(2) In this Act a dwelling-house is referred to as subject to a statutory tenancy when there is a statutory tenant of it.
(3) In subsection (1)(a) above and in Part I of Schedule 1, the phrase 'if and so long as he occupies the dwelling-house as his residence' shall be construed as it was immediately before the commencement of this Act (that is to say, in accordance with section 3(2) of the Rent Act 1968).

---

1 RA 1977 s2.
2 There is no need in these circumstances to prove a Rent Act ground for possession or that it is reasonable to make an order for possession.
3 *Boyer v Warbey (No 1)* [1953] 1 QB 234 and *Brown v Draper* [1944] KB 309; [1944] 1 All ER 246.

(4) A person who becomes a statutory tenant of a dwelling-house as mentioned in subsection (1)(a) above is, in this Act, referred to as a statutory tenant by virtue of his previous protected tenancy.

(5) A person who becomes a statutory tenant as mentioned in subsection (1)(b) above is, in this Act, referred to as a statutory tenant by succession.

16.4   There was no express requirement in the first Rent Acts[4] that a statutory tenant reside in the premises. However, in a series of cases it was decided that the protection given to a statutory tenant is 'a personal privilege which ceases when the tenant goes out of occupation'.[5] The object of the Acts was to protect tenants who occupied premises as their home,[6] not absentee tenants. The continuing importance of this principle is recognised by RA 1977 s2(3).

16.5   In determining whether or not a tenant occupies premises as a residence, the first material date is the date of termination of the contractual tenancy.[7] Whether or not the tenant was living in the premises prior to the termination of the contractual tenancy is irrelevant. However, if the tenant is not residing in the premises when the contractual tenancy is terminated, a statutory tenancy cannot arise.[8] Even if a former protected tenant resumes residence after the termination of the contractual tenancy, it is impossible to reinstate Rent Act protection as a statutory tenant; it is lost forever.[9] In addition, the tenant must remain in residential occupation throughout the statutory tenancy. Accordingly, if the tenant sublets the whole of premises rented, the protection of a statutory tenancy is lost because it is impossible for the tenant to be in residential occupation.[10] However, it is not necessary for the tenant to reside in all parts of the premises all of the time. A landlord cannot claim that a tenant has ceased to be a statutory tenant of one part only of the premises and recover

---

4   Eg, Increase of Rent and Mortgage Interest (War Restrictions) Act 1915 and Increase of Rent and Mortgage (Restrictions) Act 1920.

5   *Middleton v Baldock (TW)* [1950] 1 KB 657; [1950] 1 All ER 708.

6   *Skinner v Geary* [1931] 2 KB 546.

7   *Skinner v Geary* [1931] 2 KB 546; *John Brown v Bestwick* [1951] 1 KB 21; [1950] 2 All ER 338 and *Colin Smith Music v Ridge* [1975] 1 WLR 463.

8   *Brown v Bestwick* [1951] 1 KB 21; [1950] 2 All ER 338. Cf *Francis Jackson Developments v Hall* [1951] 2 KB 488.

9   *Brown v Bestwick* [1951] 1 KB 21; [1950] 2 All ER 338.

10 *Brown v Bestwick* [1951] 1 KB 21; [1950] 2 All ER 338 and *Ujima Housing Association v Ansah* (1998) 30 HLR 831, CA. See also RA 1977 Sch 15 case 6 below and *Regalian Securities Ltd v Ramsden* [1981] 1 WLR 611; [1981] 2 All ER 65, HL, at 74.

possession of that part.[11] Accordingly, a tenant who sublets parts of the premises from time to time, with a general intention to live in the future in the parts which are sublet, retains the statutory tenancy of the whole.[12]

16.6   'Residence' is not, however, interpreted in a narrow sense.[13] A statutory tenant need not occupy premises 24 hours per day, 365 days per year. It is accepted that tenants may be in residence for the purpose of the Rent Act even though they have been physically absent from premises for prolonged periods of 'temporary absence'. Similarly, it is well established that a tenant may maintain residence in two homes at the same time.

Temporary absence

16.7   Tenants must show two things to establish that they are still occupying, as a residence, premises from which they are temporarily absent.[14]

- *Some kind of physical presence.*[15] It is not enough merely to keep an inward intention to return. This intention must be clothed by outward and visible signs of the intention to return.[16] Tenants must leave behind deliberate symbols of their occupation and preserve the premises for their ultimate homecoming.[17] In some cases this requirement has been satisfied by tenants leaving behind furniture,[18] a caretaker to look after the premises[19] or relatives.[20] In practice, tenants intending to be absent for any length of time would be well advised to leave behind some personal items such as books, CDs, clothes, crockery and cutlery as well as furniture.

11 *Berkeley v Papadoyannis* [1954] 2 QB 149.
12 *Berkeley v Papadoyannis* [1954] 2 QB 149 and *Herbert v Byrne (No 1)* [1964] 1 All ER 882.
13 *Skinner v Geary* [1931] 2 KB 546.
14 *Brown v Brash* [1948] 2 KB 247.
15 'Corpus possessionis'.
16 *Brown v Brash* [1948] 2 KB 247.
17 *Brown v Brash* [1948] 2 KB 247.
18 *Gofor Investments Ltd v Roberts* (1975) 29 P&CR 366; *Brown v Draper* [1944] KB 309; [1944] 1 All ER 246; *Hallwood Estates v Flack* (1950) 66 TLR (Pt 2) 368 and *Dixon v Tommis* [1952] 1 All ER 725.
19 *Brown v Brash* [1948] 2 KB 247 and *Amoah v Barking and Dagenham LBC* (2001) 82 P&CR DG6; March 2001 *Legal Action* 28, ChD.
20 *Dixon v Tommis* [1952] 1 All ER 725; *Roland House Gardens v Cravitz* (1975) 29 P&CR 432; *Warriner Ltd v Wood* (1944) 144 EG 81 and *Hammersmith and Fulham LBC v Clarke* (2001) 33 HLR 77; March 2001 *Legal Action* 28, CA.

- *The tenant must at all times retain a definite intention to return.*[21] There must also be a practical possibility of the tenant fulfilling the hope of returning within a reasonable time.[22] It is not enough for this intention to be dependent on something else happening, such as the death of a parent.[23] The court should consider the tenant's intention both at the date of the expiry of the notice to quit and during the time since its expiry. It should focus on 'the enduring intention' of the tenant and not on 'fleeting changes of mind'. This is particularly true of an elderly tenant in poor health whose intentions 'may well have fluctuated from time to time and even from day to day'.[24] The reasons for a tenant's absence may be relevant and it is far easier to prove an intention to return if the initial absence is due to 'some sudden calamity' such as a sentence of imprisonment[25] or a flood.[26] Other reasons given for temporary absence have been illness of the tenant,[27] illness of relatives,[28] disrepair and pregnancy of the tenant's wife.[29] It is possible that a tenant's intention to return may override a purported assignment of the tenancy which is a nullity.[30]

16.8   It is a question of fact and degree in each case whether the absence is such that the tenant has ceased to occupy premises as a residence. The burden of proof initially lies on the landlord to show that the tenant is absent. Once a landlord has established this, it is for the tenant to show that a physical presence in the premises and an intention to return have been maintained.[31]

16.9   The following cases illustrate how long 'temporary absence' can be:

- *Wigley v Leigh*[32] – tenant's absence from 1940 to 1949. Initially she stayed with relatives because her husband was at war but she

---

21 'Animus possidendi'; *Cove v Flick* [1954] 2 All ER 441.
22 *Tickner v Hearn* [1960] 1 WLR 1406.
23 *Cove v Flick* [1954] 2 QB 326 (Note); [1954] 2 All ER 441.
24 *Hammersmith and Fulham LBC v Clarke* (2001) 81 P&CR DG20; March 2001 *Legal Action* 28, CA.
25 *Brown v Brash* [1948] 2 KB 247 and *Amoah v Barking and Dagenham LBC* (2001) 81 P&CR D12; March 2001 *Legal Action* 28, ChD.
26 *Bushford v Falco* [1954] 1 WLR 672; [1954] 1 All ER 957.
27 *Tickner v Hearn* [1960] 1 WLR 1406.
28 *Richards v Green* (1984) 11 HLR 1; (1983) 268 EG 443, CA.
29 *Atyeo v Fardoe* (1979) 37 P&CR 494.
30 *Bushford v Falco* [1954] 1 WLR 672; [1954] 1 All ER 957.
31 *Roland House v Cravitz* (1975) 29 P&CR 432 and *Amoah v Barking and Dagenham LBC* March 2001 *Legal Action* 28, ChD.
32 [1950] 2 KB 305; [1950] 1 All ER 73.

was then prevented from returning because she suffered from tuberculosis.

- *Dixon v Tommis*[33] – at the time of the hearing the tenant had been absent for six months and did not intend to return for three years. He left his furniture in the premises while his son and his son's family lived there.
- *Gofor Investments v Roberts*[34] – at the time of the hearing the tenants had been absent for five years and intended to return within 'three to five years'. They had been living in Morocco and Malta and had left their furniture and two sons in the premises.
- *Richards v Green*[35] – the tenant had been absent for two and a half years. He had been living at a house owned by his parents, initially because they had been ill, but after their death because he was clearing up the house and arranging for it to be sold.
- *Tickner v Hearn*[36] – absence of five and a half years by a tenant who was in a mental hospital suffering from schizophrenia. The mere fact that she was 'mentally unsound' did not mean that she was incapable of forming an intention to return to the premises.[37]

16.10   On the other hand, in *DJ Crocker Securities (Portsmouth) Ltd v Johal*[38] the Court of Appeal refused to overturn a judge's finding that a tenant had ceased to occupy a flat as his home. The tenant had left to look after his father in Malaysia in 1977. Since then he had lived and worked in Malaysia with his wife and children, and between 1980 and 1988 had only spent between nine and 26 days each year in the flat.

Occupation through other people

16.11   Although the presence of friends and relatives living in premises may be evidence of the absent tenant's intention to return,[39] it is not, as a general rule, possible for a tenant to maintain Rent Act protection through the residence of other people without an intention of

---

33 [1952] 1 All ER 725. See too *Brown v Draper* [1944] 1 All ER 246; *Hallwood Estates v Flack* (1950) 66 TLR (Pt 2) 368.

34 (1975) 29 P&CR 366.

35 (1984) 11 HLR 1; (1983) 268 EG 443, CA.

36 [1960] 1 WLR 1406.

37 Cf, however, *Duke v Porter* (1987) 19 HLR 1; (1986) 280 EG 633, CA – absence of ten years. Held: tenant had ceased to occupy as a residence.

38 [1989] 42 EG 103. See also *Prince v Robinson* (1999) 31 HLR 89, CA.

39 *Dixon v Tommis* [1952] 1 All ER 725, *Roland House v Cravitz* (1975) 29 P&CR 432 and *Blanway Investments Ltd v Lynch* (1993) 25 HLR 378, CA.

returning.[40] However, an exception was that a husband was deemed to be continuing to occupy premises as a residence even if he did not intend to return, if his wife was still living in the premises.[41] It was not, however, possible for a tenant who was a wife to maintain her own Rent Act protection by leaving her husband living in the premises.[42] That was changed by the Matrimonial Homes Act 1967 s1.[43] The current provision is the Family Law Act 1996 s30(4) as amended by the Civil Partnership Act 2004,[44] which provides that one spouse's or civil partner's occupation is to be treated for the purposes of the Rent Act 1977 as occupation by the other spouse (or civil partner) as the spouse's (or civil partner's) residence.[45] If the spouse (or civil partner) who is the tenant moves out and the statutory tenancy continues as a result of the non-tenant spouse's residence, the actual tenant remains liable for the rent, unless an order is made in accordance with the Family Law Act 1996 Sch 7 para 11.[46]

16.12   Rent Act protection cannot, however, be maintained by the continuing occupation of a divorced ex-spouse of the tenant,[47] although the Family Law Act 1996 Sch 7 does provide for the transfer of tenancies from one spouse to another.[48] Obviously, none of these problems of

40 *Collins v Claughton* [1959] 1 WLR 145; [1959] 1 All ER 95.

41 *Old Gate Estates v Alexander* [1950] 1 KB 311; [1949] 2 All ER 822; *Wabe v Taylor* [1952] 2 QB 735; [1952] 2 All ER 420; *Brown v Draper* [1944] KB 309; [1944] 1 All ER 246 and *Middleton v Baldock (TW)* [1950] 1 All ER 708.

42 *Collins v Claughton* [1959] 1 All ER 95.

43 Later re-enacted as Matrimonial Homes Act 1983 s1(6). Note that there is no protection unless at some time both spouses have lived in the premises as a matrimonial home: *Hall v King* (1988) 55 P&CR 307; [1987] 2 EGLR 121; (1987) 19 HLR 440, CA.

44 This provision was brought into force on 5 December 2005 by Civil Partnership 2004 (Commencement No 2) Order 2005 SI No 3175.

45 See para 12.4, where the relevant parts of the section are quoted.

46 *Griffiths v Renfree* (1989) 21 HLR 338; [1989] 2 EGLR 46, CA.

47 *Heath Estates v Burchell* (1980) 130 NLJ 548; *Metropolitan Properties Co Ltd v Cronan* (1982) 262 EG 1077 and *Crago v Julian* [1992] 1 WLR 372; [1992] 1 All ER 744; (1991) *Times* 4 December; [1991] EGCS 124, CA.

48 See also Matrimonial Causes Act 1973 s24. It is important that any application for a transfer of the tenancy is made promptly if the tenant spouse is not actually residing in the premises and the tenancy is a statutory tenancy. Occupation by a non-tenant spouse ceases to count as residence by the tenant on the making of the decree absolute unless the contrary is specifically ordered. In these circumstances the making of the decree absolute may terminate the statutory tenancy unless the order transferring the tenancy is made simultaneously. The court's power to transfer a statutory tenancy to another spouse is restricted to cases where the statutory tenancy is in existence at the date of the application for the transfer (*Lewis v Lewis* [1985] AC 828; [1985] 2 WLR 962).

continuing occupation applies if the tenancy was originally granted in joint names because occupation by one joint tenant is sufficient to maintain a statutory tenancy.[49]

16.13   A Rent Act protected tenancy does not vest in the trustee in bankruptcy if the tenant is made bankrupt. Accordingly, there is nothing to prevent a statutory tenancy arising in the ordinary way.[50]

Residence in two homes

16.14   It has been recognised since the early days of the Rent Acts[51] that it is possible for a tenant to occupy two premises as residences at the same time. A tenant may maintain Rent Act protection in both homes or, alternatively, may maintain protection in one while owning the other.

16.15   The classic example is of a tenant who has one home in the town and another in the country.[52] The question 'to be answered by ordinary common sense standards, is whether the particular premises are in the personal occupation of the tenant as his or her home, or, if the tenant has more than one home, as one of his or her homes. Occupation merely as a convenience for ... occasional visits'[53] is not sufficient. It is not merely a question of what a tenant does in particular premises; the court should look at all the circumstances and the way in which the tenant leads his or her life.[54] Comparatively limited periods of occupation may be sufficient, as in *Langford Property Co v Athanassoglou*[55] where a tenant slept in his 'town house' twice a week and rarely ate there, and *Bevington v Crawford*,[56] where tenants lived mainly in Cannes and spent approximately two or three months each year in their rented accommodation in Harrow. Tenants may occupy two homes as residences where they are in the course of moving

---

49   *Lloyd v Sadler* [1978] QB 774; [1978] 2 WLR 721, CA. For further discussion of the position of spouses, former spouses and other cohabitants, see chapter 35.

50   Insolvency Act 1986 s283(3)(a), overruling *Smalley v Quarrier* [1975] 1 WLR 938; [1975] 2 All ER 688 and *Eyre v Hall* (1986) 280 EG 193; (1986) 18 HLR 509. Note, however, that bankruptcy may provide a ground for possession: *Cadogan Estates v McMahon* [2001] AC 378; [2000] 3 WLR 1555, HL.

51   Eg, *Skinner v Geary* [1931] 2 KB 546. See too the more recent case of *Stephens v Kerr* [2006] EWCA Civ 187; [2006] All ER (D) 186 (Feb).

52   Eg, *Langford Property Co v Athanassoglou* [1948] 2 All ER 722.

53   *Beck v Scholz* [1953] 1 QB 570; [1953] 1 All ER 814 at 816.

54   *Regalian Securities Ltd v Scheuer* (1982) 263 EG 973.

55   [1949] 1 KB 29; [1948] 2 All ER 722.

56   (1974) 232 EG 191.

from one home to another.[57] It is more difficult for a tenant to claim to occupy separate premises as residences when they are close together.[58] For example, in *Hampstead Way Investments v Lewis-Weare*,[59] a tenant rented a flat half a mile from a house which he owned and in which his wife lived. He slept most nights in the rented accommodation but the House of Lords held that he did not occupy it as a residence. Similarly, the Rent Act does not provide protection for premises which are occupied only occasionally when the tenant is on holiday.[60]

---

57 *Herbert v Byrne* [1964] 1 All ER 882.

58 *Regalian Securities Ltd v Scheuer* (1982) 263 EG 973. See also *Swanbrae Ltd v Elliott* (1987) 19 HLR 86.

59 [1985] 1 WLR 164; [1985] 1 All ER 564, HL. Cf, though, *Palmer v McNamara* (1991) 23 HLR 168; (1991) 17 EG 88, CA (comparable 'occupation as a residence' under RA 1977 s12 satisfied even though no cooker and landlord did not sleep in premises).

60 *Walker v Ogilvy* (1974) 28 P&CR 288.

CHAPTER 17

Grounds for possession against Rent Act tenants

continued

Introduction

17.1   The starting point for all grounds of possession is the Rent Act (RA) 1977 s98, which provides:

> 98 (1) Subject to this Part of this Act, a court shall not make an order for possession of a dwelling-house which is for the time being let on a protected tenancy or subject to a statutory tenancy unless the court considers it reasonable to make such an order and either –
>   (a) the court is satisfied that suitable alternative accommodation is available for the tenant or will be available for him when the order in question takes effect, or
>   (b) the circumstances are as specified in any of the Cases in Part I of Schedule 15 to this Act.
> (2) If, apart from subsection (1) above, the landlord would be entitled to recover possession of a dwelling-house which is for the time being let on or subject to a regulated tenancy, the court shall make an order for possession if the circumstances of the case are as specified in any of the Cases in Part II of Schedule 15.
> ...

17.2   The main distinction between the various grounds for possession is that if landlords rely on one of the 'discretionary' grounds, they must prove not only the existence of the ground for possession but also that it is reasonable to make an order for possession (see chapter 13).

17.3   The discretionary grounds are those set out in cases 1 to 10 and in RA 1977 s98(1)(a) (ie, that 'suitable alternative accommodation' is available). The 'mandatory grounds' are those set out in cases 11 to 20 and statutory overcrowding;[1] in these cases the landlord has to prove only that the contractual tenancy has been terminated and that a ground for possession is satisfied.

Suitable alternative accommodation

17.4   This ground is fulfilled if 'the court is satisfied that suitable alternative accommodation is available for the tenant or will be available for him when the order in question takes effect'.[2]

17.5   Further guidance is given in RA 1977 Sch 15 Part IV paras 3–8, which provide:

> 3. For the purposes of section 98(1)(a) of this Act, a certificate of the local housing authority for the district in which the dwelling-house

---

1 RA 1977 s101.
2 RA 1977 s98(1)(a).

in question is situated, certifying that the authority will provide suitable alternative accommodation for the tenant by a date specified in the certificate, shall be conclusive evidence that suitable alternative accommodation will be available for him by that date.

4. Where no such certificate as mentioned in paragraph 3 above is produced to the court, accommodation shall be deemed to be suitable for the purposes of section 98(1)(a) of this Act if it consists of either –

(a) premises which are to be let as a separate dwelling such that they will then be let on a protected tenancy (other than one under which the landlord might recover possession of the dwelling-house under one of the Cases in Part II of this Schedule), or

(b) premises to be let as a separate dwelling on terms which will, in the opinion of the court, afford to the tenant security of tenure reasonably equivalent to the security afforded by Part VII of this Act in the case of a protected tenancy of a kind mentioned in paragraph (a) above,

and, in the opinion of the court, the accommodation fulfils the relevant conditions as defined in paragraph 5 below.

5. (1) For the purposes of paragraph 4 above, the relevant conditions are that the accommodation is reasonably suitable to the needs of the tenant and his family as regards proximity to place of work, and either –

(a) similar as regards rental and extent to the accommodation afforded by dwelling-houses provided in the neighbourhood by any local housing authority for persons whose needs as regards extent are, in the opinion of the court, similar to those of the tenant and of his family; or

(b) reasonably suitable to the means of the tenant and to the needs of the tenant and his family as regards extent and character; and

that if any furniture was provided for use under the protected or statutory tenancy in question, furniture is provided for use in the accommodation which is either similar to that so provided or is reasonably suitable to the needs of the tenant and his family.

(2) For the purposes of sub-paragraph (1)(a) above, a certificate of a local housing authority stating –

(a) the extent of the accommodation afforded by dwelling-houses provided by the authority to meet the needs of tenants with families of such number as may be specified in the certificate, and

(b) the amount of the rent charged by the authority for dwelling-houses affording accommodation of that extent,

shall be conclusive evidence of the facts so stated.

6. Accommodation shall not be deemed to be suitable to the needs of the tenant and his family if the result of their occupation of the accommodation would be that it would be an overcrowded dwelling-house for the purposes of Part X of the Housing Act 1985.
7. Any document purporting to be a certificate of a local housing authority named therein issued for the purposes of this Schedule and to be signed by the proper officer of that authority shall be received in evidence and, unless the contrary is shown, shall be deemed to be such a certificate without further proof.
8. In this Part 'local housing authority' and 'district' in relation to such an authority have the same meaning as in the Housing Act 1985.

A landlord may prove that alternative accommodation is suitable either by obtaining a certificate that the local authority will provide accommodation or by satisfying the various criteria set out in RA 1977 Sch 15 Part IV.

17.6   This ground for possession is very similar to Housing Act (HA) 1988 Sch 2 ground 9 (see para 12.86).

17.7   It should be noted that HA 1988 s34 provides that in possession proceedings against a protected or statutory tenant based on the availability of suitable alternative accommodation, the court should consider whether the grant of an assured tenancy (see chapter 12) would provide reasonably equivalent security. If 'in the circumstances, the grant of an assured tenancy would not afford the required security', the court may direct that the tenancy of the suitable alternative accommodation should be held on a protected tenancy. The grounds for possession against assured tenants are wider than those against Rent Act protected tenants and so tenants' representatives should try to persuade the court to direct that any new tenancy should be a protected tenancy.

17.8   So far as rent is concerned, tenants' representatives should bear in mind that if the alternative accommodation is being offered on an assured tenancy, there will be minimal rent control and after a year (or the termination of any fixed-term tenancy), the landlord will be able to seek a market rent.[3] Accordingly it may be necessary to adduce evidence about market rents (or rents for assured tenancies determined by rent assessment committees) in the area. Alternatively, a landlord may be persuaded to consent to a direction that the alternative accommodation should be held on a protected tenancy.[4]

3   HA 1988 s13.
4   HA 1988 s34.

Discretionary grounds

Case 1: Rent arrears or breach of obligations of tenancy

17.9 Where any rent lawfully due from the tenant has not been paid, or any obligation of the protected or statutory tenancy which arises under this Act, or –

(a) in the case of a protected tenancy, any other obligation of the tenancy, in so far as is consistent with the provisions of Part VII of this Act, or

(b) in the case of a statutory tenancy, any other obligation of the previous protected tenancy which is applicable to the statutory tenancy,

has been broken or not performed.

This is the most common ground for possession used by landlords of Rent Act tenants. They must prove either that there are rent arrears or that there has been a breach of a term or other obligation of the tenancy.

Rent arrears

17.10 A landlord must prove two things: first, that rent was lawfully due from the tenant and, second, that some rent remained unpaid, at the date of issue of the claim.[5] This applies only to rent which is due from the actual tenant against whom possession is claimed and not to that due from a predecessor of the present tenant (including a deceased tenant whom the present tenant has succeeded).[6] Rent becomes lawfully due at midnight on the day when it is payable.[7] If rent has been tendered to the landlord on a regular basis when it has become due, but has not been accepted by the landlord, there is a complete defence to the proceedings based on alleged rent arrears if the tenant pays into court all the rent which is due.[8] Accordingly, if a landlord refuses to accept rent, it is important that the tenant continues to tender rent regularly (for example, by sending cheques by recorded delivery) and maintains a separate bank or building society account for any rent that has been rejected so that the rent can be paid into court as soon as court proceedings are issued. If the tenant has not tendered rent regularly and there are arrears outstanding

---

5 *Bird v Hildage* [1948] 1 KB 91.
6 *Tickner v Clifton* [1929] 1 KB 207.
7 *Aspinall v Aspinall* [1961] Ch 526.
8 *Bird v Hildage* [1948] 1 KB 91 and CPR 37.3.

when proceedings are issued, the mere fact that the tenant pays all the rent arrears and fixed costs into court before the hearing date does not deprive the landlord of the ground for possession under case 1, but it is unlikely that the court will consider it reasonable to make an order for possession (see paras 13.7–13.9).

17.11 Failure to provide a rent book does not disentitle the landlord from claiming that rent is lawfully due.[9]

17.12 When advising a tenant who faces a claim for possession based on rent arrears, it is important to check exactly what rent is lawfully recoverable, and, in particular, whether the landlord has been claiming too much rent. This may happen where:

- *A landlord has been charging more than a 'fair rent' registered by the rent officer.*[10] A rent registration for furnished premises is binding even if a later tenancy of the same premises is unfurnished, and vice versa. Tenants who have paid more than the registered rent may claim back the difference for a period of up to two years before the claim.

- *A landlord has increased the rent without complying with RA 1977 s51.* In general, any agreement between a landlord and a Rent Act protected tenant to increase the rent must comply with the provisions of section 51. Any such agreement must be in writing and contain wording pointing out that a tenant's security of tenure is not affected by refusing to enter into the agreement and referring to the tenant's right to apply to a rent officer. If a landlord unilaterally increases the rent or if an agreement does not comply with section 51, the increase is irrecoverable and the tenant can claim back the difference for a period of one year.

- *A landlord has failed to serve a valid notice of increase.* In some situations (for example, where a landlord wants to increase the rent following a new rent registration) a landlord must serve a formal notice of increase. Failure to do so means that the increase is not legally recoverable.

- *A landlord has failed to furnish the tenant with an address at which notices may be served.* In such circumstances, Landlord and Tenant Act 1987 s48 provides that any rent which would otherwise be due

---

9 *Shaw v Groom* [1970] 2 QB 504.
10 RA 1977 ss44, 45 and 57. See *Rakhit v Carty* [1990] 2 QB 315; [1990] 2 WLR 1107. Cf *Metrobarn v Gehring* [1976] 1 WLR 776; *Kent v Millmead Properties Ltd* (1982) 10 HLR 13 and *Cheniston Investments Ltd v Waddock* (1990) 20 HLR 652, CA.

is to be treated as not being due before the landlord has rectified the failure.[11]

• A landlord has calculated the rent without taking into account the Rent Acts (Maximum Fair Rent) Order 1999.[12] This limits increases in registered rents by reference to an arithmetical formula. On 20 January 2000 the Court of Appeal decided that the order was ultra vires and quashed it.[13] Although the House of Lords allowed the secretary of state's appeal and found that the order was valid on 7 December 2000,[14] in the intervening period many landlords served notices of increase purporting to bring the rent up to the full uncapped registered rent. The effect of the House of Lords decision is that the Rent Acts (Maximum Fair Rent) Order has been in force throughout the period and rents have been limited accordingly.

These provisions may mean that a landlord claiming rent arrears in fact owes the tenant money rather than vice versa. In such a situation a tenant may reclaim the balance by suing (or if proceedings have already been issued, by counterclaiming) or by withholding rent until all sums due have been recovered.[15]

17.13   Advisers should also check whether there is any possibility of a set-off and counterclaim for breach of repairing obligations (see para 23.33), or whether there has been any failure by the relevant authorities to make payments of housing benefit (see para 37.23). See too the discussion of the equivalent 'rent arrears' ground relating to secure tenants (HA 1985 Sch 2 ground 1) at para 3.10.

Breach of any other tenancy obligation

17.14   This limb of case 1 is similar to HA 1988 Sch 2 ground 12 (see para 12.122) and HA 1985 Sch 2 ground 1 (second limb): see para 3.10.

17.15   It should be noted that the original provisions of the contractual tenancy continue to bind a statutory tenant so far as they are

11 See *Dallhold Estates (UK) Pty Ltd v Lindsay Trading Properties Inc* [1994] 17 EG 148, CA; *Hussain v Singh* [1993] 31 EG 75, CA but cf *Rogan v Woodfield Building Services Ltd* (1994) 27 HLR 78; [1995] 20 EG 132, CA (RA 1977 s48 complied with where address for service of notices clear from tenancy agreement) and *Drew-Morgan v Hamid-Zadeh* (2000) 32 HLR 316, [1999] 26 EG 156, CA.

12 Rent Acts (Maximum Fair Rent) Order 1999 SI No 6.

13 *R v Secretary of State for the Environment, Transport and the Regions ex p Spath Holme Ltd* [2000] 3 WLR 141.

14 *R v Secretary of State for the Environment, Transport and the Regions ex p Spath Holme Ltd* [2001] 2 AC 349; [2001] 2 WLR 15; [2001] 1 All ER 195, HL.

15 RA 1977 ss54 and 57.

consistent with the provisions of the Rent Act 1977.[16] Breach of such obligations is a ground for possession, but see para 17.17 concerning waiver.

17.16 Where a clause in a tenancy agreement gives a landlord a right of re-entry if the tenant becomes bankrupt and, after termination of the contractual tenancy, the tenant is made bankrupt, the landlord may rely upon case 1. Tenants are 'obliged' not to become bankrupt if they wish to remain in possession of their home. By becoming bankrupt, tenants break 'an obligation of the previous protected tenancy' within the meaning of case 1(b).[17]

Waiver

17.17 The acceptance of rent by a landlord who has knowledge of a breach of covenant may amount to a waiver of that breach and thus prevent the landlord from relying on case 1.[18] If the tenancy is contractual, acceptance of rent is a complete waiver of a breach even if the acceptance is qualified. However, if the tenancy is statutory, it is a question of fact in each case as to whether the breach has been waived.[19] A qualified acceptance of rent from a statutory tenant (for example, acceptance 'without prejudice') may mean that the landlord is still entitled to rely on the breach of covenant,[20] but an unqualified acceptance of rent by the landlord of a statutory tenant is as much a waiver of the breach as if it were a payment by a contractual tenant.[21]

17.18 Acceptance of rent by landlords' agents who have knowledge of a breach of covenant amounts to waiver.[22] Thus, the knowledge of a porter that there is someone other than a tenant living in the premises amounts to knowledge of the landlord.[23] See further discussion of waiver at para 14.53.

---

16 RA 1977 s3(1).

17 *Cadogan Estates Ltd v McMahon* [2001] AC 378; [2000] 3 WLR 1555, HL.

18 *Carter v Green* [1950] 1 All ER 627. See too para 14.53.

19 *Oak Property Co Ltd v Chapman* [1947] KB 886; [1947] 2 All ER 1 and *Trustees of Smith's (Henry) Charity v Willson* [1983] 1 All ER 73.

20 *Oak Property Co Ltd v Chapman* [1947] KB 886; [1947] 2 All ER 1 and *Trustees of Smith's (Henry) Charity v Willson* [1983] 1 All ER 73.

21 *Carter v Green* [1950] 1 All ER 627, cf *Trustees of Smith's (Henry) Charity v Willson* [1983] 1 All ER 73.

22 *Hyde v Pimley* [1952] 2 QB 506; [1952] 2 All ER 102.

23 *Metropolitan Properties Co Ltd v Cordery* (1979) 251 EG 567.

Case 2: Nuisance or annoyance, user for immoral or illegal purposes

17.19　Where the tenant or any person residing or lodging with him or any sub-tenant of his has been guilty of conduct which is a nuisance or annoyance to adjoining occupiers, or has been convicted of using the dwelling-house or allowing the dwelling-house to be used for immoral or illegal purposes.

Nuisance or annoyance

17.20　'Nuisance' and 'annoyance' are both used in the natural sense of the words. This ground may be satisfied by drunkenness, abusive behaviour, noise, obstructive behaviour towards other occupiers or violence.[24] Unknown people coming to the premises at all hours of the day and night may amount to an annoyance.[25] It is not necessary that the act which led to the annoyance should have taken place on the premises. For example, a married tenant who exercised 'undue familiarity' with the landlord's daughter in an alley some 200 yards away from the premises let was held to be guilty of 'annoyance'.[26] It is possible for the court to infer that annoyance or nuisance has been caused to adjoining occupants without direct evidence from them,[27] but it is more usual for the landlord to call adjoining occupants to give evidence. The word 'adjoining' does not mean that the premises must be physically touching the tenant's premises: it means that the persons affected by nuisance or annoyance must live near enough to be affected by the tenant's conduct, because, for example, they share a common entrance.[28]

Immoral or illegal purposes

17.21　'Immoral purposes' is the statutory formula for prostitution.[29] The mere fact that a tenant has been convicted of a crime which took place on the premises may not be sufficient to establish this limb of the ground for possession. It must be shown that:

> ... for the purpose of committing the crime, the premises have been used ... [It is] not enough that the tenant has been convicted of a crime

---

24　Per Wood J in *Cobstone Investments Ltd v Maxim* [1985] QB 140; [1984] 2 All ER 635.
25　*Florent v Horez* (1983) 268 EG 807.
26　*Whitbread v Ward* (1952) 159 EG 494.
27　*Platts (Frederick) Co v Grigor* [1950] 1 All ER 941, CA.
28　*Cobstone v Maxim* [1984] 2 All ER 635.
29　*Yates v Morris* [1951] 1 KB 77.

with which the premises have nothing to do beyond merely being the scene of its commission.[30]

17.22 However, the ground may be satisfied even though a tenant has been convicted of an offence which does not specifically refer to 'using premises'.[31] Depending on the circumstances, a conviction for possession of cannabis or some other unlawful drug on the premises may amount to a ground for possession. There may, however, be a difference between tenants having drugs in their immediate possession on the premises (for example, in a pocket or a handbag) and using the premises as a storage or hiding place.[32] Examples of other activities which may satisfy this ground for possession are using premises as a 'coiner's den' or as a deposit for stolen goods.[33]

Case 3: Neglect of or damage to premises

17.23 Where the condition of the dwelling-house has, in the opinion of the court, deteriorated owing to acts of waste by, or the neglect or default of, the tenant or any person residing or lodging with him or any sub-tenant of his and, in the case of any act of waste by, or the neglect or default of, a person lodging with the tenant or a sub-tenant of his, where the court is satisfied that the tenant has not, before the making of the order in question, taken such steps as he ought reasonably to have taken for the removal of the lodger or sub-tenant, as the case may be.

This ground is similar to ground 13 in HA 1988 Sch 2 (see para 12.132).

17.24 There is no need for a landlord to give advance warning of an intention to issue proceedings relying on this ground,[34] although failure to do so may be relevant when the court considers reasonableness and costs. Where allegations that the tenant has neglected premises have been substantiated, it may be unreasonable to make an order for possession without giving the tenant an opportunity to put matters right.[35]

---

30 Per Scrutton LJ in *Schneiders & Sons v Abrahams* [1925] 1 KB 301 at 311.
31 *Abrahams v Wilson* [1971] 2 QB 88.
32 *Abrahams v Wilson* [1971] 2 QB 88, per Widgery LJ. On 'reasonableness' in such cases, see *Bristol CC v Mousah* (1997) 30 HLR 32, CA and the other cases referred to at para 13.12.
33 *Schneiders & Sons v Abrahams* [1925] 1 KB 301 and *Everett v Stevens* [1957] CLY 3062.
34 *Lowe v Lendrum* (1950) 159 EG 423, CA.
35 *Holloway v Povey* (1984) 15 HLR 104; (1984) 271 EG 195, CA.

Case 4: Ill-treatment of furniture

17.25   Where the condition of any furniture provided for use under the tenancy has, in the opinion of the court, deteriorated owing to ill-treatment by the tenant or any person residing or lodging with him or any sub-tenant of his and, in the case of any ill-treatment by a person lodging with the tenant or a sub-tenant of his, where the court is satisfied that the tenant has not, before the making of the order in question, taken such steps as he ought reasonably to have taken for the removal of the lodger or sub-tenant, as the case may be.

See notes under case 3 above.

Case 5: Notice to quit by tenant

17.26   Where the tenant has given notice to quit and, in consequence of that notice, the landlord has contracted to sell or let the dwelling-house or has taken any other steps as the result of which he would, in the opinion of the court, be seriously prejudiced if he could not obtain possession.

There must be a valid tenant's notice to quit before a landlord can rely on this ground for possession.[36] The words 'notice to quit' have their normal technical meaning (see para 14.6) and the disappearance of a tenant followed by a return by him of the keys did not amount to 'notice to quit'.[37] Similarly an agreement to move out is not sufficient.[38]

17.27   There are no recent cases on the meaning of 'serious prejudice'. In an old case decided on a section with different wording, it was held that there was no prejudice to a landlord where a proposed sale of the premises 'went off' without any liability for damages on the part of the landlord.[39]

Case 6: Subletting without the landlord's consent

17.28   Where, without the consent of the landlord, the tenant has, at any time after –
(a) ...
(b) 22nd March 1973, in the case of a tenancy which became a regulated tenancy by virtue of section 14 of the Counter-Inflation Act 1973;

---

36 *De Vries v Sparks* (1927) 137 LT 441.
37 *Standingford v Bruce* [1926] 1 KB 466.
38 *De Vries v Sparks* (1927) 137 LT 441.
39 *Hunt v Bliss* (1919) 89 LJKB 174.

(bb) the commencement of section 73 of the Housing Act 1980, in the case of a tenancy which became a regulated tenancy by virtue of that section;

(c) 14th August 1974, in the case of a regulated furnished tenancy; or

(d) 8th December 1965, in the case of any other tenancy,

assigned or sublet the whole of the dwelling-house or sublet part of the dwelling-house, the remainder being already sublet.

This ground gives protection to landlords against the risk of finding someone totally unknown to them irremovably installed in the property.[40] The ground applies even if there is no prohibition against assigning or subletting in the tenancy agreement. The word 'assigned' includes a vesting assent (that is, a transfer of a lease made to implement the terms of a will) made by executors of a deceased tenant which takes effect as an assignment.[41] It does not, however, apply unless all of the premises rented have been disposed of by assigning or subletting. In practice the ground usually applies only to subletting or assignment by a contractual tenant. If a statutory tenant sublets the whole of premises, Rent Act protection is lost because the tenant can no longer occupy the premises as a residence.[42] It is not possible to assign a statutory tenancy (see para 16.4).

17.29   Consent to a subletting or assignment may be given implicitly,[43] for example, by accepting rent for some time after acquiring knowledge of the subletting.[44] Consent may be given after the subletting or assignment, at any time up to the issue of proceedings.[45] If the tenancy agreement contains a provision that the tenant cannot assign or sublet without the permission of the landlord, there is an implied proviso that consent cannot be withheld unreasonably.[46]

17.30   It is not necessary for a landlord to prove that a subtenancy or subtenancies have continued to exist right up to the date when proceedings were issued. It is enough that a tenant has at any time sublet or

---

40   *Hyde v Pimley* [1952] 2 All ER 102.

41   *Pazgate Ltd v McGrath* (1985) 17 HLR 127.

42   See para 16.2. See also *Poland v Cadogan (Earl)* [1980] 3 All ER 544, dealing with similar provisions in the Leasehold Reform Act 1967 where the comparable wording is slightly different. It seems unlikely that statutory tenants who enjoy only personal rights in premises are able to create subtenancies of the whole but compare comments of Ormrod LJ in *Trustees of Smith's (Henry) Charity v Willson* [1983] 1 All ER 73.

43   *Regional Properties Ltd v Frankenschwerth* [1951] 1 KB 631; [1951] 1 All ER 178.

44   *Hyde v Pimley* [1952] 2 All ER 102.

45   *Hyde v Pimley* [1952] 2 All ER 102.

46   Landlord and Tenant Act 1927 s19 and Landlord and Tenant Act 1988 s1.

assigned the whole of the premises.⁴⁷ However, there are likely to be strong grounds for arguing that it is unreasonable to make an order for possession if there is no subsisting subtenancy at the time when proceedings are issued. This ground for possession can enable a landlord to obtain possession against both the tenant and subtenant (notwithstanding the effect of RA 1977 s137), provided that the court is satisfied that it is reasonable to make the order.⁴⁸

17.31 Only tenants who have sublet after the various dates specified in case 6 are caught by this ground. Subparagraph (a) related to controlled tenancies and was repealed by the Housing Act 1980. Subparagraph (b) relates to tenancies which were brought into Rent Act protection by amendments to RA 1977 s4, which provides the maximum rateable values for dwelling-houses falling within full Rent Act protection. Subparagraph (bb) relates to tenancies from the Crown Estates Commission which were brought into full Rent Act protection by the Housing Act 1980.

Case 7

17.32 Case 7 was repealed by Housing Act 1980 s152 and Sch 26. It related to controlled off-licences.

Case 8: Former employees

17.33 Where the dwelling-house is reasonably required by the landlord for occupation as a residence for some person engaged in his whole-time employment, or in the whole-time employment of some tenant from him or with whom, conditional on housing being provided, a contract for such employment has been entered into, and the tenant was in the employment of the landlord or a former landlord, and the dwelling-house was let to him in consequence of that employment and he has ceased to be in that employment.

In order to succeed under this ground a landlord must prove that:⁴⁹

• *The tenant was in the employment of the landlord or a former landlord at the time when the premises were let.*⁵⁰ 'Tenant' refers to the original contractual tenant. For example, if the son of the original tenant

---

47 *Finkle v Strzelczyk* [1961] 3 All ER 409.
48 *Leith Properties Ltd v Springer* [1982] 3 All ER 731, CA.
49 *Munro v Daw* [1948] 1 KB 125; [1947] 2 All ER 360 and *Benninga (Mitcham) Ltd v Bijstra* [1946] KB 58; [1945] 2 All ER 433.
50 *Fuggle (RF) Ltd v Gadsden* [1948] 2 KB 236.

becomes a statutory tenant by succession,[51] the landlord can rely on this ground for possession if the father was in the landlord's employment at the beginning of that contractual tenancy.[52]

- *Premises were let in consequence of that employment.* This is a question of fact in each case.[53] The questions to be asked are: 'What was the reason for the landlord letting the premises to the tenant?' 'What was in the mind of the person who let the premises?' 'Was it let because of the tenant's employment or was there another reason?'[54] It is possible for premises to be let in consequence of employment even if there is no reference to the premises in the employee's contract of employment. If premises are let some time after an employee originally took the job, the letting may be in consequence of the employment or it may be treated as a separate 'independent' transaction.[55] If a former employer grants a new contractual tenancy after the tenant has stopped working for that employer, the new tenancy cannot be in consequence of that employment.[56] It is not necessary for it to be shown that the tenancy was granted as a result of any particular type of employment, only that it was in consequence of the relationship of employer and employee.[57] It is not possible for landlord and tenant to agree that a particular tenancy was not created in consequence of employment when the facts show clearly that the opposite was the case.[58]

- *Employment has ceased.* A tenant who has changed jobs (for example, from a farm worker to a laundry machine operator) but who is still employed by the same employer has not ceased to be in employment.[59]

- *The premises are reasonably required by the landlord for occupation as a residence by someone engaged in the whole-time employment of the*

---

51 Where the death occurs on or after 15 January 1989, only a spouse or civil partner will succeed to a statutory tenancy. Other members of the family will succeed to an assured tenancy: RA 1977 Sch 1 para 3.

52 *Bolsover Colliery Co Ltd v Abbott* [1946] KB 8.

53 *Long Eaton Co-op v Smith* [1949] 2 KB 144; [1949] 1 All ER 633 considering agricultural wages legislation.

54 *Braithwaite and Co Ltd v Elliot* [1947] KB 177; [1946] 2 All ER 537 at 539. Cf *Queen's Club Gardens v Bignell* [1924] 1 KB 117.

55 *Long Eaton Co-op v Smith* [1949] 2 KB 144; [1949] 1 All ER 633.

56 *Lever Brothers v Caton* (1921) 37 TLR 664.

57 *Munro v Daw* [1947] 2 All ER 360.

58 *Harvard v Shears* (1967) 111 SJ 683.

59 *Duncan v Hay* [1956] 1 WLR 1329.

landlord or someone with whom a contract of employment has been entered into which is conditional on housing being provided. When the court considers whether or not the proposed new occupant is employed or whether a contract of employment has been entered into, the relevant date is the date of the court hearing.[60] Note that the premises must be reasonably required.[61]

17.34 A tenant may be entitled to compensation if a landlord obtains an order for possession under case 8 by deceit. See para 17.43.

Case 9: Premises required for occupation by a landlord or landlord's family

17.35 Where the dwelling-house is reasonably required by the landlord for occupation as a residence for –

(a) himself, or

(b) any son or daughter of his over 18 years of age, or

(c) his father or mother, or

(d) if the dwelling-house is let on or subject to a regulated tenancy, the father or mother of his spouse or civil partner,

and the landlord did not become landlord by purchasing the dwelling-house or any interest therein after –

(i) 7th November 1956, in the case of a tenancy which was then a controlled tenancy;

(ii) 8th March 1973, in the case of a tenancy which became a regulated tenancy by virtue of section 14 of the Counter-Inflation Act 1973;

(iii) 24th May 1974, in the case of a regulated furnished tenancy; or

(iv) 23rd March 1965, in the case of any other tenancy.

This ground for possession has to be read in conjunction with RA 1977 Sch 15 Part III para 1, which provides:

> A court shall not make an order for possession of a dwelling-house by reason only that the circumstances of the case fall within Case 9 in Part I of this Schedule if the court is satisfied that, having regard to all the circumstances of the case, including the question whether other accommodation is available for the landlord or the tenant, greater hardship would be caused by granting the order than by refusing to grant it.

'Reasonably required'

17.36 Case 9 applies where the premises are reasonably required as a residence by the landlord or certain specified members of the landlord's

---

60 *Benninga (Mitcham) Ltd v Bijstra* [1945] 2 All ER 433.

61 See comments on similar wording in case 9 at para 17.36.

family. The words 'reasonably required' mean more than a 'desire' on the landlord's part, but less than 'absolute necessity'.[62] The court should consider whether this requirement is reasonable on the landlord's part, and in doing so the tenant's interests are not relevant.[63] The tenant's interests should be taken into account when the overall questions of greater hardship and reasonableness are considered: see para 13.3 (reasonableness) and para 17.40 (greater hardship). Matters which are relevant when considering whether the landlord's requirements are reasonable are, for example, the nature and place of the landlord's business, the size of the family, their actual residence or lack of it, their health, and 'innumerable other possible factors'.[64] The requirement need not be an immediate requirement.[65] It is perfectly proper for a landlord to seek possession under case 9 where the need for accommodation will exist in the ascertainable but not too far distant future.[66] However, possession has been refused in a case where a landlord stated that he required a basement for his daughter to live in on her marriage which might take place in two years' time,[67] and in a case where the trial judge had found that premises purportedly let to five surveyors were 'an investment property' which was not required by the landlord.[68] The landlord must need the premises 'with a view to living there for some reasonable period, definite or indefinite', and not for the purpose of sale[69] or for temporary accommodation while repairs are carried out in the landlord's own accommodation.[70] A landlord does, however, come within this ground for possession even if only part of the premises is required.[71]

17.37   The premises must be required for the landlord, or for the landlord's children, the landlord's parents or parents-in-law.[72] It has been said that this includes 'all normal emanations of' the landlord,[73]

---

62 *Aitken v Shaw* 1933 SLT 21 and *Kennealy v Dunne* [1977] QB 837.

63 *Funnell v Armstrong* [1962] EGD 319.

64 *Chandler v Strevett* [1947] 1 All ER 164 per Bucknill LJ.

65 Cf *Aitken v Shaw* 1933 SLT 21.

66 *Kidder v Birch* (1983) 265 EG 773. See also *Alexander v Mohamadzadeh* (1986) 18 HLR 90; (1985) 276 EG 1258 (relevant date for deciding whether premises are required is date of hearing, not date of issue of proceedings).

67 *Kissias v Lehany* [1979] CLY 1625.

68 *Ghelani v Bowie* [1988] 42 EG 119, CA.

69 *Rowe v Truelove* (1976) 241 EG 533.

70 *Johnson-Sneddon v Harper* May 1977 *LAG Bulletin* 114.

71 *Kelley v Goodwin* [1947] 1 All ER 810.

72 But not step-children: *Towns v Hole* [1956] CLY 7493 and *Harty v Greenwich LBC and Done* [1956] CLY 7494.

73 *Richter v Wilson* [1963] 2 QB 426.

including a housekeeper who lived in the same household as the landlord and was paid to look after children after the landlord had separated from his wife.[74] It has also included the son of a landlord's wife, even though he was not the landlord's son and the landlord had not adopted him.[75] It does not, however, include someone who would occupy premises as a separate household and not as part of the landlord's household, for example, where it was intended that a couple should live in a separate self-contained flat in the same building as the landlord, in order to look after him.[76] Where premises are owned by joint landlords they must reasonably be required as a residence for *all* the joint landlords.[77] Personal representatives of the deceased landlord may be a 'landlord' for the purposes of case 9. Usually, it is necessary for the personal representatives to have a beneficial interest in the premises in order to come within this ground for possession, otherwise they are acting in breach of trust. However, in exceptional cases personal representatives who do not have a beneficial interest may reasonably require possession, for example, so that children of the original, deceased landlord may live in the premises.[78]

Landlord by purchase

17.38   Landlords are not entitled to rely on case 9 if they became landlords by purchasing the premises after specified dates.[79] (Counter-Inflation Act 1973 s14 (in subparagraph (ii)) is a reference to tenancies which came within full Rent Act protection when the rateable value limits in RA 1977 s4 were increased.)

17.39   See the explanation of the equivalent wording in HA 1988 Sch 2 ground 1 at para 12.36.

'Greater hardship'

17.40   Tenants have a complete defence to possession proceedings brought under case 9 if they can prove that greater hardship would be caused

---

74 *Smith v Penny* [1947] KB 230.

75 *Theodotou v Potsos* (1991) 23 HLR 356; [1991] 2 EGLR 93, CA.

76 *Richter v Wilson* [1963] 2 QB 426 and *Bloomfield v Westley* [1963] 2 All ER 337.

77 *Baker v Lewis* [1946] 2 All ER 592; *McIntyre v Hardcastle* [1948] 2 KB 82, but see *Bostock v Tacher de la Pagerie* (1987) 282 EG 999; (1987) 19 HLR 358, CA (legal estate owned by father who sought possession as residence for daughter who was equitable tenant in common of beneficial interest). Cf also *Tilling v Whiteman* [1980] AC 1 (on case 11).

78 *Patel v Patel* [1982] 1 All ER 68, cf *Sharpe v Nicholls* [1945] KB 382; [1945] 2 All ER 55 and *Parker v Rosenberg* [1947] KB 371; [1947] 1 All ER 87.

79 See para 17.35.

to them by a possession order than would be caused to the landlord by refusing to grant the possession order. The burden of proving this lies on the tenant.[80] The court should consider how the balance of hardship will operate at the time when a possession order would take effect.[81] The 'greater hardship test' gives the court a very wide discretion to take into account all factors which may affect both landlord and tenant.[82] Matters which may be taken into consideration include:

- The availability of other accommodation for both landlord and tenant. Judges can apply their own knowledge of the difficulty in finding accommodation[83] but it is always advisable for tenants to be able to give evidence about the unsuccessful attempts which they have made to find other accommodation and any particular local accommodation difficulties. The fact that a tenant has taken no steps to look for other accommodation may be prejudicial.[84]
- The financial means of both parties, for example, the ability or inability of a tenant to buy a house.[85]
- The health of the parties, both physical and mental, and the nearness of relatives.[86]
- Hardship which may occur in the future, as well as present hardship.[87]
- The need for a tenant to sell or to store furniture on moving.[88]
- Hardship which may be caused to all people who may be affected by the grant or refusal of an order for possession including:

    ... relatives, dependants, lodgers, guests and the stranger within the gates but [the court] should weigh such hardship with due regard to the status of the persons affected and their 'proximity' to the tenant or landlord.[89]

---

80 *Smith v Penny* [1947] KB 230; *Sims v Wilson* [1946] 2 All ER 261; *Kelley v Goodwin* [1947] 1 All ER 810; *Kidder v Birch* (1983) 265 EG 773; *Robinson v Donovan* [1946] 2 All ER 731; *Chandler v Strevett* [1947] 1 All ER 164 and *Manaton v Edwards* (1985) 276 EG 1256; (1985) 18 HLR 116, CA.

81 *Wheeler v Evans* [1948] 1 KB 459 and *Kidder v Birch* (1983) 265 EG 773.

82 *Robinson v Donovan* [1946] 2 All ER 731.

83 *King v Taylor* [1954] 3 All ER 373 and *Bassett v Fraser* (1981) 9 HLR 105. See also *Manaton v Edwards* (1985) 276 EG 1256.

84 *Kelley v Goodwin* [1947] 1 All ER 810 and *Alexander v Mohamadzadeh* (1986) 18 HLR 90; (1985) 276 EG 1258.

85 *Kelley v Goodwin* [1947] 1 All ER 810.

86 *Thomas v Fryer* [1970] 2 All ER 1 and *King v Taylor* [1954] 3 All ER 373.

87 *Sims v Wilson* [1946] 2 All ER 261; *Wheeler v Evans* [1948] 1 KB 459 and *Bumstead v Wood* (1946) 175 LT 149.

88 *Sims v Wilson* [1946] 2 All ER 261.

89 *Harte v Frampton* [1948] 1 KB 73; [1947] 2 All ER 604.

The court should not, however, take into account trivial things such as 'the absence of a view of a neighbouring hill, river, tree or something pleasant of that kind'.[90]

17.41   There is a 'convention' that where the only issues before a court are questions of greater hardship and reasonableness, no order for costs should be made against the party who loses.[91]

17.42   It is hard for a landlord or tenant who is dissatisfied with a trial judge's finding in relation to greater hardship to succeed on appeal. The Court of Appeal takes the view that in all but exceptional cases greater hardship is a matter for the trial judge, and that findings made at first instance should not be upset.[92] Generally inferences made by judges about greater hardship are based on their findings of fact and no appeal can be made against such findings. There have, however, been successful appeals where tenants argued that the judge's inferences drawn from the facts were wrong and where the judge failed to consider the question of greater hardship properly. It appears that, contrary to the usual rule,[93] the Court of Appeal may be able to take into account material changes in circumstances which have occurred since the original hearing on 'greater hardship' appeals.[94]

Compensation for misrepresentation or concealment

17.43   Rent Act 1977 s102 provides:

> Where, in such circumstances as are specified in Case 8 or Case 9 in Schedule 15 to this Act, a landlord obtains an order for possession of a dwelling-house let on a protected tenancy or subject to a statutory tenancy and it is subsequently made to appear to the court that the order was obtained by misrepresentation or concealment of material facts, the court may order the landlord to pay to the former tenant such sum as appears sufficient as compensation for damage or loss sustained by the tenant as a result of the order.

This provision is similar to HA 1988 s12 (see para 12.156), but, unlike HA 1988 s12, it applies to only two grounds for possession: cases 8 and 9.

---

90   *Coplans v King* [1947] 2 All ER 393.
91   *Funnell v Armstrong* [1962] EGD 319.
92   *Coplans v King* [1947] 2 All ER 393 and *Hodges v Blee* (1987) 283 EG 1215.
93   *Goldthorpe v Bain* [1952] 2 All ER 23.
94   *King v Taylor* [1954] 3 All ER 373.

Case 10: Overcharging of subtenant

17.44   Where the court is satisfied that the rent charged by the tenant –

(a) for any sublet part of the dwelling-house which is a dwelling-house let on a protected tenancy or subject to a statutory tenancy is or was in excess of the maximum rent for the time being recoverable for that part, having regard to ... Part III of this Act, or

(b) for any sublet part of the dwelling-house which is subject to a restricted contract is or was in excess of the maximum (if any) which it is lawful for the lessor, within the meaning of Part V of this Act to require or receive having regard to the provisions of that Part.

Case 10 applies where a tenant overcharges a subtenant. It may come about in a number of ways, for example, by charging more than the registered rent,[95] where there has been a failure to comply with the statutory provisions relating to agreed increases in rent,[96] or where the tenant has charged a subtenant who enjoys a restricted contract more than the rent registered by a rent tribunal.[97] This ground for possession does not apply where the interest of the suboccupant is outside the protection of the Rent Act 1977 or where there is merely an arrangement to share the premises with other people.[98] If a subtenant is overcharged, the court may make an order for possession of the whole of the premises rented by the tenant or just that part to which the overcharging relates.[99]

17.45   There appears to be no reported authority on the position of a subtenant when a landlord has established that there has been overcharging within the meaning of case 10. In ordinary circumstances an order for possession against a tenant also operates against a subtenant, but it would seem that if the subtenancy is lawful, the subtenant would become a direct tenant of the landlord as a result of RA 1977 s137.[100]

95 RA 1977 ss44 and 45.
96 RA 1977 s51.
97 RA 1977 s88.
98 *Kenyon v Walker* [1946] 2 All ER 595.
99 *Boulton v Sutherland* [1938] 1 All ER 488.
100 It is debatable whether or not a landlord would be able to rely on this ground against the subtenant: cf *Leith Properties Ltd v Springer* [1982] 3 All ER 731, CA, where it was held that a landlord was entitled to rely on case 6 against a subtenant notwithstanding the effect of RA 1977 s137. Even if that reasoning does apply to proceedings under case 10, it is hard to imagine circumstances where it would be reasonable for the court to make an order against the tenant which would have the effect of ousting the subtenant.

Mandatory grounds

Case 11: Returning owner-occupier

17.46   Where a person (in this Case referred to as 'the owner-occupier') who let the dwelling-house on a regulated tenancy had, at any time before the letting, occupied it as his residence and –

(a) not later than the relevant date the landlord gave notice in writing to the tenant that possession might be recovered under this Case, and

(b) the dwelling-house has not, since –

  (i) 22nd March 1973, in the case of a tenancy which became a regulated tenancy by virtue of section 14 of the Counter-Inflation Act 1973;

  (ii) 14th August 1974, in the case of a regulated furnished tenancy; or

  (iii) 8th December 1965, in the case of any other tenancy,

been let by the owner-occupier on a protected tenancy with respect to which the condition mentioned in paragraph (a) above was not satisfied, and

(c) the court is of the opinion that of the conditions set out in Part V of this Schedule one of those in paragraphs (a) and (c) to (f) is satisfied.

If the court is of the opinion that, notwithstanding that the condition in paragraph (a) or (b) above is not complied with, it is just and equitable to make an order for possession of the dwelling-house, the court may dispense with the requirements of either or both of those paragraphs as the case may require.

The giving of a notice before 14th August 1974 under section 79 of the Rent Act 1968 shall be treated, in the case of a regulated furnished tenancy, as compliance with paragraph (a) of this Case.

Where the dwelling-house has been let by the owner-occupier on a protected tenancy (in this paragraph referred to as 'the earlier tenancy') granted on or after 16th November 1984 but not later than the end of the period of two months beginning with the commencement of the Rent (Amendment) Act 1985 and either –

(i) the earlier tenancy was granted for a term certain (whether or not to be followed by a further term or to continue thereafter from year to year or some other period) and was during that term a protected shorthold tenancy as defined in section 52 of the Housing Act 1980, or

(ii) the conditions mentioned in paragraphs (a) to (c) of Case 20 were satisfied with respect to the dwelling-house and the earlier tenancy,

then for the purposes of paragraph (b) above the condition in paragraph (a) above is to be treated as having been satisfied with respect to the earlier tenancy.

17.47 This ground for possession has been amended twice since the 1977 Act, first by HA 1980 s66(1) which inserted subparagraph (c), and, second, by the Rent (Amendment) Act 1985. Like cases 12 and 20 it should be read in conjunction with RA 1977 Sch 15 Part V, which was inserted by HA 1980 s66(3) and Sch 7 and which provides:

> *Provisions applying to Cases 11, 12 and 20*
>
> 1. In this Part of this Schedule – '
> mortgage' includes a charge and 'mortgagee' shall be construed accordingly;
> 'owner' means, in relation to Case 11, the owner-occupier; and
> 'successor in title' means any person deriving title from the owner, other than a purchaser for value or a person deriving title from a purchaser for value.
> 2. The conditions referred to in paragraph (c) in each of Cases 11 and 12 and in paragraph (e)(ii) of Case 20 are that –
> (a) the dwelling-house is required as a residence for the owner or any member of his family who resided with the owner when he last occupied the dwelling-house as a residence;
> (b) the owner has retired from regular employment and requires the dwelling-house as a residence;
> (c) the owner has died and the dwelling-house is required as a residence for a member of his family who was residing with him at the time of his death;
> (d) the owner has died and the dwelling-house is required by a successor in title as his residence or for the purpose of disposing of it with vacant possession;
> (e) the dwelling-house is subject to a mortgage, made by deed and granted before the tenancy, and the mortgagee –
> (i) is entitled to exercise a power of sale conferred on him by the mortgage or by section 101 of the Law of Property Act 1925; and
> (ii) requires the dwelling-house for the purpose of disposing of it with vacant possession in exercise of that power; and
> (f) the dwelling-house is not reasonably suitable to the needs of the owner, having regard to his place of work, and he requires it for the purpose of disposing of it with vacant possession and of using the proceeds of that disposal in acquiring, as his residence, a dwelling-house which is more suitable to those needs.

In Case 11, as with all the other grounds for possession in RA 1977 Sch 15 Part II (ie, cases 11 to 20) the phrase 'relevant date' is defined by Schedule 15 Part III para 2, which provides:

> 2. Any reference in Part II of this Schedule to the relevant date shall be construed as follows –
> (a) except in a case falling within paragraph (b) or (c) below, if the protected tenancy, or, in the case of a statutory tenancy, the

previous contractual tenancy, was created before 8th December 1965, the relevant date means 7th June 1966; and

(b) except in a case falling within paragraph (c) below, if the tenancy became a regulated tenancy by virtue of section 14 of the Counter-Inflation Act 1973 and the tenancy or, in the case of a statutory tenancy, the previous contractual tenancy, was created before 22nd March 1973, the relevant date means 22nd September 1973; and

(c) in the case of a regulated furnished tenancy, if the tenancy or, in the case of a statutory furnished tenancy, the previous contractual tenancy was created before 14th August 1974, the relevant date means 13th February 1975; and

(d) in any other case, the relevant date means the date of the commencement of the regulated tenancy in question.

17.48   The purpose of case 11 was to allow owner-occupiers who intended to go away and then to return to their homes to let the premises while they were away.[101] To rely on case 11 a landlord must prove that:

- *Prior to the granting of the tenancy in question, the landlord had at some time in the past occupied the premises as a residence.* The effect of the Rent (Amendment) Act 1985 is that it is not necessary for landlords to prove that they occupied the premises immediately before the granting of the tenancy.[102] Residence at any time in the past is sufficient. It is sufficient for such previous residence to have been temporary and intermittent, although visits to a house by a landlord to stay with a partner who lives there do not count as 'occupation as a residence'.[103] The landlord must previously have occupied the same premises as those which are let to the tenant whom the landlord is seeking to evict: it is not sufficient for the landlord to have lived in other rooms in the same building.

- *Notice of intention to rely on case 11 was given before the commencement of the tenancy.* The schedule provides that such notice must be in writing, although no particular form is necessary. It has been said that it is 'of the utmost importance to a tenant that he should appreciate when he takes rented property whether or

---

101 Griffiths LJ in *Bradshaw and Martin v Baldwin-Wiseman* (1985) 17 HLR 260 at 264; (1985) 49 P&CR 382; [1985] 1 EGLR 123.

102 Reversing the effect of *Pocock v Steel* [1985] 1 WLR 229. Rent (Amendment) Act 1985 operates retrospectively and applies to tenancies created before it received royal assent: *Hewitt v Lewis* [1986] 1 All ER 927, CA.

103 *Naish v Curzon* (1984) 17 HLR 220; (1984) 51 P&CR 229; [1985] 1 EGLR 117, CA; *Mistry v Isidore* (1990) 22 HLR 281; [1990] 2 EGLR 97, CA and *Ibie v Trubshaw* (1990) 22 HLR 191, CA.

not he is obtaining security of tenure'.[104] Such notice must actually be received by the tenant, otherwise it has not been given in accordance with the terms of the schedule. It is not enough for the landlord merely to say that it was sent to the tenant if a tenant's evidence that it was not received is believed.[105] Alternatively, the landlord may satisfy the court that it is just and equitable to dispense with service of the notice. The criteria which apply are the same as under HA 1988 Sch 2 Part I (see para 12.34).

- *All tenants to whom the premises have previously been let since the dates specified in case 11 have been given written notice.* Again there is a provision which entitles the court to dispense with this requirement if it is considered just and equitable to do so.

- *One of the requirements in subparagraphs (a), (c), (d), (e) or (f) in RA 1977 Sch 15 Part V is satisfied.* The most important of these is that the premises are 'required as a residence'. All that is required is that the landlord 'bona fide wants' or 'genuinely has the immediate intention' of occupying the premises.[106] The landlord need not require the premises as a permanent residence and fairly intermittent residence will be sufficient.[107] This is a question of fact in each case. It is sufficient if only one of two joint landlords requires the premises as a residence.[108] Another important use of case 11 would be where a landlord's place of work has changed and he or she wishes to sell the house with vacant possession in order to buy a new house which is more suitable, bearing in mind the place of work.[109] The other situations in which possession may be obtained under case 11 arise following the death of the landlord or relate to rights of a mortgagee.

Case 12: Retirement homes

17.49 Where the landlord (in this Case referred to as 'the owner') intends to occupy the dwelling-house as his residence at such time as he might

---

104 *Bradshaw and Martin v Baldwin-Wiseman* (1985) 17 HLR 260; (1985) 49 P&CR 382; [1985] 1 EGLR 123.
105 *Minay v Sentongo* (1983) 45 P&CR 190.
106 *Kennealy v Dunne* [1977] QB 837, cf *Ghelani v Bowie* (1988) 42 EG 119, CA.
107 *Naish v Curzon* (1984) 17 HLR 220; (1984) 51 P&CR 229; [1985] 1 EGLR 117, where it was argued by the tenant that the landlord required the premises only for holidays and short visits, and *Davies v Peterson* (1989) 21 HLR 63; [1989] 06 EG 130, CA.
108 *Tilling v Whiteman* [1980] AC 1.
109 There must be a connection within a reasonable time between the proposed sale and purchase: *Bissessar v Ghosn* (1986) 18 HLR 486, CA.

retire from regular employment and has let it on a regulated tenancy before he has so retired and –

(a) not later than the relevant date the landlord gave notice in writing to the tenant that possession might be recovered under this Case; and

(b) the dwelling-house has not, since 14th August 1974, been let by the owner on a protected tenancy with respect to which the condition mentioned in paragraph (a) above was not satisfied; and

(c) the court is of the opinion that of the conditions set out in Part V of this Schedule one of those paragraphs (b) to (e) is satisfied.

If the court is of the opinion that, notwithstanding that the condition in paragraph (a) or (b) above is not complied with, it is just and equitable to make an order for possession of the dwelling-house, the court may dispense with the requirements of either or both those paragraphs, as the case may require.

This ground for possession is similar in format to case 11. For the definition of 'relevant date' see RA 1977 Sch 15 Part III para 2 at para 17.47. Provisions about the giving of written notice and the circumstances in which notice may be dispensed with are also similar to those relating to case 11.

17.50 Case 12 may be relied on if:

- the owner has retired and requires the premises as 'a retirement home'; or

- the owner has died and the premises are required as a residence for a member of the family ('member of the family' is not defined and is wider than the limited list of relations in in case 9); or

- the owner has died and a successor in title either requires the premises as a residence or wishes to dispose of them with vacant possession; or

- in some circumstances a mortgagee requires the premises for the purpose of disposing of them with vacant possession.

Case 13: Out of season holiday lets

17.51 Where the dwelling-house is let under a tenancy for a term of years certain not exceeding 8 months and –

(a) not later than the relevant date the landlord gave notice in writing to the tenant that possession might be recovered under this Case; and

(b) the dwelling-house was, at some time within the period of 12 months ending on the relevant date, occupied under a right to occupy it for a holiday.

For the purposes of this case a tenancy shall be treated as being for a term of years certain notwithstanding that it is liable to determination by re-entry or on the happening of any event other than the giving of notice by the landlord to determine the term. This ground is almost identical to Housing Act 1988 Sch 2 ground 3 (see para 12.42). It is important to note that, unlike cases 11 and 12, the court has no power to dispense with the requirement for service of notice prior to the grant of the tenancy.[110]

Case 14: Educational institutions

17.52　Where the dwelling-house is let under a tenancy for a term of years certain not exceeding 12 months and –

(a) not later than the relevant date the landlord gave notice in writing to the tenant that possession might be recovered under this Case; and

(b) at some time within the period of 12 months ending on the relevant date, the dwelling-house was subject to such a tenancy as is referred to in section 8(1) of this Act.

For the purposes of this Case a tenancy shall be treated as being for a term of years certain notwithstanding that it is liable to determination by re-entry or on the happening of any event other than the giving of notice by the landlord to determine the term.

This ground applies to any premises which, during the period of 12 months preceding the current tenancy, were let by a specified educational institution to a student who was pursuing or intended to pursue a course of study provided by that institution or by another specified educational institution.[111] It is almost identical to HA 1988 Sch 2 ground 4 (see para 12.45). Notice in writing must have been given to the current tenant prior to the grant of the tenancy and the court has no power to dispense with service of that notice.

Case 15: Ministers of religion[112]

17.53　Where the dwelling-house is held for the purpose of being available for occupation by a minister of religion as a residence from which to perform the duties of his office and –

(a) not later than the relevant date the tenant was given notice in writing that possession might be recovered under this Case, and

(b) the court is satisfied that the dwelling-house is required for occupation by a minister of religion as such a residence.

110　Cf *Fowler v Minchin* (1987) 19 HLR 224; [1987] 1 EGLR 108, CA.
111　See RA 1977 s8 and Assured and Protected Tenancies (Lettings to Students) Regulations 1998 SI No 1967 as amended.
112　Cf HA 1988 Sch 2 ground 5, see para 12.48.

Case 16: Agricultural employees

17.54   Where the dwelling-house was at any time occupied by a person under the terms of his employment as a person employed in agriculture, and –

(a) the tenant neither is nor at any time was so employed by the landlord and is not the widow of a person who was so employed, and

(b) not later than the relevant date, the tenant was given notice in writing that possession might be recovered under this Case, and

(c) the court is satisfied that the dwelling-house is required for occupation by a person employed, or to be employed, by the landlord in agriculture.

For the purposes of this Case 'employed', 'employment' and 'agriculture' have the same meanings as in the Agricultural Wages Act 1948.

The court cannot dispense with the requirement that notice must be served prior to the commencement of the tenancy. A term in a tenancy agreement that the tenant will vacate on 28 days' notice if the premises are required for another farm worker is not sufficient,[113] but a certificate of a fair rent which was handed to the tenant before the commencement of the tenancy and which stated that the tenancy was to be subject to case 16 has been held to be sufficient.[114]

Case 17: Redundant farmhouses

17.55   Where proposals for amalgamation, approved for the purposes of a scheme under section 26 of the Agriculture Act 1967, have been carried out and, at the time when the proposals were submitted, the dwelling-house was occupied by a person responsible (whether as owner, tenant, or servant or agent of another) for the control of the farming of any part of the land comprised in the amalgamation and

(a) after the carrying out of the proposals, the dwelling-house was let on a regulated tenancy otherwise than to, or to the widow of, either a person ceasing to be so responsible as part of the amalgamation or a person who is, or at any time was, employed by the landlord in agriculture, and

(b) not later than the relevant date the tenant was given notice in writing that possession might be recovered under this Case, and

(c) the court is satisfied that the dwelling-house is required for occupation by a person employed, or to be employed, by the landlord in agriculture, and

---

113 See *Fowler v Minchin* (1987) 19 HLR 224; [1987] 1 EGLR 108, CA, where a possession order was refused.

114 *Springfield Investments v Bell* (1990) 22 HLR 440; [1991] 02 EG 157, CA.

(d) the proceedings for possession are commenced by the landlord at any time during the period of 5 years beginning with the date on which the proposals for the amalgamation were approved or, if occupation of the dwelling-house after the amalgamation contin-ued in, or was first taken by, a person ceasing to be responsible as mentioned in paragraph (a) above or his widow, during a period expiring 3 years after the date on which the dwelling-house next became unoccupied.

For the purposes of this Case 'employed' and 'agriculture' have the same meanings as in the Agricultural Wages Act 1948 and 'amalga-mation' has the same meaning as in Part II of the Agriculture Act 1967.

Case 18: More redundant farmhouses

17.56   Where –
(a) the last occupier of the dwelling-house before the relevant date was a person, or the widow of a person, who was at some time during his occupation responsible (whether as owner, tenant, or servant or agent of another) for the control of the farming of land which formed, together with the dwelling-house, an agricultural unit within the meaning of the Agriculture Act 1947, and
(b) the tenant is neither –
  (i) a person, or the widow of a person, who is or has at any time been responsible for the control of the farming of any part of the said land, nor
  (ii) a person, or the widow of a person, who is or at any time was employed by the landlord in agriculture, and
(c) the creation of the tenancy was not preceded by the carrying out in connection with any of the said land of an amalgamation approved for the purposes of a scheme under section 26 of the Agriculture Act 1967, and
(d) not later than the relevant date the tenant was given notice in writ-ing that possession might be recovered under this Case, and
(e) the court is satisfied that the dwelling-house is required for occu-pation either by a person responsible or to be responsible (whether as owner, tenant, or servant or agent of another) for the control of the farming of any part of the said land or by a person employed or to be employed by the landlord in agriculture, and
(f) in a case where the relevant date was before 9th August 1972, the proceedings for possession are commenced by the landlord before the expiry of 5 years from the date on which the occupier referred to in paragraph (a) above went out of occupation.

For the purposes of this Case 'employed' and 'agriculture' have the same meanings as in the Agricultural Wages Act 1948 and 'amalgama-tion' has the same meaning as in Part II of the Agriculture Act 1967.

Case 19: Protected shorthold tenancies

17.57   This ground for possession is now largely of historical interest only. Protected shorthold tenancies could only be granted between 1980 and 1989 for a fixed term of between one and five years. All new tenancies granted to former protected shorthold tenancies after 15 January 1989 are automatically assured shorthold tenancies.[115]

Case 20: Lettings by armed forces personnel

17.58   Where the dwelling-house was let by a person (in this Case referred to as 'the owner') at any time after the commencement of section 67 of the Housing Act 1980 and –

(a) at the time when the owner acquired the dwelling-house he was a member of the regular armed forces of the Crown;

(b) at the relevant date the owner was a member of the regular armed forces of the Crown;

(c) not later than the relevant date the owner gave notice in writing to the tenant that possession might be recovered under this Case;

(d) the dwelling-house has not, since the commencement of section 67 of the Act of 1980 been let by the owner on a protected tenancy with respect to which the condition mentioned in paragraph (c) above was not satisfied; and

(e) the court is of the opinion that –

(i) the dwelling-house is required as a residence for the owner; or

(ii) of the conditions set out in Part V of this Schedule one of those in paragraphs (c) to (f) is satisfied.

If the court is of the opinion that, notwithstanding that the condition in paragraph (c) or (d) above is not complied with, it is just and equitable to make an order for possession of the dwelling-house, the court may dispense with the requirements of either or both of these paragraphs, as the case may require.

For the purposes of this Case 'regular armed forces of the Crown' has the same meaning as in section 1 of the House of Commons Disqualification Act 1975.

17.59   Members of the regular armed forces may rely on this ground for possession only if they were members of the forces at the time when they acquired the premises and at the date when the tenancy began. The provisions relating to the giving of notice are similar to those in case 11. See para 17.47 for reasons in subparagraphs (c) to (f) of Part V which may found a claim for possession.

115 HA 1980 ss51–55 and HA 1988 s34(3). See *Defending possession proceedings*, 4th edn, 1997, pp232–233.

Other provisions entitling landlords to possession

Statutory overcrowding

17.60 Rent Act 1977 s101 concerns overcrowded dwelling-houses:

> At any time when a dwelling-house is overcrowded, within the mean-ing of Part X of the Housing Act 1985 in such circumstances as to render the occupier guilty of an offence, nothing in this Part of this Act shall prevent the immediate landlord of the occupier from obtain-ing possession of the dwelling-house.

17.61 This section in effect provides an additional mandatory ground for possession. Statutory overcrowding is defined by HA 1985 Part X, which provides:

> 324 *Definition of overcrowding*
> A dwelling is overcrowded for the purposes of this Part when the number of persons sleeping in the dwelling is such as to contravene –
> (a) the standard specified in section 325 (the room standard), or
> (b) the standard specified in section 326 (the space standard).

> 325 *The room standard*
> (1) The room standard is contravened when the number of persons sleeping in a dwelling and the number of rooms available as sleep-ing accommodation is such that two persons of opposite sexes who are not living together as husband and wife must sleep in the same room.
> (2) For this purpose –
> (a) children under the age of ten shall be left out of account, and
> (b) a room is available as sleeping accommodation if it is of a type normally used in the locality either as a bedroom or as a living room.

> 326 *The space standard*
> (1) The space standard is contravened when the number of persons sleeping in a dwelling is in excess of the permitted number, hav-ing regard to the number and floor area of the rooms of the dwell-ing available as sleeping accommodation.
> (2) For this purpose –
> (a) no account shall be taken of a child under the age of one and a child aged one or over but under ten shall be reckoned as one-half of a unit, and
> (b) a room is available as sleeping accommodation if it is of a type normally used in the locality either as a living room or as a bedroom.
> (3) The permitted number of persons in relation to a dwelling is whichever is the less of –

(a) the number specified in Table I in relation to the number of rooms in the dwelling available as sleeping accommodation, and

(b) the aggregate for all such rooms in the dwelling of the numbers specified in column 2 of Table II in relation to each room of the floor area specified in column 1.

No account shall be taken for the purposes of either Table of a room having a floor area of less than 50 square feet.

TABLE I

Number of rooms	Number of persons
1	2
2	3
3	5
4	7½
5 or more	2 for each room

TABLE II

Floor area of room	Number of persons
110 sq ft or more	2
90 sq ft or more but less than 110 sq ft	1½
70 sq ft or more but less than 90 sq ft	1
50 sq ft or more but less than 70 sq ft	½

(4) The Secretary of State may by regulations prescribe the manner in which the floor area of a room is to be ascertained for the purpose of this section; and the regulations may provide for the exclusion from computation, or the bringing into computation at a reduced figure, of floor space in a part of the room which is of less than a specified height not exceeding eight feet.

(5) Regulations under subsection (4) shall be made by statutory instrument which shall be subject to annulment in pursuance of a resolution of either House of Parliament.

(6) A certificate of the local housing authority stating the number and floor areas of the rooms in a dwelling, and that the floor areas have been ascertained in the prescribed manner, is prima facie evidence for the purposes of legal proceedings of the facts stated in it.

Responsibility of occupier

327 *Penalty for occupier causing or permitting overcrowding*

(1) The occupier of a dwelling who causes or permits it to be overcrowded commits a summary offence, subject to subsection (2).

(2) The occupier is not guilty of an offence –

    (a) if the overcrowding is within the exceptions specified in section 328 or 329 (children attaining age of 10 or visiting relatives), or

    (b) by reason of anything done under the authority of, and in accordance with any conditions specified in, a licence granted by the local housing authority under section 330.

(3) A person committing an offence under this section is liable on conviction to a fine not exceeding level 2 on the standard scale and to a further fine not exceeding one-tenth of the amount corresponding to that level in respect of every day subsequent to the date on which he is convicted on which the offence continues.

328 *Exception: children attaining age of 1 or 10*

(1) Where a dwelling which would not otherwise be overcrowded becomes overcrowded by reason of a child attaining the age of one or ten, then if the occupier –

    (a) applies to the local housing authority for suitable alternative accommodation, or

    (b) has so applied before the date when the child attained the age in question,

he does not commit an offence under section 327 (occupier causing or permitting overcrowding), so long as the condition in subsection (2) is met and the occupier does not fail to take action in the circumstances specified in subsection (3).

(2) The condition is that all the persons sleeping in the dwelling are persons who were living there when the child attained that age and thereafter continuously live there, or children born after that date of any of those persons.

(3) The exception provided by this section ceases to apply if –

    (a) suitable alternative accommodation is offered to the occupier on or after the date on which the child attains that age, or, if he has applied before that date, is offered at any time after the application, and he fails to accept it, or

    (b) the removal from the dwelling of some person not a member of the occupier's family is on that date or thereafter becomes reasonably practicable having regard to all the circumstances (including the availability of suitable alternative accommodation for that person), and the occupier fails to require his removal.

329 *Exception: visiting family member*

Where the persons sleeping in an overcrowded dwelling include a member of the occupier's family who does not live there but is sleeping there temporarily, the occupier is not guilty of an offence under section 327 (occupier causing or permitting overcrowding) unless the circumstances are such that he would be so guilty if that member of his family were not sleeping there.

17.62   It has been held that a room with no natural lighting or ventilation was not a room generally used in the locality as a living or a bed-room,[116] and so it could not be taken into account when determining the number of rooms.

17.63   A 'room' is a room which can be used for living or sleeping in.[117] The relevant date when overcrowding must exist is the date of the trial and so a tenant has a complete defence if overcrowding has ceased by the time of the court hearing.[118] It is not necessary for there to be a conviction before a landlord can rely on this 'ground'.[119] All that a landlord needs to do is to prove that the circumstances are such that a conviction for overcrowding could be obtained and that any con-tractual tenancy has been validly determined, normally by serving a notice to quit.

17.64   Where there is statutory overcrowding, the court has no power to suspend a possession order.[120]

Demolition orders, prohibiton orders etc

17.65   See para 12.151.

Restricted contracts

17.66   A significant proportion of tenants or licensees[121] who moved into premises before 15 January 1989 and who did not enjoy full Rent Act protection occupied those premises under restricted contracts.[122] Many, but not all, tenants or licensees of resident landlords whose

116 *Patel v Godal* [1979] CLY 1620.
117 *Patel v Godal* [1979] CLY 1620.
118 *Zbytniewski v Broughton* [1956] 2 QB 673; [1956] 3 All ER 348. Cf *Henry Smith's Charity v Bartosiak-Jentys* (1992) 24 HLR 627; [1991] 2 EGLR 276, CA.
119 *Zbytniewski v Broughton* [1956] 2 QB 673; [1956] 3 All ER 348.
120 *Henry Smith's Charity v Bartosiak-Jentys* (1992) 24 HLR 627; [1991] 2 EGLR 276, CA.
121 Although RA 1977 s19(2) includes a reference to rent, it is clear that the term 'restricted contract' includes licensees with exclusive occupation of premises: *Luganda v Service Hotels Ltd* [1969] 2 All ER 692 (room occupied for three years in large hotel) and *R v Battersea, Wandsworth, Mitcham and Wimbledon Rent Tribunal ex p Parikh* [1957] 1 All ER 352 (occupant described by landlord as 'paying guest'), but cf *R v Paddington and St Marylebone Rent Tribunal ex p Walston Hotels Ltd* (1948) 152 EG 449 (no exclusive occupation) and *R v South Middlesex Rent Tribunal ex p Beswick* (1976) 32 P&CR 67 (a room in a YWCA hostel).
122 See RA 1977 s19.

interests were created before 15 January 1989 and who were deprived of full Rent Act protection[123] had restricted contracts. The other principal classes of tenants who had restricted contracts were those who were excluded from Rent Act protection because their tenancies included the provision of substantial 'attendances' or small quantities of board by the landlord.[124]

17.67   Nowadays there are virtually no tenants or licensees remaining with restricted contracts.[125] Housing Act 1988 s36 not only provided that no new restricted contracts could be created on or after 15 January 1989, but also stipulated that if the rent under a restricted contract was varied by agreement, the letting should be treated as a new contract, and could therefore no longer be a restricted contract. Accordingly, only tenants or licensees whose interests were created before 15 January 1989 and whose rents have not been varied by agreement since that date can have restricted contracts. (A registration of a rent by a rent tribunal does not count as a variation by agreement.) For this reason this edition of *Defending possession proceedings* no longer deals with restricted contracts.[126]

---

123 RA 1977 s12 and Sch 2.

124 RA 1977 ss7 and 19.

125 However, for a recent case involving a tenant who originally had a restricted contract, see *Matthews v Rowe* 26 March 2001, unreported, QBD.

126 See *Defending possession proceedings*, 4th edn, 1997, chapter 16.

CHAPTER 18

Unprotected tenants and licensees

18.1 If a tenant does not come within one of the forms of statutory protection provided by the Housing Act (HA) 1985, the Housing Act 1988 or the Rent Act 1977, landlords seeking possession need only commence proceedings and prove that they have an interest in the premises and that the contractual tenancy has been determined. Such unprotected tenants include Crown tenants, tenants of fully mutual housing co-operatives,[1] student tenants of university accommodation and tenants of temporary accommodation provided by a local authority following its acceptance of a homelessness duty. It is likely that the only defence available in the short term to such a tenant is to allege that the contractual tenancy had not been determined at the date when proceedings were issued,[2] for example, because a notice to quit was defective. If the landlord is a public authority, including a 'hybrid' authority exercising a public function,[3] it may be possible to judicially review the decision to bring proceedings or to defend the claim for possession on public law grounds, although, in the current state of the law, 'human rights' arguments are likely to succeed only in exceptional cases.[4] For further discussion of human rights and public law defences, see chapters 25 and 26.

18.2 Protection from Eviction Act (PEA) 1977 s3 makes it unlawful for landlords of many unprotected tenants and licensees to enforce their right to recover possession 'otherwise than by proceedings in the court'. Landlords who fail to comply with PEA 1977 s3 commit a criminal offence contrary to section 1(2) of that Act and are liable

---

1 See *Berrisford v Mexfield Housing Co-operative Ltd* [2010] EWCA Civ 811.
2 For the termination of contractual tenancies, see chapter 14.
3 See *R (Weaver) v London & Quadrant Housing Trust* [2009] EWCA Civ 587 para 12.82.
4 *Lambeth LBC v Kay* [2006] UKHL 10; *Doherty v Birmingham CC* [2008] UKHL 57.

to a claim for damages in tort. Section 3 applies to all unprotected tenancies and licences apart from excluded tenancies and excluded licences created on or after 15 January 1989. The categories of tenancies and licences which are 'excluded' are defined in PEA 1977 s3A (see para 14.10). In brief, they are where accommodation is shared with a landlord or landlord's family, where the occupier is a former trespasser, where occupation is for a holiday, where occupation is rent-free, where the accommodation is provided to an asylum-seeker under the statutory scheme and where the occupier is a licensee of a room in a hostel provided by a social landlord. Case-law has also determined that interim accommodation provided by local authorities to homeless persons is outside the scope of section 3 (see paras 5.25 and 14.11).

18.3   An unprotected tenant or licensee has a complete defence to possession proceedings if the tenancy or licence has not been terminated by the time that proceedings are issued,[5] or if a further tenancy or licence has been created. An unprotected tenancy, if periodic, can be terminated by a valid notice to quit, which must comply with PEA 1977 s5 (see para 14.8), and the tenant can lawfully be evicted only by court order under section 3 of that Act, unless the tenancy is an 'excluded letting'. If the tenancy is excluded, a court order is not required for a lawful eviction, subject to the minimal safeguards of section 6 of the Criminal Law Act 1977. A notice to quit is still required at common law, but the period of the notice will (in the absence of any specific provision in the agreement) be the same as the rental period.[6] Thus, an excluded weekly tenancy will require one week's notice to quit which must expire on the first or last day of the rental period[7]. A common law notice to quit need not be in writing unless the tenancy stipulates otherwise.[8]

18.4   A licence may simply be a temporary agreement that someone may be on or stay on the premises. In *Thomas v Sorrell*,[9] Vaughan CJ stated, 'a dispensation or licence properly passeth no interest nor alters or transfers property in anything but only makes an action lawful, which without it has been unlawful'. It may be hard to draw the line between an owner who says, 'You can stay on the premises' and

---

5   *GLC v Jenkins* [1975] 1 WLR 155; [1975] 1 All ER 354.
6   *Doe d. Peacock v Raffan* (1806) 6 Esp. 4.
7   *Crate v Miller* [1947] KB 946.
8   *Timmins v Rowlinson* (1765) 3 Burr. 1603; *Bird v Defonvielle* (1846) 2 C. & K. 415, 420, n. (b).
9   (1673) Vaugh 330.

one who says, 'I do not agree to you staying on the premises, but I will refrain from evicting you until a certain date'.

18.5   If the licensee is a contractual licensee, the owner must observe the contractual provisions which the licence contains relating to termination. Whether or not there are contractual provisions in the licence, a licensee must be given reasonable notice:[10] there is no need for the notice itself to specify the particular time or indeed a reasonable time. However, a reasonable time must have elapsed between the giving of the notice and the issue of court proceedings.[11] The notice determines the licence immediately on service[12] but does not become operative until the expiry of such a reasonable time, even if the notice contains a specified period of time which is too short. There are no set rules about what is reasonable. The length of time depends on the circumstances in any particular case, and factors which may be taken into account are the length of time that the licensee has resided in the premises and the periods for which payments are made. A notice to terminate a licence must now comply with PEA 1977 s5 (see para 14.8) unless the licence is 'excluded'. If a licence is excluded, notice may be given orally.[13] If there are joint owners, notice may be given by one of them acting alone.[14]

18.6   A former unprotected tenant or licensee whose letting has been determined but who remains on the premises is a trespasser. Accordingly, owners are entitled to damages for trespass without bringing evidence that they could or would have relet the property if the trespasser had not been there. The measure of damages is usually either the amount of loss suffered by the owner or the value to the trespasser of the use of the property for the period of occupation, and in a usual case this is the ordinary letting value of the property.[15]

10 *Minister of Health v Bellotti* [1944] KB 298; [1944] 1 All ER 238.
11 *Minister of Health v Bellotti* [1944] KB 298; [1944] 1 All ER 238.
12 *Minister of Health v Bellotti* [1944] KB 298; [1944] 1 All ER 238.
13 *Crane v Morris* [1965] 1 WLR 1104; [1965] 3 All ER 77.
14 *Annen v Rattee* (1985) 17 HLR 323; (1984) 273 EG 503.
15 *Swordheath Properties Ltd v Tabet* [1979] 1 WLR 285; [1979] 1 All ER 240;
    Ministry of Defence v Thompson [1993] 40 EG 148; (1993) 25 HLR 552, CA and
    Ministry of Defence v Ashman (1993) 66 P&CR 195; (1993) 25 HLR 513, CA. See
    chapter 32.

CHAPTER 19

Premises occupied by employees

19.1   Employees who occupy residential premises owned by their employers may be either tenants or licensees. Where it is necessary for the employee to live in the premises for the better performance of a job or where the employee is required to live in premises as a term of his or her contract of employment, it is likely that the employee is merely a licensee of those premises.[1] If this is not the case, an employee who has exclusive possession for a term and who pays rent is a tenant.[2] If the tenancy satisfies the usual requirements for full Rent Act (RA) or Housing Act (HA) protection[3] there is security of tenure, but subject to the possibility of possession proceedings brought under RA 1977 Sch 15 case 8 (see para 17.33), HA 1985 Sch 2 ground 12 (see para 3.173) or HA 1988 Sch 2 ground 16 (see para 12.147).

19.2   If, however, employees are licensees, they have no security of tenure. Service licensees have only the limited protection that employers must bring court proceedings to evict them. Protection from Eviction Act (PEA) 1977 s8(2) provides:

> For the purposes of Part I of this Act a person who, under the terms of his employment, had exclusive possession of the premises other than as a tenant shall have been deemed to have been a tenant and the expressions 'let' and 'tenancy' shall be construed accordingly.

---

1   *Smith v Seghill Overseers* (1874–75) LR 10 QB 422; *Fox v Dalby* (1874–75) LR 10 CP 285 and *Glasgow Corporation v Johnstone* [1965] AC 609; [1965] 2 WLR 657.
2   *Royal Philanthropic Society v County* (1986) 18 HLR 83; (1985) 276 EG 1068.
3   One particular problem which tenants who are employees sometimes face is that often there is no rent payable and accordingly the tenancy is outside full Rent Act protection because of RA 1977 s5 or cannot be an assured tenancy because of HA 1988 Sch 1 para 3. See *Heslop v Burns* [1974] 1 WLR 1241 and *Montagu v Browning* [1954] 1 WLR 1039.

19.3   This means that PEA 1977 s1 (unlawful eviction and harassment of occupier) and s3 (prohibition of eviction without due process of law) apply to service licensees. Although a service licensee may not pay a quantified rent for his or her accommodation, it is likely that the value of the accommodation will be reflected in his or her wages. The letting would not therefore be an 'excluded letting' within PEA 1977 s3A, because it would be granted for 'money's worth' (see para 14.10).

19.4   Employers need prove only that they own or have an interest in the premises and that the rights of the employee (or ex-employee) to reside in the premises have been determined, in accordance with either the contract of employment or any other agreement relating to the premises. In general, the notice required to determine a service licence is the same as the notice necessary to terminate the employment, and it is not necessary to serve a separate notice to terminate the licence under PEA 1977 s5.[4]

19.5   If service licensees consider that they have been unfairly dismissed, an application may be made to an employment tribunal. Although the employment tribunal may recommend reinstatement, this is of little assistance in defending possession proceedings for tied accommodation. The employment tribunal cannot compel reinstatement and the court considering possession proceedings is generally interested in ascertaining only whether or not the contract has been terminated, not whether it has been terminated fairly or unfairly. Applications for adjournments of such possession proceedings, pending the hearing of an application to an employment tribunal, are generally unsuccessful.[5]

---

4   *Doe d Hughes v Derry* (1840) 9 C & P 494; *Ivory v Palmer* [1975] ICR 340, CA, and *Norris v Checksfield* [1991] 1 WLR 1241; [1991] 4 All ER 327; (1991) 23 HLR 425, CA.

5   See, eg, *Whitbread West Pennines Ltd v Reedy* [1988] ICR 807; (1988) 20 HLR 642, CA (manager of public house dismissed).

CHAPTER 20

Death

20.1   A contractual tenancy does not terminate on the tenant's death unless the tenancy expressly states that that is to happen.[1] If the tenant leaves a will, the tenancy passes to the tenant's executors. However, if there is no will and the tenant dies intestate, the tenancy passes to the Public Trustee until such time as letters of administration are taken out.[2] Unless there has been an automatic statutory succession, this applies to contractual Rent Act tenancies, secure tenancies, demoted and introductory tenancies, family intervention tenancies and assured and assured shorthold tenancies, but not to Rent Act (RA) statutory tenancies.

20.2   If a landlord wishes to terminate a contractual tenancy vested in executors or administrators by serving a notice to quit, that notice must be served on the executors or administrators, as the case may be. If letters of administration have not been taken out, the notice must be addressed to the personal representatives of the deceased and left at or posted to the last known place of residence of the deceased. In addition a copy must be served on the Official Solicitor and Public Trustee at PO Box 3010, London WC2B 6JS.[3]

20.3   If a deceased tenant's contractual tenancy is not determined in this way, any occupiers have a complete defence to possession proceedings which are issued before the tenancy has been determined.[4] In the long term, however, there is nothing to stop the landowner serving a valid notice to quit and then bringing new proceedings.

1 *Youngmin v Heath* [1974] 1 WLR 135.
2 Law of Property (Miscellaneous Provisions) Act 1994 s14.
3 Public Trustee (Notices Affecting Land) (Title on Death) Regulations 1995 SI No 1330. See *LS Gaz*, 17 January 2002, p31 and March 2002 *Legal Action* 16. See also *Wirral BC v Smith* (1982) 4 HLR 81; (1982) 43 P&CR 312, CA.
4 *Wirral BC v Smith* (1982) 4 HLR 81; (1982) 43 P&CR 312, CA.

20.4   Although assured and assured shorthold tenancies can be inherited by will or on intestacy, the death of an assured tenant gives the landlord a ground for possession against anyone other than the deceased tenant's spouse or civil partner or anyone living with the 'original tenant as his or her wife or husband or civil partner': these are the only persons who are entitled under the 1988 Act to succeed to the tenancy.[5]

20.5   In the ordinary course of events, a Rent Act statutory tenancy comes to an end on the death of the tenant since a dead person cannot occupy premises as a residence.[6] As a statutory tenancy is only a personal right it cannot be left to another person through the deceased tenant's will.[7] However, RA 1977 s2(1)(b) and Sch 1 Part I, as amended by the Housing Act (HA) 1988 s39, provide that a spouse or civil partner who was living with the tenant at the time of death or, if there was no such spouse or civil partner, a member of the tenant's family who had been living with the tenant for two years immediately before the death, can succeed to the tenancy. A spouse or civil partner who 'inherits' a tenancy in this way is called a 'statutory tenant by succession' and acquires a statutory tenancy. 'Spouse' is defined as including any person living with the deceased tenant as wife or husband, and 'civil partner' is defined as including any person living with the deceased as if a civil partner. Any other member of the family who succeeds to a tenancy as a result of the death of a tenant on or after 15 January 1989 acquires an assured tenancy (see chapter 12). The succession provisions apply to both contractual and statutory tenancies.[8] Rent Act 1977 Sch 1 provides that any tenancy can be passed on twice if the first successor is a spouse or civil partner, as defined.

20.6   Any spouse, civil partner or member of the original tenant's family who acquires a tenancy in this way takes the tenancy free from any rent arrears which existed at the late tenant's death: such arrears become a liability of the deceased tenant's estate. However, where the tenancy was subject to a postponed or suspended possession order, such order will continue to have effect, so that the successor may in practice become responsible for the late tenant's arrears by compliance with the terms of the order.[9]

---

5   HA 1988 s15 and Sch 4 para 2, as amended by Civil Partnership Act 2004 Sch 8 para 34. See also HA 1988 Sch 2 ground 7 (see para 12.57).
6   RA 1977 s2. See chapter 16 and *Skinner v Geary* [1931] 2 KB 546.
7   *John Lovibond and Sons Ltd v Vincent* [1929] 1 KB 687.
8   *Moodie v Hosegood* [1952] AC 61; [1951] 2 All ER 582, HL.
9   *Sherrin v Brand* [1956] 1 QB 403.

20.7   It is possible for a tenant to leave a contractual tenancy in a will to one person, but for another to be entitled to succeed to the tenancy in accordance with RA 1977 Sch 1. In this situation any person who would be entitled to succeed to the tenancy acquires a statutory tenancy by succession and the contractual tenancy goes into 'abeyance' until the statutory tenancy comes to an end.[10]

10 *Moodie v Hosegood* [1952] AC 61; [1951] 2 All ER 582, HL, overruling *Smith v Mather* [1948] 2 KB 212; [1948] 1 All ER 704 and *Thynne v Salmon* [1948] 1 KB 482; [1948] 1 All ER 49.

Rental purchase agreements

Introduction

21.1 'Rental purchase agreements'[1] are happily now almost of historical interest only. The true rental purchase agreement was, in essence, a contract for the sale of a property with the purchaser allowed into possession paying the purchase price by instalments and with completion of the sale taking place only following payment of the last instalment. It is inaccurate to describe the arrangement as a rental agreement because the purchaser was usually allowed into possession under the terms of the agreement for sale, not as tenant, but as licensee.

21.2 For a short analysis of the purchase and rental arrangements entered into within the Muslim communities to encourage home purchase without infringing Islamic principles on the payment and receipt of interest, see chapter 45.

21.3 Usually, 'rental purchase agreements' were in written form, often of a pro forma nature. The agreement provided for a specified sum to be paid before completion could be called for. It usually also specified the interest rate to be charged on the outstanding capital. A fixed weekly or monthly sum was generally specified, which went either directly towards repaying the capital borrowed or towards satisfying the accruing interest, buildings insurance and other outgoings, with only part going towards repayment of the capital. Some agreements provided for completion to take place before payment of the whole capital sum but with the vendor granting a mortgage at the date of completion of the sale for the sum outstanding at that time. There were many permutations.

Rental purchase and evasion of security of tenure

21.4 Many ostensible rental purchase agreements were prepared not with the intention of selling the property to a willing purchaser but with the sole intention of avoiding the Rent Act (RA) or Housing Act (HA) protection otherwise given to tenants, by the simple device of not creating a tenancy. Following *Street v Mountford*,[2] it was thought that, where there was a bona fide rental purchase intended by the parties,

---

1 See generally B Hoggett, 'Houses on the never-never: some legal aspects of rental purchase' (1972) 36 Conv 325; 'Houses on the never-never: some recent developments' (1975) 39 Conv 343; 'How to help the rental purchaser' June 1976 *LAG Bulletin* 133; L Burrows and R Murphy, *Rental purchase – the case for change* (1990); Shelter and National Consumer Council, *Buying a home on rental purchase; a consumer view* (1989).

2 [1985] AC 809; [1985] 2 WLR 877; [1985] 2 All ER 289, HL.

no landlord/tenant relationship would be established. However, after *Bretherton v Paton*,[3] it seems that entering into possession even with the intention of purchasing the property does not bar the application of the *Street* principle that a tenancy arises where the occupier has exclusive possession paying a specified periodic payment. Usually, in such circumstances the tenancy will be protected under the Rent Act 1977 or be an assured tenancy under the Housing Act 1988.

21.5   Where it is felt that an arrangement is not caught by the principle in *Street* and it proves necessary to consider whether an arrangement is a bona fide rental purchase, advisers should consider the following points:

- Was there any expectation that the occupier would in fact purchase the property? If not, then this is likely to be decisive. It will be necessary to check the dealings between the parties *before* the document was signed. How was the property advertised, what conversation took place, did the owner really want to sell the property?
- Was the sale price inflated above market value or was the interest rate specified in the agreement inflated as compared to the then current mortgage rate?
- Is the term of repayment unduly long, either in itself or when compared with the length of any leasehold interest granted?
- Are there any clauses inconsistent with a bona fide contract for sale, for example, a prohibition against assigning, subletting or parting with possession in the agreement?
- Was there the usual investigation of title and the property as is customary before a purchase/sale?
- Have the parties' actions since the date of the agreement been more consistent with a tenancy than a bona fide sale?
- Were solicitors instructed by the occupier before entering into the agreement?
- Does the agreement contain terms that are unfair within the meaning of the Unfair Terms in Consumer Contracts Regulations 1999?[4] Although the Unfair Contract Terms Act 1977 Sch 1 para 1 exempts land transactions from the provisions of that Act, there is no equivalent exemption from the regulations. Under the regulations an unfair term is one which, contrary to the requirement of good faith, causes a significant imbalance in the parties' rights

---

3 (1986) 18 HLR 257, CA; cf *Sharp v McArthur* (1987) 19 HLR 364, CA; see also *Martin v Davies* (1952) 7 HLR 119, CA, and *Francis Jackson Developments Ltd v Stemp* [1943] 2 All ER 601, CA.

4 SI No 2083.

and obligations to the detriment of the consumer.[5] Any term which is unfair is not binding on the consumer.[6] Schedule 2 contains 'an indicative and non-exhaustive list of terms which may be regarded as unfair'.

21.6   Where an occupier wishes to dispute his or her description in the agreement (for example, as 'purchaser' rather than as 'tenant') he or she can either apply for a declaration by the county court that he or she is a tenant with statutory protection[7] or raise that proposition as a defence to possession proceedings.

Statutory and equitable protection

21.7   Assuming that the agreement in question is a bona fide rental purchase agreement, the court has a statutory discretion to protect the occupier from eviction under HA 1980 s88:

> 88 (1) Where, under the terms of a rental purchase agreement, a person has been let into possession of a dwelling-house and, on the termination of the agreement or of his right to possession under it, proceedings are brought for the possession of the dwelling-house, the court may –
> (a) adjourn the proceedings; or
> (b) on making an order for the possession of the dwelling-house, stay or suspend execution of the order or postpone the date of possession;
> for such period or periods as the court thinks fit.

This is broadly similar to the protection given to mortgagors in default (see para 40.14) although there is no requirement that the occupier clear the arrears within a reasonable period.

21.8   The court can, but is not obliged to, grant relief on the condition that the occupier makes payments towards the arrears:

> (2) On any such adjournment, stay, suspension or postponement the court may impose such conditions with regard to payments by the person in possession in respect of his continued occupation of the dwellinghouse and such other conditions as the court thinks fit.[8]

The court has specific power to revoke or vary any condition which it has imposed.[9]

---

5   Reg 4.
6   Reg 5.
7   RA 1977 s141 and HA 1988 s40.
8   HA 1980 s88(2).
9   HA 1980 s88(3).

21.9 The definition of 'rental purchase agreement' is quite widely drafted:

> (4) In this section 'rental purchase agreement' means an agreement for the purchase of a dwelling-house (whether freehold or lease-hold property) under which the whole or part of the purchase price is to be paid in three or more instalments and the completion of the purchase is deferred until the whole or a specified part of the purchase price has been paid.[10]

The definition requires the purchase price to be paid in at least three instalments so as not to protect purchasers who are allowed into possession in the more usual transaction after exchange of contracts where usually a ten per cent deposit is paid but before completion when the second and final instalment is made.

21.10 The court has some limited equitable jurisdiction to grant relief against forfeiture for breach of any terms of the agreement although the statutory discretion is much more extensive.[11]

Necessity for possession proceedings

21.11 Where a person is let into possession under a rental purchase agreement (as defined above) and continues to reside in the property after termination of the agreement or his or her right to possession under the agreement, then the provisions of the Protection from Eviction Act 1977 will usually apply so as to require the owner to regain possession by court order.[12] An additional prohibition against eviction without court order is contained in the Consumer Credit Act 1974 s92(2) in respect of regulated conditional sale agreements.

Other points

21.12 Payments under 'an agreement for the purchase of a dwelling under which the whole or part of the purchase price is to be paid in more than one instalment and the completion of the purchase is deferred until the whole or a specified part of the purchase price has been paid' qualify as 'rent' for housing benefit purposes.[13]

---

10 HA 1980 s88(4).
11 See references at note 1 above and note at (1974) 37 MLR 705.
12 HA 1980 Sch 25 para 61.
13 Housing Benefit Regulations 2006 SI No 213 reg 12(1)(i).

CHAPTER 22

Shared ownership

22.1   The last couple of decades have seen attempts to blur the edges between owner-occupation and renting. There is every reason to believe that the blurring will continue. Great efforts have been made to ease people into owner-occupation by use of shared ownership schemes.[1] These usually allow occupiers progressively to buy tranches of the homes that they occupy until the property is owned outright, or at least owned subject to a mortgage.

22.2   There are particular problems which face occupiers under such schemes, the principal one being that where part is owned subject to a mortgage and part is rented, there are potentially two separate claims for possession if the occupier defaults. It will be necessary to service both debts simultaneously in order to retain possession.

22.3   Under a typical shared ownership scheme, a freeholder agrees to grant a long lease to the occupier in return for a premium representing, for example, a quarter or half of the capital value of the property. If the prospective occupier cannot raise the money the premium is raised by way of a mortgage from an institutional lender, or even from the freeholder. The occupier moves into the property and pays rent calculated by reference to the outstanding element not yet purchased.

22.4   In the above example the occupier will usually be an assured tenant since none of the exceptions in the Housing Act 1988 Sch 1 are likely to apply (see para 12.5). It is likely that if the freeholder is a housing association it will have specifically contracted (in the cases of shared ownership agreements entered into after 28 February 1997)

---

1   The Department for Communities and Local Government website has an analysis of all the various schemes aimed at encouraging council and social tenants, key workers and people from council waiting lists into shared ownership: www.homesandcommunities.co.uk/home_buy.

into the grant of an assured tenancy rather than the presumed assured shorthold tenancy otherwise created after that date. Only where the rent payable under the tenancy is over £25,000 per annum (£100,000 from 1 October 2010[2]) or below £250 per annum (£1,000 in London) would the tenancy fall outside the Housing Act 1988 assured tenancy regime on grounds of rent level (see para 12.5). The tenant is, accordingly, at risk of possession proceedings under all the grounds in the Housing Act 1988 Sch 2.

22.5   In *Richardson v Midland Heart Ltd*,[3] the county court granted a possession order on the basis that the occupying 'shared owner' was an assured tenant and, given the rent arrears, was liable to eviction under ground 8. The court rejected the argument that the housing association held the freehold or the lease on trust for the tenant. She was simply an assured tenant under a 99-year lease and none of the exemptions took the tenancy outside the assured tenancy regime. The implications for the future of low cost shared home ownership of this decision require consideration by the Court of Appeal.[4]

22.6   In addition, where in purchasing the lease the purchaser executed a legal charge, there is also a risk of mortgage possession proceedings in the event of default under that agreement.

22.7   Occupiers under shared ownership agreements which fall within the scope of the Housing Act 1988 and the Administration of Justice Acts will be entitled to claim relief under either legislative regime in the event of possession proceedings being brought by the relevant claimant except where proceedings are brought relying on ground 8.

22.8   Advisers will need to consider the particular agreement entered into by the individual being advised, as there are many differing forms of the shared ownership agreement.

22.9   If there is a mortgage and, in default of rent or service charge payments, the freeholder threatens to forfeit the lease, the lender will often meet those payments (to protect its security) and add the payment made to the outstanding debt owed by the mortgage borrower. Advisers will need to be alert to assess whether payments made by the mortgage-lender to the landlord who threatens forfeiture proceedings and hence the security are validly made. It is common for lenders to pay over money to the landlord simply because the landlord says that there are rent arrears and hence the risk of forfeiture. Such

---

2   Assured Tenancies (Amendment) (England) Order 2010 SI No 908.
3   [2008] L&TR 31.
4   For an analysis of the issues see S Bright, 'Low cost homeownership: legal issues of the shared ownership lease' [2009] 73 Conv 337.

payments are then recorded as mortgage arrears and, in turn, put the borrower/tenant at risk of eviction by the lender. The assertion that the borrower is in mortgage arrears should be tested in correspondence and in possession proceedings if the borrower has ceased to pay rent to the landlord for legitimate reasons. It is clear that a mortgage-lender has the right to seek relief against forfeiture if the freeholder seeks to forfeit the shared ownership lease.[5]

22.10   The Homes and Communities Agency, the Council of Mortgage Lenders and the National Housing Federation have issued joint guidance about shared ownership properties, including repossession: *Shared ownership: joint guidance for England.*[6]

Example

P agrees to buy a one-third share of a 99-year lease on a flat renovated by a housing association which has a market value of £180,000. The market rent for the flat is £1,200 per month. P takes a 99-year lease and borrows £60,000 from a bank, secured by way of legal charge on the leasehold title. P then makes mortgage repayments on the £60,000 borrowed and pays rent at the rate of £800 per month. Subsequently P agrees to purchase a further one-third share. P borrows an additional £60,000, and as a result the rent paid to the association is reduced to £400 per month but the mortgage repayments double. On buying the last third, P will then cease paying rent to the association and will continue to pay the mortgage repayments until the end of the term agreed with the bank at the time of the taking of the lease.

---

5   *Sinclair Gardens Investments (Kensington) Ltd v Walsh* [1996] QB 231; [1995] 3 WLR 524; (1996) 28 HLR 338, CA. See para 14.58 onwards on relief from forfeiture.
6   April 2010. See www.homesandcommunities.co.uk/public/documents/shared_ownership_guidance.pdf.

Possession procedure

Procedure in possession proceedings

The need for possession proceedings

23.1   It is usual for landlords who wish to evict occupiers to take possession proceedings through the courts. In many circumstances, landlords who take the law into their own hands by evicting people without first obtaining court orders risk prosecution under the Protection from Eviction Act (PEA) 1977, with a fine and/or imprisonment and/or a claim for substantial damages for breach of covenant for quiet enjoyment, trespass and/or unlawful eviction under the Housing Act (HA) 1988 ss27 and 28. However, there are exceptions which advisers should bear in mind.

Trespassers

23.2   Court proceedings are not always necessary to evict trespassers. See chapter 29.

Excluded licences and tenancies[1]

23.3   Protection from Eviction Act 1977 s3 prohibits eviction without due process of law, ie, without a court order, for lawful occupiers who would not otherwise be entitled to this safeguard. However, PEA 1977 s3A created categories of 'excluded tenancies and licences' to which the protection of section 3 does not apply. The combined effect of these sections is that if there is an excluded tenancy or licence, a landlord who evicts without a court order may not be committing a criminal offence under PEA 1977 s1 (unlawful eviction and harassment) and, if the tenancy or licence has been properly terminated (for example, by service of a valid notice to quit), the occupant has no civil redress.

23.4   A tenancy or licence is excluded if:

- under its terms the occupier shares any accommodation with the landlord or licensor and the landlord or licensor occupies as his or her only or principal home 'premises of which the whole or part of the shared accommodation formed part';
- the tenant or licensee shares accommodation with a member of the family of the landlord or licensor and the landlord or licensor has his or her only or principal home in the building where the shared accommodation is situated;
- the tenant or licensee was originally a trespasser on premises but was granted a tenancy or licence as a temporary expedient;

---

1   See chapter 18 and para 14.10.

- it confers on the tenant or licensee the right to occupy premises for a holiday only;
- it is granted otherwise than for money or money's worth;
- it is a licence of a room in a hostel provided by a social sector landlord, such as a local authority or private registered provider (PRP) or registered social landlord (RSL); or
- it is granted to provide accommodation to asylum-seekers under the Immigration and Asylum Act 1999 Part VI.[2]

Case-law has determined that other categories of letting are also excluded from section 3. Where a homeless person has been placed in interim accommodation[3] pending the local authority's decision, or in certain other kinds of temporary accommodation, such accommodation is not considered to be 'occupied as a dwelling' and so does not attract the protection of section 3. See paras 5.20–5.31.

23.5 From the point of view of landlords, it may be wise to take possession proceedings even if they believe that there is an excluded tenancy or licence. There is not only the risk that the tenancy or licence may not, in fact, be excluded, but also, if the occupants are on the premises at the time of eviction, the possibility of a prosecution under the Criminal Law Act 1977 s6 (using or threatening violence to secure entry). Prosecutions can be brought under the Criminal Law Act 1977 s6 even if the occupants are trespassers. An offence may be committed under section 6 of that Act 'whether the violence in question is directed against the person or against property'.[4]

23.6 If a landlord is threatening to evict without obtaining a possession order and the occupiers believe that they enjoy some form of security of tenure, the safest course of action is for the occupiers to seek an injunction without delay, pending an application for a declaration.

Possession procedure

23.7 Civil Procedure Rules 1998 (CPR) Part 55 applies to most claims for possession. The procedure set out in that part must be used where the claim includes a possession claim brought:

- by a landlord (or former landlord);
- by a mortgagee;

---

2 See PEA 1977 ss3 and 3A, HA 1985 s622 and Immigration and Asylum Act 1999 Sch 14 para 73.
3 Under HA 1996 s188(1).
4 Criminal Law Act 1977 s6(4)(a).

- by a licensor (or former licensor); or
- against trespassers.[5]

The full text of CPR Part 55 and its Practice Directions are set out in appendix E.

Issue of proceedings – which court?

23.8 Possession proceedings are usually started in the county court for the district where the property is situated.[6] A claimant may start proceedings in the High Court only if there are exceptional circumstances[7] such as:

- complicated disputes of fact;
- points of law of general importance; or
- where, in a claim against trespassers, there is a substantial risk of public disturbance or of serious harm to people or property which properly requires immediate determination.

23.9 The value of the property and the amount of any financial claim may be relevant circumstances, but they alone do not usually justify starting the claim in the High Court. Practice Direction 55A to CPR Part 55 points out the consequences of issuing in High Court when not justified:

> If a claimant starts a claim in the High Court and the court decides that it should have been started in the county court, the court will normally either strike the claim out or transfer it to the county court on its own initiative. This is likely to result in delay and the court will normally disallow the costs of starting the claim in the High Court and of any transfer.[8]

23.10 If a claim is issued in the High Court it must be accompanied by a certificate stating the reasons for bringing the claim in the High Court, verified by a statement of truth.[9]

23.11 In addition there are substantive law provisions which provide that landlords who initiate proceedings in the High Court may be prohibited from recovering some or all of their costs.[10]

---

5 CPR 55.2.
6 CPR 55.3(1).
7 PD 55A para 2.1.
8 PD 55A para 1.2.
9 CPR 55.3(2).
10 HA 1985 s110(3), RA 1977 s141(4) and HA 1988 s40(4).

Challenging the decision to bring proceedings

23.12 Sometimes tenants wish to challenge the decision by a local authority or another type of social landlord to bring possession proceedings – either on grounds of *Wednesbury* unreasonableness or on other conventional judicial review grounds, or because European Convention on Human Rights (ECHR/'the Convention') rights have been breached. Such challenges can in some circumstances be brought in the county court by way of a public law defence to the possession claim (see paras 25.23–25.28), but in other cases it is necessary to seek an adjournment of the claim in order to make application for judicial review in the Administrative Court: see paras 25.29–25.32. The House of Lords' judgments in *Lambeth LBC v Kay*[11] and *Doherty v Birmingham CC*[12] set out the basis for a public law defence. If there are disputes of fact, evidence may be heard in the course of the county court proceedings. Where, however, the court has a discretion concerning the making of a possession order, a county court judge is able to take into account allegations that the institution of proceedings is unlawful or contrary to regulatory guidance when considering the issue of reasonableness.[13]

Claim forms

23.13 Claim forms and Particulars of Claim in possession actions must be in the prescribed form.[14] They must be verified by a statement of truth.[15] It has been held, at first instance,[16] that a statement of truth in a possession claim form which had not been signed personally, but which bore the rubber stamp of a signature of an employee in the claimant's legal services department who had no personal knowledge of the case, had not been signed within the meaning of CPR 22.1. The requirement in CPR 22.1(a) for the statement of case to be signed is not a mere technicality or a matter of form. Courts need to

---

11 [2006] UKHL 10. See paras 26.40–26.42.

12 [2008] UKHL 57. See para 26.43.

13 *R (Mills) v Airways Housing Society Ltd* [2005] EWHC 328 (Admin); 14 January 2005.

14 PD 55A para 2.6 – forms N5 (claim form), N119 (rent claims), N120 (mortgages) and N121 (trespassers).

15 CPR 22.1.

16 *Birmingham City Council v Hosey* December 2002 *Legal Action* 20, Birmingham County Court (HHJ MacDuff QC).

be able to rely on documents bearing statements of truth. It is essential that statements of case should be properly verified. For details of who may sign a statement of truth generally, see PD 22.3.

23.14   In a claim against trespassers, if the claimant does not know the names of all the people in occupation, the claim must be brought against 'persons unknown' in addition to any named defendants.[17]

Particulars of claim

23.15   Particulars of claim must be filed and served with the claim form.[18] All particulars of claim must:

- identify the land or property to which the claim relates;[19]
- state whether it is residential property;[20]
- state the ground on which possession is claimed;[21]
- give full details of any mortgage or tenancy agreement;[22]
- give details of every person who, to the best of the claimant's knowledge, is in possession of the property;[23] and
- comply with CPR 16, ie, they must contain a concise statement of the facts relied upon, and, if interest is sought, give details of the claim for interest.

23.16   There are additional requirements for particulars of claim where the claim relates to a tenancy of residential premises.[24] If the claimant alleges that there has been non-payment of rent, the particulars of claim must state:

- The amount due at the start of proceedings.
- In schedule form, the dates when arrears of rent arose, all amounts of rent due, the dates and amounts of all payments made and a running total of the arrears. In general the schedule should cover the preceding two years, or if the first date of default occurred less than two years before the date of issue, it should cover the period from the first date of default. However, if the claimant wishes to rely on a history of arrears which is longer than two years, this

---

17 CPR 55.3(4). See chapter 29.
18 CPR 55.4.
19 PD 55A para 2.1(1).
20 PD 55A para 2.1(2).
21 PD 55A para 2.1(3).
22 PD 55A para 2.1(4).
23 PD 55A para 2.1(5).
24 PD 55A para 2.3.

should be stated in the particulars and a full schedule should be exhibited to a witness statement.

- The daily rate of any rent and interest.
- Any previous steps taken to recover arrears, with full details of any court proceedings.
- Any relevant information about the defendant's circumstances, including details about benefits and payments direct.

23.17   The particulars of claim should also give the name of any person known to be entitled to apply for relief from forfeiture. In those circumstances, the claimant must file a copy of the particulars of claim for service on any person who is entitled to apply for relief from forfeiture.[25]

23.18   If the claimant is a mortgage lender who is seeking possession of residential premises, the particulars of claim must state:[26]

- whether a Class F land charge has been registered, or a notice under the Matrimonial Homes Act 1983 has been entered, and whether a notice under the Family Law Act 1996 has been registered (and if any of these things have been done, the claimant must serve notice of proceedings upon the person named in the charge or notice);
- full details of the mortgage account, including the amount of the advance, periodic payments and interest, the amount needed to redeem the mortgage, including solicitors' costs and administration charges;
- if the mortgage is a regulated consumer credit agreement, the total amount outstanding;
- the rate of interest payable.

23.19   If the claim is based on mortgage arrears, the particulars of claim must set out:

- in schedule form, the dates when the arrears arose, all amounts due, the dates and amounts of all payments made and give a running total of the arrears;
- details of all other payments to be made and claimed (such as insurance premiums, legal costs and administrative charges);
- any relevant information about the defendant's circumstances, including details about benefits and payments direct;
- any previous steps taken to recover arrears, with full details of any court proceedings.

25   PD 55A para 2.4. See also para 12.57.
26   PD 55A para 2.5.

23.20   There are additional requirements for particulars of claim where the claim is against trespassers.[27] The particulars of claim must state:

- the claimant's interest in the land;
- the circumstances in which the land was occupied without licence or consent.

23.21   The effect of a failure by a claimant to comply with these rules depends on the circumstances. CPR 3.10 provides that, where there has been an error of procedure, such as a failure to comply with a rule or practice direction, the error does not invalidate any step taken and the court may make an order to remedy the error. So, if a landlord issues proceedings in the wrong county court, it is likely that the court will simply transfer the claim to the correct court.[28] If information is missing, it will be necessary for the claimant to seek permission to amend the particulars under CPR 17.1, either at the hearing or (depending on whether the defendant needs further time to prepare his or her case as a result of receiving the information) following an adjournment. On the other hand, if the failure to comply with the rules has been deliberate, with the intention of obtaining an unfair advantage against the defendant, the court has power to strike out the claim.[29]

23.22   Particulars of claim in the usual form are reproduced in the precedents in appendix B.[30]

Hearing dates

23.23   On the issue of a possession claim form, the court should fix a date for the first hearing.[31] The hearing date should be not less than 28 days from date of issue[32] but the standard period between issue of the claim and the hearing should be not more than eight weeks.[33] Shorter periods apply to claims against trespassers (see para 23.25).

---

27   PD 55A para 2.6. See chapter 29.
28   See, eg, *Cala Homes (South) Ltd v Chichester DC* [2000] CP Rep 28; (2000) 79 P&CR 430 and *Gwynedd CC v Grunshaw* [2000] 1 WLR 494; (2000) 32 HLR 610, CA.
29   CPR 3.4.
30   See also forms N119, N120 and N121.
31   CPR 55.5(1).
32   CPR 55.5(3)(a).
33   CPR 55.5(3)(c).

Service of the claim form

23.24   The usual Civil Procedure Rules on service apply to ordinary possession claims. CPR Part 6 allows the court to arrange personal service,
delivery by first class post, for the claim form to be left at the defendant's last known address, or service via the document exchange. Alternatively the claimant landlord may arrange service. Special rules
apply to service of claims brought against trespassers.[34]

23.25   The period between service and hearing must be at least:

- two days where there is a claim against trespassers of non-
residential land;
- five days where there is a claim against trespassers of residential
premises;
- 21 days (all other possession claims).[35]

23.26   However, those periods may be shortened.[36] Practice Direction 55A to
Part 55 states that particular consideration should be given to short-
ening the period where:

- the defendant, or a person for whom the defendant is responsible,
has assaulted or threatened to assault the landlord, a member of
the landlord's staff, or another tenant;
- there are reasonable grounds for fearing such an assault; or
- the defendant, or a person for whom the defendant is responsible,
has caused serious damage or threatened to cause serious damage
to the property or to the home or property of another resident.[37]

Defences and counterclaims

23.27   Parts I, II and IV of this book set out the substantive and technical
defences which may be raised in response to an action for possession
of residential property. The reader should refer to the main text for
consideration of the issues which must always be reviewed in planning defences.

23.28   A defendant who wishes to defend must file a defence with the
court and serve a copy on the claimant within 14 days of service of the

---

34 See CPR 55.6 and chapter 29.
35 CPR 55.5(2) and (3).
36 CPR 3.1(2)(a).
37 PD 55A para 3.2.

claim form.[38] A defendant to a possession claim who fails to file or serve a defence may still take part in the proceedings, but the failure to file or serve a defence may be taken into account when the court decides what costs order to make.[39] For example, if the first hearing is not effective and has to be adjourned because the tenant turns up without having filed or served a defence but obtains an adjournment by telling the court about a defence to the claim, the court may order the tenant to pay the wasted costs of the adjourned hearing.

23.29 Defences to possession claims must be in the prescribed form annexed to Practice Direction 55A.[40]

23.30 CPR Part 10 (acknowledgment of service) does not apply to possession claims.[41] Similarly CPR Part 12 (default judgment) does not apply to possession claims.[42] This means that it is not possible for a claimant to obtain a possession order by default if the defendant fails to file or serve a defence.

23.31 In Consumer Credit Act cases, the borrower may apply for a time order in the defence or by making an application in the proceedings.[43]

23.32 The defence should answer each of the substantive points raised in the particulars of claim, because failure to respond to a point made is taken as admission of it. Moreover, any defence and, if appropriate, counterclaim must be sufficiently accurately drafted to withstand the test of a full trial.

23.33 Often the defendant will wish to raise a grievance arising from the breach of some duty or misconduct on the part of the landlord/ owner. Most frequently this occurs in cases of disrepair and harassment. As such a complaint arises out of the subject matter of the proceedings, that is the tenancy (or other tenure), it may be raised by way of a counterclaim. For details of the law applicable to counterclaims for disrepair, readers are referred to Luba, Forster and Prevatt, *Repairs: tenants' rights*,[44] and for counterclaims for harassment to Arden, Carter and Dymond, *Quiet enjoyment*.[45] However, it should

---

38 CPR 15.2. However, this rule does not apply to claims against trespassers: see CPR 55.7(2).
39 CPR 55.7(2).
40 PD 55 para 1.5, N11, N11R or N11M.
41 CPR 55.7(1).
42 CPR 55.7(4).
43 PD 55 para 7.1.
44 4th edn, LAG, 2010.
45 6th edn, LAG, 2002.

be noted that the following heads appear most commonly in counter-claims to possession proceedings (particularly those brought for rent arrears).

Disrepair

- Breach of an express repairing covenant in the tenancy agreement (see the terms of the tenancy agreement).
- Failure to repair the structure or exterior of the premises or the common parts.[46]
- Failure to repair (or maintain in proper working order) installations in the dwelling or serving the dwelling.[47]
- Failure to take reasonable care of the tenant and the tenant's property to prevent injury to either.[48]
- Negligence in construction of the dwelling, performance of repairing works or treatment of infestation, etc.
- Nuisance (where the disrepair is caused by a problem emanating from property retained by the landlord).

Harassment

- Trespass to land/trespass to the person/trespass to goods (tort).
- Breach of the covenant for quiet enjoyment (contract).
- Breach of Protection from Eviction Act 1977 s3 (for unprotected tenants).
- Intimidation (tort).
- Breach of Housing Act 1988 ss27 and 28 (unlawful eviction).

23.34   It is best for any counterclaim to be included in the same document as the defence. If that is done, the court's permission to bring a counterclaim against a claimant is not needed. However, if a tenant wishes to bring a counterclaim at a later stage, the court's permission is needed.[49] Any counterclaim should contain full particulars of the matters complained of.

23.35   If the defendant recovers damages on his or her counterclaim, these may be set off, so as to reduce in whole or in part monies claimed by the claimant. In the case of counterclaims for disrepair, the application of a full set-off will amount to a complete defence to an action for arrears of rent. Accordingly, the body of the defence

---

46 Landlord and Tenant Act 1985 s11, as amended.
47 Landlord and Tenant Act 1985 s11, as amended.
48 Defective Premises Act 1972 s4.
49 CPR 20.4.

itself should plead the set-off, even though it is seeking to set off an as yet unliquidated claim for damages in the counterclaim.[50]

23.36   An example of a defence (including counterclaims as appropriate) is given in appendix B.

Preparation for the hearing

23.37   Apart from claims against trespassers, claimants should file and serve all witness statements at least two days before the hearing. In arrears cases these should include evidence of the arrears up to the date of the hearing, if necessary by including a daily rate. However, this does not prevent a landlord bringing the position up to date at the hearing.[51]

23.38   In mortgage possession claims, the claimant must, within five days of receiving notice of the hearing, send a notice to 'The Tenant or Occupier' of the property and also to the housing department of the local authority. The notice must give details of the parties to the proceedings and of the date and place of the hearting. The claimant must produce a copy of the notice and evidence of service at the hearing.[52] The lender's representative must also bring to the hearing two copies of a completed Mortgage Pre-action Protocol checklist (court form N123) which shows how the lender has sought to comply with the requirements of the protocol.[53]

23.39   Where the claimant has served the claim form and particulars of claim, the claimant must produce a certificate of service at the hearing.[54]

Adjournments

23.40   In view of the fact that tenants often do not seek legal advice until just before any hearing it is often necessary for their advisers to seek an adjournment at the initial hearing. Whether or not such an application is successful will depend on the particular circumstances of the case. If it is possible to draft a defence which shows that the tenant

---

50 *British Anzani (Felixstowe) v International Marine Management (UK) Ltd* [1980] QB 137; [1979] 3 WLR 451.
51 PD 55 para 5.2.
52 CPR 55.10. See chapter 43.
53 CPR PD 55A para 5.5. See also para 42.3 and appendix D.
54 CPR 55.8(6).

has a real prospect of successfully defending the claim, the court is far more likely to adjourn. Similarly, if the case is one of many listed and there is insufficient time to hear the matter, practical list management may mean that the judge has no option but to adjourn. On the other hand, if the tenant's adviser/representative is not able to point to any defence, or only to a very weak defence, the court may choose to hear the case at the first hearing. The court may want to know why (if it is the case) the tenant delayed seeking advice.

23.41 In view of the Court of Appeal decision in *North British Housing Association Limited v Matthews*,[55] there are limitations on courts' powers to adjourn where landlords are seeking possession under mandatory grounds. See para 12.67. However, these limitations do not apply where possession is sought on a discretionary ground.[56]

23.42 Other factors which should be borne in mind include:

- The overriding objective, ie, the importance of dealing with cases justly. This includes ensuring that the parties are on an equal footing, saving expense, dealing with cases proportionately, ensuring that cases are dealt with expeditiously and fairly and allocating the appropriate share of the court's resources.[57]
- Whether or not public funding has been granted to the defendant, or whether the defendant has applied for public funding.
- The risk of prejudice to either party.
- The extent to which the party applying for the adjournment has been responsible for creating the difficulty.[58]

23.43 In *Bates v Croydon LBC*,[59] a tenant facing a possession claim alleging 53 allegations of nuisance to neighbours sought an adjournment to obtain public funding. It was refused. The hearing date was then moved forward, with the result that she was given three days to read witness statements produced by the council and to prepare for the hearing. The Court of Appeal set aside the possession order. The defendant had been put on very short notice to deal with the documentation, exhibits and witness statements. She was required to respond in writing to lengthy details and then conduct her own case

---

55 [2004] EWCA Civ 1736; [2005] 1 WLR 3133; [2005] 2 All ER 667.
56 *Milecastle Housing Ltd v Walton* 14 June 2005, High Court of Justice, Newcastle upon Tyne District Registry.
57 CPR 1.1.
58 See, eg, *McShane v William Sutton Trust* (1997) 1 L & T Rev D67; December 1997 Legal Action 13, a pre-CPR case which illustrates a Woolf-type approach, and *R v Kingston upon Thames Justices ex p Martin* [1994] Imm AR 172, QBD.
59 [2001] EWCA Civ 134; (2001) 33 HLR 70.

in person. While the court accepted the desirability of conducting litigation with proper dispatch, and was reluctant to review interlocutory decisions of district judges, the decision reached in this case was wrong. An adjournment was appropriate for Ms Bates to finalise her public funding application and enable her to be represented.

Hearings in private

23.44   European Convention on Human Rights article 6 usually requires a public hearing. However, CPR 39.2(3)(c) provides that a hearing may be in private if it involves confidential information (including information relating to personal financial matters) and publicity would damage that confidentiality. The Practice Direction to CPR Part 39 paras 1.1 to 1.5 states that the decision as to whether a hearing is held in public or private must be made by the judge, having regard to representations (para 1.4) and article 6(1) of the Convention (para 1.4A). Mortgage possession claims, possession claims based on rent arrears and applications to suspend warrants should, in the first instance, be listed as hearings in private (para 1.5). Are these provisions a breach of article 6? The answer is 'no'. Like many other Convention provisions, article 6 does not provide an absolute right. It has to be balanced against other rights, such as the right to privacy given by article 8. CPR 39.2 and the Practice Direction to CPR Part 39 have been drafted specifically with article 6 in mind. They leave a discretion to the judge in each case. If that discretion is exercised reasonably, in accordance with the spirit of the Convention, it is unlikely to be criticised. Indeed, taking into account the provisions of articles 8 and 14, it is possible that a tenant defending a rent arrears case would have been able to challenge the pre-CPR position where claims against tenants were held in public and claims by lenders against borrowers based on mortgage arrears were held in private.

23.45   The legality of CPR 39.2(3)(c) and the Practice Direction to CPR Part 39, paras 1.5 to 1.7, were challenged unsuccessfully in *R (Pelling) v Bow County Court (No 2)*.[60] Dr Pelling claimed that these provisions were ultra vires and breached article 6 of the convention. Buxton LJ held that the general rule that hearings are to be in public[61] is not absolute. CPR 39.2(3) is facultative and permits certain

---

60   [2001] UKHRR 165; [2001] ACD 1, QBD (Admin Ct).
61   See *Scott v Scott* [1913] AC 417, HL.

limited exceptions. CPR 39.2 is not unlawful or ultra vires and does not breach articles 6 or 10.

At the hearing

23.46   At the first hearing, or any adjourned hearing, the court may either decide the claim or give case management directions.[62] If the claim is genuinely disputed, on grounds which appear to be substantial, directions should include allocation of the claim to a particular track or should enable it to be allocated.

Allocation to track

23.47   Possession claims should be allocated to the small claims track only if all the parties agree.[63] If a possession claim is allocated to the small claims track, the fast track costs regime applies, but the trial costs are in the discretion of the judge and should not exceed the amount of fast track costs allowable in CPR 46.2 if the value were up to £3,000, ie, currently £485.[64]

23.48   In considering the appropriate track for a possession claim, the court should take into account:

- CPR 26.8, which refers to the financial value of the claim, the nature of the remedy sought, the likely complexity of facts, law or evidence, the number of parties, the value of any counterclaim, the amount of oral evidence, the importance of the claim to people who are not parties, the views expressed by the parties and the circumstances of the parties;
- the amount of any arrears of rent or mortgage instalments;
- the importance to the defendant of retaining possession; and
- the importance of vacant possession to the claimant.[65]

The financial value of the claim is not necessarily the most important factor. A possession claim may be allocated to the fast track even though the value of the property is in excess of £25,000.

---

62   CPR 55.8(1).
63   CPR 55.9(2).
64   CPR 55.9(3).
65   PD 55 para 6.1.

Evidence at the hearing

23.49　If a possession claim has not been allocated to track, or has been allocated to the small claims track, any fact that needs to be proved may be proved by evidence in writing – ie, by a witness statement or a claim form with a statement of truth.[66] However, if that evidence is disputed and the maker of the witness statement is not present, the court will usually adjourn the claim so that oral evidence can be given.[67]

23.50　If the claim has been allocated to the fast track or the multi-track, the usual rules of evidence at trial apply – oral evidence should be given in public,[68] although it may well be that witness statements will be treated as evidence in chief and oral evidence will consist largely of cross-examination.

23.51　In *Moat Housing Group South Ltd v Harris and Hartless*[69] the Court of Appeal reviewed the use of hearsay evidence in possession claims based on anti-social behaviour and gave guidance to the lower courts. It is now well established that hearsay evidence can be given at the trial of a possession action, but 'the willingness of a civil court to admit hearsay evidence carries with it inherent dangers'. Rumours abound in small housing estates, and it is much more difficult for judges to assess the truth of what they are being told if the original makers of statements do not attend court to be cross-examined on their evidence. In this case, the large volume of hearsay evidence presented the judge with an unusually difficult problem. The Court of Appeal considered that it might have been preferable if he had started his judgment with an analysis of the direct oral evidence he received, and made more transparent his approach to the evidence of the absent named witnesses and anonymous witnesses. More attention should be paid by claimants to the need to state, by convincing direct evidence, why it was not reasonable and practicable to produce the original makers of statements as witnesses. If statements involve multiple hearsay, the route by which the original statement came to the attention of the person attesting to it should be identified as far as practicable. Anonymous hearsay is not generally admissible. See too *Solon South West Housing Association Ltd v James*.[70]

66　CPR 55.8(3).

67　PD 55A para 5.4.

68　CPR 32.2.

69　[2005] EWCA Civ 287; [2005] 3 WLR 691. See too *Washington Housing Company Ltd v Morson* [2005] EWHC 3407 (Ch) and *Wear Valley DC v Robson* [2008] EWCA Civ 1470; [2009] HLR 27.

70　[2004] EWCA Civ 1847; [2005] HLR 24.

23.52   For the general procedural rules about the admissibility of hearsay evidence and the requirement (in some circumstances) to give notice of intention to rely on hearsay evidence, see the Civil Evidence Act 1995 ss1–4 and CPR 33.1–33.5.

Interim rent

23.53   While awaiting trial of the claim for possession, a landlord may apply for an order for interim rent.[71] Tenants often respond with an undertaking to pay current rent pending trial. No such order should be made, however, if there is a genuine dispute over the sum due or if a counterclaim is being pursued.[72] Under the former County Court Rules and Rules of the Supreme Court, the court could not order that a tenant's defence be struck out merely because of failure to comply with an order to pay interim rent.[73] The position may be different under the CPR since Parts 1 and 3, when read together, give the courts a far wider discretion than the old rules.[74] Certainly failure to pay, coupled with breach of an order to file a list of documents, where there is no realistic prospect of the tenant ever paying current rent or arrears may justify striking out a defence and making a possession order[75] – although in cases involving discretionary grounds, the court should still consider the question of reasonableness.[76]

23.54   In practice, it is more common for courts to make an order for payment of current rent under their general case management powers,[77] for example, as a term of any adjournment.[78] Where financial terms are imposed as a condition of an adjournment, the onus lies on tenants to satisfy courts that they cannot comply with any condition before it is imposed.

23.55   Also, if a possession claim against a secure, assured, protected or statutory tenant is adjourned, the court must, unless it considers that to do so would cause exceptional hardship or would otherwise be unreasonable, impose conditions with regard to the payment of

---

71 CPR 25.6–25.9.
72 *Old Grovebury Manor Farm v Seymour* [1979] 1 WLR 263; [1979] 1 All ER 573.
73 *HH Property Co Ltd v Rahim* [1987] 1 EGLR 52; (1987) 282 EG 455, CA.
74 See in particular CPR 3.1(2)(m).
75 *Tower Hamlets LBC v Ellson* July 2000 *Legal Action* 28, CA.
76 See chapter 13.
77 Eg, CPR 3.1(3).
78 See, under the old rules, *Agyeman v Boadi* (1996) 28 HLR 558; [1996] EGCS 14, CA.

rent and arrears of rent (if any).[79] It would only be in an exceptional case that the court would accept a landlord's application for an interlocutory injunction and order the tenant to pay housing benefit into court, rather than require an application from the landlord for interim payments in the usual way.[80]

Possession Claims Online (PCOL)

23.56   PD 55B enables landlords and their representatives to start certain possession claims under CPR Part 55 by requesting the issue of a claim form electronically via the PCOL website. Where a claim has been started electronically, the claimant, the defendant and their representatives may take further steps in the claim electronically using PCOL. Parties may communicate with the court using the messaging service facility, available on the PCOL website. Details are available from www.possessionclaim.gov.uk.

23.57   Possession claims may be started online if:

- they are brought under Section I of CPR Part 55; and
- they include a possession claim for residential property by a landlord against a tenant, solely on the ground of arrears of rent (but not a claim for forfeiture of a lease); or
- they are brought by a mortgagee against a mortgagor, solely on the ground of default in the payment of sums due under a mortgage.

23.58   Landlords may request the issue of a claim form by completing an online claim form at the PCOL website and paying the appropriate issue fee electronically via the PCOL website or by some other means approved by Her Majesty's Courts Service. The particulars of claim must be included in the online claim form and may not be filed separately. It is not necessary for the landlord to file a copy of the tenancy agreement, mortgage deed or mortgage agreement with the particulars of claim. The particulars of claim must include a history of the rent or mortgage account in schedule form, setting out:

- the dates and amounts of all payments due and payments made under the tenancy agreement, mortgage deed or mortgage agreement either from the first date of default if that date occurred less

---

79 RA 1977 s100(3), HA 1985 s85(3) and HA 1988 s9(3).
80 *Berg v Markhill* (1985) 17 HLR 455; (1985) *Times* 10 May.

than two years before the date of issue or for a period of two years immediately preceding the date of issue; and

- a running total of the arrears.

23.59   When the court issues a claim form it should serve a printed version of the claim form and a defence form on the defendant. The claim form should have printed on it a unique customer identification number or a password by which the defendant may access the claim on the PCOL website. Tenants may file defences (and, if appropriate, counterclaims) in written form. Alternatively, they may complete the relevant online form at the PCOL website, and, if, making a counterclaim, pay the appropriate fee electronically at the PCOL website or by some other means approved by Her Majesty's Courts Service.

23.60   Some applications may be made electronically. Landlords may also request the issue of warrants electronically. Tenants may apply electronically for the suspension of warrants, by completing an online application for suspension at the PCOL website and paying the appropriate fee electronically at the PCOL website or by some other means approved by Her Majesty's Courts Service. When an online application for suspension is received, an acknowledgment of receipt should automatically be sent to the defendant by the court, but that acknowledgment does not constitute a notice that the online application for suspension has been served.

Accelerated possession proceedings

Accelerated possession proceedings

24.1   The accelerated possession procedure which landlords can use against assured shorthold tenants after service of a Housing Act (HA) 1988 section 21 notice was originally contained in the County Court Rules (CCR) Ord 49 r6A. It was introduced on 1 November 1993 and was subsequently incorporated into the Civil Procedure Rules 1998 (CPR) Part 55, with some amendments. CCR Ord 49 r6, which provided an accelerated possession procedure for use against assured tenants in certain limited circumstances, has been repealed and was not incorporated into CPR Part 55. The only possession procedure available to landlords against assured tenants is the standard one contained in CPR Part 55 Part 1.

24.2   The accelerated possession procedure applies only to claims brought under HA 1988 s21 to recover possession against assured shorthold tenants.[1] The conditions set out in CPR 55.12 must be complied with. This means that the procedure can be used only where:

- the assured shorthold tenancy was entered into on or after 15 January 1989;
- the only purpose is to recover possession – no other claim (for example, rent arrears) can be made under the accelerated procedure;
- the tenancy did not immediately follow an assured tenancy which was not an assured shorthold tenancy;
- there has been an assured shorthold tenancy in accordance with HA 1988 s19A (ie, granted on or after 28 February 1997) or s20(1)(a)–(c) (pre-28 February 1997 fixed-term tenancies granted for a term certain of not less than six months where a 'section 20' notice of assured shorthold tenancy was given prior to the grant of the tenancy);
- the tenancy is subject to a written agreement, or follows a tenancy where there was a written agreement; and
- a HA 1988 section 21(1) or section 21(4) notice has been given.

Readers should refer to chapter 11 for a detailed analysis of the rules governing assured shorthold tenancies.

24.3   Claims brought under the accelerated possession procedure must be started in the county court for the district in which the property is situated. The claim form must:

---

1 CPR 55.11.

- be in the form set out in the Practice Direction;[2]
- contain the information and be accompanied by the documents required in that form; and
- have all sections completed.

24.4 A blank reply form should accompany every claim form issued under the accelerated procedure. It is crucially important that tenants who wish to defend proceedings brought under the accelerated procedure return the N11A reply form to the court within 14 days after service of the claim form.[3] In many cases it is necessary for solicitors to use Legal Help for this purpose. If the reply form is not returned, the claim for possession will be treated as unopposed and a possession order may be made without any hearing. The defence must be set out in the reply form as specified in the Practice Direction.[4]

24.5 Common mistakes by landlords are:

- for an agent to complete the statement of truth on the claim form;[5]
- for the landlord to fail to exhibit either the HA 1988 section 20 notice (ie, notice required before the grant of an assured short-hold tenancy commencing before 28 February 1997) or the HA 1988 section 21 notice (notice requiring possession)[6] – the court has no power to dispense with either;
- to include a claim for rent arrears;
- for the HA 1988 section 20 notice[7] to be defective (see para 11.4 and the cases referred to there);
- for the HA 1988 section 21 notice to be defective (see paras 11.10–11.30 and the cases referred to there).[8]

24.6 Accelerated possession claims should be referred to a district judge, either on receipt of a defence, or on receipt of a request from the claimant after the expiry of 14 days from service of the claim form.[9]

---

2 Form N5B.
3 CPR 55.14.
4 Form N11A.
5 See *Chesters Accommodation Agency Ltd v Abebrese* (1997) 94(33) LSG 27; (1997) 141 SJLB 199; (1997) *Times* 28 July, CA and CPR 22.1(6).
6 See RA 1977 s2.
7 Note that there is no requirement for an HA 1998 section 20 notice if the tenancy was granted on or after 28 February 1997 – see HA 1988 s19A and para 11.6.
8 See HA 1988 s21(4).
9 CPR 55.15.

The judge can still consider any defence if the defence is received out of time but before the landlord's request is considered. If the defendant does not file a defence and no request for possession is received from the claimant within three months after service, the claim will be stayed automatically.

24.7   When considering accelerated possession claims, district judges should either:[10]

- make an order for possession without a hearing; or
- if they are not satisfied that the claim was served or that the claimant is entitled to possession, fix a hearing date and give case management directions – at least 14 days' notice of the hearing must be given; or
- strike out the claim if it discloses no reasonable grounds for bringing a claim.

If the claim is struck out, reasons must be given with the order. In those circumstances, the claimant landlord may apply to restore the claim within 28 days.

24.8   The Court of Appeal has stated that if a reply raises a case which, if true, would constitute an arguable defence, the judge has no discretion to make a possession order without a hearing:

> [The accelerated possession procedure] is a robust machinery. It depends upon district judges rigorously considering the documents which have been filed. Some replies may be little more than a plea, however genuine, for mercy. But if, on the face of the reply, a matter has been raised which, if true, might arguably raise a defence; or if the documents filed by the claimant might arguably disclose a defect in his claim, then the district judge must necessarily be 'not satisfied' ...[11]

24.9   It is usual for the court to order that the tenant pay the landlord's costs on the claim form. If the tenant wishes to pay costs by instalments, the appropriate box on the form N11A should be completed and returned.[12]

---

10 CPR 55.16.

11 *Manel v Memon* (2001) 33 HLR 235; [2000] 33 EG 74; (2000) *Times* 20 April, CA. Although this was a case decided under CCR Ord 49 r6A, the same principles apply to the accelerated possession procedure under CPR Part 55.

12 CPR 55.18.

Postponement of possession

24.10 Where a landlord is entitled to a possession order under the accelerated procedure, the court must make an order to take effect within
14 days, unless exceptional hardship would be caused to the tenant,
in which case the court may delay the date for the giving up of possession for a maximum of six weeks.[13] Claimants may indicate, by
not deleting the relevant paragraph in the claim form, that they are
content for the judge to consider postponing the date for possession
without a hearing. In those cases judges may fix dates for possession
up to six weeks ahead without a hearing.

24.11 Otherwise, if a defendant seeks postponement of the date for
giving up possession on the ground of exceptional hardship, the
judge must make an order for possession within 14 days, but direct
a hearing on the issue of postponement. The hearing must be before
the date on which possession is to be given up. If, at the hearing, the
judge is satisfied that there will be exceptional hardship, he or she
may vary the date on which possession must be given up, but to no
more than six weeks after the date on which the original order was
made.[14]

24.12 There is power for the court to set aside or vary a possession
order made under the accelerated procedure on an application by the
tenant within 14 days of service of the order, or on the court's own
initiative.[15]

European Convention on Human Rights

24.13 It has been suggested that the accelerated possession procedure
might fall foul of article 6 of the European Convention on Human
Rights. In view of the firm line taken by the Court of Appeal in *Manel
v Memon*,[16] it is hard to support this view. Article 6 only comes into
play if the proceedings in question are decisive for private rights and
obligations.[17] If the tenant accepts that there is no defence, there are
no civil rights to be determined. If the tenant claims that there is a
defence, there is an entitlement to a public hearing.

13 HA 1980 s89.
14 PD 55 para 8.4 and HA 1980 s89.
15 CPR 55.19.
16 (2001) 33 HLR 235; [2000] 33 EG 74, CA.
17 *Ringeisen v Austria (No 1)* (1979–1980) 1 EHRR 455, ECtHR.

CHAPTER 25

Public law defences

The public law defence: an introduction

25.1   Public bodies must respect the rule of law. They must not act unlawfully or seek to give effect to their unlawful actions. The same is true of private bodies carrying out public functions (which are, therefore, to be treated as 'public bodies' for the purposes of this chapter).

25.2   In the context of possession proceedings, a public body seeking possession must act lawfully throughout. That means that a public body must not reach an unlawful decision to terminate a tenancy or give an occupier notice to leave. It must not unlawfully decide to issue a possession claim or press it to trial. It must not make an unlawful decision to execute (that is, enforce) a possession order that it has obtained.[1]

25.3   The courts have a supervisory jurisdiction to ensure that public bodies act lawfully. In doing so, they apply a body of principles known as 'public' or 'administrative' law. Those principles, honed by the common law over decades, are now the underpinning of a distinct branch of civil law and the subject of many (large) textbooks.[2] For present purposes, it is sufficient to extract the following basic principles regarding what a public body may or may not do:

a) it must not act beyond the powers given to it;[3]

b) if it has been given a discretion whether or not to do something, it must not fetter that discretion by adopting absolute rules;

c) it must act fairly and in accordance with the rules of natural justice;

d) when making a decision about exercising its powers or performing its duties, it must take into account all relevant considerations and must exclude any irrelevant considerations;

e) it must not allow its decisions to be tainted by bias, bad faith, corruption or unlawful discrimination;

f) where there is an express or implied duty to do so, it must give reasons for what it is doing;

g) if it is under a duty to do something, it must carry out that duty;

h) if it has indicated that in particular circumstances it will act in a certain way, it will usually be required to meet a 'legitimate expectation' that it will act in the way it has indicated;

---

1   For further discussion of the decisions that may be challenged see para 25.23.

2   For examples see: Wade and Forsyth *Administrative Law*, OUP, 10th edition, 2009; Le Sueur, De Smith, Woolf and Jowell, *De Smith, Woolf and Jowell's Judicial Review of Administrative Action*, Sweet & Maxwell, 6th edition, 2007 and Craig, *Administrative Law*, Sweet & Maxwell, 6th edition, 2008.

3   In Latin, acting beyond one's powers is to act 'ultra vires'.

i) it must correctly interpret and apply any relevant laws; and

j) it must not reach a decision which is perverse or irrational, ie a decision so unreasonable that no public body properly directing itself could have reached that decision.[4]

25.4 The modern method of obtaining judicial scrutiny of the lawfulness or otherwise of the actions of a public body, measured against these principles, is called 'judicial review'.

25.5 The procedure for judicial review is set out in the Civil Procedure Rules, Part 54. Claims for judicial review are heard in the Administrative Court which is a branch of the High Court. It now sits in London and at several regional centres.[5] Cases are heard by specially 'nominated' High Court judges or their deputies. To prevent public bodies being troubled by vexatious and stale cases, the rules require that claims are made promptly following alleged unlawful action and that the permission of the court is obtained to bring the claim.[6] If a claim ultimately succeeds, the Administrative Court has power to make special orders to stop a public body doing something (a prohibition order), or require it to do something (a mandatory order) or to quash its decision (a quashing order). In certain circumstances, the court can even take for itself the decision that the public body should lawfully have taken.[7]

25.6 A defendant to a possession claim, having identified alleged unlawful action by the public body bringing that claim, could therefore invite the county court judge to adjourn the claim to enable an application for judicial review to be made in the Administrative Court. This would obviously lead to delay and, since further and separate proceedings would be involved, additional expense. The legal burden of the proceedings would switch from the claimant in the county court to the claimant in the Administrative Court. The result would be significant disruption and inconvenience.

25.7 Accordingly, even in the years before tenants of public bodies obtained security of tenure, the courts recognised that defendants in possession proceedings brought by public bodies should be able to rely on public law principles as a ground of *defence* to the possession claim itself.

---

4 Often (without great accuracy) described as the 'Wednesbury test' derived from *Associated Provincial Picture Houses Ltd v Wednesbury Corporation* [1948] 1 KB 223, CA.

5 Birmingham, Cardiff, Leeds and Manchester.

6 CPR 54.4 and 54.5.

7 CPR 54.19.

25.8   For example, in *Bristol CC v Clark*,[8] a council tenant fell into arrears of rent as a result of unemployment and illness. The council gave notice to quit and brought a possession claim. The judge refused to make a possession order and the tenant sought to uphold that decision on the basis that, before bringing the claim, the council had failed to take into account relevant considerations – a government circular on dealing with rent arrears and/or the possibility of seeking an attachment of earnings order. Although that defence failed on its facts and a possession order was made, the Court of Appeal had no difficulty with the application of public law principles in the defence of the possession claim.

25.9   Any suggestion that this decision may have been a 'one-off' was dispelled on its re-affirmation by the Court of Appeal shortly afterwards in the case of another council tenant, *Cannock Chase DC v Kelly*.[9] In the mid-1980s the House of Lords confirmed this line of cases by explicitly holding that a council tenant in a rent arrears case could – as part of his defence – mount a public law challenge to an essential ingredient of the council's possession claim. In *Wandsworth LBC v Winder (No 1)*,[10] the tenant was allowed to raise the point that the rent increase which he had refused to pay had been imposed by the council acting beyond its powers. Although that defence ultimately failed when tried on its merits,[11] the public law or '*Winder*' defence to possession was thus firmly established in possession claims over a quarter century ago.

25.10   Given the general extension of security of tenure to most tenants of social housing by the Housing Act 1980 and later legislation (as described in Part I of this book), the public law defence largely fell into abeyance. It remained in occasional use mainly in defence of those who enjoyed no security of tenure, for example, Gypsies and other Travellers[12] or non-secure licensees.[13]

25.11   The public law defence also suffered something of a temporary

8   [1975] 1 WLR 1443; [1975] 3 All ER 976, CA and see also *Bristol CC v Rawlins* (1977) 34 P&CR 12, CA.

9   [1978] 1 WLR 1; [1978] 1 All ER 152, CA and see also *Sevenoaks DC v Emmott* (1979) 78 LGR 346; (1979) 39 P&CR 404.

10 [1984] AC 461; (1984) 17 HLR 196, HL.

11 *Wandsworth LBC v Winder (No 2)* (1987) 20 HLR 400, CA.

12 *West Glamorgan CC v Rafferty* [1988] 1 WLR 45; (1986) 18 HLR 375, CA.

13 *Cleethorpes BC v Clarkson* (1978) 128 NLJ 860; July 1978 *LAG Bulletin* 166; *R v Wear Valley DC ex p Binks* [1985] 2 All ER 699, QBD; *Kensington & Chelsea RLBC v Haydon* (1984) 17 HLR 114, CA and see generally *Wandsworth LBC v A* [2000] 1 WLR 1246, CA.

setback[14] when the Court of Appeal developed a line of authority limiting its availability to those occupiers who (like Mr Winder) had a continuing private law right to remain in occupation.[15] However, in a more recent decision of the House of Lords,[16] concerned with occupiers who had no private law rights, that area of controversy was 'swept aside by the House without further ado. All seem to have accepted it as settled law … that "conventional" judicial review grounds can be raised by way of defence to possession proceedings in the county court'.[17] The Court of Appeal has rejected a suggestion that the 'sweeping aside' of this limitation was accidental or that it is not bound to follow the House of Lords on the point.[18]

25.12   With an increasing number of occupiers living in accommodation owned by public bodies but *not* enjoying full security of tenure, the public law defence was enjoying a renaissance at the time this chapter was written. It is important, however, to raise two notes of caution:

1) It will be for the occupier to prove the public law defence on the balance of probabilities. The court will presume that the public body has acted lawfully until the contrary be shown (the 'presumption of regularity').

2) Some care must be exercised in ensuring that the public law defence is only deployed in *appropriate* cases.

25.13   On the latter point, the Court of Appeal recently granted permission to appeal in a possession case specifically to enable it to discourage the taking of frivolous public law defences.[19] It said: 'The only reason we granted permission is that we considered it important to make it absolutely clear that public law attacks of the technical and over-theoretical sort advanced here have no merit whatsoever in this sort of case' and 'They were hopeless from the outset. Such defences should only be raised when they have real and obvious substance: it is not appropriate to construct intellectual edifices of public law without any proper foundations in reality.'[20]

---

14 More fully described in N Nicol, 'Public Law Defences in Possession Proceedings' [2010] JR 85.

15 See *Avon CC v Buscott* [1988] QB 656; (1988) 20 HLR 385, CA and *Manchester CC v Cochrane* [1999] 1 WLR 809; (1999) 31 HLR 810, CA.

16 *Lambeth LBC v Kay* [2006] UKHL 10; [2006] 2 AC 465.

17 *Doherty v Birmingham CC* [2006] EWCA Civ 1739; [2007] HLR 32, at [36].

18 *Salford CC v Mullen* [2010] EWCA Civ 336 at [47]–[49].

19 *London Borough of Brent v Corcoran* [2010] EWCA Civ 774.

20 At paras [12] and [26].

25.14   Although the county court does not have an explicit filter to weed out plainly unmeritorious public law defences, equivalent to the requirement of 'permission' in judicial review proceedings,[21] a public law defence should not be allowed to go to trial unless it is 'seriously arguable'.[22] The county court will not usually direct any defence to a possession claim to go for trial unless it is satisfied that the claim 'is genuinely disputed on grounds that appear to be substantial'.[23]

25.15   The following three examples of recent successful 'public law defence' appeals in the Court of Appeal may be helpful in indicating the sorts of situations in which the defence might assist an occupier:

- In *Welwyn Hatfield DC v McGlynn*,[24] the defendant was a non-secure tenant. Following complaints of anti-social behaviour the council served notice to quit. In correspondence, it made it clear that if any further anti-social behaviour occurred, it would seek possession. On receipt of further complaints, it issued a possession claim. The public law defence was that the requirements of natural justice, seen in the light of the correspondence, required the defendant at least to be told the nature of the allegations and have an opportunity to deny or respond to them before the claim was launched. The Court of Appeal held that defence to be seriously arguable and remitted the case for trial.

- In *Croydon LBC v Barber*,[25] a non-secure tenant was violent and abusive towards a resident caretaker. The council served notice to quit and issued a possession claim. In the course of the proceedings an expert medical report was obtained which indicated that the defendant had significant mental health problems and that the violent incident had been a manifestation of his disability. The public law defence was that, in deciding to press on with the possession claim, the council had failed to have regard to its own policies and procedures relating to management of anti-social behaviour by vulnerable occupiers. The Court of Appeal upheld that defence and dismissed the possession claim.

- In *Eastlands Homes Partnership Ltd v Whyte*,[26] the landlord served notice seeking possession on an assured shorthold tenant for

21 CPR 54.4
22 *Lambeth LBC v Kay* [2006] UKHL 10; [2006] 2 AC 465, HL, per Lord Hope at [110]
23 CPR 55.8(2).
24 [2009] EWCA Civ 285; [2010] HLR 10.
25 [2010] EWCA Civ 51; (2010) *Times* 24 March.
26 [2010] EWHC 695 (QB).

reasons of rent arrears and anti-social behaviour and began a possession claim. The public law defence was that the landlord had: failed to follow its own policy in relation to rent arrears; offered an appeal against its decision but failed to disclose the evidence put before the appeal panel and/or broadened the matters considered on appeal beyond the case summary it had prepared; and, having stated that it would offer a second or further appeal, failed to do so. The judge upheld the defence and dismissed the possession claim.

25.16   The House of Lords most recently sanctioned the use of public law defences to possession claims in *Doherty v Birmingham CC*.[27] That was a claim for possession of a pitch on an official Gypsy caravan site. The trial judge held that any public law challenge to the council's decision to evict could only be brought by judicial review. The House of Lords set aside his order and remitted the public law defence for trial in the possession claim. At the date of publication of this book, that trial had yet to take place.

The claimants against whom it can be deployed

25.17   The whole premise of a public law defence is that the claimant has failed to act in accordance with the public law principles described in para 25.3. However, there is no obligation on a *private* individual or company when carrying out private functions to follow or apply such principles. So the public law defence cannot usually be raised in answer to a possession claim made by a private owner or landlord. The claimant must be a *public* body or at very least a body exercising a *public* function when seeking possession.

25.18   There is no exhaustive list of those bodies which are subject to the public law principles described above. Although local authorities and other statutorily-created landlords and landowners are plainly covered, it has been left to the courts to work out, almost on a case-by-case basis, whether quasi-public landlords and landowners – particularly social landlords such as housing associations – are subject to public law principles when seeking possession.

25.19   In *R (Weaver) v London & Quadrant Housing Trust*,[28] the trust served a notice seeking possession on an assured tenant relying on mandatory Ground 8 (rent arrears). She sought judicial review of that

27 [2008] UKHL 57; [2008] HLR 45.
28 [2009] EWCA Civ 587; [2010] 1 WLR 363; [2009] HLR 40.

decision, contending that the giving of the notice breached public law principles. An issue was raised as to whether the housing trust was a body subject to such principles. By a majority, the Court of Appeal upheld a Divisional Court decision that it was. Furthermore, it held that for most social landlords the functions of letting and terminating tenancies were functions of a public nature. The majority found that:

> the following features in particular are highly relevant to the question whether the functions of the Trust are public functions (although none of them on its own is in any sense conclusive): the substantial public subsidy which enables the Trust to achieve its objectives; the way in which the allocation agreements [for nominations by local authorities] circumscribe the freedom of the Trust to allocate properties; and the nature of the regulation to which the Trust is subject. In addition, the vast majority of RSL tenants enjoy statutory protection as regards the circumstances in which a social housing tenancy may be terminated.[29]

The court was also influenced by the fact that the trust was a social landlord able to use special statutory powers to address anti-social behaviour which were not available to private landlords.

25.20   Likewise, in *R (McIntyre) v Gentoo Group*,[30] the Administrative Court held that a decision of a housing association to grant or refuse a mutual exchange was a public function for the purposes of applying public law principles. It said that

> ... the decision in *Weaver* is directly applicable. The declaration granted by the Divisional Court in that case, that the defendant was amenable to judicial review on conventional public law grounds in respect of decisions taken in the performance of its function of managing and allocating its housing stock (or perhaps more accurately, as the majority of the Court of Appeal thought, its stock of social housing), applies not merely to decisions concerning the termination of a tenancy of social housing but also to those concerned with the mutual exchange of such tenancies.[31]

25.21   These propositions were directly applied in a possession claim in *Eastlands Homes Partnership Ltd v Whyte*.[32] In that case, the landlord conceded that the court was bound by the decision of the Court of Appeal in *Weaver*. The judge said, having considered the evidence of the status and functioning of the claimant social landlord, that:

29   At para [101].
30   [2010] EWHC 5 (Admin).
31   At para [27].
32   [2010] EWHC 695 (QB).

'The claimant is in no better position than London and Quadrant, and accordingly is to be regarded as a public authority and a public body'.[33] The defendant was thus entitled to raise a public law defence.

25.22 There has, as yet, been no decision from the new Supreme Court on which public bodies are subject to public law principles. Meanwhile, the court decisions described above effectively mean that the possession claims of all private registered social landlords (PRPs and RSLs) may be met by a public law defence. For the very latest developments, reference should be made to the 'Recent developments' section of this chapter at para 25.36.

The decisions that can be challenged

25.23 The most obvious decision to be subjected to a challenge by way of a public law defence will be the decision to file the possession claim. If the defendant can demonstrate that *that* decision was unlawful, the proceedings will not have been lawfully brought and will fall to be dismissed. Dismissal of the claim is inevitable in such circumstances because the court will not allow its processes to be used unlawfully.[34]

25.24 However, as indicated above, a public body seeking possession may make a sequence or series of decisions in respect of any claim for possession. These can include decisions: to give a notice to quit; to serve notice seeking possession; to review or not to review those decisions; to issue the claim; to press on to trial having seen the defendant's defence; to press for a possession order having heard the defendant give evidence or in the light of written evidence; and (later) to seek to execute the possession order.

25.25 In *Salford CC v Mullen*,[35] the Court of Appeal decided that, in the light of previous and modern authority, a public law defence could be raised and 'apply to *any* decision of the [claimant public body] relevant to seeking possession which could be the subject of judicial review.'[36] This has added particularly useful dimensions to the public law defence. First, the defence will now be available even where the initial decisions to serve notice and bring proceedings were lawful, if

---

33 At para [5].
34 See *Lewisham LBC v Malcolm* [2008] 1 AC 1399; [2008] HLR 41, HL and *Doherty v Birmingham CC* [2008] UKHL 57, [2008] HLR 45.
35 [2010] EWCA Civ 336.
36 [2010] EWCA Civ 336 at [74].

a subsequent decision (for example, to press for a possession order) was unlawful. Second, the fact that the last challengeable decision before the making of a possession order will be the decision to seek an order from the judge at the close of the evidence means that the lawfulness of the decision-making will be tested on the most up-to-date facts rather than the facts as they were known to the public body at some much earlier stage.

25.26   This has the added advantage of enabling the county court finally to adjudicate on a public law defence *after* it has considered and re-solved (during the trial) any factual disputes. In contrast, the Administrative Court would not usually be engaged in fact-finding and would treat the relevant facts as being the facts as they had appeared to the public body at the time of its (often much) earlier decision.

25.27   The defendant's defence and argument at trial will need to identify precisely which decisions are being subject to a public law challenge. That is because the effects of success will be different depending on which decision is unlawful. For example, if the decision to give notice was lawful but the subsequent decision to bring proceedings was unlawful, the result may be that the claim is dismissed but that the original lawful notice could be used to found another claim. In *McGlynn* (see para 25.15), the only pleaded challenge in the defence was to the decision to bring the claim. On appeal, the defendant sought permission to amend the grounds of appeal (and the defence) so as to challenge the earlier decision to give notice to quit. That was refused as being too late.

25.28   Success in a challenge to the decision to bring the proceedings will sometimes leave the occupier in a legal 'limbo'. This is particularly common in situations where a notice to quit is lawfully given to end a tenancy but the subsequent possession claim is dismissed on public law grounds. The occupier will simply remain in possession as a trespasser until the public body can make a lawful decision to recover possession. It is, for example, often wrongly assumed that success for the defendants in *McGlynn* and *Barber* (see para 25.15) meant that they remained tenants. Yet, in those cases, the only success was to achieve a state of 'tolerated' trespass until another – but this time lawful – decision could be made to issue possession claims against them. In other cases, the decision successfully challenged will be the decision to serve a notice to quit. In such a case the notice will not, presumably, have lawfully determined the tenancy and it will continue.

When the defence is not available

25.29 Given that the public law defence most commonly strikes at the very root of the claimant's decision to launch the possession proceedings, it might have been thought that it would be available to the defendant in each and every possession claim.

25.30   However, a particular difficulty has arisen in the context of modern statutory schemes which expressly or by implication make the grant of a possession order mandatory, if the court is satisfied that certain pre-conditions are made out. The most obvious is the statutory scheme relating to *introductory* tenancies which provides that, unless the court is satisfied that the notice provisions have not been complied with, it shall make an order.[37]

25.31   The courts have held that the effect of such statutory provisions is to 'oust' the ability of the defendant to take a public law defence in the county court. Instead, the defendant must seek to persuade the county court to adjourn the possession claim so that a claim for judicial review can be made in the Administrative Court. Although the courts have recognised the consequent delay, expense and administrative inconvenience involved in such a procedure as described at para 25.6 above (and called for parliament to reconsider),[38] the requirement for that procedure to be followed has now been applied not only to the *introductory* tenancy regime[39] but also to *demoted* tenancy cases.[40]

25.32   At the time of writing this aspect of public law defences was under consideration by the Supreme Court and reference should be made to the 'Recent developments' section of this chapter at para 25.36.

The powers of the court

25.33 For the reasons explained above, the ordinary result of successful deployment of the public law defence will be the dismissal of the possession claim. Indeed, the court has very little room for manoeuvre.

---

37 Housing Act 1996 s127(2) and see, generally, chapter 7.
38 Expressed most starkly in the judgments in *Manchester CC v Cochrane* [1999] 1 WLR 809; (1999) 31 HLR 810.
39 See *Manchester CC v Cochrane* [1999] 1 WLR 809; (1999) 31 HLR 810, CA; *R (McLellan) v Bracknell Forest DC* [2001] EWCA Civ 1510; [2002] QB 1229 and *Salford CC v Mullen* [2010] EWCA Civ 336.
40 *Manchester CC v Pinnock* [2009] EWCA Civ 852; [2010] 1 WLR 713; [2010] HLR 7.

If the claim was unlawfully brought, it must be dismissed. There is no 'broad discretion' of the type that the Administrative Court has in deciding whether to grant relief (and what relief) to a claimant who has successfully established unlawful conduct on the part of a public body.

25.34   Unhappily, the county court cannot grant any of the orders usually available to the Administrative Court and described at para 25.5 above.[41] Although that problem could be ameliorated by regulations enabling the orders to be available in possession cases, no such regulations have been made.[42]

25.35   Accordingly, the county court cannot, for example, quash a notice to quit or a notice seeking possession. It cannot grant an order prohibiting the public body from bringing another possession claim on the same facts nor direct it to act in a particular way. Although the county court has power to make 'binding declarations',[43] the scope for making such declarations in respect of successful public law defences has yet to be fully explored.

Recent developments

25.36   As this chapter was being written, the law in relation to public law defences to possession claims was in a state of ferment. Not least, the Supreme Court has yet to be presented with an appeal which raises the question of whether these principles apply to possession claims brought by housing associations.

25.37   However, in July 2010 the Supreme Court deployed nine of its 12 justices to hear, over four days, the appeal by the tenant in *Manchester CC v Pinnock*.[44] Seven of those same justices have been assigned to hear appeals arising from *Salford CC v Mullen* [45] in late November 2010.

25.38   Between them, these appeals will require the Supreme Court to address some or all of the following questions:

1) Are the principles available to be deployed in a public law defence (set out at para 25.3) now enlarged to include the requirement that

---

41 County Courts Act 1984 s38(3).
42 County Courts Act 1984 s38(4).
43 CPR 40.20.
44 *Manchester CC v Pinnock* [2009] EWCA Civ 852; [2010] 1 WLR 713; [2010] HLR 7.
45 *Salford CC v Mullen* [2010] EWCA Civ 336.

a public body's actions must always be 'proportionate' in order to be lawful?

2) Is the public law defence open to *all* defendants – even those with no previous contractual relationship with the landlord/owner and those with no private law rights to be in occupation at all?

3) Can a public body seeking possession rely on a later 'lawful' decision to cure an earlier 'unlawful' one?

4) Do the statutory schemes for introductory and/or demoted tenants really oust the availability of the public law defence in all cases?

5) What is to happen where a possession order has been lawfully sought and obtained by a public body but it would be unlawful to enforce it, whether for the time being or at all?

25.39 Since these questions go to the heart of many of the matters reviewed in this chapter, the publishers propose to post an updating note to this chapter on their website once the decisions of the Supreme Court are available. Readers accessing this chapter in late 2010 or beyond should therefore check www.lag.org.uk for that note.

Human rights defences

The relevant rights

26.1   For over 50 years, the United Kingdom has guaranteed to those within its jurisdiction the basic protection of fundamental human rights provided by the European Convention on Human Rights (ECHR/'the Convention'). The UK is not only a signatory to the ECHR but was one of the first state signatories to allow individual complaints of infringement to be presented to the European Court of Human Rights (ECtHR).

26.2   Several of the rights protected by the ECHR potentially have direct or indirect application to housing cases, and most particularly to possession claims. These include the following provisions:

Article 6
Right to a fair trial
In the determination of his civil rights and obligations ... everyone is entitled to a fair and public hearing within a reasonable time by an independent and impartial tribunal established by law ...

Article 8
Right to respect for private and family life
(1) Everyone has the right to respect for his private and family life, his home and his correspondence.
(2) There shall be no interference by a public authority with the exercise of this right except such as is in accordance with the law and is necessary in a democratic society in the interests of national security, public safety or the economic well-being of the country, for the prevention of disorder or crime, for the protection of health or morals, or for the protection of the rights and freedoms of others.

Article 14
Prohibition of Discrimination
The enjoyment of the rights and freedoms set forth in this Convention shall be secured without discrimination on any ground such as sex, race, colour, language, religion, political or other opinion, national or social origin, association with a national minority, property, birth or other status.

Article 1 of the First Protocol
Protection of Property
Every natural or legal person is entitled to the peaceful enjoyment of his possessions. No one shall be deprived of his possessions except in the public interest and subject to the conditions provided for by law and by the general principles of international law.

26.3   Article 8, containing the right to respect for an individual's home, is obviously the right most likely to be engaged by possession proceedings. The ECtHR, the ultimate authority on the interpretation of the

Convention, has recently placed considerable emphasis on the importance of avoiding an eviction which would infringe article 8 rights. It
has repeatedly stated that:

> the loss of one's home is a most extreme form of interference with the
> right to respect for the home. Any person at risk of an interference of
> this magnitude should in principle be able to have the proportional-
> ity and reasonableness of the measure determined by an independ-
> ent tribunal in the light of the relevant principles under Article 8 of
> the Convention, notwithstanding that, under domestic law, his or her
> right of occupation has come to an end (see *McCann v the United
> Kingdom*, Application No. 19009/04, § 50, 13 May 2008, and *Paulić v
> Croatia*, Application No. 3572/06, §§ 43-45, 22 October 2009).[1]

26.4   Although these Convention rights might have theoretically been available to be relied on by tenants and other occupiers during the second
half of the 20th century, they were of limited usefulness in practice
to people in the UK. The procedure for complaint to the ECtHR in
Strasbourg was not well known and the delays at that court were such
that any occupier seeking to rely on the provisions of the Convention would long since have been evicted under the processes of the
domestic courts before the case in Strasbourg was heard. There were,
accordingly, relatively few applications, asserting a breach of the relevant rights, made by occupiers who were defending possession proceedings. Nevertheless, some UK possession cases did successfully
complete the process.

26.5   *Connors v UK*[2] provided a particularly good and recent example
of how the Convention rights described above could be used in a
possession case. The Connors are a Gypsy family who had lived for
many years on an official Gypsy caravan site provided by Leeds City
Council. When the council received complaints of anti-social behaviour, it gave notice terminating their licence to occupy the site and
sought and obtained an outright possession order on the grounds
that they were trespassers. An attempt to stop the eviction by a claim
for judicial review failed and the family were (in unpleasant circumstances) evicted from the site and onto the highway.

26.6   They complained to the ECtHR of breaches of:

1) article 6, because they had had no forum in which to dispute the
   allegations against them;
2) article 8, because no respect had been shown for their longstanding homes by the summary process of eviction;

---

1 *Belchikova v Russia* Application No 2408/06, ECtHR (First Section), 25 March 2010.
2 [2004] HLR 53; (2005) 40 EHRR 9, ECtHR.

3) article 14, because only *Gypsy* caravan sites were excluded from the protection of the Caravan Sites Act 1968 and the occupiers had none of the other statutory rights of tenants and licensees of local authorities; and

4) article 1 of Protocol 1, because items of their personal property had been interfered with, retained and later dumped in the course of the eviction.

The court focused on the article 8 complaints. It held that such serious interference with article 8 rights as summary eviction from a longstanding home required particularly weighty reasons of public interest by way of justification. The ECtHR was not persuaded that the necessity for a statutory scheme which permitted the summary eviction of the Connors family had been sufficiently demonstrated. It found that the eviction process was not attended by the requisite procedural safeguards, namely, the requirement to establish proper justification for the serious interference with article 8 rights, and consequently could not be regarded as justified by a 'pressing social need' or proportionate to the legitimate aim being pursued. There was, accordingly, a violation of article 8. The complaints of breaches of most other articles were subsumed in that finding. Mr Connors was awarded compensation.

26.7   Although the Connors family were thus ultimately successful, their case exemplified the weakness of the pre-Human Rights Act 1998 arrangements. They had been unable to rely directly on their rights in the UK courts. They had been unable to stop their eviction. Their compensation came through only many years after the relevant events and only on a complaint to the European Court of Human Rights.

26.8   Of course, although this chapter has its focus on the European Convention on Human Rights and the Human Rights Act 1998, the UK is a signatory to many other international instruments addressing housing rights. They cannot be explored in this text.[3] None of them is covered by the Human Rights Act 1998, which is considered next, and none will furnish a freestanding defence to a possession claim.

---

3 See generally Nik Nicol's helpful articles: 'Applying the Right to Housing' [2002] JHL 11; 'The Other Human Rights' [2001] *Human Rights* 156 and 'A Right to Housing' July 1998 *Legal Action* 8. See also Dr P Kenna, *Housing Rights and Human Rights* (FEANTSA, 2005).

Human Rights Act 1998

26.9 The intention of the Human Rights Act (HRA) 1998 was to 'bring rights home' by enabling the Convention rights described above to be enforced in the domestic courts. To enable the state authorities and the courts to be ready for this substantial change, the Act was not brought into force until October 2000.

26.10 This chapter cannot provide a detailed description of the content of the Human Rights Act 1998 or its application to housing cases generally. The reader is referred to other texts for that.[4] The focus here is exclusively on how the Human Rights Act 1998 may avail an occupier in a housing possession case.

26.11 In short summary, the Human Rights Act 1998 'works' by making it unlawful for any public authority to act incompatibly with an individual's Convention rights: HRA 1998 s6(1). The Convention rights are those set out in HRA 1998 Sch 1 and include all the rights extracted at para 26.2 above. The individual who is an alleged victim of an unlawful infringement of Convention rights may either bring proceedings against the relevant public authority or rely on the Convention rights in proceedings brought against him or her: HRA 1998 s7. In applying and interpreting the Convention rights in such cases, the domestic courts must take account of any relevant decisions of the Strasbourg Court (ECtHR): HRA 1998 s2.

26.12 The Human Rights Act 1998 has been carefully drawn to protect parliamentary sovereignty. Although the domestic courts must interpret legislation compatibly with Convention rights wherever possible (HRA 1998 s3) if such an interpretation proves impossible, the domestic courts cannot strike down primary legislation. The most a court can do is grant a declaration of incompatibility and leave it to parliament to address the problem: HRA 1998 s4. To avoid indirect challenges to the primacy of parliament, the acts of public authorities which have been done in compliance with incompatible legislation are not unlawful: HRA1998 s6(2).

26.13 From that short description it will be seen that a defendant to a housing possession claim might raise either or both of two possible defences based on the Human Rights Act 1998. First, it might be said that the law on which the claimant is relying for possession is itself incompatible with the Convention rights. For this form of defence

4 Baker, Dymond and Hunter, *Housing and Human Rights Law*, LAG (second edition to publish in 2011) and Luba, *Housing and the Human Rights Act*, Jordans, 2000.

see para 26.28. Second, the defendant may contend that in his or her particular case an eviction would be a breach of his or her individual Convention rights. For that form of defence see para 26.33. However, the Human Rights Act 1998 does not apply in the same way across the whole range of housing possession cases reviewed in this book. A discussion of which cases may permit a 'human rights' defence is given in the next section of this chapter.

In which possession cases will HRA 1998 apply?

Claims by 'public authorities'

26.14   A substantive *defence* to a possession claim based on Convention rights will usually arise only where it can be said that the claimant's bringing of the claim is itself unlawful (because the claim infringes the defendant's Convention rights) or that the grant of a possession order in favour of the claimant would be unlawful under the Human Rights Act 1998 (because the prospect of eviction would infringe Convention rights). For either such assertion to be made it would usually be essential that the claimant is a 'public authority' because only such an authority is subject to the provisions of HRA 1998 s6(1) making it unlawful to act in a way incompatible with Convention rights.

26.15   The Human Rights Act 1998 does not contain a list or exhaustive definition of what is a 'public authority' for section 6(1) purposes. The Act simply provides that the phrase includes every court and tribunal and also 'any person certain of whose functions are functions of a public nature': HRA 1998 s6(3). However, HRA 1998 s6(5) provides that in relation to any particular act, a person is not a public authority by virtue only of section 6(3) if the 'nature of the act is private'.

26.16   Plainly, the act of any claimant which is an arm of central or local government will be caught by that approach to the meaning of 'public authority' as will the acts of most statutorily-created bodies dealing with occupation or possession of housing. However, the last decade has been spent in teasing-out (1) which other claimants may be 'public authorities' for the purposes of enabling a 'human rights defence' to be deployed by a defendant occupier and (2) which of their acts are of a public, as opposed to private, nature. The questions have most directly arisen in possession claims brought by social landlords other than local housing authorities.

26.17   In *Poplar HARCA v Donoghue*,[5] the Court of Appeal rejected the proposition that all such landlords were automatically to be treated as public authorities for HRA 1998 s6 purposes. However, it found that Poplar HARCA (which had been set up by the local housing authority to take over parts of its housing stock in a small scale stock-transfer) was a public authority in so far as it carried out the function of making arrangements for the provision of short-term accommodation to those homeless households (such as the defendant) that the council would previously have accommodated. In the event, the human rights defence in that case failed (for reasons explored more fully in para 26.31).

26.18   Whether a particular social housing provider is or is not a 'public authority' accordingly falls to be decided in each case and turns on both the nature of the provider itself and on whether the particular function in which it is engaged is public as opposed to 'private'. The correct approach has been considered in two further recent cases.

26.19   In *R (Weaver) v London & Quadrant Housing Trust*,[6] the trust served a notice seeking possession on an assured tenant relying on mandatory Ground 8 (rent arrears). She sought judicial review of that decision, contending that the giving of the notice breached her Convention rights. An issue was raised as to whether the trust was a 'public authority' for the purposes of the Human Rights Act 1998 and whether the giving of the notice had been a private or public act. By a majority, the Court of Appeal upheld a Divisional Court decision that the trust's act in giving notice was potentially within the ambit of section 6(1). Furthermore, it held that for most social landlords the functions of letting and terminating tenancies were functions of a public nature for the purposes of section 6(3). The majority found that:

> ... the following features in particular are highly relevant to the question whether the functions of the Trust are public functions (although none of them on its own is in any sense conclusive): the substantial public subsidy which enables the Trust to achieve its objectives; the way in which the allocation agreements [for nominations by local authorities] circumscribe the freedom of the Trust to allocate properties; and the nature of the regulation to which the Trust is subject. In addition, the vast majority of RSL [registered social landlord] tenants enjoy statutory protection as regards the circumstances in which a social housing tenancy may be terminated.[7]

---

5 [2001] EWCA Civ 595; [2002] QB 48.
6 [2009] EWCA Civ 587; [2010] 1 WLR 363; [2009] HLR 40.
7 At para [101].

The court was also influenced by the fact that the housing trust was a social landlord able to use special statutory powers to address anti-social behaviour which were not available to private landlords. In the event, the claim failed on its facts.

26.20   These propositions were later directly applied in a possession claim in which a human rights defence was deployed: *Eastlands Homes Partnership Ltd v Whyte*.[8] There the landlord conceded that the court was bound by the decision of the Court of Appeal in *Weaver*. The judge said, having considered the evidence of the status and functioning of the claimant social landlord, that: 'The Claimant is in no better position than London and Quadrant, and accordingly is to be regarded as a public authority and a public body.'[9] The defendant was thus entitled to raise a human rights defence.

26.21   It should not, however, be assumed that the question of whether a social landlord seeking possession is engaged in a private or public act is finally settled. Although the Supreme Court refused permission to the trust to appeal in the *Weaver* case, it expressly recognised in its reasons for refusal that the point was of general importance. Permission was refused only on the special facts of the case (that the Trust had succeeded in defeating Ms Weaver's claim and she had pursued no appeal from the dismissal of her claim).

26.22   Even if the claimant is a public authority, or the act in seeking possession is an act of a public nature, the claimant will not be acting unlawfully – even if an eviction would contravene a Convention right – if a statutory provision prevented it from acting differently or it was acting so as to give effect to a statutory provision: HRA 1998 s6(2). Although it seems extraordinary that a claimant would ever contend that it had 'no choice' but to bring a possession claim which contravenes a Convention right, the point was taken by the local authority claimant in *Birmingham CC v Doherty*.[10] However, any other claimants are likely to be cautious about relying on section 6(2) in possession cases because the Supreme Court has been invited to depart from the reasoning of the majority of the House of Lords in *Doherty*, on that point, in the course of the recently argued appeal in *Manchester CC v Pinnock*. That invitation was extended not only by the appellant in that case but also by the two interveners – the Secretary of State for Communities and Local Government and the Equality and Human Rights Commission. The Supreme Court will

8   [2010] EWHC 695 (QB).
9   At para [5].
10 [2008] UKHL 57; [2009] 1 AC 367.

give judgment on that appeal later in 2010. See further, the recent developments section at para 26.47.

Claims by other claimants

26.23 It would be wrong to assume that human rights defences based on the Human Rights Act 1998 are not available to occupiers of *privately* owned premises. In any and every housing possession case, even in a case between private landlord and private tenant or between private mortgage lender and mortgage borrower, the courts will be obliged to interpret any relevant statutory scheme, wherever possible, in accordance with Convention rights. For example, in *Ghaidan v Godin-Mendoza*,[11] a dispute arose between a private landlord and an occupier as to whether the occupier had succeeded to the Rent Act tenancy of his late same-sex partner. Although the Rent Act provided such a right only to persons living as 'husband or wife' of the deceased, the House of Lords held that in order to avoid infringement of article 14, read with article 8, the Act should be interpreted so as to give the same right to a partner in a same-sex couple.

26.24 Therefore, where one reading of a statutory scheme would give rise to a defence in a possession claim but another would not, the occupier will obtain the benefit of that defence if the former interpretation is the one that is compatible with Convention rights and the other is not. That will apply just as much in a case between 'private' parties as in a claim brought by a 'public authority'.

26.25 Even in the absence of a defence based on statutory interpretation, private sector occupiers in possession claims might well draw attention to the fact that the court is itself a 'public authority' for Human Rights Act 1998 purposes and that it must not act unlawfully in handling the possession claim, that is, in a way which is incompatible with Convention rights: HRA 1998 ss6(1) and 6(3)(a).

26.26 In most cases, the court's ready rejoinder will be that the relevant statutory scheme in play *requires* that it makes the possession order sought and therefore it cannot be acting unlawfully in granting the order: see HRA 1998 s6(2). For example, if the defendant is an assured shorthold tenant who has been served with a valid notice given under Housing Act 1988 s21 the court will have no alternative but to grant possession within, at most, six weeks.[12] Likewise,

---

11 [2004] UKHL 30; [2004] 2 AC 557; [2004] 3 All ER 411.
12 The maximum permitted period under Housing Act 1980 s89.

if a right to possession is established on a mandatory ground under Housing Act 1988 Sch 2 or Rent Act 1977 Sch 15.

26.27　However, where the claim for possession is pursued by a private landlord or landowner, and not brought under a statutory scheme which mandates the court to grant possession, it might be suggested that the court must refuse a possession order if the grant of it would infringe Convention rights. In two recent cases brought between private parties, in which the domestic court has had to decide whether or not to grant an order leading to the recovery of possession, the ECtHR has expected the domestic court itself to apply and protect the Convention rights of the occupiers.[13] No domestic cases have yet considered such an approach.

Defences based on a challenge to the underlying law

26.28　The defendant may take the point, in defence of any possession claim, that the underlying law which enables the claimant to seek a possession order, or requires the court to grant one, is itself incompatible with a Convention right. This sort of defence was discretely identified by Lord Hope at [110(a)] of his speech in *Lambeth LBC v Kay*[14] and has become known as the 'gateway (a)' defence.

26.29　If it can be seriously argued that the legislation relied on by the claimant in a possession claim, or falling to be applied by the court in such a claim, appears incompatible with a Convention right, the first task of the court dealing with the possession claim will be to construe the legislation compatibly with the relevant Convention right if it is possible to do so: HRA 1998 s3. If such a construction seems impossible, the court should transfer the proceedings to the High Court so that it can consider making a declaration of incompatibility under section 4.

26.30　Usually only the former approach will provide any effective defence for the defendant occupier. That is because, even if a declaration of incompatibility is made, it is not binding on the parties to the proceedings in which it is made: HRA 1998 s4(6)(b). So, for example, if the High Court declares that a mandatory statutory ground for

---

13　*Zehentner v Austria*, Application No 20082/02, ECtHR (First Section), 16 July 2009 and *Belchikova v Russia* Application No 2408/06, ECtHR (First Section), 25 March 2010.

14　[2006] UKHL 10; [2006] 2 AC 465.

possession is incompatible with Convention rights, the court must still make a possession order under that ground (if the ground has been made out on the facts). It does not act unlawfully in doing so because it had no alternative (HRA 1998 s6(2)) and the parties' rights are unaffected by the declaration.

26.31   To date, no defendant has succeeded in obtaining a declaration that a statutory provision concerned with possession orders is incompatible with the Convention – although a declaration would have been granted in *Doherty v Birmingham CC*[15] in respect of the legislation concerned with possession of official Gypsy caravan sites if parliament had not already passed amending legislation which will (when brought into effect) repeal the incompatible provision.[16] The unsuccessful challenges which have so far been made to legislation relating to possession proceedings on the ground that it is incompatible include:

- *Poplar Housing and Regeneration Community Association Ltd v Donoghue.*[17] That case concerned a possession claim against an assured shorthold tenant (see chapter 11), following service of a Housing Act 1988 section 21 notice. The Court of Appeal held that, notwithstanding its mandatory terms, the right to possession contained in section 21(4) did not conflict with the tenant's rights under article 8. The section was clearly necessary in a democratic society in so far as there had to be a procedure for recovering possession of property at the end of a tenancy. The court said that it would defer to parliament as to whether the restricted power of the court in relation to possession orders sought under that section was legitimate and proportionate.

- *R (McLellan) v Bracknell Forest DC.*[18] This case concerned a possession claim against an introductory tenant (see chapter 7). It was held that the statutory procedure for recovery of possession against introductory tenants contained in the Housing Act 1996 was compliant with Convention rights.

- *Reigate & Banstead DC v Benfield* was heard with *McLellan* (above). The Court of Appeal rejected a proposition that the Housing Act 1989 s80 – which restricts the court's discretion about the time it can allow for possession to be given – was incompatible with the Convention rights.

---

15 [2008] UKHL 57; [2009] 1 AC 367.
16 Housing and Regeneration Act 2008 s318.
17 [2001] EWCA Civ 595; [2002] QB 48.
18 [2001] EWCA 1510; [2002] QB 1129.

- *Sheffield CC v Smart.*[19] The council claimed possession against non-secure tenants being accommodated under homelessness legislation following service of notices to quit (see chapter 5). The Court of Appeal held that the balance of interests arising under article 8(2) had in all its essentials been struck by the legislature when enacting the statutory scheme for the housing of homeless persons and their eviction. The legislation was not incompatible with the Convention rights.

- *Michalak v Wandsworth LBC.*[20] This was a possession claim brought against a relative of a deceased secure tenant who did not qualify to succeed to the secure tenancy because their relationship with the deceased was not in the list of 'members of a family' contained in the Housing Act 1985 s113 (reproduced at para 2.40). The Court of Appeal held that, although the provision was discriminatory in relation to a matter within the scope of article 8, and so article 14 was engaged, there was an objective justification for establishing a 'closed' list in section 113, that is, the need for certainty in determining which members of a secure tenant's family were eligible to succeed. The scheme was not incompatible.[21]

- *Southwark LBC v St Brice.*[22] The defendant applied to set aside a warrant which had been executed. The Court of Appeal held that the rules of procedure which allowed the issue of a warrant for possession and arrangements for execution following non-compliance with a suspended possession order did not infringe articles 6, 8 or 14 of the ECHR. Proportionality had been considered when the possession order was made.

- *R (Gilboy) v Liverpool CC.*[23] The Court of Appeal rejected a claim made in judicial review proceedings that the demoted tenancy scheme (see chapter 9) was incompatible with Convention rights because it made grant of a possession order mandatory if the claimant had served a notice and conducted a review, irrespective of the merits of the possession claim and in the absence of any independent scrutiny of those merits.

---

19 [2002] EWCA Civ 4; [2002] HLR 34.
20 [2002] EWCA Civ 271; [2003] 1 WLR 617.
21 See also *Sharp v Brent LBC* [2003] EWCA Civ 779; [2003] HLR 65 and *R (Gangera) v Hounslow LBC* [2003] EWHC 794 (Admin); [2003] HLR 68.
22 [2001] EWCA Civ 1138; [2002] 1 WLR 1537.
23 [2008] EWCA Civ 751; [2009] QB 699.

- *Waltham Forest LBC v Coombes.*[24] Following the death of his parents who were secure tenants, the defendant wished to remain in the family home. The council served notice to quit on the personal representatives and sought possession. The High Court dismissed a claim that the Protection from Eviction Act 1977 s3 was incompatible with Convention rights because it provided that the claim for possession must be made in a court which would inevitably grant a possession order on proof of expiry of a valid notice irrespective of the merits.

26.32 Despite these unsuccessful challenges, there are so many statutory provisions relating to possession proceedings that there may yet be a declaration of incompatibility to be made in respect of one of them.

Defences based on the facts of the particular case

26.33 An occupier may well assert that in the circumstances of his of her particular case, the seeking or making of an order for possession would be an infringement of a Convention right. Most often the right that it is asserted will be infringed by the making of a possession order is the right to respect for a home in article 8. That is hardly surprising given the ECtHR's position (see para 26.3) that eviction is an 'extreme form' of interference with that right. It is, accordingly, now well settled that a possession claim will 'engage' that right and that the claimant's case will fall to be justified within the terms of article 8(2) before an order can be made. Although the full text of article 8 is set out in para 26.2, the second paragraph of it is repeated here for convenience.

> There shall be no interference by a public authority with the exercise of this right except such as is in accordance with the law and is necessary in a democratic society in the interests of national security, public safety or the economic well-being of the country, for the prevention of disorder or crime, for the protection of health or morals, or for the protection of the rights and freedoms of others.

26.34 A claimant will have little difficulty in demonstrating obvious compliance with most of this rubric. If the claim is not brought 'in accordance with the law' it will be dismissed. It will usually be easy to establish that the claim is brought to protect one of the listed 'interests' (for example, in an anti-social behaviour case, the interests of 'public safety'

24 [2010] EWHC 666 (Admin).

or 'prevention of crime and disorder' and, in a rent arrears case, 'the economic well-being of the country'). The crucial issue will usually be whether eviction is 'necessary'. This requirement is interpreted by the ECtHR as requiring that the proposed action is 'proportionate', that is, no more than is necessary to achieve the legitimate aim being pursued.

26.35　　There is little difficulty accommodating the full requirements of justification under article 8(2) in a case in which the court dealing with a possession claim enjoys a wide discretion as to whether to make a possession order at all or what possession order to make. For example, in *Lambeth LBC v Howard*,[25] Sedley LJ said that, while article 8 should not carry county courts to materially different outcomes from those which they had been arriving at in applying the condition of reasonableness, 'it can do no harm, and may often do a great deal of good, if the exercise is approached for what it is, an application of the principle of proportionality'. Similarly, in *Kay v Lambeth LBC; Leeds CC v Price*,[26] Lord Brown said that

> where the domestic law requires the court to make a judgment (most notably perhaps in those cases under Schedule 2 to the Housing Act 1985 where repossession can only be ordered if the court considers it reasonable), or to exercise a discretion, the judge will bear in mind that he is performing this task in the context of the defendant's article 8 right to respect for his home. (at [203]).

26.36　In *Gallagher v Castle Vale Housing Action Trust*,[27] an outright possession order was made against a secure tenant following complaints of nuisance. She argued that she was not personally to blame for the offensive conduct and had not acquiesced in it; the disturbance was caused by members of the family who were about to move out, and the nuisance would therefore cease. The Court of Appeal considered that the test of 'reasonableness' takes into account most of the issues that might be raised in an attempt to show that a possession order is a 'proportionate' remedy. Nonetheless, an outright order should only be made in a very clear-cut case and only where it was 'proportionate' to do so. The outright order was set aside and a two-year suspended possession order was substituted. The court reinforced the importance, given article 8, of making an order depriving someone of his or her home only where a clear case was made out for doing so.

25　[2001] EWCA Civ 468; (2001) 33 HLR 636.
26　[2006] UKHL 10; [2006] 2 AC 465.
27　[2001] EWCA Civ 944; (2001) 33 HLR 72.

26.37 When the Human Rights Act 1998 first came into force, it was initially supposed that, in any and every housing possession case, the claimant would need to establish 'justification' for a possession order in article 8(2) terms. For example, in the early post-Human Rights Act 1998 case of *Harrow LBC v Qazi*, once the Court of Appeal was satisfied that the defendant occupied the premises as his 'home' and that article 8 was therefore engaged by the claim for possession, it remitted the article 8(2) justification for trial in the county court.[28]

26.38 But the successful appeal by the claimant landlord in that case triggered three successive decisions of the House of Lords which have cumulatively left many landlords, tenants and judges in a state of uncertainty about how and when article 8(2) now operates in the domestic courts in those cases where the general law (whether statutory or common law) usually requires that on proof of certain requirements, for example, termination of an unprotected tenancy by notice to quit, a possession order should be made.

26.39 The first of the three cases was *Harrow LBC v Qazi* itself.[29] The council brought a possession claim against a former joint secure tenant whose wife had terminated the tenancy by serving a notice to quit (see para 2.30). The House of Lords held by a majority that the law which enables a public authority landlord to exercise its unqualified right to recover possession with a view to making the premises available for letting to others on its housing list does not violate article 8. The result was that contractual and property rights to possession could not be defeated by a defence based on article 8.[30] On 11 March 2004 the ECtHR decided – without giving specific reasons – that Mr Qazi's application to that court was inadmissible.

26.40 The second decision of the House of Lords was on the appeals in *Kay v Lambeth LBC* and *Leeds CC v Price.*[31] In *Kay*, the council had licensed 'short life' premises to a trust which purported to grant licences to those allowed into occupation. In fact those 'licences' created a relationship of landlord and tenant as between the trust and the sub-occupants.[32] However, Lambeth LBC gave notice to terminate the interest of the trust and brought possession proceedings against Mr Kay and other occupiers as trespassers. Defences based

---

28 [2002] HLR 14, CA.
29 [2003] UKHL 43; [2004] 1 AC 983.
30 See also *Newham LBC v Kibata* [2003] EWCA Civ 1785; [2004] HLR 28 and *Bradney v Birmingham CC; Birmingham CC v McCann* [2003] EWCA Civ 1783; [2004] HLR 27, each applying the *Qazi* decision.
31 [2006] UKHL 10; [2006] 2 AC 465.
32 *Bruton v London and Quadrant Housing Trust* [2000] 1 AC 406, HL.

on article 8 were struck out and possession orders were made. The defendants appealed, relying on the ECtHR decision in *Connors* (see para 26.5), but the Court of Appeal[33] dismissed the appeal and held that *Connors* was only of assistance to the domestic courts in relation to cases involving Gypsies. In *Price*, the council sought possession of land which had been unlawfully occupied by the defendant trespassers, who were Gypsies. The claim was transferred to the High Court for determination of the preliminary issue of whether the defendants could rely on article 8. The judge, applying *Harrow LBC v Qazi* (see para 26.39), held that they could not and made a possession order. On appeal[34] the Court of Appeal held that:

1) *Qazi* and *Connors* were inconsistent decisions;
2) the Court of Appeal had been wrong in *Lambeth LBC v Kay* to suggest that the decision in *Connors* applied only in Gypsy cases; and
3) the domestic courts should follow and apply *Qazi* until it had been reconsidered by the House of Lords in the light of *Connors*,

and granted leave to appeal to the House of Lords.

26.41   The two appeals were joined and heard together by seven law lords. They reconsidered *Qazi* in the light of *Connors*. The appeals were dismissed in both cases. It was unanimously agreed that article 8 does not in terms give a right to be provided with a home and does not guarantee the right to have one's housing problem solved by the state authorities. But the House of Lords was divided on whether the Human Rights Act 1998 would, in exceptional cases, permit an occupier to defend the claim on the basis that a possession order would be disproportionate. Lord Hope, giving the leading speech of the majority, rejected that possibility. He said that:

> Judges in the county courts, when faced with such a defence [based on article 8 principles], should proceed on the assumption that domestic law strikes a fair balance and is compatible with the occupier's Convention rights. (at [109])

> But, in agreement with [the majority] I would go further. Subject to what I say below, I would hold that a defence which does not challenge the law under which the possession order is sought as being incompatible with article 8, but is based only on the occupier's personal circumstances, should be struck out ... [If] the requirements of the law have been established and the right to recover possession is

33   [2004] EWCA Civ 926; [2004] HLR 56.
34   [2005] EWCA Civ 289; [2005] 1 WLR 1825; [2005] 3 All ER 573.

unqualified, the only situations in which it would be open to the court to refrain from proceeding to summary judgment and making the possession order are these:

(a) if a seriously arguable point is raised that the law which enables the court to make the possession order is incompatible with article 8, the county court in the exercise of its jurisdiction under the Human Rights Act 1998 should deal with the argument in one or other of two ways: (i) by giving effect to the law, so far as it is possible to do so under section 3, in a way that is compatible with article 8, or (ii) by adjourning the proceedings to enable the compatibility issue to be dealt with in the High Court;

(b) if the defendant wishes to challenge the decision of a public authority to recover possession as an improper exercise of its powers at common law on the ground that it was a decision that no reasonable person would consider justifiable, he should be permitted to do this provided again that the point is seriously arguable: *Wandsworth LBC v Winder* [1985] AC 461. (at [110]).

26.42 The decision of the majority in *Kay* and *Price* effectively nullified any potential the Human Rights Act 1998 might have to furnish a defence based on the facts of a particular case. The first part of para [110] extracted above did no more than re-state the mechanisms provided by HRA 1998 ss3 and 4 in relation to potentially incompatible statutory schemes (see para 26.28). The second part, which became known as 'gateway (b)', was nothing more than a statement of the availability of the existing public law defence available on conventional public law principles (see chapter 25).

26.43 The third case to reach the House of Lords was *Doherty v Birmingham CC*.[35] In that claim the council sought possession of a plot on an official Gypsy caravan site. The case seemed on all fours with *Connors* (see para 26.5) in which it had been held that the statutory scheme of summary eviction of travellers from such sites without examination of the merits otherwise than in a claim for judicial review was incompatible with article 8 (see para 26.31). The defence accordingly addressed both the gateways (a) and (b) identified by Lord Hope in *Kay* and contended that, on the specific facts, an eviction would be disproportionate. The House of Lords held that the underlying statutory scheme was incompatible with article 8 and that the 'gateway (b)' defence should be remitted for trial. Although the majority were agreed that the terms of para [110] of *Kay* had to be enlarged, they were not entirely clear about how.

35 [2008] UKHL 57, [2009] 1 AC 367.

26.44   There were two almost immediate consequences of the decision in *Doherty*. The first was a rash of cases in the High Court[36] and Court of Appeal[37] each seeking to identify how, if at all, a proportionality approach could be forced into the 'enlarged' gateway (b) and then applied in individual cases. For reasons explained below, nothing is to be gained from now detailing those cases here.[38]

26.45   Second, it became even clearer than it had been before *Doherty* that the decisions of the UK courts were out of step with the approach being taken on the same issue by the ECtHR. In *McCann v UK*,[39] the Strasbourg court firmly and clearly held that where a proportionality defence was raised to a claim for a possession order in respect of an occupier's home, the terms of article 8(2) required that the court seized of the possession claim be satisfied, having regard to the aim pursued by the claimant and the circumstances of the defendant, that eviction would be proportionate. It has followed and applied that approach in a series of subsequent cases.[40] Although it has not yet determined the complaint made to it by Mr Kay, the Court has posed the following question for the parties in *Kay v UK*:[41]

> Did the applicants have the opportunity to have the proportionality of their evictions determined by an independent tribunal in light of the relevant principles under Article 8? (*McCann v the United Kingdom*, Application No. 19009/04, 13 May 2008)

26.46   The new Supreme Court has therefore been faced with a number of appeals inviting it to sort out the difficulties the domestic courts are having in applying the trio of House of Lords cases described above

---

36 *Hillingdon LBC v Collins* [2008] EWHC 3016 (Admin); *Wandsworth LBC v Dixon* [2009] EWHC 27 (Admin); *Defence Estates v JL* [2009] EWHC 1049 (Admin) and *Stokes v London Borough of Brent* [2009] EWHC 1426 (QB).

37 *Smith v Evans* [2008] 1 WLR 661, CA; *Doran v Liverpool CC* [2009] 1 WLR 2365, CA; *Central Bedfordshire v Taylor* [2010] 1 WLR 446, CA ;*Manchester CC v Pinnock* [2009] EWCA Civ 852; [2010] 1 WLR 713; [2010] HLR 7 and *Salford CC v Mullen* [2010] EWCA Civ 336.

38 For a review of how the domestic decisions have unfolded and what might be done to reconcile the approach of the domestic courts and Strasbourg see N Madge, 'Article 8: La Lutta Continua?' [2009] JHL 43 and for an analysis of how the cases might be applied in current practice see M Robinson, 'Declaration of rights' [2010] 137 *Adviser* 17.

39 (2008) 47 EHRR 40, ECtHR.

40 See *Cosic v Croatia* Application No 28261/06, 15 January 2009, ECtHR; *Zehentner v Austria* Application No 20072/02, 16 July 2009, ECtHR; *Paulić v Croatia* Application No 3572/06, 22 October 2009, ECtHR and *Belchikova v Russia* Application No 2408/06, 25 March 2010, ECtHR.

41 [2008] ECHR 1193, ECtHR.

and to find a means of reconciling them with the decisions coming from Strasbourg. Meanwhile, a great number of possession claims in the county court have been stayed or compromised awaiting clarification from the highest domestic court as to whether a 'human rights' defence can be deployed and, if so, in what terms.

Recent developments

26.47   As this chapter was being written, the law in relation to human rights defences to possession claims was – as described above – in a state of rapid evolution and change. Two developments require particular note.

26.48   First, in July 2010 the Supreme Court deployed nine of its 12 justices to hear, over four days, the appeal by the tenant in *Manchester CC v Pinnock*.[42] Seven of those same justices have been assigned to hear appeals arising from *Salford CC v Mullen*[43] in late November 2010. The cases raise again the questions of whether (1) alleged infringement of HRA 1998 s6(1) can be raised in a county court possession claim and (2) how the court is to satisfy itself – in cases where no judgment falls to be made about reasonableness – whether an order would be proportionate.

26.49   Between them, these appeals will require the Supreme Court to address many of the issues discussed in this chapter.

26.50   Second, the Supreme Court has yet to be presented with an appeal which raises the question of whether the requirements of HRA 1998 s6(1) apply to possession claims brought by housing associations (see para 26.21).

26.51   Since these developments go to the heart of many of the matters reviewed in this chapter, the publishers propose to post an updating note to this chapter on their website once the decisions of the Supreme Court are available. Anyone reading this chapter in or after late 2010 should therefore check www.lag.org.uk for that note.

42   *Manchester CC v Pinnock* [2009] EWCA Civ 852; [2010] 1 WLR 713; [2010] HLR 7.
43   *Salford CC v Mullen* [2010] EWCA Civ 336.

CHAPTER 27

Disability discrimination and possession proceedings

Possession proceedings and the Disability Discrimination Act

27.1   The possibilities of invoking the Disability Discrimination Act (DDA) 1995, as amended by the Disability Discrimination Act 2005, by way of defence to possession proceedings should be considered in appropriate cases.[1] A tenant or other occupier suffering from disability may seek to argue that the Disability Discrimination Act 1995 protects him or her from eviction. The cornerstone of this argument lies in DDA 1995 s22(3)(c), which renders it unlawful for a person managing premises to discriminate against a disabled person occupying those premises 'by evicting the disabled person or subjecting him to any other detriment'. A disabled person is defined for the purposes of the Disability Discrimination Act 1995 in section 1 as 'a person with a physical or mental impairment which has a substantial and long-term effect on his ability to carry out day-to-day activities'.[2]

27.2   Under DDA 1995 s24(1), a person discriminates against a disabled person if:

(a) for a reason which relates to the disabled person's disability, he treats him less favourably than he treats or would treat others to whom that reason does not or would not apply;[3] and
(b) he cannot show that the treatment is justified.

27.3   It is possible to justify treating a disabled person less favourably where another person (in this context, the landlord) considers that one of a number of conditions are met and that it is reasonable in all the circumstances to hold that opinion. One of these conditions (set out in DDA 1995 s24(3)) is that:

---

1   See Robert Latham and Catherine Casserley, 'Disability-related discrimination claims after *Lewisham LBC v Malcolm*' September 2008 *Legal Action* 38.

2   The definition in s1 is expanded in DDA 1995 Sch 1 and in Disability Discrimination (Meaning of Disability) Regulations 1996 SI No 1455. See also the revised *Guidance on matters to be taken into account in determining questions relating to the definition of disability*, issued by the Secretary of State for Work and Pensions (May 2006).

3   DDA 1995 requires a two-stage test: (1) What is the relevant act or omission? (2) Would a relevant comparator have been treated in the same way? Applying this test, the Court of Appeal held that a landlord was entitled to withhold consent to the installation of a stair-lift in the common parts of a block of flats, because its reasons for refusing consent were not related to the tenant's disability: *Williams v Richmond Court (Swansea) Ltd* [2006] EWCA Civ 1719; [2007] HLR 23.

(a) in any case, the treatment is necessary in order not to endanger the health or safety of any person[4] ...

27.4 Against this background, tenants in a number of cases have sought to raise a defence under the Disability Discrimination Act 1995 to possession proceedings. It should be stressed that this course is not necessary where proceedings are brought on a discretionary ground for possession, except in so far as the defendant may have a counter-claim for damages for breach of a DDA 1995 duty: in such cases, the defendant's disability, and its effect (if any) on the reason for seeking possession, are clearly relevant to the question of whether it is reason-able in all the circumstances to make a possession order.[5] Where the court has no discretion – for example, where the tenancy is a non-secure or non-assured tenancy – case-law shows that tenants raising a defence based on the Disability Discrimination Act 1995 alone are unlikely to be successful in most, though not all, cases. Such was the case in *Lewisham LBC v Malcolm*, in which the defendant, a secure tenant, was diagnosed with schizophrenia. Although he was admit-ted to hospital on numerous occasions, his condition was stabilised by medication. Later, he exercised the right to buy his flat but, be-fore completion, he sublet it, and so he ceased to be a secure tenant (Housing Act 1985 s93(2)). He said that his decision to sublet the flat related to his schizophrenia. The council gave notice to quit and issued proceedings for possession. The Court of Appeal[6] held that the tenant had been subjected to less favourable treatment because the reason for the possession claim – the unlawful subletting of his flat – 'related to' his disability, which had impaired his thought processes. However, although the House of Lords[7] accepted that an unlawful breach of the Disability Discrimination Act 1995 would amount to a complete defence to a possession claim based on such a breach, it reversed the decision of the Court of Appeal. Lord Bingham accepted that the defendant was a disabled person. The treatment alleged to constitute discrimination was the council's conduct in seeking pos-session of the flat. Applying an objective test, however, the real reason that the council, a social landlord with a limited stock of housing and a heavy demand from those on its waiting list, acted as it did was that

---

4 See *Manchester CC v Romano; Manchester CC v Samari* [2004] EWCA Civ 834; [2005] 1 WLR 2775.

5 See *North Devon Homes Ltd v Brazier* [2003] EWHC 574 (QB); [2003] HLR 59.

6 [2007] EWCA Civ 763; [2008] Ch 129.

7 [2008] UKHL 43; [2008] AC 1399.

it was not prepared to allow tenancies to continue where the tenant was not living in the property. The council's reason for seeking possession was a pure housing management decision which had nothing whatever to do with the defendant's mental disability. The correct comparator in this case was a person without a mental disability who had sublet a council flat and gone to live elsewhere.

27.5   On that basis, the House of Lords held that the defendant was not treated less favourably than other tenants in similar circumstances. He was treated in exactly the same way. Furthermore, knowledge, or at least imputed knowledge, of the disability on a landlord's part, was necessary for there to be discrimination. There was, accordingly, no defence to the possession claim. Lord Scott stated that if the physical or mental condition that constitutes the disability has played no motivating part in the decision of the alleged discriminator to inflict on the disabled person the treatment complained of, the alleged discriminator's reason for that treatment cannot relate to the disability. He too considered that the appropriate comparators were council tenants who had sublet, but whose subletting had no connection with schizophrenia or, perhaps, with any mental condition causally responsible for the subletting.[8] The defendant's schizophrenia was not known to the council and formed no part of its reason for taking proceedings.

27.6   It follows from *Malcolm* that defences to possession claims on the basis of disability discrimination under DDA 1995 s22 will now be difficult to maintain, except where it can be shown that the reason for the landlord's action relates to the disability itself (for example, because the tenant has been diagnosed with AIDS[9]) and that a non-disabled person in similar circumstances would not have been treated in the same way. However, it may be possible in some circumstances to defend a claim, or to seek an adjournment to permit an application for judicial review, on public law grounds (see chapters 25 and 26). In *Barber v Croydon LBC*,[10] where the council sought possession

---

8   The House of Lords held that *Clark v TDG Ltd (t/a Novacold)* [1999] EWCA Civ 1091; [1999] ICR 951 was wrongly decided.

9   This example is given in para 14.21 of the Disability Rights Commission code of practice *Rights of access: services to the public, public authority functions, private clubs and premises*, 2006: available at www.equalityhumanrights.com/uploaded_ files/code_of_practice_rights_of_access.pdf.

10 [2010] EWCA Civ 51. But see also *Defence Estates v JL* [2009] EWHC 1049 (Admin), in which it was held that the claimant public body was not obliged to enquire into the personal circumstances of the defendant, including her disability, before bringing possession proceedings, and that a defence relying on article 8 of the European Convention on Human Rights could not succeed.

following a single act of assault by a vulnerable tenant, it was held that the council was acting in breach of its own anti-social behaviour policy, which required it to consult specialist agencies and to consider the needs of vulnerable persons. The evidence established that the incident was associated with the appellant's medical condition. The Court of Appeal rejected an argument of unlawful discrimination under the Disability Discrimination Act 1995. It held, however, that the council had acted unlawfully in failing to liaise with relevant support services and to consider a less intrusive remedy, such as an acceptable behaviour contract. The council's approach was wrong in principle and led to a decision which no authority could reasonably have taken.

27.7   Other provisions in the Disability Discrimination Act 1995 which require a landlord to make 'reasonable adjustments' may give a tenant the means to challenge his or her landlord's conduct, whether by application to the county court for a declaration or, where relevant, by way of defence to possession proceedings. The duty to make reasonable adjustments includes a duty to take reasonable steps to provide an auxiliary aid or service.[11] It also extends to a separate duty to take reasonable steps to change a practice, policy, procedure or term of the letting which has the effect of making it impossible, or unreasonably difficult, for a disabled person to enjoy the premises or to make use of any benefit or facility.[12] However, where a tenant who suffered from bipolar mood disorder kept a dog in breach of a term prohibiting the keeping of pets in both her tenancy and in the head lease of the premises, in possession proceedings brought against the tenant it was held that the term in question did not amount to unlawful discrimination, and that the tenant could not therefore defend the possession claim on this basis. The dog was not a factor in the tenant's enjoyment of the premises, but in her state of mind while residing in the premises. The Court of Appeal contrasted the tenant's situation with that of a blind person with a guide dog: in that case, the tenant would be unable to enjoy the premises without the presence of the guide dog. There were no reasonable steps which the landlord could have taken to modify the term, since this would have put the landlord in breach of the head lease and invited forfeiture of that lease.[13]

11   DDA 1995 s24C(2).
12   DDA 1995 s24D(3). The Act provides, however, that it is never reasonable for a 'controller of let premises' to have to take steps consisting of, or including, the removal or alteration of a physical feature: DDA 1995 s24E(1).
13   *Thomas-Ashley v Drum Housing Association Ltd* [2010] EWCA Civ 265.

27.8　　Additionally, the duties on a *public body* to avoid discrimination in the carrying out of its functions or to make adjustments (DDA 1995 ss21B, 21D and 21E) as well as that body's general duty to promote disability equality and to eliminate unlawful discrimination under section 49A may also give scope for argument in appropriate cases involving local authorities and PRPs/RSLs.[14] Where a public body embarks on a consultation exercise in respect of changes which affect disabled persons, such as the proposed withdrawal of a residential warden service provided to residents in a sheltered housing scheme, it is not sufficient to focus on the needs of residents generally. In order to comply with the section 49A duty, authorities are required to give specific consideration to the impact of a decision on disabled persons and to bring that impact to the attention of the decision-maker.[15] For further discussion see chapter 25 on public law defences.

Equality Act 2010

27.9　　The Equality Act (EA) 2010 received royal assent on 8 April 2010. At the date of publication of this book, it has not yet been brought into force. It will repeal the Disability Discrimination Act 1995. Under the Equality Act 2010, disability is one of the 'protected characteristics', which also comprise: age, gender reassignment, marriage and civil partnership, pregnancy and maternity, race, religion or belief, sex, and sexual orientation.[16] A person has a disability if he or she has a physical or mental impairment which has a substantial and long-term adverse effect on his or her ability to carry out normal day-to-day activities.[17]

27.10　　Chapter 2 of the Equality Act 2010 deals with prohibited conduct. Section 13(1) prohibits direct discrimination:

> A person (A) discriminates against another (B) if, because of a protected characteristic, A treats B less favourably than A treats or would treat others.

14　See Catherine Casserley and Sue Willman, 'The equality duties and public authorities' June 2008 *Legal Action* 24, and September 2008 *Legal Action* 43.

15　*R (Boyejo and others) v Barnet LBC; R (Smith) v Plymouth CC* [2009] EWHC 3261 (Admin).

16　EA 2010 s4.

17　EA 2010 s6(1).

27.11   Section 15 creates a wider concept of disability discrimination:

(1) A person (A) discriminates against a disabled person (B) if –
(a) A treats B unfavourably because of something arising in consequence of B's disability, and
(b) A cannot show that the treatment is a proportionate means of achieving a legitimate aim.
(2) Subsection (1) does not apply if A shows that A did not know, and could not reasonably have been expected to know, that B had the disability.

27.12   Clearly, a landlord who brings possession proceedings against a disabled tenant is treating that person unfavourably. This is a different test from that of 'less favourable treatment' in the 1995 Act and does not require a comparison with the way in which another person would have been treated. The tenant may therefore have a defence to the proceedings (whatever the type of tenancy) or may be able to restrain the landlord from seeking possession where (a) the reason for the landlord's action is 'something arising in consequence of [the tenant's] disability'; and (b) the landlord cannot show that his, her or its action is proportionate and pursues a legitimate aim.

27.13   Equality Act s19(1) prohibits indirect discrimination, defined in the following terms:

A person (A) discriminates against another (B) if A applies to B a provision, criterion or practice which is discriminatory in relation to a relevant protected characteristic of B's.

Thus, as under the Disability Discrimination Act 1995, direct discrimination against a tenant on grounds of disability would afford a defence to a possession claim.

27.14   There is also a duty to make reasonable adjustments which extends to a provision, criterion or practice of the landlord; to physical features; and to the provision of an auxiliary aid, in all cases where the adjustment is required to avoid placing the disabled person at a substantial disadvantage.[18]

27.15   The above duties are applied to lettings and other disposals of property in the Equality Act 2010 Part 4 (Premises). Section 35 (Management) provides, in subsection (1):

A person (A) who manages premises must not discriminate against a person (B) who occupies the premises –
(a) in the way in which A allows B, or by not allowing B, to make use of a benefit or facility;

18 EA 2010 s20(1)–(5).

(b) by evicting B (or taking steps for the purpose of securing B's eviction);

(c) by subjecting B to any other detriment.[19]

27.16   The reference to eviction in section 35(1)(b) is in similar terms to DDA 1995 s22(3)(c) . But the tests of discrimination to be applied are those found in sections 13, 15 and 19 (see above). Where the reason for the possession proceedings derives from, or is associated with, the tenant's disability, section 15 provides the basis for a defence. Since the section 15 conditions are different from those in DDA 1995 s22, there is no need for a comparison with another person who does not possess the protected characteristic. The decision of the House of Lords in *Lewisham LBC v Malcolm* (see para 27.5) will therefore no longer apply to forestall such defences, but it must be remembered that the landlord may be able to satisfy the court that his, her or its actions are a proportionate means of achieving a legitimate aim.

---

19 Section 35(2) further prohibits harassment of an occupier or an applicant for accommodation by a manager of premises, while s35(3) prohibits victimisation by a manager in identical terms to s35(1) above. Section 36 imposes a duty to make reasonable adjustments in respect of premises, including the common parts of a multi-occupied building.

CHAPTER 28

Public funding to defend possession proceedings

Generally

28.1   In April 2000 the responsibility for the provision of public money to assist litigants of low income passed from the Legal Aid Board to the Legal Services Commission (LSC). The expression 'legal aid' ceased to be used and was replaced by the expression 'public funding'. Different levels of support are now available as part of the Community Legal Service, which the LSC is statutorily charged with managing, and are paid for out of the Community Legal Service Fund. The terms under which 'suppliers' contract with the LSC are currently contained in the Unified Contract (Civil) which expires on 13 October 2010. Suppliers of legal services will need to apply for and be awarded the new 2010 Standard Civil Contract in order to carry out any new publicly funded cases after 14 October 2010.

28.2   In the context of housing litigation there are in effect three possible levels of service. These are: Legal Help, Help at Court and Legal Representation. Legal Help and Help at Court are services provided by solicitors and not-for-profit organisations who contract with the LSC and provide advice and assistance to a predetermined number of clients by reference to the number of 'matter starts' a 'supplier' has contracted to undertake during the year. The LSC funds a separate and distinct scheme to assist defendants to possession proceedings in certain courts. The 'Housing Possession Court Duty Scheme' forms part of a supplier's contract in those courts approved for the scheme by the LSC.[1] Legal Help and Help at Court are both described as 'controlled work'. Legal Representation, by contrast, is 'licensed work' provided to a client by a solicitor under a 'public funding certificate' which is applied for and awarded on a case-by-case basis. Legal Representation may take the form of either Investigative Help or Full Representation and a solicitor can apply for either level depending on whether, at the time of the application, it is possible to estimate the prospects of successfully defending the proceedings. The most important difference between the levels of service is between Legal Help/Help at Court, on the one hand, and Legal Representation under a certificate, on the other. There is a significant overlap between work which can be carried out at either of these levels. Guidance on the full scope of Legal Help and Help at Court and Licensed

---

1   The specification for the 2010 Standard Civil Contract in relation to housing cases and the housing possession court duty scheme is available at www.legalservices.gov.uk/docs/civil_contracting/section_10_-_miscellaneous_-_dec_09.pdf.

Work is contained in the Unified Contract Civil Specification.[2] Unlike the previous General Civil Contract Specification, which regulated solicitor work under the Legal Help and Help at Court scheme before the Unified Contract, the specification provides no specific guidance relevant to possession proceedings.

Using the Legal Help and Help at Court schemes

28.3 The availability of Legal Help and Help at Court is separate from the availability of Legal Representation. The Unified Civil Contract Specification provides that the Funding Code Guidance[3] issued under the Access to Justice Act 1999 determines how assistance is to be given under the Legal Help and Help at Court scheme.

28.4 Para 19.3 of the Guidance provides:

> Examples of where it might be appropriate to provide Help at Court in housing cases are:
> (a) where the client is a defendant to mortgage possession or other possession proceedings, where rent or mortgage arrears are not in dispute, it is unlikely that an immediate order for possession would be made, and, in the absence of a defence to the proceedings, the only issue appears to be the terms on which a suspended order would be made;
> (b) where the client is a defendant to possession proceedings on the grounds of mortgage or rent arrears, where the claim for possession is not disputed, but there is a dispute over the amount of arrears owed by the defendant;
> (c) an application to suspend or further suspend a warrant for possession or execution where no substantial issue of fact or law is raised (para 19.3.1).
>
> Help at Court should not be used in any case where Legal Representation should be applied for unless Legal Representation has been applied for and refused. Where Legal Representation is refused, the case should be dealt with under Legal Help, together with Help at Court as appropriate. (para 19.3.3)

28.5 The same form (Controlled Work 1) is used for the Legal Help and Help at Court schemes and so if an adviser has been providing advice under the Legal Help scheme and it then proves necessary to

---

2 www.legalservices.gov.uk/docs/civil_contracting/081103CivilSpecification GeneralProvisionsNov08.pdf.
3 www.legalservices.gov.uk/docs/cls_main/FundingCodeDecisionMaking Guidnce-OtherGuidance(sections15-19_21-26and28)sept07.pdf.

represent at a hearing which falls within the criteria of cases for Help at Court, no further paperwork is necessary.

Using the Legal Representation scheme

28.6   Legal Representation is available to take or defend proceedings and in the context of possession proceedings is designed to provide for the defendant the full range of services available from a solicitor when defending proceedings. This includes not just the services of the solicitor but also, where relevant, the cost of experts and counsel. As noted above, Legal Representation can be authorised by the LSC either for Investigative Help or for Full Representation. Where the prospects of success are clear then it is appropriate to apply for Full Representation.

28.7   An application for Legal Representation is made to the LSC, which will consider whether to award a 'public funding certificate'. This decision is made having regard to the Funding Code[4] and subordinate Decision Making Guidance[5] issued by the LSC.

28.8   Section 10.3 of the Funding Code sets out the criteria for when Full Representation will be awarded in possession proceedings concerning the client's home:

Prospects of success
Full Representation will be refused if the client has no substantive legal defence to the proceedings or the prospects of successfully avoiding an order for possession (or, if the client is bringing proceedings, the prospects of obtaining such an order) are poor.

Cost benefit
Full representation may be refused unless the likely benefits of the proceedings to the client justify the likely costs, having regard to the prospects of success and all other circumstances.

28.9   The Funding Code Decision Making Guidance expands on the Code:

The meaning of 'home' is the client's main or only dwelling. It will include any mobile home or site that the client occupies as his or her residence. (para 19.1.2)

While housing cases within section 10 are a priority under the Code, the Commission will not fund cases which are weak or those where

---

4   Issued by the Legal Services Commission, incorporating guidance issued by the Lord Chancellor under Access to Justice Act 1999 s23.

5   www.legalservices.gov.uk/docs/cls_main/FundingCodeDecisionMaking Guidnce-OtherGuidance(sections15-19_21-26and28)sept07.pdf.

litigation is unnecessary. This is reflected in the Criteria for Full Representation which differ from those in the General Funding Code in four important respects:

(a) possession cases – because of the importance of cases concerning possession of the client's home there is no strict requirement that the client must have at least 50% prospects of success in defending such a case. Instead, funding will only be refused if the client has no substantive legal defence to the proceedings (or if the client is bringing proceedings in relation to their own home, the prospects of obtaining an order are poor) (Criterion 10.3.2 – see guidance at section 19.7 below); ... (para 19.4.1)

In relation to whether to grant Investigative Help or Full Representation the Guidance provides:

As in most other case categories, Legal Representation in housing cases can take the form of either Investigative Help or Full Representation. However the great majority of housing cases do not require extensive investigation to enable prospects of success to be determined. Few housing cases will therefore satisfy the Criteria for Investigative Help and most cases requiring a certificate will proceed straight from Legal Help/Help at Court to Full Representation. In the few cases that do fall within section 10 of the Funding Code and require substantial investigative work, there is no need to consider whether the work should be carried out privately with a view to a conditional fee agreement (Criterion 10.2.1). (para 19.3.5)

28.10 The Guidance further amplifies the terms of the Funding Code and, where relevant, advisers should quote the relevant paragraph in making an application for a public funding certificate. The Guidance says:

19.7 Cases concerning Possession of the Client's Home
Possession of Rented Property occupied by the Client
1. These cases come within section 10.3 of the Code. Legal Representation will be refused if the client has no substantive defence to the proceedings or the prospects of successfully avoiding an order for possession are poor.

2. Legal Representation will be refused in the absence of a substantive defence, (including where it applies, the defence that it would not be reasonable to make an order for possession), if the only issue to be placed before the court is whether an immediate order for possession is appropriate. If such a case Criterion 10.3.2 will not be satisfied.

3. Legal Representation to defend possession proceedings will be refused if the only defences available are technical ones. The landlord should be approached to seek a compromise. It is recognised, however, that in some cases it may be tactically advantageous to the client not to draw the defects to the landlord's attention, thus allowing the tenancy to continue longer. If no approach has been made, solicitors

must explain their decision not to do so and why Legal Representation is justified with specific reference to the costs benefit test. Where Legal Representation has been granted, and the technical defects are capable of being cured within the proceedings solicitors must report this to the Regional Office immediately so a decision may be made whether to continue funding.

4. Legal Representation is likely to be granted where there is a substantive defence to the possession action, including a defence as to reasonableness of the possession order being made, ie, where the ground for possession has been made out but where the court must also assess whether it is reasonable in all the circumstances to make an order for possession.

Suspended possession orders in rent or mortgage cases
5. Legal Representation is unlikely to be granted where the probable order is a suspended possession order, eg, where the arrears are not in dispute, reasonableness is not likely to succeed as a defence, and the only issue is the terms on which a suspended possession order would be made. In these circumstances, Legal Help or Help at Court may be appropriate.

Possession: nuisance cases
6. Where possession is sought for anti social behaviour, Legal Representation is unlikely to be granted either where the conduct is admitted, or, where the proceedings have been issued as a result of breached undertakings, unless a defence can be raised as to reasonableness. Examples of where Legal Representation may be appropriate are where the client's community care needs led directly to the breach or where the conduct complained of has ceased and is unlikely to reoccur. Legal Representation is likely to be granted where a substantive defence, including the issue of reasonableness, can be raised by the tenant.

6A. Where a demotion order is claimed in the alternative to a possession order or other than in a possession claim, the same considerations as set out in paragraph 6 above will apply to the grant of Legal Representation to defend those proceedings.

Client in rent arrears
7. Where the ground for possession is rent arrears, Legal Representation is unlikely to be granted if the arrears are the only issue, and are not in dispute, unless a defence can be raised on the issue of reasonableness. Whilst delay in payment (generated by the failure or delay of a local authority either to determine or pay housing benefit payment) is not a defence in itself, it may go to the issue of reasonableness where a reasonableness defence is being asserted.

8. Legal Representation is likely to be granted to a client who can show that no arrears of rent exist or who has a valid counterclaim

which exceeds or significantly diminishes the alleged arrears, eg, damages for disrepair or quiet enjoyment.

Service charges

9. It would not be reasonable for Legal Representation to be granted where service charges arrears are the only issue in dispute as it is unlikely that an immediate order for possession would be made and, where there is a dispute, the proceedings can be referred to the Leasehold Valuation Tribunal (LVT). Legal Representation will be refused in any case where the LVT would provide an effective way of pursuing or defending the claim. The LVT would not be appropriate in a case where a determination needs to be made as to whether the freeholder is entitled to claim for the item of work under the lease (as distinct from the reasonableness of the cost of that item).

Accelerated possession procedure

10. Legal Representation will be refused in cases which fall within the accelerated possession procedure under Civil Procedure Rules Schedule 2 CPR Order 49 Rules 6 and 6A unless, following consideration of the papers, the matter is listed by the court for an oral hearing. The decision as to whether or not to hold an oral hearing is one taken by the court on the papers. Until there is a decision that the matter should be listed for an oral hearing it would not be reasonable to grant Full Representation as there is no need for representation (Criterion 5.4.5). Once the matter has been listed for an oral hearing Legal Representation may be applied for in the usual way.

11. Where issues arise as to:
(a) the nature of the tenancy;
(b) whether the case falls within the accelerated procedure;
(c) whether there is a defence;
(d) whether there is some defect in the application
solicitors should assist the client to make representations, either by the completion of the Form N11A or by preparing an affidavit under Legal Help, if appropriate.

Anti-social injunctions

12. Legal Representation to defend an application for an anti-social injunction will generally only be granted where:
(a) There are very serious allegations;
(b) The allegations are denied wholly or substantially; and
(c) The matter cannot reasonably be dealt with by an undertaking.

However Legal Representation may be justified if there is some question of inability to defend (eg mental capacity). In such cases where the allegations made or issues raised are not sufficiently serious to justify Legal Representation or where mitigation is required at court, Help at Court may be appropriate.

Introductory tenancies

13. In relation to introductory tenancies Legal Representation will be refused unless the client can establish:

 – the tenancy was not 'introductory' at the time the proceedings were issued;
 – the section 128 notice is defective or was not served;
 – the proceedings have been commenced prematurely; or
 – that an adjournment is required under the principles set out in *Manchester CC v Cochrane* (1999) 31 HLR 810.[6]

14. In relation to an introductory tenancy an internal review should be sought before Legal Representation is applied for.

Suspension of warrants for possession

15. Legal Representation is unlikely to be granted to suspend a warrant for possession or execution if the application does not raise any significant issues of fact or law. Where there is a substantive defence to the possession proceedings or to the enforcement of the order Legal Representation may be granted. This would not include technical or procedural irregularities which only 'buy time' for the client. Examples of significant issues would be where:

(a) a non-party is trying to stop the eviction;
(b) the client is asserting that a new tenancy has been created;
(c) the landlord has waived the breach by subsequent acceptance of rent or other conduct;
(d) an application to set aside the original possession order can be made, eg, because the tenant was not present at the hearing;
(e) an application can be made to postpone the date of possession, which, if granted, would reinstate the tenancy.

Where Legal Representation is unlikely to be granted Legal Help may be available or, in appropriate cases, Help at Court.

Mortgage possession

16. Legal Representation is likely to be granted to the borrower to defend possession proceedings brought by the lender where there are substantial defences for consideration by the court, eg, where one or more of the following arise:

(a) allegations of fraud;
(b) allegations of duress or undue influence;
(c) where there are linked or (imminent) concurrent proceedings involving the borrower's spouse, co-habitee or trustee in bankruptcy;
(d) where the client is not a party but where it might be appropriate for the client to be joined to the action because the client does have a defence;
(e) where there is a substantive counterclaim.

6 *Manchester City Council v Cochrane* [1999] 1 WLR 809; (1999) 31 HLR 810.

17. Legal Representation is unlikely to be granted where:
- there is no substantive defence to a claim of arrears only;
- judgment has been entered and the representation is sought to set aside a warrant of possession in an arrears only case;
- duress or undue influence is alleged but at the relevant time the borrower received correct and appropriate legal advice from a solicitor;
- there is a procedural irregularity but no substantive defence.

18. In such cases, Legal Help should be used unless Help at Court is appropriate.

19. Legal Representation is likely to be granted to appeal if the District Judge exercised discretion unreasonably or misdirected him/herself in law. Legal Representation is likely to be refused if there is a lengthy delay before the client considered an appeal or only limited benefit to be gained.

20. Legal Representation is likely to be granted to pursue an action or counterclaim on the sale (including as to price or timing of the sale) where there are reasonable prospects of obtaining control of the sale and the quantum involved justifies the costs of representation.

...

19.11 Miscellaneous proceedings
Alleged unlawful occupiers
1. Alleged [sic] possession proceedings brought on the basis that the client is an unlawful occupier fall within section 10.3 of the Code and Legal Representation is likely to be granted where the client has a substantive defence or can show a triable issue which is likely to avoid the possession order, eg:
(a) the client asserts that a tenancy or licence exists which has not been validly determined;
(b) there is a intermediate undetermined tenancy or licence;
(c) there is a procedural irregularity which amounts to a defence;
(d) it is alleged that the occupier has acquired possessory title (twelve years' adverse possession);
(e) the client asserts that he has been given a licence to remain by the Local Authority. Legal Representation will only be justified if that licence has secure status.

NB: In the event of Legal Representation being granted a limitation to the initial summary hearing will be imposed – it is at that point that the court will decide whether there is a triable issue and only if that issue is likely to succeed will Legal Representation be continued.

2. Legal Representation is likely to be refused (unless a defence can be raised by way of estoppel) where the occupiers are within the classes of excluded occupiers in section 3(A) Protection from Eviction Act 1977, namely:

(a) persons who have entered the premises as trespassers (and their status has not changed) and an interim possession order under the Criminal Justice and Public Order Act 1994 is sought;

(b) persons occupying hostels where the status of the occupancy is not in issue;

(c) persons who have shared essential living accommodation with the landlord or the landlord's family throughout their occupancy;

(d) persons staying on in holiday lets when the holiday lease has expired and the status of the occupancy is not in issue;

(e) persons living rent free by agreement.

3. Where the dispute involving the alleged unlawful occupier does not relate to possession proceedings, the guidance for the particular issue should be followed, eg, harassment or wrongful eviction where such allegations are made.

Mobile Homes

4. Where the mobile home is being occupied by the client as his or her own home and the proceedings relate either to possession or to the landlord's obligations, they fall within section 10 of the Code. Where however the proceedings relate to other issues, such as a refusal of agreement to sale, it will fall within the General Funding Code.

5. Legal Representation may be granted to an occupant of a mobile home where the client requires a declaration relating to utilities, changing of the pitch, or refusal of agreement to a sale.

6. Legal Representation is unlikely to be granted where the applicant is a person renting a mobile home and the only issue is that of non-payment of rent where there is no substantive defence to proceedings.

7. The criteria for Legal Representation are unlikely to be satisfied if the following details are not supplied with the application:

(a) an adequate statement of case setting out the issues clearly;

(b) a copy of the agreement if an agreement has been provided by the site owner;

(c) copies of any correspondence with the site owner;

(d) details of the breach of the agreement.

8. Where there is an alternative remedy such as the referral of an issue to the local authority it would not be reasonable for Legal Representation to be granted (Criterion 5.4.5). ...

Travellers

9. Legal Representation may be available for judicial review proceedings in relation to a local authority's decision, the facilities provided or for proceedings under the Mobile Homes Act.

10. Legal Representation is not available for any criminal or civil proceedings brought in the magistrates court under the Criminal Justice and Public Order Act 1994.

Objections to a lender's costs

11. Such cases will fall within the General Funding Code. Legal Representation may be granted to cover attending the detailed assessment of the lender's solicitor's costs under section 70 of the Solicitors Act 1974 but only in cases where the costs and the reduction to be achieved are considerable. (This will be determined under Criterion 5.7.3)

28.11 It can be seen that the criteria for considering whether to grant Legal Representation to defend possession proceedings are reasonably generous. Particularly in the case of claims against tenants on discretionary grounds for possession, the grant of Legal Representation is now the norm rather than the exception.

28.12 Advisers need to apply for a public funding certificate on Forms CLSAPP1 and either CLSMEANS1 or 2. CLSMEANS2 is the financial form to be used for applicants in receipt of income support, income based jobseeker's allowance, income based employment and support allowance or guarantee credit. CLSMEANS1 is used by others. For those in employment it is necessary for the employer to complete form L17 which gives details of the applicant's income from that employment in the last three months. Where an applicant cannot provide the completed form L17 then the LSC will require six wage slips if the applicant is paid weekly or two wage slips if paid monthly. Fewer slips will usually be acceptable only if they contain cumulative information covering the previous six weeks.

28.13 In urgent cases Emergency Representation can be authorised either by a solicitor supplier if the firm has been granted authority to do so by the LSC or directly from the LSC. Emergency Representation is a form of Legal Representation and authorises work which needs to be done as an emergency before a Full Representation public-funding certificate can be obtained.

Advice to applicants for public funding

28.14 When assisting people who are considering applying for public funding it is important to advise them about any likely financial contribution which they may be required to pay to the LSC each month. This is particularly important when applying for an emergency certificate because the applicant, when signing form CLSAPP1, undertakes to accept any offer of public funding which is made to him or her. Not to accept the offer will result in the LSC revoking the certificate and looking to the applicant to pay all of the costs which are paid to the solicitor and counsel by the LSC.

28.15   Similarly, it is essential to advise the applicant to co-operate at all times with the LSC both before the grant of the full public funding certificate (if an emergency certificate has been granted) and where a substantive public funding certificate has been issued. A client should also be advised of the requirement that he or she notifies the LSC of any change in his or her financial circumstances or that of any person whose resources are aggregated with the client which might affect the terms on which funding is provided[7]. Failure to co-operate with the LSC can result in the certificate being revoked. In recent times the LSC has been much more active in seeking to recover costs paid on revocation of a certificate than was previously the case. This advice must be set out in the 'client care' letter sent to the applicant at the time of application, but there is no substitute for talking to the client about this.

Remuneration from the Legal Services Commission

28.16   Under the Legal Help and Help at Court scheme 'suppliers' are paid a fixed fee of £174 for each 'matter start'. However, where the supplier incurs costs in excess of three times the fixed fee, a claim can be made for payment as an Exceptional Case. Payment in an exceptional case will be made on the basis of specified hourly rates.[8] Currently the hourly rates are £51.05 (£54.15) for preparation, attendance and advocacy, £28.60 (£28.60) for travel and waiting and £4.05 (£4.20) for routine letters out and telephone calls. The sums in brackets are for suppliers in London. Higher rates of remuneration are payable in Exceptional Cases where the client is a defendant to possession proceedings in the county court. The relevant figures are £58.40 (£62.40), £30.05 (£30.90) and £4.20 (£4.50).[9] The sums are exclusive of VAT and disbursements (other than counsel's fees) can be claimed in addition.

28.17   Payment for work carried out under a public funding certificate is made on the basis of time spent rather than a fixed fee. The hourly rates are higher than under the Legal Help and Help at Court schemes and for that reason it is advisable to obtain a public funding certifiate as soon as possible. The relevant hourly rates for work in

---

7 Community Legal Services (Financial) Regulations 2000 SI No 516 reg 13.
8 Unified Contract Civil Specification para 7.19.
9 Civil Specification Part B Payment Annex 2008.

the county court are currently £66 (£70 in London) for preparation and attendance, £32.50 attending court or conference with counsel, £66.00 for advocacy, £29.20 travel and waiting, £6.60 per item for routine letters out and £3.65 for routine telephone calls.

28.18   In appropriate cases it is possible to claim an increased rate of payment for work done under a public funding certificate. An 'enhancement' can be claimed where (a) the work was done with exceptional competence, skill or expertise, (b) the work was done with exceptional speed or (c) the case involved exceptional circumstances or complexity.[10] The maximum uplift above the prescribed rate is 100 per cent except in cases in the High Court, Court of Appeal, Upper Tribunal or Supreme Court, where the maximum is 200 per cent.

28.19   In determining the level of any increase, the court or the LSC shall have regard to (a) the degree of responsibility accepted by the legal adviser, (b) the care speed and economy with which the case was prepared and (c) the novelty, weight and complexity of the case.

The LSC's statutory charge

28.20   Advice on the possible application of the statutory charge is important as failure properly to advise the applicant for public funding is one of the greatest causes of complaints about solicitors. It is necessary to advise mortgage-borrowers, in particular, of the possible application of the LSC's statutory charge. In summary, the statutory charge arises in favour of the LSC whenever any property is preserved or recovered in any proceedings in which a publicly funded litigant takes part, except so far as regulations provide otherwise.[11]

28.21   Accordingly, where a mortgage-borrower is successful in preserving the home, the charge arises unless he or she is awarded costs which are recovered and as a result no claim is made against the Community Legal Service fund. In *Parkes v Legal Aid Board*,[12] the Court of Appeal held that where the right to possession of property is retained or extended, the statutory charge attaches to that property notwithstanding that the beneficial interests in the property were never in issue. Certainly, the LSC's practice is now to apply the

---

10 Unified Contract Civil Specification para 7.37.

11 Access to Justice Act 1999 s10(7).

12 [1997] 1 WLR 1547; [1996] 4 All ER 271, CA. See also M Thompson, 'The Legal Aid Charge' [1997] Conv 47.

statutory charge in virtually all cases where a mortgage-borrower has been successful in preventing loss of the home in litigation where a public funding certificate has been granted.

28.22   The LSC Manual[13] states:

When is property recovered or preserved?
The courts have said that:
(a) Property has been recovered or preserved if it has been at issue in the proceedings. It is recovered by the claimant or applicant if it is the subject of a successful claim. It is preserved by the defendant or respondent if a claim fails: see *Hanlon v The Law Society* [1980] 2 All ER 199; [1980] 2 WLR 756, HL.
(b) What is at issue is a question of fact. The pleadings, affidavits and correspondence, judgment and/or order will show what property was at issue between the parties (*Hanlon*).
(c) The recovery or preservation of the **possession** of property can give rise to the charge. Even if the **title** to the property is not in issue, if the proceedings reduce it or restore it to the possession of its owner, he or she has recovered property: see *Curling v The Law Society* [1985] 1 All ER 705 and *Parkes v Legal Aid Board* [1994] 2 FLR 850. If as a result of the proceedings, the owner is able to unlock the value of the property, the charge arises.

28.23   While *Parkes* was a case involving an application for an order for sale under what is now the Trusts of Land and Appointment of Trustees Act 1996 s14, which was successfully defended, the court went on to discuss the general application of the statutory charge in possession proceedings. However, what is not clear is whether the statutory charge can apply in the common case where a deferral of an eviction is obtained in an application to stay or suspend a warrant for possession. There are inevitably grey areas where advisers will need to be careful about how court orders should be worded and diligent in subsequently disputing the LSC's view that the statutory charge applies. It is worth noting that in *Parkes* the publicly funded person had preserved the right to possession potentially until her child, who was aged two, reached majority. The right to enjoy possession must be secured for a 'substantial period' in order for any property to have been 'preserved'.

28.24   It was at one time the LSC's expressed view[14] that the statutory charge would not apply where there was a negative equity (in that the assisted person has only recovered or preserved a debt) although there appears to be a change in view, at least in some Legal Services

---

13 Vol 1 para 1D-022.
14 Letter from Legal Aid Board Area 4 to author, dated 30 June 1995.

LSC areas. It has also been suggested that the statutory charge would not arise where an order for possession was postponed to enable the borrower to sell.[15]

28.25 Regulations provide that the statutory charge does not arise in respect of the cost to the LSC of work undertaken under the Legal Help or Help at Court schemes except in relation to potential family, clinical negligence or personal injury proceedings.[16]

28.26 Where the LSC has funded Legal Representation in proceedings which it considers to have significant wider public interest and where the statutory charge would apply, the LSC has discretion to waive some or all of the amount of the statutory charge if it considers it equitable to do so.[17]

28.27 If, after getting Legal Help or Help at Court, the client goes on to receive help with Legal Representation under a public funding certificate, the statutory charge will arise in favour of the LSC in relation to property preserved after the issue of the certificate.[18]

28.28 In enforcing the statutory charge, the LSC has the same rights as are available to a chargee in respect of a charge given between parties.[19] The LSC may only postpone enforcement of the statutory charge if it appears to the LSC that it would be unreasonable for the client to repay the amount of the statutory charge immediately.[20]

28.29 Where the statutory charge does apply and providing that the LSC is satisfied that it is unreasonable for the client immediately to pay the amount of the statutory charge, it is open to the client to ask the LSC to defer the enforcement of the statutory charge:

where
(a) by order of the court or agreement it relates to property to be used as a home by the client or his dependents ...;
(b) the Commission is satisfied that the property in question will provide such security for the statutory charge as it considers appropriate; and
(c) as soon as it is possible to do so, the Commission registers a charge under the Land Registration Act 2002 to secure the amount in regulation 43 or as appropriate takes equivalent steps (whether

---

15 See letter in June 1995 *Legal Action* 27.
16 Community Legal Service (Financial) Regulations 2000 SI No 516 reg 43(3). See also 'How the Access to Justice Act 1999 will affect the statutory charge' LSC *Focus* No 29 p11.
17 Community Legal Service (Financial) Regulations 2000 SI No 516 reg 47.
18 Community Legal Service (Financial) Regulations 2000 reg 45.
19 Community Legal Service (Financial) Regulations 2000 reg 51.
20 Community Legal Service (Financial) Regulations 2000 reg 52A.

in England and Wales or in any other jurisdiction) to protect its interests in the property.[21]

28.30   It should be noted that the LSC has only very limited discretion in relation to postponement of the enforcement of the statutory charge. Unless the property preserved is adequate security for the sums to be deferred, it would appear that the client will be at risk of the LSC seeking to enforce the monies secured by the statutory charge. The LSC may review the decision to defer enforcement and again, unless it appears to the LSC that it would be unreasonable for the assisted person to repay the amount of the charge, it shall proceed to enforce the charge.[22] If the LSC continues to defer enforcement of the charge it may also do so on such terms and conditions as to repayment of the amount of the charge by way of interim payments of either capital or interest or both, as appears to the LSC to be appropriate.[23]

28.31   The adviser must notify the LSC of the preservation or recovery of property using form CLSADMIN1. Where property which is preserved is jointly owned, the LSC requires both joint owners to execute the charge deed in form CLSADMIN1 in favour of the LSC. Failing this, the LSC will defer enforcement only if the assisted person agrees to the matter being referred to the LSC's Debt Recovery Unit so that a judgment can be obtained against the assisted person. The LSC's position is then protected by a charging order which is capable of being registered as a restriction against the property.[24]

28.32   This is far from satisfactory as additional costs are incurred which will increase the amount due to the LSC. The sum secured in the LSC's favour is the amount paid out to the client's solicitor and counsel and carries flat rate interest at the rate of 8 per cent per annum from the date the charge is first registered to the date of settlement.[25] The client can make interim payments towards discharge of the sums secured by the statutory charge.[26]

28.33   Advisers are reminded of the duty to notify the LSC immediately of any property preserved so that the LSC can consider whether there are steps which need to be taken at that stage to safeguard the fund.[27]

---

21 Community Legal Service (Financial) Regulations 2000 reg 52(1).
22 Civil Legal Aid (General) Regulations 1989 SI No 339 reg 96B(1).
23 Civil Legal Aid (General) Regulations 1989 SI No 339 reg 96B(2).
24 See LSC *Focus* Issue 43, December 2003, addendum.
25 Community Legal Service (Financial) Regulations 2000 SI No 516 reg 53(1) and (3).
26 Community Legal Service (Financial) Regulations 2000 reg 53(2).
27 Community Legal Service (Costs) Regulations 2000 SI No 441 reg 20(1)(a).

Unfortunately, this obligation is not always recognised and advisers put themselves at risk if, ultimately, the statutory charge cannot be recovered because of delay in the LSC being advised of property being preserved. In such circumstances the LSC has the power to defer payment of a solicitor's costs[28].

28.34   The statutory charge will still arise where property is preserved in cases where a certificate has been discharged or revoked but where the client (or his or her personal representative or trustee in bankruptcy) has continued to defend the proceedings.[29]

28.35   Theoretically, the statutory charge may apply to contractual tenancies preserved[30] (though not to a statutory tenancy which is no more than a personal right), but only where the tenant has an interest in the property which is capable of being charged (for example, a leasehold interest).[31] In practice, there is little point in the LSC seeking to enforce the statutory charge against the vast majority of assisted tenants.

---

28 Civil Legal Aid (General) Regulations 1989 SI No 339 reg 102.
29 Community Legal Service (Financial) Regulations 2000 SI No 516 reg 49.
30 See, eg, 'Legal aid – more about the statutory charge' (1985) 82 LS Gaz 1214.
31 Letter from Legal Aid Board Area 4 to author, dated 14 October 1994.

CHAPTER 29

Possession proceedings against trespassers and other unlawful occupiers

Generally

29.1 Historically, there was no need for landowners to bring court proceedings to evict trespassers. They were entitled to use 'self-help' and to evict trespassers without a court order.[1] However, to use the words of Lord Denning, this was a course 'not to be recommended' to landowners because of the 'possible disturbance' which might be caused.[2] In addition, a landowner risks prosecution under the Criminal Law Act 1977 s6 if violence to people or property is used or threatened for the purpose of securing entry to premises when there is someone present on those premises.[3] Also, if the trespassers are former tenants or licensees who are entitled to rely on the Protection from Eviction Act (PEA) 1977 s3 as amended,[4] a landlord using self-help risks prosecution. Advisers should, however, note the Criminal Law Act 1977 s7 which creates a criminal offence where a trespasser fails to leave the premises if required to do so by or on behalf of a displaced residential occupier or a protected intending occupier of those premises.[5]

29.2 In possession proceedings against trespassers, landowners need prove only their title and an intention to regain possession.[6] If occupiers wish to claim some right of occupation which amounts to a defence (for example, a continuing licence or tenancy), the burden of proving its existence lies on them. The main defences likely to be advanced by people who face possession proceedings brought by landowners who claim that they are trespassers are:

- They have a tenancy or licence which has not been determined. On termination of tenancies and licences, see chapters 14 and 18.
- Although the people in occupation of land do not themselves have a tenancy or licence, someone else, other than the landowner, has a tenancy or licence which has not been determined. Landowners are not entitled to orders for possession unless they can prove that

1 *R v Blankley* [1979] Crim LR 166; *McPhail v Persons, Names Unknown* [1973] Ch 447; [1973] 3 All ER 393, CA.
2 *McPhail v Persons, Names Unknown* [1973] Ch 447; [1973] 3 All ER 393, per Lord Denning MR at 396.
3 Unless the landowner is a displaced residential occupier or protected intending occupier: see Criminal Law Act 1977 ss6 and 7 and Criminal Justice and Public Order Act 1994 ss75 and 76.
4 PEA 1977 as amended by HA 1988 ss30 and 31. See para 18.2.
5 See Suzanne Tarlin, 'Squatting and the criminal law' December 1977 *LAG Bulletin* 285.
6 *Portland Managements Ltd v Harte* [1977] QB 306; [1976] 1 All ER 225.

they have an immediate right to possession. This is not the case if there is an intermediate undetermined tenancy or licence. This situation most commonly arises where a tenant moves away or dies and someone else moves into the property without the land-owner's permission (see para 2.54).

- The landowner has failed to comply with the necessary procedural requirements, for example, as to service of proceedings (see para 23.24). Sometimes this may succeed in delaying matters, giving occupiers time to find other accommodation, but it is unlikely to provide a long-term defence.
- The decision by a public body, such as a local authority, to bring possession proceedings can be challenged on administrative law grounds (for example, that it has failed to take into account relevant factors or has misdirected itself in law – see para 29.13) or on Human Rights Act 1998 grounds. See chapters 25 and 26.
- Trespassers have acquired possessory title as a result of 12 years' adverse possession (Limitation Act 1980 s15(1)) or have rights under the Land Registration Act 2002 (see para 29.19).

29.3   Proceedings may be issued as ordinary possession claims. Alternatively they may be issued as 'a claim against trespassers' in accordance with the Civil Procedure Rules (CPR) 55.1(b). (The summary procedure against those who entered into or remained in occupation without licence or consent contained in the former County Court Rules (CCR) Ord 24 or Rules of the Supreme Court (RSC) Ord 113 no longer exists.) Unlike CCR Ord 24 or RSC Ord 113 the standard possession procedure contained in CPR Part 55 applies to claims against trespassers, but with some modifications. CPR 55.1(b) provides that:

> a 'possession claim against trespassers' means a claim for the recovery of land which the claimant alleges is occupied only by a person or persons who entered or remained on the land without the consent of a person entitled to possession of that land but does not include a claim against a tenant or sub-tenant whether his tenancy has been terminated or not.

This means that a 'possession claim against trespassers' under the CPR is narrower than the equivalent provision in either the CCR or the RSC, which could both be used against unlawful subtenants.[7]

29.4   The differences between a standard CPR Part 55[8] possession claim and a claim against trespassers are that in a claim against trespassers:

---

7 See *Moore Properties (Ilford) Ltd v McKeon* [1976] 1 WLR 1278; [1977] 1 All ER 262, ChD.

8 See chapter 23.

- Proceedings may be issued in the High Court if there is a substantial risk of public disturbance or of serious harm to people or property which properly requires immediate determination.
- If the claimant does not know the name of a person in occupation, the claim must be brought against 'persons unknown' in addition to any named defendants.[9]
- The particulars of claim must state the claimant's interest in the land or the basis of the right to claim possession, and the circumstances in which it was occupied without licence or consent.[10]
- Service of the claim form, particulars of claim and any witness statements must be effected against 'persons unknown' by attaching them to the main door of the property or some other part so that they are clearly visible and through the letter box in a sealed transparent envelope addressed to 'the occupiers' or by placing stakes in the land (if these methods are to be used, the claimant must supply the court with sufficient stakes and transparent envelopes).[11]
- CPR 15.2 (Defendant who wishes to defend must file defence within 14 days) does not apply.[12]
- The time between service and the hearing must be at least two days (non-residential land) or at least five days (residential premises).[13]

29.5   A licensee of premises (such as a short-life housing association) may bring a claim against trespassers provided that it has a right of effective control over land.[14]

29.6   Occasionally, after eviction, landowners are concerned that following eviction trespassers may move on to neighbouring land. In *Secretary of State for the Environment, Food and Rural Affairs v Meier and others*,[15] the defendants had set up an unauthorised encampment

---

9   CPR 55.3(4).
10   PD 55A para 2.6.
11   PD 55A para 4.1.
12   CPR 55.7(2).
13   CPR 55.5(2).
14   *Manchester Airport v Dutton* [2000] QB 133; [1999] 3 WLR 524; [1999] 2 All ER 675, CA; *Countryside Residential (North Thames) Ltd v Tugwell* [2000] 34 EG 87, CA. See also *Blackroof Community Housing Association v Charles* [1997] 6 CL 378, Lambeth County Court (nothing in CCR Ord 24 to prevent a licensee bringing summary possession proceedings). Cf *West Hampstead Housing Association v Church and others* 27 October 1983, QBD (Goulding J), unreported and *Family Housing Association v Gedge* December 1988 *Legal Action* 17. See also *Harper v Charlesworth* (1825) 4 B & C 574.
15   [2009] UKSC 11.

in woodland owned by the secretary of state and managed by the Forestry Commission. The secretary of state sought a possession order not only in respect of the land occupied by the defendants, but also in respect of other publicly owned woods in the area. The Supreme Court held, however, that a possession order could not extend to land not yet occupied by the defendants. It was not possible to recover possession of land not occupied by another because the owner already enjoyed uninterrupted possession of it.

29.7   However, in *Meier*, the Supreme Court did uphold the grant of an injunction prohibiting the defendants from occupying the other woods, in spite of the possible difficulties of enforcement. There was no evidence in the particular case that an injunction would prove to be an ineffective remedy. If necessary, such an injunction can be granted against persons unknown.[16]

29.8   Under the old summary procedure (CCR Ord 24 and RSC Ord 113) all that landowners could claim was an order for possession and costs. They could not make any claim for mesne profits or damages. In view of the fact that claims against trespassers now come within CPR Part 55, there is no apparent reason why financial claims should not also be brought, although the concept of a money judgment against persons unknown is clearly problematic.

29.9   Under the old summary procedure, a body of case-law grew up to determine what might amount to a triable issue.[17] However, none of these cases applies to the new procedure under CPR Part 55 because it is not a summary procedure. If a defendant wishes to defend a claim, the court will either try the case at the first hearing or give case management directions.[18]

29.10   At the hearing, anybody who is not a named party to the proceedings may apply to be joined and added as a defendant.[19] Unless occupants have a defence to the proceedings, there is no point in applying to be joined as a defendant since it merely opens up the likelihood of an order for costs. Orders for costs cannot be made against 'persons unknown', only against named defendants.

---

16 For other examples of injunctions granted to prevent trespass, see *Hampshire Waste Services Ltd v Persons Unknown* [2003] EWHC 1738 (ChD); September 2003 *Legal Action* 27 and *Northampton BC v Connors* [2003] All ER (D) 196; August 2003 *Legal Action* 31.

17 Eg, *Henderson v Law* (1985) 17 HLR 237; *Cooper v Varzdari* (1986) 18 HLR 299 and *Filemart Ltd v Avery* [1989] 46 EG 92, CA.

18 See para 23.46.

19 CPR 19.4.

Orders

29.11 When dealing with claims against trespassers courts should usually make an order for possession to take effect 'forthwith' (ie, immediately).[20] The court can make an order for possession to take effect on a specified later date only if all parties consent, or if the defendants are former service occupiers[21] or licensees under a rental purchase agreement (see chapters 19 and 21).

Damages for trespass

29.12 Landowners are entitled to seek orders for damages for trespass. There is no need for them to prove that they would have re-let the premises. Damages are assessed according to the loss suffered by the landowner or the value of the premises to the trespassers, and in the absence of other evidence, this will usually be the ordinary letting value.[22]

Administrative law defences

29.13 A decision of a public body, such as a local authority, may be challenged in the courts on the grounds that:

- the decision is so unreasonable that no reasonable local authority could have come to the decision;
- the local authority failed to take into account relevant material when reaching its decision;
- the local authority took into account irrelevant material in coming to the decision;
- in making the decision the local authority misdirected itself in law;
- it has fettered its discretion by adopting a blanket policy without regard to the facts of the individual case;
- it has breached its obligations under the Human Rights Act 1998.

20 *McPhail v Persons, Names Unknown* [1973] 3 All ER 393, CA; *Swordheath Properties Ltd v Floydd* [1978] 1 WLR 550; [1978] 1 All ER 721 and *Mayor and Burgesses of Camden LBC v Persons Unknown* [1987] CLY 2183, CA; June 1987 *Legal Action* 19.

21 *McPhail v Persons, Names Unknown* [1973] 3 All ER 393, CA.

22 *Swordheath Properties v Tabet* [1979] 1 WLR 285; [1979] 1 All ER 240, CA; *Ministry of Defence v Thompson* [1993] 40 EG 148; (1993) 25 HLR 552, CA and *Ministry of Defence v Ashman* (1993) 25 HLR 513; [1993] 40 EG 144, CA. See chapter 32.

29.14   A secure or assured tenant may challenge the decision to bring proceedings as an aspect of reasonableness in the possession proceedings themselves.[23] However, where the defendant is a trespasser with
no private law or contractual rights, it may be possible to challenge
the decision to evict on public law grounds. Formerly, this could be
done only by seeking an adjournment of the possession proceedings
in order to bring a claim for judicial review.[24] However, it is now
established that such challenges may be brought in the county court
by way of a public law defence to the possession claim, unless there
are particular reasons for seeking judicial review in the Administrative Court (such as where it is intended to ask the court to make a
declaration of incompatibility with European Convention on Human
Rights principles). The House of Lords' judgments in *Lambeth LBC v
Kay* and *Doherty v Birmingham CC* set out the basis on which public
law defences may be entered.[25] If there are disputes of fact, evidence
may be heard in the course of the county court proceedings. For a
more detailed discussion of public law defences and human rights
issues, see chapters 25 and 26.

29.15   Courts dealing with possession proceedings will not be sympathetic to applications for adjournments to enable a public law defence
to be filed or an application for permission to apply for judicial review
to be made unless it can be shown that there is a seriously arguable
case. Courts are particularly reluctant to allow squatters to use such
tactics merely to delay proceedings. Trespassers should make applications for emergency public funding certificates as quickly as possible after it is known that a decision to take proceedings has been
made.

29.16   The fact that a local authority is in breach of its statutory obligations (for example, to provide accommodation to homeless people
under the Housing Act 1996 Part VII) does not necessarily provide a

---

23   *Wandsworth LBC v Winder (No 1)* [1985] AC 461, HL; *Bristol DC v Clark* [1975]
1 WLR 1443; [1975] 3 All ER 976; *Cannock Chase Council v Kelly* [1978] 1 WLR 1;
[1978] 1 All ER 152, CA and para 4.49.

24   *Avon CC v Buscott and others* [1988] QB 656; [1988] 2 WLR 788; [1988] 1 All ER
841, CA and *Waverley BC v Hilden* [1988] 1 WLR 246; [1988] 1 All ER 807. See
also *R v Southwark LBC ex p Borrow* December 1988 *Legal Action* 17, but cf
Hackney LBC v Lambourne (1993) 25 HLR 172, CA, where the Court of Appeal
struck out the tenant's 'administrative law defence'.

25   [2006] UKHL 10; [2006] 2 WLR 570 (*Kay*) and [2008] UKHL 57 (*Doherty*) See too
Harrow LBC v Qazi [2003] UKHL 43; [2003] 3 WLR 792 and paras 25.23–25.32
and 26.39–26.43.

defence to possession proceedings.[26] However, breach of such statutory obligations may be important when trying to prove that a local
authority has been acting unreasonably.[27]

Enforcement

29.17   The High Court and County Courts Jurisdiction (Amendment No 2)
Order 2001[28] provides that as from 15 October 2001 a possession
order made against trespassers in a county court may be enforced
either in the High Court or in a county court.

Adverse possession

29.18   Limitation Act 1980 s15(1) provided that no action could be brought
to recover any land after the expiration of the limitation period of
12 years. 'Limitation ... extinguishes the right of the true owner to
recover the land, so that the squatter's possession becomes impreg-
nable, giving him a title superior to all others.'[29] Time ran from the
commencement of adverse possession. That required a degree of
occupation or physical control, coupled with an intention to possess
without the consent of the paper owner.[30] After 12 years' adverse
possession, the paper proprietor of the land held it on trust for the
squatter who might apply to be registered as proprietor of a new
estate, where the registered land was freehold, or as proprietor of the
registered estate where that estate was leasehold.[31]

29.19   However, where the title to land is registered, the old law of adverse possession has been replaced by the Land Registration Act 2002.
Under that Act, adverse possession of itself, for however long, does
not bar the owner's title to a registered estate in land.[32] A squatter is

---

26   *Southwark LBC v Williams* [1971] Ch 734; [1971] 2 WLR 467; *Kensington and
Chelsea RLBC v Wells* (1973) 72 LGR 289 and *R v Barnet LBC ex p Grumbridge*
(1992) 24 HLR 433, DC.

27   See, eg, *West Glamorgan CC v Rafferty* [1987] 1 WLR 457; [1987] 1 All ER 1005;
(1986) 18 HLR 375; *Tower Hamlets LBC v Rahanara Begum* [2005] EWCA Civ
116; [2006] HLR 9; *Sharp v Brent LBC* [2003] EWCA Civ 779; [2003] HLR 65 and
R v Brent LBC ex p McDonagh (1989) 21 HLR 494, DC.

28   SI No 2685.

29   *Buckinghamshire CC v Moran* [1990] Ch 623, 635; [1989] 3 WLR 152, CA.

30   *JA Pye (Oxford) Ltd v Graham* [2002] UKHL 30; [2003] 1 AC 419.

31   Land Registration Act 1925 s75.

32   Land Registration Act 2002 s96.

entitled to apply to the Land Registry to be registered as proprietor after ten years' adverse possession.[33] If the application is not opposed by any of those notified, the squatter should be registered as proprietor of the land. Otherwise, adverse possession for ten years does not by itself give a right to registration. If any of the people notified opposes the application it should be rejected, unless the adverse possessor can bring him or herself within one or more of three conditions contained in the Land Registration Act 2002 Sch 6 para 5. If the squatter's application for registration is refused but the squatter remains in adverse possession for a further two years, he or she is entitled to apply once again to be registered and should this time be registered as proprietor whether or not the registered proprietor objects. The purpose of the two-year period is to enable the paper owner to evict the squatter.

29.20   Where the registered proprietor brings proceedings to recover possession from a squatter in that intervening period, the Land Registration Act 2002 allows the squatter to establish certain limited defences. However, ten years' adverse possession by itself is not a defence. If a landowner obtains judgment for possession against someone who has been in adverse possession for ten years, that judgment ceases to be enforceable two years after the date of the judgment (section 98). If, in proceedings, a court determines that a squatter has a defence under section 98 or that a judgment for possession ceases to be enforceable under section 98(4), the court must direct the Land Registrar to register that person as proprietor of the estate. Most of the new provisions came into force on 13 October 2003.[34]

29.21   The Land Registration Act 2002 did not immediately affect the position of those who had already acquired possessory title prior to its implementation. Schedule 12 para 18 provides that where a registered estate in land is held in trust for a person by virtue of the Land Registration Act 1925 s75(1) immediately before the coming into force of section 97, he or she is entitled to be registered as the proprietor of the estate. Similarly a person has a defence to any action for the possession of land if he or she is entitled under Sch 12 para 18 to be registered as the proprietor of an estate in the land.

29.22   Schedule 12 para 7 of the 2002 Act provided that for a period of three years after 13 October 2003 the squatter's unregistered interest would be an overriding interest whether or not he or she was in actual occupation and so would be binding on purchasers (Sch 12

---

33 See s97 and Sch 6 and Land Registration Rules 2003 SI No 1417.
34 Land Registration Act 2002 (Commencement No 4) Order 2003 SI No 1725.

para 7). However, after that period any squatter who has not been registered as owner will only continue to have an overriding interest if he or she remains in occupation and Sch 3 para 2 applies.

Interim possession orders

29.23   Criminal Justice and Public Order Act 1994 ss75 and 76 and amendments to CCR Ord 24 created a new form of interim possession order (IPO) which can only be granted against trespassers. Failure to comply with an IPO is a criminal offence (see below). CCR Ord 24 has largely been repealed. The procedure for IPOs is now contained in CPR Part 55.

29.24   The IPO procedure can apply only in limited circumstances. It can be used if:

- *The landowner is claiming possession only.* An applicant cannot seek an IPO if there is a claim for another remedy (for example, damages).[35]
- *The applicant has an immediate right to possession and has had such a right throughout the period of unlawful occupation.*[36]
- *The defendants entered premises as trespassers.*[37] It cannot be used against former licensees, tenants or subtenants. Criminal Law Act 1977 s12(1)(a) defines 'premises' as 'any building, any part of a building under separate occupation, any land ancillary to a building, the site comprising any building or buildings together with any land ancillary thereto ...'.
- *The application is issued within 28 days of the date when the owner first knew, or ought reasonably to have known, that the defendants were in occupation.*[38]

29.25   Landowners seeking IPOs should use forms N5 (claim form)[39] and N130 which comprises both the application and the statement in support of the application. The written evidence (ie, the statement) must be made personally by the claimant (not by a solicitor or agent) unless the claimant is a corporate body in which case an authorised officer may make it. It includes an undertaking to re-instate the defendant and to pay damages if ordered by the court.

---

35   CPR 55.21(1)(a).
36   CPR 55.21(1)(b).
37   CPR 55.21(2).
38   CPR 55.21(1)(c).
39   See PD 55.13.

29.26　　The court should list a hearing as soon as possible after the documents have been filed, but not less than three days after the date on which the application for an IPO is issued. 'Three days' means three clear days and Saturdays, Sundays, Bank Holidays, Christmas Day and Good Friday do not count.[40]

29.27　　Service of form N5, the completed form N130 and a blank form of defendant's witness statement (form N133) must take place within 24 hours after issue. This should be done by fixing a copy to the main door or other conspicuous part of the premises, and if practicable, inserting a copy in a sealed and transparent envelope addressed to the occupiers through the letter-box in accordance with CPR 55.6. Failure to do so provides a defence to the proceedings.

29.28　　In deciding whether or not to grant an IPO the court should have regard to whether or not the owner has given the undertakings in the prescribed form N130 to reinstate the occupier and pay damages if the court subsequently finds that the IPO should not have been granted. Before making a final order, the court should have regard to whether or not the claimant has undertaken not to damage the premises or the defendant's belongings or to grant any right of occupation to any other person pending the final hearing.[41]

29.29　　The court must make an IPO if:

- it is satisfied as to service;[42]
- the claimant is only seeking possession, has an immediate right to possession and has had such a right throughout the period of unlawful occupation and the defendant entered the premises as a trespasser;[43] and
- adequate undertakings have been given.[44]

29.30　　A final hearing should be listed not less than seven days after the date on which the IPO is made.[45]

29.31　　If an IPO is made in form N134, it must be served on the trespassers with a copy of the claimant's forms N5 and N130 within 48 hours of it being sealed.[46] Under the Criminal Justice and Public Order Act 1994 s76 it is a criminal offence to be 'present on the premises as a trespasser at any time during the currency of the order' but no

40 CPR 2.8.
41 CPR 55.25.
42 See CPR 55.25(2)(a) and CPR 55.6(a).
43 See CPR 55.21.
44 See CPR 55.25(1).
45 CPR 55.25.
46 CPR 55.26.

offence is committed if the trespasser leaves the premises within 24 hours and does not return. Similarly, no offence is committed if a copy of the order is not fixed to the premises.

29.32   If an IPO is made, the court fixes a return day which is not less than seven days after the initial hearing.[47] The IPO lapses on the return day. This means that once the return day has arrived, it is no longer a criminal offence for trespassers to be on the premises. At the return day hearing, the court may either make a final possession order, dismiss the claim, give further directions or enforce any of the claimant's undertakings. A final order for possession is made in form N136.

29.33   If occupiers have vacated premises they may apply before the return day to set aside an IPO which has been made. Any such application should be supported by a witness statement.[48]

29.34   Local authorities at the initial stage of deciding whether and to whom to give a removal direction under the Criminal Justice and Public Order Act 1994 s77 have to consider the relationship of their proposed action to various statutory and humanitarian considerations and make their decision accordingly. Such decisions should be reviewed by local authorities if there is a change in circumstances. They must strike a balance between the competing and conflicting needs of those encamped illegally and of residents in the area. A removal direction once made can only apply to people who were on the land at the time when the direction was made and, therefore, can only be contravened by such people.[49]

Interim possession orders and human rights

29.35   It is arguable that the IPO procedure does not constitute access to a fair hearing within the meaning of article 6 of the European Convention on Human Rights. Key elements of a fair hearing such as the right to participate effectively, equality of arms, the right to an adversarial hearing and the right to be present are all missing. Defendants have no right to be present unless a witness statement has been served in reply. Under the IPO procedure defendants are at a substantial disadvantage and do not have a proper opportunity to present their case or to comment upon the other party's evidence.[50]

47 CPR 55.27.
48 CPR 55.28.
49 *R v Lincolnshire CC ex p Atkinson* (1996) 8 Admin LR 529; [1995] NPC 145, QBD.
    See also *R v Wolverhampton MBC ex p Dunne* (1997) 29 HLR 745; [1997] COD 210,
    QBD and *R (Ward) v Hillingdon LBC* [2001] EWHC Admin 91; [2001] HRLR 40.
50 But see *R (Ward) v Hillingdon LBC* [2001] EWHC Admin 91; [2001] HRLR 40.

requires a social landlord to consider an agreement for payment of arrears up to the date of the court hearing. Each of these factors supports the contention that a claim for possession falls within section 285(3)(a) as a 'remedy against the person or property of the bankrupt in respect of [a debt provable in the bankruptcy]'.

30.11   On this view, a claim for possession based on a rent arrears ground is in substance a remedy in respect of a debt. This further accords with the policy purpose of section 285(3), in that the landlord, as a creditor in the bankruptcy, would otherwise have an advantage over other creditors of the tenant. This is so because, in the absence of such a restriction, there would appear to be nothing to prevent a possession order being postponed or suspended on condition of payments which will over time make up the full amount provable in the bankruptcy, despite the fact that no money judgment can be obtained in respect of that amount. Even if this is not the case, the threat of proceedings may induce a pre-bankruptcy settlement to the disadvantage of the tenant's other creditors. The obligation to pay current rent due after the bankruptcy, either out of the bankrupt's own resources (by arrangement with the trustee) or by housing benefit, is not affected. In the absence of binding authority on the relationship between section 285 and possession claims, it is suggested that the possibility of a defence based on section 285(3)(a) remains open.

30.12   Even if, despite the above, section 285(3)(a) is held not to prevent the landlord from obtaining a possession order in these circumstances, it will clearly be necessary for a landlord who is also a creditor in the tenant's bankruptcy to obtain the leave of the court under section 285(3)(b) (see para 30.5) before taking possession proceedings for any reason against the tenant. It would seem that leave is required whatever the grounds on which the landlord seeks possession, not only if a rent arrears ground is used, and likewise, even where no ground for possession is necessary, for example, where a landlord/creditor is proposing to use the accelerated possession procedure to recover possession of an assured shorthold tenancy following service of a valid notice under the Housing Act 1988 s21.

Costs

Costs in possession claims

31.1   In general, and with the important exception of mortgage posses-sion claims, the usual rules about costs in the Civil Procedure Rules (CPR) apply to possession claims. This chapter accordingly consid-ers rules relating to costs in landlord and tenant possession claims, but not the costs in mortgage possession claims – for those see para 42.66.[1]

31.2   The starting point is CPR 44.3 which states:

(1) The court has discretion as to –
   (a) whether costs are payable by one party to another;
   (b) the amount of those costs; and
   (c) when they are to be paid.
(2) If the court decides to make an order about costs –
   (a) the general rule is that the unsuccessful party will be ordered to pay the costs of the successful party; but
   (b) the court may make a different order.

So, if a defendant tenant has defeated a landlord's claim, the tenant should always seek an order that the landlord pays the costs. In decid-ing about costs, the court must have regard to all the circumstances, including the conduct of the parties, whether a party has succeeded on part of his or her case, even if he or she has not been totally suc-cessful, and any payment into court or offer.[2]

31.3   Conduct includes conduct before the issue of proceedings, as well as conduct during the case. For example, failure to send a letter be-fore action, which would have informed the tenant about the land-lord's concerns and enabled him or her to respond without the need for litigation, may justify refusing an award of costs to the landlord.[3]

31.4   A pre-CPR example of circumstances in which a successful party was ordered to pay the losing party's costs occurred in *Ottway v Jones*,[4] where the claimant landlord established grounds for posses-sion based on nuisance and annoyance but failed to convince the court that it was reasonable to make an order for possession, with the result that judgment on the claim was entered for the defendant. However, in view of the finding of nuisance, the judge held that the successful defendant should pay the plaintiff's costs and this order

---

1   Detailed consideration of the law of costs is outside the scope of this book. See CPR Parts 43 to 48 and the *Practice Direction relating to Costs*.

2   CPR 44.3(4).

3   *Brent LBC v Aniedobe* January 2000 *Legal Action* 25, CA. See too the Rent Arrears Protocol (see paras 3.38–3.41 and appendix D).

4   [1955] 1 WLR 706; [1955] 2 All ER 585.

was not disturbed by the Court of Appeal. There is no reason why that case would be decided any differently under the CPR.

31.5   Costs may be awarded on either the standard basis or on the indemnity basis.[5] Where costs are awarded on the *standard* basis, the court should allow only those costs which are reasonable and proportionate to the matters in issue. Any doubt which the court may have about whether costs have been reasonably incurred or are reasonable and proportionate in amount should be resolved in favour of the paying party. Where costs are assessed on the *indemnity* basis, the court need be satisfied only that they are reasonable. Issues of proportionality do not apply. Any doubt should be resolved in favour of the receiving party.[6] CPR 44.5 provides that the court must take into account all the circumstances when deciding whether to award costs on the standard or indemnity basis. The conduct of the parties is particularly relevant.[7]

31.6   The most common type of possession claims where landlords seek indemnity costs are claims for forfeiture because leases often contain a contractual entitlement to such costs. In *Billson v Residential Apartments Ltd (No 1)*,[8] Lord Templeman stated that this practice was 'ripe for reconsideration', although, in *Church Commissioners v Ibrahim*,[9] the Court of Appeal held that landlords are not to be deprived of their contractual right to costs on an indemnity basis unless there is a good reason to do so.

31.7   When awarding costs the court may order detailed or summary assessment. If *detailed* assessment is ordered, the receiving party's solicitor (or costs draughtsman) prepares a detailed bill which is served on the paying party. If the costs are disputed and agreement is not reached, a detailed assessment hearing should be listed for a costs judge to decide the amount of costs.

31.8   If *summary assessment* is ordered, the judge who has heard the case immediately assesses costs, by considering the schedule of costs that the receiving party's solicitor should have served at least 24 hours

---

5   CPR 44.4.

6   CPR 44.4.

7   See, eg, *Wailes v Stapleton Construction and Commercial Services Ltd* [1997] 2 Lloyd's Rep 112 (conduct described as 'disgraceful or deserving of moral condemnation') and *Baron v Lovell* [1999] CPLR 630; (1999) *Times* 14 September (unreasonable conduct in litigation).

8   [1992] 1 AC 494; [1992] 01 EG 91, HL; see also *Copall v Fryxell* (1991) *Times* 31 December, QBD.

9   [1997] 1 EGLR 13; [1997] 03 EG 136, CA. See also *Gomba Holdings Ltd v Minories Finance (No 2)* [1993] Ch 171, CA and CPR 48.3.

before the hearing. Summary assessment is the norm for fast-track trials and for other hearings lasting not more than a day.[10] There are fixed advocacy costs in fast-track trials, depending on the value of the claim.[11] Summary assessment of costs is not possible where the receiving party is publicly funded.[12] It is common for judges when making a possession order against a defendant who is publicly funded, either to make no order for costs or to make an order for costs but to provide that that order should not be enforced until such time as a determination of the defendant's liability has been made in accordance with the Access to Justice Act 1999 s11, which restricts the court's powers to grant a costs order against a publicly funded litigant.

Fixed costs

31.9   Fixed costs apply to certain types of possession claims – unless the court orders otherwise. CPR 45.1 provides that fixed costs apply where:

- the defendant gives up possession and pays the amount claimed (if any) and the fixed commencement costs (CPR 45.1(2)(c));
- one of the grounds for possession is arrears of rent, the court gave a fixed date for hearing, a possession order is made (whether suspended or not) and the defendant has either failed to deliver a defence or the defence is limited to specifying proposals for payment of arrears (CPR 45.1(2)(d));
- the claim is brought under the accelerated procedure (CPR Part 55 Section 2) against an assured shorthold tenant, a possession order is made and the defendant has neither delivered a defence nor otherwise denied liability (CPR 45.1(2)(e)); or
- the claim is a demotion claim under section III of CPR Part 65 or a demotion claim is made in the same claim form in which a claim for possession is made under CPR Part 55 and that demotion claim is successful (CPR 45.1(2)(f)).

---

10 See section 13.2 of the *Practice Direction relating to Costs.*
11 CPR 46.2. Currently £485 for claims up to £3,000; £690 for claims of more than £3,000 but not more than £10,000; £1,035 for claims of more than £10,000; and £1,650 for claims in excess of £15,000, where the claim was issued after 6 April 2009.
12 See section 13.9 of the *Practice Direction relating to Costs.*

31.10 The amounts of fixed costs are set out in CPR 45.2A Table 2 and CPR 45.4A. They are presently as follows:

TABLE 2

Fixed costs on commencement of a claim for the recovery of land or a demotion claim

Where the claim form is served by the court or by any method other than personal service by the claimant	Where – ■ the claim form is served personally by the claimant; and ■ there is only one defendant	Where there is more than one defendant, for each additional defendant personally served at separate addresses by the claimant
£69.50	£77.00	£15.00

Costs on entry of judgment in a claim for the recovery of land or a demotion claim

45.4A(1) Where –
    (a) the claimant has claimed fixed commencement costs under rule 45.2A; and
    (b) judgment is entered in a claim to which rule 45.1(2)(d) or (f)[13] applies, the amount to be included in the judgment for the claimant's solicitor's charges is the total of –
        (i) the fixed commencement costs; and
        (ii) the sum of £57.25.[14]
    (2) Where an order for possession is made in a claim to which rule 45.1(2)(e) applies, the amount allowed for the claimant's solicitor's charges for preparing and filing –
    (a) the claim form;
    (b) the documents that accompany the claim form; and
    (c) the request for possession,
    is £79.50.

Proceedings begun in the High Court

31.11 If proceedings are issued in the High Court against a Rent Act protected tenant, a Housing Act assured tenant or a Housing Act secure tenant, a landlord is not entitled to recover any costs.[15]

---

13 Ie, demotion claims.
14 The total (in 2010) is generally £276.75, ie issue fee of £150 (or £100 if PCOL is used) plus costs on issue of £69.50 and £57.25 on judgment.
15 RA 1977 s141, HA 1985 s110 and HA 1988 s40.

Small claims track cases

31.12   It is rare for possession claims to be allocated to the small claims track.[16] However, if a possession claim is allocated to the small claims track, the fast track costs regime applies but the trial costs are in the discretion of the judge and should not exceed the amount of fast track costs allowable in CPR 46.2 if the value were up to £3,000 – ie, currently £485.[17]

---

16 See para 23.47.
17 CPR 55.9(3).

CHAPTER 32

Mesne profits and damages for trespass

32.1   If someone is in wrongful occupation of land, the owner of that land is entitled to damages. These may be referred to as damages for trespass, or, if the occupier is a former tenant whose tenancy has been terminated, as mesne profits. However, there can be no liability for mesne profits or damages for use and occupation until the tenancy has been determined. Until that time the tenant is liable to the landlord for rent. It is only after any tenancy has been terminated that any sub-occupier can become liable for damages for use and occupation.[1]

32.2   Until the introduction of Civil Procedure Rules (CPR) Part 55, it was not common for land owners to claim damages against trespassers because they could not be included in a claim brought under CCR Ord 24 or RSC Ord 113. This is no longer so because a claim for damages can be included in a possession claim against trespassers under CPR Part 55.[2] It has always been standard practice for landlords to claim mesne profits against former tenants from the date of termination of the tenancy until possession is given up. They are generally assessed as a lump sum figure for the period from termination of the tenancy until the date of the possession hearing and then as a daily sum until possession is actually given up. Note, however, that protected, secure and assured tenancies do not end until the tenant is actually evicted[3], or leaves voluntarily at the end of a fixed term or following a surrender or on the expiry of a tenant's notice to quit, so

---

1   *Braintree DC v Vincent* [2004] EWCA Civ 415. So, if a suspended possession order or a postponed possession order is made, in view of *Knowsley Housing Trust v White* [2008] UKHL 70; [2009] 1 AC 636 and Housing and Regeneration Act 2008 Sch 11, the usual order should now refer to 'rent at the daily rate of £X', rather than mesne profits at the daily rate of £X'.
2   See chapter 29.
3   See para 33.16.

519

that rent, rather than mesne profits, is usually payable until the tenant's departure.

32.3   The owner of land may either claim for the loss which has been suffered or for the value of the benefit which the occupier has received.[4] If the owner is claiming for the loss suffered, mesne profits are calculated according to the 'fair value of the premises'. In the absence of special circumstances, this may be calculated according to the ordinary letting value,[5] ie, the market value. The rent paid by the tenant before the tenancy was terminated may be the best evidence of this. It is not necessary for land owners to prove that they would have relet the premises if the defendant had not been on the premises.[6]

32.4   The position may be more complicated if the rent does not represent a fair value for the premises. The open market value may not be the appropriate rate for mesne profits where there are special circumstances, for example, where the property is not usually let on the open market.[7] In the case of homes provided to families of service personnel in the armed forces, more assistance may be gained by looking at what occupants would have had to pay for local authority housing than by looking at market rents.

---

4 *Ministry of Defence v Thompson* [1993] 40 EG 148; (1993) 25 HLR 552, CA and *Ministry of Defence v Ashman* (1993) 66 P&CR 195; (1993) 25 HLR 513, CA.

5 *Swordheath Properties v Tabet* [1979] 1 WLR 285; [1979] 1 All ER 240.

6 *Swordheath Properties v Tabet* [1979] 1 WLR 285; [1979] 1 All ER 240, CA and *Viscount Chelsea v Hutchinson* (1996) 28 HLR 17; [1994] 43 EG 153, CA.

7 See, eg, *Ministry of Defence v Ashman* (1993) 66 P&CR 195; (1993) 25 HLR 513, CA, where the defendants would probably never have occupied the premises if they had had to pay the full market rent and the value to the wife (after her husband had left) was no more than she would have had to pay for suitable local authority housing if she could have been immediately rehoused.

Possession orders

The effect of possession orders

Occupiers without full Rent Act or Housing Act protection

33.1   At common law judges had a discretion to allow occupiers (other than trespassers) a reasonable time before a possession order took effect even if they had no security of tenure.[1] However, this discretion was largely taken away by the Housing Act (HA) 1980. Apart from various exceptions, orders for possession must now take effect not later than 14 days after the making of the order unless that would cause exceptional hardship, in which case the order can be postponed to a date which is not more than six weeks after the making of the order. There is no definition of exceptional hardship. HA 1980 s89 provides:

> *Restriction on discretion of court in making orders for possession of land*
> (1) Where a court makes an order for the possession of any land in a case not falling within the exceptions mentioned in subsection (2) below, the giving up of possession shall not be postponed (whether by the order or any variation, suspension or stay of execution) to a date later than fourteen days after the making of the order, unless it appears to the court that exceptional hardship would be caused by requiring possession to be given up by that date; and shall not in any event be postponed to a date later than six weeks after the making of the order.
> (2) The restrictions in subsection (1) above do not apply if –
>   (a) the order is made in an action by a mortgagee for possession; or
>   (b) the order is made in an action for forfeiture of a lease; or
>   (c) the court had power to make the order only if it considered it reasonable to make it; or
>   (d) the order relates to a dwelling-house which is the subject of a restricted contract (within the meaning of section 19 of the 1977 Act); or
>   (e) the order is made in proceedings brought as mentioned in section 88(1) above.

Housing Act 1980 s89 applies as much to orders made in the High Court as to those made in the county court.[2] Where the defendant

---

1   *Air Ministry v Harris* [1951] 2 All ER 862 (six months too long); *Sheffield Corporation v Luxford* [1929] 2 KB 180 (one year too long) and *Jones v Savery* [1951] 1 All ER 820 (one month reasonable).

2   *Hackney LBC v Side by Side (Kids) Ltd* [2003] EWHC 1813 (QB); [2004] 1 WLR 363. The earlier decision of Harman J in *Bain and Co v Church Commissioners for England* [1989] 1 WLR 24; (1989) 21 HLR 29, Ch D, that 'a court' meant 'a county court', was wrongly decided.

is applying for permission to appeal, however, section 89 does not limit the court's power to grant a stay of execution of the possession order.[3]

33.2   Gathering together all possible variations (including those not referred to in HA 1980 s89), the position is as follows.

Trespassers

33.3   Courts must make an order to take effect immediately[4] unless the trespassers are former service occupiers or both parties consent to a longer period (see chapter 29).

Proceedings brought by a mortgagee for possession

33.4   Courts have a wide discretion to adjourn, or to suspend or postpone the order (see para 40.10). For discussion of general procedure in mortgage possession actions, see chapters 40 and 41.

Forfeiture of a lease

33.5   In rent arrears cases any order forfeiting a lease must be suspended for at least 28 days. In proceedings for forfeiture based on other breaches of covenant, courts have a wide discretion to grant relief from forfeiture or to suspend the order (see para 14.44 onwards).

Restricted contracts

33.6   If a restricted contract was created after 28 November 1980 the court may delay the order for possession by up to three months. The total time allowed cannot exceed three months.[5] In the case of a restricted contract created before 28 November 1980, it seems that whether or not the rent tribunal has exercised its power to delay the operation of any notice to quit, in possession proceedings courts retain their common law powers to allow a reasonable period.[6] For the reasons given in para 17.67, virtually no restricted contracts are still in existence.

---

3   *Admiral Taverns (Cygnet) Ltd v Daniel and Daly* [2008] EWHC 1688; [2009] 4 All ER 71.
4   *McPhail v Persons, Names Unknown* [1973] Ch 447; [1973] 3 All ER 393, CA.
5   See RA 1977 ss104 and 106A and *Bryant v Best* (1987) 283 EG 843, CA.
6   See, eg, *Air Ministry v Harris* [1951] 2 All ER 862; *Sheffield Corporation v Luxford* [1929] 2 KB 180 and *Jones v Savery* [1951] 1 All ER 820.

Rental purchase agreements

33.7   There is a wide discretion to adjourn, stay or suspend (see chapter 21).

Mandatory grounds against Rent Act, secure and assured tenants, and proceedings against assured shorthold, demoted and introductory tenants

33.8   If the court is satisfied that a landlord is entitled to possession on one of the mandatory grounds or because a HA 1988 section 21 notice served on an assured shorthold tenant has expired, the court must make a possession order to take effect within 14 days unless exceptional hardship would be caused, in which case six weeks may be allowed[7] (see para 33.1). The same applies to possession claims against introductory and demoted tenants (see chapters 7 and 8).

Discretionary grounds within Rent Act 1977, Housing Act 1985 and Housing Act 1988

33.9   Courts have a wide discretion to adjourn or to postpone the date for possession or to stay or suspend execution of the order (see below, paras 33.11–33.13).

All other cases

33.10   The county court's discretion is limited by HA 1980 s89 to a maximum of 14 days unless exceptional hardship would be caused.

Tenants with security of tenure: possession on discretionary grounds

33.11   Even if a landlord of a protected, statutory or assured tenant in the private or housing association sector or of a secure occupier in the public sector proves that one of the discretionary grounds for possession exists, the court may consider that it is not reasonable to make any order for possession.[8] For example, in rent arrears cases, if the arrears are low, the court may adjourn generally with liberty to restore on terms that the tenant pay current rent and a weekly or monthly

7   HA 1988 s9(6).
8   See chapter 13 and, eg, *Woodspring DC v Taylor* (1982) 4 HLR 95, CA.

sum towards the arrears, or merely make a money judgment order with a direction that the tenant pay off the arrears by instalments. Alternatively, if the court is not satisfied that it is appropriate to make an absolute order, it may make a postponed or suspended possession order. Rent Act (RA) 1977 s100, HA 1985 s85 and HA 1988 s9(2), which are in almost identical terms, give the court a wide discretion to postpone the date on which possession should be given or to stay or suspend the execution of an order.

33.12 Housing Act 1985 s85 provides:

> *Extended discretion of court in certain proceedings for possession*
> (1) Where proceedings are brought for possession of a dwelling-house let under a secure tenancy on any of the grounds set out in Part I or Part III of Schedule 2 (grounds 1 to 8 and 12 to 16: cases in which the court must be satisfied that it is reasonable to make a possession order), the court may adjourn the proceedings for such period or periods as it thinks fit.
> (2) On the making of an order for possession of such a dwelling-house on any of those grounds, or at any time before the execution of the order, the court may –
> (a) stay or suspend the execution of the order, or
> (b) postpone the date for possession,
> for such period or periods as the court thinks fit.
> (3) On such an adjournment, stay, suspension or postponement the court –
> (a) shall impose conditions with respect to the payment by the tenant of arrears of rent (if any) and rent, unless it considers that to do so would cause exceptional hardship to the tenant or would otherwise be unreasonable, and
> (b) may impose such other conditions as it thinks fit.
> (4) If the conditions are complied with, the court may, if it thinks fit, discharge or rescind the order for possession.[9]

33.13 Housing Act 1988 s9 provides:

> *Extended discretion of court in possession claims*
> (1) Subject to subsection (6) below, the court may adjourn for such period or periods as it thinks fit proceedings for possession of a dwelling-house let on an assured tenancy.
> (2) On the making of an order for possession of a dwelling-house let on an assured tenancy, or at any time before the execution of such an order, the court, subject to subsection (6) below, may –
> (a) stay or suspend execution of the order, or
> (b) postpone the date of possession,
> for such period or periods as the court thinks just.

---

9 Section 85(4) has been amended by Housing and Regeneration Act (H&RA) 2008 but the amendment has not yet been brought into force: see para 34.32.

(3) On any such adjournment as is referred to in subsection (1) above or any such stay, suspension or postponement as is referred to in subsection (2) above, the court, unless it considers that to do so would cause exceptional hardship to the tenant or would otherwise be unreasonable, shall impose conditions with regard to payment by the tenant of arrears of rent (if any) and rent and may impose such other conditions as it thinks fit.

(4) If any such conditions as are referred to in subsection (3) above are complied with, the court may, if it thinks fit, discharge or rescind any such order as is referred to in subsection (2) above.[10]

...

(6) This section does not apply if the court is satisfied that the landlord is entitled to possession of the dwelling-house –
(a) on any of the grounds in Part I of Schedule 2 to this Act; or
(b) by virtue of subsection (1) or subsection (4) of section 21 below.

Status of tenant after possession order takes effect

33.14   Absolute (or outright) orders for possession take effect on the date on which the order states possession is to be given up, but tenancies with statutory protection do not end until the order is executed, ie, until the tenant is evicted, or leaves in compliance with the order.[11]

33.15   For many years, the courts held in a series of cases that secure tenancies terminated on the date for possession specified in the order and that the tenant became a 'tolerated trespasser' from that date onwards, subject to variation or discharge of the order. Likewise, many tenants with suspended possession orders became tolerated trespassers either when they breached the terms of the order or when the date for possession in the order expired (since possession itself had been lost and what was suspended was enforcement of the order).[12] Where the court made a postponed possession order, the tenancy would continue unless or until, following a breach of its terms, the court made a further order, on the landlord's application, fixing a date for possession. As a result of the twilight status of tolerated trespasser, many people lost their tenancy rights, including rights to repair and the right to buy and, on the death of a tolerated

10 Section 9(4) has been amended by H&RA 2008 but the amendment has not yet been brought into force: see para 34.32.

11 See para 3.16.

12 See *Thompson v Elmbridge* [1987] 1 WLR 1425; *Burrows v Brent LBC* [1996] 1 WLR 1448; *Greenwich LBC v Regan* (1996) 28 HLR 469; (1996) 72 P&CR 507, CA; *Lambeth LBC v Rogers* (1999) 32 HLR 361; *Harlow DC v Hall* [2006] 1 WLR 2116 and *Bristol CC v Hassan* [2006] EWCA Civ 656; [2006] 1 WLR 2582.

trespasser, a family member would find that there was no tenancy to which they could succeed.

33.16　Tenants no longer become tolerated trespassers when the date for possession in a court order expires. In *Knowsley Housing Trust v White*,[13] the House of Lords held that assured tenancies did not terminate until the date of execution of the order (following Rent Act authority in *Sherrin v Brand*[14]) and cast doubt on the judicial reasoning that had produced the doctrine of the tolerated trespasser.[15] Then, following the coming into force of the Housing and Regeneration Act (H&RA) 2008 Sch 11 on 20 May 2009, the Housing Acts 1985, 1988 and 1996 were amended to provide that tenancies falling within those Acts do not end until the possession order is executed, ie, until actual eviction.[16] It is, of course, entirely possible for such a tenancy to be terminated voluntarily by surrender or by a tenant's notice to quit or by a tenant leaving in accordance with a possession order, but before eviction.

33.17　For any tenant who had already become a tolerated trespasser before 20 May 2009, and who still occupied the same premises as his or her only or principal home, the Housing and Regeneration Act 2008 provides that he or she, as from that date, acquired a 'replacement tenancy', provided that the parties had not already entered into another tenancy. Any outstanding liability for rent owed by the tenant to the landlord before commencement date is treated as a liability in respect of rent under the new tenancy. Likewise, the possession order under which the original tenancy ended is treated as if it applies to the new tenancy. For further details of replacement tenancies, see chapter 10.

33.18　An agreement that an occupier may remain in premises after an absolute (or outright) possession order has been made (for example, on terms that payments of rent and instalments towards arrears are made) was characterised in *Burrows v Brent LBC*[17] as a forbearance by

---

13　[2008] UKHL 70; [2009] 1 AC 636.

14　[1956] 1 QB 403.

15　[2008] UKHL 70 at paras 90–93. Further doubt on the judicial reasoning which gave rise to the concept of the tolerated trespasser was expressed by the Supreme Court in *Austin v Southwark LBC* [2010] UKSC 28, but the court declined to reverse the earlier case-law which had been assumed to be right and had been acted on in many tens of thousands of cases.

16　See new HA 1985 s82(2), substituted by H&RA 2008 Sch 11 para 2(3), in relation to secure tenancies; new HA 1988 s5(1A), inserted by Sch 11 para 6(2) (assured tenancies); HA 1988 s21(3), as amended by Sch 11 para 9(2) and s21(4A), inserted by Sch 11 para 9(3) (assured shorthold tenancies); HA 1996 s127(1A), inserted by Sch 11 para 12(3) (introductory tenancies) and HA 1996 s143D(1A), inserted by Sch 11 para 13(3) (demoted tenancies).

17　[1996] 1 WLR 144 8; [1996] 4 All ER 577.

the landlord from executing the order. After a period of compliance with the new terms, the tenant may apply to the court for a variation of the order (assuming that it was made on a discretionary ground).

Conditional (postponed or suspended) possession orders

33.19   When postponing, suspending or delaying possession orders against protected, statutory, assured or secure tenants, the court must impose conditions with regard to the repayment of arrears (if any) unless this would cause exceptional hardship or would otherwise be unreasonable. The court may impose such other conditions as it thinks fit.[18]

33.20   The effect of a conditional possession order (ie a postponed or 'suspended' order which is conditional upon the defendant's complying with certain terms) depends upon the particular form in which the order is expressed (see paras 33.27–33.37).

Criteria for postponing or suspending possession orders

33.21   The approach which the court must adopt in dealing with a claim for possession on a discretionary ground has been described as follows:

> Where, as here, the landlord relies on ... [discretionary grounds] the court has potentially three issues, although a determination of one issue in favour of the tenant may make further issues academic: first, to decide whether grounds for possession are made out, which is an issue of fact; secondly, to decide whether it is reasonable to make an order for possession, which involves the exercise of judicial discretion, but with a substantial element of judgment as to whether or not the making of the order is reasonable; and thirdly, to decide whether to postpone the date for possession or to stay or suspend execution, which involves a further exercise of judicial discretion.[19]

33.22   It is clear that the court's powers under RA 1977 s100(2), HA 1985 s85(2) and HA 1988 s9(2) must be exercised judicially, but (except in cases of immoral user, where, in general, the court's discretion to suspend should not be exercised[20] and serious anti-social behaviour/ drug dealing where a postponed or suspended order is the exception[21]) there is little guidance as to circumstances in which orders should be

---

18 RA 1977 s100(3), as inserted by HA 1980 ss75 and 87(3).
19 *West Kent Housing Association v Davies* (1998) 31 HLR 415, per Robert Walker LJ at 418.
20 *Yates v Morris* [1951] 1KB 77; [1950] 2 All ER 577, although in *Yates* the order was suspended.
21 *Bristol City Council v Mousah* (1997) 30 HLR 32, CA and the other cases referred to in para 13.12.

postponed or suspended, or the factors to be taken into account. In principle, however, an outright possession order should be made only no lesser alternative would realistically make sense.[22]

33.23   In rent arrears cases, the fundamental purpose of a postponed or suspended possession order is to enable any arrears to be paid off within a reasonable time. Any postponement or suspension should be for a definite period and should not extend into the mists of time.[23]

33.24   In practice, unless there are large rent arrears, on the first occasion that a tenant is brought to court for arrears, it is usual, if the grant of an order is appropriate at all, for a possession order to be postponed or suspended on condition that the tenant pays the current rent when due *and* a regular amount towards the arrears.[24] Even if rent arrears are high, the court may take the view that the landlord has contributed to some extent to the problem in allowing large arrears to accrue without taking any earlier action or abiding by the Rent Arrears Pre-action Protocol (see para 3.38 and appendix D) and that, accordingly, the tenant should be given the chance to pay off the arrears by instalments under a conditional possession order, although where an assured tenant owes eight weeks' or two months' rent, ground 8 is mandatory.

33.25   It is not uncommon for courts to make postponed or suspended orders which provide for arrears to be paid off over a few years.[25] The Court of Appeal has said that court practice is to be merciful to tenants and to give them a realistic opportunity to pay arrears. The question of whether it is appropriate for a tenant who owes substantial arrears to have the threat of losing his or her home hanging over him or her for years is a political question and does not go to the correctness of making an order.[26] Some courts take the realistic view that if a possession order is postponed or suspended, there is some likelihood of the landlord recovering arrears, whereas if an absolute possession order is obtained, it is unlikely in reality that the

---

22   *CDS Housing v Bellis* [2008] EWCA Civ 1315.

23   *Taj v Ali* (2001) 33 HLR 26; [2000] 43 EG 183, CA (judge wrong to make suspended possession order where arrears of £14,503 to be paid off at £5 per week) but cf *Lambeth LBC v Henry* (2000) 32 HLR 874, CA.

24   *Laimond Properties Ltd v Raeuchle* [2000] L&TR 319, CA. See too the Rent Arrears Protocol, para 3.38.

25   See, eg, *Lambeth LBC v Henry* (2000) 32 HLR 874, CA, where the Court of Appeal refused to criticise a suspended possession order which provided for payment of arrears over a period of 23 years. Cf *Taj v Ali* (2001) 33 HLR 26; [2000] 43 EG 183, CA.

26   *Lambeth LBC v Henry* (2000) 32 HLR 874, CA.

landlord will ever recover the arrears. Courts are generally, however, more prepared to postpone or suspend an order against a tenant with substantial arrears if the landlord is a local authority, rather than a private individual.

33.26   When considering what form of order should be made, the time the defendants have been tenants, their previous conduct, their age and health are all relevant factors.[27] The court should also take into account the level of arrears and the tenant's income and expenditure. Again there is little guidance about the size of such payments, but there is a strong argument where a tenant is receiving income support or jobseeker's allowance that no suspended order should require the tenant to pay more than 5 per cent[28] of the personal allowance for a single claimant aged 25 or over towards the arrears. This is the limit of the amount which a benefit officer can deduct from the claimant's benefit and pay direct to the landlord towards satisfaction of arrears.[29] The basis of the argument is that since those responsible for welfare benefits legislation consider that, taking into account the needs of claimants and the level of their benefit, it is not reasonable for more than 5 per cent of their allowance to be deducted when direct payments are made to the landlord, it would be unreasonable and contrary to RA 1977 s100(3), HA 1985 s85(3) and HA 1988 s9(3) for the court to order the payment of a greater sum. Indeed, if the Department for Work and Pensions is already making deductions to go towards the arrears, it may well be unreasonable for the court to make any possession order at all because the landlord's interests are already being adequately protected.[30]

Postponed possession orders

33.27   Two alternative forms of conditional possession order are in use by the courts in relation to protected, assured and secure tenancies, where an order is made on discretionary grounds. One is the *postponed* possession order, whereby the date for possession is not fixed by the original order. This is in effect a two-stage process. The landlord will need to apply again to the court to fix the possession date, but cannot do so as long as the tenant is complying with the

---

27   *Woodspring DC v Taylor*(1982) 4 HLR 95, CA.
28   From April 2010, £3.30 per week.
29   Social Security (Claims and Payments) Regulations 1987 SI No 1968 Sch 9 para 5(3) as amended.
30   *Woodspring DC v Taylor* (1982) 4 HLR 95, CA; *Second WRVS Housing Society v Blair* (1987) 19 HLR 104 and *Brent LBC v Marks* (1999) 31 HLR 343, CA.

terms of the order as to payment of current rent together with regular payments off the arrears. Court form N28A provides a template for the postponed possession order (see appendix B).

33.28　Where the court makes a postponed possession order in respect of a secure or assured tenancy, the procedure is governed by paragraph 10 of Practice Direction 55A to CPR 55. At least 14 days and not more than three months before applying to the court to fix a date for possession, the landlord must give written notice to the tenant. This notice must:

- state that the landlord intends to apply for an order fixing the date on which the tenant is to give up possession;
- record the current arrears and, by reference to a rent statement, state how the tenant has failed to comply with the postponed order;
- request the tenant to reply to the landlord within seven days agreeing or disputing the stated arrears; and
- inform the tenant of his or her right to apply to the court for a further postponement of the order, or to stay or suspend enforcement.[31]

33.29　In the tenant's reply to the notice, he or she must provide details of payments or credits to the account if the stated arrears are in dispute; otherwise, he or she must explain why payments have not been made.[32] If the landlord nevertheless proceeds to apply to the court for a date to be fixed, he or she must do so by filing an application notice (court form N244) under CPR Part 23. The application must state whether or not there is any outstanding claim for housing benefit by the tenant. With the application the landlord must file:

- a copy of the letter to the tenant warning of the intention to apply for a date to be fixed;
- a copy of the tenant's reply, if any, and copies of any subsequent correspondence;
- a statement of the rent account showing the arrears that have accrued since the first failure to pay in accordance with the order or the arrears that have accrued during the period of two years

31　PD 55A para 10.4.
32　Where the procedure is adapted to anti-social behaviour cases, Sedley LJ in *Wandsworth LBC v Whibley* [2008] EWCA Civ 1259; [2009] HLR 26 gave guidance on the content of the tenant's reply to the landlord's notice. It is not sufficient for the tenant to issue a bare denial of a breach. The court will expect a detailed response in order that it may establish whether there is a real triable issue concerning the alleged breach. Since the tenant has already, by definition, breached the terms of the agreement, he or she will need to have a cogent answer once there is prima facie evidence of repetition.

immediately preceding the date of the application notice, where the first such failure to pay occurs more than two years before that date.[33]

33.30   The landlord's application is then referred to a district judge, who will usually make a decision on the papers, ie, without a hearing, by fixing the date for possession as the next working day. If the tenant has responded to the landlord's notice, explaining his or her difficulties, it is likely that the district judge will wish to refer the application to a hearing at which the tenant's circumstances may be fully considered. If the judge considers that a hearing is necessary, a date should be set for the application to be heard and the tenant should be served with the application notice and supporting evidence.

33.31   Where a date for possession is fixed and expires, the landlord can request the court to issue a warrant of possession, whereupon the court bailiff will set a date for eviction. At all times, the court retains its wide discretion under HA 1985 s85(2) and HA 1988 s9(2). The tenant may still apply, at any time up to the date of eviction, to vary the possession order or to stay or suspend the warrant on terms.

Suspended possession orders

33.32   The 'suspended possession order' is something of a misnomer, since what is suspended under the standard form of the order is not possession itself, but enforcement of the order. However, the term is in common use and will be used here. Under the standard court form of suspended possession order which has been in use since October 2001 (form N28), a date is fixed for possession, but the order provides that

> this order is not to be enforced so long as the defendant pays the claimant the rent arrears and the amount for use and occupation [and costs] totalling £.... by the payments set out below in addition to the current rent.

33.33   In the event of a breach of the order, the landlord may apply for a warrant of possession, whereupon the tenant will need to apply to stay or suspend the warrant, if eviction is to be averted. In the same notice of application, the tenant may also apply for a variation of the terms of the order, if appropriate (see para 34.20). There is no requirement for the landlord to give notice to the tenant of its intention to apply for a warrant, although the court may disapprove of a landlord applying for

33   PD 55A para 10.7.

a warrant following a single missed payment or without warning the tenant about the default and inviting him or her to make up the missing payment(s). The only notice which the tenant receives is notice of the date of eviction itself, in court form N54. Use of this form is not mandatory under the Civil Procedure Rules, but it is clearly necessary to alert the tenant to the imminence of eviction. The N54 notice also notifies the tenant of his or her right to apply to the court to vary the possession order or to seek a suspension of the warrant. In *Southwark LBC v St Brice*,[34] Kennedy LJ said:

> It is important that so far as possible tenants should receive such notice in time to enable them to take advice and, if so advised, bring the matter back to the court before the date fixed for eviction.

Postponed or suspended?

33.34 The N28A form of postponed possession order was introduced in July 2006 in response to an invitation to judges by the Court of Appeal in *Bristol City Council v Hassan*[35] to use a two-stage order as a means of avoiding the creation of 'blameless tolerated trespassers', which at that time was the effect of form N28 following the expiry of the possession date. In that case, Brooke LJ stated that the form of the order was in the discretion of the judge.

33.35 Now that tolerated trespassers have been abolished, is there still a place for the postponed possession order?[36] It is suggested that the postponed order not only still has a place, but is in general preferable to the suspended order, though it is a matter for the discretion of the court in the circumstances of each case.[37] If a tenant has a particularly bad record of payment, the court may wish to make a suspended order in form N28. In other cases, the postponed possession order is likely to be the reasonable and proportionate method of disposal. A postponed order enables the court to supervise the process of enforcement in a way which does not happen where the landlord under a suspended order asks the court to issue a warrant of possession and set an eviction date as an administrative act. The use of postponed orders should also result in a reduction in the number of last-minute applications to suspend warrants.

---

34 [2001] EWCA Civ 1138; [2002] 1 WLR 1537.
35 [2006] EWCA Civ 656.
36 For a full discussion of this question, see Robert Latham, 'Conditional possession orders after *Knowsley Housing Trust v White*' March 2009 *Legal Action* 27.
37 *Bristol City Council v Hassan* [2006] EWCA Civ 656; [2006] 1 WLR 2582.

33.36   In *Leicester City Council v Aldwinckle*,[38] in which a suspended possession order was executed while the tenant was away from her flat for health reasons, Leggatt LJ unfavourably contrasted the county court procedure with that in the High Court, in which notice of the landlord's decision to apply for the order to be executed must be given to the tenant and the court's permission is required for enforcement, and expressed the view that the county court rules should be brought into line with the High Court. The requirement for the landlord to apply to fix a date enables the court to exercise a judicial scrutiny of the process, and to take account of any changes in the tenant's circumstances since the date of the order. In some cases, the landlord may be applying for a warrant some years after the suspended order was made, and the tenant's circumstances may be very different from before. Yet there is no opportunity for the court to examine whether it is still reasonable and proportionate for the landlord to proceed to eviction in the light of the changed circumstances, other than on the tenant's application for a suspension of the warrant. It is surely right that the court should take a further look at the situation at the time when the landlord wishes to execute the order, rather than that the burden should be on the tenant to apply to suspend the warrant.[39]

33.37   Form N28A (postponed possession order) contains a provision that 'this order shall cease to be enforceable when the total judgment debt is satisfied'. Thus, once the tenant has paid off the arrears and any costs in full, the order will cease to have effect and it will be necessary for the landlord to issue fresh proceedings if the tenant falls into arrears again. Form N28 (suspended possession order) does not contain such a provision. The court may be asked to add a clause of this kind to the standard order. Alternatively, once the money judgment has been satisfied, it will be necessary to ask the court to discharge the order (see para 34.29), failing which it may be re-activated if the tenant later falls into new arrears.

33.38   Where a tenancy which is subject to a suspended possession order is transferred from one spouse or civil partner to another under the Family Law Act 1996 Sch 7 (formerly the Matrimonial Homes Act 1983 Sch 1 para 3(1)), the new tenant will take the tenancy under the

38 [1992] 24 HLR 40.
39 In *Southwark LBC v St Brice* [2001] EWCA Civ 1138; [2002] 1 WLR 1537, the Court of Appeal nevertheless held that the existing procedure, whereby a warrant of possession can be obtained as an administrative act is not incompatible with articles 6, 8 and 14 of the European Convention on Human Rights. See further 'Warrants and the European Convention on Human Rights', para 34.39.

terms of the suspended order. However, in the event of a subsequent breach of those terms, the landlord would not be entitled to enforce that order against the new tenant. If landlords wish to evict in such circumstances, they would have to bring new proceedings against the new tenant.[40] The outcome would almost certainly be the same in the case of a postponed order.

33.39 Spouses and civil partners of tenants (who are not joint tenants) have the same rights as tenants themselves to seek the suspension or postponement of orders until the making of a decree absolute or termination of civil partnership provided that they are still living in the premises.[41]

33.40 Although in many cases a suspended or postponed possession order will be a favourable outcome for the tenant, it should be remembered that it is still a possession order and that if a tenant subsequently fails to comply with conditions imposed it can be difficult to argue that those conditions were not reasonable. It is therefore important to ensure that a tenant will be able to afford to make any proposed payments before agreeing to particular amounts.

Conditional orders in anti-social behaviour cases

33.41 The templates in court forms N28 and N28A are designed specifically for rent arrears cases. There are no templates specifically for possession orders based on the ground of anti-social behaviour, but such orders may follow a similar pattern, being based either on the postponement of the date for possession (whereby a further application to the court is needed to fix the date for possession) or on the suspension of enforcement, in either case on terms that the tenant abide by the terms of the tenancy and refrain from acts of a certain kind.

33.42 There is conflicting judicial guidance on which of these options is the more appropriate to nuisance cases. In *Knowsley Housing Trust v McMullen*,[42] the Court of Appeal agreed that in the particular circumstances of that case (in which the tenant had learning difficulties and the complaints were of nuisance committed by her son) there should be a clause in a postponed possession order requiring the landlord to apply for permission to issue a warrant, but Neuberger LJ suggested that this course would be appropriate only in exceptional cases.

33.43 In contrast, in *Wandsworth LBC v Whibley*,[43] Sedley LJ approved the

40 *Church Commissioners v Al-Emarah* [1996] 3 WLR 633; [1997] Fam 34, CA.
41 See chapter 35.
42 [2006] EWCA Civ 539; [2006] HLR 43.
43 [2008] EWCA Civ 1259; [2009] HLR 26.

approach of adapting Form N28A and CPR PD 55A to cases of nuisance, noting that in rent arrears cases a breach is likely to be a matter of record, while in nuisance cases there is more likely to be a dispute on the facts over whether a breach has occurred. Sedley LJ said:

> In a nuisance case there is obvious good sense in following a similar procedure: if, on being notified of the impending application and invited to respond, the defendant remains silent or puts in a plainly spurious or irrelevant response, an order may properly be made summarily. But if, as is more probable in nuisance cases, an issue is raised which is capable of affecting the court's decision, justice will require the defendant to be given an opportunity to put his or her case. The court will of course be astute not to let merely factitious or obstructive responses impede a summary disposal; but, inconvenient though it will be for the lessor and for a time nightmarish for the neighbours, it is not permissible for a tenant who has a possible tenable answer to lose his or her home unheard.

33.44　In respect of orders based on behaviour, it is suggested that a postponed order with no date fixed for possession should be the norm, since a suspended order enables the landlord to apply for a warrant on the basis of the landlord's own assessment that a breach has occurred. Where allegations of behaviour are in dispute, or where there are questions about the seriousness of the alleged acts or the degree of culpability, it is arguably essential that the court should have the opportunity to review the matter before the bailiff is instructed to evict. It is, of course, open to the tenant to apply for suspension of the warrant; but it is preferable that the court should be able to consider the issues without the pressure of an imminent eviction date. While landlords may object to postponed orders on the basis that they introduce another stage in the process and require another court fee in the event of the need to make application to fix a possession date, this must be weighed against the overwhelming importance to the tenant of not losing the roof over his or her head. In the alternative, a suspended order could be made subject to a requirement that a warrant should not issue without the permission of the court.

Consent orders

33.45　It is a well-established principle that landlords and tenants cannot 'contract out' of the statutory protection provided by the Rent Act 1977, the Housing Act 1985 or the Housing Act 1988.[44] This rule

---

44 *Barton v Fincham* [1921] 2 KB 291; *Mouat-Balthasar v Murphy* [1967] 1 QB 344; [1966] 3 WLR 695; [1966] 3 All ER 477 and *Kenyon v Walker* [1946] 2 All ER 595.

can have important consequences where occupiers with security of tenure decide to compromise possession proceedings by agreeing to a 'consent order'. The court cannot make a 'consent order' against a protected, assured or secure tenant unless there is either a concession by express admission that Rent Act or Housing Act protection does not apply or, alternatively, it is established that a ground for possession exists and, if appropriate, it is reasonable to make an order for possession.[45] Any order made without such a concession or without the establishment of a ground for possession and consideration of reasonableness, is a nullity and can be challenged by judicial review, even if both parties were legally represented and consented to it.[46] It may well be that a 'consent order' could be set aside at a later date if it were established that a concession that statutory protection did not apply was not made bona fide.[47]It will often be acceptable, however, where the terms of an order have been agreed, to include a recital in the order whereby the tenant admits the existence of a ground for possession and that it is reasonable for a possession order to be made.

33.46   In *R v Bloomsbury and Marylebone County Court ex p Blackburne*,[48] possession proceedings based on rent arrears were settled on the basis that the tenant would consent to a possession order in return for payment of £11,000 plus costs. Both parties were legally represented. Subsequently, the tenant changed his mind and successfully applied for an order of certiorari to quash the possession order.

33.47   In *Plaschkes v Jones*,[49] an unrepresented tenant went to court intending to defend possession proceedings. However, at court he agreed to a possession order, being under the impression that he would be able to obtain a council house. He later found that he was not able to get a council house and the Court of Appeal allowed his subsequent appeal because the county court had not considered the question of reasonableness.

45 *R v Bloomsbury and Marylebone County Court ex p Blackburne* (1985) 275 EG 1273, CA; *R v Newcastle upon Tyne County Court ex p Thompson* (1988) 20 HLR 430, CA; *Wandsworth LBC v Fadayomi* [1987] 1 WLR 1473; [1987] 3 All ER 474; (1987) 19 HLR 512, CA; *Hounslow LBC v McBride* (1999) 31 HLR 143, CA (suspended possession order made by consent, without evidence or concession, in anti-social behaviour case set aside after issue of warrant) and *R v Birmingham CC ex p Foley* March 2001 *Legal Action* 29, QBD.

46 *R v Bloomsbury and Marylebone County Court ex p Blackburne* (1985) 275 EG 1273, CA.

47 See, eg, Atkins LJ's references to bona fides in *Barton v Fincham* [1921] 2 KB 291.

48 (1985) 275 EG 1273, CA.

49 (1982) 9 HLR 110.

33.48   In *Hounslow LBC v McBride*,[50] a claim against a secure tenant based on non-payment of rent and serious criminal conduct causing nuisance or annoyance, the parties agreed that a suspended possession order should be made. At a brief hearing lasting no more than five minutes, which was attended by solicitors, but not the defendant, the district judge made the order sought. Before making the order she checked that the figure for the arrears was agreed and that the defendant understood the implications of the order. In a later affidavit it was stated that both solicitors 'assumed that the district judge would simply rubber stamp the order'. Later the council alleged that the defendant had broken the conditions of the suspended order and applied for a warrant of possession. Both the possession order and the warrant were set aside. Simon Brown LJ said that 'an order such as this is not in law capable of being consented to unless the terms of the Act are satisfied'. A distinction has to be drawn between a form of order which contains an admission about those matters on which the jurisdiction to make the order rests (for example, reasonableness) and an order, such as this one, which did not.

33.49   However, in *R v Worthing BC ex p Bruce*,[51] an occupier unsuccessfully appealed against the refusal of his application for judicial review of the making of a consent order in possession proceedings. He had compromised his claim for a declaration and the council's counterclaim for possession when the action was part heard on terms that he would withdraw a 'right to buy' claim and give up possession. The Court of Appeal held that the implied admission in the consent order that the tenant was not a secure tenant, taken together with the fact that the order was made by the judge after at least some evidence was heard, enabled the order to stand.

---

50 (1999) 31 HLR 143, CA.
51 [1994] 1 EGLR 116; (1994) 26 HLR 223, CA. See also *Morris v Barnet LBC* December 1995 *Legal Action* 18, CA.

CHAPTER 34

After the possession order

Appeals

34.1   If a possession order is made or refused by a district judge, an appeal lies to a circuit judge.[1] Permission to appeal is required. If permission is refused by the district judge, a further application for permission to appeal can be made to a circuit judge. Permission to appeal should be given only where the appeal has a real prospect of success or there is some other compelling reason why the appeal should be heard. The appellant's notice stating grounds of appeal should usually be filed within 21 days of the date on which the order appealed against was made.

34.2   If an order is made or refused by a circuit judge, permission to appeal to a High Court judge should be sought from the trial judge. If permission is refused by the trial judge, it may be sought from a High Court judge. However, if a possession order is made in a claim allocated to the multi-track, an appeal will be heard by the Court of Appeal (see PD 52 para 2A).

34.3   There is no right of appeal on any question of fact if the court could grant possession only on being satisfied it was reasonable to do so.[2] However, this does not exclude, in a proper case, the possibility of an appeal against a finding of reasonableness.[3] But, as indicated in the text relating to each of the main schemes for security of tenure (see paras 3.208 and 13.17), it is generally difficult to overturn any order where the issue is whether it was reasonable to award possession to the claimant.

34.4   Appeals should be allowed only where the decision of the lower court was 'wrong; or unjust because of serious procedural or other irregularity in the proceedings in the lower court'.[4] Appeals are therefore limited to a review of the decision of the lower court, although exceptionally the appeal court may consider that in the circumstances of an individual appeal it would be in the interests of justice to hold a re-hearing.[5]

34.5   Pending any appeal, an application should be made in the county court for a stay of the order for possession, because the mere lodging

1   See generally CPR Part 52.
2   County Courts Act 1984 s77(6) and RA 1977 s98(1); HA 1985 s84(2)(a) and HA 1988 s7 as it applies to grounds 9–16.
3   *Gallagher v Castle Vale Housing Action Trust* [2001] EWCA Civ 944; (2001) 33 HLR 72 and *Hounslow LBC v McBride* (1999) 31 HLR 143, CA.
4   CPR 52.11.
5   See CPR 52.11(1)(b) and *Ealing LBC v Richardson* [2005] EWCA Civ 1798; [2006] HLR 13.

of an appeal does not act as a stay.[6] If a stay is refused by the judge whose decision is being appealed, application for a stay may be made to the appeal judge.

34.6 Different provisions apply to second appeals – for example, against a High Court judge's dismissal of an appeal from a circuit judge. They are outside the scope of this book – see the Access to Justice Act 1999 and Civil Procedure Rules (CPR) 52.13.

Setting aside the possession order

34.7 CPR 39.3 sets out the circumstances in which a party who fails to attend a trial may apply to set aside an order:

> (3) Where a party does not attend and the court gives judgment or makes an order against him, the party who failed to attend may apply for the judgment or order to be set aside.
>
> (4) An application made under ... paragraph (3) must be supported by evidence.
>
> (5) Where an application is made under paragraph ... (3) by a party who failed to attend the trial, the court may grant the application only if the applicant –
>
> (a) acted promptly when he found out that the court had exercised its power to strike out or to enter judgment or make an order against him;
>
> (b) had a good reason for not attending trial; and
>
> (c) has a reasonable prospect of success at the trial.

34.8 Until the decision of the Court of Appeal in *Forcelux Ltd v Binnie*,[7] there was a general assumption that the court's powers to set aside possession orders were dependent on CPR 39.3, as above. However, this assumption has now been overturned. In *Forcelux*, following proceedings for forfeiture of a long lease on the grounds of arrears of ground rent and service charges, the landlord obtained a default judgment against the leaseholder. The leaseholder was away from his flat at the time and did not receive notification of the proceedings, and accordingly he was not present at the hearing when a possession order was made. The order was executed and the landlord took possession. Some four months after first becoming aware of the order, the leaseholder applied to set aside the possession order and for relief from forfeiture.

6 CPR 52.7.
7 [2009] EWCA Civ 854.

34.9   The landlord contended that CPR 39.3 governed the application to set aside the order, and that the leaseholder could not succeed because he had not acted promptly when he found out that an order had been made against him, However, the Court of Appeal held that CPR 39.3 does not apply unless the hearing in question was a 'trial'. A hearing in a busy undefended possession list could not be considered a trial, even if it resulted in a possession order being made. However, the court did have jurisdiction to deal with the matter under its general management powers in CPR Part 3, and in particular CPR 3.1(2)(m), under which the court may

> take any other step or make any other order for the purpose of managing the case and furthering the overriding objective.

In considering whether to exercise that power, the court should have regard to the checklist of factors in CPR 3.9 which deals with relief from sanctions, although it is not bound by these. The most relevant factors in CPR 3.9 appear to be:

- the interests of the administration of justice;
- whether the application for relief has been made promptly;
- whether there is a good explanation for the failure (which in this context may mean the general circumstances which led the court to make a possession order);
- the effect which the 'failure to comply' has had on each party; and
- the effect which the granting of relief would have on each party.

On the facts of the case it was appropriate to set aside the possession order and grant relief from forfeiture.

34.10   Earlier case-law authorities on setting aside possession orders[8] will have been decided on the basis of CPR 39.3 above, and now need to be read in the light of the judgment in *Forcelux Ltd v Binnie*. Applications to set aside which would formerly have been made in reliance on CPR 39.3 will now be made under CPR 3.1(2)(m), in that the court is being requested to 'take any other step or make any other order for the purpose of managing the case and furthering the overriding objective'. The court's powers under this limb of the rule are potentially much broader than those under CPR 39.3, in that they are not dependent on specific conditions such as the defendant having failed with good cause to attend the hearing. The guiding principle in the

---

8 *Governors of Peabody Donation Fund v Hay* (1987) 19 HLR 145, CA; *Southwark LBC v Joseph* March 2000 *Legal Action* 29; *Lewisham LBC v Gurbuz* [2003] EWHC 2078 (Ch).

exercise of the court's powers under CPR 3.1(2)(m) is the overriding objective. The overriding objective of the CPR is that of enabling the court to deal with cases justly.[9] CPR 1.1(2) provides:

> Dealing with a case justly includes, so far as practicable –
> (a) ensuring that the parties are on an equal footing;
> (b) saving expense;
> (c) dealing with the case in ways which are proportionate –
>   (i)   to the amount of money involved;
>   (ii) to the importance of the case;
>   (iii) to the complexity of the issues; and
>   (iv) to the financial position ;
> (d) ensuring that it is dealt with expeditiously and fairly; and
> (e) allotting to it an appropriate share of the court's resources, while taking into account the need to allot resources to other cases.

34.11   In the context of setting aside possession orders, the emphasis will usually be on the core principle itself, that of dealing with cases justly, rather than on procedural issues, though these may be relevant. Every effort should be made by way of witness statements and submissions, to relate the circumstances of the particular case to the overriding objective and to demonstrate how setting the possession order aside would promote that purpose of a just resolution.

34.12   Applications should be made on Form N244. The tenant must either give all necessary factual material in paragraph 10 on the application notice or (ideally) prepare a witness statement explaining why, if the court which made the order had known the full circumstances at the previous hearing (including any new evidence or later developments which might have been anticipated at that time), the outcome is likely to have been different.

34.13   Applications to set aside possession orders can be made even after execution has resulted in the eviction of the tenant.[10]

34.14   Non-service of the claim form is a ground for setting aside any possession order.[11] However, it should be remembered that posting to the tenant's 'usual or last known residence'[12] is good service, even if the tenant does not receive it. In *Nelson v Clearsprings (Management)*

---

9 CPR 1.1(1).

10 See *Governors of Peabody Donation Fund v Hay* (1987) 19 HLR 145, CA; *Grimshaw v Dunbar* [1953] 1 QB 408, CA; *Ladup Ltd v Siu* (1984) 81 LSG 283; (1983) *Times* 24 November, CA and *Tower Hamlets LBC v Abadie* (1990) 22 HLR 264.

11 *White v Weston* [1968] 2 QB 647; [1968] 2 WLR 1459; [1968] 2 All ER 842, but see *Akram v Adam* [2004] EWCA Civ 1601; [2005] 1 WLR 2782 and *Hackney LBC v Driscoll* [2003] EWCA Civ 1037.

12 CPR 6.5.

Limited,[13] a case decided under CPR 39.3 (para 34.7), as a result of the landlord's error in completing the claim form, the proceedings were posted to the property next door to the defendant's residence. The Court of Appeal held that, where a defendant had not been served with the claim form and had no knowledge of the proceedings, he or she would usually be entitled as of right to an order setting aside the judgment and for the costs of the application provided that he or she acts without undue delay on becoming aware of the judgment. On the other hand, if a claimant is served with an application to set aside a judgment in these circumstances, and believes he or she can show that the defendant has no real prospect of successfully defending the claim, then he or she may apply to the court for an order dispensing with service.

34.15   In possession proceedings against secure tenants, evidence that a local authority has failed to credit housing benefit and that, if this had been done, arrears would have been significantly lower at the time when the possession order was made should give good grounds for applying to set aside a possession order.

34.16   An application to set aside a possession order does not operate automatically as a stay of execution. If a warrant is likely to be executed before the hearing of the application to set aside, a stay of execution should be obtained pending the hearing (see para 34.47).

34.17   If a possession order is set aside, the effect is the same as if the order had never been made.[14] Usually the court will give directions about the filing of a defence and other procedural matters.

34.18   If the basis for the request to set aside an order is the availability of fresh evidence, the principles enumerated by Lord Denning in *Ladd v Marshall*[15] should be borne in mind:

> In order to justify the reception of fresh evidence for a new trial, three conditions must be fulfilled: first it must be shown that the evidence could not be obtained with reasonable diligence for use at the trial: second the evidence must be such that, if given, it would probably have an important influence on the result of the case, although it need not be decisive: third the evidence must be such as is presumably to be believed, or in other words, it must be apparently credible, although it need not be incontrovertible.

---

13 [2006] EWCA Civ 1252; [2007] 1 WLR 962.
14 See *Governors of Peabody Donation Fund v Hay* (1987) 19 HLR 145, CA and *Tower Hamlets LBC v Abadie* (1990) 22 HLR 264.
15 [1954] 3 All ER 745 at 748, CA.

34.19 Where a defendant is applying to set aside a possession order made on a discretionary ground for possession, it will often be advisable to include in the application notice an alternative application to vary the order and/or to suspend the warrant of possession (if one has been issued) on terms, in the event that the 'set aside' application is not successful.

Variation of orders

34.20 If tenants have no prospect of having a possession order set aside the court may have power to vary the order (for example, from an outright to a postponed or suspended order) or to suspend execution of the order. Where tenants enjoy statutory security of tenure and a possession order has been made under a discretionary ground, courts have wide powers to stay or suspend execution of any possession order or to postpone the date of possession (see chapter 33). Rent Act (RA) 1977 s100(2) gives such jurisdiction in the case of protected and statutory occupiers. Housing Act (HA) 1985 s85(2) applies to secure tenants while HA 1988 s9(2) gives similar rights to assured tenants. These powers can be exercised after the making of a possession order 'at any time *before the execution* of such an order', even if an absolute possession order was originally made[16] or if the original order was made by consent.[17] Such an application

> is not in any way affected or fettered by the reasons given by [the district judge who heard the possession claim] ... on such an application the district judge can take all relevant circumstances into account as they appear at the time of the application. Those will include any medical evidence which is before the court, any evidence as to the defendant's behaviour since the original order and the effect of an immediate order for possession which is not suspended upon the likelihood of the applicant being rehoused under the Housing Act 1996. ... There is a continuing remedy in the county court.[18]

16 *Plymouth CC v Hoskin* [2002] EWCA Civ 684; August 2002 *Legal Action* 32; 1 May 2002; *Payne v Cooper* [1958] 1 QB 174; [1957] 3 WLR 741; [1957] 3 All ER 335 and *Ujima Housing Association v Smith* October 2001 *Legal Action* 21, ChD, where the defendant was by the time of the application to suspend accepting her legal responsibility for serious damage to a shared kitchen and offering to pay £150 in compensation. This was a change of circumstances that justified suspension.

17 *Rossiter v Langley* [1925] 1 KB 741.

18 *Plymouth City Council v Hoskin* [2002] EWCA Civ 684; [2002] CP Rep 55; 1 May 2002.

34.21   However, in view of the words 'at any time before the execution of the order' in RA 1977 s100(2), HA 1985 s85(2) and HA 1988 s9(2), such an application cannot be granted if tenants have already given up possession without the need for execution of the order. The words 'at any time before the execution of the order' in section 85(2) have to be read subject to the qualification 'and for so long as execution is required to give effect to that order'.[19] Nor can such an application be used to obtain a complete rehearing of the case.[20] Where the court has made an absolute order under, for example, RA 1977 Sch 15 case 8 or case 9 (see paras 17.33 onwards), the power can be used to delay possession so that the tenant has more time to find other accommodation, but it cannot be used to delay indefinitely the date when possession should be given up, even if the circumstances of landlord and tenant have changed.[21]

34.22   It is possible for landlords to apply to 'convert' suspended or postponed possession orders obtained on one ground, such as rent arrears into absolute or outright possession orders where there have been other breaches of the tenancy such as anti-social behaviour. In *Manchester City Council v Finn*,[22] the Court of Appeal referred to the words 'at any time' in HA 1985 s85(2) and stated that a purposive construction has to be adopted. If a suspended order is still running, liberty to apply to the court is implicit, without the need to start new proceedings for possession. Courts can make a new order, even if the old order has not expired or if the new order would provide for possession to be given up forthwith. On such an application, the court has to bear in mind the guidance given in cases like *Sheffield City Council v Hopkins*[23] on the exercise of its discretion in such a situation, and should be astute to ensure that tenants are not taken by surprise. However, that does not necessarily extend to insisting that the proceedings be delayed by the equivalent of the extra time that would have been taken if the landlord had had to begin new proceedings. Courts can ensure that any notice of application gives the grounds and particulars which put the tenant to no greater disadvantage than envisaged by HA 1985 s84(3). Courts should determine any application to vary a possession order in exactly the same way as they would determine an original claim.

---

19 *Dunn v Bradford MDC, Marston v Leeds City Council* [2002] EWCA Civ 1137; [2003] HLR 15.
20 *Goldthorpe v Bain* [1952] 2 QB 455; [1952] 2 All ER 23 at 25.
21 *Goldthorpe v Bain* [1952] 2 QB 455; [1952] 2 All ER 23.
22 [2002] EWCA Civ 1998; [2003] HLR 41.
23 [2001] EWCA Civ 1023; [2002] HLR 12.

34.23 In view of the references to 'period or periods', it is clear that more than one application under HA 1988 s9(2), HA 1985 s85(2) or Rent Act 1977 s100(2) can be made.[24]

34.24 When postponing, suspending or staying possession orders against protected, statutory, assured or secure tenants, the court must impose conditions with regard to the repayment of arrears (if any), unless this would cause exceptional hardship or would otherwise be unreasonable.[25] Spouses and civil partners of tenants (who are not themselves joint tenants) have the same rights as the actual tenant to seek the suspension or postponement of orders until the making of a decree absolute of divorce or dissolution, provided that they are still living in the premises.[26]

34.25 The court has a comparable jurisdiction where other statutory safeguards apply. For example, where a lease has been forfeited, a lessee may apply for relief even after eviction,[27] provided that the application is made within six months of execution or the time when the landlord regained possession. In the case of mortgage borrowers Administration of Justice Act 1970 s36 provides that the court may stay or suspend execution or postpone the date for delivery of possession 'at any time before the execution of [the] judgment or order'. That power may be exercised only if 'it appears to the court that ... the mortgagor is likely to be able within a reasonable period to pay any sums due'.[28]

34.26 There is no statutory power to stay, suspend or postpone the making of a possession order where there is no security of tenure.[29]

34.27 The court has only very limited power to suspend or delay the date for giving possession where the order is made under a mandatory ground.[30] Where an order for possession is made under a mandatory ground, that ground should be stated on the face of the order.

---

24 *Sherrin v Brand* [1956] 1 QB 403; [1956] 1 All ER 194 at 204 per Birkett LJ; *Vandermolen v Toma* (1982–83) 9 HLR 91; *Westfield HA v Delin* 21 February 2002, Carlisle County Court and *Ealing LBC v Richardson* [2005] EWCA Civ 1798; [2006] HLR 13.

25 See, eg, HA 1988 s9(3).

26 See chapter 35.

27 Administration of Justice Act 1985 s55 (county court; cf *Di Palma v Victoria Square Property Co Ltd* [1986] Ch 150; [1985] 3 WLR 207, CA) or Common Law Procedure Act 1852 s210 (High Court).

28 See *Western Bank Ltd v Schindler* [1977] Ch 1; [1976] 3 WLR 341 and *Cheltenham and Gloucester BS v Norgan* [1996] 1 WLR 343; (1996) 28 HLR 443, CA. See, further, chapter 40.

29 See HA 1980 s89 (see para 33.1).

30 Eg, RA 1977 Sch 15 cases 11–19, HA 1985 Sch 2 grounds 9–11, HA 1988 Sch 2 grounds 1–8 and HA 1980 s89.

It is not proper to return to the judge at a later date to find out the grounds on which he made the order. Accordingly, where an order for possession made under one of those grounds fails to state the ground on the face of the order, it should be regarded as having been granted on uncertain grounds, leading to the assumption that the court had retained its discretion. In such circumstances, a court can revisit the exercise of discretion by the previous judge.[31]

34.28   An application to suspend or postpone possession should be made on either Form N244 or N245. It should be supported by evidence. This means that the tenant must either complete paragraph 10 of N244 as fully as possible or (ideally) prepare a witness statement dealing with all matters relied on.

Discharge of possession orders

34.29   Section 85(4) HA 1985 currently[32] provides:

> If the conditions [of a postponed or suspended order] are complied with, the court may, if it thinks fit, discharge or rescind the order for possession.

Section 9(4), in relation to assured tenancies, is in similar terms. Before the House of Lords' judgment in *Knowsley Housing Trust v White*,[33] case-law had insisted that the court's power to discharge or rescind an order was dependent on the defendant's absolute compliance with its terms, so that even a single breach would prevent the court from discharging the order.[34] Yet, under the Rent Act, the courts had accepted more general powers in relation to such orders.[35]

34.30   Since *Knowsley*, it is now clear that the court has a much wider discretion. Lord Neuberger, giving the judgment of the House, stated, in relation to section 85 of the 1985 Act:

> The section should be construed, as far as permissible, to confer as much flexibility as possible on the court, and in such a way as to minimise future uncertainty and need for further applications ... The wording of section 85(4), particularly if read with the practicalities in

---

31 *Diab v Countrywide Rentals 1 plc* (2001) *Independent* 5 November; 10 July 2001, unreported, ChD. See also *Capital Prime Plus plc v Wills* (1999) 31 HLR 926, CA.

32 See para 34.42 for the (as yet) unimplemented replacement of HA 1985 s85(4) and HA 1988 s9(4) by the Housing and Regeneration Act 2008.

33 [2008] UKHL 70; [2009] 1 AC 636.

34 See *Marshall v Bradford MDC* [2001] EWCA Civ 594; [2002] HLR 428 and *Swindon BC v Aston* [2002] EWCA Civ 1850; [2003] HLR 610.

35 *Sherrin v Brand* [1956] 1 QB 403; *Payne v Cooper* [1958] 1 QB 174.

mind, does not preclude the court from effectively committing itself in advance to discharging a suspended order, provided that (a) certain conditions are complied with, and (b) neither the landlord (by applying for a warrant of possession) nor the tenant (by applying under section 85(2)) seeks, in the meantime, reconsideration of the terms of the discharge provision.[36]

34.31 There is, accordingly, nothing to prevent the court from including a 'proleptic' discharge provision (ie, one that anticipates the discharge of the order in the event of compliance) in a postponed or suspended possession order. It is for the court to decide the extent to which compliance with the strict terms of the order will or will not be required for the order to be discharged.[37] In practice, the court is likely to make discharge conditional on full payment of the arrears and any other money due under the order, even though all payments under the order may not have been made on the due dates. It must follow that, where the order does not provide in advance for its own discharge, a tenant can apply to the court to discharge the order (under HA 1985 s85(4) or HA 1988 s9(4)) when the arrears have been paid off, on the basis that the court can decide that full payment represents compliance with the conditions of the order. Lord Neuberger also drew attention to the scope of the court's general powers of management under CPR Part 3:

> Quite apart from the wording of section 85(4), it appears to me that there is a strong argument for saying that, particularly with the advent of the CPR, it would in any event be open to a court to make an order which includes a provision that, in certain events, the order would automatically be discharged ... In this connection, it appears to me that CPR 3.1(2)(a) may be particularly in point.[38]

34.32 The Housing and Regeneration Act 2008[39] proposes to replace section 85(4) by the following provision:

> (4) The court may discharge or rescind the order for possession if it thinks it appropriate to do so having had regard to –
> (a) any conditions imposed under subsection (3), and
> (b) the conduct of the tenant in connection with those conditions.

The Act contains a similar re-enactment of HA 1988 s9(4). However, neither of these substitutions has yet been brought into force since, following the judgment in *Knowsley Housing Trust v White*, the

---

36 *Knowsley Housing Trust v White* [2008] UKHL 70; [2009] 1 AC 636 at para 97.
37 *Knowsley Housing Trust v White* [2008] UKHL 70 para 107.
38 *Knowsley Housing Trust v White* [2008] UKHL 70 para 100.
39 Sch 11 para 3(3); see also Sch 11 para 8(3) in relation to the proposed replacement of HA 1988 s9(4).

government considered that the courts have sufficiently wide powers under the existing provisions.

34.33   The courts' powers to vary or discharge possession orders were critical at a time (prior to 20 May 2009, the date of implementation of the Housing and Regeneration Act 2008 Sch 11) when tenants who became 'tolerated trespassers' could revive their tenancies by one of these means.[40] Although the tolerated trespasser is no more, and secure and assured tenancies do not end until execution of the possession order, there is still a purpose in seeking to discharge an order, since otherwise if new arrears accrue, the same order may continue to have effect. An alternative to discharge, however, is for an order to contain a provision such as the following:

> This order shall cease to be enforceable when the total judgment debt is satisfied.

34.34   The above clause appears in the standard court form N28A (postponed possession order). It does not appear in the standard suspended possession order (court form N28), but the court may be willing to add such a term to the order if requested to do so. CPR 4 provides that 'a form may be varied by the court or a party if the variation is required by the circumstances of a particular case'.

Execution of a warrant for possession

34.35   If a tenant fails to give up possession as required by an absolute order, the landlord's usual remedy is to apply for a warrant of possession.[41] In the county court, landlords follow the same procedure if they wish to enforce a suspended order for possession on a tenant's failure to comply with the terms of that order. An application for a warrant of possession is made by the landlord completing county court form N325.[42] A warrant cannot be issued before the date on

---

40   See para 33.15.

41   CCR Ord 26 r17.

42   Note that the form must be properly completed. Failure to specify the amount of arrears currently outstanding may lead to the request for the warrant being refused or, if a warrant has been issued, to the warrant being set aside: CCR Ord 26 r17(3A); *Westminster City Council v Mbah* June 1995 *Legal Action* 19; *South London Housing Association v Raxworthy* March 1996 *Legal Action* 11 (following *Hackney LBC v White* (1995) 28 HLR 219, CA); *Lambeth LBC v Johnson* December 1996 *Legal Action* 14 and *Westminster CC v Thomas* March 1997 *Legal Action* 12, but cf *Tower Hamlets LBC v Azad* (1998) 30 HLR 241, CA and *Abbey National v Gibson* September 1997 *Legal Action* 15, CA.

which it is ordered that possession be given. If a warrant is issued in such circumstances, it is a nullity.[43]

34.36 A landlord cannot enforce a suspended possession order, if a tenant fails to comply with the terms of the suspension or postponement, without making an application for a warrant,[44] but (unless the original order specified that no warrant was to be issued without the permission of the court) a warrant in the county court is issued without any prior notice to the tenant and without a hearing.[45] In this respect the county court procedure differs from that in the High Court, where leave to issue execution on a suspended order for possession on the grounds of an alleged breach of the terms of that order must not be given without allowing a tenant the opportunity to be heard.[46]

34.37 Tenants who fail to comply with possession orders theoretically commit a contempt of court. In extreme or exceptional cases landlords may apply to the court for penal notices to be attached to possession orders and, after re-service, apply to commit former tenants who still refuse to give up possession to prison for contempt of court.[47]

34.38 Although tenants are not notified in advance of landlords' applications for warrants of possession in the county court, the bailiffs should notify occupiers of the time and date when they propose to call to evict them, using form N54.

Warrants and the European Convention on Human Rights

34.39 It has been suggested that the failure of either the County Court Rules (CCR) or the CPR to provide automatic notification to a tenant of an application to issue a warrant for possession is a breach of articles 6 and 8 of the European Convention on Human Rights (ECHR/'the Convention') and article 1 of the First Protocol to the

---

43 *Tuohy v Bell* [2002] EWCA Civ 423; [2002] 1 WLR 2703.

44 *R v Ilkeston County Court ex p Kruza* (1985) 17 HLR 539 and *Hasan Hanif v Robinson* (1994) 26 HLR 386, CA, and CCR Ord 26 r17(1).

45 See, further, in relation to arguments in favour of the use of the N28A postponed possession order, para 33.34.

46 RSC Ords 45 and 46. See *Fleet Mortgage and Investment Co Ltd v Lower Maisonette 46 Eaton Place Ltd* [1972] 2 All ER 737; *Practice Direction* [1972] 1 WLR 765; [1972] 1 All ER 576; *Civil Procedure 2010*, Vol 1 para sc46.4.1. For criticism of the county court procedure, see comments by the Court of Appeal in *Leicester CC v Aldwinkle* (1992) 24 HLR 49, CA.

47 *Tuohy v Bell* [2002] EWCA Civ 423; [2002] 1 WLR 2703 and *De Grey v Ford* [2005] EWCA Civ 1223 and *Trustee in Bankruptcy of Canty v Canty* [2007] EWCA Civ 241.

Convention. Enforcement proceedings are certainly within the ambit of article 6.[48] The European Court of Human Rights has stated, albeit in a case involving rather different issues, that applicants are

> entitled to expect a coherent system that would achieve a fair balance between the authorities' interests and [their] own; in particular, [they] should have ... a clear, practical and effective opportunity to challenge an administrative act that was a direct interference with [any] right of property.[49]

34.40   It is also arguable that the absence of any requirement that the tenant be given notice of an application to issue a warrant deprives him or her of a fair hearing within the meaning of article 6. That may not be significant if the warrant is issued shortly after a possession hearing and there has been no change of circumstances. However, if many years have passed, there are often changed circumstances which are relevant. Similar arguments apply in relation to article 8 and article 1 of the First Protocol. They might be bolstered by reliance on article 14.[50] There is no apparent justification for the discrepancy between Rules of the Supreme Court (RSC) Ord 45 r3, RSC Ord 46 r3 and CCR Ord 26 r1(4), on the one hand, and CCR Ord 26 r17, on the other hand.

34.41   However, the Court of Appeal has held that the procedure which allows the issue of a warrant of possession and the arrangements for execution following breach of a suspended possession order do not infringe tenants' rights under article 6, 8 or 14. Tenants' rights to possession of premises are determined when suspended possession orders are made. The issue of the warrant of possession is simply a step authorised to be taken to enforce that order. It does not alter the legal status of the tenant or make any kind of decision in relation to his or her rights, and so is not required to be the subject of a separate hearing. Furthermore, although possession proceedings may inter-fere with tenants' right of respect for their homes, they are clearly in accordance with the law and are a legitimate and proportionate response to non-payment of rent.[51]

34.42   Bailiffs must deliver Form N54 (Notice of Eviction) to all addresses where evictions are due to take place and hand it to the defendant personally or leave it at the property in an envelope addressed to the

---

48 See, eg, *Immobiliare Saffi v Italy* (2000) 30 EHRR 756, ECtHR.

49 *De La Pradelle v France* (1992) A 253-B.

50 *Larkos v Cyprus* (1999) 7 BHRC 244.

51 *Southwark LBC v St Brice* [2001] EWCA Civ 1138; [2002] 1 WLR 1537; [2002] HLR 26.

defendant(s) by name and 'any other occupiers'. The notice points out that in some circumstances the court can decide to suspend the warrant and explains the procedure to be followed.

Effect of a warrant

34.43 When the bailiffs come to execute a county court warrant, or the sheriffs execute a High Court warrant, they can evict anyone they find on the premises, even if they were not a party to the possession proceedings or moved in after the possession order was made.[52] The only remedy for someone in the premises who was not a party to possession proceedings is to apply to be joined to the action and to set aside the order for possession. Obviously, such a course of action is likely to be successful only if there would have been a defence to the proceedings which has a real prospect of success.

34.44 At common law anyone entitled to possession, or anyone acting on his or her behalf, was entitled to use reasonable force to eject a trespasser.[53] While tenants with statutory security do not become trespassers when the date for possession in the order has passed, bailiffs are entitled to use reasonable force to execute the warrant.[54]

34.45 Permission to issue a warrant is required if six years have elapsed since the making of the possession order.[55] Applications for permission are normally made without notice with a witness statement in support, although the court may direct that the application should be served and heard on notice. Failure to obtain permission is an abuse of process and any warrant obtained in such circumstances should be set aside.[56]

34.46 A county court or High Court warrant can be executed at any time within one year after it has been issued. If landlords want to rely on a warrant after that period an application must be made for it to be renewed.[57] For a discussion of warrants for possession in mortgage actions, see chapter 42.

---

52 *R v Wandsworth County Court ex p Wandsworth LBC* [1975] 3 All ER 390.
53 *McPhail v Persons Unknown* [1973] Ch 447; [1973] 3 WLR 71, CA.
54 For a case in which the Court of Appeal held that an occupier may authorise the police to evict a trespasser, see *Porter v Commissioner of Police of the Metropolis* 20 October 1999, unreported, CA. See also dictum of Cockburn CJ in *R v Roxburgh* (1871) 12 Cox CC 8.
55 CCR Ord 26 rr5 and 17(6) and RSC Ord 46 r2.
56 *Hackney LBC v White* (1996) 28 HLR 219, CA.
57 County Courts Act 1984 s111(2), CCR Ord 26 rr6 and 17.

Staying and suspending warrants

34.47   The mere fact that an application has been made to set aside a possession order or to suspend its operation does not automatically prevent a court from enforcing a warrant for possession. In some courts bailiffs may agree not to evict if an application to set aside or suspend a possession order has been made, although as a matter of law a landlord may insist on the execution of a warrant unless a judge has ordered a stay. In the absence of clear written confirmation from the landlord or the court that a warrant will not be executed, tenants should apply to stay the warrant if eviction is likely to take place before the hearing of the application to set aside or suspend the order. CPR 3.1(2)(f) gives the court jurisdiction to stay execution. In addition County Courts Act 1984 s88 provides that:

> If at any time it appears to the satisfaction of the court that any party to any proceedings is unable from any cause to pay any sum recovered against him ... or any instalment of such a sum, the court may, in its discretion, stay any execution issued in the proceedings for such time and on such terms as the court thinks fit, and so from time to time until it appears that the cause of inability has ceased.

34.48   CCR Ord 25 r8 provides that the power to stay execution of a warrant may be exercised by a district judge, or, in some circumstances, by a proper officer of the court. Generally applications to suspend warrants for possession are heard by district judges. Form N245 is designed for such an application, but in practice Form N244 is often used with a witness statement in support.

34.49   In accordance with the usual procedure governing applications, an application for a stay should be made on at least three days' notice to the landlord, unless it is particularly urgent (for example, the warrant is about to be executed). In general, if possible, it is better for time to be abridged under CPR 3.1(2)(a), allowing short notice to the landlord, than for the application to be made without notice.

34.50   If there is a substantial dispute over the amount of rent claimed to be owing and the tenant's compliance with the order, the application should be adjourned so that the up-to-date position can be established.[58] One cause of tenants' failures to comply with the financial provisions of suspended or postponed orders may be delays in receiving housing benefit. Where the tenant has provided all the information necessary to enable the claim for housing benefit to be

58   *Haringey LBC v Powell* (1996) 28 HLR 798, CA.

determined, it may be that the service of a witness summons[59] on a senior official responsible for administering the scheme (in the local authority) compelling him or her to attend at the application and to explain the cause of the delay will not only be of assistance in making the application, but will also cause any benefit due to be paid rather rapidly.

34.51　The court exercising its discretion to stay, suspend or postpone the date for possession under RA 1977 s100(2), HA 1985 s85 or HA 1988 s9(2) may, subject to the necessary procedural safeguards, take account of matters (for example, breaches of the terms of the tenancy agreement or anti-social behaviour) other than those relied on as grounds for making the original possession order.[60] There is no limit to the number of applications that can be made to suspend a warrant.[61] While not attempting to fetter the discretion of district judges, the Court of Appeal has stated[62] that the following points are relevant:

- The discretion should be used so as to further the policy of the legislation, reinforced by ECHR article 8. The policy is to evict only after a serious breach of an obligation, where it is reasonable to do so, and where the tenant is proved to have breached any condition of suspension.

- The overriding objective of the CPR, especially the need for applications to be dealt with in a summary and proportionate way, means that it may not be possible to deal with wider issues on an application to suspend or vary. They may need to be dealt with in some other way.

- The tenant should have clear evidence of what is alleged, especially where the allegations were not contained in the original proceedings.

- The fact that the landlord had or had not included the allegations as part of the original proceedings is relevant.

- The discretion to consider other allegations should generally be exercised more readily in respect of matters occurring after commencement of the proceedings.

59　CPR 34.3.
60　*Sheffield City Council v Hopkins* [2001] EWCA Civ 1023; [2002] HLR 12. Cf *Hammersmith and Fulham LBC v Brown* [2000] 5 CL 350 and *Islington LBC v Reeves* [1997] CLY 2715.
61　In *Ealing LBC v Richardson* [2005] EWCA Civ 1798; [2006] HLR 13, the tenant succeeded in a further application after eight previous applications to suspend warrants.
62　*Sheffield CC v Hopkins* [2001] EWCA Civ 1023; [2002] HLR 12.

- The court should also consider the practicalities of dealing with matters on the execution of a warrant.
- The fact that the tenant is at the mercy of the court and the responsibilities of a public landlord to its other tenants.

34.52   The list is not exhaustive. District judges have to exercise their discretion, bearing in mind the importance of the issue to the tenant, at risk of losing his or her home, and the responsibilities of social landlords to their other tenants. However, it would appear that the court cannot take into account allegations which have not been proved or admitted by the tenant.

34.53   Tenants outside the protection of the Rent Act 1977, the Housing Act 1985 and the Housing Act 1988 cannot apply to suspend the execution of a warrant for possession once it has been issued.[63]

After eviction

34.54   If execution has taken place, former tenants are unable to rely on the county court's general powers to suspend or stay judgments or orders[64] or to extend time or to allow for payment by instalments.[65]

34.55   Similarly, once eviction has taken place, the court no longer has any power to stay, suspend or set aside a warrant under RA 1977 s100(2), HA 1985 s85(2) or HA 1988 s9(2), since those powers are expressly limited by the words 'at any time before the execution of the order'.[66] An application to set aside a warrant in these circumstances can only succeed if the possession order itself is set aside (see above), the warrant has been obtained by fraud or there has been an abuse of process or oppression in its execution. In *Hammersmith and Fulham LBC v Hill*,[67] the Court of Appeal held that there was an arguable case of oppression where representations by a housing officer deterred

---

63   HA 1980 s89.
64   County Courts Act 1984 s71.
65   CPR 3.1(2)(a) and (f). See *Moore v Registrar of Lambeth County Court* [1969] 1 All ER 782.
66   See *Scott-James v Bass Chehab* [1988] 41 EG 75, CA; *Leicester City Council v Aldwinkle* (1991) 24 HLR 49, CA; *Hammersmith and Fulham LBC v Hill* (1994) 27 HLR 368; [1994] 35 EG 124, CA and *Tower Hamlets LBC v Azad* (1998) 30 HLR 241, CA, but cf *Islington LBC v Harridge* (1993) *Times* 30 June, CA, where it was held that an application was 'made' on the day before eviction when the application was lodged with the court and accordingly the court had power to hear it even though eviction had taken place prior to the hearing.
67   (1995) 27 HLR 368.

the tenant from seeking legal help or advice or otherwise making an application to stay the warrant before execution.[68]

34.56 The Court of Appeal has stated that:

[O]ppression may be very difficult if not impossible to define, but it is not difficult to recognise. It is the insistence by a public authority on its strict rights in circumstances which make that insistence manifestly unfair. The categories of oppression are not closed because no-one can envisage all the sets of circumstances which could make the execution of a warrant oppressive.[69]

34.57 Recent years have seen a number of cases in which courts have decided what amounts to and what does not amount to 'oppression'. For example, in *Saint v Barking and Dagenham LBC*,[70] a secure tenant failed to comply with the terms of a suspended possession order during a short period while he was held on remand in custody. Although he notified the council about his detention and whereabouts, without notice to him, the council applied for a warrant which was executed during his absence. The Court of Appeal set aside the warrant and directed his reinstatement. Peter Gibson LJ held that the conduct of the council in obtaining and executing the warrant had, in the circumstances, been 'oppressive'. First, the council had been under a duty 'promptly' to invite the applicant to renew his claim for housing benefit. That obligation required the council to send the renewal form to an address where it was likely to come to the applicant's attention (ie, his prison address). The council was relying on its own wrong-doing in obtaining the warrant to the extent that non-payment of housing benefit had caused the suspended order to be breached. Second, before the applicant's arrest his level of arrears had fallen below the level required to comply with the suspended

---

68 See also *Hackney LBC v Gabriel* December 1994 *Legal Action* 14 (warrant executed more than a year after issue); *Lewisham LBC v Clarke* December 1994 *Legal Action* 14 (where the council had misrepresented correspondence from the DSS which had affected payment of housing benefit); *Greenwich LBC v Minnican* December 1994 *Legal Action* 14 (local authority failed to arrange direct deductions from income support payments, as envisaged when the suspended possession order was made); *Haringey LBC v Innocent* June 1995 *Legal Action* 19 (bailiffs executing warrant gained entry to the former secure tenant's home but tenant re-entered using her back door key and resumed possession; held: the warrant had not been executed and the court still had power to stay or suspend the warrant) and *Westminster CC v Mbah* June 1995 *Legal Action* 19 (warrant set aside because application failed to state the amount of money remaining due (CCR Ord 26 r17(3A)).

69 *Southwark LBC v Sarfo* (2000) 32 HLR 602 at 609, CA, per Roch LJ.

70 (1999) 31 HLR 620, CA.

order and when the warrant was applied for his outstanding debt was small (£336). In these circumstances, if he had been given an opportunity to apply to suspend the warrant of possession he should have succeeded.

34.58   Other examples of oppressive behaviour have included:

- Continuing with execution of a warrant even though the tenant had paid the full amount of the arrears to the housing officer who attended with the bailiffs to execute the warrant.[71]
- Execution of a warrant when the tenant was entitled to conclude that no further step would be taken until her housing benefit applications had been decided, against a background of maladministration that had been manifestly unfair.[72]
- A housing officer not telling the defendant that a warrant had been applied for, even though the tenant had said that she was going abroad and had paid court costs and provided evidence of the renewal of her housing benefit claim.[73]
- Eviction of a tenant amounted to oppression after (a) a letter claiming that the defendant was behind with his payments under the court order when he was in fact ahead of schedule; (b) the issue of a warrant of possession one day before the expiry of the time allowed for the defendant to produce documents in support of his claim for housing benefit; (c) the issue of a warrant for possession at a time when the arrears which had accrued on the account were simply the result of an administrative decision to suspend the defendant's housing benefit; and (d) the failure to inform the defendant of his right to apply under section 85(2) at the time when the warrant was applied for.[74]
- Eviction of a tenant who was making irregular payments towards the arrears, which stood at £274. The council had failed to have regard to its own rent arrears policy requiring it to use eviction only as a last resort. In particular, it had failed to consider applying for an attachment of earnings order against the tenant, who was in work.[75]

34.59   In some circumstances misleading information from a third party, such as a member of court staff, which deprives a tenant of the chance

---

71 *East Staffs BC v Brady* January 1999 *Legal Action* 26.
72 *Southwark LBC v Sarfo* (2000) 32 HLR 602, CA.
73 *William Sutton HT v Breen* March 2000 *Legal Action* 29.
74 *Barking and Dagenham LBC v Marquis* October 2002 *Legal Action* 28, Ilford County Court.
75 *Southwark LBC v Augustus* February 2007 *Legal Action* 29, Lambeth County Court.

of taking steps to have execution of a warrant for possession stayed prior to execution may equally amount to oppression, thereby entitling the court to set aside execution of the warrant.[76]

34.60   On the other hand, in *Jephson Homes Housing Association v Moisejevs*,[77] the Court of Appeal decided that, if a possession warrant is obtained and executed against a secure tenant without fault on anyone's part, it cannot properly be set aside as oppressive or an abuse of process. Oppression cannot exist without the unfair use of court procedures. Something more than the mere use of the eviction process – that is, some action on someone's part which was open to criticism – is required before the court's procedures can be said to have been unfairly used. An eviction cannot be regarded as oppressive or abusive merely because it is appreciated after the event that the tenant might have applied to stay or suspend execution of the warrant. There is no requirement that a tenant should be given notice of a request for the issue of a possession warrant in all cases.[78] The absence of such a provision in the CCR was noted in *Peachey Property Corp Ltd v Robinson*.[79] There have been two new sets of rules since then, without any such requirement being thought necessary. However, cases may arise when the landlord can properly be held to have acted oppressively if the tenant never received any notice whatever of the impending eviction.

34.61   Other examples where it has been held that execution of a warrant has *not* been oppressive include cases where:

• Shortly before the council made an application for a warrant the tenant took a lump sum of £400 to the council. A housing officer received it with the words 'that will do for now'. The tenant took no further step and made no further payment because he thought that the council would be in touch with him. The court found it 'difficult to believe' in all the circumstances that the tenant had genuinely formed the belief that he had simply to wait for the council to contact him. The judge preferred the evidence of the

76 *Hammersmith and Fulham LBC v Lemeh* (2001) 33 HLR 231; [2001] L&TR 423, CA (tenant who attended court to apply for suspension wrongly told by court staff that there was no warrant) and *Lambeth LBC v Hughes* (2001) 33 HLR 350, CA (council wrote to the defendant stating that the only way to stop eviction would be to pay all the arrears in full; bailiff's letter giving date of eviction sent by second-class post arrived as the eviction was taking place).

77 [2001] 2 All ER 901; (2001) 33 HLR 594; [2001] 41 EG 186; (2001) *Times* 2 January; [2000] EGCS 123, CA. See too *Circle 33 Housing Trust v Ellis* [2005] EWCA Civ 1233; [2006] HLR 7.

78 But see form N54, referred to at para 34.38.

79 [1967] 2 QB 543; [1966] 2 WLR 1386.

housing officer and rejected the allegation of 'oppressive' conduct. The Court of Appeal dismissed the tenant's appeal.[80]

- There was a dispute over housing benefit. The tenant had a poor rent record and there had been substantial non-compliance with a possession order.[81]

Warrants of restitution

34.62   Sometimes, particularly in squatting cases, occupiers move into premises after a warrant has been executed or the landlord has in some other way regained possession in accordance with the provisions of an order for possession. Unless there is some connection between the new occupiers and the people who were originally evicted, the landlord cannot apply for a further warrant in the same proceedings, but must issue further proceedings for possession. Once an order has been executed the proceedings are over and cannot be reactivated.[82]

34.63   The position is different if there is a 'close nexus' between the new occupiers and any people who were dispossessed in earlier proceedings. If the further occupation is 'part and parcel of the same transaction'[83] the landlord is entitled to apply without notice for a warrant of restitution in the county court or a writ of restitution in the High Court.[84] The effect of a warrant of restitution is to enable the bailiff or sheriff to evict any person in unlawful occupation of premises again without the landowner having to issue new proceedings. A warrant of restitution may be issued even though not all of the new occupiers of the land were among the original defendants.[85] It is theoretically possible for a landowner to apply to court to commit for contempt a person who has re-entered premises unlawfully after an earlier eviction, but such an order should be made in only the most exceptional circumstances.[86]

---

80   *Camden LBC v Akanni* (1997) 29 HLR 845, CA.

81   *Hackney LBC v Asik* March 2000 *Legal Action* 29, CA.

82   *Thomas v Metropolitan Housing Corp* [1936] 1 All ER 210; *Ratcliffe v Tait* (1664) 1 Keble 216; *Lovelace v Ratcliffe* (1664) 1 Keble 785; *Doe d Pait v Roe* (1807) 1 Taunton 55; *Clissold v Cratchley* [1910] 2 KB 244 and *Brighton BC v Persons Unknown* June 1991 *Legal Action* 13.

83   *Wiltshire CC v Frazer (No 2)* [1986] 1 WLR 109; [1986] 1 All ER 65 per Simon Brown J.

84   CCR Ord 26 r17(4) and RSC Ord 46 r3.

85   *Wiltshire CC v Frazer (No 2)* [1986] 1 WLR 109; [1986] 1 All ER 65.

86   *Alliance Building Society v Austen* [1951] 2 All ER 1068, where such an order was in fact granted.

CHAPTER 35

Domestic relationship breakdown in a rented home

Introduction

35.1   This chapter outlines briefly the steps which may be taken to maintain occupation of the family home where there has been a breakdown of the domestic relationship between the adult occupiers – most commonly between spouses or other cohabitants – and the home is rented. (For the parallel position on relationship breakdown where the family home is held on a mortgage, see chapter 44.) These few pages are only intended to highlight some of the issues.

35.2   Often a crisis in relation to occupation of the rented home (for example, the service of possession proceedings) arises at the same time as, or shortly after, a breakdown in the domestic relationship between occupiers. For example, as a result of the relationship breakdown one partner may have moved out, jeopardising security of tenure and/or leaving the other facing financial difficulties in paying the rent, which will put the home at risk.

35.3   Where the landlord has not yet threatened possession proceedings there is usually time to get advice about immediate entitlement to remain in the home and any rights to obtain a transfer of the tenancy. Where very urgent action is needed (for example, to prevent violence or to prevent the loss of the tenancy), the client should be immediately directed to a source of specialist advice on family law.

Preserving the tenancy[1]

35.4   The following paragraphs are concerned with the situation in which not only has the relationship broken down but also one of the partners has *left* the family home.

Sole tenant in occupation

35.5   If the partner remaining in the family home is the sole tenant there should be little difficulty in preserving the home until the issues arising from the relationship breakdown are resolved. Where the breakdown of the relationship has caused financial difficulties this may trigger entitlement for the tenant to housing benefit or to higher payments of such benefit. If, however, possession proceedings are

---

1   See Conway, 'Protecting tenancies on marriage breakdown' [2001] Fam Law 208 and Da Costa, 'Keeping alive the tenancy in the matrimonial home' [1995] Fam Law 622.

threatened or have been launched, the appropriate chapters of this book should assist in avoiding dispossession.

Sole tenant has left

35.6   In this scenario there are twin concerns for the partner remaining in possession. The first is to prevent the departed tenant from ending the tenancy. The second is to ensure that the tenancy retains any security of tenure and survives any possession proceedings brought by the landlord. In the longer term, once those matters have been addressed, the partner remaining may seek to have the tenancy transferred into his or her sole name as part of the legal arrangements made to resolve the consequences of the relationship breakdown.

35.7   If the remaining occupier is a *spouse* or *civil partner* of the sole tenant he or she enjoys legal rights of occupation (and associated benefits) by virtue of the 'home rights' conferred by the Family Law Act 1996 s30 for as long as the marriage or civil partnership lasts. Any question of occupation thereafter should be addressed in the legal proceedings to end the marriage or partnership.

35.8   The *cohabitant* of the departed tenant who remains in occupation, by contrast, has no such automatic rights to continue to occupy the home but can apply to the court for an 'occupation order' under the Family Law Act 1996 s36. If granted, that confers rights equivalent to the home rights enjoyed by a spouse or civil partner.[2]

35.9   If there is any risk that the departed sole tenant may end the tenancy without other arrangements being in place for the continued occupation of the former family home, the non-tenant partner may need to move very quickly to obtain a court order to prevent the tenant from either giving notice to quit or surrendering the tenancy. Such a pre-emptive injunction is – for obvious reasons – usually sought without notice to the tenant until after the injunction is granted. Where the partners are married, the family court has jurisdiction to grant such an injunction under the Matrimonial Causes Act 1973 s37(2)(a). Where the partners are unmarried, the jurisdiction will be based on the court's power to grant interim relief in proceedings under the Family Law Act 1996 or the Children Act 1989 (brought to obtain an occupation order or to achieve a transfer of the tenancy from the tenant partner).[3]

2   *Gay v Enfield LBC* [2000] 1 WLR 673; [1999] 3 All ER 795, CA.
3   *Greenwich LBC v Bater* [1999] 4 All ER 944; [1999] 2 FLR 993, CA and *Re F (Minors)* [1994] 1 WLR 370; (1993) 26 HLR 354, CA.

35.10   If no such protection is obtained from the court, the sole tenant could simply end the tenancy by giving notice to quit or by agreeing a surrender with the landlord (although the latter would be unusual as the presence of the former partner will prevent the tenant giving vacant possession).[4] This may happen very fast – for example, because the landlord is prepared to waive any requirements as to length or formality of the notice to quit.[5] Once the tenancy has been ended it will plainly not be available for the purpose of being transferred from one partner to the other. It will also be too late for even a spouse or civil partner to set aside the termination of the tenancy.[6] The owner would be able to seek possession against the remaining former partner as a trespasser.

35.11   If the departed tenant's tenancy is continuing, the remaining partner needs to ensure that the tenancy is safeguarded until other arrangements can be made. For example, if the tenant's rent is not being paid, the remaining partner could pay it. If the remaining partner is a spouse or civil partner, any payments he or she makes are treated by law as though they had been made by the tenant and must be accepted as such.[7] Likewise, a payment of rent made by a cohabitant with an occupation order is treated as being made by the tenant.[8] Housing benefit may be claimed by the occupying partner if the person legally liable to pay for the family home is not paying.[9]

35.12   Although the sole tenant is not physically present, the continued occupation by the former partner may operate to preserve any security of tenure the tenant enjoyed. Where the remaining occupier is the tenant's spouse or civil partner, his or her own occupation is deemed to be occupation by the tenant for the purposes of preserving security of tenure as a protected, assured, secure, demoted or introductory tenant.[10] The same 'deemed occupation' arises if the remaining partner is a cohabitant who has successfully applied for an occupation order.[11]

---

4   But see *Sanctuary Housing Association v Campbell* [1999] 1 WLR 1279; (2000) 32 HLR 100, CA.

5   *Hackney LBC v Snowden* (2001) 33 HLR 554; [2001] L&TR 6, CA.

6   *Harrow LBC v Johnstone* [1997] 1 WLR 459; (1997) 29 HLR 475, HL and *Newlon Housing Association v Al-Sulaimen* [1999] 1 AC 313; [1998] 4 All ER 1; (1998) 30 HLR 1132, HL.

7   Family Law Act 1996 s30(3).

8   Family Law Act 1996 s36(13).

9   Housing Benefit Regulations 2006 SI No 213 reg 8.

10   Family Law Act 1996 s30(4).

11   Family Law Act 1996 s36(13).

35.13   The remaining partner may also have to intervene in any possession proceedings taken against the sole tenant in order to preserve
the home.

35.14   If those possession proceedings are based on the proposition that
any security of tenure has been lost by failure of the sole tenant – who
has left – to occupy the premises as his or her home, the remaining
partner may be able to defend successfully on the basis that there
is continuing deemed occupation by a spouse or civil partner with
home rights or by a cohabitant with an occupation order (see para
35.8).

35.15   If the possession proceedings are based on one of the grounds
for possession which requires the court to be satisfied that suitable
alternative accommodation is available, this may involve (consequent
on a relationship breakdown) the provision of separate units of housing for the tenant and his or her partner. Any spouse, civil partner or
cohabitant anxious that he or she should be adequately housed if possession is ordered against the tenant in these circumstances should
apply to be joined as a party to the proceedings.[12]

Joint tenant remaining in occupation[13]

35.16   The first priority for the joint tenant who remains in occupation of a
family home held on a joint tenancy is to ensure that the other joint
tenant does not bring the joint tenancy to an end. Although the other
joint tenant, acting alone, cannot end the joint tenancy by means
of a surrender, a joint tenancy can be ended by that tenant giving
the landlord a notice to quit. The other joint tenant need not even
inform or consult the one in occupation before giving such notice.[14]
The effect of a valid notice to quit is to bring the whole joint tenancy
to an end,[15] which obviously leaves the former partner in occupation
as a trespasser and entitles the landlord to possession.[16] See chapter 26 on whether article 8 of the European Convention on Human
Rights might provide protection to the former partner remaining in
occupation.

35.17   If there is any risk that the departed joint tenant may end the
tenancy without other arrangements being in place for the continued

---

12 *Wandsworth LBC v Fadayomi* [1987] 1 WLR 1473; [1987] 3 All ER 474, CA.
13 Jenrick and Bretherton, 'Joint tenancies: continuing implications for housing
    and family law' [2000] JHL 8.
14 *Notting Hill Housing Trust v Brackley* [2001] EWCA Civ 601; [2002] HLR 10, CA.
15 *Hammersmith and Fulham LBC v Monk* [1992] 1 AC 478; [1990] 3 WLR 1144, HL.
16 *Greenwich LBC v McGrady* (1983) 81 LGR 288; (1983) 46 P&CR 223, CA.

occupation of the former family home, the joint-tenant partner may need to move very quickly to obtain a court order to prevent the other joint tenant from giving notice to quit. Such a pre-emptive injunction is – for obvious reasons – usually sought without notice to the other joint tenant until after the injunction is granted. Where the partners are married, the family court has jurisdiction to grant such an injunction under the Matrimonial Causes Act 1973 s37(2)(a). Where the partners are unmarried, the jurisdiction may be based on the court's power to grant interim relief in proceedings under the Family Law Act 1996 or the Children Act 1989 (brought to obtain an occupation order or to achieve a transfer of the tenancy from joint to sole names).[17]

35.18   If a joint tenant has already given a notice to quit, it should be checked for validity. A notice not complying with the relevant contractual or statutory requirements is not effective to terminate the tenancy (because the agreement of all joint tenants is needed to waive any defect).[18] If it is a valid notice, it terminates the tenancy and cannot be set aside, even in matrimonial proceedings.[19] See para 14.6 onwards for further discussion concerning the validity of notices to quit.

35.19   Of course, if the landlord is prepared to grant the remaining party a new sole tenancy with equivalent security of tenure, there is no difficulty caused by either partner giving notice to quit.

35.20   It may be possible for the two joint tenants to 'regularise' matters either by the departed tenant completing a deed of release or by both joint tenants assigning the tenancy into the sole name of one of them. In either case, the remaining joint tenant becomes the sole tenant. However, these options may not be available in respect of some tenancies. There have been particular difficulties with secure joint tenancies in this regard.[20]

35.21   If the departing joint tenant fails to make any contribution towards the rent, the remaining joint tenant may obtain assistance from the housing benefit scheme both towards his or her own 'share' of the rent and towards the share of the former partner (see chapter 37).

---

17 *Greenwich LBC v Bater* [1999] 4 All ER 944; [1999] 2 FLR 993, CA.

18 *Hounslow LBC v Pilling* [1993] 1 WLR 1242; (1993) 25 HLR 305, CA.

19 *Harrow LBC v Johnstone* [1997] 1 WLR 459; (1997) 29 HLR 475, HL and *Newlon Housing Association v Al-Sulaimen* [1999] 1 AC 313; [1998] 4 All ER 1; (1998) 30 HLR 1132, HL.

20 *Burton v Camden LBC* [2000] 2 AC 399; [2000] 2 WLR 427, HL and Blandy, 'Secure Tenancies and Relationship Breakdown Revisited' [2000] JHL 47.

35.22　The joint tenant may rely on his or her own occupation as meeting any necessary conditions of residence for retention of security of tenure (for example, the continued occupation by one of several joint secure tenants maintains the 'security of tenure' of a secure or assured tenancy).[21]

35.23　In any possession proceedings, the joint tenant may defend in just the same way as a sole tenant.

Transferring the tenancy[22]

35.24　In the longer term, the sensible outcome following a relationship breakdown is often the making of a court order for transfer of the tenancy (if that is needed) into the sole name of the partner remaining in the home. Jurisdiction to make such orders is available both in the Matrimonial Causes Act 1973 s24 (for spouses) and in the Family Law Act 1996 s53 (for spouses, civil partners and cohabitants). Alternatively, where the parties are parents, an order can be made for a transfer of the tenancy for the benefit of a child.[23] Procedural rules make provision for notice to be given to the landlord. The housing statutes themselves make provision for the consequences of such transfer orders being made (see, for example, HA 1985 s91(3)(b) in relation to orders for transfer of secure tenancies). Any competent family law specialist should be familiar with the process involved in securing an order for the transfer of the tenancy.

21　HA 1985 s81 and HA 1988 s1.
22　See Bridge, 'Transferring tenancies of the family home' [1998] Fam Law 26.
23　Children Act 1989 Sch 1 para 1(2)(e).

CHAPTER 36

Homelessness

Introduction

36.1   A full description of the law relating to homelessness is beyond the scope of this book. Readers seeking a detailed treatment are referred to Andrew Arden QC, Emily Orme and Toby Vanhegan *Homelessness and Allocations*[1] and Jan Luba and Liz Davies *Housing Allocation and Homelessness: Law and Practice*.[2] The following pages describe how homelessness law affects those people subject to actual or potential possession proceedings.

36.2   The substantive law relating to homelessness is contained in the Housing Act (HA) 1996 as amended. All statutory references in this chapter are accordingly to HA 1996 Part VII (Homelessness) unless otherwise stated.

36.3   In outline, HA 1996 Part VII requires the local housing authority to 'secure that accommodation is available' to a homeless person who is eligible for assistance and in priority need, unless the authority is satisfied, following the making of enquiries, that the person became homeless intentionally.[3]

36.4   In the exercise of their functions under HA 1996 Part VII, authorities are bound to have regard to guidance given by the secretary of state. The current *Homelessness code of guidance* was published in July 2006.[4] Although authorities are expected to comply with the guidance in the code, they may depart from it if such departure is justified in a particular case.[5]

Eligibility

36.5   The scope of HA 1996 Part VII is restricted to 'eligible persons', which is defined to debar most 'persons subject to immigration control' and some other 'persons from abroad' from help under the Act.[6]

---

1   8th edition, 2010, Legal Action Group.
2   2nd edition, 2010, Jordans.
3   HA 1996 s193(2).
4   Obtainable from the Communities and Local Government website: www.communities.gov.uk/publications/housing/homelessnesscode.
5   *R v Croydon LBC ex p Jarvis* (1994) 26 HLR 194, QBD. Cf *R v Newham LBC ex p Ugbo* (1993) 26 HLR 263, QBD.
6   HA 1996 ss185 and 186, together with Allocation of Housing and Homelessness (Eligibility) (England) Regulations 2006 SI No 1294.

Preventing homelessness

36.6 Each housing authority is required to have its own homelessness advisory service or to contract with others to provide such a service.[7] A primary function of such a service is to provide the advice and information necessary to prevent homelessness. The Department for Communities and Local Government (CLG) has issued guidance on ways of preventing homelessness, for example, by negotiation with the applicant's landlord or by exploring the scope for mediation.[8] The guidance emphasises (para 2.11) that local authority approaches to homelessness prevention should not be inspired by a 'gatekeeping' mentality. Advice on other housing options should never replace or delay a statutory homelessness assessment where the authority has reason to believe that someone may be homeless or threatened with homelessness.

36.7 In addition, sections 1–3 of the Homelessness Act 2002 require authorities to conduct homelessness reviews and formulate homelessness strategies. These reviews and strategies must be available for inspection and purchase[9] and must address the prevention of homelessness in the council's district.[10]

Threatened homelessness

36.8 All those against whom possession proceedings are initiated ultimately run the risk of homelessness. Local housing authorities have a statutory duty to assist people who apply to them for accommodation and are 'threatened with homelessness'. Where an applicant who is in priority need is threatened with homelessness, the authority is obliged to take reasonable steps 'to secure that accommodation does not cease to be available for his occupation'[11] unless it can satisfy itself that the applicant became threatened with homelessness intentionally. For the duty to be triggered it must be likely that a person will become homeless within 28 days.[12] However, authorities are required to consider taking action at an earlier stage where possible.

---

7 HA 1996 s179(1).
8 *Homelessness prevention: a guide to good practice*, CLG, June 2006.
9 Homelessness Act 2002 ss2(3) and 3(9).
10 Homelessness Act 2002 ss2(2)(a) and 3(1)(a).
11 HA 1996 s195(2).
12 HA 1996 s175(4).

36.9   It is for the authority to decide whether the occupier is threatened with homelessness within the meaning of HA 1996 s175(4). In
calculating whether the occupier is within 28 days of homelessness,
authorities must work back from the hypothetical or actual future
date on which the occupier may or will be evicted.[13] If an occupier is
not threatened with homelessness a negative decision on an application will be premature.[14]

36.10   Even if there are more than 28 days to go before any possession
order could be executed, an occupier faced with prospective or actual
proceedings might be accepted as threatened with homelessness on
the ground that it will shortly become unreasonable for him or her
to remain in possession.[15] Some authorities are prepared to accept
that those faced with possession proceedings on mandatory grounds,
or an inevitable possession order in other circumstances, are threatened with homelessness before a possession order will take effect or
following the expiry of a valid notice.

36.11   Once the occupier is accepted as threatened with homelessness
the authority must either 'take reasonable steps to secure that accommodation does not cease to be available for his occupation' (where
the occupier is in priority need and not intentionally threatened with
homelessness) or 'furnish advice and assistance' to help maintain
accommodation (where the occupier is not in priority need or became threatened with homelessness intentionally).[16] There is also a
power to take steps to secure that accommodation does not cease to
be available to a person unintentionally threatened with homelessness who does *not* have a priority need.[17]

36.12   The first of those duties is usually interpreted as a duty initially to
try to keep for the applicant his or her existing accommodation and
then, if that fails, to secure alternative accommodation.[18]

36.13   Where the possession proceedings are taken or threatened by a
private owner or PRP or RSL, the advice and assistance which an
authority is required to provide by HA 1996 s195 might include legal
advice on the merits of the claim, possible defences, other legal advice, the provision of representation in court by the council's own

---

13   *R v Newham LBC ex p Khan* (2001) 33 HLR 29, QBD (Admin Ct).
14   *R v Rugby BC ex p Hunt* (1994) 26 HLR 1, QBD.
15   HA 1996 s175(3).
16   HA 1996 s195(2) and (5).
17   HA 1996 s195(6), inserted by Homelessness Act 2002 s5.
18   HA 1996 s195(4).

lawyers,[19] counselling, mediation, financial assistance, welfare benefits advice and much else besides.

36.14   If the possession proceedings have been initiated by the local authority, the occupier can at least expect some assistance about what steps should be taken if a possession order is made, including making a homelessness application to the authority itself.

Homelessness

36.15   In essence, a person is homeless if there is no accommodation which that person is entitled to occupy.[20] However, the definition of statutory homelessness also provides:

> A person shall not be treated as having accommodation unless it is accommodation which it would be reasonable for him to continue to occupy.[21]

The Act provides that it is not reasonable for a person to continue to occupy accommodation if it is probable that this will lead to violence against him or her, or another member of the household.[22] But in other cases, in assessing whether it is reasonable for a person to remain in accommodation, the authority may have regard to the general housing circumstances in its area.[23]

36.16   In some situations an occupier involved in possession proceedings may in fact already be statutorily homeless and therefore entitled to some immediate assistance from the local authority. Occupiers are homeless unless the authority is satisfied that it is reasonable for them to continue in occupation of their accommodation.[24] The authority might accept that it is not reasonable to continue in occupation if faced by a strong case for mandatory possession and the risk of court costs (see para 36.10).

36.17   Where a person's existing accommodation is not affordable – for example, because of a housing benefit restriction or because of a severe deterioration in a mortgage borrower's financial circumstances – he or

19 Local Government Act 1972 s222.
20 HA 1996 s175(1).
21 HA 1996 s175(3).
22 HA 1996 s177(1) and (1A).
23 HA 1996 s177(2).
24 HA 1996 s175(3). In *Moran v Manchester CC* [2009] UKHL 36, the House of Lords held that the applicant, who was fleeing domestic violence and had found shelter in a women's refuge, was homeless because it was not reasonable for a woman to occupy a room in a refuge indefinitely.

she may be statutorily homeless even before possession proceedings have been initiated or completed.[25] Where, following a careful assessment of the applicant's financial situation, it is evident that the loss of the home is inevitable, then it is strongly arguable that it is not reasonable for him or her to continue to occupy the property and that he or she is already statutorily homeless. Subject to the questions of eligibility, priority need and intentionality being resolved in the applicant's favour, a local authority would then find itself obliged to provide alternative accommodation before proceedings have been concluded or even started. In this context it is worth reminding local authorities of the following observation by Kennedy J in *R v Hillingdon LBC ex p Tinn*:

> As a matter of commonsense, it seems to me that it cannot be reasonable for a person to continue to occupy accommodation when they can no longer discharge their financial obligations in relation to that accommodation ... without so straining their resources as to deprive themselves of the ordinary necessities of life, such as food, clothing, heat, transport and so forth.[26]

36.18   An application for homelessness assistance should be made at the earliest opportunity to try to resolve the question of what rehousing duty, if any, falls on the housing authority. In this way, the legal costs of possession proceedings may be avoided, not to mention the trauma of the applicant being evicted.

36.19   All squatters (ie, those occupying property without authorisation of the owner) are already homeless persons within the meaning of HA 1996 s175. The fact that the owner has chosen to evict them by court proceedings rather than by physically dispossessing them does not alter their status.

36.20   A possession order cannot usually be enforced other than by execution by a court bailiff acting on a warrant for possession. It has been held in both the High Court[27] and the Court of Appeal[28] that homelessness occurs at the point of actual eviction, rather than the date when the possession order takes effect. In the 28 days prior to the eviction the occupier is 'threatened' with homelessness (see para 36.8).

36.21   The type of assistance the authority must provide to a homeless person varies depending on whether the applicant is in priority need[29] and/or intentionally homeless.[30]

25 Homelessness (Suitability of Accommodation) Order 1996 SI No 3204.
26 (1988) 20 HLR 305 at 308.
27 *R v Newham LBC ex p Khan* (2001) 33 HLR 269.
28 *R v Newham LBC ex p Sacupima* [2001] 1 WLR 563; (2001) 33 HLR 2, CA.
29 HA 1996 s189.
30 HA 1996 s191.

Priority need

36.22 The following persons (in England) have a priority need for accommodation:[31]

- a pregnant woman or a person with whom she resides or might reasonably be expected to reside;
- a person with whom dependent children reside or might reasonably be expected to reside;
- a person who is homeless or threatened with homelessness as a result of an emergency such as flood, fire or other disaster;
- a person aged 16 or 17 (with certain exceptions where the young person is already owed a duty by social services[32]);
- a person under 21 who was (but is no longer) looked after, accommodated or fostered by children's services at any time between the ages of 16 and 18;
- a person who is vulnerable as a result of:
  - old age, mental illness or handicap or physical disability or other special reason (or a person with whom such a person resides or might reasonably be expected to reside);
  - having been looked after, accommodated or fostered while under 18;
  - having been a member of Her Majesty's regular naval, military or air forces;
  - having been imprisoned or held in custody;
  - ceasing to occupy accommodation because of violence from another person or threats of violence from another person which are likely to be carried out.

36.23 A person is considered 'vulnerable' for the purpose of priority need if he or she is less able when homeless to fend for him/herself than an ordinary homeless person, so that injury or detriment would result to him or her when a less vulnerable person would be able to cope without harmful effects.[33] The assessment is a composite one, but there

---

31 HA 1996 s189(1) together with Homelessness (Priority Need for Accommodation) (England) Order 2002 SI No 2051 and Homeless Persons (Priority Need) (Wales) Order 2001 SI No 607. Note that there are some differences between the classes of priority need under the England and the Wales Orders.

32 See *R (G) v Southwark LBC* [2009] UKHL 26; [2009] 1 WLR 1299.

33 *R v London Borough of Camden ex p Pereira* (1999) 31 HLR 317, CA and *R v Waveney DC ex p Bowers* [1983] QB 238; (1983) 4 HLR 118, CA.

must be a risk of injury or detriment. The assessment is carried out on the assumption that the applicant is street homeless.[34]

Interim accommodation

36.24   Where the authority has *reason to believe* that an applicant *may be* homeless, eligible for assistance and in priority need, it has an immediate statutory duty to provide suitable interim accommodation pending the outcome of its enquiries[35] and to take reasonable steps to prevent the loss of or damage to the applicant's personal property if he or she is unable to protect or deal with it.[36] The threshold of proof necessary to trigger the interim accommodation duty is a low one. The test is not whether the authority is 'satisfied' that the three conditions exist, only that it has reason to believe that they may exist.

Intentional homelessness

36.25   The homeless (including those in priority need) do not qualify for the 'full' housing duty if they are found to have become homeless 'intentionally'. In these circumstances the duty is limited to securing accommodation for the applicant's use for such period as the authority considers will give him or her 'a reasonable opportunity of securing accommodation for his occupation'.[37] At most the applicant will receive short-term accommodation together with advice and assistance in looking for alternative accommodation.[38] In those circumstances it is clearly important to avoid, where possible, the prospect of the person faced with possession proceedings being found intentionally homeless.

36.26   A person is intentionally homeless:

> ... if he deliberately does or fails to do anything in consequence of which he ceases to occupy accommodation which is available for his occupation and which it would have been reasonable for him to continue to occupy.[39]

34   *Osmani v LB Camden* [2004] EWCA Civ 1706; [2005] HLR 22.
35   HA 1996 s188(1).
36   HA 1996 s211.
37   HA 1996 s190(2).
38   HA 1996 s190. In deciding how long a period will give the applicant a 'reasonable opportunity', the authority must consider the particular needs and circumstances of the applicant: *Conville v LB Richmond upon Thames* [2006] EWCA Civ 718; [2006] 1 WLR 2808.
39   HA 1996 s191(1).

36.27   This definition is, however, qualified so that:

> ... an act or omission in good faith on the part of a person who was unaware of any relevant fact shall not be treated as deliberate.[40]

The 'good faith' test is a subjective one, that is, whether the applicant honestly had no knowledge of the circumstances, not whether or not another person acting reasonably would have done so. The distinction was made by the Court of Appeal in the context of a mortgage default case:

> It is not enough simply to find that he was a hopeless businessman or that the venture was ill advised, but it is necessary to look at all the circumstances to decide whether on the one hand, he honestly believed he was acting sensibly, or on the other, he knew perfectly well the risk he was taking, namely that his house might be repossessed.[41]

Only in the latter case can the applicant be classified as intentionally homeless.

36.28   A person can be found intentionally homeless only if he or she satisfies all limbs of the definition at para 36.26 above. He or she must have deliberately done or failed to do something in consequence of which accommodation is lost. If it would not have been reasonable to have continued to occupy the property, then the applicant cannot be intentionally homeless.

36.29   Where a person has lost his or her home because of financial difficulties, authorities must pay careful attention to the question of whether the accommodation was affordable. An applicant's actions may not amount to intentional homelessness where he or she has lost his or her home, or was obliged to sell it, because of rent or mortgage arrears resulting from particular financial difficulties, and the applicant was genuinely unable to keep up the rent or mortgage payments even after claiming benefits. In relation to mortgage borrowers, Communities and Local Government has issued *Supplementary guidance on intentional homelessness*,[42] which gives specific guidance in assessing homeowners who have lost their home as a result of mortgage arrears, in relation to intentional homelessness.

36.30   Advisers must be aware that local authorities are given a 'very substantial measure of appreciation' in deciding whether a person who has been evicted for non-payment of housing costs has become homeless intentionally or whether the failure to pay was genuinely

---

40   HA 1996 s191(2).
41   *R v Wandsworth LBC ex p Onwudiwe* (1994) 26 HLR 302.
42   www.communities.gov.uk/documents/housing/pdf/1304826.

attributable to inadequacy of resources to cover the necessities of life.[43] It is vital therefore to be able to justify every item of the applicant's expenditure.

36.31   Where it is feared that the partner with financial control in a relationship may be found intentionally homeless, it is advisable for a clearly separate application to be made to the authority under HA 1996 Part VII by the 'non-responsible' partner. The authority is required to investigate whether the partner had acquiesced in the deliberate failure to make the appropriate payments before he or she can be found to be 'intentionally' homeless.[44]

36.32   Similar difficulties can arise where a mortgage borrower decides to sell the property in advance of the lender taking possession proceedings, where the borrower knows or believes that there is no prospect of defending the lender's claim at court. Many authorities find applicants who sell the property in such circumstances intentionally homeless. It should be stressed, in representations to the authority, that the borrower had no reasonable prospect of preventing dispossession and reference should be made to the test of whether it would have been reasonable to continue to occupy the property.[45] It is wise before sale of the property to approach the authority to explain the financial circumstances and discuss any alternative options.

36.33   Three further points of importance arise. First, it is obvious that any form of 'consent' order should be avoided in possession proceedings (even if it is possible for such an order to be made – see paras 3.5 and 33.45) since this at least raises a suspicion for the authority that the homeless person has brought about his or her own homelessness.[46]

36.34   Second, it does not automatically follow that an occupier against whom a possession order has been made on a 'fault' ground is intentionally homeless; the authority is required to make its own enquiries[47] and to satisfy itself as to the true facts of the case. For example, if the ground on which possession was granted was 'nuisance', the authority must itself investigate who caused or was responsible for the

---

43 *R v Brent LBC ex p Baruwa* [1997] 3 FCR 97; (1997) 29 HLR 915, CA.

44 *R v North Devon DC ex p Lewis* [1981] 1 WLR 328; [1981] 1 All ER 27.

45 See *R v Eastleigh BC ex p Beattie (No 1)* (1982–83) 10 HLR 134 and *(No 2)* (1984) 17 HLR 168; *R v Hammersmith and Fulham LBC ex p Duro-Rama* (1983) 9 HLR 71; 81 LGR 702 and *R v Hillingdon LBC ex p Tinn* (1988) 20 HLR 305.

46 *R v Wandsworth LBC ex p Henderson* (1986) 18 HLR 522, QBD.

47 HA 1996 s184.

nuisance.[48] The council cannot fetter its discretion in the application of the definition of intentionality[49] by unquestioningly adopting the findings of the court which dealt with the possession action.

36.35　　Third, occupiers frequently panic and leave the premises before they are legally required to do so. This may occur either at the stage at which possession proceedings are threatened or under way or otherwise before the time allowed by the possession order has expired. If in leaving they bring to an end their interest in the property (for example, by notice to quit or surrender) they become homeless. In such circumstances it may be open to a local authority to find that, notwithstanding that the applicants would have become homeless in due course, they are 'intentionally homeless' because it would have been reasonable for them to have remained in the property at the date they left it.[50] Consideration should, however, be given to the possibility of challenging any such finding.

36.36　　Acts or omissions made in good faith where someone was genuinely unaware of a relevant fact must not be regarded as deliberate.[51] A general example would be a situation where a person gave up possession of accommodation in the belief that they had no legal right to continue to occupy the accommodation and, therefore, it would not be reasonable for them to continue to occupy it. See para 36.27.

36.37　　A more acute illustration of the 'early departure' problem arises where the local authority has actually advised the tenant to stay in possession and resist the possession proceedings. Although the authority cannot properly advise defending in hopeless cases,[52] it may assert that a person renders him or herself intentionally homeless as a result of ignoring appropriate advice to 'stay put' until the court has made a possession order or until enforcement of that order.[53]

36.38　　If met with a decision of 'intentionally homeless' the applicant should be immediately referred to an adviser specialising in housing law.

48　*Devenport v Salford City Council* (1983) 8 HLR 57, CA.
49　HA 1996 s191.
50　*Din v Wandsworth LBC* [1983] 1 AC 657; [1981] 3 WLR 918; [1981] 3 All ER 881; (1982) 1 HLR 73, HL.
51　HA 1996 s191(2).
52　*R v Portsmouth City Council ex p Knight* (1983) 10 HLR 115, QBD and *R v Surrey Heath BC ex p Li* (1984) 16 HLR 79, QBD.
53　*R v Penwith DC ex p Hughes* August 1980 *LAG Bulletin* 187.

Local connection

36.39   In certain limited circumstances an authority which has accepted a
duty to house an unintentionally homeless person in priority need
may refer him or her to a different authority which will provide the
accommodation. The conditions for referral of the case to another
authority are met if (and only if) the applicant (and any household
member) has no local connection with the authority; the applicant (or
any household member) has a local connection with the district of a
second authority; and the applicant (or any household member) will
not run the risk of violence in that other district.[54]

36.40   A person has a local connection with the district of a local housing
authority if any of the following circumstances apply:

- because he or she is, or in the past was, normally resident there,
  and that residence is or was of his or her own choice;
- because he or she is employed there;
- because of family associations; or
- because of special circumstances.[55]

36.41   The Local Authority Association *Joint local connection agreement*[56] offers an interpretation of the factors relevant to local connection, as
follows:

   (1) A working definition of 'normal residence' should be that the
   household has been resident in the area for at least six out of the
   previous 12 months, or for not less than three out of the previous
   five years. Time spent in hospital or in emergency accommodation (such as refuges or some hostels) may be disregarded. Time
   spent in the service of the armed forces, or in prison, is also to be
   disregarded.
   (2) Employment in the area 'of a casual nature' will not normally
   count.
   (3) Family associations normally arise where an applicant, or member of his/her household as parents, adult children or brothers or
   sisters currently residing in the area and these relatives have been
   resident for a period of at least five years and the applicant indicates a wish to be near them.
   (4) Special circumstances: the fact that an applicant seeks to return to
   an area where s/he was brought up or had lived for a considerable
   period of time in the past may be a basis for finding a local connection because of special circumstances.

54 HA 1996 s198.
55 HA 1996 s199(1).
56 *Homelessness Code of Guidance for Local Authorities*, 2006, annex 18.

The terms of the Local Authority Agreement are not conclusive, and in some aspects are too restrictive, for example, the confinement of 'family associations' to close relatives with five years' residence. It would be unlawful for an authority to base its decision solely on the working definitions set out in the Agreement.

36.42   If a person has no local connection with any authority in England, Wales or Scotland, the authority to which he or she has applied must take responsibility for discharging the housing duty.[57] The assessment of local connection is not made on the basis that the applicant has a stronger local connection with another borough: if the applicant has a sufficient local connection with the authority to which he or she has applied, that authority cannot refer him or her to another authority.

36.43   The local connection provisions may be invoked only when the first authority has accepted that it owes a duty to house the homeless person. It would be unlawful for an authority to refuse to entertain an application on the basis of a want of local connection, and the authority must continue to accommodate the applicant pending a referral to another borough. Authorities must consider in each case whether in all the circumstances it is appropriate to make the referral and should always be prepared to consider special circumstances for not referring to another authority.[58]

Protection of property

36.44   It is important to note that local authority duties towards the homeless extend to the protection of property and powers are available to assist the non-priority homeless in this respect.[59] Assistance should be sought once loss of possessions has become inevitable. The effect of a possession order will be that the defendant loses a home, while these duties and powers to protect property prevent the defendant's loss of all his or her belongings too.[60] Of course, the council is entitled to levy a reasonable charge for transport and storage.[61]

---

57 *R v Hillingdon LBC ex p Streeting (No 2)* [1980] 1 WLR 1425; [1980] 3 All ER 413, CA.
58 *R v Harrow LBC ex p Carter* (1994) 26 HLR 32, QBD.
59 HA 1996 s211.
60 See *Deadman v Southwark LBC* (2001) 33 HLR 75; (2000) *Times* 31 August, CA.
61 HA 1996 s211(4).

Housed as homeless

36.45   Local authorities and others may seek to recover possession of accommodation into which a homeless person has been placed in discharge of statutory duties arising under HA 1996 Part VII. For the limited 'security of tenure' of such people see paras 5.20–5.31.

36.46   All accommodation provided to homeless persons under HA 1996 Part VII must be 'suitable'. The Homelessness (Suitability of Accommodation) Order 1996[62] provides that, in determining whether accommodation is suitable for a person, there shall be taken into account whether or not the accommodation is *affordable*, and in particular

- the financial resources available to that person;
- the costs of the accommodation;
- that person's other reasonable living expenses.

Reviews and appeals

36.47   An applicant has the right to request a review of any decision made by a local housing authority on what duty (if any) is owed to him or her, or a local connection referral, or the suitability of the accommodation provided.[63]

36.48   A request for review must be made within *21 days* of the date when the applicant is notified of the authority's decision (unless the authority allows a longer period).[64] The review must be completed and notified to the applicant within 56 days,[65] unless the applicant and the authority jointly agree an extension in writing.

36.49   If the decision on review is unfavourable to the applicant, the authority must notify him or her of the reasons for the decision. It must also inform the applicant of his or her right to appeal to the county court on a point of law, and of the time limit for appealing.

36.50   Where an applicant has requested a review of an authority's decision and he or she is

- dissatisfied with the decision on the review, or
- not notified of the review decision within the prescribed time,

---

62   SI No 3204.
63   HA 1996 s202(1).
64   HA 1993 s202(3).
65   Allocation of Housing and Homelessness (Review Procedures) Regulations 1999 SI No 71 reg 5.

he or she may appeal to the county court on any point of law arising from the decision.[66] An appeal must be brought within 21 days of notification of the decision.[67]

36.51   The procedure, as with other statutory appeals, is governed by Part 52 of the Civil Procedure Rules.

66 HA 1996 s204(1).
67 HA 1996 s204(2). Some relief for late appellants may be available through s204(2A), which provides that the court may give permission for an appeal to be brought after the 21-day deadline, but only if satisfied that the applicant had a good reason for being unable to bring the appeal in time and for any delay in applying for permission.

Housing benefit

Introduction

37.1   Many occupiers faced with possession proceedings are in that situation as a result of failure to make rental or other payments to the landlord or licensor.

37.2   The housing benefit scheme is designed to assist those on low incomes in meeting their liabilities for housing costs. The benefit is claimed from – and payable by – the local housing authority for the area in which the property is situated. Housing benefit is not available to owner-occupiers (financial assistance for mortgage borrowers is outlined in chapter 41).

37.3   In outline, the statutory scheme[1] provides that recipients of income support, income-based jobseeker's allowance, income-related employment and support allowance or guarantee credit are eligible for assistance with up to 100 per cent of their housing costs and others on low income are eligible to receive proportionate help. For many occupiers of private sector housing, however, housing benefit is paid on the basis of a flat-rate 'local housing allowance'. This book does not have scope for a full description of the workings of the housing benefit scheme, for which see Zebedee, Ward and Lister *Guide to housing benefit and council tax benefit*.[2] However, there are a number of aspects of the housing benefit scheme which touch directly on possession proceedings.

Eligible rent

37.4   A tenant's 'eligible rent' is the sum used to calculate his or her housing benefit entitlement. It may be equal to the actual rent, but in many cases it is not. The rules are complex, and the reader is referred to chapter 7 of the *Guide to housing benefit and council tax benefit*.

37.5   In most cases, the eligible rent is determined either on the 'standard basis' or by reference to the local housing allowance (LHA). In all cases, however, a deduction is made for certain ineligible service charges before the amount of housing benefit is assessed. Thus, where the rent on a tenancy is inclusive of water charges and heating charges for the accommodation itself, the amounts attributable to those expenses will not be payable by housing benefit.

---

1   Contained in Social Security Contributions and Benefits Act 1992 and Housing Benefit Regulations 2006 (HB Regs 2006) SI No 213.
2   Obtainable from Shelter and the Chartered Institute of Housing.

Standard cases

37.6   In these cases, the eligible rent will usually be the actual rent less any ineligible service elements such as water charges. The following cases are dealt with on the standard basis of assessment:

- council tenancies, where housing benefit is paid by way of a rent rebate;
- tenancies from a housing association or other PRP (provided that the local authority accepts that the rent and the size of the accommodation are not unreasonable);
- Rent Act protected and statutory tenancies with a registered fair rent.

Local housing allowance cases

37.7   The LHA is the means by which housing benefit is paid to private sector tenants. It originated in the Welfare Reform Act 2007 and applies where a tenant pays rent to a private landlord and either makes a new claim for housing benefit or changes his or her address on or after 7 April 2008.[3] Where a private tenant has been in occupation and in receipt of housing benefit since a date before 7 April 2008, his or her rent is referred to a rent officer for an assessment of whether it is reasonable: the assessment involves comparing the rent with the 'local reference rent'. In LHA cases, the claimant is paid a standard housing allowance. The LHA is the maximum rent that will be payable by housing benefit for dwellings of different sizes in a particular area. It is based on the number of bedrooms that each household is deemed to require. The Valuation Service compiles a list of market rents for each size of property within a *broad rental market area* (BRMA). The LHA is the median rent which is calculated from these lists. The levels of LHA are set monthly by the rent officer and are publicly available at https://lha-direct.voa.gov.uk.

37.8   A BRMA is the area within which a person could reasonably be expected to live having regard to facilities and services for the purposes of health, education, recreation, personal banking and shopping, taking account of the distance of travel, by public and private transport, to and from those facilities and services.

37.9   Once the LHA has been fixed it applies from the date of claim for 12 months unless there is a change of circumstances which requires a reassessment, such as a change in the number of household

---

3   HB Regs 2006 regs 12D and 13C–13E. See also the DWP's *Housing benefit local housing allowance manual.*

members or a material change in age, for example, a child reaching his or her 16th birthday. An increase in the rent actually charged does not qualify for a reassessment.

37.10   Some private tenants, mainly those who have been claiming housing benefit continuously in the same property since 1 January 1996, are exempt from both the LHA and local reference rent schemes.

37.11   The LHA will not apply to claims in the following categories:[4]

- where the landlord is a housing association or other PRP;
- certain excluded tenancies, including protected and statutory tenancies under the Rent Act 1977;[5] and
- houseboats, caravans, mobile homes, hostels, or tenancies where a substantial amount of the rent is attributable to board and attendance.

Non-dependants

37.12   A tenant's eligible rent will be reduced if he or she has a 'non-dependant' living in the same property. A non-dependant is someone who lives with the tenant as a member of the household, but who is not the tenant's partner or dependent child. Often, this will be a grown-up son or daughter. It does not include joint owners, sub-tenants, or lodgers. A set deduction from the tenant's housing benefit is made for each non-dependant according to their circumstances, irrespective of what contribution the non-dependant actually makes to the household finances. A failure to declare a non-dependant is a frequent cause of a claim by the local authority for an overpayment. Often, the tenant does not realise the obligation to notify the authority, especially where, for example, a young person leaves full-time education and commences employment.

Making a claim for housing benefit

37.13   A claim for housing benefit (HB) can be made in one of the following ways:

- On a local authority housing benefit claim form. Each local authority has its own claim forms, as there is no national template.
- If the claimant is also claiming income support, income-based jobseeker's allowance, employment and support allowance or

---

4 HB Regs 2006 reg 13C(5).
5 HB Regs 2006 Sch 2 paras 4–10.

pension credit, he or she will usually complete a form HCTB1. The claimant may later be asked to provide further information and/or to complete the authority's standard claim form.

- By letter from the claimant, his or her solicitor or adviser, or someone acting on the claimant's behalf, stating that they want to claim HB. The local authority will then usually send out its standard claim form for completion.

37.14 The Housing Benefit Regulations 2006[6] provide that a claim for HB in writing: 'may be sent or delivered to the appropriate Department for Work and Pensions (DWP) office where the claimant or his partner is also claiming income support, incapacity benefit, state pension credit or a jobseeker's allowance'; and that where the claim is sent or delivered to a 'gateway office', the date of claim for housing and council tax benefits is the first day of entitlement to jobseeker's allowance (or other benefit).[7] Regulation 2(1) defines a 'gateway office' as including an appropriate DWP office. Even where the claim is defective, it can be rectified. The Court of Appeal has held that there is no need for the benefit being claimed to be expressly named, provided that a reasonable official could understand that there was an intention to claim the relevant benefit.[8]

37.15 Under the Housing Benefit and Council Tax Benefit (Amendment) Regulations 2008,[9] claimants may make a telephone claim for housing and council tax benefit, at the same time as they make a telephone claim for pension credit, income support, jobseeker's allowance, incapacity benefit or employment and support allowance. Their details will then be sent on to the local authority for processing.

37.16 Regulation 86(1) of the Housing Benefit Regulations 2006 provides:

> ... a person who makes a claim, or a person to whom housing benefit has been awarded, shall furnish such certificates, documents, information and evidence in connection with the claim or the award or any question arising out of the claim or the award, as may reasonably be required by the relevant authority in order to determine that person's entitlement to, or continuing entitlement to, housing benefit, and shall do so within one month of the relevant authority requiring him, or the Secretary of State requesting him, to do so, or such longer period as the relevant authority may consider reasonable ...

---

6 HB Regs 2006 reg 83(4)(a).
7 HB Regs 2006 reg 84.
8 *Novitskaya v Brent LBC and Secretary of State for Work and Pensions* [2009] EWCA Civ 1260.
9 SI No 2299.

37.17   Most local authorities adopt the DWP's Verification Framework as a means of requiring and checking evidence in support of claims. The Framework is often a source of delays because, among other security measures, it calls for the originals of all relevant documents. However, its status is only that of guidance, and advisers should press for the authority to dispense with unrealistic demands for certain kinds of written evidence. Although there are close links between housing benefit and Jobcentre Plus offices, claimants are often called on to take the same documents to different offices.

Maximising housing benefit to clear arrears

37.18   If there are arrears and the occupier is presently (or has recently been) on a low income, the starting point should be to check that housing benefit is being paid or has been paid and that the correct amount is being, and has been, received.

37.19   Once the appropriate current housing benefit entitlement has been established, it may be possible to use the housing benefit scheme to make inroads into the outstanding arrears.

37.20   First, *backdating* should be considered. If there has been some potential entitlement in the past for which the occupier failed to claim, application should be made for the backdating of the current award of benefit. This may produce a lump sum of arrears of housing benefit which can be applied to meeting the debt. The local authority has power to backdate for up to six months if good cause is shown for not having initiated a claim at an earlier date.[10] 'Good cause' is undefined and might be established by a variety of circumstances ranging from ill-health to earlier inaccurate advice. The adviser should not hesitate to present the individual claimant's explanation as one amounting to good cause.

37.21   Second, the occupier may be able to apply for a *discretionary housing payment*. The scheme for payment of discretionary housing payments (which are strictly not housing benefits) is contained in the Discretionary Financial Assistance Regulations 2001[11] made under the Child Support, Pensions and Social Security Act 2000.

---

10 HB Regs 2006 reg 83(12). For claimants over 60, good cause need not be shown for the previous three months, and authorities should automatically consider eligibility for that period.
11 SI No 1167.

Guidance[12] issued to local authorities by the DWP sets out both a description of the scheme and an indication of the breadth of the discretion to assist with unmet housing costs. A discretionary housing payment may be made in respect of rent arrears.[13]

37.22 If possession proceedings have already been started, they should be adjourned pending the outcome of an application for backdating of housing benefit or for discretionary housing payments if that is possible. It is not generally possible to secure such an adjournment where a court is satisfied that mandatory ground 8 of the Housing Act 1988 Sch 2 is satisfied in respect of an assured tenant. If the requisite level of rent arrears has been proved in such a case, the court must order possession even if the arrears have accumulated for want of housing benefit to which the tenant is entitled, subject however to the possibility of a public law defence in these circumstances (see para 12.74).[14] The Protocol for Possession Claims based on Rent Arrears requires social landlords to make direct contact with the relevant housing benefit department and to ensure that difficulties are resolved wherever possible without court proceedings. The full text of the Protocol is set out in appendix D. See also paras 3.38–3.40.

'Arrears' resulting from delayed payment

37.23 Landlords frequently initiate possession proceedings based on arrears which are entirely, or mainly, the result of late or delayed payment of housing benefit to the occupier by the local authority. Once a claim has been submitted, it is essential for the claimant, or someone acting on his or her behalf, to check that it has been received by the authority, that it is being processed and that all necessary evidence of personal and financial circumstances has been provided. All too often, claims are 'lost' in the system and it is essential to keep track of them. Where the claimant supplies documents (such as wages slips) in connection with the claim, he or she should obtain a note of acknowledgment from the housing benefit office to confirm receipt.

12 *Guidance for local authorities on the operation of discretionary housing payments,* DWP (formerly DSS), March 2001, and *Discretionary housing payments: best practice guide,* DWP, March 2008: both obtainable from www.dwp.gov.uk/docs/ dhpguide.

13 Discretionary Financial Regulations 2001 SI No 1167; *R (Gargett) v Lambeth LBC* [2008] EWCA Civ 1450; [2009] LGR 527.

14 *North British Housing Association v Matthews* [2004] EWCA Civ 1736; [2005] 1 WLR 3133.

37.24   Once the occupier has claimed housing benefit from the local authority, the latter should, within 14 days, make a decision on the claim (provided that the claimant has provided all necessary evidence).[15] If it is not possible to determine a claim for benefit in respect of a private tenant or tenant of a PRP or RSL within 14 days, provided that the claimant has not without good cause failed to provide evidence of his or her circumstances, the local authority should make payments on account of prospective entitlement.[16] Each of these duties on the authority is mandatory and capable of enforcement in proceedings for judicial review.[17]

37.25   Where the claimant in such a case is the local authority itself, the occupier may be properly advised to respond to any possession proceedings based on arrears either by inviting the court to strike out the proceedings as an abuse of process[18] or by entering a defence and counterclaiming for breach of statutory duty. The private law duty in respect of which breach can be asserted arises only after a decision to make a payment of housing benefit has been taken.[19] If the problem is in securing such a decision, the tenant may seek to defend the claim on the basis that it is an improper exercise of power for the authority to bring proceedings in these circumstances, or alternatively request an adjournment of the possession claim and apply for judicial review.[20]

37.26   Where the claimant is a private landlord or PRP or RSL, the local authority could be joined as a third party (under Part 20 of the Civil Procedure Rules 1998 (CPR)) if there has been an actionable breach of duty.[21] Alternatively, the senior officer responsible for housing benefit could be summonsed to give evidence relating to the occupier's entitlement to housing benefit and reasons for non-payment of it.[22] Either step should prompt the authority into payment of the correct benefit and a back payment. If the entire proceedings have been caused by local authority failures in dealing with the defendant's housing benefit claim, that authority could be joined as a third

---

15 HB Regs 2006 reg 89(2).
16 HB Regs 2006 reg 93(2).
17 See *R v Liverpool City Council ex p Johnson* 23 June 1994, unreported, QBD, and *R v Haringey LBC ex p Ayub* (1993) 25 HLR 566, QBD.
18 *Lambeth LBC v Tagoe* August 2000 *Legal Action* 24.
19 *Haringey LBC v Cotter* (1997) 29 HLR 682, CA.
20 *Wandsworth LBC v Winder* [1985] AC 461; *Kay v LB Lambeth, Leeds CC v Price* [2006] UKHL 10; [2006] 2 AC 465, para 110.
21 CPR Part 19.
22 CPR Part 34.

party simply for the purpose of obtaining an order that it pay all the costs.[23]

'Arrears' resulting from overpayment

37.27 Since the introduction of the modern housing benefit scheme in 1988, local authorities have had the power to recover overpayments of housing benefit from both the claimant *and* any other person to whom such benefit was paid (which may include the landlord – see para 37.33).[24] If recovery is made by deducting an amount from future benefit entitlement, the tenant faces the possibility of being unable to pay the rent in full and of subsequent arrears arising. However, many authorities seek to recover the past overpayment in a lump sum. The issue then arises as to whether the 'debt' in such cases can constitute 'arrears' in any proceedings for possession based on rent arrears. The answer depends on whether the landlord is the local authority.

37.28 An overpayment of housing benefit is defined as

> ... any amount which has been paid by way of housing benefit and to which there was no entitlement under these Regulations (whether on the initial decision or as subsequently revised or superseded ...) and includes any amount paid on account under regulation 93 (payment on account of a rent allowance) which is in excess of the entitlement to housing benefit as subsequently decided.[25]

A 'payment' in these terms includes payment to the claimant, the landlord, the landlord's agent or any other person, and includes credits being made to a local authority's own rent account where the tenancy is a council tenancy.

37.29 Where claims for overpayments are concerned, tenants may need advice from a specialist welfare benefits adviser about whether a particular overpayment is recoverable. Local authorities may sometimes fail to follow proper decision-making procedures, and fail to notify claimants of decisions in relation to overpayments.

37.30 Decisions not to award housing benefit or to make deductions from housing benefit or to recover overpayments may be reviewed by the local authority on request, and ultimately would be subject to

---

23 CPR 48.2 and *Asra Greater London Housing Association v Cooke* June 2001 *Legal Action* 31.

24 HB Regs 2006 regs 99–107.

25 HB Regs 2006 reg 99.

challenge, either by judicial review or by appeal to an independent tribunal.

Council tenants

37.31   Typically, a local authority pays housing benefit to its own tenants by way of credit to the rent account (ie, a 'rent rebate'). The rent due is directly 'paid'[26] in this way in whole or in part and the occupier's rent liability is met at least to the extent of that credit or payment. Inevitably, there are errors or mistakes and tenants are paid too much benefit or paid benefit to which they are not entitled. The regulations prescribe careful procedures to regulate recovery and ensure notification in such cases.[27] However, local authorities, on discovering an overpayment, not infrequently 'seize' back from the occupier's rent account the benefit overpaid and then issue rent account statements showing tenants 'in arrears' by that amount. This activity is improper for the following reasons:

- Some overpayments are irrecoverable[28] and the authority has a discretion as to whether to recover any overpayment even if it is recoverable.[29]
- Before taking any recovery action, the authority is obliged to issue written notification of the decision that there has been an overpayment and that it should be recovered and details of the method selected for recovery.[30]
- The permitted methods of recovery of overpaid housing benefit do not include debiting the amount of the overpayment to the occupier's rent account.

37.32   If possession proceedings are initiated against an occupier for such 'paper arrears', the defence should be that the alleged arrears are not 'rent lawfully due' but are overpaid housing benefit (see para 3.30), and that possession proceedings are not the appropriate means of recovery. The effect of the statutory definition of 'payment' in this context is that the amount of benefit awarded extinguishes liability for that much rent, ie, the rent lawfully due is and has been paid in that amount. The council cannot resurrect a liability for rent which has

---

26 See the definition of 'pay' in Social Security Administration Act 1992 s134(2).
27 HB Regs 2006 reg 102.
28 HB Regs 2006 reg 100.
29 Social Security Administration Act s75(1).
30 HB Regs 2006 reg 90 and Sch 9 para 15.

been extinguished. For that reason the DWP's *HB/CTB Overpayments guide*[31] emphasises the distinction between a recoverable overpayment of housing benefit and arrears of rent (see paras 4.150–4.153 of the *Guide*). An overpayment can, however, be recovered by deductions from ongoing HB entitlement.

Other tenants

37.33　Similar difficulties can occur when housing benefit payments have been made direct to private landlords or housing associations or other PRPs/RSLs and are subsequently discovered to have been overpayments. If a local authority exercises its power to seek recovery from the landlord,[32] and the landlord repays the money, the tenant's adviser needs to consider carefully the legal consequences. Regulation 95(2) of the Housing Benefit Regulations 2006 provides that:

> Any payment of rent allowance made to a landlord pursuant to this regulation or to regulation 96 (circumstances in which payments may be made to a landlord) shall be to discharge, in whole or in part, the liability of the claimant to pay rent to that landlord in respect of the dwelling concerned, except in so far as –
> (a) the claimant had no entitlement to the whole or part of that rent allowance so paid to his landlord; and
> (b) the overpayment of rent allowance resulting was recovered in whole or in part from that landlord.

It is arguable that this provision is ultra vires in so far as it seeks to regulate a contractual liability between landlord and tenant; but it must be acknowledged that the provision (with its predecessor in the 1987 Regulations) has been in effect for many years without challenge.[33]

37.34　Whether the occupier is a social or private sector tenant or licensee, the authority is required properly to notify a decision to recover an overpayment. Until such notification is given the overpayment is not legally recoverable.[34]

31　Available from www.dwp.gov.uk/docs/op-guide-amd2.pdf.
32　Social Security Administration Act 1992 s75(3)(a) and HB Regs 2006 reg 101.
33　See CPAG's *Housing benefit and council tax benefit legislation* 18th edn, p447 (in relation to the equivalent provision in reg 93(1) of Housing Benefit (General) Regulations 1987, now superseded by Housing Benefit Regulations 2006).
34　*Warwick DC v Freeman* (1995) 27 HLR 616, CA and *R v Thanet DC ex p Warren Court Hotels Ltd* (2001) 33 HLR 32, QBD (Admin Ct).

Direct payments of housing benefit

37.35   Tenants of housing associations or other PRPs/RSLs can elect that housing benefit be paid direct to the landlord. Where housing benefit is in the form of the LHA, the general rule is that the LHA is paid to the tenant, and not directly to the landlord. However, in some circumstances, the authority *must* make direct payments to the landlord:

- where the rent is eight weeks or more in arrears,[35] unless the authority considers it to be in the tenant's overriding interest not to make direct payments; or
- where direct payments toward rent arrears are already being made by the DWP by deduction from income support, income-based jobseeker's allowance, pension credit or employment and support allowance.[36]

37.36   The authority has a discretion to make direct payments in the following situations:

- the tenant has difficulty managing his or her own affairs; or
- it is improbable that the tenant will pay the rent; or
- the authority was making direct payments to the landlord at the tenant's previous address.

37.37   The availability of direct payments is obviously relevant to possession proceedings because:

- Failure by a landlord to seek direct payments may be helpful in establishing that it is not 'reasonable in all the circumstances' for the court to make a possession order in proceedings based on rent arrears on a discretionary ground.
- An offer may be made to the court that the tenant or the tenant's advisers will make an approach to the authority with a view to direct payments being made in the future, and the court may be invited to adjourn the proceedings accordingly.

37.38   Where direct payments are to be made, both the occupier and the landlord are informed in writing by the authority.[37]

---

35   Rent is in arrears once the contractual date for payment has passed without payment being made, irrespective of whether rent is due in advance or in arrear (Circular HB/CTB A26/2009). Thus, where rent is payable monthly in advance, and no payment has been made, the tenant will be in eight weeks' arrears after one month and one day.

36   See para 37.40.

37   HB Regs 2006 reg 90 and Sch 9 para 11.

37.39 Usually, on receipt of the direct payment, the landlord applies the housing benefit in satisfaction of all or part of the occupier's rent liability. Difficulties can arise if subsequently it is discovered that the amount of housing benefit has been overpaid (see para 37.33).

Direct deductions from other benefits

37.40 Direct deductions may be made by the DWP from a tenant's weekly income support, income-based jobseeker's allowance, employment and support allowance or pension credit to be paid to the landlord towards arrears of rent.[38]

37.41 The landlord may request direct deductions if the tenant is in at least four weeks' rent arrears and has been in arrears over a period of at least eight weeks. The DWP may also make its own decision to make direct deductions if the tenant is in at least four weeks' rent arrears, though he or she has been in arrears for less than eight weeks, and in its opinion it is in the overriding interest of the family that direct deductions should be made. The tenant can him or herself also make a request to the DWP.

37.42 Where a claimant is in receipt of housing benefit, the DWP also has power to make direct deductions from these benefits to pay water charges and heating charges which are not covered by housing benefit.[39]

---

38 Social Security (Claims and Payments) Regulations 1987 SI No 1968 Sch 9 para 5(1) and (6).

39 Social Security (Claims and Payments) Regs 1987 Sch 9 para 5(3).

Mortgages

Mortgages

Introduction

38.1   In 1904, an appeal judge said, 'No one, I am sure, by the light of nature ever understood an English mortgage of real estate'.[1] In 1986, the Law Commission, in more reserved tone, commented in its introduction to Working Paper No 99 on reform of land mortgages:[2]

> The English law of land mortgages is notoriously difficult. It has never been subjected to systematic statutory reform, and over several centuries of gradual evolution it has acquired a multi-layered structure that is historically fascinating but inappropriately and sometimes unnecessarily complicated.

38.2   It is clear that the current state of the English law of mortgages is inadequate. This was recognised by the Law Commission as long ago as November 1991 when it published its recommendations for the reform of the law regulating land mortgages.[3] In July 2009 in a white paper, *A better deal for consumers – delivering real help now and change for the future,*[4] the then government indicated that the Law Commission had been asked to conduct a review of the fundamental principles of residential mortgage law with a view to bringing it up to date.

38.3   The defects in the law have become all the more important given the great social impact of its subject matter. In 2008 it was estimated that there were 14.6 million owner-occupiers representing 68.3 per cent of all households in England.[5] Almost 60 per cent of owner-occupiers have one or more mortgages.[6] Between 1980 and 2008 the number of mortgage possession actions started in the county courts in England and Wales rose from 27,105 to 142,046.[7] In 2009 93,463 mortgage possession actions were started.[8] The number of repossessions by members of the Council of Mortgage Lenders (CML), which comprises all the major lenders, in 2009 came to 46,000 and at the end of that year some 188,300 mortgage borrowers were in

---

1   *Samuel v Jarrah Timber and Wood Paving Corporation* [1904] AC 323 at 326 per Lord MacNaughten.
2   *Land Mortgages*, Law Commission Working Paper No 99, HMSO, 1986.
3   *Transfer of Land – Land Mortgages*, Law Com No 204 HC5, HMSO, 1991.
4   www.berr.gov.uk/files/file52072.pdf.
5   *Housing in England 2007–08*, Communities and Local Government, from www.tsoshop.co.uk.
6   *Social Trends 37* (2007 edn London) 133 (Table 10.8).
7   Lord Chancellor's Department, *Judicial Statistics: Annual Report 1991*, Cm 1990 and Ministry of Justice Press Release, 20 February 2009.
8   www.justice.gov.uk/publications/docs/stats-mortgage-land-q4-09.pdf.

arrears equivalent to at least 2.5 per cent of their outstanding mortgage balance.[9]

38.4   It is against this backdrop that this Part is written, to try to explain the law and practice of mortgage possession actions and how advisers can help prevent loss of occupation by borrowers and their families.

Nature of legal mortgages

38.5   A lender who has secured its loan on property by way of mortgage has a considerable advantage over an unsecured lender and is not solely dependent on the solvency of the borrower to recover the money lent. A mortgagee (ie, lender) has a number of options open as methods of enforcing the security. The lender may sue the borrower on the personal covenant in the mortgage deed, appoint a receiver to collect rent due from any tenants in the property, or seek a foreclosure order from the court. However, in practice, large institutional lenders usually seek to obtain possession of the property and sell with vacant possession to recover the money owed to them.[10] This part of this book primarily deals with the law and practice related to this last method of enforcement. Throughout, the terms 'lender' and 'borrower' will be used in place respectively of the more technical terms 'mortgagee' and 'mortgagor', except where a term of art is to be used. The lender will, of course, almost invariably be a bank, building society or similar institution rather than an individual.

38.6   Since 1925, legal mortgages have been capable of being made in only one of two ways.[11] The first is the granting of a lease by the freehold owner to the lender for a term of 3,000 years. Where the property is leasehold, the lease granted in favour of the lender is for a term equivalent to the owner's interest, less one day. In both cases there is included a provision for 'cesser on redemption', that is for the lease to terminate on redemption of the loan. The second (and much more usual) way is a charge by deed expressed to be by way of

---

9   CML Press Release, 11 February 2010.

10   See *Alliance & Leicester plc v Slayford* [2000] EWCA Civ 257; [2001] 1 All ER (Comm) 1 and M Thompson, 'The cumulative range of mortgagee's remedies' [2002] Conv 53 for a discussion of the interrelationship between the different remedies open to a lender.

11   Law of Property Act 1925 ss85(1) and 86(1). See also *Lavin v Johnson* [2002] EWCA Civ 1138 and C McNall, 'Truth suppressed? "Purported conveyance by way of mortgage"' [2003] Conv 326.

legal mortgage. This is commonly known as a legal charge. Although the borrower remains the holder of the legal estate, with the lender obtaining no legal term as such, the lender is by statute given the same powers and remedies as a lender whose loan is protected by the creation of a lease in the lender's favour.[12]

38.7   In practice, modern institutional lenders invariably rely on mortgages by way of legal charge because they are simpler to use. The legal charge is an agreement whereby a particular property is used as security to ensure that a borrower complies with the terms of a loan from the lender without the transfer of possession or title by the borrower to the lender. In the event of default by the borrower, the lender is given various statutory powers in respect of the property and, generally, additional contractual powers are reserved to the lender in the mortgage deed. The borrower is usually made responsible in the charge deed for the maintenance and insurance of the building, and is made personally liable for payment of the mortgage money and the lender's legal costs and expenses in enforcing the security. Advisers should look at the terms of the charge deed (and any collateral agreement) for the details in each case. In the cases of loans from fringe banks and similar lenders, it is essential to obtain a copy of the loan agreement as well as the legal charge so that all the terms of the loan are clear. Usually, a copy will be forthcoming on request.

Types of mortgage

38.8   There are, most commonly, two different forms of modern mortgage used by individuals for the securing of a loan, whether for the initial purchase of a property or for a subsequent loan. It is important for advisers to clarify which the borrower has entered into.

38.9   The first is the *capital repayment* (or annuity) mortgage. This usually requires a monthly repayment to the lender, part of which is repayment of the capital borrowed and the balance of which is interest. In this way the capital is repaid gradually over the term of the loan.

38.10   The second common form of mortgage is the *interest-only* mortgage in which, usually, two monthly payments are required: one is to the lender and comprises interest on the capital borrowed, and the other is to a financial institution which over the term of the mortgage

12 Law of Property Act 1925 s87(1).

(through investment) accumulates a lump sum payment which should be adequate to pay off the capital sum borrowed.

38.11   Perhaps the most common of these 'capital vehicles' is the endowment insurance policy. During the term, the benefit of the policy is sometimes formally assigned to the lender and it is a condition of the loan that the premiums are paid on the policy. However, the policy may not have been the subject of a deed of assignment when the mortgage was taken out and as a result the policy remains the borrower's and can be disposed of at the borrower's discretion. Some endowment insurance policies are 'with profits' and are designed to give the borrower a small additional lump sum at the end of the term, over and above the money needed to pay off the loan and redeem the mortgage. A 'with profits' endowment mortgage requires higher monthly instalments. Unfortunately, in recent years, a significant number of borrowers have been told by their endowment policy companies that the policies will be inadequate to pay off the capital sum borrowed. Borrowers in this situation should be encouraged to contact the Financial Services Authority (FSA) for advice.[13]

38.12   Other forms of interest-only mortgage are now available. One is the *pension* mortgage, where the owner's private retirement pension is used as security for repayment of the capital borrowed. Personal equity plans (PEPs) and individual savings accounts (ISAs) can also be used as investment 'wrappers' to secure a mortgage. In all cases the capital needed to repay the mortgage is paid out of the lump sum which becomes payable to the borrower when the pension plan, PEP or ISA matures. No formal assignment of the pension, PEP or ISA can be made, and so lenders are really relying on their right to possession as security in the event of the capital not being repaid at the end of the agreed term. As with endowment mortgages, the borrower is required to pay interest on the outstanding capital throughout the term. Numerically, these types of mortgage are becoming more significant as the push to develop private pension and personal finance plans continues.

38.13   Many interest-only mortgages are taken out with no 'repayment vehicle' in place from the outset of the loan. Usually the borrower will rely on an increase in the value of the security as a basis for their later ability to make repayment of the loan. Often the loan will have started as an interest only loan with an endowment or other similar facility in place. Commonly this is often the first thing that is stopped being paid for when money becomes tight.

---

13   See www.fsa.gov.uk.

38.14   In 2007, 32.1 per cent of mortgages were approved on an 'interest-only' basis.[14] Advisers will need to identify whether a 'repayment vehicle' was taken out at the start of the mortgage and, if so, whether that is still available.

38.15   A further variant is the *flexible* mortgage, which seeks to blur the distinction between capital repayment and interest-only loans. In essence this is usually an interest-only mortgage which allows the borrower to make capital payments ostensibly at any time, with the capital payment instantly reducing the balance due and on which interest payments are calculated. Some of these 'flexible' mortgage 'products' are designed to combine the borrower's other personal finances with the mortgage debt, in effect so that the mortgage is used as a bank account. The aim is to ensure maximum financial benefit for the borrower. However, in this way all of the borrower's indebtedness is secured in favour of the lender by the mortgage. Such mortgages commonly also include provisions whereby the borrower is permitted to have mortgage payment 'holidays' where no payments are required for a specified period.

38.16   Traditionally, banks and building societies have been responsible for mortgage lending for people to be able to buy their own homes. More recently the banks in particular have been advancing significantly in the 'buy-to-let' mortgage market. This is where the loan is specifically given for the purpose of a landlord letting the property to tenants. In November 2009 'buy-to-let' mortgages represented 11 per cent of the residential mortgage market.[15]

14 FSA *Mortgage market review* DP09/3 October 2009 para 2.6.
15 CML Press Release, 12 November 2009.

CHAPTER 39

The lender's common law right to possession

39.1   As a legal charge gives the lender a notional lease of the property, the lender is, subject to any agreement to the contrary in the deed, entitled to take possession of the property as soon as the deed has been executed.[1] It is not necessary for the borrower to be in default. However, if someone other than the borrower has a right to possession in priority to that of the lender, the latter would be prevented from taking possession (see para 46.2). The fact that a borrower may have entered into a sub-charge does not strip the lender, as principal chargee, of its right to possession. Both principal chargee and sub-chargee have rights to possession.[2]

39.2   Obviously modern institutional lenders do not want possession of the property as they would prefer that they receive the regular repayments agreed with the borrower. The exercise of this right to possession is usually only a preliminary step to enforcing the security by way of sale with vacant possession in case of financial or other default under the mortgage.

39.3   Unless the mortgage deed requires it, at common law, notice of proceedings for possession need not be given,[3] although a number of warning letters are usually sent by a lender. However, lenders must have regard to the Mortgage Arrears Protocol, see paras 42.3–42.13 and appendix D. It is not necessary for lenders to obtain a possession order in order to take possession,[4] except in cases regulated by the Consumer Credit Act 1974.

1   Law of Property Act 1925 s95(4) and *Four-maids Ltd v Dudley Marshall (Properties) Ltd* [1957] Ch 317; [1957] 2 All ER 35 and generally R J Smith 'The mortgagee's right to possession – the modern law' [1979] Conv 266.

2   *Credit & Mercantile plc v Marks* [2004] EWCA Civ 568; [2005] Ch 81.

3   *Jolly v Arbuthnot* (1859) 4 De G & J 224.

4   *Ropaigealach v Barclays Bank plc* [2000] QB 263; [1999] 3 WLR 17; [1999] 4 All ER 235, CA.

39.4   In *Horsham Properties Group Ltd v Clark and Others*,[5] it was held that the exercise of the power of sale by receivers acting on behalf of the lender (which enables a lender to sell the security without first seeking a possession order) did not amount to a deprivation of a possession contrary to article 1 of the 1st Protocol of the European Convention on Human Rights.

39.5   Any occupier of the security can be evicted as a trespasser. However, where a property is occupied, a lender would be guilty of an offence under the Criminal Law Act 1977 s6 if it recovered possession other than through the courts. In practice, to ensure an ability to sell as mortgagees in possession, lenders do seek orders for possession. The extent to which parliament has modified this common law right to possession is discussed in chapter 40.

39.6   Some charge deeds contain a clause effectively creating a notional tenancy between the lender and the borrower. This is now not common. Such a clause is called an 'attornment clause'. If the agreement contains such a clause then the lender must first terminate the tenancy before exercising its right to possession.[6] Such clauses are not used in modern institutional mortgage deeds. The legal charge may expressly state when the lender is able to seek possession from the borrower.

---

5 [2008] EWHC 2327 (Ch); [2008] 3 EGLR 75; [2009] 1 P&CR 8.
6 *Hinckley and Country Building Society v Henny* [1953] 1 WLR 352.

CHAPTER 40

Courts' powers to allow borrowers to remain in their homes

continued

Legal regulation of mortgages – overview

40.1 On 31 October 2004 major changes were introduced to the legal regulation of residential mortgages. The Financial Services and Markets Act (FSMA) 2000 brought significant elements of mortgage lending and mortgage administration under the control of the Financial Services Authority (FSA). Regulations issued under the 2000 Act introduced the concept of the 'regulated mortgage contract'. For full details see para 40.72 onwards. The 2000 Act also set up the Financial Ombudsman Service (FOS) as a dispute resolution body whose function is to investigate and resolve complaints about regulated activities as an alternative to the courts, including those relating to the sale, granting and administration of mortgages. The 2000 Act does not, however, apply to mortgages which are not 'regulated mortgage contracts', such as 'buy-to-let' mortgages or second charges, nor to mortgages that were entered into before 31 October 2004.

40.2 Mortgages entered into before 31 October 2004 remain regulated solely by the provisions of the Administration of Justice Acts (AJA) 1970 and 1973 unless they fall within the definition of 'regulated agreement' within the meaning of the Consumer Credit Act (CCA) 1974, in which case they will be regulated by that legislation.[1]

40.3 Mortgages entered into after 31 October 2004 which fall within the definition of 'regulated mortgage contract' are regulated by the FSA. In the event of possession proceedings, the courts also have the powers available in the Administration of Justice Acts 1970 and 1973, again unless the agreement falls within the Consumer Credit Act 1974, in which case that legislation will apply. The Consumer Credit Act 2006 made significant changes to the powers available to the courts when dealing with possession proceedings by lenders.

40.4 The small residue of residential mortgages which do not qualify as 'regulated mortgage contracts' and which also fall outside the provisions of the Consumer Credit Act 1974 will have possession proceedings regulated by the 1970 and 1973 Acts.

40.5 In December 2009 the then government issued a consultation document proposing that the control by the FSA should be extended to include all secured loans and 'buy-to-let' mortgages.[2]

40.6 As has been indicated above (see chapter 39), the lender has an immediate legal right to possession of the mortgaged property. The

1 AJA 1970 s38A, inserted by CCA 1974 Sch 4 para 30.
2 *Mortgage regulation: a consultation*, see www.hm-treasury.gov.uk/d/consult_mortgage_regulation.pdf.

court, when considering an application by the lender for an order for possession, has only limited inherent and statutory power to prevent the lender from obtaining possession or to delay repossession.

Inherent powers and equitable relief

40.7   The High Court has an inherent discretion in possession proceedings to grant a short adjournment only (for example, 28 days) so as to allow any default to be remedied or for the loan to be paid off.[3] It has also been stated that the court's equitable powers extend to preventing a lender from taking possession 'except when it is sought bona fide and reasonably for the purpose of enforcing the security and then only subject to such conditions as the court thinks fit to impose'.[4]

40.8   This is a proposition of equity articulated by Lord Denning MR in 1979, which has since been approved in the Court of Appeal[5] and gives scope for borrowers to argue, for instance, that if there is some other method of enforcing payment of arrears (such as an attachment of earnings order) then no order for possession should be granted. This would be particularly useful in cases where the lender's interests are not significantly at risk because there is plenty of equity in the property (ie, the sale value of the property substantially exceeds the outstanding debt). The extent of this equitable jurisdiction has yet to be fully assessed.

40.9   The courts have also accepted an equitable jurisdiction, which potentially may assist borrowers, through the doctrine of 'unconscionable bargain'. Under this jurisdiction the court can set aside the legal charge or clauses within a charge on the basis that they are 'unconscionable', 'unfair' or 'unreasonable', where the lender 'has imposed the objectionable terms in a morally reprehensible manner ... in a way which affects his conscience'.[6] Browne-Wilkinson J gave as the classic example of such a bargain, a case 'where advantage has been taken of a young, inexperienced or ignorant person to introduce such a term which no sensible well-advised person or party would have accepted'.[7]

---

3   *Birmingham Citizens' Permanent Building Society v Caunt* [1962] Ch 883. See too *Cheltenham & Gloucester plc v Booker* (1997) 29 HLR 634, CA.

4   *Quennel v Maltby* [1979] 1 WLR 318; [1979] 1 All ER 568, CA, at 571e.

5   *Albany Homes Loans v Massey* [1997] 2 All ER 609; (1997) 29 HLR 902, CA. See also M P Thompson, 'The Powers and Duties of Mortgagees' [1998] Conv 391.

6   *Multiservice Bookbinding Ltd v Marden* [1979] Ch 84 at 110F.

7   *Multiservice Bookbinding Ltd v Marden* [1979] Ch 84.

40.10   It seems that there has to be some element of morally reprehensible behaviour, involving abusive inequality of bargaining power such as to 'shock the conscience of the court'.[8] There is obviously a very clear overlap between this, the unfair relationship provisions of the Consumer Credit Act 1974 and the Unfair Terms in Consumer Contracts Regulations 1999[9] (see para 40.64 onwards). While of obviously limited application, in appropriate cases this equitable jurisdiction may prove to be an additional basis of defence to a possession claim.[10]

Statutory powers

40.11   There are two mutually exclusive statutory regimes which may be available to assist a borrower in default under the mortgage. In the case of residential mortgages, the court has powers to grant relief either by virtue of the Administration of Justice Acts 1970 and 1973 or, alternatively, under the Consumer Credit Act 1974. A regulated mortgage contract within the meaning of the Financial Services and Markets Act 2000 which is entered into after 31 October 2004 is an 'exempt agreement' and as such is outside the scope of the Consumer Credit Act 1974 and hence will be governed by the Administration of Justice Acts 1970 and 1973.[11] Where the mortgage is a 'regulated agreement' within the meaning of the Consumer Credit Act 1974 (for which see para 40.37), the provisions of that Act apply in place of those of the Administration of Justice Acts.[12] Where the mortgage relates to non-residential property, then there is statutory power to grant relief only if the agreement in question is 'a regulated agreement' within the Consumer Credit Act 1974.

---

8 See *Creswell v Potter* [1978] 1 WLR 255; *Backhouse v Backhouse* [1978] 1 All ER 1158; *Lloyds Bank Ltd v Bundy* [1974] 3 All ER 757, CA and *Alec Lobb (Garages) Ltd v Total Oil GB Ltd* [1983] 1 All ER 944.

9 SI No 2083.

10 See *Credit Lyonnais Bank Nederland v Burch* [1997] 1 All ER 143, CA. Cf, *Portman Building Society v Dusangh* [2000] 2 All ER (Comm) 221, CA. See also L McMurty, 'Unconscionability and undue influence: an interaction?' [2000] 64 Conv 573.

11 Financial Services and Markets Act 2000 (Regulated Activities) Order 2001 SI No 544 reg 90.

12 AJA 1970 s38A, inserted by CCA 1974 Sch 4 para 30, Consumer Credit Act 1974 (Commencement No 8) Order 1983 SI No 1551 and County Courts Act 1984 s21(9).

40.12   Occasionally, the court may make the mistake of treating consumer credit loans in the same way as loans to which the Administration of Justice Acts apply. It is important to remind district judges of the difference when dealing with consumer credit loans and to emphasise the fact that the court's powers under the Consumer Credit Act 1974 are wider than those under the Administration of Justice Acts.

Administration of Justice Acts 1970 and 1973

40.13   Administration of Justice Act 1970 Part IV, together with AJA 1973 s8, sets out the court's principal powers to assist borrowers who are in default.[13] It has been said that the Administration of Justice Act 1970 represents a form of 'social legislation' in which 'Parliament has attempted to give legislative shelter to a wide class of owner-occupiers'.[14]

40.14   Administration of Justice Act 1970 s36(1) provides:

> Where the mortgagee under a *mortgage* of land which consists of or includes a *dwelling-house* brings an action in which he claims possession ... not being an action for *foreclosure* in which a claim for possession ... is also made, the court may exercise any of [its] powers ... if it appears to the court that in the event of its exercising the power the mortgagor *is likely* to be able within a *reasonable period* to pay any *sums due* under the mortgage or to remedy a default consisting of a breach of any other obligation arising under or by virtue of the mortgage. [Authors' emphasis: the italicised phrases are considered below.]

Section 36(2) provides that the court:

> (a) may adjourn the proceedings, or
> (b) on giving judgment, or making an order, for delivery of possession ... or at any time before execution of such judgment or order may:
> (i) stay or suspend execution of the judgment or order, or
> (ii) postpone the date for delivery of possession,
> for such period or periods as the court thinks reasonable.

By AJA 1970 s36(3) any order made in exercise of any section 36(2) powers may be made:

> ... subject to such conditions with regard to payment by the mortgagor of any sum secured by the mortgage or the remedying of any default as the court thinks fit.

---

13   See generally R J Smith, 'The mortgagee's right to possession – the modern law' [1979] Conv 266 and A Clarke, 'Further implications of s36 of the Administration of Justice Act' [1983] Conv 293.

14   *Centrax Trustees Ltd v Ross* [1979] 2 All ER 952 at 955f per Goulding J.

The court is empowered by AJA 1970 s36(4) to vary or revoke any condition imposed under section 36(3) but not the period of any postponed possession order.[15]

40.15   Administration of Justice Act 1970 s36 is qualified by AJA 1973 s8(2) which states:

> A court shall not exercise ... the powers conferred by section 36 ... unless it appears to the court not only that the mortgagor is likely to be able within a reasonable period to pay any amounts regarded ... as due on account of the principal sum secured, together with the interest on those amounts, but also that he is likely to be able by the end of that period to pay any further amounts that he would have expected to be required to pay by then on account of that sum and of interest on it ...

40.16   In effect, before exercising any of its powers it must appear to the court not only that the borrower is likely to be able to pay off the missed monthly payments within a reasonable period, but also that it is likely that by the end of that reasonable period the borrower will also have paid off the payments which will have fallen due during that period. This will usually mean being able to show that the borrower can resume payment of the current instalments and can also make regular payments towards the arrears so that at the end of the reasonable period all the arrears will have been discharged. However, section 36 would also be satisfied if the borrower can pay off the arrears over the reasonable period and discharge the payments that have fallen due over that period by a payment made at the end of that period,[16] for example, by way of a lump sum payment. It may be reasonable to adjourn proceedings in order to determine, at some later date, whether there has emerged in the interim any prospect of the borrower being able, within a reasonable period, to pay sums due under the mortgage,[17] for example, where a student borrower who is currently studying for qualifications could later obtain employment which would enable the arrears to be discharged.

40.17   The court's powers apply equally to endowment mortgages, where there is no obligation to repay the capital originally borrowed until the end of the loan period, as they do to annuity (or capital repayment) mortgages, where part of each monthly repayment is capital

---

15 *Secured Residential Funding v Greenhill* noted at *Current Law Week* 22 October 1993, Bournemouth County Court, HHJ Darwell-Smith.

16 *Governor & Company of the Royal Bank of Scotland v Elmes* April 1998 *Legal Action* 11.

17 *Skandia Financial Services Ltd v Greenfield* [1997] CLY 4248.

and part interest.[18] By analogy, interest-only loans would also be included. Administration of Justice Act 1970 s36 powers can also be exercised whether or not there is default under the mortgage deed itself, for example, breach of some collateral agreement.[19]

40.18   Administration of Justice Act 1973 s8(1) restricts the way in which the court can exercise its AJA 1970 section 36 powers. It provides that only where a borrower is entitled to repay the capital by instalments or otherwise to defer payment of it in whole or in part and there is also provision for earlier payment of the capital either on default by the borrower or demand by the lender, then the court may treat as due in respect of capital such sums as the borrower would have been expected to repay but for the provision in the mortgage for earlier repayment. Section 8(1) will not apply where deferral is granted as a mere indulgence by the lender, lacking contractual force, unless it is enforceable by estoppel.[20] Where an agreement to secure a bank overdraft provides that money owed shall become payable only on demand, then there is no agreement to defer payment and so the agreement falls outside the scope of AJA 1973 s8.[21] These are sometimes described as 'all monies' charges. In such cases the court retains the more limited power under AJA 1970 s36 to suspend enforcement of a possession order to enable the borrower to pay off the entire debt over a reasonable period. However, in such cases the court has no contractual term to consider by way of guidance as to what the reasonable term should be and therefore will have to determine this in isolation.

40.19   A reasonable time must be given to the borrower to comply with a demand for repayment before the lender is permitted to claim possession unless it is clear that, even if given a reasonable period, the borrower will not be able to pay off the mortgage debt.[22]

'Mortgage'

40.20   As indicated in chapter 38 there is no significant practical difference between a legal mortgage and a legal charge. Administration

---

18 *Bank of Scotland v Grimes* [1985] QB 1179; [1985] 3 WLR 294, CA.

19 *Western Bank Ltd v Schindler* [1977] Ch 1; [1976] 3 WLR 341; [1976] 2 All ER 393, CA and generally C Harpum, 'A mortgagee's right to possession and the mischief rule' (1977) 40 MLR 356.

20 *Rees Investments Ltd v Groves* [2002] 1 P&CR DG9; 27 June 2001, unreported, ChD, Neuberger J, noted at April 2002 *Legal Action* 22.

21 See *Habib Bank Ltd v Tailor* [1982] 1 WLR 1218; [1982] 3 All ER 561, CA.

22 *Sheppard & Cooper v TSB Bank plc (No 2)* [1996] 2 All ER 654, ChD.

of Justice Act 1970 s39(1) confirms that the expression 'mortgage' includes a 'charge' and that 'mortgagor' and 'mortgagee' should be similarly construed.

'Dwelling-house'

40.21 Administration of Justice Act 1970 s39(1) defines 'dwelling-house' as meaning 'any building or part thereof which is used as a dwelling'. Section 39(2) of the Administration of Justice Act 1970 amplifies this by expressly providing that this may include premises some of which are used 'as a shop or office or for business, trade or professional purposes'. It follows, therefore, that a mixed business/residential user is covered by the 1970 Act. The relevant time for determining whether land consists of, or includes, a dwelling-house is the date the lender claims possession.[23] The fact that the property may be used as a dwelling for someone other than the borrower does not prevent the security from being a dwelling-house and so within scope of the 1970 Act. However, if the non-borrower occupier is in occupation in breach of a term of the mortgage, this amounts to a breach within the meaning of AJA 1970 s36(1).

'Foreclosure'

40.22 Although it is often said that a property is being foreclosed by a lender for mortgage default, in practice the common form of enforcement is that of taking possession and subsequent sale. The court's powers are not available where the lender's claim includes a claim for foreclosure.

40.23 Foreclosure of residential mortgages is very rare as it is more complex than enforcement by possession and sale. The latter is usually sufficient as a method of enforcement. Foreclosure is technically quite different from the obtaining of possession and subsequent sale in that it involves the extinction of the borrower's equitable right to redeem the mortgage on the property and the vesting of the legal estate absolutely in the lender. An example will illustrate the difference.

---

23 *Royal Bank of Scotland v Miller* [2001] EWCA Civ 344; [2002] QB 255; [2001] 3 WLR 523.

Example

X borrows £220,000 by way of a mortgage from C Ltd. X repays £40,000 before C Ltd obtains possession and sells it for £240,000. X would receive £60,000 after redemption of the existing mortgage of £180,000. If C Ltd foreclosed on the property, instead of taking possession and selling, X would lose the equity of £60,000. C Ltd would become the absolute owner of the property worth £240,000 and X would receive nothing.

40.24   In view of the draconian nature of foreclosure, the courts are reluctant to grant foreclosure orders and they put procedural obstacles in the way of a lender seeking such an order. Briefly, the procedure to obtain such an order is as follows. Once repayment of the mortgage money has fallen due, for example, on breach of any term in the mortgage or after calling-in by the lender (ie, an express and unconditional demand is made for payment) and it remains unpaid, the lender can apply for a foreclosure decree *nisi*. This order directs the taking of accounts between the lender and the borrower as to money paid during the term of the mortgage, and provides that if the borrower pays the remaining outstanding money by a particular date then the mortgage is redeemed and the debt discharged. If the mortgage is not redeemed by that date, then the lender can apply to be granted a foreclosure order *absolute*. The lender then becomes the legal owner and the property is transferred to it. At the request of any person interested the court has the power[24] to order sale of the property instead of foreclosure. Usually, such an order for 'judicial sale' would be granted so as to ensure that the borrower receives the balance of the sale price once the lender has been paid off. The court's dislike of foreclosure is such that, on occasion, even after a foreclosure order absolute has been made, it will 'open' the foreclosure. As a result of this, and the efficacy of other methods of enforcement, foreclosure is rarely used by lenders[25] although it may be pleaded as part of the lender's claim for relief in addition to claims for sale and/or possession. It may also be that the remedy of foreclosure amounts to a breach of the borrower's rights under article 1 of Protocol No 1 of the European Convention on Human Rights.

---

24 Law of Property Act 1925 s91(1) and (2).
25 For a note on foreclosure in commercial mortgages, see E Bannister, 'Foreclosure – a remedy out of its time?' (1992) EG 28 March.

40.25   It seems likely that foreclosure is no longer possible in the case of 'regulated agreements' within the meaning of the Consumer Credit Act 1974 (see para 40.37) as section 113(1) of that Act prevents a lender from obtaining any greater benefit by enforcing any security provided in relation to a regulated agreement than would be the case if no such security had been given. No authority on the point has been found but, in view of the very restricted use of foreclosure, happily the point may remain academic.

40.26   The Administration of Justice Acts add, to some limited degree, to the court's powers in cases where foreclosure is claimed. In effect, where foreclosure alone is claimed, the only statutory (as opposed to common law or inherent) power is adjournment. If the claim is for foreclosure and possession, there appears to be power to adjourn the foreclosure claim and then to adjourn the possession claim or stay, suspend execution or postpone any order for possession.[26]

'Is likely'

40.27   The question of whether a borrower is likely to be able to pay any sums due within a reasonable time is one of fact for the judge on the evidence before him or her, whether in a witness statement or given by way of oral evidence.[27] For this reason it is essential that the borrower(s) attend the possession hearing, otherwise it is likely that there will be no evidence before the district judge to allow him or her to exercise the court's statutory powers, although the district judge may of his or her own volition ask about the last payments or in some other way seek evidence from the lender's representative. It may be reasonable to adjourn proceedings in order to determine, at a later date, whether there has emerged in the interim any prospect of the borrower being able within a reasonable period to pay sums due under the mortgage, for example, where a student borrower is studying for qualifications which would result in employment adequate to enable the borrower to discharge the arrears.[28] The court cannot suspend an order for possession, however hard the circumstances, if there is no prospect of the borrower reducing the arrears.[29]

26 AJA 1970 s36 and AJA 1973 s8(3). See generally S Tromans, 'Mortgages: possession by default' [1984] Conv 91.

27 *Royal Trust Company of Canada v Markham* [1975] 1 WLR 1416; [1975] 3 All ER 433, CA and *Western Bank Ltd v Schindler* [1977] Ch 1; [1976] 2 All ER 393, CA.

28 *Skandia Financial Services Ltd v Greenfield* [1997] CLY 4248, Horsham County Court.

29 *Abbey National Mortgages v Bernard* (1996) 71 P&CR 257, CA.

'Reasonable period'

40.28 One crucial question which has to be asked in each case is: what is the 'reasonable period'? It has been stated, obiter, that in making the assessment the court must 'bear in mind the rights and obligations of both parties, including [the lender's] right to recover the money by selling the property, if necessary, and the whole past history of the security'.[30] More important, however, is the approach to the length of the period during which arrears are to be cleared.

40.29 However, in *Cheltenham & Gloucester Building Society v Norgan*,[31] the Court of Appeal reviewed the authorities and concluded that, when assessing a 'reasonable period', it was appropriate for the court to take account of the whole of the remaining part of the original term of the mortgage. The court stated that in determining the 'reasonable period' the court 'should take as its starting point the full term of the mortgage and pose at the outset the question: would it be possible for the mortgagor to maintain payment-off of the arrears by instalments over that period?'[32] The court listed a number of considerations which are likely to be relevant when establishing what is a reasonable period. They are:

(a) How much can the borrower reasonably afford to pay, both now and in the future?
(b) If the borrower has a temporary difficulty in meeting his obligations, how long is the difficulty likely to last?
(c) What was the reason for the arrears which have accumulated?
(d) How much remains of the original term?
(e) What are the relevant contractual terms, and what type of mortgage is it, ie when is the principal due to be repaid?
(f) Is it a case where the court should exercise its power to disregard accelerated payment provisions (section 8 of the 1973 Act)?
(g) Is it reasonable to expect the lender, in the circumstances of the case, to recoup the arrears of interest: (1) over the whole of the original term, or (2) within a shorter period, or even (3) within a longer period, ie by extending the repayment period? Is it reasonable to expect the lender to capitalise the interest or not?
(h) Are there reasons affecting the security which should influence the length of the period for payment?[33]

30 *Centrax Trustees v Ross* [1979] 2 All ER 952 at 957, per Goulding J.
31 [1996] 1 WLR 343; [1996] 1 All ER 449, CA. See also J Morgan, 'Mortgage arrears and the family home' (1996) 112 LQR 553 and M Thompson, 'Back to square two' [1996] Conv 118. See too *First Middlesbrough Trading and Mortgage Co Ltd v Cunningham* (1974) 28 P&CR 69, CA and *Western Bank v Schnider* [1977] Ch 1; [1976] 3 WLR 34.
32 [1996] 1 All ER 449 at 458.
33 [1996] 1 All ER 449 at 463a.

40.30 It is clear from the judgment that the existence of equity in the security to protect the lender is a significant factor in determining whether the court will exercise its discretion in the borrower's favour. Following this case, district judges have tended to adopt a much more generous interpretation of the reasonable period. Although, no doubt mindful of certain obiter dicta in *Norgan* to the effect that the court should be less sympathetic if a borrower has once failed to meet payments calculated by reference to the balance of the contractual term, it is not universal practice to use the balance of the term as the starting point in assessing the reasonable period. In the case of regulated mortgage contracts (for which see para 40.75) the FSA's stated position is that in appropriate cases the remaining term of the mortgage will be the reasonable repayment period.[34]

40.31 Where there is sufficient equity in the property (ie, the surplus value of the property arrived at after deducting the money outstanding under any mortgages), it is hard to see what risk there is to the lender in deferring possession. Therefore it can be useful to clarify with the lender before the hearing whether it accepts that there is equity or to produce evidence to prove the amount of equity to show that the lender is not at risk. The Legal Help scheme (see para 28.3 for further discussion) can be used to pay for the cost of an expert's report on the valuation. An estate agent's valuation may be helpful as a guide although the Court of Appeal has commented that such valuations should be treated with 'reserve'.[35] Institutional lenders often have property valuations which bear little relationship to a genuine valuation based, as they are, on general statistics relating to market trends or even 'drive by' valuations. Where there is likely to be a dispute about the value of the property, and therefore the level of equity, then this of itself may be sufficient to persuade the Legal Services Commission to grant a public funding certificate for representation (see chapter 28). In such cases it should be pointed out that in practice the courts are influenced greatly by the valuation evidence.

40.32 Where, however, there is no equity (ie, there would be a shortfall if the property were sold) it is possible to argue that the lender's interests are better served by a delay in possession being given up, particularly where there is some prospect of the market improving. The contrary view is that on a falling market it is in the lender's interest to allow sale to proceed at the earliest opportunity so that the loss to the lender is minimised.

---

34 Mortgage Conduct of Business Sourcebook (MCOB) 2003 13.3.6, see para 40.96.
35 *Bristol & West Building Society v Ellis* (1997) 29 HLR 282; 73 P&CR 158, CA.

40.33   See chapter 48 for the situation where the borrower wishes to sell the property in order to pay off the loan.

'Sums due'

40.34   Most mortgage deeds enable the lender to 'call in' the loan at any time or else provide that the capital money in total becomes immediately payable in the event of any default. As originally drafted, Administration of Justice Act 1970 s36 enabled the court to give relief to the borrower only if it were likely that he or she could pay any sums due under the mortgage. The court's power to give relief was therefore available in such cases only if the borrower could pay off any arrears *and* the outstanding capital which had invariably also become payable. To resolve this anomaly, AJA 1973 s8(1) redefined 'sums due' to make it clear that in the case of instalment mortgages or mortgages where payment was deferred in whole or part, the financial default to be considered at the hearing was limited to the normal instalments due but unpaid and that the provision for earlier repayment of capital contained in the mortgage deed was to be ignored.

40.35   It is not clear from the wording of AJA 1970 s36 and AJA 1973 s8, when read together, whether it is proper for the court in 'instalment mortgage' cases to take into account interest which accrues on arrears (and other payments which fall due as a result of being in arrears) in determining a borrower's ability to pay off 'any sums due' over the reasonable period. It is suggested that, given the wording of AJA 1973 s8(1), the borrower should be required to show only that he or she is likely to be able to pay off the arrears built up by the hearing date and not that he or she can pay off those arrears plus any interest and other payments which may accrue over the reasonable period.[36]

Administration of Justice Acts and European Convention on Human Rights

40.36   The Court of Appeal has said that AJA 1970 s36 strikes the right balance between the rights of the borrower to remain in his or her home and the rights of the lender to repayment within a reasonable period. There is no breach of the European Convention on Human Rights article 8 or article 1 of the First Protocol.[37]

---

36 For an interesting article on this and other points relating to the practice of mortgage possession proceedings, see District Judge Parmiter, 'Wrongly dispossessed?' LS Gaz 29 April 1992.

37 *Barclays Bank plc v Alcorn* [2002] EWCA Civ 817.

Consumer Credit Act 1974

40.37 Where a 'regulated agreement' within the meaning of the Consumer Credit Act 1974 is secured by a legal charge, then the provisions of that Act apply in place of those in the Administration of Justice Acts.[38] Basically, a regulated agreement is a consumer credit agreement under which an individual is supplied with credit of any amount unless the agreement falls within the Act's 'exempt agreement' provisions.[39] A consumer credit agreement is 'an agreement between an individual ('the debtor') and any other person ('the creditor') by which the creditor provides the debtor with credit of any amount'.[40]

40.38 Amendments made to the Consumer Credit Act 1974 by the Consumer Credit Act 2006 s2,[41] effective from 6 April 2008, removed the previous financial limit of £25,000, rendering all loans under regulated agreements within the provisions of the 1974 Act.

40.39 A consumer credit agreement is a regulated agreement within the meaning of the 1974 Act if it is not an 'exempt' agreement within the meaning of sections 16, 16A, 16B or 16C. Loans which otherwise would be within scope of the Consumer Credit Act 1974 are 'exempt agreements' in the following circumstances:

- *All loans by local authorities secured on land.*[42] Also, loans by building societies and the various banks, insurance companies, friendly societies and charities specified in the Consumer Credit (Exempt Agreements) Order 1989[43] are exempt provided the loans are secured on land and are for the purchase of land, or the provision of a dwelling or business premises. Additionally, loans by these lenders are exempt where they are for:
  – the alteration, enlargement, repair or improvement of a dwelling or business premises, provided the lender has already lent for the purchase of land or the provision of a dwelling or business premises; or, alternatively,
  – the alteration, enlargement, repair or improvement of a dwelling, such work to be undertaken by a housing association or other specified body.

---

38 AJA 1970 s38A.
39 See CCA 1974 ss8, 16, 16A, 16B and 16C.
40 CCA 1974 s8(1).
41 See generally 'The Consumer Credit Act 2006: real additional mortgagor protection?' [2007] 71 Conv 316.
42 CCA 1974 s16.
43 SI No 869, as substantially amended.

In either case, to be exempt, the loan must be secured on the property in question.

- A *'regulated mortgage contract'* or a *'regulated home purchase plan'* *within the meaning of the Financial Services and Markets Act*[44] (see para 40.75).
- *The borrower is a 'high net worth' individual.*[45] Individuals who have a 'high net worth', ie, had an income or had assets in the previous financial year in excess of a prescribed amount, can exempt themselves from the provisions of the 1974 Act by completing a declaration in prescribed form.[46] Currently the respective figures are no less than £150,000 and £500,000.
- *A consumer credit agreement where the borrower is provided with credit exceeding £25,000 which is provided wholly or predominately for the purpose of a business carried on, or intended to be carried on by the borrower.*[47]
- *Secured loans for the purchase of investment properties.*[48] The loan must be secured on land provided also that less than 40 per cent of the property is used or intended to be used as a dwelling for the borrower or his or her spouse or civil partner, parent, sibling, child, grandparent or grandchild.

The 'unfair relationship' provisions of the Consumer Credit Act 1974 (see para 40.58) have application to these loans which otherwise are outside scope of the 1974 Act.

40.40   Happily, in practice it is usually clear whether a loan falls within scope of the Consumer Credit Act 1974 because of the explicit references to the Act in the documentation. In July 2009 HM Treasury issued a consultation paper *Reforming financial markets*, which proposed bringing the regulation of second charges and buy-to-let mortgages under the authority of the FSA.[49]

40.41   The provisions of the Consumer Credit Act 1974 are notoriously complicated, dealing as they do with a multitude of different types of credit transaction. The Act seeks to prescribe the way in which regulated agreements are entered into. Failure to observe any of these rules renders the agreement 'improperly executed' and so unenforce-

---

44   CCA 1974 s16(6C).
45   CCA 1974 s16A.
46   CCA 1974 s16A and Consumer Credit (Exempt Agreements) Order 2007 SI No 1168.
47   CCA 1974 s16B.
48   CCA 1974 s16C, inserted by the Legislative Reform (Consumer Credit) Order 2008 SI No 2826 art 3(1).
49   www.hm-treasury.gov.uk/d/reforming_financial_markets080709.pdf.

able without a court order.[50] In addition, the loan agreement must be in a prescribed form[51] and the Act lays down provisions for copies of the unexecuted agreement to be given to the borrower and a prescribed procedure for the execution of the agreement.[52] The sanction for non-compliance with the formality provisions of the Act is that the agreement is deemed not to have been 'properly executed' and is enforceable only by way of a court order under CCA 1974 s127.[53] A lender seeking to enforce an agreement which breaches these formality requirments must apply for an enforcement order. The court has discretion to allow enforcement but only if it is considered just to do so.[54] The provisions of the 1974 Act are not simple and reference should be made to the standard works on consumer credit law for details.[55]

40.42　　In the context of possession proceedings, the Consumer Credit Act 1974 affords a borrower some protection from enforcement of the loan and mortgage if it is within the protection of the Act. The lender can only enforce through a particular procedure in which the court has specific powers to give relief. The lender under a regulated agreement must serve a default notice before being entitled 'to recover possession of any ... land' or 'to enforce any security'. The default notice must be in a prescribed form and specify the nature of the breach of the agreement being alleged.[56] If the borrower complies with the notice, the breach is treated as never having occurred.[57] The terms of the default notice must be accurate. If the amount claimed by the creditor to remedy non-payment was in excess of the sum necessary to remedy such a breach, that default notice would be invalid and any subsequent proceedings liable to be struck out.[58]

Time orders

40.43　Receipt of a default notice by the borrower entitles him or her to apply to the court for a time order by means of which the court can

---

50　CCA 1974 s65.

51　CCA 1974 s60 and Consumer Credit (Agreements) Regulations 1983 SI No 1553.

52　CCA 1974 ss58, 61, 62 and 63.

53　CCA 1974 s65(1).

54　CCA 1974 s127, as amended by CCA 2006 s15.

55　See Goode, *Consumer credit law & practice* (5 Vols), Butterworths, and Goode, *Consumer credit reports* (3 vols), Butterworths.

56　CCA 1974 ss87 and 88 and Consumer Credit (Enforcement, Default and Termination Notices) Regulations 1983 SI No 1561.

57　CCA 1974 s89.

58　*Worcester Lease Management Services Ltd v Swain & Co* [1999] 1 WLR 263, CA.

reschedule payment of money owed under the agreement. Follow-ing a default notice, application for a time order[59] is by way of a Part 8 claim under the Civil Procedure Rules (CPR). Alternatively, the borrower can seek a time order in any possession action which the lender brings, following the expiry of the default notice, either in his or her defence or by application notice in the proceedings.[60] In most cases it will be advisable to seek a time order at the earliest possible opportunity.[61]

40.44   Assuming that the borrower does not pay off the arrears or remedy any other default within the period specified in the default notice, then the lender will be at liberty to issue a possession claim against the borrower. A mortgage securing a regulated agreement is specifically enforceable only by an order of the court.[62] The time order provisions,[63] together with the supplementary powers contained in CCA 1974 ss135 and 136, give the court powers to assist the borrower greatly in excess of those in the Administration of Justice Acts.

40.45   Consumer Credit Act 1974 s129(1) provides:

If it appears to the court just to do so –

...

(b) on an application made by a debtor ... under this paragraph after service on him of –

(i) a default notice, or ...

(c) in an action brought by a creditor ... to enforce a regulated agree-ment or security, or recover possession of any ... land to which a regulated agreement relates,

the court may make an order under this section (a 'time order').

It is clear from the wording of the section that, in the case of proceed-ings brought by the lender to recover possession, the court has the discretion to make a time order even if the borrower has not sought one or even if the borrower is not present in court. The only require-ment is that it should appear to the court 'just to do so'. Form N440 in CPR Part 4 may be used to make a time order application. See prece-dent at appendix B for a consumer credit defence and Part 20 claim.

---

59 CCR Ord 49 r4(5).

60 CPR PD 55A para 7.1.

61 See generally D McConnell, 'Time orders on loans secured against property' January 1990 *Legal Action* 19; R Leszczyszyn, 'Time orders revisited' (1990) *Adviser* No 20 p22; E James, 'Time orders and the Consumer Credit Act' March 1991 *SCOLAG* p40 and F Ratcliffe, 'Tinkering with time orders' September 2005 *Legal Action* 6.

62 CCA 1974 s126.

63 CCA 1974 ss129 and 130.

40.46   Consumer Credit Act 1974 s129(2) provides:

> A time order shall provide for one or both of the following, as the
> court considers just –
> (a) the payment by the debtor ... of any sum owed under a regulated
>   agreement or a security by such instalments, payable at such
>   times, as the court, having regard to the means of the debtor ...
>   and any surety, considers reasonable;
> (b) the remedying by the debtor ... of any breach of a regulated agree-
>   ment (other than non-payment of money) within such period as
>   the court may specify.

40.47   The court is required by the section to order payment of any money
owed by instalments or the remedying of other default if it wishes
to make a time order. However, having determined to exercise its
discretion to grant a time order, the court must have regard only to
the means of the debtor (and any surety) when considering the size
and rate of instalments. It is not legitimate to look to possible hardship caused to the lender or its investors. Equally, there is no requirement that the arrears or any other monies owed be paid off within a
'reasonable period' or even by the end of the original contractual loan
period. The court is given absolute discretion.

40.48   The court's power under CCA 1974 s129(2)(a) enables it to order
payment by instalments of 'any sum owed', ie, already owed. Only in
the cases of hire-purchase and conditional sale agreements may the
courts deal with sums which fall due for payment in the future.[64]

40.49   In mortgage cases, this seemed to rule out the rescheduling of
anything other than the total of instalments missed by the date of the
hearing. However, many legal charges provide that, as soon as default
occurs, the whole loan becomes immediately payable. Alternatively,
in cases where the whole loan does not automatically become due on
default, lenders may have 'called-in' the loan before issuing proceedings. In other words, demand by letter for immediate payment of the
outstanding loan may have been made in pursuance of rights given
to the lender in the legal charge. This calling-in letter is distinct from
the statutory default notice. If the whole loan has been called in by
any of these means, a time order can deal with the total debt.

40.50   Allied to the time order provisions is the related but distinct power
to impose conditions or to suspend operation of an order. Section
135 of the 1974 Act provides:

> (1) If it considers it just to do so, the court may in an order made by it
>   in relation to a regulated agreement include provisions –

---

64   CCA 1974 s130(2).

(a) making the operation of any term of the order conditional on the doing of specified acts by any party to the proceedings;
(b) suspending the operation of any term of the order either –
(i) until such time as the court subsequently directs, or
(ii) until the occurrence of a specified act or omission.

40.51   This subsection empowers the court to suspend any order for possession it may make, whether conditionally on payment of specified instalments by the borrower or until a particular event (for example, default in an instalment order, or the date the property is sold or the borrower rehoused by a local authority). Where a court finds it appropriate to make a time order, the enforcement of any order for possession granted can be suspended so long as payment of the instalments under the time order is made.

40.52   It is specifically stated that any person, 'affected by a time order'[65] or 'affected by a provision'[66] included in an order under CCA 1974 s135 may apply to the court for a variation or revocation in the case of a time order or a variation in the case of a section 135 order. These are particularly useful provisions because they allow a lender to make application to the court for a variation of the terms of a time order where, for example, a time order has been granted on favourable terms to allow the borrower to overcome temporary difficulties. In this way it can be argued that the lender would not be prejudiced by the granting of a time order on terms generous to the borrower, as the lender would be able to come back to court to have those terms varied.

40.53   Finally, Consumer Credit Act 1974 contains a rather cryptic provision in section 136 under the heading of 'Power to vary agreements and securities'. The section reads:

> The court may in an order made by it under this Act include such provision as it considers just for amending any agreement or security in consequence of a term of the order.

40.54   For some years it was not clear how the time order provisions were to be construed. However, in *Southern & District Finance plc v Barnes*,[67] the Court of Appeal (in hearing three linked appeals and in reviewing conflicting county court decisions) gave general guidance on the time order provisions:

---

65   CCA 1974 s130(6).
66   CCA 1974 s135(4).
67   (1995) 27 HLR 691; [1995] Con Cred LR 62, CA. See also A Dunn, 'Footprints on the sands of time: sections 129 and 136 Consumer Credit Act 1974' [1996] 60 Conv 209 and R Rosenberg, 'Calling Time' *Quarterly Account* Issue 63 p11.

- When a time order is applied for, the court must first consider whether it is just to make it. This involves consideration of all of the circumstances of the case including the position of the lender as well as that of the borrower.
- When a time order is made it should usually be made only for a stipulated period on account of temporary financial difficulty.
- The court must consider what instalments would be reasonable, both in amount and their timing, having regard to the borrower's means.
- If, despite being given more time, the borrower will be unable to resume payment of the total indebtedness by at least the amount of the contractual instalments, no time order should be made. In such circumstances it is more equitable to allow the regulated agreement to be enforced.
- When a time order is made following financial default, the 'sum owed' means every sum which is due and owing; in the context of possession proceedings, that usually comprises the total indebtedness (for the reasons given in para 40.49).
- The court may vary the contractual interest rate under CCA 1974 s136.
- Where a time order is made governing the whole of the outstanding balance due under the loan, there will be consequences for the term of the loan, the rate of interest or both.
- If justice requires the making of a time order, the court should suspend any possession order so long as the terms of the time order are complied with.

40.55　Some further guidance can be gleaned from the judgments. Once it is accepted that it is just to make a time order, it appears to be legitimate to assess what the borrower can afford in the temporary period of relief which he or she is being given and to fix this as the rate of payment due to the lender. Variation of the interest rate to give efficacy to this rate of payment is permissible. It is worth noting that the Court of Appeal in *Barnes*[68] expressly approved the approach of one circuit judge who reduced the interest rate under the loan agreement to nil and ordered the total indebtedness to be repaid over a period exceeding the original contractual term. In *Director General of Fair Trading v First National Bank plc*,[69] the circuit judge's approach was approved.

68　*Southern & District Finance plc v Barnes* (1995) 27 HLR 691; [1995] Con Cred LR 62, CA.
69　[2001] UKHL 52; [2002] 1 AC 481; [2001] 3 WLR 1297.

However, it was also observed that 'time orders extending over long periods of time are usually better avoided'.

40.56   It is important to recognise that the time order provisions are distinct from the 'unfair relationship' provisions contained in CCA 1974 ss140A–140C (described at para 40.58). It is possible for the 'unfair relationship' provisions to be used in addition to an application for a time order in the same proceedings or independently from a time order application.

40.57   It is sensible to emphasise to district judges hearing possession actions relating to regulated agreements that they have these powers which are distinct from and much wider than those under the Administration of Justice Acts with which they are more familiar. In particular, the absence of any requirement to clear arrears within the 'reasonable period' should be stressed. It is important to reflect on the fact that loans taken out for the initial purchase of a property (which is the case with the majority of first mortgages) have been seen by parliament to warrant different treatment from loans taken out for consumer purposes which happen to be secured on a borrower's home.

Unfair relationships

40.58   The 'extortionate credit bargain' provisions of the Consumer Credit Act 1974, as originally enacted, were replaced by the 'unfair relationship' provisions of the Consumer Credit Act 2006 and are found at CCA 1974 ss140A–140D. They now apply to credit agreements whenever they were enterd into.[70] Section 140A provides:

> *Unfair relationships between creditors and debtors*
> (1) The court may make an order under section 140B in connection with a credit agreement if it determines that the relationship between the creditor and the debtor arising out of the agreement (or the agreement taken with any related agreement) is unfair to the debtor because of one or more of the following –
>> (a) any of the terms of the agreement or of any related agreement;
>> (b) the way in which the creditor has exercised or enforced any of his rights under the agreement or any related agreement;
>> (c) any other thing done (or not done) by, or on behalf of, the creditor (either before or after the making of the agreement or any related agreement).

---

70 See B Say, 'Unfair relationships under the Consumer Credit Act' *Quarterly Account* Autumn 2008 p4 for an introduction to the provisions.

(2) In deciding whether to make a determination under this section the court shall have regard to all matters it thinks relevant (including matters relating to the creditor and matters relating to the debtor).[71]

(3) For the purposes of this section the court shall (except to the extent that it is not appropriate to do so) treat anything done (or not done) by, or on behalf of, or in relation to, an associate or former associate of the creditor as if done (or not done) by, or on behalf of, or in relation to, the creditor.

(4) A determination may be made under this section in relation to a relationship notwithstanding that the relationship may have ended.

(5) An order under section 140B shall not be made in connection with a credit agreement which is an exempt agreement by virtue of section 16(6C).

40.59   Section 16(6C) exempts regulated mortgage contracts (see para 40.75) from the provisions of the Consumer Credit Act 1974.[72]

40.60   However, even 'exempt agreements' within the meaning of the Consumer Credit Act 1974 s16 fall within scope of the 'unfair relationship' provisions.[73] Section 140B provides:

Powers of court in relation to unfair relationships

(1) An order under this section in connection with a credit agreement may do one or more of the following –

(a) require the creditor, or any associate or former associate of his, to repay (in whole or in part) any sum paid by the debtor or by a surety by virtue of the agreement or any related agreement (whether paid to the creditor, the associate or the former associate or to any other person);

(b) require the creditor, or any associate or former associate of his, to do or not to do (or to cease doing) anything specified in the order in connection with the agreement or any related agreement;

(c) reduce or discharge any sum payable by the debtor or by a surety by virtue of the agreement or any related agreement;

(d) direct the return to a surety of any property provided by him for the purposes of a security;

(e) otherwise set aside (in whole or in part) any duty imposed on the debtor or on a surety by virtue of the agreement or any related agreement;

---

71 Deceit by the debtor or non-disclosure of all relevant facts tends to be fatal to any possible challenge: *First National Securities Ltd v Bertrand* [1980] Consumer Credit Law Reports 5 and *Premier Finance Co v Gravesande* [1985] Consumer Credit Law Reports 22.

72 Financial Services and Markets Act 2000 (Regulated Activities) Order 2001 SI No 544 art 90.

73 CCA 1974 s16 (7A), inserted by CCA 2006 s22(2).

(f) alter the terms of the agreement or of any related agreement;

(g) direct accounts to be taken, or (in Scotland) an accounting to be made, between any persons.

(2) An order under this section may be made in connection with a credit agreement only –

(a) on an application made by the debtor or by a surety;

(b) at the instance of the debtor or a surety in any proceedings in any court to which the debtor and the creditor are parties, being proceedings to enforce the agreement or any related agreement; or

(c) at the instance of the debtor or a surety in any other proceedings in any court where the amount paid or payable under the agreement is relevant.

(3) An order under this section may be made notwithstanding that its effect is to place on the creditor, or any associate or former associate of his, a burden in respect of an advantage enjoyed by another person ...

40.61   If the borrower or surety alleges that the relationship is unfair it is for the lender to prove to the contrary.[74] The Consumer Credit Act 1974 also entitles a party to any proceedings mentioned in section 140B(2) to have any person who might be the subject of an order under section 140B made a party to the proceedings.[75] An application by the borrower or surety under section 140B(2)(a) may be made only in the county court.[76]

40.62   It is thought that, as with the previous extortionate credit bargain provisions, the borrower will need to show much more than the transaction was 'unwise.'[77] It may also be the case, as before, that there is a need to show 'at least a substantial imbalance in bargaining power of which one party has taken advantage'.[78] Under the unamended 1974 Act the rate of interest charged was highly relevant and will clearly remain an issue.[79] The amended 1974 Act does, however, allow the court to take into account events and circumstances which occurred after the transaction was entered into, effectively side-stepping *Paragon Finance plc v Nash*,[80] which had concluded that in assessing

---

74   CCA 1974 s140B(9).

75   CCA 1974 s140B(8).

76   CCA 1974 s140B(2) and (4).

77   *Wills v Wood* [1984] Consumer Credit Law Reports 7 and *Paragon Finance plc v Nash* [2002] 1 WLR 685.

78   See *Wills v Wood* [1984] Consumer Credit Law Reports 7.

79   *Davies v Directloans Ltd* [1986] 1 WLR 823 and *Patel v Patel* [2009] EWHC 3264 (QB).

80   [2002] 1 WLR 685.

the 'credit bargain' it was permissible to look at the original terms only. Under the unfair relationship provisions the court is entitled to assess the fairness of the relationship between the borrower and lender as at the date of trial or, if the relationship has ended, as at that date. The fact that a loan agreement was entered into more than 12 years earlier is not a bar.[81]

40.63   The unfair relationship provisions have been deliberately drafted in a way which gives the county court considerable discretion and it remains to be seen how the courts will develop the jurisprudence. The Office of Fair Trading has issued some guidance on 'unfair relationships'.[82]

Unfair contract terms

40.64   The Unfair Terms in Consumer Contracts Regulations 1999[83] can in some ways be seen as complementing the powers available to the court under the 'unfair relationship' provisions of the Consumer Credit Act 1974. The regulations are made pursuant to the European Communities Act 1972 and were introduced in order to comply with EC Directive 93/13. The purpose of the Directive was 'to approximate the laws, regulations and administrative provisions of the Member States relating to unfair terms in contracts concluded between a seller or supplier and a consumer'. The 1999 Regulations came into effect on 1 October 1999 and apply to consumer contracts concluded on or after that date.

40.65   Regulation 4 of the 1999 Regulations applies the regulations 'in relation to unfair terms in contracts concluded between a seller or supplier and a consumer'. However, the regulations do not apply if the contractual term reflects a mandatory statutory or regulatory provision. The term 'consumer' is defined as meaning 'any natural person who, in contracts covered by these Regulations, is acting for purposes which are outside his trade, business or profession'.[84]

40.66   Regulation 5(1) of the 1999 Regulations provides:

> A contractual term which has not been individually negotiated shall be regarded as unfair if, contrary to the requirements of good faith,

---

81 *Patel v Patel* [2009] EWHC 3264 (QB).

82 See *Unfair relationships: enforcement action under Part 8 of the Enterprise Act 2002* OFT, December 2006.

83 SI No 2083. See J Holbrook, 'Unfair terms in housing contracts' September 1999 *Legal Action* 26.

84 Unfair Terms in Consumer Contracts Regulations 1999 reg 3.

it causes a significant imbalance in the parties' rights and obligations arising under the contract, to the detriment of the consumer.

The criteria by which the assessment as to 'good faith' is to be made is not defined in the 1999 Regulations. However, Schedule 2 of the predecessor 1994 Regulations provided that:

regard shall be had in particular to:

(a) the strength of the bargaining positions of the parties;

(b) whether the consumer had an inducement to agree to the term;

(c) whether the goods or services were sold or supplied to the special order of the consumer; and

(d) the extent to which the seller or supplier has dealt fairly and equitably with the consumer.

Given that these matters are contained in the preamble to the Directive they must remain a good aid to construction.

40.67   Unfair Terms in Consumer Contracts Regulations 1999 reg 5(2) states:

[a] term shall always be regarded as not having been individually negotiated where it has been drafted in advance and the consumer has therefore not been able to influence the substance of the term.

Regulation 8 provides that 'an unfair term in a contract concluded with a consumer by a seller or supplier shall not be binding on the consumer' and goes on to say that '[t]he contract shall continue to bind the parties if it is capable of continuing in existence without the unfair term'.

40.68   Schedule 2 para 1 to the 1999 Regulations contains 'an indicative and non-exhaustive list of terms which may be regarded as unfair'. In the context of mortgage lending the following are worthy of note:

Terms which have the object or effect of ...

(e) requiring any consumer who fails to fulfil his obligation to pay a disproportionately high sum in compensation;

...

(i) irrevocably binding the consumer to terms with which he had no real opportunity of becoming acquainted before the conclusion of the contract;

(j) enabling the seller or supplier to alter the terms of the contract unilaterally without a valid reason which is specified in the contract ...

Schedule 2 to the 1999 Regulations qualifies this latter term so as to allow a supplier of financial services to

alter the rate of interest payable by the consumer or due to the [supplier], or the amount of other charges for financial services without notice where there is a valid reason, provided that the supplier is required to inform the other contracting party or parties thereof at the earliest opportunity and that the latter are free to dissolve the contract immediately.

40.69 Apart from providing that an unfair term is not binding on a borrower, the regulations also enable the Director General of Fair Trading to seek an injunction against anyone using or recommending the use of unfair terms.[85]

40.70 These regulations, particularly in relation to secured loans from secondary lenders, have not perhaps been considered enough by advisers and it is hoped that there will be greater development in this area. Provisions which have been found unfair by the courts include:

- dual interest rates where a concessionary rate is lost;
- computation of interest on a flat-rate basis over the term of a loan irrespective of the amounts paid off the capital;
- the calculation of a redemption figure by applying the Rule of 78;[86] and
- the provision of a deferred settlement date of six months.[87]

40.71 Unfair Terms in Consumer Contracts Regulations apart, while a lender has considerable discretion as to the rate of interest charged in relation to a loan, the mortgage agreement is subject to an implied term that this discretion will not be exercised for an improper purpose, dishonestly, capriciously, arbitrarily or so unreasonably that no lender would have acted in that way.[88] The OFT's *Unfair contract terms guidance* was issued in September 2008.[89]

---

85 Unfair Terms in Consumer Contracts Regulations 1999 reg 12. See *Director General of Fair Trading v First National Bank plc* [2001] UKHL 52; [2002] 1 AC 481; [2001] 3 WLR 1297.

86 CCA 1974 s95 and Consumer Credit (Rebate on Early Settlement) Regulations 1983 SI No 1562 provide for a statutory rebate in cases where a regulated agreement is repaid before the end of the contract period. With effect from 31 May 2005 the 'Rule of 78' was replaced by the formula set out in the Consumer Credit (Early Settlement) Regulations 2004 SI No 1483. See also R Rosenberg, 'Good-bye to Rule of 78' *Quarterly Account* Issue 76 p4.

87 See *Falco Finance Ltd v Gough* April 1999 *Legal Action* 13; cf, *Kindlance Ltd v Murphy* (1997) unreported, No 625, High Court Northern Ireland. See also S Bright, 'Attacking unfair mortgage terms' [1999] Conv 360.

88 *Paragon Finance plc v Staunton* [2001] EWCA Civ 1466; [2002] 1 All ER 248.

89 www.oft.gov.uk/shared_oft/reports/unfair_contract_terms/oft311.pdf.

Regulation of mortgage lending by the Financial Services Authority

40.72   The Financial Services Authority (FSA) was established by the Financial Services and Markets Act 2000 to regulate the activities of persons involved in financial services in the UK. In January 2000 it was announced that the FSA would be responsible for mortgage regulation and in 2001 this was extended to cover those advising and arranging mortgages as well as the conduct of lenders. The regime set up by the FSA for the regulation of residential mortgages came into effect on 31 October 2004.[90] The Financial Services and Markets Act 2000 also set up the Financial Ombudsman Service[91] (FOS) for the resolution of some types of dispute 'quickly and with a minimum of formality'.[92]

40. 73   The regulatory role of the FSA and the FOS is not a simple alternative to the use of the courts. Advisers will need to have regard to the statutory regimes of the Administration of Justice Acts 1970 and 1973 and the Consumer Credit Act 1974 which set out the courts' powers in relation to possession claims by lenders. The authority of the FSA and the power of the FOS may, however, be an important adjunct when seeking to influence the way that a mortgage lender is responding to a borrower whose loan falls within the scope of the 2000 Act.

40.74   Financial Services and Markets Act 2000 ss19 and 22 impose a 'general prohibition' on any person carrying on an activity regulated by the Act without appropriate authorisation from the FSA. An activity is a 'regulated activity' within the meaning of the 2000 Act if it is carried on by way of a business and if it is a 'specified' activity.

40.75   The Financial Services and Markets Act (Regulated Activities) Order 2001[93] Chapter XV deals with 'Regulated Mortgage Contracts'. Entering into a 'regulated mortgage contract' as a lender is a 'specified' activity.[94] 'Administrating' a regulated mortgage contract is also a specified kind of activity.[95]

---

90   Mortgages: Conduct of Business Sourcebook (Amendment) Instrument 2004 and Financial Services and Markets Act (FSMA) 2000 ss138, 145, 156 and 159(1).
91   FSMA 2000 Part XVI.
92   FSMA 2000 s225.
93   SI 2001 No 544.
94   FSMA 2000 (Regulated Activities) Order 2001 art 61(1).
95   FSMA 2000 (Regulated Activities) Order 2001 art 61(2).

40.76   A 'regulated mortgage contract' means a contract under which –

(i) a person ('the lender') provides credit to an individual or to trustees ('the borrower'); and

(ii) the obligation of the borrower to repay is secured by a first legal mortgage on land (other than timeshare accommodation in the United Kingdom) at least 40 per cent of which is to be used, or is intended to be used, as or in connection with a dwelling by the borrower or (in the case of credit provided to trustees) by an individual who is a beneficiary of the trust, or a related person.[96]

40.77   'Administrating' a regulated mortgage contract means:

either or both of –

(i) notifying the borrower of changes in interest rates or payments due under the contract, or of other matters of which the contract requires him to be notified; and

(ii) taking any necessary steps for the purposes of collecting or recovering payments due under the contract from the borrower;

but a person is not treated as administering a regulated mortgage contract merely because he has, or exercises, a right to take action for the purposes of enforcing the contract (or to require that such action is or is not taken).[97]

'Credit' includes a cash loan and any other form of financial accommodation.[98]

40.78   In terms of the requirement that the borrower must use or intend to use at least 40 per cent of the property '… the area of any land which comprises a building or other structure containing two or more storeys is to be taken to be the aggregate of the floor area of each of those storeys'.[99]

40.79   A 'related person' is defined as being the borrower or beneficiary's spouse or civil partner or 'a person (whether or not of the opposite sex) whose relationship with that person has the characteristics of the relationship between husband and wife' or the borrower or beneficiary's parent, brother, sister, child, grandparent or grandchild.[100]

40.80   The Regulated Activities Order[101] also engages with 'home purchase plans' which are in nature similar to mortgages but are intended not to contravene Islamic law against payment of *riba* or interest (see chapter 45). In essence, a home purchase plan is where a

96 FSMA 2000 (Regulated Activities) Order 2001 art 61(3)(a).
97 FSMA 2000 (Regulated Activities) Order 2001 art 61(3)(b).
98 FSMA 2000 (Regulated Activities) Order 2001 art 61(3)(c).
99 FSMA 2000 (Regulated Activities) Order 2001 art 61(4)(b).
100 FSMA 2000 (Regulated Activities) Order 2001 art 61(4)(c).
101 FSMA 2000 (Regulated Activities) Order 2001 art 63F(3).

purchaser buys a property on the basis that it will be held on trust for the purchaser and an individual(s) as beneficial tenants in common. The transaction must also provide that the individual(s) or a 'related person' is entitled to occupy more than 40 per cent of the property in question and that there is an obligation on the individual(s) to purchase the property during the course of or at the end of a specified period.

40.81   It follows that loans secured on commercial properties, 'buy-to-let' mortgages, loans to limited companies and second mortgages are outside scope of regulation by the 2000 Act.[102] A regulated mortgage contract which would otherwise fall within the scope of the Consumer Credit Act 1974 is an 'exempt agreement' for the purposes of the 1974 Act and as such outside the provisions of that legislation save for the requirement that the mortgage is enforceable only following court order.[103]

40.82   Part III of the 2000 Act sets up a requirement for persons engaged in mortgage lending activities to be authorised by the FSA. Part V enables the FSA to regulate the performance of authorised persons. An agreement entered into in relation to a regulated activity by a person when not authorised is unenforceable by that person and any money paid or property transferred to that person is recoverable.[104]

40.83   The FSA is charged with regulatory control of a myriad of different financial services and has issued a *Handbook* which contains over 30 'sourcebooks' setting out the rules governing regulated persons in different fields. The *Handbook* and its regulations are issued pursuant to powers given to the FSA under the 2000 Act.[105] If a lender fails to comply with the rules it runs the risk of regulatory and disciplinary action by the FSA. A borrower who can show that he or she has suffered loss as a result of a contravention of a rule may sue the authorised person for damages.[106] However, such a contravention does not render the transaction void or unenforceable.[107]

40.84   In the *Handbook*, *Rules* issued by the FSA are identified by a suffix 'R' to a particular paragraph. *Guidance* issued by the FSA is identified by a suffix 'G'. Guidance is generally designed to throw light

---

102 In December 2009 HM Treasury issued a consultation paper, *Mortgage regulation: a consultation*, proposing the bringing of second charge and buy-to-let mortgages under FSA regulation.

103 FSMA 2000 (Regulated Activities) Order 2001 art 90(2).

104 FSMA 2000 s26.

105 FSMA 2000 ss138, 139, 145, 149, 156 and 157(1).

106 FSMA 2000 s150(1).

107 FSMA 2000 s151(2).

on a particular aspect of regulatory requirement but is not of itself binding. The *Handbook* also contains commentary which identifies evidential provisions which tend to show compliance with a particular rule. These paragraphs contain suffix 'E'.[108]

40.85   The *Mortgages and Home Finance: Conduct of Business sourcebook*[109] (MCOB) was issued in its final form in October 2003 and came into effect on 31 October 2004[110] affecting mortgages entered into on or after that date. It governs the relationships between the lender and borrower including any intermediaries. It consists of 13 chapters governing every facet of the life of a mortgage. Chapter 13 of MCOB deals with arrears and repossession.

The Mortgage Conduct of Business (MCOB) rules

40.86   The MCOB rules cover all aspects of the mortgage lender/borrower relationship effectively from the cradle to the grave and, indeed, beyond, since they also regulate mortgage shortfalls. Advisers would do well to create a link to the MCOB sourcebook on their computer as a 'favourite' for easy access. The most relevant chapters in relation to mortgage repossession cases are chapter 11, which deals with 'Responsible lending', chapter 12 on 'Charges' and, more importantly, chapter 13, which deals with 'Arrears and repossessions'.

40.87   In relation to 'responsible lending', MCOB 11.3.1 R requires a lender to 'be able to show that before deciding to enter into a regulated mortgage contract with a customer or, on making a further advance on a regulated mortgage contract, account was taken of a customer's ability to pay'. Furthermore, a lender 'must make an adequate record that it has taken account of the customer's ability to pay for each regulated contract that it enters into and each further advance that it provides on a regulated contract. The record must be retained for a year from the date at which the regulated mortgage contract is entered into or the further advance provided.' Particular guidance is given in relation to cases involving self-certification of income in MCOB 11.3.2 R.

40.88   MCOB 11.3.4 R deals in more detail with the requirements for a 'responsible lending policy'. A lender must put in place, and operate

---

108 See generally *Reader's Guide: an introduction to the FSA Handbook*, chapter 6: status of provisions, July 2005.

109 http://fsahandbook.info/FSA/html/handbook/MCOB.

110 *Mortgages: conduct of business sourcebook instrument 2003* issued by FSA under FSMA 2000 s153(2).

in accordance with, a written policy setting out the factors it will take into account in assessing a customer's ability to pay. Further, more detailed guidance is given in MCOB 11.3.5 G to 11.3.8 G as to the evidence needed to satisfy a lender that the borrower has the ability to repay the loan being sought. The lender should take account of a prospective borrower's actual or reasonably anticipated income or both when deciding whether to enter into the loan. The lender should consider whether the borrower will still be able to meet the payments at the end of any initial discounted repayment period and whether the borrower can service the debt payments due on any associated repayment vehicle such as an endowment policy.

40.89   MCOB 12 seeks to regulate 'early repayment charges', 'arrears charges' and 'excessive charges'. Guidance at 12.2.1 G reaffirms earlier obligations in MCOB about appropriate disclosure at pre-application stage and at offer stage and general product disclosure to make charges transparent to customers. Paragraph 12.2.1 is expressly intended to reinforce 'these requirements by preventing a [lender] from imposing unfair and excessive charges'.

40.90   MCOB 12.3.1 R deals with 'early repayment charges'. It requires a lender to 'ensure that any regulated mortgage contract that it enters into does not impose, and cannot be used to impose, an early repayment charge other than one that is (1) able to be expressed as a cash value and (2) a reasonable pre-estimate of the costs as a result of the customer repaying the amount due under the regulated mortgage contract before the contract has terminated'.

40.91   MCOB 12.4.1 R regulates 'arrears charges':

> [A lender] must ensure that any regulated mortgage contract that it enters into does not impose, and cannot be used to impose, a charge for arrears on a customer except where that charge is a reasonable estimate of the cost of additional administration required as a result of the customer being in arrears.

However, this would not prevent a mortgage term under which a defaulting borrower may be transferred from a fixed or discounted interest rate to some other generally applicable standard variable interest rate.[111] The levying of a charge on arrears where the lender and borrower have come to an agreement about repayment of the arrears which is being met by the borrower would be taken by the FSA as breach of the MCOB 12.4.1 R.[112] In addition, lenders are required to

---

111 MCOB 12.4.1 R(2).
112 MCOB 12.4.1A E.

allocate payments received from the borrower towards payment of arrears rather than towards any interest or charges on the arrears.[113]

40.92   MCOB 12.5.1 R requires a lender 'to ensure that any regulated mortgage contract that it enters into does not impose, and cannot be used to impose, excessive charges upon a customer'. The concept of 'excessive charge' is not further defined.

40.93   MCOB 13 deals with 'Arrears and repossessions'. The chapter seeks to control both the administration of a regulated mortgage contract during its lifetime and also the recovery of any mortgage shortfall debt after repossession and sale.

MCOB 13.1 'Dealing fairly with customers in arrears: policy and procedures'

40.94   A lender is obliged to 'deal fairly with any customer who (a) is in arrears on a regulated mortgage contract; or (b) has a mortgage shortfall debt'.[114] A lender must also 'put in place, and operate in accordance with, a written policy (agreed by its governing body) and procedures for complying with [its duty to deal fairly]'.[115] Guidance provides that:

> A *firm* must, when dealing with any *customer* in payment difficulties:
> (1) make reasonable efforts to reach an agreement with a *customer* over the method of repaying any payment shortfall or *sale shortfall*, in the case of the former having regard to the desirability of agreeing with the *customer* an alternative to taking possession of the property;
> (2) liaise, if the *customer* makes arrangements for this, with a third party source of advice regarding the payment shortfall or *sale shortfall*;
> (3) allow a reasonable time over which the payment shortfall or *sale shortfall* should be repaid, having particular regard to the need to establish, where feasible, a payment plan which is practical in terms of the circumstances of the *customer*;
> (4) grant, unless it has good reason not to do so, a *customer's* request for a change to:
>   (a) the date on which the payment is due (providing it is within the same payment period); or
>   (b) the method by which payment is made;
>   and give the *customer* a written explanation of its reasons if it refuses the request;

113 MCOB 12.4.1B R.
114 MCOB 13.3.1R (1).
115 MCOB 13.3.1 R (2).

(5) where no reasonable payment arrangement can be made, allow the *customer* to remain in possession for a reasonable period to effect a sale; and

(6) not repossess the property unless all other reasonable attempts to resolve the position have failed.[116]

40.95   The duty to have an adopted policy to deal with arrears and mortgage shortfall debts 'does not oblige a [lender] to provide customers with a copy of the written policy and procedures. Nor, however, does it prevent a [lender] from providing customers with either these documents or a more customer-orientated version'.[117]

40.96   In relation to the obligation not to seek repossession unless all other reasonable attempts to resolve the position have failed:

(1) a *firm* must consider whether, given the individual circumstances of the *customer*, it is appropriate to do one or more of the following in relation to the *regulated mortgage contract* or *home purchase plan* with the agreement of the *customer*:

(a) extend its term; or

(b) change its type; or

(c) defer payment of interest due on the *regulated mortgage contract* or of sums due under the *home purchase plan* (including, in either case, on any *sale shortfall*); or

(d) treat the payment shortfall as if it was part of the original amount provided (but a *firm* must not automatically capitalise a payment shortfall); or

(e) make use of any Government forbearance initiatives in which the *firm* chooses to participate;

(2) a *firm* must give *customers* adequate information to understand the implications of any proposed arrangement; one approach may be to provide information on the new terms in line with the *annual statement provisions*.[118]

Lenders are advised that these options are not exhaustive and that the FSA would expect lenders to be able to justify a decision to offer a particular option.[119] Lenders are also required to make borrowers aware of any applicable Government scheme available to assist borrowers in difficulty with their payments.[120]

40.97   In terms of the requirement to adopt a reasonable approach to the length of time a borrower should be given to clear arrears, MCOB guidance provides:

116 MCOB 13.3.2A.
117 MCOB 13.3.3 G.
118 MCOB 13.3.4A R.
119 MCOB 13.3.AC G.
120 MCOB 13.3.AB R.

... The FSA takes the view that the determination of a reasonable repayment period will depend upon the individual circumstances. In appropriate cases this will mean that repayments are arranged over the remaining term of the regulated mortgage contract.[121]

40.98 Lenders are advised that if they intend to outsource aspects of customer relationships (including debt collection) the FSA will hold them responsible for the way in which this work is carried out.[122]

MCOB 13.3 'Record keeping: arrears and repossessions'

40.99 A lender which is also involved in the administration of a regulated mortgage contract is obliged to make and retain an adequate record of its dealings with borrowers in arrears (or who have a mortgage shortfall debt) to enable it to show that it has complied with the obligations imposed by MCOB chapter 13. A lender is required to retain a record of its dealings with the borrower in arrears[123] for three years, including a recording of all telephone conversations between the lender and borrower where the arrears are discussed.

The record should contain, or provide reference to, matters such as:
(1) the date of first communication with the customer after the account was identified as being in arrears;
(2) in relation to correspondence issued to a customer in arrears, the name and contact number of the employee dealing with that correspondence, where known;
(3) ... [*This paragraph deals with business mortgages*]
(4) information relating to any new payment arrangements proposed;
(5) the date of issue of any legal documents;
(6) the arrangements made for the sale after the repossession (whether legal or voluntary);
(7) the date of any communication summarising the customer's outstanding debt after sale of the repossessed property[124] and
(8) the date and time of each call for the purposes of MCOB 13.3.9R(1).

---

121 MCOB 13.3.6 G.
122 MCOB 13.3.8 G.
123 MCOB 13.3.9 R.
124 MCOB 13.3.10 G.

MCOB 13.4.1 R 'Arrears: provision of information to the customer'

40.100 A lender is required to provide a comprehensive package of information to a borrower in arrears.

> If a customer falls into arrears on a regulated mortgage contract, a [lender] must as soon as possible, and in any event within 15 business days of becoming aware of that fact, provide the customer with the following in a durable medium:
> (1) the current FSA information sheet on mortgage arrears;
> (2) a list of the due payments either missed or only paid in part;
> (3) the total sum of the payment shortfall;
> (4) the charges incurred as a result of the payment shortfall;
> (5) the total outstanding debt, excluding charges that may be added on redemption; and
> (6) an indication of the nature (and where possible the level) of charges the customer is likely to incur unless the payment shortfall is cleared.[125]

MCOB 13.4.5 R 'Steps required before action for repossession'

40.101 Before issuing possession proceedings a lender must provide the information listed in para 40.100, ensure that the borrower is informed of the need to contact the local housing authority to establish whether he or she is 'eligible' for local authority housing if the property is repossessed and 'clearly state the action that will be taken with regard to repossession'.[126] It is far from clear what this last requirement means in practice.

MCOB 13.5 R 'Statements of charges'

40.102 Many lenders have adopted punitive policies of levying additional charges on borrowers in arrears and the MCOB seeks to ensure that at least the borrower is made aware of the extent of the charging.

> Where an account is in arrears, and the payment shortfall or sale shortfall is attracting charges, a [lender] must provide the customer with a regular written statement (at least once a quarter) of the payments due, the actual payment shortfall, the charges incurred and the debt.[127]

---

125 MCOB 13.4.1 R.
126 MCOB 13.4.5 R.
127 MCOB 13.5.1 R.

40.103 Charges that trigger the requirement for regular statements include all charges and fees levied directly as a result of the account falling into arrears. This includes charges such as monthly administrative charges, legal fees and interest. If interest is applied to the amount of the arrears, as it is applied to the rest of the mortgage, a lender need not send a written statement, unless other charges are also being made. If interest is applied to the amount of the arrears in a different manner to the rest of the mortgage then a written statement will be required.[128]

MCOB 13.5 R 'Pressure on customers'

40.104 MCOB also seeks to protect borrowers from the more unpleasant forms of debt collection: 'The rules state that a [lender] must not put pressure on a customer through excessive telephone calls or correspondence, or by contact at an unreasonable hour'.[129] Guidance suggests that a reasonable hour will usually fall between 8 am and 9 pm. Putting pressure on a borrower includes the use of documents which resemble a court summons or other official document, or are intended to lead the borrower to believe that they have come from or have the authority of a court. It also includes the use of documents containing unfair, unclear or misleading information intended to coerce the borrower into paying.[130]

MCOB 13.6 R 'Repossessions'

40.105 Lenders are required to dispose of repossessed properties and to deal with the consequences of sale in a reasonable manner.

> A [lender] must ensure that, whenever a property is repossessed (whether voluntarily or through legal action) and it administers the regulated mortgage contract or home purchase plan in respect of that property, steps are taken to:
> (1) market the property for sale as soon as possible; and
> (2) obtain the best price that might reasonably be paid, taking account of factors such as market conditions as well as the continuing increase in the amount owed by the customer under the regulated mortgage contract.[131]

---

128 MCOB 13.5.2 G (1).
129 MCOB 13.5.3 R.
130 MCOB 13.5.5 G.
131 MCOB 13.6.1 R.

40.106 Guidance suggests that:

> ... it is recognised that a balance has to be struck between the need to sell the property as soon as possible, to reduce or remove the outstanding debt, and other factors which might prompt the delay of the sale. These might include market conditions ... but there may be other legitimate reasons for deferring action. This could include the expiry of a period when a grant is repayable on re-sale, or the discovery of a title defect that needs to be remedied if the optimal selling price is to be achieved.[132]

40.107 Guidance further provides that a lender is not required to recover a shortfall on sale and may not wish to recover a shortfall in some situations 'for example where the sums involved make action for recovery unviable'.[133] It then deals with two scenarios:

'If the proceeds of sale are less than the debt'

40.108 A lender is obliged to ensure that, as soon as possible after the sale of a repossessed property, the borrower is informed in a 'durable medium' of the size of the mortgage shortfall and, where relevant, whether the debt might be pursued by another person, for example a mortgage indemnity insurer.[134] Durable medium is defined as paper or electronic medium such as a floppy disc, CD Roms etc.

40.109   If a lender intends to seek to recover the shortfall the borrower must be told of this fact and this notification must take place within six years of the date of sale.[135]

'If the proceeds of sale are more than the debt'

40.110 A lender is obliged to ensure that reasonable steps are taken, as soon as possible after the sale, to inform the borrower in a durable medium of the surplus and subject to the rights or any other lender to pay the surplus to the borrower.[136]

---

132 MCOB 13.6.2 G.
133 MCOB 13.6.5 G.
134 MCOB 13.6.3 R.
135 MCOB 13.6.4 R.
136 MCOB 13.6.6 R.

Sale and rent back

40.111 Following consultation,[137] the FSA brought under its jurisdiction the regulation of agreements whereby a home owner sells his or her property and simultaneously rents it back from the buyer.[138] An interim regulatory regime was introduced on 1 July 2009 with the 'full regime' effective on 30 June 2010.[139] The provisions bring under FSA control persons who carry on the business of arranging or advising in relation to a 'regulated sale and rent back transaction'. This is an arrangement whereby:

- a person (the agreement provider) buys all or part of a 'qualifying interest' in land from an individual or trustees (the agreement seller) who is an individual or beneficiary under a trust or a 'related person' who is entitled to occupy at least 40 per cent of the land in question as a dwelling and
- the agreement seller is granted or any member of that person's family is granted a right to occupy the land in question as, or in connection with, a dwelling and intends to occupy it.

For the definition of 'related person' see para 40.79. Under the full regime, the FSA prohibits exploitative advertising and cold calling, provides for a 14-day cooling off period to provide owners time to reflect on the proposed transaction, provides for a minimum five year tenancy and ensures that the risks associated are made clear to the owner.

Dispute resolution

40.112 The Financial Services and Markets Act 2000 s225 provides for the setting up of the FOS to investigate complaints about lenders (although it also covers those involved in the administration of regulated mortgage contracts). Complaints are to be determined according to what the Ombudsman considers to be 'fair and reasonable in all

---

137 FSA *Regulating sale and rent back: an interim regime* February 2009.
138 FSMA 2000 (Regulated Activities) (Amendment) Order 2009 SI 1342 and *Interim Permitted Regulated Sale and Rent Back Activities Instrument* 2009 – see http://fsahandbook.info/FSA/handbook/LI/2009/FOS_2009_3.pdf. For HM Treasury's explanatory statement, see www.opsi.gov.uk/si/si2009/em/uksiem_20091342_en.pdf.
139 www.fsa.gov.uk/pubs/cp/cp10_04.pdf.

the circumstances of the case'.[140] The FSA Handbook sets out an elaborate complaints dispute resolution procedure entitled 'Dispute Resolution: Complaints'.[141]

40.113   The procedure provides that a complainant must first seek redress through the lender's internal complaint's procedure. The FOS cannot look into a complaint until either the lender has issued its final response to the complaint or eight weeks have elapsed from the date the complaint was received by the lender.[142] The FOS complaint form which needs to be used can be downloaded from the FOS website.[143] If the FOS upholds a complaint, it may either make a monetary award against the lender (to a maximum of £100,000) or a direction that the lender takes such steps in relation to the complaint as the FOS considers just and appropriate (whether or not a court could order those steps to be taken) or both.[144] Unfortunately the FOS does take time to determine complaints to it, with investigations taking months rather than weeks. It remains to be seen to what extent the court dealing with possession will itself grant a stay of proceedings, under CPR 26.4(2)(b), to allow negotiations to take place between the parties or to allow the FOS time to investigate a complaint. In *Derbyshire Home Loans Ltd v Keaney*,[145] a stay on proceedings was granted to enable a complaint to the Financial Ombudsman Service to be processed if necessary, given the claimant's failure to deal with proposals put to it by the borrowers. It is worth noting in this context that the Mortgage Arrears Protocol provides at paragraph 8.1:

> The lender should consider whether to postpone the start of a possession claim where the borrower has made a genuine complaint to the Financial Ombudsman Service (FOS) about the potential possesion claim.

40.114 For the purpose of awards, financial loss includes consequential or prospective loss.[146] The FOS can also award a sum which reflects some or all of the costs reasonably incurred by the complainant although 'it is not anticipated that awards of costs will be common since in most cases complainants should not need to have professional advisers to

---

140 FSMA 2000 s228.

141 http://.fsahandbook.info/FSA/html/handbook/DISP.

142 Dispute Resolution: Complaints para 2.3.1 R.

143 www.financial-ombudsman.org.uk.

144 Dispute Resolution: Complaints para 3.9.1.G.

145 April 2007 *Legal Action* 28, Bristol County Court.

146 Dispute Resolution: Complaints para 3.9.3 G.

bring complaints to the Financial Ombudsman Service'.[147] The FOS website can be found at www.financial-ombudsman.org.uk and the FOS Technical Advice Desk on 020 7964 1400 (open 10 am to 4 pm).

40.115   There is a clear tension between the powers given to the courts under the Administration of Justice Acts 1970 and 1973 and the Consumer Credit Act 1974 and the statutory regime set up under the Financial Services and Markets Act 2000. It is to be hoped that an early opportunity can be taken to rationalise into one statutory code the law protecting mortgage borrowers who are in difficulty with their payment.

147 Dispute Resolution: Complaints para 3.9.11 G.

CHAPTER 41

Preventing the lender from obtaining possession

Introduction

41.1　In practice, mortgage possession actions can usually be successfully defended only by raising enough money to satisfy the lender or, failing that, by persuading the court that it is right to exercise one of the statutory powers to deny possession or restructure the loan, described in chapter 40. In common with most debt cases, this involves minimising the borrower's expenditure and maximising the borrower's income.

41.2　Where the borrower is working, the question of income maximisation is largely one of ensuring that he or she is in receipt of any possible relevant additions to wages, income support, working tax credit, child tax credit, maintenance and child support payments, child benefit, etc. If the borrower is unemployed, it is important to ensure that: benefit payments are correct and complete; any potential tax rebates have been claimed; and any unfair dismissal, redundancy or discrimination claims have been considered.

41.3　It is also worth checking whether the borrower is protected by any mortgage protection plan (where an insurance company has agreed to make part or all of the mortgage repayments for a limited period of time following the borrower becoming sick or unemployed). See para 41.6. Detailed consideration of these options is really outside the scope of this chapter and readers are encouraged to go online to National Debtline,[1] which has a range of leaflets and advice on all aspects of debt. However, a brief synopsis of options relating to cutting mortgage costs and increasing relevant income may be useful here.

Reducing mortgage costs

41.4　Although in law most lenders have quite wide-ranging powers to lend money as they wish, lenders often say that options for rescheduling the loan are not available, possible or practical. It will be necessary to persevere and show that by the lender reducing the current mortgage costs, for example, by rescheduling over a longer term (see para 41.7) or by altering the level and/or frequency of repayment, it will be possible for the borrower to meet future commitments.

1　www.nationaldebtline.co.uk; tel: 0808 808 4000.

Reduction of repayments

41.5 Lenders (especially 'responsible lenders' such as local authorities, building societies and banks) should be prepared to accept interest-only payments and defer capital repayments within repayment mortgages at least in the short term. This should prevent further arrears accruing providing payments are made, although the lender may require that the unpaid capital elements be paid off when normal repayments are resumed. In relation to regulated mortgage contracts (see para 40.75) the Financial Services Authority (FSA) requires lenders to deal fairly with any borrower in arrears.[2] Lenders must also operate within their written policy for complying with this obligation. FSA guidance suggests that lenders may wish to defer payment of interest due on a regulated mortgage contract or treat any arrears as if they were part of the original amount borrowed.[3] An unreasonable response to such a request might found the basis for a complaint to the Financial Ombudsman Service (FOS).[4] See para 40.112. Many financial institutions are also sensitive to bad media publicity where the lender is obviously acting insensitively.

41.6 Where the borrower took out a mortgage protection policy (to pay the mortgage instalments in the event of unemployment or sickness), it is important to lodge the necessary claim form with insurers as soon as possible. Many of these policies set down a very short time-scale within which a claim should be made. Do not, however, be put off lodging the claim after the time specified, because the insurers can extend the time at their discretion. Complaints about mortgage protection policies can be lodged with the FOS. Mortgage protection policies are commonly taken out with second mortgages or 'secured loans'. Payments received under a mortgage protection policy which are then used by a claimant receiving income support or income-based jobseeker's allowance to pay housing costs not covered by the Department for Work and Pensions (DWP) are not treated as the claimant's income.[5] Similarly, payments which these claimants receive from other sources (rather than being paid directly by a third party to the lender), which are actually used to make payments

---

2 Mortgage: Conduct of Business sourcebook (MCOB) 13.3.1 R (1)(b). See para 40.94 of this book.

3 MCOB 13.3.4 G (1)(c) and (d).

4 www.financial-ombudsman.org.uk.

5 Income Support (General) Regulations (IS Regs) 1987 SI No 1967 Sch 9 para 29 and Jobseeker's Allowance Regulations (JSA Regs) 1996 SI No 207 Sch 7 para 30.

towards a secured loan which does not qualify for assistance under the benefit regulations, are ignored unless the claimant has used insurance policy payments for the same purpose.[6]

Extension of term

41.7   In any repayment mortgage case, it may be possible to extend the term of the loan so as to reduce the capital element and thus the amount of the monthly repayment. This option need not be pursued if the lender is prepared to accept interest-only payments for a period. Extending the term of the loan involves entering into a new mortgage arrangement and it may be possible, as part of that process, to have the existing arrears 'capitalised' by the lender wiping out the arrears and increasing the outstanding capital by an equivalent amount. In this way, the borrower can be given a fresh start. Care, however, should be taken in pre-October 1995 loan cases to try to ensure that the new agreement will not be treated as a post-October 1995 loan in the case of future claims for income support and jobseeker's allowance. See para 41.18.

41.8   Again the FSA encourages lenders in relation to regulated mortgage contracts[7] to consider extending the term of the regulated mortgage contract.[8]

Changing type of mortgage

41.9   In the case of an endowment mortgage, it is worth considering whether there would be a reduction in monthly payments by switching to a repayment mortgage. The amount of interest paid each month would remain the same but the monthly repayments of the capital (over the remainder of the term or over an extended term) may be less than the payments of the endowment insurance premium. The amount of capital originally borrowed from the lender could be reduced by the surrender or sale value of the endowment policy. If the endowment policy has been going for some years, more will be raised by selling the policy to an endowment policy investor. The borrower should contact a reputable insurance broker for details of how the policy could be

6   IS Regs 1987 Sch 9 para 30(a)–(d) and JSA Regs 1996 Sch 7 para 31.
7   Para 40.76.
8   MCOB 13.3.4 G (1)(a).

sold on. It can be difficult to sell policies which have been in existence for only a few years. If the lender agrees to a new loan, a mortgage protection policy may have to be taken out to cover the possibility of the borrower's death before the end of the loan term.

41.10   Where an endowment mortgage borrower is told by the endowment policy insurance company that the sums likely to be realised at the end of the term of the policy are less than the amount needed to pay off the mortgage loan, the borrower would probably be better advised to negotiate with the lender to make additional payments towards the shortfall, as if those payments were capital repayments, rather than taking out an additional endowment or similar policy cover to pay off the shortfall. Again the FSA advice in relation to regulated mortgage contracts[9] is that lenders may wish to consider changing the type of the regulated mortgage contract.[10] Borrowers who have been advised that their endowment policy is unlikely to be enough to pay off the capital borrowed and who feel that they may have been missold the policy should contact the FSA.[11]

41.11   The Mortgage Arrears Protocol (see paras 42.3–42.10 and appendix D) expressly identifies four of these options for consideration by the lender and borrower, namely extending the term of the loan, changing the type of loan, deferring payment of interest and capitalising the arrears.

Remortgaging

41.12   Where there are two or more mortgages (one of which is likely to be with a 'fringe' mortgage company which charges high rates of interest), or even where there is one high interest rate loan, it is worth trying to persuade one of the mainstream lenders (such as a bank or building society[12]) to 'remortgage' the loan. This involves redemption of the existing loan(s) and replacement with a new mortgage agreement. It is easier to persuade a building society or bank to remortgage the property if, at the time of the new mortgage, the borrower's local housing authority agrees to enter into a form of mortgage guarantee which would indemnify the lender in the event of the bank or building society suffering a loss because of any default.[13] It is worth

9   Para 40.76.
10   MCOB 13.3.4 G(1)(b).
11   See www.fsa.gov.uk.
12   Building Societies Act 1986 Part I.
13   See Housing Act (HA) 1985 s442, as amended by HA 1996.

arguing that the lender has in the future nothing to lose, as the money will be recovered either following repossession and sale or, if there is any shortfall, by the local authority meeting the shortfall under the terms of the guarantee.

41.13   Extreme caution should be exercised when considering whether to remortgage with institutions other than building societies (or other similar lenders) because the terms offered may well be disadvantageous over a period of time. The fees for remortgaging may also be considerable, as they include not only surveyors' and solicitors' fees but also the commission charged by the mortgage broker who arranges the remortgage. However, it is worth seeking specialist advice from a reputable mortgage broker as lenders are keen to attract new customers, often on initially advantageous terms.

41.14   Where a borrower is 'threatened with homelessness', ie, it is 'likely that he will be homeless within 28 days',[14] it is useful to remind the housing authority of its duty[15] to 'take reasonable steps to secure that accommodation does not cease to be available for [the borrower's] occupation'. It is arguable that this duty may extend to requiring the authority to use one or more of its powers in Housing Act (HA) 1996 Part VII to try to prevent dispossession. This duty, however, arises only where the local housing authority is satisfied that the borrower is in priority need and not intentionally threatened with homelessness. See chapter 36.

Repurchase by local authorities

41.15   In practice, it is quite common for a defaulting borrower who has purchased his or her previously council-owned property to ask the local authority to buy the property back. Local authorities purchasing properties which have previously been bought under the 'right to buy' provisions of the Housing Act 1985 receive government subsidy.[16]

Financial help from the Department for Work and Pensions

41.16   For a detailed analysis of the rules relating to mortgage interest payments by the DWP for people eligible for income support,

14   HA 1996 s175(4).
15   HA 1996 s195(2).
16   Local Authorities (Capital Finance) (Amendment) Regs 1999 SI No 501.

income-based jobseeker's allowance, income-related employment and support allowance and pension credit, reference should be made to the current year's edition of the Child Poverty Action Group's *Welfare benefits and tax credit handbook*. Alternatively, in summary, the following help is available.

41.17   The DWP is required in most cases to pay interest on loans for the purchase or repair or improvement (as defined) of the home, where the borrower is in receipt of income support or income-based jobseeker's allowance.[17] Claimants receiving income-related employment and support allowance and pension credit can also receive assistance. There is no obligation on the DWP to pay the capital element in the monthly loan repayment or the monthly premium on the insurance policy in endowment mortgages, or to assist in maintaining the private pension contribution in cases of pension mortgages.

41.18   The DWP makes reduced payments during the first weeks of the claim unless the claimant or his or her partner is aged over 60. For loans taken out before 2 October 1995 nothing is paid for the first eight weeks, 50 per cent of the housing costs are paid for the next 18 weeks, and full housing costs are met after 26 weeks. For loans taken out after 1 October 1995 nothing used to be paid for the first 39 weeks but full housing costs were paid after 39 weeks. However, as a temporary measure from 5 January 2009 relevant claimants are entitled to mortgage interest payments after 13 weeks from the start of the claim for benefit.[18] The maximum loan on which mortgage interest is met has been increased from £100,000 to £200,000. Complicated 'add back' provisions apply to those who were receiving financial assistance before 2 October 1995.

41.19   Interest is payable by the DWP by reference to a standard interest rate (SIR), which is usually calculated as the Bank of England base rate plus 1.58 per cent. However, since November 2008 the SIR has been frozen at 6.08 per cent. From 1 October 2010 the SIR will be abolished and mortgage interest will be paid by reference to the Bank of England's average mortgage rate, which is currently 3.09 per cent.[19]

41.20   Payments are made to the lender every four weeks in arrears even if the contractual payments are monthly.

---

17 IS Regs 1987 regs 17(e) and 18(f) and Sch 3 paras 7 and 8 and JSA Regs 1996 reg 83(f) and Sch 2 paras 14 and 15.
18 Social Security (Housing Costs Special Arrangements) (Amendment and Modification) Regs 2008 SI No 3195.
19 Social Security (Housing Costs) (Standard Interest Rate) (Amendment) Regs 2010 SI No 1811.

41.21   Since 8 April 2010, where payments are made to a lender which exceed the borrower's liability in respect of mortgage interest payable, the excess is required to be applied first towards discharge of any arrears or, if there are no arrears, towards discharging the capital debt or any other sum payable in respect of the loan.[20]

Other government support

41.22   Following the financial credit crunch in late 2008, central government has introduced a number of measures to try to prevent a repetition of the level of repossession experienced in the early 1990s when the numbers of home owners evicted was recognised as politically unacceptable.

41.23   The lead initiative of the UK government is the *Mortgage Rescue Scheme for England*, which is designed to allow homeowners to remain in possession of their homes either as tenants of registered social landlords (RSL) or alternatively as shared owners. The scheme became nominally effective in January 2009 and is intended to be completed by March 2011. The scheme has been criticised for its slow delivery and complexity. The *Government Mortgage to Rent* scheme involves the purchase of a property by an RSL and the continued occupation by the occupiers as tenants. For the detail of the scheme see 'Government mortgage to rent'.[21] The alternative is the *Shared Equity* scheme which allowes an RSL to purchase a share in the property so as to reduce the mortgage repayments to a level which the owner can afford. For details see 'Shared Equity'.[22] The *Homeowners Mortgage Support Scheme* provides a central government guarantee for lenders who agree to allowing borrowers to pay less than the contractual instalments where after a period of two years the borrower is expected to resume full payment.[23]

41.24   The Welsh Assembly government has issued its own *Mortgage Rescue Scheme for Wales*.[24]

---

20 Social Security (Claims and Payments) Amendment Regulations 2010 SI No 796.

21 www.cfg.homesandcommunities.co.uk/government-mortgage-to-rent.htm.

22 www.cfg.homesandcommunities.co.uk/se-shared-equity.htm.

23 www.communities.gov.uk/housing/buyingselling/mortgagesupportscheme.

24 http://wales.gov.uk/docs/desh/publications/091119housingmortgagerescueen.doc.

Procedure and tactics

Venue for proceedings

42.1   Proceedings for possession of a dwelling-house must be brought in the county court for the district in which the house is situated unless an enactment provides otherwise or the claimant believes that there are exceptional circumstances warranting the issue of the proceedings in the High Court.[1] Where the loan is one regulated by the Consumer Credit Act (CCA) 1974, proceedings must be brought in the county court.[2] The claim for possession in a new Consumer Credit Act case may be brought in the High Court if the claimant files, with the claim form, a certificate stating the reasons for bringing the proceedings in the High Court verified by a statement of truth. Circumstances may, in an appropriate case, justify starting a claim in the High Court if:

- there are complicated disputes of fact;
- there are points of law of general importance; or
- the claim is against trespassers and there is a substantial risk of public disturbance or of serious harm to people or property which properly require immediate determination.[3]

The value of the property and the amount of any financial claim may be relevant circumstances but these factors alone will not usually justify starting the claim in the High Court.[4]

42.2   If a claimant starts a claim in the High Court and the court decides that it should have been started in the county court, the court will usually either strike out the claim or transfer it to the county court of its own initiative. The court will usually disallow the costs of starting the claim in the High Court or of any transfer.[5] In practice, it is much more common for proceedings to be brought in the county court and the procedure and tactics discussed in this chapter apply to proceedings in that court unless otherwise indicated.

Mortgage arrears protocol

42.3   Since 18 November 2008 the *Pre-Action Protocol for Possession Claims based on Mortgage or Home Purchase Plan Arrears in respect*

---

1 CPR 55.3 but see CPR 3.10 and *Gwynedd County Council v Grunshaw* [2000] 1 WLR 494; (2000) 32 HLR 610, CA.
2 CCA 1974 s141(1).
3 CPR PD 55 para 1.3.
4 PD 55 para 1.4.
5 PD 55 para 1.2.

of Residential Property[6] ('Mortgage Arrears Protocol') has had effect. The full text is set out in appendix D. The aims of the protocol are to ensure that the lender and borrower 'act fairly and reasonably with each other' and to 'encourage more pre-action contact' in an effort to seek an agreement between the parties and, where that cannot be reached, for court time to be used efficiently.

42.4   The protocol applies to residential mortgages regulated by the Financial Services Authority (FSA) under the Financial Services and Markets Act 2000, charges regulated under the Consumer Credit Act 1974 and 'unregulated mortgages'. Its application to 'buy-to-let' mortgages is uncertain.

42.5   The lender 'should respond promptly' to any proposal for payment of the arrears and, if the offer is rejected, to give written reasons within ten business days of the proposal (para 5.5).

42.6   The protocol counsels against the issuing of proceedings in three sets of circumstances:

> A lender should consider not starting a possession claim for mortgage arrears where the borrower can demonstrate to the lender that the borrower has –
> (1) submitted a claim to
>   (a) the Department for Works and Pensions (DWP) for Support for Mortgage Interest (SMI); or
>   (b) an insurer under a mortgage payment protection policy; or
>   (c) a participating local authority for support under a Mortgage Rescue Scheme,
>   and has provided all the evidence required to process a claim;
> (2) a reasonable expectation of eligibility for payment from the DWP or from the insurer or support from the local authority; and
> (3) an ability to pay a mortgage instalment not covered by a claim to the DWP or the insurer in relation to a claim under paragraph 6.1(1)(a) or (b). (para 6.1)

Where none of those three circumstances applies, proceedings should not be issued in these further situations:

> If a borrower can demonstrate that reasonable steps have been or will be taken to market the property at an appropriate price in accordance with reasonable professional advice, the lender should consider postponing starting a possession claim. The borrower must continue to take all reasonable steps actively to market the property where the lender has agreed to postpone starting a possession claim.

6 www.justice.gov.uk/civil/procrules_fin/contents/protocols/prot_mha.htm.

Where the lender has agreed to postpone starting a possession claim the borrower should provide the lender with a copy of the particulars of sale, the Home Information Pack and (where relevant) details of purchase offers received within a reasonable period of time specified by the lender. The borrower should give the lender details of the estate agent and the conveyancer instructed to deal with the sale. The borrower should also authorise the estate agent and the conveyancer to communicate with the lender about the progress of the sale and the borrower's conduct during the process. (paras 6.2 and 6.3)

The third situation where the protocol advises forbearance by a lender is as follows:

The lender should consider whether to postpone the start of a possession claim where the borrower has made a genuine complaint to the Financial Ombudsman Service (FOS) about the potential possession claim. (para 8.1)

42.7　Emphasis is placed on alternative dispute resolution. The protocol provides that '[t]he court takes the view that staring a possession claim is usually a last resort and that such a claim should not normally be started when a settlement is still actively being explored' (para 7.1). The protocol identifies four options which the parties may wish to consider:

- extending the term of the mortgage;
- changing the type of mortgage;
- deferring payment of interest due under the mortgage; or
- capitalising the arrears. (para 7.1(1)–(4))

See para 41.5 onwards.

42.8　Compliance with the protocol can be monitored by inviting the court to ask the lender to demonstrate how it has complied. The protocol provides that the parties 'should be able, if requested by the court, to explain the actions that they have taken to comply with this protocol' (para 9.1). This has been supplemented since October 2009 by the requirement that the lender must bring to court two completed copies of form N123, which is a checklist requiring the lender to identify how it has in the previous three months complied with the protocol.[7] A blank copy of form N123 is at appendix D.

42.9　Critics of the protocol point to the changes introduced to the draft protocol, which was more regulatory in nature.[8] The protocol's aspirational provisions (for example, the lender '*should consider*' whether to

---

7　PD 55A para 5.5.

8　See L Whitehouse, 'The mortgage arrears pre-action protocol: an opportunity lost' (2009) 72(5) MLR 793.

postpone proceedings) do not impose any real obligation. That said, experience of the protocol in practice suggests that lenders are having to justify their conduct more often and that some district judges are prepared to protect borrowers against the worst excesses of some lenders.

42.10   Issued at the same time as the protocol was implemented was the Council of Mortgage Lenders (CML)'s *Industry guidance on arrears and possessions to help lenders comply with MCOB 13 and TCF principles.*[9] The guide sets out in tabular form examples of good practice in policy and procedure and might be of some benefit to advisers seeking to demonstrate non-compliance with the protocol.

42.11   While the protocol does not contain specific sanctions for non-compliance, paragraph 9 clearly requires the lender to be able to explain the actions they have taken to comply with the protocol. However the general 'Practice Direction – Pre-Action Conduct'[10] states

- The court may take into account the extent of a party's compliance with a relevant pre-action protocol when giving directions for the managements of claims and when making costs orders. (para 4.1)
- The court will expect the parties to have complied with any relevant pre-action protocol and may ask the parties to explain what steps were taken to comply prior to the start of the claim. (para 4.2)
- When deciding whether to impose sanctions, the court will look at the overall effect of non-compliance. (para 4.5)

42.12   If in the opinion of the court there has been non-compliance, the sanctions available under the 'Practice Direction – Pre-Action Conduct' include:

- staying the proceedings until steps which ought to have been taken have been taken;
- imposing an order that the party at fault pays costs (including indemnity costs);
- imposing against a claimant who has been granted a monetary judgment an order depriving it of interest or awarding interest at a lower rate.

42.13   Institutional lenders issuing possession proceedings which include a claim for a monetary judgment should, prior to issuing such proceedings, in a letter before claim provide the information contained at annex B to the Practice Direction on how to access debt advice.

---

9 www.cml.org.uk/cml/policy/issues/1629#1.
10 www.justice.gov.uk/civil/procrules_fin/contents/practice_directions/pd_pre-action_conduct.htm.

Claim form

42.14   Mortgage possession proceedings are brought by claim form with attached particulars of claim. The claim form is endorsed with the hearing date.[11] The hearing date cannot be less than 28 days from the date of issue[12] and the standard period between the issue of the claim form and the hearing should not be more than eight weeks.[13] The defendant must be served with the claim form and the particulars of claim not less than 21 days before the hearing.[14] The stage of borrower default at which lenders issue proceedings varies but can be when as little as two months' arrears have accrued. In practice, proceedings are brought to enforce payment with the deterrent that failure to pay will result in possession being lost. The proceedings are in the same form whether the claimant is a first or subsequent mortgagee.

42.15   Depending on the terms of the mortgage deed, before issuing the claim the lender may send a 'calling-in' letter (see para 40.34). This specifies the amount required to be paid by the borrower to redeem the loan. The mortgage deed may require the lender to make such a formal demand for the outstanding loan before it becomes payable in whole. Alternatively, the mortgage deed may provide that the whole outstanding loan becomes due immediately on default in which case the calling-in letter is not necessary.

42.16   The particulars of claim attached to the claim form are required[15] to set out certain details relating to the loan including, among others, the amount of the loan, any periodic payment and any payment of interest required to be made and in schedule form to show the dates and amounts of all payments due and payments made under the mortgage agreement for the period of two years immediately preceding the date of issue of the proceedings.[16] If the lender wishes to rely on a history of arrears which is longer than two years, this must be stated in the particulars of claim and a full (or longer) schedule exhibited to a witness statement.[17]

42.17   In the case of claims issued using 'Possession Claims Online' (PCOL) the lender does not need to provide a schedule showing the

11   CPR 55.4 and 55.5.
12   CPR 55.5(3)(a).
13   CPR 55.5(3)(b).
14   CPR 55.5(3)(c).
15   PD 55A para 2.5 and form N120.
16   PD 55A para 2.5(3).
17   PD 55A para 2.5A.

arrears from the date of default or for two years if default exceeds that period, provided that such a schedule has been served before issue. Instead, the lender need only provide a summary of the arrears in the claim form but must, not more than seven days from the issue of proceedings, serve on the defendant a schedule of arrears if they exceed two years or from the date of default if less than two years. In a PCOL case a lender which has only provided a summary of arrears in the claim form must also make a witness statement or provide oral evidence at the hearing that the appropriate schedule was served on the defendant before the proceedings were issued.[18]

42.18   Details of any other payments required to be made as a term of the mortgage (such as for insurance premiums, legal costs, default interest, penalties, administrative or other charges) must also be specified, as must details of any other sums claimed, stating the nature and amount of any such charge. The lender must also specify whether any of those payments are in arrears and whether these are included in the amount of any periodic payment. However, failure to provide the required information may not justify refusal to grant a possession order.[19] The claim form must be verified by a statement of truth.[20] In the usual way, the defendant(s) has 14 days within which to file any defence. An acknowledgment of service is not required.[21]

42.19   Generally, the only defence available will be to seek the benefit of the court's powers under the Administration of Justice Acts or the Consumer Credit Act 1974 (see chapter 40). See appendix B for a precedent defence. Although it is important to file a formal defence if any unusual point is to be argued, the courts should allow a defendant to seek such relief without any formal pleadings being served.[22] It remains to be seen to what extent the courts will stay proceedings under CPR 26.4 to allow any complaint concerning a regulated mortgage contract (see para 40.75) to be investigated by the Financial Ombudsman Service.

42.20   It is not possible to obtain a default judgment in possession proceedings.[23] Form N11M, the defence form which is sent out by the court with the possession summons, must be used.[24] This enables

18 PD 55B para 6.3–6.3C
19 *Nationwide Anglia Building Society v Shillibeer* [1994] CLY 3295.
20 CPR 22.1.
21 CPR 55.7.
22 See *Redditch Benefit Building Society v Roberts* [1940] Ch 415; [1940] 1 All ER 342, CA and CPR 55.7(3).
23 CPR 55.7(4).
24 PD 55A para 1.5.

the borrower to give a complete picture of his or her finances because the form is really little more than an income and expenditure statement. An application for a time order under CCA 1974 s129 may be made in the defence or by application notice in the proceedings.[25]

42.21   Where, after proceedings have been issued, the borrower pays off the arrears, the proper course is to adjourn the proceedings generally so that the lender can apply to reinstate the proceedings if further arrears accrue. This saves further legal costs which are likely to be added to the borrower's mortgage debt.[26]

Parties to proceedings

42.22   It is, it seems, necessary to join as defendants not only the borrower(s) but also those people in occupation who are known to claim a right to remain.[27] An occupier who is not a legal owner (the property being in the sole name of the borrower) does not have the absolute right to be joined as defendant. Where a spouse or civil partner has registered a Class F land charge, or a notice or caution pursuant to the Family Law Act 1996 s31, he or she has the right to be notified of the action being brought by the lender against his or her spouse, and should be sent a copy of the particulars of claim.[28] He or she does not have to be joined as defendant by the lender from the outset. Whether or not any such charge, notice or caution has been registered, a 'connected person' who is not a defendant may apply to be joined as a defendant 'at any time before the action is finally disposed of in that court' and shall be made a defendant with a view to meeting the borrower's liabilities provided that the court 'does not see any special reason against it' and the court is satisfied that he or she may be able to persuade the court to exercise any of its powers under the Administration of Justice Act 1970.[29] The expression 'connected person' in relation to any person means that person's spouse, former spouse, civil partner, former civil partner, co-habitant or former co-habitant.[30] In the case of a former spouse, former civil partner or former cohabitant, the right to apply to be joined as a defendant applies only

---

25 PD 55A para 7.1. See also form N440.
26 *Halifax plc v Taffs* April 2000 *Legal Action* 15; [2000] CLY 4385, CA. See also *Greyhound Guaranty Ltd v Caulfield* [1981] CLY 1808.
27 *Brighton and Shoreham Building Society v Hollingdale* [1965] 1 All ER 540.
28 Family Law Act 1996 s56.
29 Family Law Act 1996 s55.
30 Family Law Act 1996 s54(5).

where that person has the benefit of a court order conferring rights of occupation. In such circumstances, the court can only refuse the application to be joined if there are 'special reasons' against the applicant being joined in the action. Where a person has registered his or her rights of occupation under the Family Law Act 1996 as a land charge or at the Land Registry then the lender is also obliged to serve notice of the claim on that person.[31]

42.23   Obviously, it is quite possible that a deserted spouse or civil partner may not hear about the proceedings until the bailiffs come to execute a warrant for possession, but it would be possible for him or her to apply at that stage to be joined as a defendant and to claim relief. Occupiers (such as tenants) who wish to be joined as defendants to argue any point should apply without notice by letter to the court and attend the hearing.[32] Alternatively, they could simply attend the hearing and ask to be joined as a defendant then. CPR 55.10(2) requires the lender within five days of being notified by the court of the hearing date to send to the mortgaged property a notice addressed to the 'tenant or the occupier' as well as to the housing authority for the district where the property is located, and to the registered proprietor of any other legal charge, stating that possession proceedings have been issued and giving details of the parties to the proceedings the court and the hearing date. The lender is also required to produce at the hearing a copy of the notice and evidence that the notice has been served.[33]

42.24   An occupying tenant (who may well have no right to remain as against the lender) may need to apply to be joined as defendant so as to obtain a possession order for the purpose of application to the local housing authority for assistance under the homelessness provisions of the Housing Act 1996 Part VII. Advisers should consider the practice of the local housing authority before making any application because a tenant renders himself or herself at risk as to costs. It is likely, however, that a lender would not usually take steps to recover costs against the tenant but would rely on recovery of costs against the security of the property (see para 42.78). However, a tenant wishing to be joined in the proceedings as a named defendant should be advised of this theoretical risk.

42.25   The Mortgage Repossessions (Protection of Tenants etc) Act 2010 gives the court power to suspend an order for possession on application by a tenant. The Act is due to come into force on 1 October

31 Family Law Act 1996 s56.
32 CPR 19.3.
33 CPR 55.10(4).

2010.[34] Where a mortgage lender brings possession proceedings against a property which consists of or includes a dwelling-house and there is an unauthorised tenancy of all or part of the property, the court may *on making an order for possession*, on application of the tenant, postpone delivery of possession for up to two months.[35]

42.26   There is an 'unauthorised tenancy' only if:

(a) an agreement has been made which, as between the parties to it (or their successors in title) is or gives rise to –
(i) an assured tenancy (within the meaning of the Housing Act 1988), or
(ii) a protected or statutory tenancy (within the meaning of the Rent Act 1977), and
(b) the lender's interest in the property is not subject to the tenancy. (s1(8))

42.27   Subsequently the court may, on application of the tenant, *stay or suspend execution of the order* for a period not exceeding two months if –

(a) the court did not exercise its powers to suspend on application of the tenant when making the order for possession or if it did the tenant applicant was not the tenant when it exercised those powers,
(b) the tenant has asked the lender to give an undertaking in writing not to enforce the order for two months beginning with the date the undertaking is given, and
(c) the lender has not given such an undertaking. (s1(4))

The court's powers under s1(4) arise only where an order for possession has been made but not executed.[36]

42.28   In considering whether to execute its powers the court must have regard to:

(a) the circumstances of the tenant, and
(b) if there is an outstanding breach by the tenant of a term of the unauthorised tenancy –
(i) the nature of that breach, and
(ii) whether the tenant might reasonably be expected to have avoided breaching that term or to have remedied the breach.[37]

42.29   Any postponement, stay or suspension may be made conditional on the making of payments to the lender in respect of occupation of the

---

34 See Dwelling Houses (Execution of Possession Orders by Mortgagees) Regulations 2010 SI No 1809.
35 Section 1(1) and (2).
36 Section 1(3).
37 Section 1(5).

property.[38] The making of these payments pursuant to an undertaking given by a lender under section 1(4)(c) or a condition imposed by the court on the tenant is not to be regarded as creating (or as evidence of the creation of) any tenancy or other rights to occupy the property.[39]

42.30 Enforcement of a possession order by a lender in respect of a dwelling-house may take place only following the service of a prescribed form giving the tenant/occupier no less than 14 days' notice of the date for the eviction. See para 42.66.

42.31 The fact that the borrower is bankrupt does not mean that he or she has no right or power to address the court in possession proceedings. Both the order and warrant are directed to the named defendants and as such they have locus standi to raise issues which are relevant to the exercise of any Administration of Justice Act discretion.[40] The trustee in bankruptcy of a bankrupt borrower should be joined as party only if the court so directs.[41]

Evidence

42.32 The claim for possession is heard in private (unless the court directs to the contrary).[42] The evidence in support of the claim will be set out in the particulars of claim and verified by a statement of truth (CPR PD 55A para 5.1). Additional evidence may be given by witness statement without specific court order except where the case is allocated to the fast track or multi-track or the court otherwise orders.[43] Usually, institutional lenders make use of this facility as it is easier and more cost-effective to give evidence by witness statement than to incur the expense of attendance at court of management personnel. Pro forma witness statements are generally produced, which do little more than confirm the contents of the particulars of claim. The mortgage deed is usually exhibited to the witness statement, as is any calling-in letter. Where relevant, an up-to-date search certificate of HM Land Registry or Land Charges Department will also be exhibited to ascertain if any notice, caution or Class F land charge has been registered to protect a civil partner or spouse's rights of occupation under family legislation.

38 Section 1(6).
39 Section 1(7).
40 *Nationwide Building Society v Purvis* [1998] BPIR 625, CA.
41 *Alliance Building Society v Shave* [1952] Ch 581.
42 PD 39 para 1.5.
43 CPR 55.8(3).

42.33   However, it is possible on the application of any party to obtain an order requiring the maker of the witness statement to attend court for cross-examination. If the maker of a witness statement does not attend the hearing and the borrower disputes material evidence in the statement, the court 'will normally adjourn the hearing so that oral evidence can be given'.[44] The borrower may wish to require attendance of the maker of the witness statement where, for example, the lender is claiming arrears of payments which include separate interest charges on missed monthly payments so as to have this clarified for the court. Advisers can then argue that only bona fide missed payments should be taken into account in considering whether to postpone an order or not. Borrowers should seek the attendance of the makers of witness statements only if there is some good reason, in view of the formidable position which lenders have in connection with costs and expenses (see para 42.78). The witness statement is usually sent by post to the borrower before the hearing and must be served at least two days before the hearing.[45]

42.34   Well advised borrowers will prepare their witness statements for the hearing and serve then two days in advance of the hearing date. In practice this is unusual. The court is entitled to accept material adduced as evidence informally by the borrower or his or her representative even if that does not strictly comply with the laws of evidence.[46] If the lender disputes what the borrower has said then formal evidence would need to be called.

42.35   Advisers may wish to request, in place of the attendance of the maker of the witness statement, an order from the court that the claimant file a detailed witness statement setting out all sums claimed to be due and a copy of the account from the inception of the loan so as to expose to the court the full details of the claim.

Hearings and orders for possession

42.36   As stated above (para 42.32), the hearing of the claim is usually in private and before the district judge.[47] Given the numbers of possession claims being listed for hearing, in practice the court may well expect

---

44   PD 55A para 5.4.
45   CPR 55.8(4).
46   *Cheltenham & Gloucester Building Society v Grant* (1994) 26 HLR 703, CA. See also M Thompson, 'A very wide discretion?' [1995] Conv 51.
47   Originally Administration of Justice Act 1970 s38(3) (repealed by County Courts Act 1984 s148(3)) and now CPR PD 39 para 1.5.

to be able to spend only a matter of minutes on each case.[48] If any substantive argument is raised, then it is likely that the case will be adjourned to another date. In such cases the borrower should offer to make some payment towards the mortgage in the interim. If the case is to be defended then the court should proceed to deal with the case or give case management directions to include, 'where the claim is disputed on grounds which appear to be substantial', allocating to track.[49]

42.37   In deciding allocation to track, the matters to which the court shall have regard include, under CPR 26.8, the level of arrears, the importance to the defendant of retaining possession and the importance of vacant possession to the claimant.[50] The financial value of the property is not necessarily the most important factor in deciding the track for a possession claim and the court may direct a possession claim to be allocated to the fast track even though the value of the property is in excess of £25,000.[51] In practice, it is rare for an 'undefended' claim to be allocated to a track.

42.38   As with many hearings in private, practice and procedure vary. Usually, the lender's solicitor outlines the history of the case and advises on any change in circumstances since the date of the witness statement. The original legal charge and a search for the purpose of identifying any rights registered under the Family Law Act 1996 may be produced for examination by the district judge and a certificate of service if, unusually, the claimant has served the claim form and particulars of claim.[52] There is strictly no need for the *original* charge certificate to be produced because office copies of the register and documents filed at the Land Registry are admissible under the Land Registration Act 2002 s67.[53] The lender is obliged to produce at the hearing a copy of the 'Dear Occupier' notice as well as evidence that the notice has been served.[54] Failure to produce these can be grounds for an adjournment. Where no valid search has been made it is for the claimant to satisfy the court that there are no people who should be notified in accordance with the Family Law Act 1996 s56. The lender's representative should 'present' form N123 in accordance with that

---

48 For a study of possession proceedings see J Nixon et al, *Housing cases in county courts*, Policy Press, 1996.
49 CPR 55.8(1) and (2).
50 CPR 55.9.
51 PD 55A para 6.1.
52 CPR 55.8(6).
53 Civil Evidence Act 1995 s9.
54 CPR 55.10(4)(b).

form's guidance notes. It is essential before the hearing starts for the lender's representative to be asked for a copy of N123. Advisers will need to take immediate instructions from the borrower on what is asserted there about compliance with the protocol (see para 42.3).

42.39   The borrower should then be asked to comment on the lender's case and to justify the court's exercise of any statutory power to postpone the giving up of possession. It is important to ensure that the court has the essential information needed to assess the case, including: the current balance outstanding; the arrears; the monthly instalment; the remaining term of the mortgage; and the last payment made and the amount. Where there is equity available to protect the lender, then this should be made clear. It is obviously essential that the borrower attends the hearing so as to give evidence to support any claim for statutory relief. Evidence which can be of use includes a letter of confirmation from the Department for Work and Pensions concerning payment of mortgage interest, evidence of future regular employment from a new employer, or a loan from friends or relatives, proof of remortgage facilities and an estate agent's valuation of the property. Where relief by way of a time order is being sought, realistic statements of income and expenditure should be available if not provided in N11M.

42.40   If, when arranging the mortgage, the borrower was required to pay for a mortgage indemnity policy, taken out by the lender to protect it in the event of a shortfall on sale following the borrower's eviction, this should be made clear to the district judge if there is any doubt about extent of the security. Since such a policy indemnifies the lender (either entirely or to a pre-set figure), the lender will not usually be prejudiced by giving any benefit of the doubt to the borrower in deciding whether to delay possession. The existence of such a policy should be clear from the mortgage offer letter which would have been sent to the borrower at the time the loan was taken out (as paying for the policy would have been one of the 'special' conditions of the advance).

42.41   As stated above, local practice varies but the courts since *Norgan*,[55] when considering possible orders for postponed possession, are now much more flexible in assessing how long to give the borrower to pay off the arrears. Advisers should obviously seek to argue for as long a period as is viable so that the amount of money required to be paid monthly towards the arrears is minimised. That said, advisers need

---

55   *Cheltenham & Gloucester Building Society v Norgan* [1996] 1 WLR 343; [1996] 1 All ER 449, CA and see para 40.29.

to bear in mind observations in the judgment in *Norgan* that if the borrower is given the period most favourable to the borrower and still defaults, it will be easier for the lender to argue against the borrower being given a further postponement, in any future application by the borrower.[56]

42.42   In cases falling within the Consumer Credit Act 1974, it is important to ensure that the district judge is aware that, when considering an application for a possession order, there is no statutory restriction requiring the arrears to be paid off within a 'reasonable period' (see para 40.57). In addition, it is important also to ask him or her to consider making a time order (see para 40.43) as well as suspending any order for possession granted in favour of the lender.

42.43   Any order giving statutory relief is likely to require the borrower to pay a stated amount per month in addition to the normal monthly instalment. The usual postponed order for possession in mortgage cases is set out as county court form N31. Effectively, the number of months it will take to clear off the arrears at £x per month is the 'reasonable period' referred to in the Administration of Justice Act 1970 s36(1) (see para 40.29).

42.44   Courts generally lean against making absolute orders for possession unless the borrower either fails to attend the hearing or is unable to make any proposals which meet the statutory criteria. Usually the court will, unless the security is insufficient or threatened, be concerned not to grant an absolute order in favour of the lender unnecessarily. Where the court does not feel able to exercise its discretion, then an order for possession in 28, or possibly 56, days is given in favour of the lender.

42.45   Where the borrower's financial position is uncertain (for example, where he or she has recently applied for a job or where a fresh claim has been made for income support and the amount of help to come from the Department for Work and Pensions by way of income support is not clear), it is possible to ask for an adjournment for a short period to allow the issues to be clarified. Borrowers should, if at all possible, offer to make some payments in the interim.

42.46   Where an endowment mortgage borrower has defaulted in maintaining payments under the endowment policy it is common for lenders, where they become aware of this, to 'switch' the mortgage from an interest-only loan to a capital and interest loan. This, particularly where the mortgage has been running for some time, results in a

---

56   *Cheltenham & Gloucester Building Society v Norgan* [1996] 1 All ER 449 at 459, although in *Norgan*, the Court of Appeal granted a fourth suspension.

substantial increase in the monthly payments expected from the borrower. Advisers must check carefully whether the legal charge provides for this. A lender will no doubt seek to argue that there must be a term implied into the mortgage agreement that allows for this 'switching'. Where the legal charge does specifically regulate the circumstances in which this conversion can take place it is difficult to see how such a term can be implied if the particular circumstances of the borrower's case do not meet the requirements of the express term in the legal charge. In any event it is arguable that, even if there is no 'capital vehicle' (see para 38.11) in place to repay the original loan, the loan could be repaid from the sale of the security if there were insufficient funds available to the borrower at the end of the mortgage term. It would be open to the lender to make application to the court if there was a change in circumstances such as to put the lender at risk.[57]

42.47   If the borrower is not able to persuade the district judge to grant a postponed order for possession because the borrower is not able to meet the current payments and clear the arrears over a reasonable period, some district judges have adopted a practice of granting an order for possession effective some time in the future. This might be, for instance, an order for possession in three months' time. The rationale would seem to be that this gives a borrower who is not able to meet the statutory criteria for relief a period of time in order to improve his or her situation. If this proves to be the case, the borrower can apply to the court at that stage for a variation of the order for possession so that it is then postponed on terms. Alternatively, the court may direct that there be a review hearing in, say, three months to ensure that the case is reassessed automatically.

42.48   In general, an order for possession should not be made against only one of two borrowers where it would not advantage the lender because the other borrower is entitled to remain in possession. This will, for example, arise where a husband has no defence to the claim but the wife has an arguable defence based on her consent to the charge being obtained by undue influence. In such circumstances, the court should not grant a possession order against the husband alone but should adjourn the proceedings as against the husband with liberty to restore should the wife leave the property or an order for possession be made against her.[58]

---

57 See *Household Mortgage Corporation plc v Etheridge* April 1997 *Legal Action* 13.
58 *Albany Home Loans Ltd v Massey* [1997] 2 All ER 609, CA. See also M P Thompson, 'The powers and duties of mortgagees' [1998] 62 Conv 391.

42.49   Where it is clear that some form of statutory relief is to be given to the borrower, advisers should argue, where the Administration of Justice Acts apply, for an adjournment on terms as to specified monthly payments by the borrower instead of a postponed order for possession. The advantage is that in the event of default a further hearing would be required if an adjournment was originally ordered; whereas a lender would be able to apply immediately for a warrant for possession without further hearing if the terms of a postponed order were breached. Many district judges are unwilling to adjourn on terms as they feel that this is insufficient by way of incentive to the borrower to pay and/or that by building in this extra step in the proceedings all that is being done is to increase the legal costs which will usually be added to the mortgage debt.

42.50   By contrast, in the High Court, execution of an order for possession because of a breach of a suspensory term cannot take place without the defendant being given an opportunity to be heard.[59]

42.51   In a mortgage claim the court should not usually attach to a postponed order for possession a requirement that the warrant for possession should not be executed without permission of the court,[60] although in practice it is not unknown for such a requirement to be added.

42.52   A borrower is not barred from making an application for a further postponement of an order or warrant just because a similar application has been refused before, although the court can dismiss such an application if it is an abuse of process.[61]

42.53   Where a borrower is not able to satisfy the court that it should grant him or her any statutory relief, then the lender is entitled to possession of the property. This may put the borrower in practical difficulty if some time is required to obtain alternative accommodation (either privately or from the local housing authority) and the lender is not willing to defer, by consent, the obtaining of physical possession. The county court has sufficient jurisdiction to postpone execution of the warrant for possession for a reasonable period.[62] However, it is clear that this power must be used judicially and the limits of this jurisdiction are unclear.

59 *Fleet Mortgage and Investment Co v Lower Maisonette 46 Eaton Place Ltd* [1972] 2 All ER 737 and *Practice Direction* [1972] 1 All ER 576.
60 *Royal Trust Co of Canada v Markham* [1975] 3 All ER 433, CA.
61 *Abbey National Mortgages v Bernard* (1996) 71 P&CR 257; [1995] NPC 118, CA.
62 See *Kelly v White, Penn Gaskell v Roberts* [1920] WN 220.

Counterclaims

42.54 The existence of a counterclaim for damages against a lender does not prevent the latter from exercising its common law right to possession. Even where a meritorious counterclaim exists (for example, for negligence or breach of warranty arising out of a survey report on the condition of the mortgaged property), this does not allow the court to exercise its Administration of Justice Act discretion any differently, because damages received by virtue of the counterclaim would not necessarily extinguish arrears by the end of a 'reasonable period'.[63] The position may be different, however, where the counterclaim against the lender is by way of a set-off and if the existence and prospects of success can be regarded as enabling the sums due to be paid within a reasonable period[64] or where the counterclaim is for rescission of the mortgage.[65] The situation of mortgages governed by the Consumer Credit Act 1974 may be different, in that the court's power to assist the borrower is not qualified by having to be satisfied that the arrears and accruing payments will be paid up to date by the end of a 'reasonable period' (see para 40.57).

Money judgments

42.55 The practice of the major institutional lenders varies but some lenders include, as part of the relief claimed, a request for judgment for the entire debt due at the date of the hearing. The particulars of claim and witness statement in support forms the evidence for that claim as well as for the order for possession. The rationale behind this is that a money judgment makes it easier for the lender to take subsequent enforcement action (if, for example, the property is sold for less than the money judgment obtained). However, the court has the discretion under the County Courts Act 1984 s71(2) to suspend payment of the entire debt. In the usual case the

---

63 See *National Westminster Bank plc v Skelton* [1993] 1 All ER 242, CA, *Citibank Trust v Ayivor* [1987] 1 WLR 1157; *Barclays Bank plc v Tennet* CAT 242, 6 June 1984, noted at [1985] CLY 5; *Midland Bank plc v McGrath* [1996] EGCS 61, CA and A Pugh-Thomas, 'Mortgagees and counterclaims' LS Gaz 27 April 1988, p28.

64 See *Ashley Guarantee plc v Zacaria* [1993] 1 All ER 254, CA and *Royal Bank of Scotland v O'Shea* April 1998 *Legal Action* 11, CA.

65 See *Barclays Bank plc v Waterson* (1988) Manchester County Court, noted at [1989] CLY 2505.

money judgment is postponed on the same terms as the order for possession.[66]

42.56 There are instances where it would be right to depart from the practice of granting a money judgment (where, for example, the borrower produces evidence of the sale of the mortgaged property taking place within a reasonable period).[67] The money judgment, in cases where a postponed order for possession is also obtained, does not appear on the judgment register as a county court judgment unless and until terms of the suspension are breached and the lender takes steps to enforce the order for possession. The Register of Judgments, Orders and Fines Regulations 2005[68] reg 9(d) exempts from registration as a county court judgment 'an order for the payment of money arising from an action for the recovery of land (whether for costs, payments due under a mortgage, arrears of rent or otherwise) until the creditor takes any step to enforce the order ...'.

42.57 It is not an abuse of process for a lender to seek possession first before subsequently choosing the alternative remedy of seeking a money judgment.[69] Accordingly, it is not improper for a lender who has been met with a successful *Barclays Bank v O'Brien*[70] defence (for which see para 47.4) choosing after disclaiming the security of the legal charge to sue on the personal covenant in the legal charge with a view as an unsecured creditor to bankrupt the mortgage borrower, even if this might result in the trustee in bankruptcy applying for an order for sale.[71]

42.58 A lender's claim for a money judgment is not res judicata simply because no money judgment was requested in previous unopposed proceedings in which a possession order was obtained where in those proceedings a money claim was made.[72] However, a claimant who had obtained a money judgment as well as a possession order based on an 'all monies' legal charge cannot subsequently issue fresh proceedings against the defendant seeking a money judgment in relation to a guarantee entered into by the defendant before the previous

---

66 *Cheltenham & Gloucester Building Society v Grattidge* (1993) 25 HLR 454, CA.
67 *Cheltenham & Gloucester Building Society v Johnson* (1996) 28 HLR 885, CA.
68 SI No 3595.
69 *Zandfarid v BCCI* [1996] 1 WLR 1420.
70 [1994] 1 AC 180, HL.
71 *Alliance & Leicester plc v Slayford* [2000] EWCA Civ 257; [2001] 1 All ER (Comm) 1; (2001) 33 HLR 66.
72 *UCB Bank plc v Chandler* [1999] EGCS 56, CA.

proceedings. The claimant's cause of action had merged in the earlier judgment.[73]

Appeals

42.59   Appeals from a district judge lie to the circuit judge.[74] The procedure is set out in CPR Part 52 and Practice Direction 52. Appeals from the circuit judge lie to the High Court in most cases. The old distinction between interlocutory and final orders has now gone and, accordingly, it can now in practice be more difficult to appeal certain orders by district judges, such as refusals to suspend warrants. CPR 52.11(3) provides that

> [t]he appeal court will allow an appeal where the decision of the lower court was (a) wrong or (b) unjust because of a serious procedural or other irregularity in the proceedings in the lower court.

However, an appeal court will be reluctant to interfere with the exercise of discretion unless it can be shown that the judge had:

- misunderstood the facts;
- taken account of irrelevant matters;
- failed to exercise the discretion; or
- made a decision that no reasonable judge could have made.

42.60   Permission to appeal is required from the judge whose order it is proposed to appeal or from the appeal court. The appellant's notice of appeal must be filed within 21 days of the order under appeal. The lodging of an appellant's notice does not stay enforcement of the order under appeal unless the appeal court or the lower court orders otherwise.[75] An undertaking not to seek to enforce the order under appeal should be sought from the claimant or a stay should be sought from the district judge or the circuit judge pending appeal. There are special rules relating to second appeals, that is an appeal from a circuit judge hearing a case on appeal from the district judge.

---

73   *Lloyds Bank plc v Hawkins* [1998] Lloyd's Rep Bank 379, CA. See also P Mostyn, 'No interest for mortgagees after money judgment' [1998] NLJ 1728 for a discussion of the case and an argument that lenders are, post-judgment, restricted to interest on the judgment debt at the statutory judgment rate rather than any contractual rate. See also *Director General of Fair Trading v First National Bank plc* [2001] UKHL 52; [2002] 1 AC 481; [2001] 3 WLR 1297.

74   See Access to Justice Act 1999 (Destination of Appeals) Order 2000 SI No 1071.

75   CPR 52.7.

42.61 Where a borrower has unsuccessfully applied to a district judge for the suspension of a warrant and has been evicted, if subsequently the borrower is successful on appeal to the circuit judge, he or she is entitled to be reinstated into the property. A circuit judge hearing an appeal can exercise all the jurisdiction which the district judge had. If the circuit judge reverses the decision of the district judge, he or she should restore, as near as possible, the position as it would have been had the district judge made the order now made by the circuit judge.[76]

Warrants for possession

Pre-execution

42.62 Where an immediate order for possession has been granted at the hearing or any period of postponement has expired or where the terms of any postponed order have been broken, the lender is free to apply without notice for the issue and execution of a warrant for possession. No further hearing is required and this does not breach European Convention on Human Rights article 6.

42.63 It is often only when the occupiers receive notification of the proposed eviction by the bailiffs that advice is sought. At this stage, where there has been a trial, advisers should consider applying to set aside the original possession order, if there are grounds for doing so under CPR 39.3, before execution of the warrant, for example, where the borrower did not attend the hearing because of non-receipt of the summons or illness. See para 34.7. Applications should be made in form N244, preferably with a supporting witness statement and if possible with a draft defence to the original claim (see precedent at appendix B).

42.64 The first hearing of a possession claim is not a trial within the meaning of the Civil Procedure Rules. It follows that if a defendant does not attend the first hearing an application to set aside the possession order can be made under CPR 3.1(2) and not CPR 39.3.[77]

42.65 The requirements for the enforcement of a possession order by a lender in respect of a dwelling-house will be changed with effect from 1 October 2010 with the coming into force of the Mortgage

---

76 *Hyde Park Funding Ltd v Ioannou* [1999] CLY 4382, County Court.
77 *Forcelux Ltd v Binnie* [2009] EWCA Civ 854.

Repossessions (Protection of Tenants etc) Act 2010.[78] This legislation was intended to give unauthorised tenants (see paras 42.25–42.26) the right to apply to the court to defer eviction by their landlord's lender. However, the provisions go wider than affecting tenants and put in place a further step for lenders wishing to enforce a possession order against properties. Execution of a possession order may take place:

(a) only if the lender gives notice at the property of any prescribed step taken for the purpose of executing the order, and
(b) only after the end of the prescribed period beginning with the day on which such notice is given. (s2(2))

42.66   Regulations provide that the prescribed period is 14 calendar days and the prescribed step as being the service on the tenant or occupier of a prescribed form advising of the lender's intention to enforce the possession order no fewer than 14 days before the date for the eviction. A copy of the notice is contained in appendix A to this book. While the 2010 Act enables 'unauthorised tenants' to make application to the court, it does not widen the legal options open to other occupiers – although confusingly the statutory notice is addressed to 'tenant/occupier'.

42.67   Where occupiers are not parties to the proceedings, they may wish to make an application to be joined as defendants as well as applying to have the order for possession set aside. An application to be joined as a party may be made on notice using form N244 and should also be supported by evidence setting out the occupier's interest in or connection with the claim.[79] Where a tenant occupies part of the property he or she may be able to have judgment set aside only in respect of the part he or she occupies. See paras 42.22–42.31.

42.68   A borrower in breach of a conditional order for possession can apply to have the order itself further postponed and the condition varied, or alternatively to have the warrant for possession suspended on terms. Administration of Justice Act 1970 s36 may be used to stay or suspend execution of an order for possession 'at any time before execution of such … order'.[80] Similar scope is given to the court in respect of regulated agreements within the meaning of the Consumer

---

78   Dwelling Houses (Execution of Possession Orders by Mortgagees) (England and Wales) Regulations 2010 SI No 1809.

79   PD 19 paras 1.3 and 1.4.

80   See *R v Bloomsbury and Marylebone County Court ex p Villerwest Ltd* [1976] 1 All ER 897, CA; *R v Ilkeston County Court ex p Kruza* (1985) 17 HLR 539 and *Hawtin v Heathcote* [1976] CLY 371, County Court.

Credit Act 1974.[81] Any application for such a further stay or suspension should usually be made on notice to the lender on form N244. It is advisable to make such an application (see precedent at appendix B) pending negotiations if there is any doubt as to whether a lender will agree to a stay.

Post-execution

42.69   Once the bailiff has executed the warrant and the borrower has been displaced, the court's statutory powers are exhausted.[82] However, the court's power to set aside judgment granting the order for possession and the subsequent warrant for possession or to suspend the warrant for possession may still be of assistance.[83] See para 34.55 for a discussion of the circumstances where the warrant for possession will be set aside on grounds of fraud, oppression or abuse of process by the lender. A party to proceedings who through no fault of his or her own did not have notice of a hearing until after it had already commenced, but who then made no attempt to apply to have the hearing recommenced could not later expect the court to set aside judgment given against him or her.[84] Where the borrower can raise the money to redeem the mortgage prior to exchange of contracts on the lender's sale, the court may restrain the lender from selling although separate proceedings for an injunction to restrain sale would need to be brought.

42.70   The borrower's equity of redemption is extinguished when the lender enters into a contract for sale, rather than at the time of completion, although it is unclear what the situation would be where the borrower has grounds to have the original order set aside or where the warrant was obtained by fraud or there has been abuse of the process or oppression in its execution such as to justify the warrant being set aside.[85] Where a lender is concerned about the risk of a borrower making some sort of application to the court which would have the effect of putting off a prospective buyer, the appropriate step is

---

81   CCA 1974 s135.

82   *Cheltenham & Gloucester Building Society v Obi* (1996) 28 HLR 22, CA and *Mortgage Agency Services Number Two Ltd v Bal* [1998] EWCA Civ 1186; (1998) 95(28) LSG 31.

83   CPR 39.3. See also *Governors of Peabody Donation Fund v Hay* (1987) 19 HLR 145, CA; *Hammersmith and Fulham LBC v Hill* (1995) 27 HLR 368, CA and *Cheltenham & Gloucester Building Society v Obi* (1996) 28 HLR 22, CA.

84   CPR 39.3 and *National Counties Building Society v Antonelli* [1995] NPC 177, CA.

85   *National Provincial Building Society v Ahmed* [1995] 38 EG 138, CA.

for the lender to apply for an order for sale under the Law of Property Act 1925 s91 where taking the property by virtue of the court order would protect the buyer absolutely.[86]

42.71   Where, however, an occupier is evicted by the bailiff and claims to have an independent right to remain as against the lender, for example, as an occupier with a tenancy binding on the lender or as an occupier with a superior equitable interest (for which see paras 43.3 and 46.7), he or she may apply to have judgment set aside or stayed so far as he or she is concerned and to be allowed to defend the proceedings.[87]

Responsibilities of mortgagee in possession

42.72   In the context of residential mortgages, the lender will be seeking possession of the borrower's home with a view to evicting the borrower and selling with vacant possession. For a discussion on the responsibilities imposed on the lender when selling, see para 48.16. A borrower will be concerned about the time it takes for the sale to be concluded and the fact that interest continues to accrue until the final payment of the mortgage following sale. The common law 'Duty to account' imposed on a mortgagee in possession may be of some assistance to borrowers in these circumstances. The extent of this liability has not been considered recently by the courts, and many of the old cases do not readily lend themselves to giving guidance on the position where modern institutional lenders take possession for the sole purpose of disposing of the premises with vacant possession. The duty to account operates in the borrower's favour by allowing the borrower, on redeeming the mortgage, to set off against monies due to the lender under the mortgage any rent or other profits received during the period of the lender's possession of the mortgaged property. If necessary, the court can order the taking of accounts in redemption proceedings.

42.73   A mortgagee who goes into possession of the mortgaged property, and thereby excludes the mortgagor from control of it, is bound to account to the mortgagor, not only for the rents and profits which he or she actually receives, but also for the rents and profits which, but for his or her wilful default or neglect, he or she might have received; ie, for everything which he or she has received, or might or ought to have received, while he or she continued in possession.[88]

---

86   *Arab Bank plc v Mercantile Holdings* [1994] Ch 71.
87   *Minet v Johnson* (1890) 63 LT 507 and *Hawtin v Heathcote* [1976] CLY 371.
88   *Halsbury's Laws* Vol 32 para 698.

42.74   A lender who refuses to rent out the property will be liable to account for rent that could have been received. In the seventeenth-century case of *Anon*[89] it was held that the lender's liability to account on the basis of wilful default included the refusal to rent to a tenant who was capable of paying the going rent for the property. The short note of the case states:

> A Mortgagee shall not account according to the value of the land, viz. He shall not be bound by any proof that the land was worth so much, unless you can likewise prove that he did actually make so much of it or might have done so, had it not been for his wilful default: as if he turned out a sufficient tenant, that held it at so much rent, or refused to accept a sufficient tenant that would have given so much for it.

The burden of proof is on the person alleging wilful default in not letting the property,[90] and the onus shifts to the lender where that person shows that the property can be let or has been let, and it is then up to the lender to show that he or she has been vigilant in attempts to let the property.

42.75   While the leading textbook on the law of mortgages considers that this duty to account for notional rent does not arise where possession has been taken with a view to sale within a reasonable period,[91] the authority on which the proposition is based does not in fact support that assertion.[92]

42.76   The courts have been more restrictive in terms of imposing obligations on a mortgagee in possession in relation to repair of the property. It appears that there is some general obligation not to be negligent in relation to protection of the repossessed property, with the lender being under a duty to take reasonable steps to protect the property against vandalism.[93]

42.77   One of the practical problems which can be a cause of further animosity between the lender and borrower is in deciding what items in the property are fixtures and hence should be left in situ when the borrower leaves, and what items are the borrower's and can lawfully be removed when the borrower gives up possession. In *TSB Bank*

---

89 (1682) 1 Vern 45.

90 *Brandon v Brandon* (1862) 10 WR 287.

91 W Clark, *Fisher and Lightwood's law of mortgages*, 12th edn, Butterworths, 2006, and 1st supplement, 2008.

92 *Norwich General Trust v Grierson* [1984] CLY 2306.

93 See generally *Fisher and Lightwood*, note 83; *Norwich General Trust v Grierson* [1984] CLY 2306 and H Markson, 'Liability of lenders in possession' (1979) 129 NLJ 334.

plc v Botham,[94] the Court of Appeal gave guidance on whether tap fittings, extractor fans, mirrors, 'white goods' and the like were part of the fixtures and as such the lender's to dispose of with the security on sale or were the borrower's to remove.

Costs

42.78   Advisers assisting borrowers should, throughout, be conscious of the advantageous position which lenders have concerning legal and other costs. In other types of litigation the usual rule is that costs follow the event. In mortgage cases the lender is, prima facie, entitled to all its 'costs, charges and expenses' reasonably and properly incurred in preserving the security or recovering the mortgage debt, including the costs of possession proceedings.[95] Costs of possession proceedings themselves will be allowed as being part of these 'just allowances',[96] even without mention of an order for costs in the court order. However, where the court orders detailed assessment of the lender's costs in a possession action that assessment will be on a standard basis and then it seems that the lender is restricted, in the absence of terms to the contrary in the deed, to those standard basis costs.[97] Usually, however, the lender's position is strengthened by such contractual terms in the mortgage deed. The court has no authority to assess the lender's costs unless requested to do so by the lender.[98]

42.79   In practice, lenders usually seek a specific order that there be 'no order as to costs' (or 'costs to be added to security') or simply make no reference to the costs at the hearing, relying on a mortgagee's apparent right to add costs to the security. It appears that a mortgagee may be entitled to charge, in addition to any standard basis costs, the sum required to make them up to the solicitor and own client costs which it will be charged by its solicitor (if there is a right to do so in the mortgage deed).[99]

94   [1996] EGCS 149; 73 P&CR (D) 1, CA. See also S Elwes, 'When do chattels form part' (1995) 11 IL & P 141.

95   *Drydon v Frost* (1838) My & C 670; *National Provincial Bank of England v Games* (1886) 31 Ch D 582, CA and *Sandon v Hooper* (1843) 6 Beav 246.

96   *Wilkes v Saunion* (1877) 7 Ch D 188.

97   *Re Adelphi Hotel (Brighton)* [1953] 2 All ER 498 and *Re Queen's Hotel Co Cardiff Ltd* [1900] 1 Ch 792.

98   *Principality Building Society v Llewellyn* [1987] CLY 2940 and *Bank of Ireland Home Mortgages Ltd v Bissett* [1999] 11 CL 53.

99   *Gomba Holdings (UK) Ltd v Minories Finance Ltd (No 2)* [1993] Ch 171; [1992] 3 WLR 723, CA.

42.80   However, it is arguable that a lender is entitled to recover only what its own solicitor could properly charge following an assessment under the Solicitors Act 1974. Under that Act[100] the amount which may be allowed in the county court on assessment must not exceed the amount which would have been allowed in respect of that item on a standard basis. Where the rights of the lender to costs are extended by the terms of the mortgage deed, then that agreement may be un-affected by the Solicitors Act 1974 and assessment of the lender's costs conducted on the basis specified in the mortgage deed.[101] How-ever, where the court assesses a lender's bill in accordance with an indemnity provision in the legal charge this can only fix the upper limit of the borrower's liability. In separate proceedings the borrower may be able to have that sum reduced if costs were unreasonable or improperly incurred and any clause providing to the contrary would be contrary to public policy.[102] In practice, it is usual for lenders to secure indemnification of all costs and expenses (including all solici-tors' and estate agents' costs) from sale receipts when the mortgage is redeemed on sale.

42.81   While it is clear from the above that the lender is in a strong posi-tion as regards costs, the borrower can ask the court to restrict the lender's claim for costs in a number of ways. CPR PD 48 para 1.3 effectively restates the decision in the leading case of *Gomba Hold-ings (UK) Ltd v Minories Finance Ltd (No 2)*[103] and sets out the prin-ciples which apply. The lender's prima facie entitlement to the costs of the possession proceedings does not exclude the court's jurisdic-tion to regulate the payment of litigation costs. Even where the mort-gage deed provides for the lender's costs to be paid on the indemnity basis, the court has the discretion to override that contractual pro-vision and to disentitle the lender from receiving those costs. This can be done where the costs proposed to be claimed by the lender have been unreasonably incurred or where they are unreasonable in amount.

42.82   Walton J put it this way:

> The court might very well take the view that, in the circumstances of any particular case, [the contractual right to costs on an indemnity

100 Solicitors Act 1974 s74(3).

101 *Tarrant v Speechly Bircham* [1986] CLY 3193. See also 'Costs' (1992) EG 4 April for a short commentary on *Primeridge Ltd v Jean Muir Ltd* [1992] 1 EGLR 273 on the importance of the correct wording in mortgage deeds if the lender is to ensure that costs will be paid on an indemnity basis.

102 *McLeod v Royal Bank of Scotland* LS Gaz, 29 November 1995, p27.

103 [1993] Ch 171; [1992] 3 WLR 723, CA.

basis] was a contractual provision which it ought to overlook and it ought not to give effect to.[104]

42.83   The court may order that the disputed costs are assessed under CPR 48.3.[105]

42.84   Where the lender has acted unreasonably in relation to the bringing of proceedings or in relation to some aspect of the proceedings, it is advisable to ask at the hearing for the court expressly to direct, as part of the order, that the lender 'be not at liberty to add any costs to the security' in relation to the proceedings or the particular hearing in question. Where it is clear that the lender has flouted the Mortgage Arrears Protocol advisers should seek such an order. See paras 42.3 and 42.11.

42.85   In addition, the borrower, as the paying party to the proceedings, is entitled to ask the court to subject the lender's solicitor's costs to detailed assessment under the Solicitors Act 1974 s70. The borrower has the absolute right to ask the court to subject the bill to detailed assessment if objection is made within one month of delivery of the bill.[106] Outside this period the court may grant an order for detailed assessment on such terms as it thinks fit.[107] However, no order for assessment will be granted after the expiry of 12 months from the bill's delivery in the absence of 'special circumstances',[108] and no order can be made at all more than 12 months after payment.[109] This would seem to be the case under the Solicitors Act 1974 even if the borrower has not been told of the amount of the costs claimed by the lender's solicitors. Unfortunately, borrowers are very often not told of the fact that the bill has been delivered, or of the amount claimed and debited to the borrower's account. However, it has been held that a paying client against whom a solicitor brings proceedings for non-payment of a bill is at common law entitled to challenge the reasonableness of the bill even if the 12-month period allowed by the Solicitors Act 1974 has elapsed.[110]

104   *Bank of Baroda v Panessar* [1987] Ch 335; [1987] 2 WLR 208 at 224D. See also *Gomba Holdings (UK) Ltd v Minories Finance Ltd (No 2)* [1993] Ch 171; [1992] 3 WLR 723; [1992] 4 All ER 588, CA and C Evans, 'The new rules are working!' [2000] *Adviser* 79.

105   PD 48 para 50.4(3).

106   Solicitors Act 1974 s70(1).

107   Solicitors Act 1974 s70(2).

108   Solicitors Act 1974 s70(3).

109   Solicitors Act 1974 s70(4).

110   *Turner & Co v O Palomo SA* [2000] 1 WLR 37, CA.

42.86 An application under the Solicitors Act 1974 s70 should be made by claim form unless it is made in pending proceedings, in which case it should be made by application within those proceedings. The county court has jurisdiction where the amount of the bill does not exceed £5,000 and all or part of the work to be the subject of court scrutiny was carried out in the county court. Otherwise the High Court has jurisdiction.[111]

42.84 Under the Solicitors Act 1974 the party asking for the assessment of the costs will have to pay for the costs of the assessment proceedings unless he or she is able to persuade the court to reduce the amount of the costs to be paid by one-fifth of the sum claimed.[112] However, it is possible to identify a part only of the bill for scrutiny by the court and so restrict the risk of the consequences of the 'one-fifth rule'. It would, however, seem that the district judge has some discretion under the Solicitors Act 1974 s70(10) to disregard the one-fifth rule where there are 'any special circumstances'.

42.88 It is advisable to ask the lender to provide details of its solicitor's bill of costs as soon as it is received by the lender, itemising the number of letters written and received, phone calls made and received by the lender, the time spent, the status of the fee earner in the case and the hourly rate claimed as well as the work undertaken. Details of the amount of the disbursements involved should also be identified. From this it may be possible to assess whether Solicitors Act 1974 assessment is advisable.

42.89 Subject to the terms of the mortgage deed, a borrower is not personally liable for such costs[113] and does not have to pay them directly. They will be added to the security as part of the mortgage and paid out of the proceeds of the sale.[114] Lenders are entitled to add costs to the security even against a borrower with a public funding certificate and this will not be contrary to the Access to Justice Act 1999 s11 which restricts awards of costs against publicly funded parties,[115] because technically the costs are recovered from the security and not the borrower.

---

111 Solicitors Act 1974 s69(3).
112 Solicitors Act 1974 s70(9).
113 *Sinfield v Sweet* [1967] 3 All ER 479.
114 *National Provincial Bank of England v Games* (1886) 31 Ch D 582, CA.
115 *Saunders v Anglia Building Society (No 2)* [1971] 1 All ER 243, HL.

Tenants of borrowers

Introduction

43.1   At common law, a borrower had no power to grant a tenancy which was binding on the mortgage lender. Since 1925 borrowers have had statutory power to grant certain types of lease.[1] However, this statutory power can be excluded by the terms of the mortgage deed and in practice the power to grant tenancies is invariably excluded either absolutely or on terms that the property cannot be let without prior written approval. Where a borrower seeks consent from the lender to let out the security, it may in exceptional circumstances be possible to imply a term that the lender's consent would not be unreasonably refused.[2]

43.2   Providing a borrower remains in control of the property and does not get into arrears, the lender may not be interested in any third party occupation. In recent years, many institutional lenders have advanced money under 'buy-to-let' mortgages specifically to enable their borrowers to rent out properties. It is clear that, irrespective of whether the tenancy is binding on the lender, as between the borrower/landlord and the tenant, the tenancy will be binding on the former, if only by estoppel.[3] However, when a lender seeks possession, the position of a tenant is usually dependent on whether the tenancy was granted before or after the mortgage deed was executed.[4]

Tenancies granted before the date of the mortgage

Registered land

43.3   In common with any other purchaser of a legal interest, a mortgagee takes the property subject to any interests which qualify as 'overriding interests' within the meaning of the Land Registration Act 2002 Sch 3 para 2. Certain tenancies qualify as overriding interests.

---

1 Law of Property Act 1925 s99.
2 *Starling v Lloyds TSB Bank plc* [2000] EGLR 101, CA and *Citibank International plc v Kessler* [1999] Lloyd's Rep Bank 123.
3 *Dudley and District Benefit Society v Emerson* [1949] 2 All ER 252, CA and *Chatsworth Properties v Effiom* [1971] 1 All ER 604, CA.
4 For an inventive article on the possibility of civil and criminal action against lenders for harassment of residential tenants, see D Barnsley, 'Harassment of tenants by mortgagees' [1991] JSWL 220; see also S Robinson, 'Helping tenants of defaulting landlords' (1991) March *Adviser* 23. See also *Berkshire Capital Funding Ltd v Street* (2000) 32 HLR 373, CA and *Woolwich Building Society v Dickman* [1996] 3 All ER 204; (1996) 28 HLR 661, CA.

43.4   A lease granted for a term not exceeding three years where the tenant is in possession is effective to create a legal interest.[5] Such a tenancy need not be registered at HM Land Registry to bind the lender and will qualify as an overriding interest being the right of a person in actual occupation unless enquiries have been made and these rights are not disclosed.[6] The fact that a tenant may have signed a form of consent subordinating his or her rights as tenant to those of the lender to enable the borrower landlord to obtain the mortgage does not prevent the tenant subsequently relying on his or her tenancy as an overriding interest which binds the lender.[7]

43.5   In addition, a lease for a term not exceeding seven years also qualifies as an overriding interest[8] and, provided it is in writing, will be valid and binding on the lender whether or not the tenant is in occupation. In the case of registered land, the mortgage is completed and becomes effective on the date it is executed, although tenancies which are created after completion of the advance but before registration at HM Land Registry will be binding on the lender.[9] This applies even if the tenancy is granted in breach of a term of the legal charge.[10]

Unregistered land

43.6   The tenancy of a person who went into occupation before the mortgage was granted will be binding on the lender if validly created, that is if the tenancy either was created formally by deed or was one capable of being created orally, ie, for a term not exceeding three years taking effect in possession at the best rent which can be reasonably obtained without taking a fine.[11] This will include weekly and monthly tenancies. Given the provisions of the Land Registration Act 2002 in relation to compulsory registration of land, in practice it is uncommon to find unregistered titles.

5   Law of Property Act 1925 s54(2).
6   Land Registration Act 2002 Sch 3 para 2; *Barclays Bank Ltd v Stasek* [1957] Ch 28, *Bolton Building Society v Cobb* [1965] 3 All ER 814; [1966] 1 WLR 1; *Woolwich Equitable Building Society v Marshall & Long* [1952] Ch 1; [1951] 2 All ER 769, ChD and *Barclays Bank plc v Zaroovabli* [1997] Ch 321; [1997] 2 All ER 19, ChD.
7   *Woolwich Building Society v Dickman* [1996] 3 All ER 204, CA. See also J Morgan, 'Mortgages v Occupiers: overriding interest in an age of consent' [1997] Conv 402.
8   Land Registration Act 2002 Sch 3 para 1.
9   *Abbey National Building Society v Cann* [1991] 1 AC 56; [1990] 1 All ER 1085; [1991] 1 AC 56, HL and *Pourdanay v Barclays Bank plc* [1997] Ch 321, ChD.
10 *Barclays Bank plc v Zaroovabli* [1997] Ch 321.
11 Law of Property Act 1925 s54(2) and *Universal Permanent Building Society v Cooke* [1952] Ch 95, CA.

Pre-mortgage binding tenancies

43.7 Although it is conceivable that a borrower may have been able to allow tenants into a property in anticipation of the completion of the initial purchase, in practice cases where a tenant has an interest binding on a lender are more likely to arise with second or subsequent mortgages. The effect of a binding tenancy is that the lender cannot take possession as against the tenant unless, for example, the tenancy was granted following a notice under the Housing Act 1988 Sch 2 ground 2 (for which see para 12.39). So long as the borrower is allowed to retain the property as against the lender, he or she is entitled to claim the rent and to sue for possession against the tenant.[12] If the lender claims possession in accordance with its common law right then the tenant is bound to pay the rent to the lender.[13] This includes any rent due but unpaid to the borrower at the time of the lender's demand.[14] Where the lender takes possession and gives notice to the tenant requiring rent to be paid to it, the tenant cannot set off against the rent a personal claim he or she has against the borrower.[15] A borrower executing a second mortgage deed, after the granting of a tenancy, to correct the terms of an earlier deed entered into before the granting of the tenancy does not replace the earlier deed so as to result in the tenancy being binding on the lender.[16]

Tenancies granted after the date of the mortgage

43.8 As indicated above (see para 43.1), most mortgage deeds exclude the borrower's statutory power to grant leases, either absolutely or without the lender's specific permission. It has been held that a tenancy granted in breach of such a term in the mortgage deed is not binding on the lender under the Rent Act 1977 although it remains binding as such on the borrower.[17] The principle applies equally to tenancies under the Housing Act 1988. The statutory tenant's 'status of irremovability' granted to a protected tenant on the ending of the contractual tenancy does not bind the lender if the original contractual

---

12 Law of Property Act 1925 ss99 and 141 and *Trent v Hunt* (1853) 9 Exch 14.
13 *Rogers v Humphreys* (1835) 4 Ad & El 299.
14 *Moss v Gallimore* (1779) 1 Doug KB 279.
15 *Reeves v Pope* [1914] 2 KB 284.
16 *Walthamstow Building Society v Davies* (1990) 22 HLR 60, CA.
17 *Dudley and District Benefit Society v Emerson* [1949] Ch 707; [1949] 2 All ER 252, CA. Cf *Abbey National plc v Yusuf* June 1993 *Legal Action* 12.

tenancy was granted in breach of a term in the mortgage deed.[18] As a result, the occupying tenant has no claim to remain once the lender exercises its right to possession. Until and unless something takes place to change the relationship, the tenant is, as against the lender, a trespasser. With effect from 1 October 2010, unauthorised tenants have the right to apply to the court for an order postponing enforcement of a possession order for up to two months. See para 42.25. Where a tenant is required by the lender to pay rent to it, the tenant can raise this recognition of a tenancy as a defence to any claim by the borrower for the payment of rent.[19]

43.9 The fact that the lender knew that a borrower was proposing to rent out the property for which mortgage finance was being sought does not prevent the lender from relying on a clause prohibiting the granting of a tenancy.[20]

43.10 The occupier's tenancy, however, becomes binding on the lender if the lender does something expressly or by implication to recognise the tenant as its tenant.[21] As the original tenancy between the borrower and the tenant is a nullity so far as the lender is concerned, any tenancy created between the tenant and the lender must take effect as a new tenancy. An example of this arose where a lender's solicitor wrote to the borrower's tenant informing him that he should not pay any more rent to his 'former landlords' and making new arrangements for payment of rent.[22] The test is not one of intention but of objectivity – what would a reasonable person understand the relationship to be? In this case the court held that, by writing to the borrower's tenant in such terms, the lender was estopped from denying that it had accepted him as its tenant.

43.11 Mere knowledge of an unauthorised post-mortgage tenancy, coupled with a failure to take steps to evict the tenant, does not have the effect of creating a new tenancy with the lender.[23] Acceptance of rent by the lender from the borrower's tenant creates a tenancy between the two parties, although the terms of the tenancy are not necessarily the same as the tenancy from the borrower but are such

18 *Britannia Building Society v Earl* [1990] 2 All ER 469; [1990] 1 WLR 422, CA. For a commentary see S Bridge, 'The residential tenant and the mortgaged reversion' [1990] Conv 450. See also *Mann v Nijar* (2000) 32 HLR 223, CA and *Sadiq v Hussain* [1997] NPC 19, CA.

19 *Underhay v Read* (1888) 20 QBD 209, CA.

20 *Lloyds Bank plc v Doyle* April 1996 *Legal Action* 17, CA.

21 See *Stroud Building Society v Delamont* [1960] 1 All ER 749.

22 *Chatsworth Properties v Effiom* [1971] 1 All ER 604, CA.

23 *Taylor v Ellis* [1960] Ch 368 and *Parker v Braithwaite* [1952] 2 All ER 837.

as are agreed or inferred from conduct.[24] However, a lender's requirement that payment of rent should in future be made to a receiver
appointed under a legal charge as a formal agent for the borrower
(as is usually the case with receivers) does not create a landlord and
tenant relationship between tenant and landlord.[25]

43.12   The mere fact, however, that a receiver has been appointed does
not in an appropriate factual context prevent a court from concluding
that a tenancy has arisen with the lender as landlord.[26] Where a first
mortgagee has acted in such a way as to have created a tenancy between itself and occupying tenants, a second mortgagee in possession
proceedings is entitled to a possession order but subject to the rights
of the tenants until such time as those rights are determined.[27]

43.13   It has been argued that the lender may act in such a way that,
although falling short of creating a tenancy at common law, an equitable estoppel is raised precluding it from treating the tenant as a trespasser, relying on the usual equitable principles relating to estoppel.[28]
It is thought that, for this to happen, a lender who knew of the tenancy
would have to act or refrain from acting at a time when the tenant was
prejudicing him or herself (over and above paying rent) in reliance on
that action or inaction. The essence of this would be that the lender
was giving the tenant a false sense of security which resulted in the
tenant acting reasonably in the circumstances but to his or her detriment. No direct authority is, however, known on the point.

43.14   The definition of 'mortgagor' in the Administration of Justice
Acts as including 'any person deriving title under the original mortgagor'[29] does not include the borrower's tenant so as to enable that
tenant to seek the protection of the Acts as if he or she were the borrower.[30] Where, however, a tenant does pay the rent to the lender to
avoid eviction, he or she may deduct the amount actually paid to the
lender from any future rental payments to the borrower.[31]

43.15   Under the Consumer Credit Act 1974 it would be open to a tenant
who is joined as a defendant to seek to persuade the court to exercise

---

24 *Keith v R Gancia & Co Ltd* [1904] 1 Ch 774, CA.
25 *Lever Finance Ltd v Needleman's Property Trustee* [1956] Ch 357 and Law of
     Property Act 1925 s109(2).
26 *Mann v Nijar* (2000) 32 HLR 223, CA.
27 *Berkshire Capital Funding Ltd v Street* (1999) 78 P&CR 321, CA.
28 See A Walker, 'Tenants of mortgagors' (1978) 128 NLJ 773.
29 Administration of Justice Act 1970 s39(1).
30 See *Britannia Building Society v Earl* [1990] 2 All ER 469, CA.
31 *Johnson v Jones* (1839) 9 Ad and El 809 and *Underhay v Read* (1887) 20 QBD
     209, CA.

its discretion to make a time order and to postpone any order for possession. The court is empowered[32] to make a time order and to postpone a possession order of its own volition where it is 'just to do so' in actions brought for possession of land to which a regulated agreement relates. It is clear that a time order must be directed at the borrower, requiring payment by the borrower. However, in the face of potential proceedings by the tenant for breach of covenant for quiet enjoyment (see para 43.18), the borrower may be persuaded to meet the payments required under the time order.

43.16 A tenant whose tenancy is invalid as against the lender is still, during the period of a contractual as opposed to a statutory tenancy, a person interested in the equity of redemption and has the right to take a transfer of the mortgage on paying off the loan.[33] Similarly, as a person entitled to redeem the mortgage, the tenant can ask the court to order sale of the property with a view to buying it.[34]

43.17 Where occupiers are occupying the property under a tenancy which is not binding on the lender, it has been held to be inappropriate for the lender to use the special procedure (now Civil Procedure Rules 1998 (CPR) Part 55) to obtain an order for possession against trespassers. The correct procedure is by way of an orthodox possession claim.[35]

43.18 A tenant evicted by a lender as a result of possession being obtained against the borrower may be able to sue the borrower landlord for breach of the covenant for quiet enjoyment ordinarily implied into the tenancy agreement.[36] A similar right to claim damages for breach of an express covenant for quiet enjoyment may arise where there is a written lease.[37] However, there may well be practical difficulties in enforcing a monetary judgment against the borrower/landlord unless other assets can be identified.

43.19 Tenants threatened with eviction in these circumstances should consider applying to be joined as defendants to the possession proceedings with a view to claiming damages against the landlord/borrower within those proceedings under CPR 19.1. Where an expedited hearing resulting in judgment can be arranged, or where it is possible to

---

32 CCA 1974 ss129(1), (2) and 135.

33 *Tarn v Turner* (1888) 39 Ch D 456, CA as considered in *Britannia Building Society v Earl* [1990] 2 All ER 469; [1990] 1 WLR 422, CA.

34 Law of Property Act 1925 s91(2) and *National Westminster Home Loans v Riches* [1995] 43/95 CLW 2.

35 *London Goldhawk Building Society v Eminer* (1977) 242 EG 462. See CPR 55.5.

36 *Stalker v Karim* June 1994 *Legal Action* 12 and *Sutherland v Wall* [1994] CLY 1448.

37 *Carpenter v Parker* (1857) 3 CBNS 206.

obtain judgment in default, it would be possible to register a charging order against the title. Assuming that there is sufficient equity, the judgment would be satisfied on the lender selling the property.

43.20   The Council of Mortgage Lenders has issued advice to its members on appropriate practice involving 'buy-to-let' tenants, unauthorised tenants and repossessions see *Industry guidance on buy-to-let arrears and possessions* (June 2009).[38]

Assured tenancies

43.21   The Housing Act (HA) 1988 introduced a mandatory ground for possession available to a borrower/landlord or a lender against assured tenants.[39] There is no corresponding ground under the Rent Act 1977. The ground provides that the court must make an order for possession where:

- the mortgage was granted before the beginning of the tenancy;
- the lender is entitled to exercise a power of sale conferred by the deed or under the Law of Property Act 1925 s107;
- the lender requires possession of the dwelling-house for the purpose of disposing of it with vacant possession;

and either:

- notice was given by the landlord not later than the beginning of the tenancy that possession might be required under this ground; or
- the court considers it is just and equitable to dispense with the requirement of notice.

For further discussion see paras 12.40–12.41.

43.22   Assured tenancies created after the mortgage and in breach of a prohibition on the granting of tenancies are not binding on the lender but are, however, binding on the borrower (see para 43.8). This ground for possession specifically envisages a lender permitting a borrower to create a tenancy without running the risk of the tenant claiming security of tenure by virtue of the lender's permitting the tenancy to arise.

43.23   From 1 October 2010 unauthorised tenants have the right to apply to the court for a postponement of enforcement of a possession order for up to two months. See para 42.25.

---

38 www.cml.org.uk/cml/policy/issues/5002.
39 HA 1988 Sch 2 ground 2: see para 12.39.

CHAPTER 44

Domestic relationship breakdown in mortgaged homes

Introduction

44.1   The two most common causes of mortgage default are reduction of income following loss of employment and relationship breakdown. Where partners separate, it may be inevitable that the home has to be sold if neither can afford to maintain the property on his or her sole income. However, where it is possible for one partner to maintain the property there are two additional problems for the remaining partner to consider over and above the continuing problem of paying for any existing mortgage. The first is preventing sale of the property by the other party and the second is preventing the property being used as security for further loan finance with the corresponding increased risk of eviction by a new lender.

Sole ownership

44.2   Where the property is in the sole legal ownership of the departed partner the latter is free to sell the property or raise further mortgage finance on it. As a result, where the couple are married or have entered into a civil partnership under the Civil Partnership Act 2004, it is important for the remaining spouse or civil partner to register his or her statutory right to occupy the home ('home rights') under the Family Law Act 1996 s30 as soon as possible. The statutory 'home rights' are quite distinct from any rights of occupation which a person may have as a beneficiary under any trust of land under the Trusts of Land and Appointment of Trustees Act 1996.

44.3   In the case of registered land this should be done by way of a notice registered at HM Land Registry, or a class F land charge if the title is unregistered. If in doubt, an index map search should be made to check if the property is registered or not. This is done by sending District Land Registry Form SIM to the Land Registry for the area in which the property is situated. Land Registry Practice Guide 10, 'Official Searches of the Index Map', provides more information on the process.[1] No fee is payable on filing Form SIM. Land Registry Practice Guide 11 deals with obtaining a copy of the register in relation to any title.

44.4   Application for the registration of home rights is made on form HR1. No fee is payable. Since 28 May 2001, HM Land Registry practice has been automatically to notify the registered proprietor that an

---

1   See www.landreg.gov.uk.

entry relating to the family home has been made. This is, according to HM Land Registry, to ensure compliance with the registered proprietor's rights under the Human Rights Act 1998. Advisers must therefore ensure that people registering home rights are aware of this process.

44.5 The effect of registration of home rights is, in practice, that the legal owner is unable to sell or mortgage the property until the notice or charge is vacated. It is important to note that taking this step has no effect on any prior mortgage and any arrears which may accrue under that loan. However, where such home rights have been registered, a lender is required to give notice to the remaining spouse or civil partner of any possession proceedings brought,[2] to name that person in the particulars of claim and to file at court a copy for service on that person. Such a person may then apply to be joined as defendant with a view to persuading the court to exercise its statutory powers.[3]

44.6 A 'connected person' has the right to make the mortgage repayments to the lender in respect of the home and should do so if he or she can, in order to avoid loss of possession.[4] 'Connected person' in relation to any person means that person's spouse, former spouse, civil partner, former civil partner, co-habitant or former co-habitant.[5] He or she has the right to seek to be joined as a party to any possession proceedings 'at any time before the action is finally disposed of in that court'[6] and will be made a party if the court does not see 'a special reason' against him or her being joined *and* if the court is satisfied that he or she may be able to meet the legal owner's mortgage liabilities either with or without the court exercising its Administration of Justice Acts powers.

44.7 An occupier who does not fall within the definition of 'connected person' has no right to contest the possession proceedings or to pay the mortgage instalments on behalf of the legal owner. Where, however, he or she has an equitable interest in the property which has priority over the interest of the lender, this protects him or her against dispossession (see chapter 46) and possession proceedings brought by a lender can be defended on this basis.

---

2 Family Law Act 1996 s56.
3 Family Law Act 1996 s55.
4 Family Law Act 1996 s30(3).
5 Family Law Act 1996 s54(5).
6 Family Law Act 1996 s55(3).

Joint ownership

44.8   Where the property is in joint legal ownership, the departed partner obviously cannot lawfully sell or obtain further mortgage finance
without the remaining partner's agreement because he or she would
have to execute the necessary mortgage deed or transfer form. It
would, however, be open to the departed partner to seek a court order
requiring sale of the property or, indeed, any other order that the
court may think fit to make in relation to the property.[7] Given the abolition by the Trusts of Land and Appointment of Trustees Act 1996[8]
of the presumption of a trust for sale where land is owned jointly, the
court is given wide discretion as to whether, on application following
relationship breakdown, the home should be sold or its occupation
regulated. For an analysis of the law on this topic see para 48.29.

44.9   In the case of married couples the court has the usual wide-ranging power to transfer property as part of its matrimonial jurisdiction
on divorce or judicial separation and similar powers are available to
civil partners under the Civil Partnership Act 2004.[9] As joint owners,
both partners remain equally liable under the mortgage deed and are
usually both joined as defendants in any proceedings brought by a
lender.

44.10   Difficulties can arise where one joint legal owner forges the signature of the other on a deed creating a legal charge. In the case of unregistered land the beneficial interest of the owner who has created
the forgery passes to the lender, leaving the legal estate being held on
trust by the joint legal owners for the innocent legal owner and the
lender. The lender would be able to seek a court order for sale under
the Trusts of Land and Appointment of Trustees Act 1996. With registered land, the legal charge is effective if registration at HM Land
Registry is completed. The innocent joint legal owner's beneficial interest may, however, qualify as an overriding interest if he or she is in
actual occupation. See para 46.9. For further detail reference should
be made to one of the major works on land law.[10]

7   Trusts of Land and Appointment of Trustees Act 1996 s14.
8   Trusts of Land and Appointment of Trustees Act 1996 ss4 and 5 and Sch 2.
9   Civil Partnership Act 2004 ss66 and 72 and Sch 5.
10   See K Gray and S Gray, *Elements of land law* 5th edn, Oxford University Press,
    2009.

CHAPTER 45

Islamic property finance

45.1 Shariah law prohibits the charging or receipt of interest. As a result, followers of Islam have had to devise ways of being able to purchase properties with the assistance of loans from commercial lenders without the requirement to pay interest. This chapter is intended to give an overview of the types of transaction available to assist in house purchase consistent with Islamic principles.

45.2 There are three main types of financial arrangement. Under the *Murabaha*, a customer finds a property for sale and agrees a purchase price with the seller. The provider (usually a bank) buys the property and then re-sells it to the customer at an agreed higher price, ie, the original purchase price plus an agreed profit margin. The total cost to the customer and the repayment term is agreed at the outset, although provision may be made for the customer to discharge the debt at any time. The higher price is calculated depending on the purchase price paid for by the provider, the amount of any initial contribution made by the customer and the repayment term. The provider takes a first charge on the property. The customer takes possession and starts making fixed monthly payments to the provider. This transaction has the approval of Shariah scholars in that this amounts to trading (ie, the buying and selling of houses at a profit) and not lending. Under this scheme it is usual for the customer to have to provide a significant down payment, usually 20 per cent of the higher figure. In this model, because the customer is the home owner subject to a mortgage, the usual powers available to the court will apply in case of default and repossession.

45.3 Under the *Ijara* scheme, the provider buys the property that the customer wants to acquire. The property is then leased to the customer by the provider for a specified period at an agreed rent. During the period of the lease the title remains with the provider.

The customer enters into a 'promise to purchase' agreement under which the property is transferred to the tenant at the end of the lease. There is also a tenancy agreement which regulates the rights of occupation. The customer makes fixed monthly payments during the term of the lease calculated so that part of the payment is rent and part goes towards the purchase price. The rental element is calculated based on the amount of the property that has not been 'bought' through the customer's initial downpayment. The monthly payments are reassessed usually every six months with the rental element being recalculated with reference to market interest rates. The customer is usually allowed to repay the purchase price early and to make payments in excess of the agreed monthly instalment. Title to the property is transferred to the customer at the end of the agreed term when the agreed purchase price has been paid. While this arrangement has all the markings of a 'shared ownership' arrangement (see chapter 22), the customer would be either an assured or an assured shorthold tenant and would appear to have the protection available to rental purchasers. See para 21.1.

45.4   The third variant is the *Ijara with diminishing Musharaka*. Under this model, the customer agrees a price for the purchase of a property. The customer puts down a significant deposit, for example, 20 per cent, with the provider paying the balance. The title is acquired in the provider's name with the property being held on express trust for the customer and the provider. The customer enters into a 'promise to purchase' agreement and a tenancy agreement. The provider's share is divided into smaller units (for exmple, eight units worth 10 per cent of the higher purchase price) and over the agreed term the customer buys these units. As the provider's share in the property diminishes so do the customer's rental payments. At the end of the term the title is transferred to the customer. Again the customer would be either an assured or an assured shorthold tenant until the title is transferred on final payment of the purchase price. However, it would appear to be the case that application could be made to the court under the Trusts of Land and Appointment of Trustees Act 1996 for orders in relation to the property because it is held on trust.

45.5   Whilst the Murabaha scheme has always fallen within the control of the Financial Services Authority, regulation of the Ijara 'home purchase plans' was brought within the control of the Financial Services Authority with effect from 6 April 2007.[1] The 'Mortgage Arrears

---

1   Financial Services and Markets Act 2000 (Regulated Activities) (Amendment) (No 2) Order 2006 SI No 2383.

Protocol' has application in relation to any possession proceedings brought in respect of a 'home purchase plan' which consists of a 'method of purchasing a property by way of a sale and lease arrangement that does not require the payment of interest.[2]

2 Mortgage Arrears Protocol para 4.1.

Rights of equitable owners

Introduction

46.1   This chapter considers those cases where the legal title to a property is vested in the name of one or more people (the legal owners) but where another person has an interest in the property which is recognised in equity but falls short of being a legal interest. The most common example of this is where a matrimonial home is in the sole legal ownership of one spouse but where the other has an equitable interest. Such an occupier, who is not a legal owner, may defeat a mortgage lender's possession claim by relying on an equitable interest.

46.2   A legal charge is treated as a legal interest in land. So a mortgage lender who advances money secured by a legal charge is treated as a purchaser of a legal interest in the property which is being used as the security. In the case of *unregistered* land it is a basic principle of English land law that a bona fide purchaser for value of a legal estate (which includes a mortgage lender) takes that estate subject to any equitable interests in the property of which the lender has notice, whether actual or constructive.[1] In the case of *registered* land, a purchaser takes the property subject to entries on the land register and any 'overriding interests', which can include the rights of people in actual occupation except where enquiry is made of those people and they do not disclose their rights in circumstances where they could reasonably have been expected to do so.[2] The application of these general principles in the context of residential mortgages is considered in more detail below. In certain circumstances, therefore, occupiers who are not legal owners but who have some form of equitable interest in the property can effectively prevent the lender from obtaining possession. In this way the defaulting legal owner may retain occupation under the protection of the equitable owner, without even making any further financial payments. However, advisers should be aware that a lender is likely to respond to continued non-payment by applying for an order for sale and possession under the Trusts of Land and Appointment of Trustees Act 1996. The following is a brief outline only of what is a complicated area of residential land law.

Creation of equitable interests

46.3   The courts have found it difficult to be consistent when deciding whether an occupying non-owner has acquired an equitable interest

---

1   Law of Property Act 1925 ss199(1) and 205(1).
2   Land Registration Act 2002 Sch 3 para 2(b).

in a property. Many of the cases seem to depend on whether the judge feels that the justice of the situation demands intervention as against the legal owner and third parties.

46.4   No apology is made for not analysing the extensive case-law in detail; for a full explanation, reference must be made to the standard works on land law as well as family law (many of the decisions have been reached in the context of relationship breakdown). However, by way of example only, the courts have held that a non-legal owner can have acquired an equitable interest by:

- paying directly for the purchase of a property which was conveyed into the legal owner's sole name;[3]
- contributing towards the deposit paid on the purchase;[4]
- helping with the construction of the house;[5]
- making regular and substantial direct financial contributions to the mortgage.[6]

46.5   Great weight is attached to the making of a financial contribution or a direct contribution of money's worth.[7] Indirect financial contribution to the purchase of the property may result in the acquisition of an equitable interest, for example, where the non-owner has contributed to pooling of resources from which payments for the property are made or has in some other way relieved the legal owner from expenditure on the property.[8] Alternatively, where the non-legal owner has acted to his or her detriment on the basis of assumed joint ownership,

---

3   *Pettitt v Pettitt* [1970] AC 777, HL. A resulting trust does not, however, arise from the fact that money was lent to facilitate a purchase: see *Hussey v Palmer* [1972] 1 WLR 1286, CA and *Pettitt v Pettitt* [1970] AC 777; [1969] 2 All ER 385, HL. See also *Midland Bank plc v Cooke* [1995] 4 All ER 562, CA, where the court held that where an equitable owner had established an interest by direct contribution the court will assess the assumed beneficial proportion by investigating the whole course of dealings between the parties.

4   See *Gissing v Gissing* [1971] AC 886, HL and *Burns v Burns* [1984] Ch 317; [1984] 1 All ER 244, CA at 264.

5   *Cooke v Head* [1972] 1 WLR 518, CA.

6   *Gissing v Gissing* [1971] AC 886, HL.

7   See *Lloyds Bank plc v Rosset* (1990) 22 HLR 349; [1991] 1 AC 107, HL; M P Thompson, 'Establishing an interest in the home' [1990] Conv 314; S Gardner, 'A woman's work' (1991) 54 MLR 126; D Hayton, 'Equitable rights of cohabitants' [1990] Conv 370 and P Sparkes, 'The quantification of beneficial interests: problems arising from contributions to deposits, mortgage advances and mortgage instalments' [1991] OJLS 39. See also *Ivin v Blake* [1995] 1 FLR 70 and A Lawson, 'Direct and indirect contributions to the purchase price of a home' [1996] Conv 462.

8   *Grant v Edwards* [1986] 2 All ER 426, CA and J Warburton, 'Interested or not?' [1986] Conv 291.

then the court may be prepared to recognise some equitable interest under a constructive trust.[9] In *Stack v Dowden*,[10] the House of Lords determined that where the legal title to a property is held jointly the presumption is that the joint owners also hold the property jointly for themselves in equity.

Nature of equitable interests

46.6   The courts have also not been consistent in defining the nature of the interest accruing to the occupying non-owner who successfully argues that he or she has some form of equitable interest. The court may hold that the occupier is a beneficiary under a resulting or constructive trust. If this is the case, the legal owner holds the property jointly on his or her behalf and on behalf of the non-legal owner.[11] An alternative basis for granting relief may be to find that the non-legal owner has rights under an irrevocable licence conferring some form of interest that is binding on the legal owner and lender.[12]

Binding equitable interests

Legal ownership in one name

46.7   The legal considerations to be applied in deciding whether an equitable owner's interest in a property (which is vested legally in another person) binds third parties differ, depending on whether the land is registered or unregistered.

46.8   In the case of *registered* land, a lender taking a legal charge takes it subject to the interests specified in the Land Register and to any overriding interests.[13]

---

9   *Midland Bank Ltd v Dobson* [1986] 1 FLR 171; *Coombes v Smith* [1986] 1 WLR 808, *Re Basham (decd)* [1986] 1 WLR 1498; M P Thompson, 'Estoppel and clean hands' [1986] Conv 406 and J Montgomery, 'A question of intention' [1987] Conv 16. See also *Drake v Whipp* [1996] 1 FLR 826, CA.

10   [2007] 2 AC 432. See also *Kernott v Jones* [2010] EWCA Civ 578.

11   *Oxley v Hiscock* [2004] EWCA Civ 546; [2004] 3 WLR 715; 'Resulting and constructive trusts of land: the mist descends and rises' [2005] Conv 79; *Kingsnorth Finance Co v Tizard* [1986] 2 All ER 54; [1986] 1 WLR 783 and *Grant v Edwards* [1986] 2 All ER 426; [1986] Ch 638.

12   *Re Sharpe* [1980] 1 WLR 219 and see *Bristol and West Building Society v Henning* [1985] 2 All ER 606; [1985] 1 WLR 778, CA, and noted at [1985] Conv 361. See generally references at note 9.

13   Land Registration Act 2002 s29(1) and (2) and Sch 3.

46.9   Land Registration Act 2002 Sch 3 para 2 defines which interests that have *not* been specified in the Land Register can constitute an overriding interest of a person in occupation, and includes:

Interests of persons in actual occupation

2 An interest belonging at the time of the disposition to a person in actual occupation, so far as relating to land of which he is in actual occupation, except for –

(a) ...

(b) an interest of a person of whom inquiry was made before the disposition and who failed to disclose the right when he could reasonably have been expected to do so;

(c) an interest –

(i) which belongs to a person whose occupation would not have been obvious on a reasonably careful inspection of the land at the time of the disposition, and

(ii) of which the person to whom the disposition is made does not have actual knowledge at that time.

46.10   The wording differs slightly from the comparable provision in the previous legislation.[14] The aim of the legislation is clearly to protect occupiers of property where the fact of their occupation would alert a purchaser to the possibility of unrecorded interests on the land register and, as a result, the necessity to make further enquiry. It follows that the interests of an actual occupier 'override' the legal charge taken by the lender except in cases where either the actual occupier has unreasonably failed, on enquiry, to disclose his or her own entitlement or the relevant occupation was neither reasonably discoverable by nor actually known to the lender. The inclusion of the wording 'could reasonably have been expected to do so', which did not appear in the previous legislative definition of 'overriding interest', would seem to suggest that there is now some duty of candour on an occupier to assert a right (but still only if enquiry is made).

46.11   In *Williams & Glyn's Bank Ltd v Boland*,[15] the House of Lords held that the beneficial interest under a trust of an occupying spouse, acquired by way of substantial contribution to the initial purchase price of the house, is an overriding interest capable of binding a lender. Whether someone is in 'actual occupation' is a question of fact.[16] Occupation must not only be actual but should be apparent or patent such as to 'put a person inspecting the land on notice that there was

---

14   Land Registration Act 1925 s70(1)(g).

15   [1981] AC 487; [1980] 3 WLR 138, HL.

16   *Lloyds Bank plc v Rosset* [1989] Ch 350, CA and *Link Lending Ltd v Bustard* [2010] EWCA Civ 424.

some person in occupation'.[17] Vicarious occupation through, for ex-ample, a spouse or other relative or even a limited company[18] quali-fies.[19] Protection only applies to the part actually occupied although in the context of residential mortgages this provision might have limited impact. A child cannot be a person in occupation for this purpose.[20] The relevant date for considering whether someone is in occupation is the date of execution of the mortgage, not the date of its registration at HM Land Registry.[21]

46.12　　Where the mortgage financed the initial purchase of the property and the purchase and the mortgage were simultaneous, the courts have been loath to allow an equitable owner's rights to take prece-dence over the lender's legal interest where the equitable owner knew, at the time, that the mortgage was being taken out. In such circum-stances the courts have concluded that the equitable owner intended that his or her interest be postponed to that of the lender and so is estopped from claiming priority.[22] This postponement of the equit-able owner's interest applies even to a subsequent remortgage taken out by the legal owner without the equitable owner's knowledge but limited to the extent of the original mortgage.[23] Where, however, the mortgage was genuinely granted, after the property's acquisition, to a borrower in whom the legal estate had already vested, where the bene-ficial owner was unaware of the creation of the legal charge, then that occupier's equitable interest binds the lender.[24]

46.13　　In the case of *unregistered* land, a mortgage lender advancing money on land by way of legal charge takes the security subject to any equitable interests in the property of which it has notice, whether actual, constructive or imputed.[25] Actual notice is self-explanatory. Constructive notice is notice which the lender would have obtained

17　*Malory Enterprises Ltd v Cheshire Homes Ltd* [2002] Ch 216.

18　*Stockholm Finance Ltd v Garden Holdings Inc* [1995] NPC 162.

19　*Abbey National Building Society v Cann* [1991] 1 AC 56, HL.

20　*Hypo-Mortgage Services Ltd v Robinson* [1997] 2 FLR 71, CA.

21　See Land Registration Act 2002 Sch 3 para (2)(i) and *Abbey National Building Society v Cann* [1991] 1 AC 56; (1990) 22 HLR 360, HL.

22　See *Paddington Building Society v Mendelsohn* (1985) 50 P&CR 244, CA; M P Thompson, 'The retreat from Boland' [1986] Conv 57 and *Bristol and West Building Society v Henning* [1985] 2 All ER 606; [1985] 1 WLR 778, CA. See also M Welstead, 'The mistress and the mortgage' [1985] CLJ 354.

23　*Equity Home Loans Ltd v Prestridge* [1992] 1 WLR 137; (1992) 24 HLR 76, CA and *Locobail (UK) Ltd v Waldorf Invstment Corpn* (1999) *Times* 31 March.

24　*Williams and Glyns Bank v Boland* [1981] AC 487; [1980] 2 All ER 408; [1980] 3 WLR 138, HL and *HSBC v Dyche* [2009] EWHC 2954 (Ch).

25　Law of Property Act 1925 s199.

'if such enquiries and inspections had been made as ought reasonably to have been made' by the lender.[26] Imputed notice is the actual or constructive notice of the lender's agent, although only so far as notice was received by the agent in the case of the lender granting the mortgage.[27] It is not clear when a lender is fixed with constructive notice or the lengths to which a lender has to go to discharge its duty to make reasonable enquiry. However, it seems that the courts require considerable enquiries to be made. In one case it was held that a lender's agent visiting the property at a prearranged time was insufficient enquiry to discharge an obligation to find out whether a matrimonial home was occupied by a spouse who might have an equitable interest.[28] As with registered land, the courts have proved unwilling to allow a beneficial owner to bind a lender where he or she knowingly was to benefit from the legal owner's borrowing money by way of mortgage, although the courts' reasoning is open to question.[29]

46.14   In practice, however, the question of whether an equitable owner's interest or right binds a lender is most likely to arise in cases of mortgages entered into *after* the initial purchase of the property.

46.15   Where a lender has granted a mortgage on a property which is subject to equitable rights in priority to its rights under the mortgage, the lenders will often dispute the assertion that there is a binding equitable interest on the assumption that the claim is being fabricated in an attempt to prevent eviction.[30] Advisers should therefore test the evidence supporting the claim of the equitable interest at an early stage.

46.16   Similarly advisers will need to assess whether there would be any basis for a lender to be able to argue that the beneficial owner's conduct constitutes an estoppel so as to resurrect the lender's rights.[31] If these are not viable responses, it would remain open to the lender to apply for an order for sale under Trusts of Land and Appointment of Trustees Act 1996 s14.[32] Alternatively, it is open to the lender to sue the legal owner for repayment of the loan by virtue of any covenant to

---

26 Law of Property Act 1925 s199(1)(ii)(a).

27 Law of Property Act 1925 s199(1)(ii)(b).

28 *Kingsnorth Finance Co v Tizard* [1986] 2 All ER 54; [1986] 1 WLR 783. See also P Luxton, 'Clandestine co-owners: an occupational hazard for mortgagees?' (1986) NLJ 771 and M P Thompson, 'The purchaser as private detective' [1986] Conv 283. See also *Lloyds Bank plc v Carrick* [1996] 4 All ER 630, CA.

29 See *Bristol and West Building Society v Henning* [1985] 2 All ER 606; [1985] 1 WLR 778, CA and M P Thompson, 'Relief for first mortgagees?' (1986) 49 MLR 245.

30 *Midland Bank plc v Dobson* [1986] 1 FLR 171.

31 *Barclays Bank plc v Goff* [2001] EWCA Civ 685.

32 *Bank of Baroda v Dhillon* (1997) 30 HLR 845; [1998] 1 FLR 524, CA and S Pascoe, 'The further decline of overriding interests' [1998] Conv 415.

repay contained in the mortgage deed. If the borrower is made bankrupt, his or her trustee in bankruptcy could seek a court order for sale of the property under Trusts of Land and Appointment of Trustees Act 1996 s14.[33] See para 49.15.

Legal ownership in several names

46.17   Different legal considerations apply where the title to the mortgaged property is held legally in joint names. Although there was initially some doubt, following the decision in *Williams & Glyn's Bank Ltd v Boland*,[34] the House of Lords, in *City of London Building Society v Flegg*,[35] confirmed that a lender who advances money on the security of a property where the legal title is vested in two or more people as trustees or a trust corporation, is free from the concern of whether or not other people may have equitable interests under such a trust.[36] By virtue of the 'overreaching' provisions of the Law of Property Act 1925,[37] such a lender takes its interest by virtue of the mortgage free from all beneficial claims. The value of an equitable owner's interests theoretically attach to the capital money realised when the property is sold. Notice of beneficial interests in unregistered land and actual occupation in registered land is irrelevant. Equitable owners under a trust of registered land are generally entitled to register a 'restriction' on the relevant register of title but this will not prevent those rights being 'overreached' by the sale of the property or the grant of a mortgage.

46.18   It has been argued that a distinction needs to be drawn between people who have a beneficial interest behind a trust (where 'overreaching' will apply) and people who have a right to occupy the property under a form of estoppel licence (where overreaching would not apply).[38]

---

33 See *Alliance & Leicester plc v Slayford* [2000] EWCA Civ 257; [2001] All ER (Comm 1); (2001) 33 HLR 66 and M P Thompson, 'The cumulative range of a mortgagee's remedies' [2002] Conv 53.

34 [1981] AC 487; [1980] 3 WLR 138, HL.

35 [1988] AC 54; (1987) 19 HLR 484, HL. See also W Swadling, 'The conveyancer's revenge' [1987] Conv 451 and S Gardner, 'Bleak House latest – Law Lords dispel fog?' (1988) 51 MLR 365.

36 Law of Property Act 1925 ss2 and 27.

37 Law of Property Act 1925 s36(1). See M P Thompson, 'Dispositions by trustees for sale' [1988] Conv 108; M P Thompson, *Co-ownership*, Sweet & Maxwell, 1988, p136; *Re Sharpe* [1980] 1 WLR 219.

38 See M P Thompson, 'Dispositions by trustees for sale' [1988] Conv 108; M P Thompson, *Co-ownership*, Sweet & Maxwell, 1988, p136; *Re Sharpe* [1980] 1 WLR 219.

Mortgage consent forms

46.19 In an effort to avoid the risk of being landed with a binding equitable owner, most lenders now require adult occupiers (intending
or actual) who are not to be joined as parties to the mortgage deed
to execute forms of consent or undertaking prior to completion of
the mortgage. These are intended to postpone any legal or equitable
rights they may have, until after those of the lender. Executing such
a form may act either as an estoppel preventing the equitable owner
from seeking to rely on his or her interest or have the effect of postponing such rights to those of the lender.[39]

---

39 *Woolwich Building Society v Plane* [1997] EWCA Civ 2372; *Woolwich Building
Society v Dickman* [1996] 3 All ER 204, CA; Le Foe v Le Foe and Woolwich plc
[2001] 2 FLR 970 and *Skipton Building Society v Clayton* (1993) 25 HLR 596.

Undue influence

Introduction

47.1   Historically, the courts have sought to protect people who have acted to their detriment because of undue pressure put on them. In recent years there has been a burgeoning trend of borrowers (or sureties) claiming that a mortgage is voidable, and hence unenforceable, because of misrepresentation or because of 'undue influence' put on them, either by the lender directly or more commonly by a third party for whose benefit finance is being sought. The wrongdoing which is relevant is any conduct which has 'misled' the surety as to relevant facts of a proposed transaction or has caused the surety's will to be overborne or coerced. In this context the expression 'surety' is intended to include joint owners who allow their interest in property to be used as security for another joint owner for whose benefit a loan is taken out, as well as a person who puts up property as security for another where that person is not him or herself putting anything forward as security for the loan.

47.2   Litigation in this field has been extensive since the 1980s. The House of Lords has had cause to consider the law on two separate occasions in the leading cases of *Barclays Bank v O'Brien* and *CIBC Mortgages v Pitt*[1] in 1994 and *Royal Bank of Scotland v Etridge (No 2)*[2] in 2001. This chapter is simply designed to introduce advisers to the issues. For a comprehensive analysis of the law reference should be made to leading texts on land law and mortgages.[3]

Lender misconduct

47.3   The instances where a surety will allege that a bank or other mortgage lender has misrepresented or pressured a borrower or surety into signing a legal charge are limited. Before the transaction will be set aside, it will be necessary to show that unfair advantage has been taken in the sense that the transaction was to the manifest disadvantage of the victim.[4] Where, however, there is actual undue influence (as contrasted with constructive undue influence, for which see below) then manifest disadvantage does not need to be shown.[5]

---

1   [1994] 1 AC 180 and 200, HL.

2   [2002] AC 773, HL.

3   K Gray and S Gray, *Elements of land law*, 5th edn, Oxford University Press, 2009 and W Clark, *Fisher and Lightwood's law of mortgage*, 12th edn, Butterworths, 2006.

4   *National Westminster Bank plc v Morgan* [1985] AC 686, HL.

5   *O'Hara v Allied Irish Banks Ltd* [1985] BCLC 52.

There is no general duty on a bank to advise a potential surety as to the nature of a relevant transaction although the situation is likely to be different where the surety is an existing customer.[6] Where the lender is taken to be under a duty and its explanation is inadequate, the security may not be enforceable.[7] Where the principal debtor was acting as the lender's agent, the lender is fixed with the misrepresentation or undue influence practised by him or her.[8] In practice, however, cases are rare in which the lender simply leaves the principal debtor to extract his or her signature from the surety by whatever means he or she may choose.

Misconduct of principal debtor

47.4   In recent years, the courts have in some cases sought to impose liability on lenders for the misconduct of a principal debtor where that person could reasonably have been expected to have had influence over a prospective mortgage borrower or surety. Most of the cases have involved wives being prevailed on to enter into second mortgages of the matrimonial home, with the principal debtor being their husband. This development culminated in the leading cases of *Barclays Bank plc v O'Brien* and *CIBC Mortgages v Pitt*.[9] Here the House of Lords sought to define the circumstances in which a lender will be deemed to be on notice of undue influence or misrepresentation perpetrated in order to induce a borrower to enter into the mortgage or a joint owner to put up his or her interest as surety, such as to enable the borrower or surety to apply to the court to have the transaction declared ineffective to charge that person's interest in the property used as security. While, commonly, such cases involve second

6 *Cornish v Midland Bank plc* [1985] 3 All ER 513, CA. See generally A Ward, 'The liability of UK banks for financial advice – recent developments' (1996) 11 JIBL 472; *Barclays Bank v Khaira* [1992] 1 WLR 623; *Midland Bank v Perry* (1987) Fin LR 237; *Verity v Lloyds Bank* [1995] NPC 148 and L Wise, 'Biting the hand that lends?' SJ, 9 February 1996.

7 *Barclays Bank plc v O'Brien* [1994] 1 AC 180, HL.

8 *Kings North Trust Ltd v Bell* [1986] 1 WLR 119 and *Barclays Bank plc v Kennedy* (1989) 58 P&CR 221, CA.

9 [1994] AC 200. See generally M Thompson, 'The enforceability of mortgages' [1994] Conv 140; J Lehane, 'Undue influence, misrepresentation and third parties' (1994) 100 LQR 167; B Fehlberg, 'The husband, the bank, the wife and her signature' (1994) 57 MLR 467; P Sparkes, 'The proprietary effect of undue influence' [1995] Conv 250; B Fehlberg, *Sexually transmitted debt*, Clarendon Press, 1997 and S Gardner, 'Wives' guarantees of their husbands' debts' [1999] LQR 1.

mortgages on jointly owned property, the principles apply equally where a sole owner or a beneficial co-owner is prevailed on by a principal debtor to secure finance made available to that person.

47.5   Where the lender is taken to be on notice of the principal debtor's misconduct then the lender is not able to enforce the mortgage. However, the lender's rights against the principal debtor remain unaffected. In this way the surety may be able to resist possession proceedings by the lender although advisers should be aware that where the surety and the principal debtor are joint owners then, ultimately, possession is at risk if the principal debtor is bankrupted and an order for sale sought by the trustee in bankruptcy or where the lender may be able independently to seek an order for sale under the Trusts of Land and Appointment of Trustees Act 1996.[10] See para 49.14.

47.6   The following is an attempt to summarise the situation following *O'Brien* and *Pitt* in the light of the refinements of the principles superimposed by the House of Lords in *Etridge (No 2)*.[11] A mortgage may be unenforceable against the innocent party for misrepresentation by the principal debtor to the innocent party so long as the misrepresentation would have been sufficient to make a contract voidable if that misrepresentation had been made by the lender. An innocent misrepresentation suffices.[12]

47.7   The mortgage may also be unenforceable or set aside if there has been undue influence exercised resulting in the surety entering into the transaction. Undue influence is unacceptable behaviour which 'arises out of a relationship between two persons where one has acquired over another a measure of influence, or ascendancy, of which the ascendant person takes unfair advantage'.[13] Undue influence may be actual undue influence (for example, threats) or presumed undue influence which is treated as tainting a transaction either because of a particular type of relationship (for example, solicitor and client) or because of an actual relationship where the surety trusted and relied on the abuser. A lender having actual knowledge of the facts entitling the surety to apply to set aside is very rare. A lender is put on enquiry wherever a person offers to stand as surety for the debts of a spouse or any other person involved in some non-commercial relationship

---

10 *First National Bank plc v Achampong* [2003] EWCA Civ 487; [2004] 1 FCR 18, CA. See M P Thompson, 'Undue influence before Etridge' [2003] Conv 314.

11 *Royal Bank of Scotland v Etridge (No 2)* [2002] 2 AC 773, HL.

12 *TSB v Camfield* [1995] 1 All ER 951; (1995) 27 HLR 206, CA.

13 *Royal Bank of Scotland v Etridge (No 2)* [2002] 2 AC 773, HL at [8].

(whether heterosexual, homosexual or platonic, whether or not involving cohabitation[14]) of which the lender is aware. The relationship of employer–employee falls within this definition.[15] The transaction must not appear to be to the surety's advantage.[16]

47.8   The requirement that the transaction is not to the innocent borrower/surety's financial advantage will often be fulfilled in the case where the borrower is being asked to stand as surety for the principal debtor's debts and where no direct financial gain is being obtained by the former. This was the case in *O'Brien* and such cases are described in the case-law as 'surety cases'. Where, however, the transaction is ostensibly a joint borrowing by the borrower/surety and the principal debtor, then there will be no constructive notice to the lender even if the stated purpose (as in *Pitt*) was false. These are called 'joint loan cases'. Cases where a spouse becomes surety for the debts of a company whose shares are held by her and her husband, even when the surety is a director or secretary, cannot be equated with joint loans.[17]

47.9   A lender may be put on notice, even if the loan being sought is ostensibly a joint borrowing, if the advantage to be gained by the borrower/surety is out of proportion to the risk being undertaken.[18] Knowledge possessed by solicitors acting for a lender, the principal debtor and surety in a remortgage (as to the purpose for which monies were to be used) is not imputed to the lender. The knowledge has not come to the solicitors as solicitors for the lender as such.[19]

47.10   Where the lender is put on enquiry it must take 'reasonable steps' to bring home to the surety the risks involved in the transaction proposed.[20] The usual way to disprove undue influence is for the lender to ensure that the surety had full access to independent professional

---

14 *Massey v Midland Bank plc* [1995] 1 All ER 929.

15 *Credit Lyonnais Bank Nederland NV v Burch* [1997] 1 All ER 144, CA. See H Tijo, 'O'Brien and Unconscionability' (1997) 113 LQR 10.

16 *Royal Bank of Scotland v Etridge (No 2)* [2002] AC 773, HL. See M P Thompson, 'Wives, sureties and banks' [2002] Conv 174 and G Andrews, 'Undue influence – where's the disadvantage?' [2002] Conv 456.

17 *Royal Bank of Scotland v Etridge (No 2)* [2002] AC 773, HL.

18 *Goode Durrant Administration v Biddulph* (1994) 26 HLR 625; *Barclays Bank v Sumner* [1996] EGCS 65 and *Bank of Scotland v Bennett* [1997] 1 FLR 801.

19 *Halifax Mortgage Services Ltd v Stepsky* [1996] Ch 207; (1996) 28 HLR 522, CA, *Scotlife Home Loans (No 2) v Hedworth* (1996) 28 HLR 771; *National Westminster Bank plc v Beaton* (1997) 30 HLR 99, CA; *Woolwich plc v Gomm* (2000) 79 P&CR 61, CA; S Nield, 'Imputed Notice' [2000] Conv 196; *Northern Rock Building Society v Archer* (1999) 78 P&CR 65, CA and M P Thompson, 'Constructive notice of undue influence' [1999] Conv 510.

20 *Royal Bank of Scotland v Etridge (No 2)* [2002] 2 AC 773, HL.

advice. However, the essential question is not whether the surety understood the implicatons of what was being proposed but whether he or she was free of pressures which might threaten to override independent judgment.[21] In *Etridge (No 2)* the House of Lords drew a distinction between transactions entered into before the ruling in that case (ie, 11 October 2001) and those after.

47.11   In pre-*Etridge* transactions Lord Nicholls, in *Etridge (No 2)*, indicated that the duty on lenders was as set out in *O'Brien*. Reasonable steps would have been taken if the lender had received from a solicitor confirmation that the surety had been advised of the risks involved in the transaction. The lender would also have satisfied the requirement by advising that the surety obtain independent legal advice or by insisting that the surety attend a private meeting (without the third party being present) with a representative of the lender at which the surety was warned about the risks. However, the lender cannot simply rely on an honest belief that the surety was advised by a solicitor. The lender must have taken active steps not only to ensure that a solicitor was retained but also that the solicitor was instructed to give the surety independent advice on the transaction.[22]

47.12   In post-*Etridge (No 2)* transactions, a more taxing protocol is required to be followed, involving again the requirement for advice from a solicitor. The steps to be taken by a lender are:

- The lender must make direct contact with the surety to identify the solicitor whom the surety will instruct and to advise that the role of that solicitor will be to ensure that any later consent to the transaction cannot be disputed.
- The lender must receive the surety's nomination of solicitor.
- The lender must disclose to the solicitor all relevant information in respect of the principal debtor's financial position and the extent, purpose and terms of the proposed transaction. A copy of the loan application form should be provided to the solicitor.
- The solicitor and the surety must meet in the absence of the principal debtor. At that meeting, the solicitor must advise in suitably non-technical language about the nature and implications of the transaction. The relevant documents must be explained, as must the implications if the lender has to take enforcement action – for example, repossession and/or bankruptcy. The advice must cover the extent of the surety's liability under the transaction and the

---

21 *Royal Bank of Scotland v Etridge (No 2)* [2002] 2 AC 773 at [20] and *Niersmansv Pesticcio* [2004] EWCA Civ 372 at [23].

22 *Yorkshire Bank v Tinsley* [2004] 1 WLR 2380 at [29].

fact that the transaction is optional. The solicitor must check that the surety wishes to proceed and indicate to the surety that the lender will be advised that these issues have been covered and that the transaction is being entered into in the knowledge of this.

47.13   Receipt by the lender of written confirmation that these steps have been taken from the solicitor in question protects the lender from any future allegation of undue influence or misrepresentation. Clearly, however, the solicitor involved in this process runs the risk of a claim of negligence if the surety suffers loss as a result of the transaction because he or she will owe a duty of care to the surety.

The relief available to the surety

47.14   A surety who successfully raises an *O'Brien* defence will be able to resist the claim for possession based on the legal charge.

47.15   It is not possible to 'partly' escape from the consequences of a transaction where, for example, a surety knew that he or she was guaranteeing a certain sum whereas the mortgage which he or she was induced to enter into secured a much larger debt.[23] In such circumstances, the whole transaction must be set aside. Where, however, a loan arrangement comprises several transactions, for example, a loan agreement with a separate later side letter, it is possible to sever the objectionable transaction leaving the other uncontaminated part enforceable.[24] A lender granting a remortgage which would otherwise be voidable by the surety has a 'right of subrogation' in relation to a previous charge which was not voidable and can claim possession based on the element of the remortage referrable to the previous mortgage.[25] Where a further remortgage takes place that lender is also protected on the principle of 'sub-subrogation'.[26] A remortgaging lender in such circumstances is entitled to the same security as the original lender but cannot be subrogated to an amount greater than the mortgage which has been discharged by the remortgage.[27] Where a mortgage which is voidable because of undue influence is

---

23   *TSB Bank plc v Camfield* [1995] 1 WLR 430; [1995] 1 All ER 951, CA. See A Phang, 'Partial rescission for misrepresentation rejected' [1995] 111 LQR 555.

24   *Barclays Bank plc v Caplan* [1998] 1 FLR 532, ChD.

25   *Halifax plc v Omar* [2002] EWCA Civ 121; [2002] 2 P&CR 377 and *Halifax Mortgage Services Ltd v Muirhead* (1997) 76 P&CR 418, CA.

26   *UCB Group Ltd v Hedworth* [2003] EWCA Civ 1717.

27   *Cheltenham & Gloucester plc v Appleyard* [2004] EWCA Civ 291; [2004] 13 EGCS 127.

discharged and a new mortgage created between the same parties, the new mortgage is itself voidable.[28]

The lender's response

47.16   A surety who delays asserting an *O'Brien* defence (for example, by acknowledging the legal charge in matrimonial ancillary relief proceedings) may be barred from raising it in subsequent possesssion proceedings brought by the lender.[29] There is nothing improper in a lender, met with an *O'Brien* defence, seeking a money judgment against the principal debtor with a view to bankruptcy of the principal debtor and subsequent sale by the trustee in bankruptcy of the security.[30]

Taking instructions from the innocent borrower/ surety

47.17   Obviously much will depend on the circumstances of each case, although there are a number of common issues which will need to be addressed when considering an *O'Brien* defence:

* Was the mortgage granted before or after 11 October 2001, ie, pre- or post-*Etridge (No 2)?*
* Did the principal debtor exert real pressure or misrepresent matters to the borrower/surety? What exactly was said and done? Did the borrower/surety rely on the principal debtor for financial decisions and rely unquestioningly on him or her?
* What educational or business background does the borrower/surety have?
* How was the transaction explained by the principal debtor? Were half-truths or inaccuracies involved?
* Where, when, how and before whom was the document signed? Is there a certificate confirming that the implications were made known to the borrower/surety?

28   *Yorkshire Bank plc v Tinsley* [2004] EWCA Civ 816; [2004] 1 WLR 2380. See M P Thompson, 'Replacement mortgages' [2004] Conv 399.
29   *First National Bank plc v Walker* [2001] 1 FCR 21, CA.
30   *Alliance & Leicester plc v Slayford* [2000] EWCA Civ 257; [2001] 1 All ER (Comm) 1. See M P Thompson, 'The cumulative range of a mortgagee's remedies' [2002] Conv 53.

- Did the client have any advice from the lender or from anyone else and, if so, who and what was the advice? Was the extent of present and prospective future financial liability made clear? Was the principal debtor present when the advice was given? Did the borrower/surety understand the advice?
- Did the lender insist on legal advice being obtained as a precondition to the loan?
- Did the borrower/surety receive legal advice, and if so from whom and what was that advice?
- Did the borrower/surety understand the nature of the transaction?
- Was the transaction in relation to a guarantee or a joint loan? What did the lender believe it to be for and what did the loan application say it was for?
- Obtain on disclosure the correspondence between the lender and the solicitor/adviser to clarify who, and in relation to what, the solicitors were expected to advise about.

47.18   Armed with this information, advisers will be able to make a clearer judgment of the strengths of the potential defence. It should be remembered that it is be open to the disadvantaged surety to take the initiative and, as a claimant, to seek a declaration that the mortgage was voidable as against him or her. There is no need to wait for the lender to seek possession.

Sale of the home

Introduction

48.1   For the vast majority of borrowers in difficulty with their mortgage, the aim will be to try to preserve their occupation of the home. In possession proceedings, the lender will usually be looking to force the borrower into making increased payments to pay off arrears with the sanction that eviction will follow if sufficient payments are not made. Very often this threat will be backed by an order for possession postponed for as long as the stipulated payments are made.

48.2   However, where it is clear that dispossession is inevitable then a borrower may seek the opportunity of selling the home, ie, the property mortgaged to the lender. Alternatively, where the borrower has given up possession either voluntarily in the face of possession proceedings or following eviction after proceedings, the borrower will be concerned about the sale of the home by the lender. This would be either because there may be a surplus due to the borrower after the mortgage has been redeemed or because the lender will wish to recover the amount of any shortfall if the sale proceeds are not sufficient to discharge the mortgage debt in total. Occupiers of a mortgaged property may also face a claim by the lender for a specific order from the court for the property to be sold. This may arise where the lender is unable to rely on the mortgage in order to obtain possession with a view to sale as mortgagee in possession. This may occur where, for instance, the lender is faced with an occupier who has successfully raised a *Barclays Bank v O'Brien*[1] defence (for which see para 47.4) or where a joint owner has forged the signature of the other joint owner.[2] In such a case the lender will be seeking an order for sale and possession under the Trusts of Land and Appointment of Trustees Act 1996. Such an order may be sought, as an alternative, in possession proceedings.

Sale by the borrower

48.3   As the owner of the mortgaged property, the borrower is at liberty to sell the property at any time. The lender's consent is not required. However, the purchaser will not usually complete the purchase until the seller's solicitors give a formal undertaking that they will provide either the receipted legal charge in the case of unregistered land or,

---

1   [1994] 1 AC 180, HL.
2   *First National Securities Ltd v Hegerty* [1985] QB 850.

where the title is registered, a form DS1 duly receipted by the lender. In turn, the seller's solicitors will not give such an undertaking, for which the partners of the solicitor's firm in question would be personally liable, until they are satisfied that the sale proceeds will be sufficient to redeem the mortgage or, if there is more than one, all the mortgages secured against the property. Where the seller is acting in person, the buyer will want to ensure that some other arrangement is in place to ensure that any mortgage debt is paid off on completion.

48.4 It is usually in both the lender's and the borrower's interests for the borrower to remain in occupation until the home is sold. In this way it is likely that the sale price will be higher than would be obtained by the lender if the home is empty following the borrower leaving. In addition, any income support or other benefits payable on account of mortgage interest will continue to be paid direct to the lender while the borrower is in occupation, reducing the ultimate mortgage debt.

Where the whole mortgage debt can be paid from the sale proceeds

48.5 Where, before proceedings have been started, it is clear to the borrower that sale of the home is inevitable, the borrower should advise the lender of the decision to sell. The lender should be asked to agree to delay issuing proceedings on the basis of the borrower showing that reasonable steps are being taken to sell the home at the appropriate market price as advised by an estate agent. The borrower should agree to keep the lender advised about progress. The Mortgage Arrears Protocol requires the lender in these circumstances to consider delaying proceedings and, if it decides none the less to issue proceedings, to give the borrower its reasons at least five business days before starting proceedings.[3] This might entitle the borrower to refer the lender's decision by way of a complaint to the Financial Ombudsman Service (see para 40.112).

48.6 If the sale proceeds are sufficient to pay off the whole mortgage debt, it is open to the borrower to argue, where proceedings are issued, that the arrears would be paid off out of the sale proceeds and that therefore the Administration of Justice Act 1970 s36(1) would be available to assist the borrower providing that the court is satisfied that the sale would take place within a reasonable period. It is a question of fact for the court in each case whether the borrower will be

---

3 Mortgage Arrears Protocol paras 6.2 and 6.4.

able to sell within a reasonable period.[4] See para 40.16. However, it is important to produce some evidence to support the assertion that a sale is likely within the proposed period.[5] Certainly, in the initial stages of the sale process a simple letter from an estate agent as to the likely time-scale should be sufficient. There is no reason why the reasonable period should not be six or nine or even 12 months, but in one case the Court of Appeal postponed a possession order for only three months to enable the borrowers to try to sell.[6]

48.7　The length of time which the borrower might expect to be given by the court will obviously depend on the particular circumstances. However, the Court of Appeal has given some general guidance.[7] Where the home was already on the market and there was some indication of delay on the part of the borrower, it might be that a short period of postponement of only a few months would be reasonable. Where there was likely to be considerable delay in selling the property and/or its value was close to the total of the mortgage debt and arrears (so that the lender was at risk as to the adequacy of the security), immediate possession or only a short period of postponement might be reasonable. Where there had already been considerable delay in realising a sale and/or the likely sale proceeds were unlikely to cover the mortgage debt and arrears, or there was simply not sufficient evidence about the sale value, the usual order would be for immediate possession. It can be seen from these observations that the level of equity is of considerable significance.

48.8　It remains unclear whether Administration of Justice Act 1970 s36 can be relied on in order to stay enforcement in relation to part of the security where, for instance, part of the property can be sold to pay off the mortgage.[8]

4　*National and Provincial Building Society v Lloyd* [1996] 1 All ER 630, CA. See generally M P Thompson, 'When mortgaged property should be sold' [1998] Conv 125.

5　*Bristol & West Building Society v Ellis* (1997) 29 HLR 282; (1997) 73 P&CR 158, CA.

6　*Target Home Loans v Clothier* [1994] 1 All ER 439; (1993) 25 HLR 48, CA.

7　*Bristol & West Building Society v Ellis* (1997) 29 HLR 282; (1997) 73 P&CR 158, CA.

8　*Barclays Bank plc v Alcorn* [2002] EWHC 498 (Ch); [2002] P&CR (D) 10; October 2002 *Legal Action* 29.

Where the whole mortgage debt cannot be paid from the sale proceeds

48.9   Where the sale price is likely to be insufficient to discharge the mortgage debt in total then, in practice, the lender can prevent a sale by the borrower from proceeding. This is because the seller will be unable to redeem the legal charge on completion. In such circumstances it is open to the borrower to apply to the High Court for an order directing, at the court's instigation, the sale of the property under the Law of Property Act (LPA) 1925 s91.[9] Section 91(2) provides:

> In any action, whether for foreclosure, or for redemption, or for sale, or for the raising and payment in any manner of mortgage money, the court, on the request of the mortgagee, or of any person interested either in the mortgage money or in the right of redemption, and, notwithstanding that –
>
> (a) any other person dissents; or
> (b) the mortgagee or any person so interested does not appear in the action;
>
> and without allowing any time for redemption or for payment of any mortgage money, may direct a sale of the mortgaged property, on such terms as it thinks fit, including the deposit in court of a reasonable sum fixed by the court to meet the expenses of sale and to secure performance of the terms.

48.10   The court is given wide discretion whether to direct a sale and, if so, on what terms. Under LPA 1925 s91 the court has the discretion to order sale and to allow the borrower to remain in occupation pending sale, even where there is a negative equity.[10] However, where the sale proceeds would fall substantially below the amount of the mortgage debt, an order for sale will not be made save in exceptional circumstances.[11] The court is not limited to considering purely financial matters when exercising its discretion and is fully entitled to take into account the pressing social needs of the borrower.[12] In cases where the lender is pressing for possession with a view to sale, the county court has no discretion to suspend a warrant for possession to enable an application to be made in the High Court for an order for sale

---

9   *Palk v Mortgage Services Funding plc* [1993] Ch 330; [1993] 2 WLR 415; (1993) 25 HLR 56, CA. See also *Polonski v Lloyds Bank Mortgages Ltd* [1998] 1 FLR 896; (1999) 31 HLR 721, ChD.

10 *Barrett v Halifax Building Society* (1996) 28 HLR 634, ChD.

11 See *Palk v Mortgage Services Funding plc* [1993] Ch 330; [1993] 2 WLR 415; (1993) 25 HLR 56, CA and *Pearn v Mortgage Business plc* (1998) LSG 4 February, ChD.

12 *Polonski v Lloyds Bank Mortgages Ltd* [1998] 1 FLR 896; (1999) 31 HLR 721, ChD.

under LPA 1925 s91 except where there are funds available to the borrower to make up the shortfall on sale.[13] A borrower wishing to seek an order for sale must ensure that the application is determined before the lender seeks to enforce a possession order.

48.11   The county court does nevertheless have discretion under Administration of Justice Act 1970 s36, in appropriate cases, to give conduct of the sale to the lender while postponing the execution of a warrant for possession and so allowing the borrower to remain in possession pending sale, even where there is little (if any) equity in the property.[14] This can be done where the court is satisfied that:

- possession would not be required by the lender pending completion of the sale but only by the purchasers on completion;
- the presence of the borrowers pending completion would enhance, or at least not depress, the sale price;
- the borrowers would co-operate in the sale; and
- they would give possession to the purchasers on completion.

48.12   Both those claiming to have a beneficial interest in the security[15] and tenants[16] have been held to have the right to apply for an order for sale under LPA 1925 s91.

48.13   Where the amount owing under the mortgage is in excess of £30,000 the county court has no jurisdiction to consider an application under LPA 1925 s91 and the application must be made in the High Court.[17] However, the High Court is likely to transfer the case to the county court for trial.

48.14   In the case of regulated mortgage contracts (see para 40.75) lenders are obliged to give 'consideration, where no reasonable payment arrangement can be made, to the [borrower] being allowed to remain in possession to effect a sale'.[18] Failure to give such consideration may be relied on as tending to show contravention of the lender's obligation to deal fairly with the borrower[19] and as such form the basis of a complaint to the Financial Ombudsman Service (see para 40.112).

---

13 *Cheltenham & Gloucester plc v Krausz* [1996] 1 WLR 1558; [1997] 1 All ER 21, CA. See A Kenny, 'No postponement of evil day' [1998] Conv 223 and M Dixon, 'Combating the mortgagee's right to possession: new hope for the mortgagor in chains?' [1998] *Legal Studies* 279.

14 *Cheltenham & Gloucester plc v Booker* (1997) 73 P&CR 412; (1997) 29 HLR 634, CA.

15 *Halifax Building Society v Stansfield* [1993] EGCS 147, CA. See chapter 46.

16 *National Westminster Home Loans v Riches* [1995] CLW 43/95. See chapter 43.

17 High Court and County Courts Jurisdiction Order 1991 SI No 724 art 2(4).

18 Mortgage: Conduct of Business sourcebook (MCOB) para 13.3.2 E (1) (e). See para 40.86.

19 MCOB para 13.3.2 E (2).

Sale by the lender

48.15 Borrowers will be concerned about a sale by the lender in two circumstances. The first is where the lender has taken possession and is seeking (as mortgagee in possession) to sell and to recoup the outstanding mortgage debt from the sale proceeds. The second is where the occupier has raised a defence which prevents the lender from obtaining an order for possession. In such circumstances, the lender has the option of applying to the court for an order for sale.

Lender selling as mortgagee in possession

48.16 In the context of residential mortgages, the lender will be seeking possession of the borrower's home with a view to evicting the borrower and selling with vacant possession. As a disincentive to the taking of possession, the common law imposes some fairly ill-defined obligations on the lender after possession has been taken. In practice, particularly in a depressed property market, disputes between the lender and the borrower tend to arise over, first, the timing of the sale and, second, the sale price.

48.17 As mortgagee in possession, the common law imposes an obligation on the lender to 'take reasonable precautions to obtain the true market value of the mortgaged property at the date on which he decides to sell'.[20] However, it is clear that while there is an obligation to obtain the best price at the date of sale, the timing of that sale is left to the judgment of the lender,[21] although in choosing the time a reasonable degree of care must be exercised.[22]

48.18 The lender must ensure that the property is fairly and properly exposed to the market.[23] This duty is owed both to the borrower and any guarantor[24] although it does not extend to people claiming as

---

20 *Cuckmere Brick Co Ltd v Mutual Finance Ltd* [1971] Ch 949, CA, at 968H. See generally P Devonshire, 'The mortgagee's power of sale: a case for the equitable standard of good faith' (1995) 46 NILQ 182; L Bentley, 'Mortgagee's duties on sale – no place for tort?' [1990] Conv 431; J Marriott, 'Sell and be sued? The mortgagee's duty on sale' LS Gaz 30 September 1987 p2756; H Wilkinson, 'The mortgagee's duty to mortgagors and guarantors' [1982] NLJ 883 and *Meftah v Lloyds TSB Bank plc (No 2)* [2001] 2 All ER (Comm) 741, ChD.

21 *Bank of Cyprus v Gill* [1979] 2 Lloyd's Rep 508, CA.

22 *Standard Chartered Bank Ltd v Walker* [1982] 1 WLR 1410, CA.

23 *Silven Properties Ltd v Royal Bank of Scotland plc* [2004] 1 WLR 997.

24 *Standard Chartered Bank v Walker* [1982] 1 WLR 1410, CA and *American Express International Banking Corp v Hurley* [1985] 3 All ER 564. See also *Skipton Building Society v Stott* [2001] QB 261; [2000] 3 WLR 1031, CA.

beneficiaries under constructive, resulting or other trusts.[25] The borrower may bring an action for breach of duty against the lender, but a separate action in negligence may lie also against the lender's selling agents.[26] The lender cannot discharge the duty of care by merely putting the sale in the hands of apparently competent estate agents and the lender will be liable for the negligence of the agents even if the lender may be able to recover damages payable to the borrower from the agents.[27] Provisions in a legal charge purporting to exclude the lender's duty to take reasonable care do not exempt the lender if loss arises from the lender's failure to take such reasonable care.[28]

48.19　　In the case of a 'regulated mortgage contract' (see para 40.75) where a property is repossessed (either voluntarily or through legal action) a lender must take steps to market the property for sale as soon as possible and obtain the best price that might reasonably be paid, taking account of factors such as market conditions as well as the continuing increase in the amount owed by the borrower to the lender.[29] Where a lender chooses to sell by auction, it is under a duty to ensure that the auction is preceded by appropriate advertisement.[30]

48.20　　Where the lender has sold at an undervalue then the borrower's usual remedy will be a claim for damages based on the estimated under-value.[31] However, in most cases the remedy will be by way of a set-off or counterclaim in an action by the lender for a money judgment against the borrower for the shortfall on sale.[32] It would be possible in the alternative, where the property has still to be sold, to seek an injunction to prevent the sale. It is open to a borrower to seek such an injunction even after exchange of contracts but before completion.[33]

48.21　　Borrowers concerned about the possibility of a sale at an undervalue will wish to consider a number of issues, including:

25　*Parker-Tweedale v Dunbar Bank plc (No 1)* [1991] Ch 26; [1990] 3 WLR 780; [1990] 2 All ER 588, CA.

26　See *Garland v Ralph Pay and Ransom* (1984) 271 EG 106 and *Minah v Bank of Ireland* [1995] EGCS 144.

27　*Tomlin v Luce* (1890) 43 ChD 191, CA.

28　See *Bishop v Bonham* [1988] 1 WLR 742, CA and see para 40.86.

29　MCOB para 13.6.1 R.

30　*Pendlebury v Colonial Mutual Life Assurance Society Ltd* (1912) 13 CLR 676.

31　Law of Property Act 1925 s104(2). See *Michael v Miller* [2004] EWCA Civ 282; [2004] 2 EGLR 151, CA and *Mortgage Express v Mardner* [2004] EWCA Civ 1859. M P Thompson, 'Irregular sales of mortgaged property' [2004] Conv 49.

32　*Platts v TSB Bank plc* [1998] 2 BCLC 1.

33　*Shercliff v Engadine Acceptance Corporation Pty Ltd* [1978] 1 NSWLR 729.

- Was the property sold at auction? Sale at an auction is legitimate but the property must be properly described in sale particulars, sufficient notice of the auction should be given and the reserve price should not be unusually low.
- How does the sale price compare with earlier valuations? What can the borrower say about other similar properties being sold in the area?
- Where was the sale advertised? Was this adequate exposure?
- Who was the buyer and was the property then resold soon afterwards?
- Did the sale price just cover the mortgage debt?
- Did the lender sell following one or more competent surveyor's recommendations about the method of sale?
- In the case of a specialised property was expert advice taken as to how and where to market the property?

48.22   It will, in any case where litigation is contemplated, be essential to obtain an expert's report on the value of the property. This should be done as soon as possible. Whether there is the possibility of successful litigation against the lender will ultimately depend on the strength of the expert evidence available.

48.23   On completion of the sale the borrower will be entitled to be paid the balance of the purchase monies after the mortgage(s) has been redeemed. For that reason the borrower should notify the lender of his or her whereabouts so that any balance can be forwarded to him or her where there are surplus proceeds of sale.

48.24   In the case of a 'regulated mortgage contract' a lender is obliged to take reasonable steps (as soon as possible after the sale) to inform the borrower of the surplus and, subject to the rights of any other secured lender, to pay it to the borrower.[34]

48.25   However, where the sale proceeds are insufficient to pay off the mortgage in full, there is nothing to prevent the lender suing the borrower for the shortfall on the personal covenant in the mortgage deed.[35] If this is likely, it is important to try to identify whether a mortgage indemnity guarantee policy was taken out at the time of the initial mortgage advance. A mortgage indemnity guarantee policy is simply an insurance policy taken out by the lender (although paid for by the borrower) to protect itself in part from any financial loss suffered when a mortgaged property is repossessed and sold.

---

34 MCOB 13.6.6 R. See para 40.86.
35 *Gordon Grant and Co Ltd v Boos* [1926] AC 781, PC.

Such policies are commonly taken out when the mortgage advance is anything over (usually) 75 per cent of the value of the property which is the security for the loan. The policy is taken out for the benefit of the lender and not the borrower.[36] Many borrowers are unaware of whether such a policy has been taken out because the cost of the insurance premium may well have not been paid for by the borrower at the outset of the loan but merely debited to the mortgage account. It is, however, important that the borrower is aware that the insurance company with whom the policy was taken out is, in law, entitled to seek to recover from the borrower any payment made by it. This is not, however, common in practice.[37]

48.26 The relevant limitation period for the recovery of the outstanding balance on the mortgage is 12 years (and six years for the interest) from the date of the accrual of the lender's right to the debt.[38] It is essential to consider the terms of the legal charge in question to assess when the right arose.[39] In the case of a 'regulated mortgage contract' (see para 40.75) a lender is obliged, as soon as possible, after the sale of the repossessed property to inform the borrower of the amount of the shortfall, and (where relevant) that the debt may be pursued by another company (for example, a mortgage indemnity insurer).[40] Any decision to recover the mortgage shortfall must be notified to the borrower within six years.[41] In addition, members of the Council of Mortgage Lenders have agreed that (with effect from 11 February 2000) no enforcement action will be taken unless within six years from the sale of a property at a shortfall a borrower has been contacted about recovery of the outstanding debt.[42]

48.27 It is worth noting that there is no need to obtain an order from the court authorising sale of the property after possession is obtained.

---

36 See *Woolwich Building Society v Brown* [1996] CLC 625. See R Del Tufo, 'Mortgage indemnity guarantees: the litigation implications' [1996] SJ 612 and D Ohrenstein, 'MIGS come under fire' LS Gaz 15 May 1996. See also D Falkowski, 'Mortgage indemnity insurance: are the terms unfair?' [1996] SJ 1080 for an interesting discussion of whether lenders could face a challenge to this orthodoxy under the Unfair Terms in Consumer Contracts Regulations 1994 SI No 3159 and 1999 SI No 2083.

37 See P Madge, 'A false security' (1991) *Adviser* May 1991 p28.

38 *Bristol & West plc v Bartlett* [2002] EWCA Civ 1181; [2002] 4 All ER 544.

39 *West Bromwich Building Society v Wilkinson* [2005] UKHL 44; [2005] 1 WLR 2303, HL.

40 MCOB 13.6.3 R. See para 40.86.

41 MCOB 13.6.4 R. See para 40.86.

42 *Debt following mortgage possession*, see www.cml.org.uk/cml/consumers/guides/debt#3.

The lender's right to sell the property will have arisen either under the terms of the mortgage deed or under the Law of Property Act 1925.

Lender seeking order for sale

48.28 Where land is held on trust (for example, by the defaulting borrower and a person with an overriding beneficial interest), the Trusts of Land and Appointment of Trustees Act 1996 enables the court, among other things, to order its sale and the eviction of any occupiers. 'Trust of land' is widely defined and comprises 'any trust of property which consists of or includes land' irrespective of the date of creation or origin of that trust.[43] This will include express, implied, resulting or constructive trusts.

48.29 Trusts of Land and Appointment of Trustees Act 1996 s14(1)–(2) give the court jurisdiction to make such order as it 'thinks fit' in resolution of any dispute over whether trust land should be sold or retained for occupation by the trust beneficiaries. The county court is the relevant court irrespective of the value of the property which is the subject of the application for sale.[44] A mortgage lender, having an interest in the trust property, is able to apply to the court for an order for sale. The matters to which the court is expressly to have regard when determining whether to make an order for sale include:

- the intention of the person(s) who created the trust;
- the purposes for which the trust property is held;
- the welfare of any minor who occupies or might reasonably be expected to occupy the trust property as a home; and
- the interests of any secured creditor of any beneficiary.[45]

48.30 The initial case-law was unsympathetic to occupiers notwithstanding the clear policy change introduced by the 1996 Act's abolition of the statutory 'trust for sale'. A lender in possession proceedings faced with a binding overriding interest is able to apply successfully for an order for sale.[46] However, in *Mortgage Corporation Ltd v Shaire*,[47]

---

43 Trusts of Land and Appointment of Trustees Act 1996 s1(2).
44 High Court and County Courts Jurisdiction Order 1991 SI No 724 art 2(1)p.
45 Trusts of Land and Appointment of Trustees Act 1996 s15(1).
46 *Bank of Baroda v Dhillon* [1998] 1 FLR 524, CA.
47 [2001] Ch 743; [2001] 4 All ER 364; [2000] 1 FLR 973, ChD. See also S Pascoe, 'Section 15 of the Trusts of Land and Appointment of Trustees Act 1996 – a change in the law?' [2000] Conv 315 and M P Thompson, 'Secured creditors and sales' [2000] Conv 329.

the court observed that the presumption of sale contained within the concept of the trust for sale had been abolished by the 1996 Act. Section 15(1) contains four factors to be taken into account with the interests of the secured lender being but one. There is no suggestion that those interests should be given any greater weight than the interests of children residing in the house. The court concluded that parliament had intended to relax the law so as to enable the courts to have more discretion in favour of families and against banks and other chargees. On the facts of the case, an order for sale was made but was suspended on Ms Shaire paying interest on the sum effectively charged on the property in favour of the claimant. While her signature had been forged on the legal charge, the claimant had a valid charge on the other joint owner's interest in the property. Providing the claimant was compensated in interest, the family's occupation of the home could be preserved and the lender was adequately protected pending the eventual sale of the property.

48.31   Whether, in any particular case, an order for sale will be refused or postponed depends to what extent a secured creditor is at risk and if it can be compensated financially pending sale of the property[48] and repayment of the monies secured at that time. Case-law since *Shaire* has seen a hardening in judicial attitude. Issues such as ill health may be relevant when considering the duration of any period of postponement of sale but may be irrelevant (in the absence of any compensatory payments to the lender) when considering whether to allow a lender's application for sale.[49]

---

48   *Bank of Ireland Home Mortgages Ltd v Bell* [2000] EWCA Civ 426; [2001] 2 All ER (Comm) 920; *Edwards v Lloyds TSB Bank plc* [2004] EWHC 1745 (Ch); [2005] 1 FCR 139 and *First National Bank plc v Achampong* [2003] EWCA Civ 487; [2005] 1 FCR 18. See R Probert, 'Creditors and section 15 of the Trusts of Land and Appointment of Trustees Act 1996: first among equals?' [2002] Conv 61 and M P Thompson, 'Undue influence before Etridge' [2003] Conv 314.

49   *Bank of Ireland Home Mortgages Ltd v Bell* [2001] 2 All ER (Comm) 920; *Edwards v Lloyds TSB Bank plc* [2005] 1 FCR 139 and *Edwards v Bank of Scotland* [2010] EWHC 652 (Ch).

Possession claims by unsecured creditors

Introduction

49.1   Owner-occupiers are, in certain circumstances, at risk of possession claims by creditors who were, at least initially, unsecured creditors. Advisers should be alert to these possible actions when advising owner-occupiers in relation to their debts. The two ways in which owners can be evicted are by way of a successful application for an order for sale (1) following a creditor obtaining a charging order, and (2) on application by the owner's trustee in bankruptcy. The two possibilities need to be looked at separately.[1]

Charging orders

49.2   Under the Charging Orders Act 1979 a creditor may, after obtaining a money judgment against a debtor, apply to the court for a charging order and then register a charge in relation to property owned legally or beneficially by a judgment debtor, whether alone or jointly with others. The procedure is regulated by the Civil Procedure Rules (CPR) Part 73.

49.3   The relevant court for an application for a charging order is the county court except where the judgment debt is a High Court judgment in excess of £5,000,[2] in which case the judgment creditor has the option of using either the High Court or county court.

49.4   Following the judgment for the debt, application is made without notice to the court for an interim charging order (previously known as a charging order nisi). Where the charge relates to *registered* land held legally and beneficially by the judgment debtor, the creditor can enter a 'notice' in the charges register of the debtor's title or, in the case of *unregistered* land, under the Land Charges Act 1972. Where the order relates to the debtor's beneficial interest under a trust of land a 'restriction' can be entered in the proprietorship register of the registered title. It appears that no similar protection is available to a creditor in unregistered land where the debtor has only a beneficial interest. The debtor is then served with notice of the hearing of the application for the charging order to be made final. The onus is on the debtor to show cause why the order should not be made final.[3]

---

1   See generally W Boyce and J Middleton, *Debt and insolvency on family breakdown*, 2nd edn, Family Law, 2001.

2   Charging Orders Act 1979 s1(2) and County Courts Jurisdiction Order 1981 SI No 1123.

3   *Roberts Petroleum Ltd v Bernard Kenny Ltd* [1983] 2 AC 192; [1982] 1 WLR 305, HL and *United Overseas Bank Ltd v Iwuanyanwu* (2001) 5 March, unreported, CA.

49.5   The court has discretion whether to grant the charging order and is required to take into account

> all the circumstances of the case and, in particular, ... (a) the personal circumstances of the debtor, and (b) whether any other creditor of the debtor would be likely to be unduly prejudiced by the making of the order.[4]

The court should not grant the charging order where the size of the debt is small compared with the value of the property,[5] where the judgment creditor is in competition with other creditors[6] or where a county court judgment has been ordered to be paid by instalments (unless and until the debtor has defaulted in payments).[7]

49.6   Where the charging order is being sought against the legal estate of a sole owner or all the joint legal owners advisers should point out the limited powers described above that the court has to prevent an order for sale on the creditor's application. In practice, however, it is not difficult for a creditor to obtain a final charging order.

49.7   The court-imposed charge made by a charging order becomes enforceable 'in the same manner as an equitable charge created by the debtor by writing under his hand'.[8] Variation or discharge of a charging order is possible on application by 'any person interested in any property to which the order relates'.[9]

49.8   Proceedings to enforce a charging order by sale of the legal interest are regulated by CPR 73.10 and PD 73.[10] Where a charging order has been granted against the beneficial interest of only one of two or more joint owners, the judgment debtor will need to apply under the Trusts of Land and Appointment of Trustees Act 1996 for an order for sale.[11] It has been held that the power to enforce a charging order under

---

4   Charging Orders Act 1979 s1(5); *Harman v Glencross* [1985] Fam 49; [1986] 1 All ER 545, CA and *Roberts Petroleum Ltd v Bernard Kenny Ltd* [1983] 2 AC 192, HL. For the exercise of the court's powers in the context of simultaneous divorce proceedings see also *Harman v Glencross* (above); *Austin-Fell v Austin-Fell and Midland Bank plc* [1990] Fam 172; [1990] 3 WLR 33; [1990] 2 All ER 455 and J Warburton, 'Victory for the sprinter' [1986] Conv 218.

5   *Robinson v Bailey* [1942] 1 All ER 498.

6   See *Harman v Glencross* [1986] Fam 81 at 93A.

7   *Mercantile Credit Co Ltd v Ellis* [1987] CLY 2917; (1987) *Times* 2 April, CA.

8   Charging Orders Act 1979 s3(4). See *Bland v Ingrams Estates Ltd* [2001] Ch 767.

9   Charging Orders Act 1979 s3(5).

10 See M Buckley, 'Enforcing a charging order by way of an application for an order for sale' *Quarterly Account* Winter 2008/09 p8.

11 Charging Orders Act 1979 s2. See also *National Westminster Bank plc v Stockman* [1981] 1 WLR 67.

the 1996 Act is compliant with the European Convention on Human Rights.[12] For an analysis of the law in this area see para 48.30.

49.9   Where the charging order is against the legal estate of either a sole owner or of all the joint owners the court has none of the discretion available under the 1996 Act. There is no trust of land in this situation. The court is simply dealing with an application by a creditor who has the benefit of an equitable charge. The court's powers would seemingly be limited to its inherent jurisdiction in mortgage cases. See para 40.7.

49.10   Under CPR 73.10 the creditor can apply for an order for sale and for an order for possession using a Part 8 claim form with supporting witness statement, setting out the charging order which it is sought to enforce, the amount still outstanding to the creditor, details of prior mortgagees, the sums outstanding and the estimated sale price. This application has to be made by issuing a new claim and cannot be made in existing proceedings. An application for an order for sale based on a charging order is an application to enforce an equitable charge. The county court has jurisdiction where the sum owing is under £30,000.[13] Otherwise the application must be in the High Court, although it is likely that the High Court will transfer the case to the county court even if the sum involved exceeds the county court financial limit.[14] Appendix A to PD 73 contains an optional form of order for sale. The application is heard in the county court by a district judge. In practice, district judges are often unwilling to grant the creditor's application for sale and possession because they consider that the security of the charging order is adequate protection for a creditor who was originally unsecured.

49.11   When seeking to contest the application for sale, it is important to emphasise the fact that the creditor is already well protected and to point out the detriment which will result to innocent members of the family if the sale is allowed to proceed, particularly where the sale would result in insufficient funds to enable the family to be rehoused.[15] If the debtor is able to offer alternative ways of discharging the judgment debt, these should be put forward.[16]

---

12   *National Westminster Bank plc v Rushmer* [2010] EWHC 554 (Ch).
13   County Courts Act 1984 s23 and High Court and County Courts Jurisdiction Order 1991 SI No 724.
14   *National WestminsterBank plc v King* [2008] EWHC 280 (Ch).
15   See generally *Harman v Glencross* [1985] Fam 49; [1984] 2 All ER 577, CA.
16   See generally M Sullivan, 'Charging orders and their enforcement in the county courts' (1999) 52 *Quarterly Account* p4, and P Madge, 'Charging interest' (1999) 76 *Adviser* p32.

49.12   When a judgment creditor obtains a charge on a property as security for a judgment debt, the creditor's security extends also to interest on the debt even if interest is not expressly mentioned in the order. In equity, the creditor is also entitled to add the costs of enforcing the charge to the security. The amount of interest recoverable under the charging order is not restricted by the Limitation Act 1980.[17] Similarly, the judgment creditor is entitled to the costs of enforcing the charging order including the costs of fending off claims by third parties that they had beneficial interests in the proceeds of sale of the property subject to the charging order.[18]

49.13   The rights of a creditor who has a charging order are not statute barred after 12 years under the Limitation Act 1980 because the holder does not have a right to possession such that time can run against it under section 15 and extinction of title cannot therefore occur under section 17.[19]

Trustees in bankruptcy

49.14   When a person becomes bankrupt, his or her property vests in the trustee in bankruptcy as soon as that person is appointed. The property is vested in the trustee without the necessity of any deed of transfer.[20] The trustee's duty is then 'to get in, realise and distribute'[21] the bankrupt's assets and to distribute the estate in accordance with the Insolvency Act 1986.

49.15   Where the legal and beneficial estate is in the sole name of the bankrupt, then the trustee is at liberty to dispose of that asset without the need to consider the position of others. However, where the legal estate is in the joint names of the bankrupt and a third party, or where the bankrupt and a third party have beneficial interests, then the trustee is a 'person interested' who can apply under the Trusts

---

17 *Ezekiel v Orakpo* [1997] 1 WLR 340, CA.
18 *Holder v Supperstone* [2000] 1 All ER 457, ChD.
19 *Yorkshire Bank Finance Ltd v Mulhall* [2008] EWCA Civ 1156.
20 Insolvency Act 1986 s306(1) and (2). See generally Thompson, *Co-ownership*, p103; E Bailey and C Berry, 'The matrimonial home in bankruptcy' (1987) 137 NLJ 310; E Bailey and C Berry, 'Applications by the trustee for possession and sale' (1987) 137 NLJ 347; M Cohen, 'Homes and other assets in bankruptcy' (1996) *Money Advice* 28.
21 Insolvency Act 1986 s305(2).

of Land and Appointment of Trustees Act 1996 s14 for an order for sale. The bankruptcy of a 'beneficial joint tenant' operates as an act of severance, resulting in the property being held by the owners as a 'tenancy in common'.[22] Where there is a spouse or civil partner in occupation (but not a mere cohabitant) who has no legal or beneficial interest, then he or she will have to rely on any rights of occupation under the Family Law Act 1996. A cohabitant who has neither a legal nor beneficial interest in the property will not be able to resist an application for an order for possession in advance of sale.

49.16   Insolvency Act 1986 s335A[23] provides that, when considering applications for sale and possession of property by the trustee under the Trusts of Land and Appointment of Trustees Act 1996 s14, the court shall make such order as it thinks just and reasonable having regard to:

(a) the interests of the bankrupt's creditors;
(b) where the application is made in respect of land which includes a dwelling-house which is or has been the home of the bankrupt or the bankrupt's spouse or civil partner or former spouse or former civil partner –
   (i) the conduct of the spouse, civil partner, former spouse or former civil partner, so far as contributing to the bankruptcy,
   (ii) the needs and financial resources of the spouse, civil partner, former spouse or former civil partner, and
   (iii) the needs of any children; and
(c) all the circumstances of the case other than the needs of the bankrupt.[24]

49.17   The usual criteria by which the court assesses an application for sale under the Trusts of Land and Appointment of Trustees Act 1996 are expressly excluded where the trustee in bankruptcy is the claimant.[25] The application for an order for sale is made to the bankruptcy court.[26]

49.18   The Insolvency Act 1996 provides for a statutory presumption in favour of making the order for possession and sale for the benefit of the creditors *after* a 12-month period:

22   *Re Gorman* [1990] 1 WLR 616; [1990] 1 All ER 717.
23   Inserted by Trusts of Land and Appointment of Trustees Act 1996 s25(1) and Sch 3 para 23.
24   Insolvency Act 1986 s335A(2). See generally G Miller, 'Applications by a trustee in bankruptcy for sale of the family home' (1999) 15(6) IL & P 76.
25   Trusts of Land and Appointment of Trustees Act 1996 s15(4).
26   Insolvency Act 1986 s335A(1).

... after the end of the period of one year beginning with the first vesting ... of the bankrupt's estate in a trustee, the court shall assume, unless the circumstances of the case are exceptional, that the interests of the bankrupt's creditors outweigh all other considerations.[27]

49.19 While this statutory presumption would seem to favour the creditors 12 months after the bankruptcy, it does not prevent an application for sale/possession by the trustee during that period. However, faced with the prospect of a defended application during the initial period, many trustees will prefer to wait for this statutory period to elapse before making the application. It is, however, arguable that this statutory presumption that the property is to be sold after the end of the 12 months infringes article 8 (and article 1 of the First Protocol) of the European Convention on Human Rights.[28]

49.20 The Insolvency Act 1986, therefore, allows for the enforcement of the interests of creditors to be delayed, but not indefinitely. The statutory period of 12 months will, in most cases, allow a breathing space for the third party to seek alternative accommodation. However, the Insolvency Act 1986, in effect, does allow this period to be exceeded where there are 'exceptional circumstances'. The fact that innocent third parties will be made homeless is not such an 'exceptional circumstance' as to prevent a sale being ordered.[29] In *Re Citro*,[30] it was held, by a majority, that the interests of the creditors will usually prevail over the interests of a spouse and children, and that more than the ordinary consequences of debt and improvidence would be necessary before the court would be able to postpone sale for a substantial period.

49.21 Where relevant, it is important to emphasise the personal circumstances of the debtor's family, including, for example, the effect on the children's education, particularly if they are shortly to take examinations. If this is the case, it may be possible to have the order for possession postponed until after the examination date.[31] In cases where there is severe ill health it may be possible to argue that this is an exceptional circumstance such as to enable the court to delay sale

---

27 Insolvency Act 1986 s335A(3).

28 *Jackson v Bell* [2001] EWCA Civ 387; [2001] BPIR 612 and *Barca v Mears* [2004] EWHC 2170; [2005] 2 FLR 1. See also 'Trusts of land, bankruptcy and human rights' [2005] Conv 161.

29 *Re Lowrie* [1981] 3 All ER 353.

30 [1991] Ch 142; [1990] 3 WLR 880, CA. Cf *Re Holliday* [1981] Ch 405; [1981] 2 WLR 996.

31 See generally D Brown, 'Insolvency and the matrimonial home – the sins of the fathers: *In re Citro (A Bankrupt)*' (1992) 55 MLR 284.

of the property until either death of the family member or his or her departure from the home.[32]

49.22   It follows that advisers are often left with little scope for manoeuvre when advising the bankrupt or other occupiers affected by the bankruptcy. It is, however, worth arguing that it is open to the trustee to apply under the Insolvency Act 1986 s313 for a charging order over property in favour of the bankrupt's estate. If made, then such a charging order becomes subject to the Charging Orders Act 1979 s3, and the court will have the power to impose conditions as to when the charge becomes enforceable. In addition, the bankrupt may be allowed to remain living in the property notwithstanding the bankruptcy, conditionally on him or her making payments towards the mortgage and the other outgoings. The bankrupt would not, however, by virtue of this acquire any interest in the property.[33]

49.23   A joint owner who remains in the property following the date of the other owner's bankruptcy is entitled to be repaid (out of the bankrupt's share) for half of the mortgage payments made by him or her but this sum must be set off against an 'occupation rent' in favour of the bankrupt's trustee.[34]

49.24   With effect from 1 April 2004, where the property which vests in the trustee was the home of the bankrupt or his or her spouse or previous spouse, the trustee has three years from the date of bankruptcy to start an action to realise the interest by sale or the property automatically revests in the bankrupt.[35] During that period the trustee must either realise the interest or apply for an order for sale or possession to avoid the revesting in the bankrupt. These provisions apply to pre-commencement bankruptcies resulting in automatic revesting of the bankrupt's interest in the bankrupt unless the trustee took one of the steps mentioned above to avoid reverting by 1 April 2007.[36]

---

32   See *Re Bremner (A Bankrupt)* [1999] 1 FLR 912, ChD and *Claughton v Charalambous* [1999] 1 FLR 740; [1998] BPIR 558, ChD. See also *In the matter of Haghighat (a bankrupt) sub nom Brittain (Trustee of the property of the bankrupt) v Haghighat* [2009] EWHC (Ch) Case no 189 of 2002. Cf *Nicholls v Lan* [2006] EWHC 1255 (Ch).

33   Insolvency Act 1986 s338.

34   *Re Byford; Byford v Butler* [2003] EWHC 1267 (Ch); [2004] 1 FLR 56. See also H Conway, 'Co-ownership, equitable accounting and the trustee in bankruptcy' [2003] Conv 533.

35   Insolvency Act 1986 s283A, inserted by Enterprise Act 2004 s261(1) and Enterprise Act 2004 (Commencement No 4 and Transitional Provisions & Savings) Order 2003 SI No 2093.

36   Enterprise Act 2004 s261(8). See also M P Thompson, 'A bankrupt home for a spouse' [2004] Conv 255.

49.25 The court must also dismiss a trustee's application for sale or possession where the net value of the bankrupt's interest in the property is below an amount prescribed in secondary legislation,[37] currently £1,000.[38] The value of the bankrupt's interest is calculated after deducting the value of any loans secured by mortgage or any other third party interests and the reasonable costs of sale.[39]

49.26 The procedure for applying for an order for sale is as set out above dealing with charging orders in the text (see para 49.10).

49.27 When ordering sale, the court has the power to impose conditions on the sale, including a requirement to reimburse the joint beneficial owner who has paid the instalments to a mortgage lender (so preventing earlier eviction and the sale of the property) to recompense him or her for the increase in the house value during the period in which he or she has repaid the loan.[40]

---

37 Insolvency Act 1986 s313A, inserted by Enterprise Act 2004 s261 and Enterprise Act 2004 (Commencement No 4 and Transitional Provisions and Savings) Order 2003 SI No 2093.

38 Insolvency Proceedings (Monetary Limits) (Amendment) Order 2004 SI No 547 art 2.

39 2004 SI No 547 art 3.

40 *McMahon's Trustee v McMahon* 1997 SLT 1090, CtS.

APPENDICES

Statutory notices and forms[1]

This section contains the following notices and forms:

1 Notice of seeking possession of a secure tenancy
2 Notice requiring possession of a property let on a periodic assured shorthold tenancy
3 Notice seeking possession of a property let on an assured tenancy
4 Notice to quit
5 Notice under Mortgage Repossessions (Protection of Tenants etc) Act 2010

---

1 Forms 1–4 are reproduced for illustrative purposes only by kind permission of The Solicitors' Law Stationery Society Limited. Forms can be obtained from www. oyezformslink.co.uk.

1 Notice of seeking possession of a secure tenancy

Secure Tenancies (Notices) Regulations 1987,
Schedule, Part I as amended.

This Notice is the first step towards requiring you to give up possession of your dwelling. You should read it very carefully.

HOUSING ACT 1985

Section 83

Notice of Seeking Possession

(1) Name(s) of
Secure Tenant(s).

1. To (1)

If you need advice about this Notice, and what you should do about it, take it as quickly as possible to a Citizens' Advice Bureau, a Housing Aid Centre, or a Law Centre, or to a Solicitor. You may be able to receive Legal Aid but this will depend on your personal circumstances.

(2) Insert name.

2. The landlord (2)
intends to apply to the Court for an Order requiring you to give up possession of:

(3) Address of
property.

(3)

If you are a secure tenant under the Housing Act 1985, you can only be required to leave your dwelling if your landlord obtains an order for possession from the Court. The order must be based on one of the Grounds which are set out in the 1985 Act (see paragraphs 3 and 4 below).

If you are willing to give up possession without a Court order, you should notify the person who signed this Notice as soon as possible and say when you would leave.

(4) Give the text
in full of each Ground
which is being
relied on.

3. Possession will be sought on Ground(s)
of Schedule 2 to the Housing Act 1985 which read(s) (4):

Whatever Grounds for possession are set out in paragraph 3 of this Notice, the Court may allow any of the other Grounds to be added at a later stage. If this is done, you will be told about it so you can argue at the hearing in Court about the new Ground, as well as the Grounds set out in paragraph 3, if you want to.

[P.T.O.

HA1/1

(5) Give a full explanation of why each Ground is being relied upon.

4. Particulars of each Ground are as follows (5):

Before the Court will grant an order on any of the Grounds 1 to 8 or 12 to 16, it must be satisfied that it is reasonable to require you to leave. This means that, if one of these Grounds is set out in paragraph 3 of this Notice, you will be able to argue at the hearing in Court that it is not reasonable that you should have to leave, even if you accept that the Ground applies.

Before the Court grants an order on any of the Grounds 9 to 16, it must be satisfied that there will be suitable alternative accommodation for you when you have to leave. This means that the Court will have to decide that, in its opinion, there will be other accommodation which is reasonably suitable for the needs of you and your family, taking into particular account various factors such as the nearness of your place of work, and the sort of housing that other people with similar needs are offered. Your new home will have to be let to you on another secure tenancy or a private tenancy under the Rent Act of a kind that will give you similar security. **There is no requirement for suitable alternative accommodation where Grounds 1 to 8 apply.**

If your landlord is not a local authority, and the local authority gives a certificate that it will provide you with suitable accommodation, the Court has to accept the certificate.

One of the requirements of Ground 10A is that the landlord must have approval for the redevelopment scheme from the Secretary of State (or, in the case of a landlord of a property in England which is a private registered provider of social housing, from the Regulator of Social Housing). The landlord must have consulted all secure tenants affected by the proposed redevelopment scheme.

[P.T.O.

HA1/2

(6) Cross out this paragraph if possession is being sought on Ground 2 of Schedule 2 to the Housing Act 1985 (whether or not possession is also sought on another Ground)

5.   (6) **The court proceedings for possession will not be begun until after** (7)

- Court proceedings cannot be begun until after this date, which cannot be earlier than the date when your tenancy or licence could have been brought to an end. This means that if you have a weekly or fortnightly tenancy, there should be at least 4 weeks between the date this Notice is given and the date in this paragraph.

(7) Give the date after which Court proceedings can be brought.

- After this date, Court proceedings may be begun at once or at any time during the following twelve months. Once the twelve months are up this Notice will lapse and a new Notice must be served before possession can be sought.

(8) Cross out this paragraph if possession is not being sought on Ground 2 of Schedule 2 to the Housing Act 1985

5.   (8) **Court proceedings for possession of the dwelling-house can be begun immediately. The date by which the tenant is to give up possession of the dwelling-house is** (9)

(9) Give the date by which the tenant is to give up possession of the dwelling-house.

- Court proceedings may be begun at once or at any time during the following twelve months. Once the twelve months are up this Notice will lapse and a new Notice must be served before possession can be sought.

- Possession of your dwelling-house cannot be obtained until after this date, which cannot be earlier than the date when your tenancy or licence could have been brought to an end. This means that if you have a weekly or fortnightly tenancy, there should be at least 4 weeks between the date this Notice is given and the date possession is ordered.

Signed

On behalf of

Address

Tel No.

Date 1st August 2010

HA1/3

2 Notice requiring possession of a property let on a periodic assured shorthold tenancy

HOUSING ACT 1988
Section 21(4)(a)

Assured Shorthold Tenancy : Notice Requiring Possession: Periodic Tenancy
(Note 1)

(1) Name and address of tenant.

To(¹)

of

(2) Name and address of landlord (Note 2 overleaf).

From(²)

of

(3) Address of dwelling.

I give you notice that I require possession of the dwelling-house known as(³)

(4) Date of expiry (Note 3 overleaf).

after(⁴)   or, if later, the day on which a complete period of your tenancy expires next after the end of two months from the service of this notice

(5) Note 3 overleaf.

Dated(⁵) 1st August 2010

Landlord

(6) Name and address.

[Landlord's agent](⁶)

[P.T.O.

© 2001 Oyez 7 Spa Road, London SE16 3QQ.
Tel 020 7556 3200

8.2002
downloaded from www.formalink.co.uk

HA 21A

HA21A/1

NOTES

1. Where an assured shorthold tenancy has become a periodic tenancy, a court must make an order for possession if the landlord has given proper notice in this form.

2. Where there are joint landlords, at least one of them must give this notice.

3. The date specified must be:
   (a) the last day of a period of the tenancy;
   (b) at least two months after this notice is given; and
   (c) no sooner than the earliest day on which the tenancy could ordinarily be brought to an end by a notice to quit.

HA21A/2

Note: This is an *example* of a notice under Housing Act 1988 s21; the above notes on the form are not obligatory and there is no prescribed form which must be used.

3 Notice seeking possession of a property let on an assured tenancy

OYEZ Form No. 3 of the Assured Tenancies and Agricultural Occupancies (Forms) Regulations 1997

HOUSING ACT 1988

Section 8 as amended by Section 151 of the Housing Act 1996

Notice Seeking Possession of a Property Let on an Assured Tenancy or an Assured Agricultural Occupancy

- Please write clearly in black ink.
- Please tick boxes where appropriate and cross out text marked with an asterisk (*) that does not apply.
- This form should be used where possession of accommodation let under an assured tenancy, an assured agricultural occupancy or an assured shorthold tenancy is sought on one of the grounds in Schedule 2 to the Housing Act 1988.
- Do not use this form if possession is sought on the "shorthold" ground under section 21 of the Housing Act 1988 from an assured shorthold tenant where the fixed term has come to an end or, for assured shorthold tenancies with no fixed term which started on or after 28th February 1997, after six months has elapsed. There is no prescribed form for these cases, but you must give notice in writing.

(1) Name(s) of tenant(s)/ licensee(s).

1. To (¹):

(2) Address of premises.

2. Your landlord/licensor* intends to apply to the court for an order requiring you to give up possession of (²):

(3) Give the full text (as set out in the Housing Act 1988 as amended by the Housing Act 1996) of each ground which is being relied on. Continue on a separate sheet if necessary.

3. Your landlord/licensor* intends to seek possession on ground(s) in Schedule 2 to the Housing Act 1988, as amended by the Housing Act 1996, which read(s) (³):

(4) Continue on a separate sheet if necessary.

4. Give a full explanation of why each ground is being relied on (⁴):

Notes on the grounds for possession:

- If the court is satisfied that any of grounds 1 to 8 is established, it must make an order (but see below in respect of fixed term tenancies).
- Before the court will grant an order on any of grounds 9 to 17, it must be satisfied that it is reasonable to require you to leave. This means that, if one of these grounds is set out in section 3, you will be able to suggest to the court that it is not reasonable that you should have to leave, even if you accept that the ground applies.
- The court will not make an order under grounds 1, 3 to 7, 9 or 16, to take effect during the fixed term of the tenancy (if there is one) and it will only make an order during the fixed term on grounds 2, 8, 10 to 15 or 17 if the terms of the tenancy make provision for it to be brought to an end on any of these grounds.
- Where the court makes an order for possession solely on ground 6 or 9, the landlord must pay your reasonable removal expenses.

[P.T.O.
HA 32/1

(5) Give the earliest date on which court proceedings can be brought.

5. The court proceedings will not begin until after([9]):

- Where the landlord is seeking possession on grounds 1, 2, 5 to 7, 9 or 16, court proceedings cannot begin earlier than 2 months from the date this notice is served on you (even where one of the grounds 3, 4, 8, 10 to 13, 14A, 15 or 17 is specified) and not before the date on which the tenancy (had it not been assured) could have been brought to an end by a notice to quit served at the same time as this notice.

- Where the landlord is seeking possession on grounds 3, 4, 8, 10 to 13, 14A, 15, or 17, court proceedings cannot begin earlier than 2 weeks from the date this notice is served (unless one of grounds 1, 2, 5 to 7, 9 or 16 is also specified in which case they cannot begin earlier than two months from the date this notice is served).

- Where the landlord is seeking possession on ground 14 (with or without other grounds), court proceedings cannot begin before the date this notice is served.

- Where the landlord is seeking possession on ground 14A, court proceedings cannot begin unless the landlord has served, or has taken all reasonable steps to serve, a copy of this notice on the partner who has left the property.

- After the date shown in section 5, court proceedings may be begun at once but not later than 12 months from the date on which this notice is served. After this time the notice will lapse and a new notice must be served before possession can be sought.

6. Name and address of landlord/licensor*.

To be signed and dated by the landlord or licensor or his agent (someone acting for him). If there are joint landlords each landlord or the agent must sign unless one signs on behalf of the rest with their agreement.

Signed: Date:

Please specify whether: landlord ☐   licensor ☐   joint landlords ☐   landlord's agent ☐

Name(s): (BLOCK CAPITALS)

Address

Telephone: Daytime: Evening:

What to do if this notice is served on you.

- This notice is the first step requiring you to give up possession of your home. You should read it very carefully.

- Your landlord cannot make you leave your home without an order for possession issued by a court. By issuing this notice your landlord is informing you that he intends to seek such an order. If you are willing to give up possession without a court order, you should tell the person who signed this notice as soon as possible and say when you are prepared to leave.

- Whichever grounds are set out in section 3 of this form the court may allow any of the other grounds to be added at a later date. If this is done, you will be told about it so you can discuss the additional grounds at the court hearing as well as the grounds set out in section 3.

- If you need advice about this notice, and what you should do about it, take it immediately to a citizens' advice bureau, a housing advice centre, a law centre or a solicitor.

HA 32   HA 32/2

4 Notice to quit

NOTICE TO QUIT

(BY LANDLORD OF PREMISES LET AS A DWELLING)

Name and
Address of
Tenant.

To

of

Name and
Address of
Landlord.

[I] [We] [as] [on behalf of] your landlord[s],

of

*Me/them or as
appropriate.

give you **NOTICE TO QUIT** and deliver up possession to*

†Address of
premises.

of†

‡ Date for
possession.

on‡   , or the day on which a complete period of your

tenancy expires next after the end of four weeks from the service of this notice.

Date of notice.

Dated

Signed

Name and
Address of
Agent if Agent
serves notice.

INFORMATION FOR TENANT

(See Note 2 overleaf)

1.   If the tenant or licensee does not leave the dwelling, the landlord or licensor must get an order for possession from the court before the tenant or licensee can lawfully be evicted. The landlord or licensor cannot apply for such an order before the notice to quit or notice to determine has run out.

2.   A tenant or licensee who does not know if he has any right to remain in possession after a notice to quit or a notice to determine runs out can obtain advice from a solicitor. Help with all or part of the cost of legal advice and assistance may be available under the Legal Aid Scheme. He should also be able to obtain information from a Citizens' Advice Bureau, a Housing Aid Centre or a Rent Officer.

[P.T.O.

Oyez 7 Spa Road, London SE16 3QQ
© Crown copyright.

5.1999 MM
L&T61/1

Landlord and Tenant 61

NOTES

1. Notice to quit premises let as a dwelling must be given at least four weeks before it takes effect, and it must be in writing (Protection from Eviction Act 1977, s. 5 as amended).

2. Where a notice to quit is given by a landlord to determine a tenancy of any premises let as a dwelling, the notice must contain this information (The Notices to Quit etc. (Prescribed Information) Regulations 1988).

3. Some tenancies are excluded from this protection: see Protection from Eviction Act 1977, ss. 3A and 5(1B).

L&T61/2

5 Notice under Mortgage Repossessions (Protection of Tenants etc) Act 2010[1]

Notice that your home is at risk
If you are paying rent to live in this property, please read the following carefully.
If you are an owner occupier, please seek advice on your
position as different rules apply

This notice is given under Section 2(4) of the Mortgage Repossessions (Protection of Tenants etc) Act 2010.

I give you notice that the Lender/the Lender's Agent has applied/will apply (delete as appropriate) to the court for a warrant for possession against this property on:......................................

(Insert the date on which the application for the warrant for possession was made or will be made. The order will only be executed after the end of the 14 day prescribed period.)

At:..

Tel:...

Address:...
....
(Insert the name, address and telephone number of the court at which the application has been or will be made.)

1. This notice advises you that **you could be evicted from your home.** For tenants, be advised that your landlord's Lender has obtained an order for possession against the property. It is now seeking to enforce that order through the courts. Please read this notice carefully. If you need advice you should contact any of the following:

—a Citizens' Advice Bureau;
—a housing advice organisation, or charity such as Shelter;
—a housing aid centre;
—a Law Centre;
—a solicitor.

2. The law gives certain tenants the right to apply to the Lender to ask it not to enforce the order for a period of two months. You should contact the Lender or its Agent on the number given to ask for this delay if you require it. This is to give you time to find somewhere else to live. If you are unsure whether you may qualify, you should seek advice immediately from one of the organisations listed, or a similar organisation. If the Lender agrees to your request, they must confirm this to you in writing. If the Lender refuses your request, or if you receive no reply, you may be able to make an application to court for a similar delay. The Lender may make any agreement with you conditional on you continuing to pay to live at the property. An application to the Lender or to the court should be accompanied by any evidence you have to prove the existence of your tenancy.

3. This notice is not directed at owner occupiers. If you pay a mortgage to live at the property, you should urgently seek advice on your position as you have different rights.

4. If you do not ask for a delay, the Lender can go ahead to obtain possession of this property. Although the warrant for possession cannot be executed earlier than 14 days after the date on which the Lender sent you this notice **you must act quickly if you are seeking the delay, otherwise you may run out of time.**

1   © Crown Copyright. This form can be found in the Schedule to the Dwelling Houses (Execution of Possesssion Orders by Mortgagees) Regulations 2010 SI No 1809.

Served on:...
(Insert address of the property. Address to: "Tenant/Occupier" or name of tenant(s) if
known).

Served by::...("the
Lender")

Tel:..

Address:...
....
....
(Insert full name of Lender, telephone number and address where enquiries about this notice
can be made.)

If served by Lender's Agent:

Served on:...
(Insert address of the property. Address to: "Tenant/Occupier" or name of tenant(s) if
known).

Served by:...("the Lender's
Agent")

On behalf of:...("the Lender")

Tel:..

Address:...
....
....
(Insert full name of Lender's Agent, telephone number and address where enquiries about
this notice can be made.)

Signed.. Date......................................

To be signed and dated by the Lender or the Lender's Agent

Statements of case and applications

This section contains the following statements of case and application:

1 Claim form for possession of property (form N5)
2 Particulars of Claim for rented residential premises (form N119)
3 Defence form for rented residential premises (form N11R) with additional defence form
4 Particulars of Claim for mortgaged residential premises (form N120)
5 Defence form for mortgaged residential premises (form N11M) with additional defence form
6 Application notice (form N244) to set possession order aside
7 Witness statement in support of application to set possession order aside
8 Application notice (form N244) to suspend warrant for possession
9 Witness statement in support of application to suspend warrant
10 Order for possession with no date fixed (form N28A)
11 Order adjourning on terms

1 Claim form for possession of property (form N5)

Claim form for possession of property	In the Anytown County Court
	Claim No.	AN10 09601

SEAL

Claimant
(name(s) and address(es))

Rainbow District Council
Town Hall
Anytown AN1 1DA

Defendant(s)
(name(s) and address(es))

Wayne Ross
32 Small Street
Anytown AN1 7DG

The claimant is claiming possession of :

32 Small Street
Anytown AN1 7DG

which (includes) (~~does not include~~) residential property. Full particulars of the claim are attached.
(The claimant is also making a claim for money).

This claim will be heard on: 21 July   20 10 at   am/~~pm~~

at Anytown County Court, Castle Street, Anytown AN1 2GH

At the hearing
• The court will consider whether or not you must leave the property and, if so, when.
• It will take into account information the claimant provides and any you provide.

What you should do
• Get help and advice immediately from a solicitor or an advice agency.
• Help yourself and the court by **filling in the defence form** and **coming to the hearing** to make sure the court knows all the facts.

Defendant's name and address for service	Wayne Ross 32 Small Street Anytown AN1 7DG		
		Court fee	£ 100.00
		Solicitor's costs	£ 69.50
		Total amount	£ 169.50
		Issue date	12 June 2010

N5 Claim form for possession of property (08.05)   HMCS

Claim No.	AN10 09601

Grounds for possession

The claim for possession is made on the following ground(s):

- ☑ rent arrears
- ☐ other breach of tenancy
- ☐ forfeiture of the lease
- ☐ mortgage arrears
- ☐ other breach of the mortgage
- ☐ trespass
- ☐ other *(please specify)* _____

Anti-social behaviour

The claimant is alleging:

- ☐ actual or threatened anti-social behaviour
- ☐ actual or threatened use of the property for unlawful purposes

Is the claimant claiming demotion of tenancy? ☐ Yes ☑ No

Is the claimant claiming an order suspending the right to buy? ☐ Yes ☑ No

See full details in the attached particulars of claim

Does, or will, the claim include any issues under the Human Rights Act 1998? ☐ Yes ☑ No

Statement of Truth

*~~(I believe)~~(The claimant believes) that the facts stated in this claim form are true.
* I am duly authorised by the claimant to sign this statement.

signed _____ date 6 June 2010 _____

*~~(Claimant)(Litigation friend~~ *(where the claimant is a child or a patient)*)(Claimant's solicitor)
**delete as appropriate*

Full name John Smith

Name of claimant's solicitor's firm Legal Services, Rainbow District Council

position or office held Head of Legal Services
(if signing on behalf of firm or company)

Claimant's or claimant's solicitor's address to which documents or payments should be sent if different from overleaf.

John Smith
Legal Services
Rainbow District Council
Town Hall
Anytown

Postcode AN1 1DA

if applicable

Ref. no.	
fax no.	
DX no.	
e-mail	
Tel. no.	

2   Particulars of Claim for rented residential premises (form N119)

Particulars of claim **for possession** (rented residential premises)	Name of court Anytown County Court	Claim No. AN10 09601
	Name of Claimant Rainbow District Council	
	Name of Defendant Wayne Ross	

1. The claimant has a right to possession of:

   32 Small Street Anytown AN1 7DG

2. To the best of the claimant's knowledge the following persons are in possession of the property:

   The Defendant, his wife Ann Ross and their children.

About the tenancy

3. (a) The premises are let to the defendant(s) under a(n) secure   tenancy which began on 7 July 2008

   (b) The current rent is £98   and is payable each (week) (fortnight) (month). (other   )

   (c) Any unpaid rent or charge for use and occupation should be calculated at £ 13.96   per day.

4. The reason the claimant is asking for possession is:

   (a) because the defendant has not paid the rent due under the terms of the tenancy agreement. *(Details are set out below)(Details are shown on the attached rent statement)*
   Rent Arrears at 7 November 2009 - £912.62
   Rent Arrears at 6 March 2010 - £1103.16

   (b) because the defendant has failed to comply with other terms of the tenancy. *Details are set out below.*

   (c) because: (including any (other) statutory grounds)

N119 Particulars of claim for possession (rented residential premises) (08.05)   HMCS

5. The following steps have already been taken to recover any arrears:
   Repeated correspondence with the Defendant and a Home Visit

6. The appropriate (~~notice to quit~~) (~~notice of breach of lease~~) (notice seeking possession) (~~notice seeking a demotion order~~) (*other.* ~~ ~~) was served on the defendant on 8 Novembr 20 09 .

About the defendant

7. The following information is known about the defendant's circumstances:
   The Defendant is believed to be working and in receipt of tax credit.

About the claimant

8. The claimant is asking the court to take the following financial or other information into account when making its decision whether or not to grant an order for possession:
   The Claimant is a local authority responsible for the management of its housing stock upon which there are considerable demands. There are 11,500 families awaiting accommodation and identified as living in housing need.

Forfeiture

9. (a) There is no underlessee or mortgagee entitled to claim relief against forfeiture.

   ~~or (b)~~   ~~of~~

   ~~is entitled to claim relief against forfeiture as underlessee or mortgagee.~~

What the court is being asked to do:

10. The claimant asks the court to order that the defendant(s):

    (a) give the claimant possession of the premises;

    (b) pay the unpaid rent and any charge for use and occupation up to the date an order is made;

    (c) pay rent and any charge for use and occupation from the date of the order until the claimant recovers possession of the property;

    (d) pay the claimant's costs of making this claim.

11. In the alternative to possession, is the claimant asking the court to make a demotion order or an order suspending the right to buy?

    ☐ Yes   ☑ No

Demotion/Suspension claim
This section must be completed if the claim includes a claim for demotion of tenancy or suspension order in the alternative to possession

12. The (demotion) (suspension) claim is made under:

    ☐ section 82A(2) of the Housing Act 1985

    ☐ section 6A(2) of the Housing Act 1988

    ☐ section 121A of the Housing Act 1985

13. The claimant is a:

    ☑ local authority   ☐ housing action trust

    ☐ registered social landlord   ☐ other please specify (suspension claims only)

    [   ]

(Demotion claims only)
14. Has the claimant served on the tenant a statement of express terms of the tenancy which are to apply to the demoted tenancy?

    ☐ Yes   ☐ No

    If Yes, please give details:

15. The claimant is claiming delete as appropriate (demotion of tenancy) (and) (an order suspending the right to buy) because: *State details of the conduct alleged and **any** other matters relied upon.*

Statement of Truth

*(I believe)(The claimant believes) that the facts stated in these particulars of claim are true.
* I am duly authorised by the claimant to sign this statement.

signed _____ date 9 June 2010 _____

*(Claimant)(Litigation friend(where claimant is a child or a patient))(Claimant's solicitor)
*delete as appropriate

Full name John Smith _____

Name of claimant's solicitor's firm Legal Services, Rainbow District Council _____

position or office held Head of Legal Services _____
              (if signing on behalf of firm or company)

3 Defence form for rented residential premises (form N11R) with additional defence form

Defence form
(rented residential premises)

Name of court	Claim No.
Anytown County Court	An10 09601

Name of Claimant
Rainbow District Council

Name of Defendant
Wayne Ross

Date of hearing
21 July 2010

Personal details

1. Please give your:

    Title ☑Mr ☐Mrs ☐Miss ☐Ms ☐Other Wayne

    First name(s) in full
    Wayne

    Last name
    Ross

    Date of birth 2 7 1 0 1 9 7 5

    Address *(if different from the address on the claim form)*

    Postcode

Disputing the claim

2. Do you agree with what is said about the premises and the tenancy agreement?   ☑Yes   ☐No

    If No, set out your reasons below:

    Did you receive the notice from the claimant referred to at paragraph 6 of the particulars of claim?   ☐Yes   ☑No

3. If Yes, when: _____

N11R Defence form (rented residential premises) (04.06)   HMCS

4. Do you agree that there are arrears of rent as stated in the particulars of claim? ☐ Yes ☑ No

If No, state how much the arrears are: £_____ ☑ None

5. If the particulars of claim give any reasons for possession other than rent arrears, do you agree with what is said? ☐ Yes ☐ No

If No, give details below:

6. Do you have a money or other claim (a counterclaim) against your landlord? ☑ Yes ☐ No

If Yes, give details:

Arrears

7. Have you paid any money to your landlord since the claim was issued? ☐ Yes ☑ No

If Yes, state how much you have paid and when: £_____ date_____

8. Have you come to any agreement with your landlord about repaying the arrears since the claim was issued? ☐ Yes ☑ No

I have agreed to pay £_____ each (week)(month)

9. If you have not reached an agreement with your landlord, do you want the court to consider allowing you to pay the arrears by instalments? ☑ Yes ☐ No

10. How much can you afford to pay in addition to the current rent? £ 3.10_____ per (week)(month)

About yourself

State benefits

11. Are you receiving Income Support? ☑ Yes   ☐ No

12. Have you applied for Income Support? ☐ Yes   ☑ No

If Yes, when did you apply?   _____

13. Are you receiving housing benefit? ☐ Yes   ☑ No

If Yes, how much are you receiving?   £_____ per (week)(month)

14. Have you applied for housing benefit? ☐ Yes   ☑ No

If Yes, when did you apply?   _____

15. Is the housing benefit paid   ☐ to you   ☐ to your landlord

Dependants *(people you look after financially)*

16. Have you any dependant children? ☑ Yes   ☐ No

If Yes, give the number in each age group below:

[2] under 11   [ ] 11-15   [ ] 16-17   [ ] 18 and over

Other dependants

17. Give details of any other dependants for whom you are
financially responsible:

Other residents

18. Give details of any other people living at the premises for
whom you are not financially responsible:

Money you receive

		Weekly	Monthly
19. Usual take-home pay or income if self-employed *including overtime, commission, bonuses*	£_____	☐	☐
Job Seekers allowance	£_____	☐	☐
Pension	£_____	☐	☐
Child benefit	£ 33.70	☑	☐
Other benefits and allowances	£ 160.32	☑	☐
Others living in my home give me	£_____	☐	☐
I am paid maintenance for myself (or children) of	£_____	☐	☐
Other income	£_____	☐	☐
Total income	£ 194.02	☐	☐

Bank accounts and savings

20. Do you have a current bank or building society account?   ☑ Yes   ☐ No

If Yes, is it

  ☐ in credit? If so, by how much?   £_____

  ☑ overdrawn? If so, by how much? £ 250.00

21. Do you have a savings or deposit account?   ☐ Yes   ☑ No

If Yes, what is the balance?   £_____

Money you pay out

22. Do you have to pay any court orders or fines?

Court	Claim/Case number	Balance owing	Instalments paid
Antown Magistrates	ATN 01611	£870.00	£20.00

		Total Instalments paid £20.00	per month

23. Give details if you are in arrears with any of the court payments or fines:

Not applicable

24. Do you have any loan or credit debts?   ☐ Yes   ☑ No

Loan/credit from	Balance owing	Instalments paid
	Total Instalments £	per month

25. Give details if you are in arrears with any loan / credit repayments:

Regular expenses

(Do not include any payments made by other members of the household out of their own income)

26. What regular expenses do you have?

(List below)

		Weekly	Monthly
Council tax	£15.00	☑	☐
Gas	£ 30.00	☑	☐
Electricity	£ 30.00	☑	☐
Water charges	£ 10.00	☑	☐
TV rental & licence	£ 12.00	☑	☐
Telephone	£ 25.00	☑	☐
Credit repayments	£	☐	☐
Mail order	£	☐	☐
Housekeeping, food, school meals	£ 60.00	☑	☐
Travelling expenses	£ 20.00	☑	☐
Clothing	£ 5.00	☑	☐
Maintenance payments	£	☐	☐
Other	£	☐	☐
Total expenses	£ 207.00	☑	☐

Priority debts

27. This section is for **arrears** only. **Do not** include regular expenses listed at Question 26.

		Weekly	Monthly
Council tax arrears	£_____	☐	☐
Water charges arrears	£_____	☐	☐
Gas account	£_____	☐	☐
Electricity account	£_____	☐	☐
Maintenance arrears	£_____	☐	☐
Others *(give details below)*			
	£ 20.00	☐	☑
	£_____	☐	☐
	£_____	☐	☐

28. If an order for possession were to be made, would you have somewhere else to live?   ☐ Yes   ☑ No

If Yes, say when you would be able to move in: _____

29. Give details of any events or circumstances which have led to your being in arrears of rent *(for example divorce, separation, redundancy, bereavement, illness, bankruptcy)* or any other particular circumstances affecting your case. If there are any reasons why the date any possession order takes effect should be delayed, give them here. If you believe you would suffer exceptional hardship by being ordered to leave the property immediately, say why.

See attached additional defence form.

You need only answer question 30 if the claim form includes a claim for demotion or suspension of right to buy.

30.   Do you agree with what is said about your conduct or use of   ☐ Yes   ☐ No
        the property?

        If No, set out your reasons below:

Statement of Truth

*(I believe)(~~The defendant(s) believe(s)~~) that the facts stated in this defence form are true.
* I am duly authorised by the defendant(s) to sign this statement.

signed_____   date _18 July 2010_____

*(Defendant)(~~litigation friend~~ *(where defendant is a child or a patient)*)(~~Defendant's solicitor~~)

delete as appropriate

Full name Wayne Ross_____

Name of defendant's solicitor's firm _Rainbow Law Centre_____

position or office held _____
                          (if signing on behalf of firm or company)

IN THE ANYTOWN COUNTY COURT   CASE NO: AN10 09601

BETWEEN

RAINBOW DISTRICT COUNCIL   Claimant

and

WAYNE ROSS   Defendant

ADDITIONAL DEFENCE FORM

---

1. This Additional Defence Form is filed to supplement the Defence Form filed in this action by the Defendant.

2. The Defendant admits that he occupies 32 Small Street Anytown ('the property') with his family under a secure tenancy within the meaning of the Housing Act 1985. The Defendant denies that the Claimant is entitled to termination of that tenancy and possession of the property as claimed.

3. The Defendant denies being served with the Notice Seeking Possession referred to at paragraph 6 of the Particulars of Claim.

4. The Defendant admits that he has failed to make some rent payments as they have fallen due but is not able to comment on the level of underpayment. The Claimant is put to strict proof as to the level of any rent underpayments. The Defendant asserts that in any event he is entitled to set off against any rent otherwise due the sums Counterclaimed as set out below.

5. In the alternative the Defendant claims the protection of Housing Act 1985 Section 84 and denies that in all the circumstances it would be reasonable for an Order for Possession to be made.

COUNTERCLAIM

---

6. The Defendant repeats paragraphs 1 to 5 above.

7. The Defendant is entitled to the benefit of the repairing covenant implied by Landlord and Tenant Act 1985 Section 11 in respect of which the Claimant is in breach. Further and in the alternative the Claimant is in breach of the express repairing obligations set out in paragraph 5 of the Tenancy Agreement.

8. In breach of these covenants the Claimant has since in or about January 2003 failed to keep the property in repair.

PARTICULARS OF DISREPAIR

(i)   Roof leak to main roof
(ii) Rot to kitchen windowsill
(iii) Defective pointing to front wall
[........ *Set out the detail of the other defects complained about*]

9. The Claimant has had notice of these defects by reason of numerous verbal

complaints to its employees since January 2003, a complaint made to the Local Government Ombudsman by the Defendant in October 2004 and by visits by various employees of the Claimant on various dates.

10. Because of the breaches of covenant the Defendant has suffered loss, damage, injury and inconvenience.

PARTICULARS

(i)   Due to damp penetration the Defendant has been unable to use the first floor rear bedroom since March 2003.

(ii) Decorations have been ruined in the front first floor bedroom because of damp penetration with the result that the Defendant has spent £750 on decorating materials.

(iii) By reason of the dampness the Defendant spent additional sums on heating which he estimates at £500 for each Winter quarter.

(iv) The Defendant's wife has been depressed and a strain has been placed on their marriage.

[*Set out the detail of other consequences of the defects complained about*]

11. Further and in the alternative the Claimant is in breach of the Defective Premises Act 1972 Section 4.

PARTICULARS OF BREACH OF DUTY

---

12. The Defendant repeats the Particulars set out in paragraph 10 above.

13. The Defendant claims interest pursuant to County Courts Act 1984 Section 69 at such rate and for such period as the Court will allow.

14. The Defendant Counterclaims for:

(1) Damages limited to £5000.

(2) A Mandatory Order or Order for specific performance to remedy such of the defects mentioned above as are outstanding at the date of the trial.

(3) Interest pursuant to County Courts Act 1984 Section 69.

(4) Costs.

Dated   18 July 2010

STATEMENT OF TRUTH

I believe that the facts stated in this Defence and Part 20 Counterclaim are true.

W.Ross
....
WAYNE ROSS

c/o Jenny Brown, Rainbow Law Centre, 1 Lavender Close, Anytown

To the Court Manager
And to the Claimant

4 Particulars of Claim for mortgaged residential premises (form N120)

Particulars of claim for possession
(mortgaged residential premises)

In the
Anytown County Court

Claim No.
AN10 09615

Equitable Secured Home Loan Ltd

Claimant

Stephen and Josie Neill

Defendant

1. The claimant has a right to possession of:

    1 Cedar Street Anytown

About the mortgage

2. On 19 February 2008 the claimant(s) and the defendant(s) entered into a mortgage of the above premises.

3. To the best of the claimant's knowledge the following persons are in possession of the property:
    The Defendants

[Delete (a) or (b) as appropriate]

4. (a) The agreement for the loan secured by the mortgage (or at least one of them) is a regulated consumer credit agreement. Notice of default was given to the defendant(s) on 9 December 20 09.

    ~~(b) The agreement for the loan secured by the mortgage is not (or none of them is) a regulated consumer credit agreement.~~

5. The claimant is asking for possession on the following ground(s):

    (a) the defendant(s) ~~(has)~~(have) not paid the agreed repayments of the loan and interest.
    Give details (as required under paragraph 2.5 of Practice Direction accompanying Part 55 of the Civil Procedure Rules):
    The arrears amount to £2100.06. See attached schedule of arrears.

N120 Particulars of claim for possession (mortgaged residential premises)(10.05)

HMCS

(b) because:

6.   (a) The amount loaned was £ 18,000.00

    (b) The current terms of repayment are: *(include any current periodic repayment and any current payment of interest)*

      Monthly payments of £450.00 are payable on the 8th of each month.

    (c) The total amount required to pay the mortgage in full as at 19 June   20 10 (not more than 14 days after the claim was issued) would be £ 21,080.99   taking into account any adjustment for early settlement. This includes £ 750.00   payable for solicitor's costs and administration charges.

    (d) The following additional payments are also required under the terms of the mortgage:

      £   for   [not] included in 6(c)

      £   for   [not] included in 6(c)

      £   for   [not] included in 6(c)

    (e) Of the payments in paragraph 6(d), the following are in arrears:

      arrears of £

      arrears of £

      arrears of £

    [(f) The total amount outstanding under the regulated loan agreement secured by the mortgage is £   ]

    (g) Interest rates which have been applied to the mortgage:

      (i) at the start of the mortgage   8.00 % p.a.

      (ii) immediately before any arrears were accrued   12.00 % p.a.

      (iii) at the start of the claim   12.00 % p.a.

7. The following steps have already been taken to recover the money secured by the mortgage:

Letters sent to the Defendants, telephone calls and a home visit by a debt counsellor.

About the defendant(s)

8. The following information is known about the defendant's circumstances:
(*in particular say whether the defendant(s) (is)(are) in receipt of social security benefits and whether any payments are made directly to the claimant*)

The Defendants are believed to be employed.

[Delete either (a) or (b) as appropriate]

9. (a) There is no one who should be given notice of these proceedings because of a registered interest in the property under section 31(10) of the Family Law Act 1996 or section 2(8) or 8(3) of the Matrimonial Homes Act 1983 or section 2(7) of the Matrimonial Homes Act 1967.

~~(b) Notice of these proceedings will be given to~~ ~~who has a registered~~ ~~interest in the property.~~

Tenancy

[Delete if inappropriate]

~~10.~~ ~~A tenancy was entered into between the mortgagor and the mortgagee on~~
~~A notice was served on~~

What the court is being asked to do

11.   The claimant asks the court to order that the defendant(s):

(a) give the claimant possession of the premises;

(b) pay to the claimant the total amount outstanding under the mortgage.

Statement of Truth

*~~(I believe)~~(The claimant believes) that the facts stated in these particulars of claim are true.
* I am duly authorised by the claimant to sign this statement.

signed_____ date _____
*~~(Claimant)(Litigation friend~~ *~~where claimant is a child or a patient)~~*(Claimant's solicitor)
delete as appropriate

Full name Jayne Osborne_____

Name of claimant's solicitor's firm Mammon & Co _____

position or office held Solicitor_____
                         (if signing on behalf of firm or company)

5 Defence form for mortgaged residential premises (form N11M) with additional defence form

Defence form
(mortgaged residential premises)

Name of court	Claim No.
Anytown County Court	AN10 09615

Name of Claimant
Equitable Secured Home Loan Ltd

Name of Defendant
Stephen and Josie Neill

Date of hearing
21 July 2010

Personal details

1. Please give your:

    Title ☑ Mr ☐ Mrs ☐ Miss ☐ Ms ☐ Other

    First name(s) in full
    Stephen

    Last name
    Neill

    Date of birth | 1 | 8 | 0 | 5 | 1 | 9 | 8 | 5 |

    Address *(if different from the address on the claim form)*

    Postcode

Disputing the claim

2. Do you agree with what is said about the property and the
    mortgage agreement in the particulars of claim? ☑ Yes ☐ No

    If No, set out your reasons below:

3. Do you agree that there are arrears of mortgage repayments as
    stated in the particulars of claim? ☑ Yes ☐ No

    If No, state how much the arrears are: £_____ ☐ None

N11M Defence form (mortgaged residential premises) (04.06)   HMCS

4. If the particulars of claim give any reasons for possession
    other than arrears of mortgage repayments, do you agree with   ☐ Yes   ☐ No
    what is said?

    If No, give details below:

    (Only answer these questions if the loan secured by the mortgage (or part
    of it) is a regulated consumer credit agreement)

5. Do you want the court to consider whether or not the terms of   ☑ Yes   ☐ No
    your original loan agreement are fair?

6. Do you intend to apply to the court for an order changing the   ☑ Yes   ☐ No
    terms of your loan agreement (a time order)?

Arrears

7. Have you paid any money to your mortgage lender since the   ☑ Yes   ☐ No
    claim was issued?

    If Yes, state how much you have paid and when: £ 150.00   date 2 July 2010

8. Have you come to any agreement with your mortgage lender   ☐ Yes   ☑ No
    about repaying the arrears since the claim was issued?

    I have agreed to pay £_____ each (week)(month).

9. If you have not reached an agreement with your mortgage   ☑ Yes   ☐ No
    lender, do you want the court to consider allowing you to pay
    the arrears by instalments?

10. How much can you afford to pay in addition to the current   £ 100.00   per (week)(month)
    instalments?

About yourself

State benefits

11. Are you receiving Income Support? ☐ Yes ☑ No

12. Have you applied for Income Support? ☐ Yes ☑ No

   If Yes, when did you apply? _____

13. Does the Department of Social Security pay your mortgage interest? ☐ Yes ☑ No

Dependants (people you look after financially)

14. Have you any dependant children? ☑ Yes ☐ No

   If Yes, give the number in each age group below:

   [2] under 11   [ ] 11-15   [ ] 16-17   [ ] 18 and over

Other dependants

15. Give details of any other dependants for whom you are financially responsible:

   Josie Neill

Other residents

16. Give details of any other people living at the premises for whom you are not financially responsible:

Money you receive		Weekly	Monthly
17. Usual take-home pay or income if self-employed *including overtime, commission, bonuses*	£ 1,100.00	☐	☑
Job Seekers allowance	£_____	☐	☐
Pension	£_____	☐	☐
Child benefit	£ 146.03	☐	☑
Other benefits and allowances	£_____	☐	☐
Others living in my home give me	£_____	☐	☐
I am paid maintenance for myself (or children) of	£_____	☐	☐
Other income	£_____	☐	☐
Total income	£ 1,246.03	☐	☐

Bank accounts and savings

18. Do you have a current bank or building society account?   ☑ Yes   ☐ No

    If Yes, is it

        ☐ in credit? If so, by how much?   £_____

        ☑ overdrawn? If so, by how much? £ 800.00 ____

19. Do you have a savings or deposit account?   ☐ Yes   ☑ No

    If Yes, what is the balance?   £_____

Money you pay out

20. Do you have to pay any court orders or fines?   ☑ Yes   ☐ No

Court	Claim/Case number	Balance owing	Instalments paid
Anytown Magistrates	ATN 65491	£500	£80

Total instalments paid £80.00   per month

21. Give details if you are in arrears with any of the court payments or fines:

22. Do you have any loan or credit debts?   ☑ Yes   ☐ No

Loan/credit from	Balance owing	Instalments paid
Better Furnishings Ltd	£1300	£100

Total instalments paid £ 100.00   per month

23. Give details if you are in arrears with any loan / credit repayments:

Regular expenses
(Do not include any payments made by other members of the household out of their own income)

24. What regular expenses do you have?
(List below)

		Weekly	Monthly
Council tax	£ 15.00	☐	☑
Gas	£ 80.00	☐	☑
Electricity	£ 60.00	☐	☑
Water charges	£ 50.00	☐	☑
TV rental & licence	£ 60.00	☐	☑
Telephone	£ 80.00	☐	☑
Credit repayments	£	☐	☐
Mail order	£	☐	☐
Housekeeping, food, school meals	£ 450.00	☐	☑
Travelling expenses	£ 100.00	☐	☑
Clothing	£	☐	☐
Maintenance payments	£	☐	☐
Other mortgages	£	☐	☐
Other	£	☐	☐
Total expenses	£ 895.00	☐	☑

Priority debts

25. This section is for arrears only. Do not include regular expenses listed at Question 24.

		Weekly	Monthly
Council tax arrears	£	☐	☐
Water charges arrears	£	☐	☐
Gas account	£	☐	☐
Electricity account	£	☐	☐
Maintenance arrears	£	☐	☐

Others (give details below)

		Weekly	Monthly
	£	☐	☐
	£	☐	☐
	£	☐	☐

26. If an order for possession were to be made, would you have somewhere else to live?   ☐ Yes   ☑ No

    If Yes, say when you would be able to move in: _____

27. Give details of any events or circumstances which have led to your being in arrears with your mortgage (for example divorce, separation, redundancy, bereavement, illness, bankruptcy). If you believe you would suffer exceptional hardship by being ordered to leave the property immediately, say why.

    See Additional Defence Form attached.

Statement of Truth

*(I believe)(The defendant believes) that the facts stated in this defence form are true.
* I am duly authorised by the defendant to sign this statement.

signed _____ date _____
*(Defendant)(Litigation friend(where defendant is a child or a patient))(Defendant's solicitor)
*delete as appropriate

Full name John Dobson

Name of defendant's solicitor's firm Rainbow Law Centre

position or office held Solicitor
          (if signing on behalf of firm or company)

IN THE ANYTOWN COUNTY COURT

BETWEEN

EQUITABLE SECURED HOME LOAN LIMITED   <u>Claimant</u>

and

STEPHEN and JOSIE NEILL   <u>Defendant</u>

ADDITIONAL DEFENCE FORM

---

1. This Additional Defence Form is filed to supplement the Defence Form filed in this action by the Defendants.
2. The Defendants admit that the agreement for the loan secured by the mortgage in favour of the Claimant is one regulated by the Consumer Credit Act 1974. The Defendants claim the protection of the provisions of that Act and in particular the provisions relating to Time Orders contained in Consumer Credit Act 1974 Sections 129–136.
3. The Defendants do not dispute the information provided in the Particulars of Claim relating to the mortgage and to the Defendants.

COUNTERCLAIM

---

4. The Defendants repeat their Defence set out above.
5. In November 2005 the Defendant Josie Neill was dismissed from her employment because of ill health. Because of the loss of her salary the Defendants were unable to meet the payments under the agreement with the Claimant. The Defendants expect Josie Neill to return to work in October 2010. Attached to this Defence Form is a letter from the employer confirming that as soon as she is fit to resume work she will be re-employed on the same terms as previously. At that time the Defendants would then be able to resume payments in accordance with the terms of the agreement with the Claimant.
6. The Defendants ask that the Court make a 'Time Order' providing for the monthly instalments due under the agreement to be reduced to £140 with effect August 2010 until November 2010 and that pursuant to that Time Order the interest rate provided for in the agreement to be reduced to an annual rate of 8%.
7. The Defendants Counterclaim for:
   (1) Relief pursuant to Consumer Credit Act 1974 Sections 129–136.
   (2) Further or other relief.

Dated   18 July 2010

STATEMENT OF TRUTH

We believe that the facts stated in this Defence and Part 20 Counterclaim are true.

....
STEPHEN & JOSIE NEILL

c/o Rainbow Law Centre, 1 Lavender Close, Anytown

To the Court Manager
And to the Claimant

6 Application notice (form N244) to set possession order aside

Application notice

For help in completing this form please read the notes for guidance form N244Notes.

Name of court	Anytown County Court
Claim no.	AN10 09601
Warrant no. (if applicable)	
Claimant's name (including ref.)	Rainbow District Council
Defendant's name (including ref.)	Wayne Ross
Date	3 August 2010

1. What is your name or, if you are a solicitor, the name of your firm?

   Wayne Ross

2. Are you a   ☐ Claimant   ☑ Defendant   ☐ Solicitor

   ☐ Other *(please specify)*

   If you are a solicitor whom do you represent?

3. What order are you asking the court to make and why?

   The Order for Possession dated 21 July 2010 be set aside as it was obtained in my absence and I have a good reason for not attending the hearing.

4. Have you attached a draft of the order you are applying for?   ☐ Yes   ☑ No

5. How do you want to have this application dealt with?   ☑ at a hearing   ☐ without a hearing   ☐ at a telephone hearing

6. How long do you think the hearing will last?   ☐ Hours   15 Minutes

   Is this time estimate agreed by all parties?   ☐ Yes   ☑ No

7. Give details of any fixed trial date or period   None

8. What level of Judge does your hearing need?   District Judge

9. Who should be served with this application?   The Claimant

N244 Application notice (05.08)   1   © Crown copyright 2008

10. What information will you be relying on, in support of your application?

☑ the attached witness statement

☐ the statement of case

☐ the evidence set out in the box below

If necessary, please continue on a separate sheet.

Statement of Truth

(I believe) (~~The applicant believes~~) that the facts stated in this section (and any continuation sheets) are true.

Signed _____   Dated 3 August 2010 _____

Applicant('s ~~Solicitor~~)('s ~~litigation friend~~)

Full name Wayne Ross _____

Name of applicant's solicitor's firm Rainbow Law Centre _____

Position or office held _____
(if signing on behalf of firm or company)

11. Signature and address details

Signed _____   Dated 3 August 2010 _____

Applicant('s ~~Solicitor~~)('s ~~litigation friend~~)

Position or office held _____
(if signing on behalf of firm or company)

Applicant's address to which documents about this application should be sent

Rainbow Law Centre 1 Lavender Close Anytown Postcode	If applicable	
	Phone no.	
	Fax no.	
	DX no.	
	Ref no.	

E-mail address	

2

Application Notice (Form N244) – Notes for Guidance

Court Staff cannot give legal advice. If you need information or advice on a legal problem you can contact Community Legal Service Direct on 0845 345 4 345 or www.clsdirect.org.uk, or a Citizens Advice Bureau. Details of your local offices and contact numbers are available via their website www.citizensadvice.org.uk

Paying the court fee
A court fee is payable depending on the type of application you are making. For example:

- To apply for judgment to be set aside
- To apply to vary a judgment or suspend enforcement
- To apply for a summons or order for a witness to attend
- To apply by consent, or without service of the application notice, for a judgment or order.

No fee is payable for an application by consent for an adjournment of a hearing if it is received by the court at least 14 days before the date of the hearing.

What if I cannot afford the fee?
If you show that a payment of a court fee would involve undue hardship to you, you may be eligible for a fee concession.

For further information, or to apply for a fee concession, ask court staff for a copy of the combined booklet and form EX160A - Court fees - Do I have to pay them? This is also available from any county court office, or a copy of the leaflet can be downloaded from our website www.hmcourts-service.gov.uk

Completing the form

Question 3
Set out what order you are applying for and why; e.g. to adjourn the hearing because..., to set aside a judgment against me because... etc.

Question 5
Most applications will require a hearing and you will be expected to attend. The court will allocate a hearing date and time for the application. Please indicate in a covering letter any dates that you are unavailable within the next six weeks.

The court will only deal with the application 'without a hearing' in the following circumstances.

- Where all the parties agree to the terms of the order being asked for;
- Where all the parties agree that the court should deal with the application without a hearing, or
- Where the court does not consider that a hearing would be appropriate.

Telephone hearings are only available in applications where at least one of the parties involved in the case is legally represented. Not all applications will be suitable for a telephone hearing and the court may refuse your request.

Question 6
If you do not know how long the hearing will take do not guess but leave these boxes blank.

Question 7
If your case has already been allocated a hearing date or trial period please insert details of those dates in the box.

Question 8
If your case is being heard in the High Court or a District Registry please indicate whether it is to be dealt with by a Master, District Judge or Judge.

Question 9
Please indicate in the box provided who you want the court to send a copy of the application to.

Question 10
In this section please set out the information you want the court to take account of in support of the application you are making.
If you wish to rely on:

- **a witness statement**, tick the first box and attach the statement to the application notice. A witness statement form is available on request from the court office.

- **a statement of case**, tick the second box if you intend to rely on your particulars of claim or defence in support of your application.

- **written evidence** on this form, tick the third box and enter details in the space provided. You must also complete the statement of truth. Proceedings for contempt of court may be brought against a person who signs a statement of truth without an honest belief in its truth.

Question 11
The application must be signed and include your current address and contact details. If you agree that the court and the other parties may communicate with you by Document Exchange, telephone, facsimile or email, complete the details

Before returning your form to the court
Have you:
- signed the form on page 2,
- enclosed the correct fee or an application for fee concession,
- made sufficient copies of your application and supporting documentation. You will need to submit one copy for each party to be served and one copy for the court.

7 Witness statement in support of application to set possession order aside

Defendant;
W Ross
First

3 August 2010

IN THE ANYTOWN COUNTY COURT   CASE NO: AN10 09601

BETWEEN

RAINBOW DISTRICT COUNCIL   <u>Claimant</u>

and

WAYNE ROSS   <u>Defendant</u>

WITNESS STATEMENT OF WAYNE ROSS

I Wayne Ross of 32 Small Street Anytown, currently unemployed, will say as follows:

1. I am the Defendant in this case and make this statement in support of my application to have the Order for Possession dated 21 July 2010 set aside having been obtained in my absence. The facts set out in this statement are within my own knowledge or are based on information provided to me by my Solicitors and which I believe to be true.

2. I am the tenant of 32 Small Street Anytown which I rent from the Claimant.

3. On 31 July 2010 I received a copy of the Order for Possession that had been granted to the Claimant on 21 July 2010. This was the first that I had heard about the proceedings that had been brought against me. At no stage have I received any Claim for Possession from the Court nor have I been told by anyone on the Claimant's behalf that proceedings had been started. I should add that I have experienced other problems with postal deliveries. In May and June 2010 a series of letters sent to me at home went missing in the post. My local sorting office accepted that this was their mistake.

4. I can only assume that if the Claim for Possession was posted by the Court (which I understand from my Solicitor is the usual practice) and that the -envel-ope has gone missing somewhere in the postal system.

5. I wish to defend the proceedings brought against me and to Counterclaim against the Claimant for damages for breach of repairing obligation and for a Mandatory Order to require the Claimant to undertake repairs for which it is responsible. I refer to the draft Defence and Counterclaim marked WR 1 which is attached to this statement which I serve in these proceedings.

[Alternatively, a brief synopsis of the Grounds for Possession and Counterclaim should be set out]

6. I would respectfully suggest that I have shown that I had a good reason for not attending the hearing and that I have a good defence to the claim brought against me by the Claimant. I would ask that the Possession Order dated 21 July 2010 be set aside and that the Court give Case Management Directions for the service of my Statement of Case and consequential Directions for the disposal of this claim.

7. I believe the facts stated in this Witness Statement are true.

W.Ross   Date... *3 August 2010*
....
WAYNE ROSS

To the Court Manager
And to The Claimant

8 Application notice (form N244) to suspend warrant for possession

Application notice

For help in completing this form please read
the notes for guidance form N244Notes.

Name of court	Anytown County Court
Claim no.	AN10 09601
Warrant no. (if applicable)	TR 2978N
Claimant's name (including ref.)	Rainbow District Council
Defendant's name (including ref.)	Wayne Ross
Date	27 August 2010

1. What is your name or, if you are a solicitor, the name of your firm?

2. Are you a   ☐ Claimant   ☑ Defendant   ☐ Solicitor

     ☐ Other *(please specify)*

     If you are a solicitor whom do you represent?

3. What order are you asking the court to make and why?

     The warrant for possession due to be enforced on 3 September 2010 be suspended on terms.

4. Have you attached a draft of the order you are applying for?   ☐ Yes   ☑ No

5. How do you want to have this application dealt with?   ☑ at a hearing   ☐ without a hearing
     ☐ at a telephone hearing

6. How long do you think the hearing will last?   ☐ Hours   15 Minutes

     Is this time estimate agreed by all parties?   ☐ Yes   ☑ No

7. Give details of any fixed trial date or period   None

8. What level of Judge does your hearing need?   District Judge

9. Who should be served with this application?   Claimant

N244 Application notice (05.08)   1   © Crown copyright 2008

10. What information will you be relying on, in support of your application?

☑ the attached witness statement

☐ the statement of case

☐ the evidence set out in the box below

If necessary, please continue on a separate sheet.

Statement of Truth

(I believe) (The applicant believes) that the facts stated in this section (and any continuation sheets) are true.

Signed _____   Dated 27 August 2010 _____

Applicant(~~'s Solicitor~~)(~~'s litigation friend~~)

Full name Wayne Ross _____

Name of applicant's solicitor's firm _____

Position or office held _____
(if signing on behalf of firm or company)

11. Signature and address details

Signed _____   Dated 27 August 2010 _____

Applicant(~~'s Solicitor~~)(~~'s litigation friend~~)

Position or office held _____
(if signing on behalf of firm or company)

Applicant's address to which documents about this application should be sent

32 Small Street Anytown	If applicable	
	Phone no.	
	Fax no.	
Postcode	DX no.	
A N 1 7 D G	Ref no.	
E-mail address		

2

9 Witness statement in support of application to suspend warrant

IN THE ANYTOWN COUNTY COURT   Claim No: AN10 09601

BETWEEN

RAINBOW DISTRICT COUNCIL   <u>Claimant</u>

and

WAYNE ROSS   <u>Defendant</u>

APPLICATION NOTICE (in Form N244)

TAKE NOTICE that the Defendant intends to apply to the Court at

      on   day the   day of   2010

for an order:

1. That the warrant for possession issued in this matter be suspended on such terms as the Court thinks fit;

2. That the order for possession dated 25th March 2010 be varied so as to postpone the date for possession on compliance with the terms in paragraph 1 and otherwise on such terms as the Court thinks fit; and

3. That the costs of this application may be provided for.

Dated, etc,

IN THE ANYTOWN COUNTY COURT   Claim No: AN10 09601

BETWEEN

RAINBOW DISTRICT COUNCIL   Claimant

and

WAYNE ROSS   Defendant

WITNESS STATEMENT

I, WAYNE ROSS, of 32 Small Street Anytown will say as follows:

1. I am the Defendant in this matter. I make this Witness Statement in support of my application for a suspension of the warrant and for a variation of the suspended possession order granted to the Claimant by this Court on 21 July 2010.

2. Under that order, the Court granted possession of 32 Small Street Anytown to the Claimant on 18 August 2010, but suspended enforcement of the order on terms that I should pay the current weekly rent plus the sum of £3.30 per week towards the arrears, which at that date stood at £1,599.93.

3. Following the order of 21 July 2010, I requested the Department for Work and Pensions to deduct the sum of £3.30 from my weekly income support entitlement and to make these payments directly to the Claimant. I understood that this arrangement would come into effect immediately, but I realised that this was not the case when my housing officer wrote to me informing me that no payments had been received. I contacted the Department for Work and Pensions, and was informed that they had no record of the arrangement. I therefore had to complete another form of request. I understand that direct deductions came into operation several weeks later, and that they have continued to be paid at four weekly intervals in arrear.

4. At all times since the order was made, I have been in receipt of income support. I have also claimed housing benefit throughout, but my contributions towards the rent have changed frequently. At first, my full rent was covered by housing benefit, apart from the sum of £6.50 in respect of water rates and service charges. I have paid at least this sum every week, with the exception of six weeks in August/September 2010. I missed those payments because I was under extreme financial pressure at the time. The electricity company were threatening to cut off my supply because of an outstanding bill of £224. I incurred other debts to friends and family in borrowing the money to pay off that account.

5. Difficulties have also arisen because my son James Ross, who is aged 20 and who now lives with me, started employment in August 2010, and has had three different jobs in the last two months. This has led to a non-dependant deduction being applied to my housing benefit entitlement, resulting in my weekly contribution to the rent increasing at intervals. I did not realise

at first that James's wages would affect my housing benefit, so I did not understand the need to provide evidence of his income to the Claimant's housing benefit office. This resulted in an overpayment of benefit of £324, and this is being recovered from me by deductions of £8.00 each week from my ongoing -benefit.

6. James has been in and out of work during this period. On each occasion that he has started work again, I have declared his income to the housing benefit office, but it has taken several weeks for them to inform me how much I should be paying towards the rent because of the non-dependant deduction.

7. I am currently paying a total of £29.30 towards my weekly rent, together with the weekly instalments of £3.30 off the arrears which are paid by direct deduction.

8. I have not always understood the correspondence which I have received from the housing benefit office, and in particular I did not understand at first that a deduction was being made from my housing benefit because of James's employment.

9. I was informed by my housing officer that unless I made up the shortfall in my payments under the order, a warrant for possession of my flat would be issued. I could not afford to make up these payments in a lump sum.

10. My household now consists of myself, together with James, my other son Jon, who is aged 9, and my daughter Kate, who is aged 10. I suffer from agora-phobia and depression and I am unable to work. I have done my best to comply with the terms of the court order

11. In the circumstances, I respectfully ask the Court to suspend the warrant of possession on terms that I will continue to pay the current rent plus the sum of £3.30 off the arrears.

I believe that the facts set out in this Statement are true.

Dated: *17 October 2010*

Signed *W. Ross*
           Wayne Ross
           Defendant

To the Court and to the Claimant

10 Order for possession with no date fixed (form N28A)

IN THE ANYTOWN COUNTY COURT   CASE NO: AN10 09601

BETWEEN

RAINBOW DISTRICT COUNCIL   <u>Claimant</u>

and

WAYNE ROSS   <u>Defendant</u>

ORDER

---

1. The defendant is to give up possession of 32 Small Street Anytown to the claimant.
2. The date on which the defendant is to give up possession of the property to the claimant is postponed to a date to be fixed by the court on an application by the claimant. The defendant's tenancy of the property will continue until that date.
3. The defendant must pay the claimant £1,599.93 for rent arrears and £276.75 for costs. The total judgment debt is £1,876.68 to be paid by instalments as specified in paragraph 4 below.
4. The claimant shall not be entitled to make an application for a date to be fixed for the giving up of possession and the termination of the defendant's tenancy so long as the defendant pays the claimant the current rent together with instalments of £3.30 per week towards the judgment debt.
5. The first payment of the current rent and the first instalment must be made on or before 31 July 2010.
6. Any application to fix the date on which the defendant is to give up possession may be determined on the papers without a hearing (unless the district judge considers that such a hearing is necessary).
7. This order shall cease to be enforceable when the total judgment debt is satisfied.

Dated   21 July 2010

DISTRICT JUDGE

To the defendant

The court has ordered that **unless you pay the arrears** and costs at the rate set out above **in addition to your current rent**, you must leave the premises.

Payments should be made to the claimant, not to the court. If you need more information about making payments, you should contact the claimant.

If you do not make the payments or leave the premises, the claimant can ask the court, **without a further hearing**, to fix a date for you to leave the premises and if you do not do so, to authorise a bailiff or High Court Enforcement Officer to evict you. (You can apply to the court to stay the eviction; a judge will decide if there are grounds for doing so.)

(If there is an order to pay money)

If you do not pay the money owed when it is due and the claimant takes steps to enforce payment, the order will be registered in the Register of Judgments, Orders and Fines. This may make it difficult for you to get credit. Further information about registration is available in a leaflet which you can get from any court office.

11 Order adjourning on terms

IN THE GREENFIELD COUNTY COURT   CASE NO: GF10 06111

BETWEEN

GREENFIELD DISTRICT COUNCIL   <u>Claimant</u>

and

CHRIS URBAN   <u>Defendant</u>

ORDER

Upon hearing the Solicitors for the Claimant and Defendant

It is Ordered that:

1. The Claimant's claim for possession be adjourned generally with liberty to restore on terms that the Defendant do pay the current rent plus £3.30 each week off the arrears of £1836.54 with the first payment towards the arrears to be made by 4 pm on 7 August 2010.

2. The Claimant have permission on written request to the Court to restore this action if the Defendant fails to comply with the terms set out in paragraph 1 above.

3. There be no order as to costs other than detailed assessment of the Defendant's costs pursuant to the Community Legal Service (Costs) Regulations 2000.

Dated   28 July 2010

DISTRICT JUDGE

Instructions checklist

Social and private rented sector occupiers

Occupiers
Full name, address, dates of birth, phone number, occupation, income and savings, national insurance numbers, relationships between.

Name of tenant(s)
Name and address and relationship to occupier.

Status
Protected/statutory/secure/assured tenant/assured shorthold/demoted/ introductory/unprotected/successor tenant/assignee/family intervention.

Details of accommodation
Room/flat/house, shared facilities, location in house.

Landlord/ agent/ solicitor
Name, address, telephone number, DX, e-mail, reference number.

Rent
Amount (inclusive/exclusive of services), rent registration, any irrecoverable rent, arrears, agreement as to level of arrears, is landlord accepting rent, method of payment.

Documents
Tenancy agreement, rent receipts, rent book.

Date of commencement of tenancy

Date of commencement of occupancy

Housing benefit
Amount received/date of claim/possible backdated claim/paid to tenant or landlord/housing benefit shortfall.

Notice to quit/ notice of intention to seek possession
Date received/method of service.

Court proceedings
Previous proceedings, current proceedings, hearing date, date of receipt of claim form.

Causes of action against landlord or other
Set-off for disrepair and evidence of landlord's knowledge of disrepair, third party action against local authority over housing benefit.

Correspondence

Details of any previous arrangements to remedy default

Proposals to pay off arrears
Amount/method of payment.

Regular financial commitments
Maintenance, court orders, credit agreement, etc.

Rehousing obligations
Children, pregnancy, vulnerability, community care issues.

Mortgage borrowers
Occupiers
Full name, address, dates of birth, phone number, occupations, income and savings, relationships between, date of commencement of occupation.

Legal owner
Name and address, relationship to occupier.

Mortgagee/solicitors
Name, address, telephone and reference numbers, priority (first, second, etc).

Type of mortgage
Repayment/endowment/pension/other.

Date of mortgage

Legal title
Freehold/leasehold, registered/unregistered land.
Joint owner/sole/trustee.

Payments
Monthly instalments (interest and capital/endowment), arrears, date of last payment.

Date of commencement of occupancy

Equitable owners
Previous properties occupied as such, details of contribution to purchase or mortgage payments, financial/other detriment.

Correspondence

Court proceedings
Previous/current proceedings, hearing dates, date of receipt of summons.

Details of any previous arrangements to remedy default

Amount required to redeem mortgage

Value of property with vacant possession

Insurance cover
Mortgage indemnity policy, mortgage protection policy.

Regular financial commitments
Maintenance, court orders, credit agreement etc.

Rehousing obligations
Children, pregnancy, vulnerability, community care issues.

Causes of action against lender or other
Misrepresentation, negligence against surveyor/solicitor.
Undue influence.

Mortgage rescue scheme eligibility

Mortgage interest payments for Department for Work and Pensions

Pre-Action Protocols for possession claims[1]

Pre-action Protocol for possession claims based on rent arrears

Pre-Action Protocol for possession claims based on mortgage or home purchase plan arrears in respect of residential property

Mortgage Pre-action Protocol checklist

Pre-action Protocol for possession claims based on rent arrears

Aims and scope of the protocol

This protocol applies to residential possession claims by social landlords (such as local authorities, Registered Social Landlords, Housing Action Trusts and private registered providers of social housing) and private registered providers of social housing which are based solely on claims for rent arrears. The protocol does not apply to claims in respect of long leases or to claims for possession where there is no security of tenure.

The protocol reflects the guidance on good practice given to social landlords and private registered providers in the collection of rent arrears. It recognises that it is in the interests of both landlords and tenants to ensure that rent is paid promptly and to ensure that difficulties are resolved wherever possible without court proceedings.

Its aim is to encourage more pre-action contact between landlords and tenants and to enable court time to be used more effectively.

Courts should take into account whether this protocol has been followed when considering what orders to make. Registered Social Landlords, private registered providers of social housing and local authorities should also comply with guidance issued from time to time by the Housing Corporation and the Department for Communities and Local Government.

Initial contact

1 The landlord should contact the tenant as soon as reasonably possible if the tenant falls into arrears to discuss the cause of the arrears, the tenant's financial circumstances, the tenant's entitlement to benefits and repayment of the arrears. Where contact is by letter, the landlord should write separately to each named tenant.

2 The landlord and tenant should try to agree affordable sums for the tenant to pay towards arrears, based upon the tenant's income and expenditure (where such information has been supplied in response to the landlord's enquiries). The landlord should clearly set out in pre-action correspondence any time limits with which the tenant should comply.

3 The landlord should provide, on a quarterly basis, rent statements in a comprehensible format showing rent due and sums received for the past 13 weeks. The landlord should, upon request, provide the tenant with copies of rent statements in a comprehensible format from the date when arrears first arose showing all amounts of rent due, the dates and amounts of all payments made, whether through housing benefit or by the tenant, and a running total of the arrears.

4 (a) If the landlord is aware that the tenant has difficulty in reading or understanding information given, the landlord should take reasonable steps to ensure that the tenant understands any information given. The landlord should be able to demonstrate that reasonable steps have been taken to ensure that the information has been appropriately communicated in ways that the tenant can understand.

(b) If the landlord is aware that the tenant is under 18 or is particularly vulnerable, the landlord should consider at an early stage –

   (i) whether or not the tenant has the mental capacity to defend possession proceedings and, if not, make an application for the appointment of a litigation friend in accordance with CPR 21;

   (ii) whether or not any issues arise under Disability Discrimination Act 1995; and

   (iii) in the case of a local authority landlord, whether or not there is a need for a community care assessment in accordance with National Health Service and Community Care Act 1990.

5 If the tenant meets the appropriate criteria, the landlord should arrange for arrears to be paid by the Department for Work and Pensions from the tenant's benefit.

6 The landlord should offer to assist the tenant in any claim the tenant may have for housing benefit.

7 Possession proceedings for rent arrears should not be started against a tenant who can demonstrate that he has –

(a) provided the local authority with all the evidence required to process a housing benefit claim;

(b) a reasonable expectation of eligibility for housing benefit; and

(c) paid other sums due not covered by housing benefit.

The landlord should make every effort to establish effective ongoing liaison with housing benefit departments and, with the tenant's consent, make direct contact with the relevant housing benefit department before taking enforcement action.

The landlord and tenant should work together to resolve any housing benefit problems.

8 Bearing in mind that rent arrears may be part of a general debt problem, the landlord should advise the tenant to seek assistance from CAB, debt advice agencies or other appropriate agencies as soon as possible.

After service of statutory notices

9 After service of a statutory notice but before the issue of proceedings, the landlord should make reasonable attempts to contact the tenant, to discuss the amount of the arrears, the cause of the arrears, repayment of the arrears and the housing benefit position.

10 If the tenant complies with an agreement to pay the current rent and a reasonable amount towards arrears, the landlord should agree to postpone court proceedings so long as the tenant keeps to such agreement. If the tenant ceases to comply with such agreement, the landlord should warn the tenant of the intention to bring proceedings and give the tenant clear time limits within which to comply.

Alternative dispute resolution

11 The parties should consider whether it is possible to resolve the issues between them by discussion and negotiation without recourse to litigation. The parties may be required by the court to provide evidence that alternative

means of resolving the dispute were considered. Courts take the view that litigation should be a last resort, and that claims should not be issued prematurely when a settlement is still actively being explored.

The Legal Services Commission has published a booklet on 'Alternatives to Court', CLS Direct Information Leaflet 23 (http://www.communitylegaladvice.org.uk/en/legalhelp/leaflet23_1.jsp), which lists a number of organisations that provide alternative dispute resolution services.

Court proceedings

12 Not later than ten days before the date set for the hearing, the landlord should –
  (a) provide the tenant with up to date rent statements;
  (b) disclose what knowledge he possesses of the tenant's housing benefit position to the tenant.

13 (a) The landlord should inform the tenant of the date and time of any court hearing and the order applied for. The landlord should advise the tenant to attend the hearing as the tenant's home is at risk. Records of such advice should be kept.
  (b) If the tenant complies with an agreement made after the issue of proceedings to pay the current rent and a reasonable amount towards arrears, the landlord should agree to postpone court proceedings so long as the tenant keeps to such agreement.
  (c) If the tenant ceases to comply with such agreement, the landlord should warn the tenant of the intention to restore the proceedings and give the tenant clear time limits within which to comply.

14 If the landlord unreasonably fails to comply with the terms of the protocol, the court may impose one or more of the following sanctions –
  (a) an order for costs;
  (b) in cases other than those brought solely on mandatory grounds, adjourn, strike out or dismiss claims.

15 If the tenant unreasonably fails to comply with the terms of the protocol, the court may take such failure into account when considering whether it is reasonable to make possession orders.

Pre-Action Protocol for possession claims based on mortgage or home purchase plan arrears in respect of residential property

I INTRODUCTION

1 Preamble

1.1 This Protocol describes the behaviour the court will normally expect of the parties prior to the start of a possession claim within the scope of paragraph 3.1 below.

1.2 This Protocol does not alter the parties' rights and obligations.

1.3 It is in the interests of the parties that mortgage payments or payments under home purchase plans are made promptly and that difficulties are resolved wherever possible without court proceedings. However in some cases an order for possession may be in the interest of both the lender and the borrower.

2 Aims

2.1 The aims of this Protocol are to–

(1) ensure that a lender or home purchase plan provider (in this Protocol collectively referred to as 'the lender') and a borrower or home purchase plan customer (in this Protocol collectively referred to as 'the borrower') act fairly and reasonably with each other in resolving any matter concerning mortgage or home purchase plan arrears; and

(2) encourage more pre-action contact between the lender and the borrower in an effort to seek agreement between the parties, and where this cannot be reached, to enable efficient use of the court's time and resources.

2.2 Where either party is required to communicate and provide information to the other, reasonable steps should be taken to do so in a way that is clear, fair and not misleading. If the lender is aware that the borrower may have difficulties in reading or understanding the information provided, the lender should take reasonable steps to ensure that information is communicated in a way that the borrower can understand.

3 Scope

3.1 This Protocol applies to arrears on –

(1) first charge residential mortgages and home purchase plans regulated by the Financial Services Authority under the Financial Services and Markets Act 2000;

(2) second charge mortgages over residential property and other secured loans regulated under the Consumer Credit Act 1974 on residential property; and

(3) unregulated residential mortgages.

3.2 Where a potential claim includes a money claim and a claim for possession this protocol applies to both.

4 Definitions

4.1 In this Protocol–

(1) 'possession claim' means a claim for the recovery of possession of property under Part 55 of the Civil Procedure Rules 1998 ('CPR');

(2) 'home purchase plan' means a method of purchasing a property by way of a sale and lease arrangement that does not require the payment of interest;

(3) 'bank holiday' means a bank holiday under the Banking and Financial Dealings Act 1971;

(4) 'business day' means any day except Saturday, Sunday, a bank holiday, Good Friday or Christmas day; and

(5) 'Mortgage Rescue Scheme' means the shared equity and mortgage to rent scheme established either –

(a) by the UK Government to help certain categories of vulnerable borrowers avoid repossession of their property in England, announced in September 2008 and opened in January 2009; or

(b) by the Welsh Assembly Government to help certain categories of vulnerable borrowers avoid repossession of their property in Wales, first announced in June 2008.

II ACTIONS PRIOR TO THE START OF A POSSESSION CLAIM

5 Initial contact and provision of information

5.1 Where the borrower falls into arrears the lender should provide the borrower with–

(1) where appropriate, the required regulatory information sheet or the National Homelessness Advice Service booklet on mortgage arrears; and

(2) information concerning the amount of arrears which should include–

(a) the total amount of the arrears;

(b) the total outstanding of the mortgage or the home purchase plan; and

(c) whether interest or charges will be added, and if so and where appropriate, details or an estimate of the interest or charges that may be payable.

5.2 The parties should take all reasonable steps to discuss with each other, or their representatives, the cause of the arrears, the borrower's financial circumstances and proposals for repayment of the arrears (see 7.1). For example, parties should consider whether the causes of the arrears are temporary or long term and whether the borrower may be able to pay the arrears in a reasonable time.

5.3 The lender should advise the borrower to make early contact with the housing department of the borrower's Local Authority and, should, where necessary, refer the borrower to appropriate sources of independent debt advice.

5.4 The lender should consider a reasonable request from the borrower to change the date of regular payment (within the same payment period) or the method by which payment is made. The lender should either agree to such a request or, where it refuses such a request, it should, within a reasonable period of time, give the borrower a written explanation of its reasons for the refusal.

5.5 The lender should respond promptly to any proposal for payment made by the borrower. If the lender does not agree to such a proposal it should give reasons in writing to the borrower within 10 business days of the proposal.

5.6 If the lender submits a proposal for payment, the borrower should be given a reasonable period of time in which to consider such proposals. The lender should set out the proposal in sufficient detail to enable the borrower to understand the implications of the proposal.

5.7 If the borrower fails to comply with an agreement, the lender should warn the borrower, by giving the borrower 15 business days notice in writing, of its intention to start a possession claim unless the borrower remedies the breach in the agreement.

6 Postponing the start of a possession claim

6.1 A lender should consider not starting a possession claim for mortgage arrears where the borrower can demonstrate to the lender that the borrower has–

(1) submitted a claim to–

(a) the Department for Works and Pensions (DWP) for Support for Mortgage Interest (SMI); or

(b) an insurer under a mortgage payment protection policy; or

(c) a participating local authority for support under a Mortgage Rescue Scheme,

and has provided all the evidence required to process a claim;

(2) a reasonable expectation of eligibility for payment from the DWP or from the insurer or support from the local authority; and

(3) an ability to pay a mortgage instalment not covered by a claim to the DWP or the insurer in relation to a claim under paragraph 6.1(1)(a) or (b).

6.2 If a borrower can demonstrate that reasonable steps have been or will be taken to market the property at an appropriate price in accordance with reasonable professional advice, the lender should consider postponing starting a possession claim. The borrower must continue to take all reasonable steps actively to market the property where the lender has agreed to postpone starting a possession claim.

6.3 Where the lender has agreed to postpone starting a possession claim the borrower should provide the lender with a copy of the particulars of sale, the Home Information Pack and (where relevant) details of purchase offers received within a reasonable period of time specified by the lender. The borrower should give the lender details of the estate agent and the conveyancer instructed to deal with the sale. The borrower should also authorise the estate agent and the conveyancer to communicate with the lender about the progress of the sale and the borrower's conduct during the process.

6.4 Where the lender decides not to postpone the start of a possession claim it should inform the borrower of the reasons for this decision at least 5 business days before starting proceedings.

7 Alternative dispute resolution

7.1 The court takes the view that starting a possession claim is usually a last resort and that such a claim should not normally be started when a settlement is still actively being explored. Discussion between the parties may include options such as:

(1) extending the term of the mortgage;

(2) changing the type of a mortgage;

(3) deferring payment of interest due under the mortgage; or

(4) capitalising the arrears.

8 Complaints to the Financial Ombudsman Service

8.1 The lender should consider whether to postpone the start of a possession claim where the borrower has made a genuine complaint to the Financial Ombudsman Service (FOS) about the potential possession claim.

8.2 Where a lender does not intend to await the decision of the FOS it should give notice to the borrower with reasons that it intends to start a possession claim at least 5 business days before doing so.

9 Compliance

9.1 Parties should be able, if requested by the court, to explain the actions that they have taken to comply with this protocol.

Mortgage Pre-action Protocol checklist

Mortgage pre-action protocol checklist

Name of court		Claim no.	
Name of claimant			
Name of defendant			
Mortgage account number			

You must produce two copies of the Checklist on the day of the hearing.

Checklist

1. Is the possession claim within the scope of the Protocol? ☐ Yes ☐ No

2. Have you provided the defendant with the information/notice in the Protocol —

   (a) paragraph 5.1(1) ☐ Yes ☐ No If Yes, date provided: ☐☐/☐☐/☐☐☐☐

   (b) paragraph 5.1(2) ☐ Yes ☐ No If Yes, date provided: ☐☐/☐☐/☐☐☐☐

   (c) paragraph 5.7 ☐ Yes ☐ No If Yes, date of notice: ☐☐/☐☐/☐☐☐☐

3. Do you have evidence that the defendant has made a claim for —

   • Support for Mortgage Interest (SMI) ☐ Yes ☐ No

   • Mortgage Rescue Scheme (MRS), or ☐ Yes ☐ No

   • mortgage payment protection. ☐ Yes ☐ No

   If Yes, please explain why possession proceedings are continuing.

4. Is there an unresolved complaint by the defendant to the Financial Ombudsman Service that could justify postponing the possession claim? ☐ Yes ☐ No

   If Yes, please explain why possession proceedings are continuing.

5. Summarise the number and dates, in the three months prior to the date of this checklist, you attempted to discuss with the defendant ways of repaying the arrears.

6. In the three months prior to the date of this checklist have you rejected any proposals   ☐ Yes ☐ No
    by the defendant to change the date or method of regular payments?

    If Yes, did you respond in accordance with paragraph 5.4 of the Protocol?   ☐ Yes ☐ No

    If No, please explain why.

7. Have you rejected a proposal for repayment by the defendant in the three months   ☐ Yes ☐ No
    prior to the date of this checklist?

    If Yes, have you responded in accordance with paragraph 5.5 of the Protocol?   ☐ Yes ☐ No

    If No, please explain why.

8. Has the defendant indicated that the property will be or is being sold?   ☐ Yes ☐ No

    If Yes, explain why possession proceedings are proceeding.

Statement of Truth

*I believe that the facts stated in this Checklist are true.

*I am duly authorised by the claimant to sign this statement.

Signed _____   Date _____

Full name

Name of claimant's solicitor's firm

Position or office held

*Delete as appropriate

Guidance for the mortgage pre-action protocol checklist

The Checklist

This guidance is provided for those using the new Mortgage Pre-Action Protocol Checklist. Use of the Checklist came into effect on 1 October 2009 for all claims issued on or after that date in order to provide a uniform format for the provision of information to demonstrate compliance with the Protocol.

This guide must be read with the Mortgage Pre-Action Protocol, the Civil Procedure Rules and Practice Direction 55.

The Checklist (form N123), must be completed by all claimants (lenders) or their representatives making a possession claim. The claimant or their representative should be able to explain to the court the actions taken or not by the claimant, and the reason for issuing a possession claim.

Once the claimant and defendant (borrower) have been notified by the court of the date of the hearing, a Checklist must be completed indicating the action taken by the claimant within the previous three months to reach an agreement with the defendant, and comply with the Protocol.

The claimant must present two copies of the Checklist on the day of the hearing. No additional documents are necessary unless an issue arises.

Claimants can copy this form onto their systems but the form must not go beyond two sides.

Scope

The following mortgages fall within the scope of the Protocol and Checklist –

(i) first charge residential mortgages and home purchase plans regulated by the Financial Services Authority under the Financial Services and Markets Act 2000;

(ii) second charge mortgages over residential property and other secured loans regulated under the Consumer Credit Act 1974 on residential property; and

(iii) unregulated residential mortgages.

Where a potential claim includes a money claim and a claim for possession, these are also within scope.

Q1 – requires confirmation of the type of mortgage and whether it is within scope of the Protocol as indicated above. If the answer is No, there is no need to compete the rest of the form. However, you must be prepared to explain to the court why you consider that the mortgage does not fall within the scope of the Protocol.

If the answer to Q1 is Yes, all the remaining questions must be answered in full.

Q2 – answer the questions Yes or No, as appropriate, and insert the dates where relevant. Where you have not complied with one or more of these requirements, you must be prepared to explain to the court in full why that is the case.

Q3 – answer the questions Yes or No, as appropriate. Where a claim, either for Support for Mortgage Interest (SMI), Mortgage Rescue Scheme (MRS) or under a mortgage payment protection policy, has been made, you must set out clearly and succinctly why you are proceeding with a claim for possession.

Q4 – answer the question Yes or No, as appropriate. If the defendant has an unresolved complaint you must set out clearly and succinctly why you are proceeding with a claim for possession.

Q5 – you should provide here a list of dates and details of the associated media (for example, letter, telephone, etc). Where use has been made of automated diallers, which do not necessarily keep an individual record of each attempted call, you should confirm the number of attempts and frequency that your system is programmed to make.

Q6 – answer the question Yes or No, as appropriate. Where you have answered:

- No, then no further information is required.

- Yes, you must also confirm whether or not you have complied with the requirements of paragraph 5.4 of the Protocol when notifying the defendant of your decision. If the answer to that question is:

  o Yes – then no further information is required on the Checklist but you must be prepared to explain to the court what action you took if requested to do so.

  o No – you should set out your reasons for non-compliance clearly and succinctly.

Q7 – answer the question Yes or No, as appropriate. Where you have answered:

- No, then no further information is required.
- Yes, you must also confirm whether or not you have complied with the requirements of paragraph 5.5 of the protocol when notifying the defendant of your decision. If the answer to that question is:
  - o Yes – then no further information is required on the Checklist but you must be prepared to explain to the court what action you took if requested to do so.
  - o No – you should set out your reasons for non-compliance clearly and succinctly.

Q8 – answer the question Yes or No, as appropriate. Where the defendant is trying to sell their property you need to explain clearly and succinctly why you are bringing proceedings including, specifically, whether or not the defendant has complied with the requirements of paragraphs 6.2 and 6.3 of the Protocol.

The statement of truth
The statement of truth must be signed and completed by the claimant or representative. This section must be completed in order to validate the information provided.

Service of the Checklist
Two copies of the Checklist must be brought to the hearing.

CPR Part 55 and Practice Directions[1]

CPR Part 55: Possession claims

Part 55A Practice Direction: Possession claims

Part 55B Practice Direction: Possession claims online

CPR Part 55: Possession claims

55.1 Interpretation

In this Part–

(a) 'a possession claim' means a claim for the recovery of possession of land (including buildings or parts of buildings);

(b) 'a possession claim against trespassers' means a claim for the recovery of land which the claimant alleges is occupied only by a person or persons who entered or remained on the land without the consent of a person entitled to possession of that land but does not include a claim against a tenant or sub-tenant whether his tenancy has been terminated or not;

(c) 'mortgage' includes a legal or equitable mortgage and a legal or equitable charge and 'mortgagee' is to be interpreted accordingly;

(d) 'the 1985 Act' means the Housing Act 1985;

(e) 'the 1988 Act' means the Housing Act 1988;

(f) 'a demotion claim' means a claim made by a landlord for an order under section 82A of the 1985 Act or section 6A of the 1988 Act ('a demotion order');

(g) 'a demoted tenancy' means a tenancy created by virtue of a demotion order; and

(h) 'a suspension claim' means a claim made by a landlord for an order under section 121A of the 1985 Act.

I General rules

55.2 Scope

(1) The procedure set out in this Section of this Part must be used where the claim includes –

(a) a possession claim brought by a –

(i) landlord (or former landlord);

(ii) mortgagee; or

(iii) licensor (or former licensor);

(b) a possession claim against trespassers; or

(c) a claim by a tenant seeking relief from forfeiture.

(Where a demotion claim or a suspension claim (or both) is made in the same claim form in which a possession claim is started, this Section of this Part applies as modified by rule 65.12. Where the claim is a demotion claim or a suspension claim only, or a suspension claim made in addition to a demotion claim, Section III of Part 65 applies).

(2) This Section of this Part

(a) is subject to any enactment or practice direction which sets out special provisions with regard to any particular category of claim;

(b) does not apply where the claimant uses the procedure set out in Section II of this Part; and

(c) does not apply where the claimant seeks an interim possession order under Section III of this Part except where the court orders otherwise or that Section so provides.

55.3 Starting the claim

(1) The claim must be started in the county court for the district in which the land is situated unless paragraph (2) applies or an enactment provides otherwise.

(2) The claim may be started in the High Court if the claimant files with his claim form a certificate stating the reasons for bringing the claim in that court verified by a statement of truth in accordance with rule 22.1(1).

(3) Practice Direction 55A refers to circumstances which may justify starting the claim in the High Court.

(4) Where, in a possession claim against trespassers, the claimant does not know the name of a person in occupation or possession of the land, the claim must be brought against 'persons unknown' in addition to any named defendants.

(5) The claim form and form of defence sent with it must be in the forms set out in Practice Direction 55A.

55.4 Particulars of claim

The particulars of claim must be filed and served with the claim form.

(Part 16 and Practice Direction 55A provide details about the contents of the particulars of claim)

55.5 Hearing date

(1) The court will fix a date for the hearing when it issues the claim form.

(2) In a possession claim against trespassers the defendant must be served with the claim form, particulars of claim and any witness statements –

(a) in the case of residential property, not less than 5 days; and

(b) in the case of other land, not less than 2 days,

before the hearing date.

(3) In all other possession claims –

(a) the hearing date will be not less than 28 days from the date of issue of the claim form;

(b) the standard period between the issue of the claim form and the hearing will be not more than 8 weeks; and

(c) the defendant must be served with the claim form and particulars of claim not less than 21 days before the hearing date.

(Rule 3.1(2)(a) provides that the court may extend or shorten the time for compliance with any rule)

55.6 Service of claims against trespassers

Where, in a possession claim against trespassers, the claim has been issued against 'persons unknown', the claim form, particulars of claim and any witness statements must be served on those persons by –

(a) (i) attaching copies of the claim form, particulars of claim and any witness statements to the main door or some other part of the land so that they are clearly visible; and

(ii) if practicable, inserting copies of those documents in a sealed transparent envelope addressed to 'the occupiers' through the letter box; or

(b) placing stakes in the land in places where they are clearly visible and attaching to each stake copies of the claim form, particulars of claim and any witness statements in a sealed transparent envelope addressed to 'the occupiers'.

55.7 Defendant's response

(1) An acknowledgment of service is not required and Part 10 does not apply.

(2) In a possession claim against trespassers rule 15.2 does not apply and the defendant need not file a defence.

(3) Where, in any other possession claim, the defendant does not file a defence within the time specified in rule 15.4, he may take part in any hearing but the court may take his failure to do so into account when deciding what order to make about costs.

(4) Part 12 (default judgment) does not apply in a claim to which this Part applies.

55.8 The hearing

(1) At the hearing fixed in accordance with rule 55.5(1) or at any adjournment of that hearing, the court may –

(a) decide the claim; or

(b) give case management directions.

(2) Where the claim is genuinely disputed on grounds which appear to be substantial, case management directions given under paragraph (1)(b) will include the allocation of the claim to a track or directions to enable it to be allocated.

(3) Except where –

(a) the claim is allocated to the fast track or the multi-track; or

(b) the court orders otherwise,

any fact that needs to be proved by the evidence of witnesses at a hearing referred to in paragraph (1) may be proved by evidence in writing.

(Rule 32.2(1) sets out the general rule about evidence. Rule 32.2(2) provides that rule 32.2(1) is subject to any provision to the contrary)

(4) Subject to paragraph (5), all witness statements must be filed and served at least 2 days before the hearing.

(5) In a possession claim against trespassers all witness statements on which the claimant intends to rely must be filed and served with the claim form.

(6) Where the claimant serves the claim form and particulars of claim, he must produce at the hearing a certificate of service of those documents and rule 6.17(2)(a) does not apply.

55.9 Allocation

(1) When the court decides the track for a possession claim, the matters to which it shall have regard include –

(a) the matters set out in rule 26.8 as modified by the relevant practice direction;

(b) the amount of any arrears of rent or mortgage instalments;

(c) the importance to the defendant of retaining possession of the land;

(d) the importance of vacant possession to the claimant; and

(e) if applicable, the alleged conduct of the defendant

(2) The court will only allocate possession claims to the small claims track if all the parties agree.

(3) Where a possession claim has been allocated to the small claims track the claim shall be treated, for the purposes of costs, as if it were proceeding on the fast track except that trial costs shall be in the discretion of the court and shall not exceed the amount that would be recoverable under rule 46.2 (amount of fast track costs) if the value of the claim were up to £3,000.

(4) Where all the parties agree the court may, when it allocates the claim, order that rule 27.14 (costs on the small claims track) applies and, where it does so, paragraph (3) does not apply.

55.10 Possession claims relating to mortgaged residential property

(1) This rule applies where a mortgagee seeks possession of land which consists of or includes residential property.

(2) Within 5 days of receiving notification of the date of the hearing by the court, the claimant must send a notice to –

(a) the property, addressed to 'the tenant or the occupier';

(b) the housing department of the local authority within which the property is located; and

(c) any registered proprietor (other than the claimant) of a registered charge over the property.

(3) The notice referred to in paragraph (2)(a) must –

(a) state that a possession claim for the property has started;

(b) show the name and address of the claimant, the defendant and the court which issued the claim form; and

(c) give details of the hearing.

(3A) The notice referred to in paragraph 2(b) must contain the information in paragraph (3) and must state the full address of the property.

(4) The claimant must produce at the hearing –

(a) a copy of the notice; and

(b) evidence that he has served it.

55.10A Electronic issue of certain possession claims

(1) A practice direction may make provision for a claimant to start certain types of possession claim in certain courts by requesting the issue of a claim form electronically.

(2) The practice direction may, in particular –

(a) provide that only particular provisions apply in specific courts;

(b) specify –

(i) the type of possession claim which may be issued electronically;

(ii) the conditions that a claim must meet before it may be issued electronically;

(c) specify the court where the claim may be issued;

(d) enable the parties to make certain applications or take further steps in relation to the claim electronically;

(e) specify the requirements that must be fulfilled in relation to such applications or steps;

(f) enable the parties to correspond electronically with the court about the claim;

(g) specify the requirements that must be fulfilled in relation to electronic correspondence;

(h) provide how any fee payable on the filing of any document is to be paid where the document is filed electronically.

(3) The Practice Direction may disapply or modify these Rules as appropriate in relation to possession claims started electronically.

II Accelerated possession claims of property let on an assured shorthold tenancy

55.11 When this section may be used

(1) The claimant may bring a possession claim under this Section of this Part where –

(a) the claim is brought under section 21 of the 1988 Act to recover possession of residential property let under an assured shorthold tenancy; and

(b) subject to rule 55.12(2), all the conditions listed in rule 55.12(1) are satisfied.

(2) The claim must be started in the county court for the district in which the property is situated.

(3) In this Section of this Part, a 'demoted assured shorthold tenancy' means a demoted tenancy

where the landlord is a registered social landlord.

(By virtue of section 20B of the 1988 Act, a demoted assured shorthold tenancy is an assured shorthold tenancy)

55.12 Conditions

(1) The conditions referred to in rule 55.11(1)(b) are that –

(a) the tenancy and any agreement for the tenancy were entered into on or after 15 January 1989;

(b) the only purpose of the claim is to recover possession of the property and no other claim is made;

(c) the tenancy did not immediately follow an assured tenancy which was not an assured shorthold tenancy;

(d) the tenancy fulfilled the conditions provided by section 19A or 20(1)(a) to (c) of the 1988 Act;

(e) the tenancy –

(i) was the subject of a written agreement;

(ii) arises by virtue of section 5 of the 1988 Act but follows a tenancy that was the subject of a written agreement; or

> (iii) relates to the same or substantially the same property let to the same tenant and on the same terms (though not necessarily as to rent or duration) as a tenancy which was the subject of a written agreement; and
>
> (f) a notice in accordance with sections 21(1) or 21(4) of the 1988 Act was given to the tenant in writing.

(2) If the tenancy is a demoted assured shorthold tenancy, only the conditions in paragraph (1)(b) and (f) need be satisfied.

55.13 Claim form

(1) The claim form must –

> (a) be in the form set out in the relevant practice direction; and
>
> (b) (i) contain such information; and
>
> (ii) be accompanied by such documents,
>
> as are required by that form.

(2) All relevant sections of the form must be completed.

(3) The court will serve the claim form by first class post (or an alternative service which provides for delivery on the next working day).

55.14 Defence

(1) A defendant who wishes to –

> (a) oppose the claim; or
>
> (b) seek a postponement of possession in accordance with rule 55.18,
>
> must file his defence within 14 days after service of the claim form.

(2) The defence should be in the form set out in Practice Direction 55A.

55.15 Claim referred to judge

(1) On receipt of the defence the court will –

> (a) send a copy to the claimant; and
>
> (b) refer the claim and defence to a judge.

(2) Where the period set out in rule 55.14 has expired without the defendant filing a defence –

> (a) the claimant may file a written request for an order for possession; and
>
> (b) the court will refer that request to a judge.

(3) Where the defence is received after the period set out in rule 55.14 has expired but before a request is filed in accordance with paragraph (2), paragraph (1) will still apply.

(4) Where –

> (a) the period set out in rule 55.14 has expired without the defendant filing a defence; and
>
> (b) the claimant has not made a request for an order for possession under paragraph (2) within 3 months after the expiry of the period set out in rule 55.14,
>
> the claim will be stayed.

55.16 Consideration of the claim

(1) After considering the claim and any defence, the judge will –
- (a) make an order for possession under rule 55.17;
- (b) where he is not satisfied as to any of the matters set out in paragraph (2) –
  - (i) direct that a date be fixed for a hearing; and
  - (ii) give any appropriate case management directions; or
- (c) strike out the claim if the claim form discloses no reasonable grounds for bringing the claim.

(2) The matters referred to in paragraph (1)(b) are that –
- (a) the claim form was served; and
- (b) the claimant has established that he is entitled to recover possession under section 21 of the1988 Act against the defendant.

(3) The court will give all parties not less than 14 days' notice of a hearing fixed under paragraph (1)(b)(i).

(4) Where a claim is struck out under paragraph (1)(c) –
- (a) the court will serve its reasons for striking out the claim with the order; and
- (b) the claimant may apply to restore the claim within 28 days after the date the order was served on him

55.17 Possession order

Except where rules 55.16(1)(b) or (c) apply, the judge will make an order for possession without requiring the attendance of the parties.

55.18 Postponement of possession

(1) Where the defendant seeks postponement of possession on the ground of exceptional hardship under section 89 of the Housing Act 19801, the judge may direct a hearing of that issue.

(2) Where the judge directs a hearing under paragraph (1) –
- (a) the hearing must be held before the date on which possession is to be given up; and
- (b) the judge will direct how many days' notice the parties must be given of that hearing.

(3) Where the judge is satisfied, on a hearing directed under paragraph (1), that exceptional hardship would be caused by requiring possession to be given up by the date in the order of possession, he may vary the date on which possession must be given up.

55.19 Application to set aside or vary

The court may
- (a) on application by a party within 14 days of service of the order; or
- (b) of its own initiative,

set aside or vary any order made under rule 55.17.

III Interim possession orders

55.20 When this section may be used

(1) This Section of this Part applies where the claimant seeks an Interim Possession Order.

(2) In this section –

    (a) 'IPO' means Interim Possession Order; and

    (b) 'premises' has the same meaning as in section 12 of the Criminal Law Act 1972.

(3) Where this Section requires an act to be done within a specified number of hours, rule 2.8(4) does not apply.

55.21 Conditions for IPO application

(1) An application for an IPO may be made where the following conditions are satisfied –

    (a) the only claim made is a possession claim against trespassers for the recovery of premises;

    (b) the claimant –

        (i) has an immediate right to possession of the premises; and

        (ii) has had such a right throughout the period of alleged unlawful occupation; and

    (c) the claim is made within 28 days of the date on which the claimant first knew, or ought reasonably to have known, that the defendant (or any of the defendants), was in occupation.

(2) An application for an IPO may not be made against a defendant who entered or remained on the premises with the consent of a person who, at the time consent was given, had an immediate right to possession of the premises.

55.22 The application

(1) Rules 55.3(1) and (4) apply to the claim.

(2) The claim form and the defendant's form of witness statement must be in the form set out in Practice Direction 55A.

(3) When he files his claim form, the claimant must also file –

    (a) an application notice in the form set out in Practice Direction 55A; and

    (b) written evidence.

(4) The written evidence must be given –

    (a) by the claimant personally; or

    (b) where the claimant is a body corporate, by a duly authorised officer.

    (Rule 22.1(6)(b) provides that the statement of truth must be signed by the maker of the witness statement)

(5) The court will –

    (a) issue –

        (i) the claim form; and

        (ii) the application for the IPO; and

    (b) set a date for the hearing of the application.

(6) The hearing of the application will be as soon as practicable but not less than 3 days after the date of issue.

55.23 Service

(1) Within 24 hours of the issue of the application, the claimant must serve on the defendant –

(a) the claim form;

(b) the application notice together with the written evidence in support; and

(c) a blank form for the defendant's witness statement (as set out in Practice Direction 55A) which must be attached to the application notice.

(2) The claimant must serve the documents listed in paragraph (1) in accordance with rule 55.6(a).

(3) At or before the hearing the claimant must file a certificate of service in relation to the documents listed in paragraph (1) and rule 6.17(2)(a) does not apply.

55.24 Defendant's response

(1) At any time before the hearing the defendant may file a witness statement in response to the application.

(2) The witness statement should be in the form set out in Practice Direction 55A.

55.25 Hearing of the application

(1) In deciding whether to grant an IPO, the court will have regard to whether the claimant has given, or is prepared to give, the following undertakings in support of his application –

(a) if, after an IPO is made, the court decides that the claimant was not entitled to the order to –

(i) reinstate the defendant if so ordered by the court; and

(ii) pay such damages as the court may order; and

(b) before the claim for possession is finally decided, not to –

(i) damage the premises;

(ii) grant a right of occupation to any other person; and

(iii) damage or dispose of any of the defendant's property.

(2) The court will make an IPO if –

(a) the claimant has –

(i) filed a certificate of service of the documents referred to in rule 55.23(1); or

(ii) proved service of those documents to the satisfaction of the court; and

(b) the court considers that –

(i) the conditions set out in rule 55.21(1) are satisfied; and

(ii) any undertakings given by the claimant as a condition of making the order are adequate.

(3) An IPO will be in the form set out in the relevant practice direction and will

require the defendant to vacate the premises specified in the claim form within 24 hours of the service of the order.

(4) On making an IPO the court will set a date for the hearing of the claim for possession which will be not less than 7 days after the date on which the IPO is made.

(5) Where the court does not make an IPO –

(a) the court will set a date for the hearing of the claim;

(b) the court may give directions for the future conduct of the claim; and

(c) subject to such directions, the claim shall proceed in accordance with Section I of this Part.

55.26 Service and enforcement of the IPO

(1) An IPO must be served within 48 hours after it is sealed.

(2) The claimant must serve the IPO on the defendant together with copies of

(a) the claim form; and

(b) the written evidence in support, in accordance with rule 55.6(a).

(3) CCR Order 26, rule 17 does not apply to the enforcement of an IPO.

(4) If an IPO is not served within the time limit specified by this rule, the claimant may apply to the court for directions for the claim for possession to continue under Section I of this Part.

55.27 After IPO made

(1) Before the date for the hearing of the claim, the claimant must file a certificate of service in relation to the documents specified in rule 55.26(2).

(2) The IPO will expire on the date of the hearing of the claim.

(3) At the hearing the court may make any order it considers appropriate and may, in particular –

(a) make a final order for possession;

(b) dismiss the claim for possession;

(c) give directions for the claim for possession to continue under Section I of this Part; or

(d) enforce any of the claimant's undertakings.

(4) Unless the court directs otherwise, the claimant must serve any order or directions in accordance with rule 55.6(a).

(5) CCR Order 24, rule 6 applies to the enforcement of a final order for possession.

55.28 Application to set aside IPO

(1) If the defendant has left the premises, he may apply on grounds of urgency for the IPO to be set aside before the date of the hearing of the claim.

(2) An application under paragraph (1) must be supported by a witness statement.

(3) On receipt of the application, the court will give directions as to –

(a) the date for the hearing; and

(b) the period of notice, if any, to be given to the claimant and the method of service of any such notice.

(4) No application to set aside an IPO may be made under rule 39.3.

(5) Where no notice is required under paragraph (3)(b), the only matters to be dealt with at the hearing of the application to set aside are whether –

    (a) the IPO should be set aside; and

    (b) any undertaking to re-instate the defendant should be enforced, and all other matters will be dealt with at the hearing of the claim.

(6) The court will serve on all the parties –

    (a) a copy of the order made under paragraph (5); and

    (b) where no notice was required under paragraph (3)(b), a copy of the defendant's application to set aside and the witness statement in support.

(7) Where notice is required under paragraph (3)(b), the court may treat the hearing of the application to set aside as the hearing of the claim.

Practice Direction 55A: Possession claims

This Practice Direction supplements Part 55

Section I – General rules

55.3 Starting the claim

1.1 Except where the county court does not have jurisdiction, possession claims should normally be brought in the county court. Only exceptional circumstances justify starting a claim in the High Court.

1.2 If a claimant starts a claim in the High Court and the court decides that it should have been started in the county court, the court will normally either strike the claim out or transfer it to the county court on its own initiative. This is likely to result in delay and the court will normally disallow the costs of starting the claim in the High Court and of any transfer.

1.3 Circumstances which may, in an appropriate case, justify starting a claim in the High Court are if –

(1) there are complicated disputes of fact;

(2) there are points of law of general importance; or

(3) the claim is against trespassers and there is a substantial risk of public disturbance or of serious harm to persons or property which properly require immediate determination.

1.4 The value of the property and the amount of any financial claim may be relevant circumstances, but these factors alone will not normally justify starting the claim in the High Court.

1.5 The claimant must use the appropriate claim form and particulars of claim form set out in Table 1 to Part 4 Practice Direction. The defence must be in form N11, N11B, N11M or N11R, as appropriate.

1.6 High Court claims for the possession of land subject to a mortgage will be assigned to the Chancery Division.

1.7 A claim which is not a possession claim may be brought under the procedure set out in Section I of Part 55 if it is started in the same claim form as a possession claim which, by virtue of rule 55.2(1) must be brought in accordance with that Section. (Rule 7.3 provides that a claimant may use a single claim form to start all claims which can be conveniently disposed of in the same proceedings)

1.8 For example a claim under paragraphs 4, 5 or 6 of Part I of Schedule 1 to the Mobile Homes Act 1983 may be brought using the procedure set out in Section I of Part 55 if the claim is started in the same claim form as a claim enforcing the rights referred to in section 3(1)(b) of the Caravan Sites Act 1968 (which, by virtue of rule 55.2(1) must be brought under Section I of Part 55).

1.9 Where the claim form includes a demotion claim, the claim must be started in the county court for the district in which the land is situated.

55.4 Particulars of claim

2.1 In a possession claim the particulars of claim must:

(1) identify the land to which the claim relates;

(2) state whether the claim relates to residential property;

(3) state the ground on which possession is claimed;

(4) give full details about any mortgage or tenancy agreement; and

(5) give details of every person who, to the best of the claimant's knowledge, is in possession of the property.

Residential property let on a tenancy

2.2 Paragraphs 2.3 to 2.4B apply if the claim relates to residential property let on a tenancy.

2.3 If the claim includes a claim for non-payment of rent the particulars of claim must set out:

(1) the amount due at the start of the proceedings;

(2) in schedule form, the dates and amounts of all payments due and payments made under the tenancy agreement for a period of two years immediately preceding the date of issue, or if the first date of default occurred less than two years before the date of issue from the first date of default and a running total of the arrears;

(3) the daily rate of any rent and interest;

(4) any previous steps taken to recover the arrears of rent with full details of any court proceedings; and

(5) any relevant information about the defendant's circumstances, in particular:

(a) whether the defendant is in receipt of social security benefits; and

(b) whether any payments are made on his behalf directly to the claimant under the Social Security Contributions and Benefits Act 1992

2.3A If the claimant wishes to rely on a history of arrears which is longer than two years, he should state this in his particulars and exhibit a full (or longer) schedule to a witness statement.

2.4 If the claimant knows of any person (including a mortgagee) entitled to claim relief against forfeiture as underlessee under section 146(4) of the Law of Property Act 1925 (or in accordance with section 38 of the Supreme Court Act 1981, or section 138(9C) of the County Courts Act 1984):

(1) the particulars of claim must state the name and address of that person; and

(2) the claimant must file a copy of the particulars of claim for service on him.

2.4A If the claim for possession relates to the conduct of the tenant, the particulars of claim must state details of the conduct alleged.

2.4B If the possession claims relies on a statutory ground or grounds for possession, the particulars of claims must specify the ground or grounds relied on.

Land subject to a mortgage

2.5 If the claim is a possession claim by a mortgagee, the particulars of claim must also set out:

(1) if the claim relates to residential property whether:

(a) a land charge of Class F has been registered under section 2(7) of the Matrimonial Homes Act 1967;

(b) a notice registered under section 2(8) or 8(3) of the Matrimonial Homes Act 1983 has been entered and on whose behalf; or

(c) a notice under section 31(10) of the Family Law Act 1996 has been registered and on whose behalf; and if so, that the claimant will serve notice of the claim on the persons on whose behalf the land charge is registered or the notice or caution entered.

(2) the state of the mortgage account by including:

(a) the amount of:

    (i)   the advance;

    (ii) any periodic repayment; and

    (iii) any payment of interest required to be made;

(b) the amount which would have to be paid (after taking into account any adjustment for early settlement) in order to redeem the mortgage at a stated date not more than 14 days after the claim started specifying the amount of solicitor's costs and administration charges which would be payable;

(c) if the loan which is secured by the mortgage is a regulated consumer credit agreement, the total amount outstanding under the terms of the mortgage; and

(d) the rate of interest payable:

    (i)   at the commencement of the mortgage;

    (ii) immediately before any arrears referred to in paragraph (3) accrued;

    (iii) at the commencement of the proceedings.

(3) if the claim is brought because of failure to pay the periodic payments when due:

(a) in schedule form, the dates and amounts of all payments due and payments made under the mortgage agreement or mortgage deed for a period of two years immediately preceding the date of issue, or if the first date of default occurred less than two years before the date of issue from the first date of default and a running total of the arrears;

(b) give details of:

    (i)   any other payments required to be made as a term of the mortgage (such as for insurance premiums, legal costs, default interest, penalties, administrative or other charges);

    (ii) any other sums claimed and stating the nature and amount of each such charge; and

    (iii) whether any of these payments is in arrears and whether or not it is included in the amount of any periodic payment.

(4) whether or not the loan which is secured by the mortgage is a regulated consumer credit agreement and, if so, specify the date on which any notice required by sections 76 or 87 of the Consumer Credit Act 1974 was given;

(5) if appropriate details that show the property is not one to which section 141 of the Consumer Credit Act 1974 applies;

(6) any relevant information about the defendant's circumstances, in particular:

  (a) whether the defendant is in receipt of social security benefits; and
  (b) whether any payments are made on his behalf directly to the claimant under the Social Security Contributions and Benefits Act 1992;

(7) give details of any tenancy entered into between the mortgagor and mortgagee (including any notices served); and

(8) state any previous steps which the claimant has taken to recover the money secured by the mortgage or the mortgaged property and, in the case of court proceedings, state:

  (a) the dates when the claim started and concluded; and
  (b) the dates and terms of any orders made.

2.5A If the claimant wishes to rely on a history of arrears which is longer than two years, he should state this in his particulars and exhibit a full (or longer) schedule to a witness statement.

Possession claim against trespassers

2.6 If the claim is a possession claim against trespassers, the particulars of claim must state the claimant's interest in the land or the basis of his right to claim possession and the circumstances in which it has been occupied without licence or consent.

Possession claim in relation to a demoted tenancy by a housing action trust or a local housing authority

2.7 If the claim is a possession claim under section 143D of the Housing Act 1996 (possession claim in relation to a demoted tenancy where the landlord is a housing action trust or a local housing authority), the particulars of claim must have attached to them a copy of the notice to the tenant served under section 143E of the 1996 Act.

55.5 Hearing date

3.1 The court may exercise its powers under rules 3.1(2)(a) and (b) to shorten the time periods set out in rules 55.5(2) and (3).

3.2 Particular consideration should be given to the exercise of this power if:

(1) the defendant, or a person for whom the defendant is responsible, has assaulted or threatened to assault:

  (a) the claimant;
  (b) a member of the claimant's staff; or
  (c) another resident in the locality;

(2) there are reasonable grounds for fearing such an assault; or

(3) the defendant, or a person for whom the defendant is responsible, has caused serious damage or threatened to cause serious damage to the property or to the home or property of another resident in the locality.

3.3 Where paragraph 3.2 applies but the case cannot be determined at the first hearing fixed under rule 55.5, the court will consider what steps are needed to finally determine the case as quickly as reasonably practicable.

55.6 Service in claims against trespassers

4.1 If the claim form is to be served by the court and in accordance with rule 55.6(b) the claimant must provide sufficient stakes and transparent envelopes.

55.8 The hearing

5.1 Attention is drawn to rule 55.8(3). Each party should wherever possible include all the evidence he wishes to present in his statement of case, verified by a statement of truth.

5.2 If relevant the claimant's evidence should include the amount of any rent or mortgage arrears and interest on those arrears. These amounts should, if possible, be up to date to the date of the hearing (if necessary by specifying a daily rate of arrears and interest). However, rule 55.8(4) does not prevent such evidence being brought up to date orally or in writing on the day of the hearing if necessary.

5.3 If relevant the defendant should give evidence of:

(1) the amount of any outstanding social security or housing benefit payments relevant to rent or mortgage arrears; and

(2) the status of:

(a) any claims for social security or housing benefit about which a decision has not yet been made; and

(b) any applications to appeal or review a social security or housing benefit decision where that appeal or review has not yet concluded.

5.4 If:

(1) the maker of a witness statement does not attend a hearing; and

(2) the other party disputes material evidence contained in his statement,

the court will normally adjourn the hearing so that oral evidence can be given.

5.5 The claimant must bring 2 completed copies of Form N123 to the hearing.

Consumer Credit Act claims relating to the recovery of land

7.1 Any application by the defendant for a time order under section 129 of the Consumer Credit Act 1974 may be made:

(1) in his defence; or

(2) by application notice in the proceedings.

Enforcement of charging order by sale

7.2 A party seeking to enforce a charging order by sale should follow the procedure set out in rule 73.10 and the Part 55 procedure should not be used.

Section II – Accelerated possession claims of property let on an assured shorthold tenancy

55.18 Postponement of possession

8.1 If the judge is satisfied as to the matters set out in rule 55.16(2), he will make an order for possession in accordance with rule 55.17, whether or not the defendant seeks a postponement of possession on the ground of exceptional hardship under section 89 of the Housing Act 1980.

8.2 In a claim in which the judge is satisfied that the defendant has shown exceptional hardship, he will only postpone possession without directing a hearing under rule 55.18(1) if –

(1) he considers that possession should be given up 6 weeks after the date of the order or, if the defendant has requested postponement to an earlier date, on that date; and

(2) the claimant indicated on his claim form that he would be content for the court to make such an order without a hearing.

8.3 In all other cases if the defendant seeks a postponement of possession under section 89 of the Housing Act 1980, the judge will direct a hearing under rule 55.18(1).

8.4 If, at that hearing, the judge is satisfied that exceptional hardship would be caused by requiring possession to be given up by the date in the order of possession, he may vary that order under rule 55.18(3) so that possession is to be given up at a later date. That later date may be no later than 6 weeks after the making of the order for possession on the papers (see section 89 of the Housing Act 1980).

Section III – Interim possession orders

9.1 The claim form must be in form N5, the application notice seeking the interim possession order must be in form N130 and the defendant's witness statement must be in form N133.

9.2 The IPO will be in form N134 (annexed to this practice direction).

Section IV – Orders fixing a date for possession

10.1 This paragraph applies where the court has made an order postponing the date for possession under section 85(2)(b) of the Housing Act 1985 (secure tenancies) or under section 9(2)(b) of the Housing Act 1988 (assured tenancies).

10.2 If the defendant fails to comply with any of the terms of the order which relate to payment, the claimant, after following the procedure set out in paragraph 10.3, may apply for an order fixing the date upon which the defendant has to give up possession of the property. Unless the court further postpones the date for possession, the defendant will be required to give up possession on that date.

10.3 At least 14 days and not more than 3 months before applying for an order under paragraph 10.2, the claimant must give written notice to the defendant in accordance with paragraph 10.4.

10.4 The notice referred to in paragraph 10.3 must –

(1) state that the claimant intends to apply for an order fixing the date upon which the defendant is to give up possession of the property;

(2) record the current arrears and state how the defendant has failed to

comply with the order referred to in paragraph 10.1 (by reference to a statement of the rent account enclosed with the notice);

(3) request that the defendant reply to the claimant within 7 days, agreeing or disputing the stated arrears; and

(4) inform the defendant of his right to apply to the court :

(a) for a further postponement of the date for possession; or

(b) to stay or suspend enforcement.

10.5 In his reply to the notice, the defendant must –

(1) where he disputes the stated arrears, provide details of payments or credits made;

(2) where he agrees the stated arrears, explain why payments have not been made.

10.6 An application for an order under paragraph 10.2 must be made by filing an application notice in accordance with Part 23. The application notice must state whether or not there is any outstanding claim by the defendant for housing benefit.

10.7 The claimant must file the following documents with the application notice:

(1) a copy of the notice referred to in paragraph 10.3;

(2) a copy of the defendant's reply, if any, to the notice and any relevant subsequent correspondence between the claimant and the defendant;

(3) a statement of the rent account showing:

(a) the arrears that have accrued since the first failure to pay in accordance with the order referred to in paragraph 10.2; or

(b) the arrears that have accrued during the period of two years immediately preceding the date of the application notice, where the first such failure to pay occurs more than two years before that date.

10.8 Rules 23.7 (service of a copy of an application notice), and 23.10 (right to set aside or vary an order made without service of the application notice) and paragraphs 2.3, 2.4 and 2.5 of Practice Direction 23A do not apply to an application under this section.

10.9 On being filed, the application will be referred to the District Judge who –

(1) will normally determine the application without a hearing by fixing the date for possession as the next working day; but

(2) if he considers that a hearing is necessary:

(a) will fix a date for the application to be heard; and

(b) direct service of the application notice and supporting evidence on the defendant.

10.10 The court does not have jurisdiction to review a decision that it was reasonable to make an order for possession.

Part 55B Practice Direction: Possession claims online

This Practice Direction supplements CPR rule 55.10A.

Scope of this practice direction

1.1 This practice direction provides for a scheme ('Possession Claims Online') to operate in specified county courts –

(1) enabling claimants and their representatives to start certain possession claims under CPR Part 55 by requesting the issue of a claim form electronically via the PCOL website; and

(2) where a claim has been started electronically, enabling the claimant or defendant and their representatives to take further steps in the claim electronically as specified below.

1.2 In this practice direction –

(1) 'PCOL website' means the website www.possessionclaim.gov.uk which may be accessed via Her Majesty's Courts Service website (www.hmcourts-service.gov.uk) and through which Possession Claims Online will operate; and

(2) 'specified court' means a county court specified on the PCOL website as one in which Possession Claims Online is available.

Information on the PCOL website

2.1 The PCOL website contains further details and guidance about the operation of Possession Claims Online.

2.2 In particular the PCOL website sets out –

(1) the specified courts; and

(2) the dates from which Possession Claims Online will be available in each specified court.

2.3 The operation of Possession Claims Online in any specified court may be restricted to taking certain of the steps specified in this practice direction, and in such cases the PCOL website will set out the steps which may be taken using Possession Claims Online in that specified court.

Security

3.1 Her Majesty's Courts Service will take such measures as it thinks fit to ensure the security of steps taken or information stored electronically. These may include requiring users of Possession Claims Online –

(1) to enter a customer identification number or password;

(2) to provide personal information for identification purposes; and

(3) to comply with any other security measures,

before taking any step online.

Fees

4.1 A step may only be taken using Possession Claims Online on payment of the prescribed fee where a fee is payable. Where this practice direction provides for a fee to be paid electronically, it may be paid by –

(1) credit card;

(2) debit card; or

(3) any other method which Her Majesty's Courts Service may permit.

4.2 A defendant who wishes to claim exemption from payment of fees must do so through an organisation approved by Her Majesty's Courts Service before taking any step using PCOL which attracts a fee. If satisfied that the defendant is entitled to fee exemption, the organisation will submit the fee exemption form through the PCOL website to Her Majesty's Courts Service. The defendant may then use PCOL to take such a step.

(Her Majesty's Courts Service website contains guidance as to when the entitlement to claim an exemption from payment of fees arises. The PCOL website will contain a list of organisations through which the defendant may claim an exemption from fees).

Claims which may be started using possession claims online

5.1 A claim may be started online if –

(1) it is brought under Section I of Part 55;

(2) it includes a possession claim for residential property by –

(a) a landlord against a tenant, solely on the ground of arrears of rent (but not a claim for forfeiture of a lease); or

(b) a mortgagee against a mortgagor, solely on the ground of default in the payment of sums due under a mortgage, relating to land within the district of a specified court;

(3) it does not include a claim for any other remedy except for payment of arrears of rent or money due under a mortgage, interest and costs;

(4) the defendant has an address for service in England and Wales; and

(5) the claimant is able to provide a postcode for the property.

5.2 A claim must not be started online if a defendant is known to be a child or patient.

Starting a claim

6.1 A claimant may request the issue of a claim form by –

(1) completing an online claim form at the PCOL website;

(2) paying the appropriate issue fee electronically at the PCOL website or by some other means approved by Her Majesty's Courts Service.

6.2 The particulars of claim must be included in the online claim form and may not be filed separately. It is not necessary to file a copy of the tenancy agreement, mortgage deed or mortgage agreement with the particulars of claim.

6.2A In the case of a possession claim for residential property that relies on a statutory ground or grounds for possession, the clamant must specify, in section 4(a of the oinline claim form, the ground or grounds relied on.

6.3 Subject to paragraphs 6.3A and 6.3B, particulars of claim must include a history of the rent or mortgage account, in schedule form setting out –

(1) the dates and amounts of all payments due and payments made under the tenancy agreement, mortgage deed or mortgage agreement either from the first date of default if that date occurred less than two years

before the date of issue or for a period of two years immediately preceding the date of issue; and

(2) a running total of the arrears.

6.3A Paragraph 6.3B applies where the claimant has, before commencing proceedings, provided the defendant in schedule form with –

(1) details of the dates and amounts of all payments due and payments made under the tenancy agreement, mortgage deed or mortgage account –

    (a) for a period of two years immediately preceding the date of commencing proceedings; or

    (b) if the first date of default occurred less than two years before that date, from the first date of default; and

(2) a running total of the arrears.

6.3B Where this paragraph applies the claimant may, in place of the information required by paragraph 6.3, include in his particulars of claim a summary only of the arrears containing at least the following information –

(1) The amount of arrears as stated in the notice of seeking possession served under either section 83 of the Housing Act 1985 or section 8 of the Housing Act 1988, or at the date of the claimant's letter before action, as appropriate;

(2) the dates and amounts of the last three payments in cleared funds made by the defendant or, if less than three payments have been made, the dates and amounts of all payments made;

(3) the arrears at the date of issue, assuming that no further payments are made by the defendant.

6.3C Where the particulars of claim include a summary only of the arrears the claimant must –

(1) serve on the defendant not more than 7 days after the date of issue, a full, up-to-date arrears history containing at least the information required by paragraph 6.3; and

(2) either –

    (a) make a witness statement confirming that he has complied with sub-paragraph (1) or (2) of paragraph 6.3A as appropriate, and including or exhibiting the full arrears history; or

    (b) verify by way of oral evidence at the hearing that he has complied with sub-paragraph (1) or (2) of paragraph 6.3A as appropriate and also produce and verify the full arrears history.

(Rule 55.8(4) requires all witness statements to be filed and served at least 2 days before the hearing.)

6.4 If the claimant wishes to rely on a history of arrears which is longer than two years, he should state this in his particulars and exhibit a full (or longer) schedule to a witness statement.

6.5 When an online claim form is received, an acknowledgment of receipt will automatically be sent to the claimant. The acknowledgment does not constitute notice that the claim form has been issued or served.

6.6 When the court issues a claim form following the submission of an online claim form, the claim is 'brought' for the purposes of the Limitation Act 1980 and any other enactment on the date on which the online claim form is received by the court's computer system. The court will keep a record, by electronic or other means, of when online claim forms are received.

6.7 When the court issues a claim form it will –

(1) serve a printed version of the claim form and a defence form on the defendant; and

(2) send the claimant notice of issue by post or, where the claimant has supplied an e-mail address, by electronic means.

6.8 The claim shall be deemed to be served on the fifth day after the claim was issued irrespective of whether that day is a business day or not.

6.9 Where the period of time within which a defence must be filed ends on a day when the court is closed, the defendant may file his defence on the next day that the court is open.

6.10 The claim form shall have printed on it a unique customer identification number or a password by which the defendant may access the claim on the PCOL website.

6.11 PCOL will issue the proceedings in the appropriate county court by reference to the post code provided by the claimant and that court shall have jurisdiction to hear and determine the claim and to carry out enforcement of any judgment irrespective of whether the property is within or outside the jurisdiction of that court.

(CPR 30.2(1) authorises proceedings to be transferred from one county court to another.)

Defence

7.1 A defendant wishing to file –

(1) a defence; or

(2) a counterclaim (to be filed together with a defence) to a claim which has been issued through the PCOL system,

may, instead of filing a written form, do so by –

(a) completing the relevant online form at the PCOL website; and

(b) if the defendant is making a counterclaim, paying the appropriate fee electronically at the PCOL website or by some other means approved by Her Majesty's Courts Service.

7.2 Where a defendant files a defence by completing the relevant online form, he must not send the court a hard copy.

7.3 When an online defence form is received, an acknowledgment of receipt will automatically be sent to the defendant. The acknowledgment does not constitute notice that the defence has been served.

7.4 The online defence form will be treated as being filed –

(1) on the day the court receives it, if it receives it before 4 p.m. on a working day; and

(2) otherwise, on the next working day after the court receives the online defence form.

7.5 A defence is filed when the online defence form is received by the court's computer system. The court will keep a record, by electronic or other means, of when online defence forms are received.

Statement of truth

8.1 CPR Part 22 requires any statement of case to be verified by a statement of truth. This applies to any online claims and defences and application notices.

8.2 CPR Part 22 also requires that if an applicant wishes to rely on matters set out in his application notice as evidence, the application notice must be verified by a statement of truth. This applies to any application notice completed online that contains matters on which the applicant wishes to rely as evidence.

8.3 Attention is drawn to –

(1) paragraph 2 of the practice direction supplementing CPR Part 22, which stipulates the form of the statement of truth; and

(2) paragraph 3 of the practice direction supplementing CPR Part 22, which provides who may sign a statement of truth; and

(3) CPR 32.14, which sets out the consequences of making, or causing to be made, a false statement in a document verified by a statement of truth, without an honest belief in its truth.

Signature

9.1 Any provision of the CPR which requires a document to be signed by any person is satisfied by that person entering his name on an online form.

Communication with the court electronically by the messaging service

10.1 If the PCOL website specifies that a court accepts electronic communications relating to claims brought using Possession Claims Online the parties may communicate with the court using the messaging service facility, available on the PCOL website ('the messaging service').

10.2 The messaging service is for brief and straightforward communications only. The PCOL website contains a list of examples of when it will not be appropriate to use the messaging service.

10.3 Parties must not send to the court forms or attachments via the messaging service.

10.4 The court shall treat any forms or attachments sent via the messaging service as not having been filed or received.

10.5 The court will normally reply via the messaging service where –

(1) the response is to a message transmitted via the messaging service; and

(2) the sender has provided an e-mail address.

Electronic applications

11.1 Certain applications in relation to a possession claim started online may be made electronically ('online applications'). An online application may be made if a form for that application is published on the PCOL website ('online application form') and the application is made at least five clear days before the hearing.

11.2 If a claim for possession has been started online and a party wishes to make an online application, he may do so by –

(1) completing the appropriate online application form at the PCOL website; and

(2) paying the appropriate fee electronically at the PCOL website or by some other means

approved by Her Majesty's Courts Service.

11.3 When an online application form is received, an acknowledgment of receipt will automatically be sent to the applicant. The acknowledgment does not constitute a notice that the online application form has been issued or served.

11.4 Where an application must be made within a specified time, it is so made if the online application form is received by the court's computer system within that time. The court will keep a record, by electronic or other means, of when online application forms are received.

11.5 When the court receives an online application form it shall –

(1) serve a copy of the online application endorsed with the date of the hearing by post on the claimant at least two clear days before the hearing; and

(2) send the defendant notice of service and confirmation of the date of the hearing by post; provided that

(3) where either party has provided the court with an e-mail address for service, service of the application and/or the notice of service and confirmation of the hearing date may be effected by electronic means.

Request for issue of warrant

12.1 Where –

(1) the court has made an order for possession in a claim started online; and

(2) the claimant is entitled to the issue of a warrant of possession without requiring the permission of the court

the claimant may request the issue of a warrant by completing an online request form at the PCOL website and paying the appropriate fee electronically at the PCOL website or by some other means approved by Her Majesty's Courts Service.

12.2 A request under paragraph 12.1 will be treated as being filed –

(1) on the day the court receives the request, if it receives it before 4 p.m. on a working day; and

(2) otherwise, on the next working day after the court receives the request.

(CCR Order 26 rule 5 sets out certain circumstances in which a warrant of execution may not be issued without the permission of the court. CCR Order 26 rule 17(6) applies rule 5 of that Order with necessary modifications to a warrant of possession.)

Application to suspend warrant of possession

13.1 Where the court has issued a warrant of possession, the defendant may apply electronically for the suspension of the warrant, provided that:

(1) the application is made at least five clear days before the appointment for possession; and

(2) the defendant is not prevented from making such an application without the permission of the court.

13.2 The defendant may apply electronically for the suspension of the warrant, by –

(1) completing an online application for suspension at the PCOL website; and

(2) paying the appropriate fee electronically at the PCOL website or by some other means approved by Her Majesty's Courts Service.

13.3 When an online application for suspension is received, an acknowledgment of receipt will automatically be sent to the defendant. The acknowledgment does not constitute a notice that the online application for suspension has been served.

13.4 Where an application must be made within a specified time, it is so made if the online application for suspension is received by the court's computer system within that time. The court will keep a record, by electronic or other means, of when online applications for suspension are received.

13.5 When the court receives an online application for suspension it shall –

(1) serve a copy of the online application for suspension endorsed with the date of the hearing by post on the claimant at least two clear days before the hearing; and

(2) send the defendant notice of service and confirmation of the date of the hearing by post; provided that

(3) where either party has provided the court with an e-mail address for service, service of the application and/or the notice of service and confirmation of the hearing date may be effected by electronic means.

Viewing the case record

14.1 A facility will be provided on the PCOL website for parties or their representatives to view –

(1) an electronic record of the status of claims started online, which will be reviewed and, if necessary, updated at least once each day; and

(2) all information relating to the case that has been filed by the parties electronically.

14.2 In addition, where the PCOL website specifies that the court has the facility to provide viewing of such information by electronic means, the parties or their representatives may view the following information electronically –

(1) court orders made in relation to the case; and

(2) details of progress on enforcement and subsequent orders made.

Index

Housing Law Casebook

Fourth edition

Nic Madge and Claire Sephton

'An essential addition to any housing practitioner's library.' *Independent Lawyer*

'An indispensable purchase.' *Adviser*

'an immensely important book for practitioners.' *Civil Justice Quarterly*

2008 Pb 978 1 903307 45 8
1192pp £55

*This edition comes with a free, fully searchable CD-Rom containing the full text of the *Housing Law Casebook*

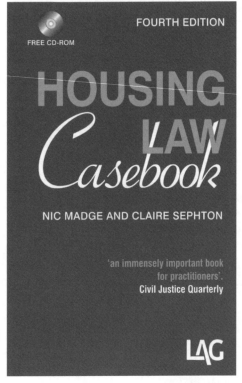

FOURTH EDITION

FREE CD-ROM

HOUSING

Casebook

NIC MADGE AND CLAIRE SEPHTON

'an immensely important book for practitioners'.
Civil Justice Quarterly

www.lag.org.uk/books